Relation of the Directors

to the Work and Publications

of the National Bureau of Economic Research

1. The object of the National Bureau of Economic Research is to ascertain and to present to the public important economic facts and their interpretation in a scientific and impartial manner. The Board of Directors is charged with the responsibility of ensuring that the work of the National Bureau is carried on in strict conformity with this object.

2. To this end the Board of Directors shall appoint one or more Directors of Research.

3. The Director or Directors of Research shall submit to the members of the Board, or to its Executive Committee, for their formal adoption, all specific proposals concerning researches to be instituted.

4. No report shall be published until the Director or Directors of Research shall have submitted to the Board a summary drawing attention to the character of the data and their utilization in the report, the nature and treatment of the problems involved, the main conclusions and such other information as in their opinion would serve to determine the suitability of the report for publication in accordance with the principles of the National Bureau.

5. A copy of any manuscript proposed for publication shall also be submitted to each member of the Board. For each manuscript to be so submitted a special committee shall be appointed by the President, or at his designation by the Executive Director, consisting of three Directors selected as nearly as may be one from each general division of the Board. The names of the special manuscript committee shall be stated to each Director when the summary and report described in paragraph (4) are sent to him. It shall be the duty of each member of the committee to read the manuscript. If each member of the special committee signifies his approval within thirty days, the manuscript may be published. If each member of the special committee has not signified his approval within thirty days of the transmittal of the report and manuscript, the Director of Research shall then notify each member of the Board, requesting approval or disapproval of publication, and thirty additional days shall be granted for this purpose. The manuscript shall then not be published unless at least a majority of the entire Board and a two-thirds majority of those members of the Board who shall have voted on the proposal within the time fixed for the receipt of votes on the publication proposed shall have approved.

6. No manuscript may be published, though approved by each member of the special committee, until forty-five days have elapsed from the transmittal of the summary and report. The interval is allowed for the receipt of any memorandum of dissent or reservation, together with a brief statement of his reasons, that any member may wish to express; and such memorandum of dissent or reservation shall be published with the manuscript if he so desires. Publication does not, however, imply that each member of the Board has read the manuscript, or that either members of the Board in general, or of the special committee, have passed upon its validity in every detail.

7. A copy of this resolution shall, unless otherwise determined by the Board, be printed in each copy of every National Bureau book.

(Resolution adopted October 25, 1926 and revised
February 6, 1933 and February 24, 1941)

NATIONAL BUREAU OF ECONOMIC RESEARCH

Fiscal Studies

THE NATURE AND
TAX TREATMENT OF
CAPITAL GAINS AND LOSSES

LAWRENCE H. SELTZER
Professor of Economics, Wayne University

With the assistance of
SELMA F. GOLDSMITH
and
M. SLADE KENDRICK

NATIONAL BUREAU OF ECONOMIC RESEARCH, INC.

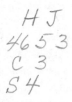

HJ
4653
C 3
S 4

PREFACE

Whether the profits a man realizes by selling stocks, bonds, land, houses, or other property not a part of his stock-in-trade for more than they cost him should be taxed as income or exempted in whole or in part has long been a moot question in the United States. Broadly known as capital gains, such profits, and the correlative capital losses, have been subjected to frequent changes in tax treatment since the beginning of the federal income tax. At all times the American treatment has differed materially from that of Great Britain and most Continental countries. Wide differences of opinion still exist regarding not only the most desirable policy but also the underlying facts and their interpretation and even the theoretical principles involved.

In view of the continuing public interest in the question, the Conference on Research in Fiscal Policy decided in 1943, under the chairmanship of W. L. Crum, to sponsor an objective investigation of the facts, as far as they could be made accessible, and of the main issues. The Directing Committee consisted of Lawrence H. Seltzer of Wayne University, Chairman, Selma F. Goldsmith, then of the Bureau of Agricultural Economics, now of the Department of Commerce, and M. Slade Kendrick of Cornell University.

While the major portion of the study and the setting down of its findings fell to me, my associates lightened the task considerably. Mrs. Goldsmith not only assembled, coordinated, and refined the figures on capital gains and losses from *Statistics of Income* but also, with great skill and resourcefulness, filled gaps and revealed many significant relations or their absence. Nearly all the statistical appendix is her work. She contributed also a preliminary draft of a substantial segment of Chapter 5, in which the figures are reviewed, as well as related materials used in several other chapters. Her chief assistant was Bella Shapiro; others were Marion Gillim and Merton Miller.

Professor Kendrick supplied several preliminary memoranda, including a survey of the tax treatment of capital gains and losses in other countries before World War II and various materials on real estate and corporations, and made helpful suggestions for refining the language in the final manuscript.

Professor Crum took a continuous active interest in the project from its inception, reading the drafts of every chapter with conscientious care and making numerous fruitful suggestions.

Robert Murray Haig of Columbia University, besides giving me the benefit of his own searching criticism, transmitted comments of members of his graduate seminar in public finance who reviewed the manuscript in the spring of 1949.

In addition, various members of the National Bureau's Research Staff and of its Committee on Fiscal Research read parts or all of the manuscript and offered valuable criticisms and suggestions: Arthur F. Burns, C. Lowell Harriss, Carl S. Shoup, and George J. Stigler of Columbia University; Dan Throop Smith of Harvard University, Milton Friedman of the University of Chicago, and Daniel M. Holland and Geoffrey H. Moore.

Many others have aided the enterprise. In writing Chapter 10 on the tax treatment of capital gains and losses abroad, I had the advantage not only of examining Professor Kendrick's materials on the prewar situation but also a manuscript by Paul Wueller of Pennsylvania State College, covering the same period. In bringing these studies up to date, I received valuable aid from Percival Brundage, senior partner of Price, Waterhouse and Co., who communicated with the foreign offices and correspondents of his firm on my behalf. Officials of various embassies and legations in Washington, and in some instances, their home offices as well, were also very cooperative.

Among others to whom I am indebted for their counsel and criticism are Harold M. Groves of the University of Wisconsin, Roswell H. Magill of Columbia University, Stanley S. Surrey of Harvard University, J. K. Lasser of J. K. Lasser & Co., George O. May of Price, Waterhouse and Co., Arthur H. Kent of the California Bar, Harry J. Rudick of the New York Bar, and Bayre Levin, Benjamin E. Jaffe, and A. J. Seltzer of the Michigan Bar. Needless to say, none of those mentioned necessarily shares my interpretations or is responsible for any errors.

Martha Anderson, Editor of the National Bureau of Economic Research, did much to smooth the text. H. Irving Forman made the charts.

Although the study lies primarily in the field of tax policy, I hope it will have some value outside. The economic nature of capital gains and losses has hitherto received remarkably little attention in the literature, and the discussion in Chapter 3 may challenge the unqualified acceptance of some widely held views. Students of national income may be interested in this discussion as well as in the continuous series on American capital gains and losses in Appendix Two.

Lawrence H. Seltzer

CONTENTS

I BASIC DATA FOR 1917-1946

Federal Individual and Taxable Fiduciary Income Tax Returns

III   ADDITIONAL DATA FOR 1936

Federal Individual and Taxable Fiduciary Income Tax Returns

XXI

Chapter 1

BACKGROUND OF THE CONTROVERSY

1 WHAT ARE CAPITAL GAINS AND LOSSES?

In every decade a considerable number of able, venturesome, and/or lucky persons experience substantial additions to their private fortunes not by receiving, saving, and investing ordinary income but through increases in the market value of investments they have made in real estate, business enterprises, or other property. Such gains are known as 'capital gains' or 'capital profits'. Landowners may make fortunes because a new highway or bus line is built or an urban area becomes fashionable for specialty shops or apartment houses. For example, land values in the Sutton Place area of Manhattan (York Avenue, between East 54th and 59th Streets, New York) soared from $300 a front foot in 1924 to $2,000 in 1929.[1] An investor who bought 100 feet for $30,000 in 1924, perhaps with a down payment of $10,000, could sell it for $200,000 five years later. Similar examples of Dame Fortune's goodwill, as well as appalling illustrations of her illwill, can be cited by real estate men in most of the large cities of the country. Various examples of both can be found in the value changes of selected sites in New York City and Cleveland presented in Chart I and Table 91. While some sites rose in value upwards of 300 percent, others rose only moderately, and still others lost heavily.

The stock market offers endless illustrations of such gains and losses. A man who bought 200 shares of Pepsi Cola Company common stock at $6 a share in 1939 could sell his holdings for more than $225,000 in 1945. A man who invested $3,000 in American and Foreign Power Company $7 cumulative second preferred stock in 1941 could have sold out for more than $100,000 in 1945. The market value of 2,500 shares of Northern States Power Company Class A stock rose from $5,000 in 1942 to more than $180,000 in

---

[1] As measured by assessment values, which tend to lag behind market changes in both directions, and are often only rough approximations to market values.

1

Chart 1

Change in Assessed Values of Various Groundsites
New York City, 1909-42; Cleveland, 1910-42

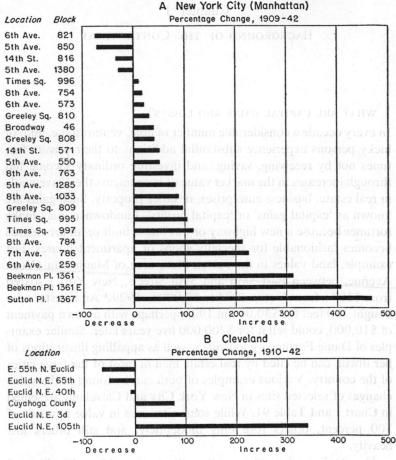

A New York City (Manhattan)

Location *Block*   Percentage Change, 1909-42

Location	Block
6th Ave.	821
5th Ave.	850
14th St.	816
5th Ave.	1380
Times Sq.	996
8th Ave.	754
6th Ave.	573
Greeley Sq.	810
Broadway	46
Greeley Sq.	808
14th St.	571
5th Ave.	550
8th Ave.	763
5th Ave.	1285
8th Ave.	1033
Greeley Sq.	809
Times Sq.	995
Times Sq.	997
8th Ave.	784
7th Ave.	786
6th Ave.	259
Beekman Pl.	1361
Beekman Pl.	1361 E
Sutton Pl.	1367

-100   0   100   200   300   400   500
Decrease   Increase

B Cleveland

Location   Percentage Change, 1910-42

Location
E. 55th N. Euclid
Euclid N.E. 65th
Euclid N.E. 40th
Cuyahoga County
Euclid N.E. 3d
Euclid N.E. 105th

-100   0   100   200   300   400   500
Decrease   Increase

Source: Table 91.

May 1946, the price per share rising from $2 to $73. A prescient or lucky investor could have multiplied his capital by 12 during 1945 alone by investing in the $4 preferred stock of Standard Gas & Electric Company.

On the other hand, some investors paid $300 a share in 1929 for Northern States Power Class A stock which fell to $2 a share by 1942. The common stock of Philip Morris & Company fell 30 percent in the 6 months ended March 1, 1946. In the 4 months ended September 30, 1946, the aggregate market value of all stocks listed on the New York Stock Exchange fell $18 billion or a fifth; between September 1929 and March 1933, in the most disastrous decline on record, from $90 to $20 billion.

Capital gains vs. ordinary profits

In both law and common speech, capital gains are generally regarded as the profits realized from increases in the market value of any assets that are not a part of the owner's stock-in-trade or that he does not regularly offer for sale; and capital losses, as the losses realized from declines in the market value of such assets. *Ordinary* profits and losses, in contrast, are realized on the sale of goods and services that *are* a part of the seller's stock-in-trade or that he regularly offers for sale. The profit earned by a manufacturing company through the operation of its plants and machinery may be contrasted with the gain it would make if it sold some of its investment securities for more than they had cost it. The former is an ordinary business profit, the latter a capital gain.

Ordinary profits are commonly the result of buying goods in one market and selling them in another, that is, in a different form, in different quantities, at a different season, or in a different place. The manufacturer earns ordinary profits by converting raw materials and semifinished goods into new forms, which he sells to other manufacturers, wholesalers, retailers, or consumers. The wholesaler buys in large quantities from the manufacturer and relieves the latter of the task of finding and supplying scores of retail outlets. The retailer earns ordinary income by buying his wares from wholesalers, jobbers, and manufacturers, and selling them to his customers in much smaller unit-quantities, together with packaging, and perhaps delivery and credit services. Capital gains or losses, on the other hand, are most commonly the result of changes in prices in the same market. They are realized most characteristically when one investor or speculator sells his holdings to another. The profit made by a real estate company that buys raw acreage, subdivides it into streets and building lots, and sells plots, is regarded as an ordinary business profit; but the gain made by the farmer or long term speculator who sells the acreage to the real estate company, or by the factory worker who purchases a single lot and subsequently resells it, is regarded as a capital gain.

The major sources of capital gains and losses are capital assets; that is, property acquired for income-making rather than consumption purposes — corporation securities, real estate, government bonds, and interests in partnerships, leases, and contracts. In 1936, the only year for which the relevant data are available, approximately four-fifths of the aggregate net capital gains reported on federal income tax returns were derived from stocks and bonds (Table 69). In the broadest sense, personal and other nonbusiness possessions such as jewelry, paintings, and houses may also give rise to capital gains and losses. During World War II and the period immediately following, many persons were able to sell automobiles, houses, cameras, and certain other articles they had previously purchased for their own use at much higher prices than these goods had cost them. The United States recognizes capital gains so derived and taxes them as such, but it does not allow deductions from taxable income for losses sustained on assets not acquired for a 'gainful', i.e., money-making, purpose.

Realized vs. unrealized capital gains and losses
Most commonly, in both law and ordinary speech, a distinction is made between 'realized' and 'unrealized' capital gains or losses. An owner who does not sell or enter into an exchange legally equivalent to a sale is said not to 'realize' a capital gain or loss, however big the change in the market value of his holdings, however marketable they are, and regardless how long he has owned them. The change in market value, commonly referred to as an 'unrealized' capital gain or loss, is not taken into account in computing taxable income. Very substantial proportions of the increases in the value of lands and corporate securities are never 'realized' in the current legal sense because the law does not regard transfers of property at death as occasioning 'realization'. The difference between the cost of the property to a decedent and its value on the date of his death is not regarded as a capital gain or loss to either the decedent or his heirs. The latter put the property on their books at the value on the date of transfer (or other date chosen by the executor for the purpose of the estate tax) and measure their capital gains or losses on it from the value on that date.

Distinction between capital gains and ordinary income often blurred
While the broad distinction we have made between capital gains and ordinary profits is useful in a general way, it cannot be pressed far for purposes of either economic analysis or law. As we shall find upon further examination, ordinary business profits often contain large amounts of what are essentially capital gains, while large amounts of so-called capital gains are little or no different from

ordinary profits, or arise indirectly from the accumulation of ordinary income.

Moreover, although the general distinction offers a rough guide to the legal concept of capital gains and losses, the effective legal definition has varied from time to time in the United States and in other countries. The profits and losses arising from short term transactions in capital assets, for example, have frequently been excluded from the legal category of capital gains and losses. In addition, the dividing line between short and long term transactions has at different times been 24, 18, 12, and 6 months in the United States. In Sweden the dividing line is 10 years for real estate and 5 years for other capital assets. The point at which the owner of any kind of capital assets ceases to be merely an investor and becomes, in the eyes of the law, engaged in buying and selling them (and his capital gains become, for tax purposes, ordinary profits), is by no means always clear and has been the subject of much litigation. What constitutes 'realization' has also been altered by the statutes and courts from time to time. The legal form of the transaction rather than its substance is sometimes decisive. The successive changes in the statutory definition of capital assets in the United States are described briefly at the end of this chapter.

2 CAPITAL GAINS AN IMPORTANT SOURCE OF PRIVATE FORTUNES

For many persons capital gains have supplied prodigious short-cuts to tremendous riches. Some of the biggest family fortunes in the United States — the Astor, Goelet, Rhinelander, Schermerhorn, and Marshall Field — have come mainly from increases in land values. These fortunes were not due primarily to the receipt and accumulation of land rents and other forms of ordinary income but to the growth in the earning power of real estate that had been acquired at prices reflecting a much smaller earning power. If the market was appraising similar properties at ten times their annual earnings, a rise in the net rent of a piece of real estate from $10,000 to $100,000 a year was equivalent to an increase of $900,000 in the owner's fortune. If the owner sold, he formally 'realized' a capital gain; if he did not, he was nevertheless worth $900,000 more. Large capital gains came to men who discovered or exploited various mineral resources of the country, such as coal mines, gold, copper, silver, lead, and other mineral ores, and oil and natural gas formations. Other men acquired huge fortunes from the capital gains arising from the creation or expansion of the earning power of public utility and industrial enterprises. The fortunes accumulated by Rockefeller, Harriman, Mellon, Guggenheim, Carnegie, Morgan, Baruch, and many others were not built primarily by the year by year receipt, saving, and reinvestment of ordinary income, but by 'realized' and 'unrealized' capital gains. In fact, capital gains have played such an outstanding role in the creation of large fortunes as to suggest that they have been their main source.

Nor have they been insignificant elsewhere. They have been major sources of wealth for numerous farmers and their heirs whose lands happened to lie close to the centers of growing towns and cities; for many urban land speculators and investors; and for many active and passive investors in big and small enterprises. The capital gains arising in connection with the enlargement of corporate earning power did not all accrue to the dominant personalities whose enterprise, daring, energy, imagination, and other personal qualities were often immediately responsible for them, but were shared by numerous less active risk-takers and investors.

Realized capital gains a major source of large incomes
The records provide us with only fragmentary information on the amounts of capital gains and losses that occurred before figures from the federal income tax became available. We know that appreciation in the value of real estate was enormous. According to the Federal Trade Commission, the value of privately owned taxable land exclusive of improvements was approximately $100 billion in 1922.[2] A very large part of this entire sum, which by itself constituted nearly one-third of the estimated total private wealth of the country in 1922, was clearly due to increases in market value from the time the land was first purchased or appropriated from the Indians. Some was doubtless due to draining, grading, and similar cost-entailing actions by the owners; and a good deal more, to the construction of roads, railroads, schools, factories, etc. whose costs were borne only in part by those who owned the surrounding land; but the mere scarcity of land in all sections that became thickly settled was doubtless a potent factor causing values to rise. In any event, considerable amounts of the total appreciation were enjoyed by individuals whose investment of effort and money was relatively small.

The realized capital gains minus realized capital losses reported

[2] *National Wealth and Income,* 69th Cong., 1st Sess., Senate Document 126, p. 34.

each year by individuals filing income tax returns are analyzed in considerable detail in several subsequent chapters and Appendix One. For 1917-46 the net gains of those with net incomes totaled $50 billion, about 11 percent of their total income from property, i.e., sources other than wages and salaries, before deductions, and 5 percent of their aggregate net income including wages and salaries.[3] In

[3] 'Net capital gains' refers to the sum of the annual excesses of capital gains over capital losses of all individuals who reported such an excess in any year. The figure cited does not cover the net capital gains of those who were not required to file income tax returns because their gross or net incomes were smaller than the minima for which returns had to be filed under the successive statutes, or 'unrealized' gains and losses, such as those embodied in property transferred at death or received in tax-free exchanges, or in property that did not change hands.

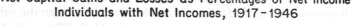

Chart 2

Net Capital Gains and Losses as Percentages of Net Income Individuals with Net Incomes, 1917-1946

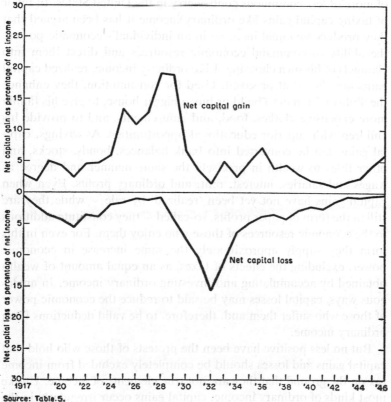

Source: Table.5.

boom years net capital gains were sometimes very much larger. They constituted approximately 19 percent of the aggregate net income of those filing tax returns with net income in 1928 and 1929, and about 13 percent in 1925 and 1927 (Chart 2 and Table 5).

Capital gains have regularly been a bigger proportion of larger than of smaller incomes, on the average. For the 30 years as a whole they were a major source of very large incomes, accounting for about a third of the aggregate net income of individuals with statutory net incomes of $100,000 or over, and for half of the aggregate net income of those reporting $1 million or over (Chart 3 and Table 6). The individuals comprising these groups were not the same, of course, throughout the period.

3 ARE CAPITAL GAINS INCOME?

Whether capital gains should be taxed as ordinary income, taxed at lower rates, or excluded from taxable income has been the subject of more or less continuous controversy in the United States. In favor of taxing capital gains like ordinary income it has been argued that they produce an equal increase in an individual's economic power: the ability to command economic resources and direct them into channels of his own choosing. Like ordinary income, realized capital gains may be spent or saved. Used for consumption, they enhance the ability of a man to build or buy a bigger house, to give his family more expensive clothes, food, and amusements, and to provide his children with superior educational opportunities. As savings, capital gains can be converted into bank balances, bonds, stocks, and other titles to wealth in precisely the same manner and degree as wages and salaries, interest, rent, and ordinary profits. Even when capital gains have not yet been 'realized' by sale — while they are still in the form of paper profits, so-called — they constitute additions to the economic resources of those who enjoy them. For even in this form they supply approximately the same increase in economic power, excluding the effects of taxes, as an equal amount of wealth obtained by accumulating and investing ordinary income. In analagous ways, capital losses may be said to reduce the economic power of those who suffer them and, therefore, to be valid deductions from ordinary income.

But no less positive have been the protests of those who hold that capital gains and losses should be completely excluded from income tax on the ground that they are not true elements of income. Unlike most kinds of ordinary income, capital gains occur irregularly in the

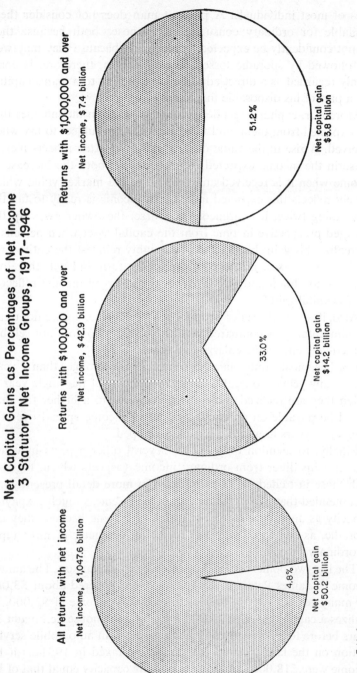

Chart 3

Net Capital Gains as Percentages of Net Income
3 Statutory Net Income Groups, 1917–1946

All returns with net income
Net income, $1,047.6 billion

Net capital gain
$50.2 billion

4.8%

Returns with $100,000 and over
Net income, $42.9 billion

Net capital gain
$14.2 billion

33.0%

Returns with $1,000,000 and over
Net income, $7.4 billion

Net capital gain
$3.8 billion

51.2%

Source: Table 6.

lives of most individuals. A prudent man does not consider them available for ordinary consumption purposes both because they cannot confidently be expected to recur and because they may well be followed by sporadic losses. A capital gain, therefore, is commonly regarded as a direct addition or accretion to a man's capital, not a part of his disposable income.

Moreover, capital assets derive their value from the incomes that are expected from them, and these incomes are subject to tax when received. A rise in the value of a capital asset often reflects merely a rise in the income expected from it. To tax both the increase in income when it is received and the rise in the market value which merely reflects this expected increase in income is really to tax the same thing twice, it is argued. Of course, the owner gives up the enlarged prospective income from the capital asset when he sells it to 'realize' his gain; but he will presumably reinvest the entire proceeds, minus taxes, at the going rate of return and will therefore continue to obtain and pay taxes on the enlarged income reflected by his capital gain.

Also, if we tax the seller's capital gain as income, are we not treating him unfairly as compared with the owner who does not sell but who equally enjoys the enlarged income?

Further, most capital gains arise over periods longer than 1 year, often many years. To treat them as the income of the single year in which they are realized subjects the recipient to a higher tax than would be payable on an equal amount of income spread over the number of years in which the gain developed.

Finally, to mention only one of several other aspects in which capital gains differ from ordinary income (aspects which, together with those just cited, will be discussed in more detail presently), it is contended that capital gains do not represent as much taxpaying capacity as an equal amount of ordinary income because they are sporadic, as compared with the recurring character of most types of ordinary income.

The last two points can be illustrated by a comparison. The annual income of James Peters of Cleveland, Ohio hovered about $3,000 for many years. In 1951, besides his ordinary income of $3,000, he realizes a capital gain of $15,000 by selling the house he bought 30 years before to a company that plans to erect an automobile service station on the land. Should Mr. Peters be taxed in 1951 as if his income were $18,000? Does his taxpaying capacity equal that of his sister whose 1951 income of $18,000 was derived wholly from $720,000 par value of 2½ percent Treasury bonds bequeathed her by her husband?

Powerfully supporting the view that capital gains and losses are not true elements of income has been the example of Great Britain, Canada, Australia, and most European countries with respect to capital gains realized by individuals outside the course of their ordinary business activities. A long tradition in European thought and law has excluded most casual and irregular gains, particularly from the sale of capital assets, from the prevailing concept of personal income and, therefore, from the taxable income of individuals. Besides the force of example, some of the same historical influences and logical considerations that produced this attitude in Europe have been influential in the United States.

But some capital gains are different only in form from ordinary income. An investor who buys a 30-year 3 percent corporation bond at 90 is actually getting an interest return of about 3.55 percent annually; but his return will take the *form* of an interest income of 3 percent a year and a capital gain of about $100 per $1,000 bond at maturity.

Reinvested corporate profits

Capital gains that appear to reflect the direct reinvestment of profits by corporations have raised an especially troublesome question. Because the law conceives a business corporation as an entity separate and distinct from its stockholders, corporate profits are not regarded as the income of the latter unless and until they receive them in dividends. Consequently, stockholders can postpone or avoid the ordinary personal income taxes upon their proportionate shares of retained corporate earnings. But if these retained earnings are profitably employed by the corporation, stockholders can reasonably expect to obtain some proportion of them — though often only a surprisingly small proportion — in the form of a capital gain taxable at a preferentially low rate when they sell the stock. Meanwhile, they can expect to enjoy a rise in the earning power and market value of their holdings. Even the capital gains tax will be avoided and the share of these stockholders in the accumulated earnings of the corporation will never be subjected to personal income taxes if they never sell the stock but leave it to their heirs or give it away during their lifetimes to charitable or other tax-exempt institutions or to persons who leave it to *their* heirs. (Persons who sell property received by gift are subject to tax on the proceeds over the excess of the donor's cost or other basis.)

On the other hand, some reinvestment of earnings may be essential to enable an enterprise merely to maintain its competitive position and its earning power. Accounting charges for obsolescence are often absent or insufficient, with the consequence that the reported earnings often overstate what later are seen to have been the true earnings. Most individual shareholders in large corporations cannot expect to influence dividend policies greatly. They seldom regard their *pro rata* share in the undistributed earnings of their corporations as a part of their individual incomes. They cannot confidently expect their holdings to increase in market value by the exact amount of earnings reinvested on their behalf. Even if such an increase occurs, the stockholder may find it impracticable to convert it into disposable income by selling one or a few shares and regarding the enhanced market value of the remainder as a measure of the maintenance of the principal of his investment. The scale of brokers' commission charges makes the sale of a few shares of stock relatively expensive, and the market value of a single share may greatly exceed the amount of corporate earnings being reinvested on behalf of the remainder of the investor's holdings. For these and other reasons, the market is likely in many cases to appraise reinvested corporate earnings at less than face value.[4] The question of the proper tax treatment of capital gains comes into contact at this point with the whole question of the tax treatment of corporate profits.

4 SPECIAL TREATMENT OF CAPITAL GAINS IN INCOME TAXATION

One major practical effect of the distinction between capital gains and ordinary income is that many countries exempt the former from income taxes under certain conditions or, like the United States, tax them at very much lower rates. In Great Britain, Canada, Australia, and South Africa capital gains are exempt from income tax, whether realized by individuals or corporations, unless they are received "in the ordinary course of trade."

In Belgium they are exempt when realized by individuals outside the course of their business but are taxable as ordinary income when received by corporations or by firms or individuals in the course of

---

[4] Cf. John Burr Williams, *Theory of Investment Value* (Harvard University Press, 1938), pp. 80-1; Alfred Cowles, 3rd, and Associates, *Common Stock Indexes* (Principia Press, 1938), pp. 40-3.

business. This is also the situation in the Netherlands, except that the nonbusiness capital gains of individuals are counted as ordinary income if from sales of real estate held less than 2 years or marketable securities held less than 1 year.

Capital gains in France were treated substantially the same as in Belgium until 1949, when France adopted the recent American practice of subjecting half of the net capital gains of individuals to the regular schedule of income surtaxes, though without the American ceiling rate of 25 percent. The capital gains of business enterprises and those realized by individuals in the course of their business remain taxable in full.

In Norway they are exempt for both individuals and corporations unless derived from property that had been purchased with the intention of reselling or from property used in business or from patents, copyrights, or building sites, or from other real estate held less than 10 years.

In Sweden they are exempt for both individuals and corporations if derived from real estate held 10 years or more, or from securities or other property held 5 years or more.

Capital losses are usually treated similarly; that is, when the gains are fully taxable, the losses, in most countries, are fully deductible, and when the gains are exempt, the losses are not permitted to be deducted from ordinary income for the purposes of the income tax.[5]

In the United States capital gains were taxed as ordinary income in the first several income tax laws enacted after the adoption of the 16th Amendment in 1913.[6] But in 1922, when the ordinary income of individuals was subject to tax rates ranging up to 70 percent, Congress placed an upper limit of 12½ percent upon the rates applicable to their gains from capital assets held more than 2 years, regardless of the amount of ordinary income or capital gains of the taxpayer, and in 1924 Congress limited the allowance for the net losses of individuals on capital assets held more than 2 years to a maximum of 12½ percent of the loss. These ceilings remained in force until the end of 1933. For corporations the original full taxation of capital gains was continued until 1942, and the full deductibility of capital losses from ordinary income until 1932.

[5] See Chapter 10 for a fuller discussion of the tax treatment of capital gains and losses in these and other countries.

[6] The 16th Amendment reads: "The Congress shall have power to lay and collect taxes on incomes, from whatever source derived, without apportionment among the several States, and without regard to any census or enumeration."

In 1934-37 the preferential tax treatment of capital gains reported by individuals took the form of excluding varying proportions from taxable income. The excluded fraction ranged from 10 percent for capital assets held more than 1 but less than 2 years to 70 percent for those held more than 10 years. In 1938-41 this method, with altered proportions and time periods, was combined with the reestablishment of a ceiling rate on capital gains — this time 15 percent. In 1942-50 individuals were given the option of including in taxable income only half of their net gains from capital assets held more than 6 months or of separately computing the tax on such capital gains at the flat rate of 25 percent,[7] regardless of the amount of their ordinary income, if by so doing they would pay a smaller tax. At the same time, a ceiling rate — of 25 percent — was for the first time extended to the capital gains of corporations.

The markedly preferential tax treatment of long term capital gains as compared with ordinary income in 1922-50, particularly for individuals with sizeable incomes, is illustrated in Table 88 and Chart 4. For a man with a net income of $100,000 from ordinary sources, the effective tax rate on a capital gain from an asset held more than 2 years was less than a third the rate on an additional dollar of ordinary income in 18 of the 29 years 1922-50, and was in no year more than three-fifths of the ordinary rate. In 1922 a married man with 2 dependents and an ordinary net income of $100,000 was subject to a tax rate of 56 percent on the next dollar of ordinary income, but could realize any amount of capital gains at a tax cost of only 12½ percent. By reason of successive reductions in surtax rates during the 'twenties, the disparity between taxes on capital gains and on ordinary income was reduced for a time, but even when the top surtax rate reached its lowest level, 20 percent in 1929, the combined normal and surtax of 24 percent was nearly twice as high as the maximum capital gains tax rate. Since 1937 the effective tax rates on an additional dollar of ordinary income for individuals with statutory net incomes of $5,000 or more have been from 2 to 5 times as high as those on capital gains.

The successive tax ceilings and partial exemptions for capital gains have usually been accompanied by similar ceilings and partial exclusions for capital losses. Beyond such parallel treatment, however, the deductibility of net capital losses from taxable income

---

[7] Nominally, the flat rate was 50 percent but was applicable only to half of long term net gains minus the entire amount of short term net losses.

Chart 4

Capital Gains Tax Rate as a Percentage of
Tax Rate on Ordinary Income, 3 Income Levels

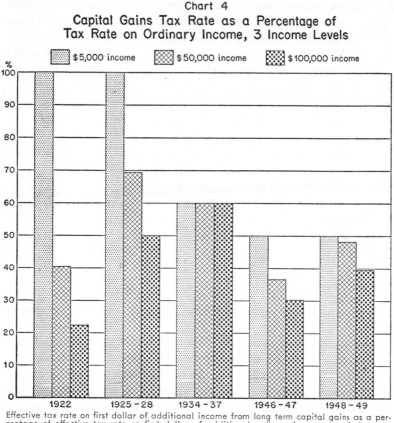

$5,000 income $50,000 income $100,000 income

Effective tax rate on first dollar of additional income from long term capital gains as a percentage of effective tax rate on first dollar of additional ordinary income; married person with 2 dependents besides his wife and with maximum earned income credit.
Rates assume assets had been held 2-5 years in 1934-37 and that joint returns were filed in 1948-49.
Source: Table 88.

(losses in excess of gains) has been arbitrarily limited at various times since 1934 to $2,000 or $1,000 or, for short term net losses, has at times been eliminated altogether.

In consequence of their preferential tax treatment, capital gains appear to enjoy a privileged status as a source of funds for both the taxpayer's current consumption spending and his accumulation of wealth. A business man with a net income of $50,000 in 1947 from salaries, dividends, and other forms of ordinary income could add more, for current spending or savings, after paying his income tax, from a capital gain of $50,000 than from an increase of $225,000 in his salary, dividends, and ordinary profits. Similarly, a $50,000 capital gain would net a $25,000 a year man more than an $185,000 increase in ordinary income. Even the $5,000 a year man would realize more after income tax from a capital gain of $50,000 than from an increase of nearly 3 times that amount in his ordinary income. The change in the tax law, beginning in 1948, that permitted husbands and wives to divide their combined incomes equally on joint returns, materially reduced the effective rates of tax on larger incomes, and, therefore, diminished the preference accorded capital gains in the middle and upper income brackets. Nevertheless, the superior tax position of capital gains remained substantial. In 1950 a married taxpayer with ordinary net income of $50,000 who filed a joint return could retain more after taxes from a long term capital gain of $50,000 than from an increase of more than $100,000 in salaries, dividends, interest, etc. If his income was otherwise $25,000, a long term capital gain of $50,000 would be worth more to him than an increase of over $83,000 in ordinary income; and if his income was otherwise $5,000, he could keep as much from a long term capital gain of $50,000 as from an increase of something more than $65,000 in ordinary income.

5 DOES THE TAXATION OF CAPITAL GAINS HAVE BAD PRACTICAL EFFECTS?

As we have noted, under the prevailing concept of realization, a capital gain or loss is not recognized by the law until the asset is sold. Hence by deferring its sale the taxpayer can postpone incurring a tax liability on the appreciation in value. If he realizes the gain, the tax absorbs a portion of his resources. If he defers the realization, he is permitted to retain without cost the use of funds that would otherwise go to the government in taxes. If he never sells, the income tax liability will be avoided altogether, for transfers at death do not legally constitute realization, and neither his estate nor the heirs will be liable for income tax on the gain.[8] As a result, any substantial taxation of capital gains gives taxpayers a motive for avoiding sales.

Ordinarily an individual taxpayer to whom wages and salaries, interest, rents, and profits are due has only limited opportunities to choose the year in which to take them into his income account. Usually he becomes subject to taxation on these types of income in the

[8] If the amount of the income tax avoided is not spent or given away during the life of the decedent, the taxable estate will be correspondingly larger (if the total exceeds the statutory exemption), and a higher estate tax will be levied. But as long as the rate of the estate tax is less than 100 percent, the addition to the estate tax cannot equal the saving in income tax.

year he obtains the right to receive them.[9] But the taxpayer commonly has unrestricted power to choose whether and when to convert an 'unrealized' rise in the market value of an investment into a realized capital gain — subject to the risk, however, that the gain will shrink or vanish if he delays. Moreover, he may obtain many of the advantages of this increase in value without selling the assets and paying a tax on the gain. If the rise reflects an actual or prospective increase in dividend income, the larger dividends will be his to enjoy without payment of a capital gains tax. If it reflects merely an improvement in the stability and security of the prospective dividends, he will similarly enjoy this enhanced security. Meanwhile, his ability to sell his asset at the new market price gives him substantially the same enlarged command over cash for contingency needs or for future investment opportunities as he would obtain by actually selling his asset now. It is true that by retaining his asset he subjects his capital to investment risks. If he sells, he obtains a new range of choice. He may retain the proceeds in liquid form, after providing for the capital gains tax. But if he expects to reinvest the proceeds, he faces new investment risks that may differ only in small degree, if at all, from his present ones. Hence any substantial tax on realized capital gains may readily dissuade him from selling assets he would otherwise be disposed to sell.

Because of this factor, it has been repeatedly contended, the capital gains taxes that have actually been in force in the United States have seriously impaired the mobility of capital assets and the efficiency with which they are used. For somewhat similar reasons, taxes on capital gains and allowances for capital losses are also charged with causing sharper fluctuations in the prices of securities

[9] If he can arrange to have these incomes technically earned by a corporation that he controls, he can regulate the flow of income to himself in considerable measure by regulating the dividend policy of the corporation, though at the expense of corporate income and other taxes and at the risk of violating the law against the improper accumulation of surplus. Individuals who receive fees and related compensation on the basis of bills to their clients, patients, or other purchasers of their services can, by delaying the presentation of the bills until after the end of the calendar or fiscal year, defer the receipt of such income by one tax year. Individuals operating a business enterprise can affect the timing of income to some extent by arranging shipments and billings so that collections will occur before the expiration of a tax year or just after it. The receipt of interest can be postponed and converted into a capital gain by buying a bond at a discount from its redemption value and refraining from amortizing the discount before redemption. For other examples, see Chapter 9.

and other capital assets than would otherwise occur. The ability of an investor or speculator to avoid the tax by refraining from selling when he has a profit is said to cause a scarcity in the supply of stocks when prices are rising, thereby accentuating the rise; while the allowance for losses accentuates a decline by encouraging selling when prices are falling. In addition, the charge generally made against all substantial taxes on profits, that they seriously impair incentives to risky investment, is made also against the tax on capital gains. We shall examine the evidence and the considerations bearing upon these contentions in Chapters 6-7.

6 ARE THE FEDERAL REVENUES FROM CAPITAL GAINS WORTH THEIR ADMINISTRATIVE COST?

The federal government's net revenues from its capital gains taxes and loss allowances have been highly erratic, bulking large at times and dwindling to relatively small proportions or negative figures at other times. They averaged $380 million a year, considering taxable returns alone, during the great stock market boom, 1926-29. In the next 3 years a net revenue loss averaging $61 million annually is estimated to have been sustained. In the decade 1935-44 the net revenues are estimated to have averaged $90 million annually (Table 90). The estimated net revenues for 1926-34 are overstated as compared with those for later years because cruder statistical procedures were employed in the earlier period and because returns reporting net deficits were excluded.

Since capital gains are realized mainly in years of high prosperity, and capital losses in years of depression, it has been argued that the inclusion of capital gains and losses in taxable income not only contributes little net revenue in the long run but also accentuates fluctuations in the government's revenues and is undesirable (though to some desirable) on this account as well.

Moreover, it is charged that even the modest revenue that has been obtained is attributable to arbitrary and inequitable limitations upon the recognition of capital losses. This argument starts with the contention that capital gains and losses tend to be equal over a period of years, for both individual taxpayers and taxpayers as a whole. In this event, the revenues produced by taxation of capital gains would be roughly offset in the long run by the revenue reductions from capital losses, if full deductibility were allowed for the latter. The complete exclusion of capital gains and losses from taxable income would be a great boon on the added account, some contend, that it would enormously reduce the litigation and administrative difficulties now encountered by the government and by taxpayers because of the difficulty of drawing a clear line between ordinary income and capital gains and losses.

7 OTHER ISSUES

In addition to the central questions whether capital gains can logically and equitably be taxed as income, and whether in any event the bad practical effects of taxing them calls for their exemption or highly preferential treatment, a number of subsidiary questions merit attention:

1) Is the taxation of capital gains an appropriate and effective method of reaching the shares of stockholders in the reinvested earnings of corporations, which are not now counted as part of the income of their stockholders?

2) How long a holding period, if any, should be required before the gain from the sale of a capital asset is treated as a capital gain rather than as ordinary income?

3) How can tax avoidance through the deliberate conversion of ordinary income into capital gains be prevented?

4) Should the tax treatment of capital losses always parallel that of capital gains, or may it properly differ in important respects?

5) Should the capital gains and losses of corporations and of individuals be treated differently?

6) If capital gains are to be taxed in some measure, should they be included in whole or in part in the ordinary income tax schedule or should they be taxed separately.

7) Should the effective tax rates for capital gains vary inversely with the period the asset is held?

8) Should any attempt be made to tax unrealized capital gains and allow deductions for unrealized capital losses?

8 AIM OF THE BOOK

We shall attempt in the following pages to throw what light we can on both the central and subsidiary questions. In connection with many points our detailed survey of the records should enable the reader to substitute knowledge for guesses or mere assertions, and in this way improve his understanding of the problems. In connection with some questions comprehensive quantitative and other factual data are not available. In these cases, as well as in those in which our quantitative data are serviceable, we seek to present an objective, critical analysis of the opposing contentions. Our purpose is not to arrive at specific recommendations concerning public policy but to provide the reader with the kind of analysis upon which he can come to a more informed judgment of his own.

NOTE: STATUTORY DEFINITION OF CAPITAL ASSETS UNDER THE
SUCCESSIVE REVENUE ACTS, 1913-1950

1913-1921

From 1913 to 1921 capital assets were not expressly distinguished in the income tax laws from other kinds of property. Gains from the sale of all kinds of property were taxable in full as ordinary income. But losses from sales of property were deductible in 1913-15 only if the property had been used in the trade or business of the taxpayer. In 1916 this limitation was somewhat liberalized to provide that losses from sales of property were deductible if the transaction had been entered into for profit.

1922-1933

The Revenue Act of 1921 (which was applicable to the income years 1922-23) was the first to define capital assets and to provide a special treatment for gains realized upon their sales by individuals. These special provisions did not affect corporations, whose capital gains continued to be treated as ordinary income until 1942.[10] Capital assets were defined as property acquired and held by the taxpayer for profit or investment more than 2 years (whether or not connected with his trade or business), exclusive of property held for the personal use or consumption of the taxpayer or his family, and exclusive of stock-in-trade or other property of a kind that would properly be included in the inventory of the taxpayer if on hand at the close of the taxable year.

In 1924 Congress modified this definition by eliminating the requirement that the property must be held for profit or investment, and the previous exclusion of property held for personal use or consumption. These changes permitted individuals to obtain the benefit of the preferentially low capital gains tax rates on their gains from sales of houses and other property purchased for reasons other than profit. This definition remained in force from 1924 through 1933.

[10] Under the Revenue Act of 1932 and subsequent revenue acts, however, corporations became subject to limitations upon the deductibility of their capital losses.

1934-1937

In 1934 Congress narrowed the exclusions from the category of capital assets. Instead of excluding all "property held by the taxpayer primarily for sale in the course of his business" it excluded "property held by the taxpayer primarily for sale *to customers* in the ordinary course of his business." (Italics ours.) At the same time, the previous exclusion of assets held 2 years or less was removed. A major purpose of these changes was to take away from professional traders and speculators in securities and commodities their former right to deduct their trading losses in full as ordinary losses. The assets in which they regularly traded had been ruled to constitute noncapital assets under the definition in effect in 1924-33 (*Donander Co.,* 29 B.T.A. 312; *Oil Shares, Inc.,* 29 B.T.A. 664). This status of their trading assets permitted them not only to deduct their trading losses in full as ordinary losses (*Ignaz Schwinn,* 9 B.T.A. 1304), but also to avoid, partly or wholly, the special disallowance of all short term net losses from securities contained in the Revenue Act of 1932, applicable to the income years 1932 and 1933. Under it losses from sales of stocks and bonds held 2 years or less were allowed only to the extent of gains from such securities. Professional traders could avoid this limitation in varying measure by offsetting their gains on their 'noncapital' assets held more than 2 years against their losses on securities held 2 years or less which were also 'noncapital' assets (*Charles Wesley Purdy,* 36 B.T.A. 572). The changed wording in the Revenue Act of 1934 had the effect of subjecting the losses of professional traders and speculators to the limited deductibility of net capital losses. On the other hand, the change did not make their gains eligible for the preferential treatment accorded long term capital gains, in most cases, because the preferential treatment was confined to gains on assets held more than 1 year, whereas the gains of professional traders and speculators are characteristically realized on assets held a shorter period.

1938-1941

From the time of the imposition of severe restrictions upon the deductibility of net capital losses, in the Revenue Act of 1934, protests were made against applying such restrictions to depreciable property. It was argued that the loss limitation unfairly penalized taxpayers who took conservative depreciation deductions and tended to prolong the use of antiquated or obsolete factories, machinery, and equipment. Before 1934 any loss incurred on the sale of machinery or buildings at a price below the depreciated value could be deducted in full from corporate income. Under the Revenue Act of 1934 such losses were allowable only up to $2,000 plus capital gains. Refusal to allow a loss upon the sale of depreciable property, while permitting depreciation to be claimed in full if the property was retained, was inconsistent and unfair, it was charged. In the Revenue Act of 1938, in response to protests of this character, Congress added depreciable property used in the trade or business of the taxpayer to the classes of goods excluded from the statutory category of capital assets. In consequence, both corporations and individuals were permitted to charge off against ordinary income the full amount of losses on the sale of buildings, machinery, and other depreciable property used in the taxpayer's trade or business. Land, however, including sites on which business buildings stood, continued to be classed as a capital asset.

The separate and unlike tax treatment of land and buildings under the Revenue Act of 1938 aroused considerable dissatisfaction. Administrative difficulties, as well as some attempts to evade taxes, resulted from the necessity of allocating the proceeds of a sale of improved property between the building, a noncapital asset, and the land, a capital asset. A loss allocated to the site could be deducted only up to $2,000 plus capital gains; a loss allocated to the building, on the contrary, could be deducted in full. In hearings before the House Ways and Means Committee during the consideration of the Revenue Act of 1939 the National Association of Manufacturers urged that the law be amended to treat all capital gains and losses of corporations as ordinary income and loss for the purpose of taxation. Other representatives of business urged that the $2,000 limitation on capital losses of corporations be removed; this position was supported by the Treasury.[11]

Congress did not adopt either proposal but provided that, beginning in 1940, the long term capital losses of corporations (losses on capital assets held more than 18 months) should be fully deductible under the corporate income tax. This provision, which applied until it was revised by the Revenue Act of 1942, did not alter the separate classification of land and real estate improvements but made the tax treatment of long term losses therefrom uniform for corporations. In addition, the Second Revenue Act of 1940, which imposed the Excess Profits Tax, provided that excess profits net income should

[11] *Revenue Revision — 1939*, Hearings, Ways and Means Committee, 76th Cong., 1st Sess., pp. 6, 148, 251, and 265.

exclude both long term net capital gains and net gains from sales of depreciable assets held more than 18 months, although net losses from sales of such depreciable assets were made fully deductible.

Since 1942

The continued necessity of determining separately the gain or loss on a building and on its site, and the continued taxability in full of any gain ascribed to buildings and other depreciable improvements to real property, led to renewed protests. Sales involving gains on such property had been relatively few in the bad business climate of 1938, but became much more conspicuous in the rearmament and war conditions of 1941 and 1942. Many properties were changing hands for conversion into armament and related production, but it was feared that other transfers were being discouraged by the full taxability of any gain ascribed to the buildings and other depreciable assets. Moreover, many sales were taking place under conditions akin to government seizure or requisition, for in addition to direct requisition of various properties under the government's war powers, the sale of others were only a little less compulsory when their owners were denied essential materials and supplies under priority and rationing restrictions.

Congress met these problems in the Revenue Act of 1942 by enacting Sections 117 (a)(1) and 117 (j) of the Internal Revenue Code. The former provided that depreciable property and real property used in a trade or business are not capital assets; hence, a net loss realized on the sale, exchange, or involuntary conversion of such an asset was made fully deductible for both income and excess profits tax purposes. The latter nevertheless provided that if the taxpayer realizes a net gain, on the whole, from sales, exchanges, or involuntary conversions of depreciable and real property used in a trade or business and owned longer than 6 months, and from long term capital assets, the gain shall be taxed as a capital gain; i.e., be subject to a maximum income tax rate of 25 percent and be exempt from excess profits tax.

The depreciable property affected by these provisions consists only of such property as is used in a trade or business of a taxpayer or is held for the production of income. The provisions do "not apply to inventories or stock in trade, or to land apart from the improvements or physical development added to it" (*Reg.* 111, Sec. 29.23) (1)-2. Nor do they apply "to bodies of minerals which through the process of removal suffer depreciation". Depreciable property includes not merely tangible assets that are subject to wear and tear — building, plant, machinery, and transportation facilities — but also certain intangible assets with a limited life — patents, licenses, copyrights, and franchises. It does not include securities or goodwill, neither of which may be depreciated (Internal Revenue Bulletin 'F', rev. Jan. 1942, pp. 85 and 88). Livestock used for draft, breeding, or dairy purposes is depreciable property.

Property 'used' in the taxpayer's trade or business is restricted to property so used at the time of the sale, exchange, or involuntary conversion. However, the property need not be in active use when sold: it may be in current use as a reserve even if it is physically idle. In stipulating that the use must be current, the Regulation merely aims to exclude properties that may once have been used in the taxpayer's trade or business but are currently not so used or are currently devoted to a different use, such as a former factory subsequently devoted to a nonbusiness use. The use qualification means also that a given article may be subject to depreciation in the hands of one owner but not in the hands of another: finished machines produced by a concern making them for sale comprise a part of the inventories of the producer, while similar machines may be part of the depreciable property of another concern.

Trade or business seems never to have been defined in the income tax statutes or the regulations issued by the Bureau of Internal Revenue. In *Ignaz Schwinn v. Commissioner,* 9 B.T.A. 1304 (1928), the Board of Tax Appeals declared: "When the expression 'trade or business' is used in the statutes in connection with losses it would seem to refer to a regular occupation or calling of the taxpayer for the purpose of livelihood or profit. . . .

It has been recognized by the courts and the Bureau of Internal Revenue that a person can be engaged in more than one trade or business."

Chapter 2

ORIGINS OF THE SPECIAL LEGAL STATUS OF CAPITAL GAINS

1 THE HARVEST TRADITION OF INCOME

The concept of income that has come down to us from the past took its character from agriculture as practiced in the Temperate Zone. In a predominantly agricultural economy, income appears to be a physical fact and to consist of the annual harvest or its worth in money. Capital too appears to be a physical fact: it is the land, predominantly.

The formal concepts of income evolved by economists during the eighteenth and most of the nineteenth centuries, though generalized in form, were based squarely upon the nature of agricultural income.[1] Income arises from purposeful economic activity, such as farming, and recurs fairly regularly with the lapse of time, e.g., with the passage of the seasons. It arises from a fixed and continuing source, such as a farm or landed estate. Like the annual harvest, it is given off by or separated from this fixed source and becomes available for independent disposition or consumption without depleting the source. Strongest of all these traditional earmarks of income is the tendency to recur at more or less regular intervals.

Casual, sporadic, and unexpected gains, whether from the sale of land, other property not ordinarily dealt in by the recipient, gifts, or otherwise derived, did not fit into this concept of income. They appeared to be the result of good luck, not the usual product of purposeful activity. Lacking a continuing source, such as a farm or business enterprise, they arose from discrete events. Hence they could not reliably be expected to recur at regular intervals. A prudent man, the conclusion was, will therefore regard them differently from ordinary income. He will treat them as additions to his capital, not available for ordinary consumption. Capital gains in this view included all unexpected receipts.

[1] See P. H. Wueller, Concepts of Taxable Income, a series of four articles in the *Political Science Quarterly,* March, June, September, and December 1938.

2 EARLY JUDICIAL CONCEPT OF INCOME DESIGNED FOR ENTAILED
   AND TRUST ESTATES

The need for a legal concept of income first arose in connection with
the common practice of landowners in England and on the Conti-
nent of entailing their estates; that is, of limiting the inheritance of
an estate to a specified line of heirs so that the estate could not be
sold by any one of them or bequeathed at his pleasure. In effect,
each succeeding heir was entitled only to the income from the estate
during his lifetime, not to any part of the principal. The courts had
to distinguish between income and principal in the sense of what
could be rightfully consumed by the life-tenant as against what
belonged to the *corpus* or body of the estate.

The resulting legal concepts of capital and income were evolved
at a time when landed property comprised the bulk of all durable
property. The courts adopted the view that a man's capital or
estate, usually a farm or group of farms, was a physical entity, and
the income from it, its separable fruit or harvest. Increases in the
capital value of an entailed estate could not be regarded as income
of the life-tenant. What had been left to him was a life-interest in
specific pieces of physical property, not in a given capital value.
He did not have a right to sell any part of the estate and therefore
could not 'realize' a gain in value if it occurred. Hence there was
no useful sense in which appreciation in the value of the estate
could be considered income. For similar reasons, declines in value
did not reduce the income allotted to the life-tenant.

Where property was not entailed or transferred in trust, the
question whether a rise or fall in value, realized or unrealized, should
be regarded as an element of income was of small practical importance because of the general immobility of ownership and the
absence of income taxes.

Since the estates of the propertied classes in postfeudal Europe
were commonly entailed, a man's wealth was better measured by his
income than by the capital value of the property from which he
drew it. And the kind of income that was significant for this purpose
was the income that could be reasonably expected, the more or
less recurring income, not unforeseen, sporadic gains. Hence in
England and in Europe generally it became traditional to measure a
man's economic position by the amount of his recurring annual
income, not by the principal amount of his estate. 'Smith is worth
£5,000 a year' illustrates the type of measure of wealth that persists
in England to this day.

3 THE PHYSICAL CONCEPT OF INVESTMENT APPLIED TO SECURITIES

When securities and saleable real estate came to constitute large parts of trust estates, the courts had to choose between assigning to the life-tenant as income or to the remainderman as principal the profits realized on sales of assets. Had it been common to think of capital or principal as a pecuniary quantity, the estate to be safeguarded might have been conceived as consisting of a given capital value, with all additions being viewed as income available for consumption. Even unrealized changes in the market value of the items comprising the estate might conceivably have been taken into account in arriving at the income available for the holder of a life-interest.

But this, we have seen, was not the case. The dominant position long held by landed property had fostered the concept of capital as a physical thing. As against the fairly elaborate accounting practices needed to administer a pecuniary or quantitative concept of capital, most owners of property until a century or so ago kept only primitive and scanty financial accounts. Although government bonds and some other securities were bought and sold to a limited extent through stockbrokers long before the organization of the London Stock Exchange in 1773, they were only a tiny and unrepresentative fraction of accumulated private wealth. For most capital assets, primarily landed properties, ready markets did not exist and sales were infrequent.

In these circumstances it is not surprising that, instead of regarding securities as quantities of pecuniary value, measured by cost or market price, the courts applied the same physical concept of capital or principal that they had long applied in the administration of landed estates.[2] A government bond in which the purchaser had invested £1,000 was regarded as a *res,* a thing. The capital investment was not the quantity of money that had been paid for the bond or its market value, but the bond itself. Hence a rise or fall in the value of the bond did not change the investment and was not an element of income. If gains were realized on the sale, they were regarded as nonincome 'accretions to capital' in much the same way as an accretion was said to take place to a piece of land when, in the course of time, a water boundary receded. Since the capital investment was regarded as a thing, not a pecuniary quantity, the

[2] See Nathan Isaacs, Principal — Quantum or *Res,* 46 *Harvard Law Review,* 776 ff. (1933); Roswell Magill, *Taxable Income* (Ronald Press, rev. ed. 1945), p. 29, 40-2.

'maintenance of capital' did not require the maintenance of its value. The entire receipts from interest payments constituted income even if the value of the bond fell below its cost and it was sold at a loss. The retention of the *res* concept of capital in the administration of various trust estates, despite a clear recognition of its alternative, was emphasized by an American court in 1927 (*Hayes v. St. Louis Union Trust Co.,* 317 Mo. 1028, 1043, 298 S. W. 91, 97): "What is the principal or corpus of the estate in cases of this kind? Is it the corporate stock, itself, or its *value* at a given time? Undoubtedly the former. If the trust estate were land, the fact would be clear."

By dint of long usage the concept of a capital investment as a *res* or thing and the correlative view that a rise or fall in its value, realized or unrealized, is not relevant for determining income became thoroughly embedded in the law and traditions of England and various other countries. When the use of incomes as a base for taxes was gradually introduced into Great Britain and Europe, mainly during the 19th century, taxable income was commonly limited to the yields from specific continuing sources. The early European income taxes were not levied upon the total incomes of *persons,* but upon the net yields of various *sources* of income, the rates often varying with the source. Net yield taxes of this type, though now usually supplemented by general personal income taxes, are still levied in most European countries.

When Great Britain inaugurated income taxation in 1798 and when she adopted her present income tax system in 1842, the *form* of the tax was that of a levy on the yields from stated sources, but the effect was that of a *personal* income tax because the same rates were applied to incomes from all sources and because nearly all kinds of income were covered. Consistent with the *res* concept of an investment, though doubtless for other reasons as well, capital gains were excluded. By long tradition capital gains were not regarded as ordinary income, and the British early adopted, and still retain, the principle that taxable income is to be determined by the practices of the business community when these do not conflict with express provisions of the law.[3]

Before World War I British practice also excluded from income tax the profits from isolated or infrequent transactions. This exclusion was in keeping with the agricultural tradition that confined the concept of income to regularly recurring receipts. It appeared to be in keeping, too, with the wording of the law, which applied to

[3] See George O. May, *Financial Accounting* (Macmillan, 1943), Ch. IV.

'annual' income. The British Revenue Act does not expressly define income as such and does not cover all forms of income. It applies only to the types described in 5 'schedules.' Schedules A, B, C, and E deal with income from specified sources, such as the rental value of lands and buildings, and interest on government bonds. Schedule D applies to "the annual profits or gains arising . . . from any kind of property whatever . . . from any trade, profession, employment or vocation," to interest annuities, "and other annual profits or gains not charged under Schedule A, B, C, or E, and not specially exempted from tax. . . ." The word 'annual' had long been interpreted to exclude occasional isolated profits. Opportunities to make sporadic, nonrecurring gains were exceptionally abundant during and immediately after World War I, and much indignation was aroused by the fact that such profits were escaping taxation.[4] The Royal Commission on the Income Tax (Par. 91) was "of the opinion that any profit made on a transaction recognizable as a business transaction, i.e., a transaction in which the subject matter was acquired with a view to profit-seeking, should be brought within the scope of the income tax, and should not be treated as an accretion of capital simply because the transaction lies outside the range of the taxpayer's ordinary business, or because the opportunities of making such profits are not likely, in the nature of things, to occur regularly at short intervals."

But the Commission distinguished such profits from those realized by "ordinary changes of investments" (Par. 90): "Profits that arise from ordinary changes of investments should normally remain outside the scope of the tax but they should nevertheless be charged if and when they constitute a regular source of profit."

The Commission's recommendations were not formally embodied in law. Instead, the Board of Inland Revenue made a vigorous and successful effort to reach the profits from single ventures of an obviously trading nature and those from a series of transactions, each of which separately would not have constituted the carrying on of a trade.[5]

4 AMERICAN CONDITIONS DIFFERED

While the economy of the United States was predominantly agricultural in its early years, realized capital gains quickly took on a more

[4] See George O. May, The British Treatment of Capital Gains, *Journal of Accountancy,* June 1942.
[5] *Ibid.*

conspicuous role than they had abroad. Land was so plentiful and cheap that its ownership did not carry the social prestige it did abroad. The strong desire to keep the descent of land ownership along family lines, so conspicuous in Europe, was relatively weak here. The purchase and sale of land and the accumulation of private fortunes through the profits from such transactions became common early in our history. On the other hand, long established and stable incomes from land rents and bond interest were rare. Later, the quick succession of economic changes created by the rapid growth of population and the discovery and exploitation of natural resources produced frequent large increases in the market values of countless business enterprises and pieces of real estate. By reason of a high degree of mobility of business men and their capital, a considerable part of such value increases was converted into realized gains.

In many transactions gains from sales of capital assets constituted the major type of profit contemplated. With little regard for the niceties of accrual accounting, profits were commonly sought and calculated on the basis of specific transactions. Opportunities for capital gains were in fact recurring. It became not uncommon for some business men to meet a part or even all of their consumption requirements from capital gains. In some sections of the country farmers acquired the reputation of buying their farms with one eye on the income to be obtained from farming and the other on the trend of land values.

In this environment capital gains became scarcely distinguishable from ordinary business profits for many business men and a familiar source of private wealth. At the same time, unlike the situation in England, the value of a man's principal or capital, rather than the income he derived from it, was generally adopted as the measure of his wealth. For these reasons the sharp distinction between ordinary income and capital gains that still prevails in England never obtained as strong a hold in the United States.

5 AMERICAN JURISPRUDENCE INHERITED THE BRITISH CONCEPTS BUT WAS GOVERNED BY DIFFERENT STATUTES

American jurisprudence inherited from the British common law the tendency to regard a capital investment as a thing, rather than as a quantity of pecuniary value equal to the original cost or market value. But when Congress expressly included the gains from capital assets in taxable income, the Supreme Court did not find this unconstitutional. The Court did, however, establish the requirement that, to be taxable as income, the gains must be 'realized.' And in ruling on the earmarks of realization, it has tended to apply the *res* as against the value concept of capital investment.

The Revenue Act of 1862, the first tax measure of the Civil War period to become effective, introduced an income tax "upon the annual gains, profits, or income of every person residing in the United States, whether derived from any kind of property, rents, interest, dividends, salaries, or from any profession, trade, employment, or vocation carried on in the United States or elsewhere, or from any other source whatever, except as hereinafter mentioned, if such annual gains, profits, or income exceed the sum of six hundred dollars. . . ."[6] Neither the Act nor the regulations referred specifically to capital gains and losses, though the language of the form for reporting the tax appeared to be broad enough to include them.[7] That profits on sales of real estate were taxable is known from the objections raised in Congress during the discussion of the Revenue Act of 1864 to a ruling of the Commissioner of Internal Revenue that profits from real estate were income in the year of sale even though they had accrued over a long period.[8] The 1864 Act altered this treatment by providing that gains and losses from sales of real estate should be taken into account in determining taxable income only when realized from property that had been acquired within the preceding year, but expressly included in "the annual gains, profits, or income" to be taxed "all income or gains derived from the purchase and sale of stocks or other property, real or personal. . . ."[9] In 1867 the law was amended (14 *Stat. L.* 471-87) by dropping the word 'annual' from the general definition of "the gains, profits or income" to be taxed; by omitting the clause quoted in the preceding sentence under which gains from the purchase and sale of stocks or other property were specifically included; and by including gains from real estate acquired during the preceding two years.

[6] The first act passed, that of 1861, never went into effect. Revenue Act of 1862, Sec. 89, Public No. 97, 37th Cong., 2d Sess., Ch. 119, 12 statutes.

[7] For a copy of the income tax regulations and an outline of the form for reporting, see C. F. Estee, *The Excise Tax Law* (Fitch, Estee, and Co., New York, 1863).

[8] J. S. Seidman, *Legislative History of the Federal Income Tax Laws, 1861-1938* (Prentice-Hall, 1938), p. 1028, cites to this effect the *Congressional Globe,* 38th Cong., 1st Sess., p. 2516.

[9] 13 *Stat. L.* 223.

In a famous case interpreting the Civil War Income Tax Act of 1867 — *Gray v. Darlington,* decided in 1872 (15 Wall. 63) — the Supreme Court declared that profits of $20,000 realized by an investor in 1869 on the sale of United States government bonds he had owned for four years were not taxable as income.

"The statute looks, with some exceptions, for subjects of taxation only to annual gains, profits, and income. Its general language is 'that there shall be levied, collected, and paid *annually* upon the gains, profits, and income of every person. . . .' This language has only one meaning, and that is that the assessment, collection, and payment prescribed are to be made upon the annual products or income of one's property or labor, or such gains or profits as may be realized from a business transaction begun and completed during the preceding year. There are exceptions, as already intimated, to the general rule of assessment thus prescribed. One of these general exceptions is expressed in the statute and relates to profits upon sales of real property, requiring, in the estimation of gains, the profits of such sales to be included where the property has been purchased, not only within the preceding year, but within the two preceding years. . . . Except, however, in these and similar cases, and in cases of sales of real property, the statute only applies to such gains, profits, and income as are strictly acquisitions made during the year preceding that in which the assessment is levied and collected.

The mere fact that the property has advanced in value between the date of its acquisition and sale does not authorize the imposition of the tax on the amount of the advance. Mere advance in value in no sense constitutes the gains, profits, or income specified by the statute. It constitutes and can be treated merely as increase of capital.

The rule adopted by the officers of the revenue in the present case would justify them in treating as gains of one year the increase in the value of property extending through any number of years, through even the entire century. The actual advance in value of property over its cost may, in fact, reach its height years before its sale; the value of the property may, in truth, be less at the time of the sale than at any previous period in ten years, yet, if the amount received exceed the actual cost of the property, the excess is to be treated, according to their views, as gains of the owner for the year in which the sale takes place. We are satisfied that no such result was intended by the statute."

Although some of the language of the opinion, particularly in the second of the three paragraphs reproduced above, reflects the traditional British distinction between income and an accretion to capital, the actual decision appears to have been based squarely upon the wording of the statute.[10] Except for gains from real estate acquired within 2 years, the statute was interpreted to apply only to annual or recurring gains. It is noteworthy that the Court did not condemn the inclusion of the specified real estate gains in taxable income.

The Revenue Act of 1870 (16 *Stat. L.,* 256-62), nearly identical with that of 1867 in its definition of income, was the last of the Civil War income tax laws. After it expired in 1873, Congress did not reimpose an income tax until 1894, when it enacted a measure (28 *Stat. L.,* 553-69) under which taxable income was defined, in part, as in the 1867 Act, as "the gains, profits, and income . . . whether said gains, profits, or income be derived from any kind of property, rents, interest, dividends, or salaries . . . or from any source whatever." Gains from the sale of real estate acquired within 2 years and the money value of gifts and inheritances were specifically included. But the Supreme Court, by a five to four decision in *Pollock v. Farmers' Loan and Trust Company,* held the Act unconstitutional on the ground that the tax was a direct tax which could be valid only if apportioned among the states in proportion to population.[11]

Fourteen years later Congress accommodated itself to this decision, as far as a tax on corporation incomes was concerned, by enacting the Corporation Excise Tax Act of 1909 (36 *Stat. L.,* 13-8) under which the tax was nominally imposed for the privilege of doing business in corporate form, but the amount of the tax was measured by 1 percent of the net income in excess of $5,000. This law was found constitutional.[12] In a leading decision interpreting it, the Supreme Court enunciated a definition of taxable income that it subsequently repeated many times: "Income may be defined as the gain derived from capital, from labor, or from both combined."[13]

In three other decisions under the 1909 Act, all handed down

[10] Magill, *op. cit.,* pp. 103-4.
[11] 157 U. S. 429, 15 Sup. Ct. 673 (1895); on rehearing 158 U. S. 601, 15 Sup. Ct. 912 (1895).
[12] *Flint v. Stone-Tracy Company,* 220 U. S. 107, 31 Sup. Ct. 342 (1911).
[13] *Stratton's Independence, Ltd. v. Howbert,* 231 U. S. 399, 34 Sup. Ct. 136 (1913).

on the same day in 1918, the Supreme Court upheld the inclusion in taxable income of realized gains derived from the appreciation of property values. In *Doyle v. Mitchell Brothers Company,* in which a lumber dealer contended that the proceeds of its sales largely represented a rise in the value of its capital assets, not a taxable gain, the Court said:[14]

"The suggestion that the entire proceeds of the conversion should be still treated as the same capital, changed only in form and containing no element of income although including an increment of value, we reject at once as inconsistent with the general purpose of the act. Selling for profit is too familiar a business transaction to permit us to suppose that it was intended to be omitted from consideration in an act for taxing the doing of business in corporate form upon the basis of the income received 'from all sources'.

. . . In order to determine whether there has been gain or loss, and the amount of the gain, if any, we must withdraw from the gross proceeds an amount sufficient to restore the capital value that existed at the commencement of the period under consideration."

In *Hays v. Gauley Mountain Coal Company,* the defendant company had realized a gain of $210,000 in 1911 on the sale of stock in another company acquired nine years before.[15] The Court held that the excess of the sales price over the value on December 31, 1908, constituted a taxable profit, and a decision to the same effect was rendered in *U. S. v. Cleveland, C., C. & St. L. Ry. Co.*[16]

6 STATUTORY PROVISION FOR TAXING REALIZED CAPITAL GAINS AS INCOME UNDER THE 16TH AMENDMENT SQUARELY UPHELD

The 16th Amendment to the Constitution was ratified on February 25, 1913. The present-day series of income tax laws begins with the first Act passed under it, that approved on October 3, 1913, effective as of March 1, 1913 (38 *Stat.* 166). Net income was defined in the following paragraph, the substance of which has been repeated in the subsequent Acts:

"That, subject only to such exemptions and deductions as are hereinafter allowed, the net income of a taxable person shall include gains, profits, and income derived from salaries, wages, or compensation, or personal service of whatever kind and in whatever form paid, or from professions, vocations, businesses, trade, commerce, or sales, or dealings in property whether real or personal, growing out

[14] 247 U. S. 179, 38 Sup. Ct. 467 (1918).
[15] 247 U. S. 189, 38 Sup. Ct. 470 (1918).
[16] 247 U. S. 195, 38 Sup. Ct. 472 (1918).

of the ownership or use of or interest in real or personal property, also from interest, rent, dividends, securities, or the transaction of any lawful business carried on for gain or profit, or gains or profits, and income derived from any source whatever."

In a series of notable decisions in 1920 and 1921 the Supreme Court crystallized its interpretation that the word 'income' includes capital gains. In *Eisner v. Macomber,* Justice Pitney, speaking for the majority, declared:[17]

"For the present purpose, we require only a clear definition of the term 'income' as used in common speech, in order to determine its meaning in the Amendment; . . . after examining the dictionaries in common use . . . we find little to add to the succinct definition adopted in two cases arising under the Corporation Act of 1909. 'Income may be defined as the gain derived from capital, from labor, or from both combined,' provided it be understood to include profit gained through a sale or conversion of capital assets."

In the *Merchant's Loan and Trust Company v. Smietanka* the Court held that the word 'income' in the 16th Amendment included a gain from a single isolated sale as well as profits from sales by one engaged in buying and selling as a business.[18] The Court said:

"It is sufficient to say of this contention, that no such distinction was recognized in the Civil War Income Tax Act of 1867, c. 169, 14 Stat. 471, 478, or in the Act of 1894, c. 349, 28 Stat. 509, 553, declared unconstitutional on an unrelated ground; that it was not recognized in determining income under the Excise Tax Act of 1909, as the cases cited, *supra,* show; that it is not to be found, in terms, in any of the income tax provisions of the Internal Revenue Acts of 1913, 1916, 1917, or 1919; that the definition of the word 'income' as used in the Sixteenth Amendment, which has been developed by this Court, does not recognize any such distinction; that in departmental practice, for now seven years, such a rule has not been applied; and that there is no essential difference in the nature of the transaction or in the relation of the profit to the capital involved, whether the sale or conversion be a single, isolated transaction or one of many. The interesting and ingenious argument, which is earnestly pressed upon us, that this distinction is so fundamental and obvious that it must be assumed to be a part of the 'general understanding' of the meaning of the word 'income' fails to convince us

[17] 252 U. S. 189, 40 Sup. Ct. 189 (1920).
[18] 255 U. S. 509, 41 Sup. Ct. 386 (1921).

that a construction should be adopted which would, in a large measure, defeat the purpose of the Amendment.

. . . In determining the definition of the word 'income' thus arrived at, this court has consistently refused to enter into the refinements of lexicographers or economists and has approved, in the definitions quoted, what it believed to be the commonly understood meaning of the term which must have been in the minds of the people when they adopted the Sixteenth Amendment to the Constitution.

The British income tax decisions are interpretations of statutes so wholly different in their wording from the acts of Congress which we are considering that they are quite without value in arriving at the construction of the laws here involved."

7 ACCRUED BUT UNREALIZED CAPITAL GAINS AND LOSSES EXCLUDED FROM DETERMINATION OF TAXABLE INCOME

On the question whether an unrealized appreciation in the value of an asset may be taxed as income the Supreme Court has consistently ruled in the negative. In *Towne v. Eisner* a unanimous court declared that Congress had not intended, when it passed the Revenue Act of 1913, to tax stock dividends as income.[19] The 1916 Act specifically included the cash value of stock dividends in taxable income. When the Standard Oil Company of California distributed a 50 percent stock dividend in 1916, charging the dividend against its accumulated surplus account, one stockholder paid under protest a personal income tax on the part of the value of the dividend that represented corporate profits accumulated after March 1, 1913, and sued to recover the amount on the ground that the stock dividend was not income. In a famous five to four decision in *Eisner v. Macomber* (see note 17), the Supreme Court held on constitutional grounds that income, to be taxable, must be realized, and that a stock dividend is not a realization. The Court declared: "Neither under the Sixteenth Amendment nor otherwise has Congress power to tax without apportionment a true stock dividend made lawfully and in good faith, or the accumulated profits behind it, as income of the stockholder.

We are clear that not only does a stock dividend really take nothing from the property of the corporation and add nothing to that of the shareholder, but that the antecedent accumulation of profits evidenced thereby, while indicating that the shareholder is

[19] 245 U. S. 418, 38 Sup. Ct. 158 (1918).

the richer because of an increase of his capital, at the same time shows he has not realized or received any income in the transaction.

. . . without selling, the shareholder, unless possessed of other resources, has not the wherewithal to pay an income tax upon the dividend stock. Nothing could more clearly show that to tax a stock dividend is to tax a capital increase, and not income, than this demonstration that in the nature of things it requires conversion of capital in order to pay the tax.

. . . Secondly, and more important for present purposes, enrichment through increase in value of capital investment is not income in any proper meaning of the term."

The Court made liberal use of italics to emphasize that to constitute income the gain must be separated from the capital:

"Here we have the essential matter: *not* a gain accruing to capital, not a *growth* or *increment* of value *in* the investment; but a gain, a profit, something of exchangeable value *proceeding from* the property, *severed from* the capital however invested or employed, and *coming in,* being *derived,* that is, received or *drawn by* the recipient (the taxpayer) for his *separate* use, benefit and disposal; — *that* is income derived from property."

As Professor Magill has pointed out, the decision does not explain the Court's reasons for holding why a mere growth in the value of an investment cannot be regarded as income; why a gain, to be income, must be severed from capital (*op. cit.,* p. 18). Professor T. R. Powell, in an often-quoted comment upon this decision, declared:

"Nothing in the nature of things makes separation from capital one of the requisites of income from capital. From a practical commonsense point of view, there is something strange in the idea that a man may indefinitely grow richer without being subject to an income tax."[20]

In accordance with the Court's decision, Congress expressly provided in the Revenue Act of 1921 and in subsequent revenue acts until 1936 that "a stock dividend shall not be subject to tax". The Treasury interpreted this to mean that a corporation might issue any class of its own stock as a dividend to its stockholders without subjecting the latter to income tax on it.[21] The common stockholders might receive a tax-free dividend of 6 percent preferred

[20] Income from Corporate Dividends (1922), 35 *Harvard Law Review,* 363, 376.
[21] Articles 115-8, Treas. *Reg.* 86 (1934).

stock, for example. But in 1936, in *Koshland v. Helvering* (298
U. S. 441, 56 Sup. Ct. 767), the Supreme Court declared: "where
a stock dividend gives the stockholder an interest different from
that which his former stock holdings represented, he receives income," and "the latter type of dividend is taxable under the Sixteenth
Amendment". Congress promptly removed the blanket statutory
exemption it had apparently granted to stock dividends since the
Macomber decision of 1920, and replaced it with one reading:

"A distribution made by a corporation to its shareholders in
its stock or in rights to acquire its stock shall not be treated as a
dividend to the extent that it does not constitute income to the
shareholder within the meaning of the Sixteenth Amendment to
the Constitution."

The Treasury Department soon brought a case before the
Supreme Court in which the issues decided in *Eisner v. Macomber*
might be reconsidered.[22] The Court, however, on the ground that
Congress had not intended to tax the stock dividends in question,
refused to reconsider the Macomber decision. A minority of the
Court, nevertheless, was ready to do so. Speaking for the minority
of three justices, Mr. Justice Douglas declared (pp. 409-11):

"The wealth of stockholders normally increases as a result of the
earnings of the corporation in which they hold shares. I see no
reason why Congress could not treat that increase in wealth as
'income' to them. . . . The notion that there can be no 'income' to
the shareholders in such a case within the meaning of the Sixteenth
Amendment unless the gain is 'severed from' capital and made
available to the recipient for his 'separate use, benefit and disposal'
. . . will not stand analysis. . . . The narrow question here is whether
Congress has the power to make the receipt of a stock dividend
based on earnings an occasion for recognizing that accrual of wealth
for income tax purposes."

8 RATIONALE OF THE REALIZATION DOCTRINE

The Supreme Court's insistence that a capital gain must be realized
in order to be taxable as income is consistent with the traditional
judicial view that a taxpayer's capital investment consists of the
thing, the *res,* rather than its value, the land or factory building or
share of stock or bond, not its money cost or its market price. As
long as the gain is embodied in the same investment entity, the
taxpayer is said not to have anything more than he had before.

[22] *Helvering v. Griffiths,* 318 U. S. 371, 63 Sup. Ct. 636 (1943)

When it is separated from this entity or when the investment is sold, the gain constitutes taxable income. In holding that realized capital gains are income, however, the Supreme Court has applied the *res* concept in less extreme form than the British. The latter have continued to regard realized, like unrealized gains, as mere 'accretions to capital': what the seller receives is only the money value of the investment entity he possessed before; the entire proceeds of the sale merely replaces the capital investment he gives up.

As we have observed, the *res* concept was convenient in an agricultural economy with only rudimentary accounting practices. Under present conditions it is much less so. A landed estate could once be presumed to last forever. But much of present-day capital equipment has a relatively short life. To determine net income now requires pecuniary appraisals of the amounts of capital value used up through the depreciation and obsolescence of assets, even when the latter retain the same physical dimensions as before. Stocks and bonds now form a major part of private property, and these are passed frequently from hand to hand by transient owners, quite unlike the landed estates of postfeudal England. Their market value is often their most significant aspect for the investor. A rise in their value gives him the same addition to his command over economic goods and services as an equal addition to his savings from other sources; a fall, the same decrease.

For these reasons, outside the courts, the physical aspects of capital and income have receded into the background and the pecuniary or value aspects have assumed predominance. A man's capital today tends to be regarded as a quantity of pecuniary value that may be shifted from one investment to another. And because the investment is viewed as a quantity of value, not as a thing or series of things, the ancient judicial distinction between income and an 'accretion to capital' now sounds archaic to laymen and is not always intelligible to them. The *res* concept of capital gives rise to such anomalies in England as the nonallowance of depreciation in the determination of taxable income from buildings other than factories, and the nonrecognition of deductions for depletion. In the modified form in which the concept has been applied in the United States such anomalies are greatly reduced. But the requirement that gains must be 'realized' to be taxable frequently produces highly unequal tax treatment as between individuals who realize and those who do not realize their gains. For example, a man whose $5,000 investment in an industrial enterprise becomes worth $5 mil-

lion during his lifetime may leave his fortune to his children without
ever paying an income tax on the amount of the increase by merely
not selling the stock or trading it in a taxable exchange. (Of course
he will have been subject to income tax on any cash dividends and
certain stock dividends he may have received.)

In accordance with the value concept of a capital investment,
some economists contend that income in the sense of a man's
capacity to contribute to the support of government properly
includes both the amount of his consumption expenditures and all
net additions to the value of his property during a given period.
R. M. Haig's definition, "Income is the money value of the net
accretion to one's economic power between two points of time" is
of this character.[23] So is Henry Simons' view: "Personal income
may be defined as the algebraic sum of (1) the market value of
rights exercised in consumption and (2) the change in the value
of the store of property rights between the beginning and the end
of the period in question."[24] Georg Schanz proposed a similar view
in Germany in 1896.[25]

Nevertheless, no one can contend that the popular conception of
income includes unrealized or 'paper' profits and losses. The income
tax statute depends for its successful administration upon the cooperation of millions of individual and corporate taxpayers, each
of whom is responsible for making out his tax return. The legal
concept of income should therefore approximate that of the intelligent layman. Even if the popular conception were altered through
education and experience to include unrealized gains and losses, the
difficulties of administering a concept of income that required an
appraisal of every taxpayer's assets each year would be forbidding.
The liquidation of capital assets is often costly, and the market value
of a small amount of a given asset, say 100 shares of X Company
common stock, is sometimes not a reliable measure of the price
that could be obtained if a much larger amount had to be sold. For
these and other reasons, the valuations would in many cases have to
be conjectural and therefore subject to dispute; and the accounting
and auditing requirements of both taxpayers and tax enforcement
officials would be multiplied.

[23] The Concept of Income, *The Federal Income Tax* (Columbia University
Press, 1926), Ch. 1.
[24] *Personal Income Taxation* (University of Chicago Press, 1938), p. 50.
[25] Der Einkommenbegriff und die Einkommensteuergesetze, *Finanz Archiv*,
XIII (1896), 23.

Nor is the popular conception without merit. Changes in the market values of capital assets are often transitory. To take account of all changes might entail much burdensome bookkeeping with little net result. Even when a rise in value appears to be more lasting, the taxpayer who does not sell might be gravely inconvenienced or injured if he had to pay a tax on his imputed gain under the income tax in the year in which it arises. To sell a portion of his asset to raise funds to pay the tax might be impractical or unduly costly. In short, we might wholly agree with the general validity of the position taken by Haig, Simons, Schanz, and some others, but still hold that the appropriate and convenient time to take account of changes in the value of a man's property is when he realizes the gains or losses.

What constitutes 'realization', however, is a critical question. If only sales for cash were deemed to occasion realization for tax purposes, the door would be opened wide for avoiding taxes on capital gains. Since many if not most sellers of capital assets sooner or later reinvest rather than consume the proceeds, they could contrive, possibly with the aid of third parties, to have their sales take the form of exchanges of some types of capital assets for others. A man might exchange a parcel of real estate for marketable securities having a value several times the cost of the real estate to him, without technically realizing a gain. If an investor wanted to take his profits in General Motors common stock and to shift his funds to Bethlehem Steel common, he might have a broker arrange an exchange, instead of a sale and purchase, and so avoid realizing a taxable gain. Or a corporation might distribute its accumulated profits as dividends consisting of marketable shares of preferred and common stocks in subsidiary or affiliated or even unrelated corporations, without making its stockholders liable to income taxes on the distributions.

But the Supreme Court, by a broad construction of 'realization', removed most of these possibilities of avoiding income taxes on capital gains. In *Peabody v. Eisner* it held that the gain need not be realized in money but might occur in connection with the receipt of property having an exchangeable value.[26] Exchanges of property, no less than sales, may give rise to taxable gains. The Court's rulings in 1920, that the receipt of a stock dividend in the Macomber case did not constitute taxable income to the stockholder even though the dividend represented accumulated profits, has been of

[26] 247 U. S. 347, 38 Sup. Ct. 546 (1918).

much narrower application than was at first supposed. In a series of leading cases concerning new securities received by stockholders in connection with corporate reorganizations, decided between 1921 and 1925,[27] it held that the stockholders realized taxable income when they received securities differing in kind or extent from their previous holdings.[28] When a gain previously accrued was realized by being separated from the investment, it was held to be taxable income even if the value of the investment declined by an amount corresponding to the gain. This was the situation of the stockholders of the Prairie Oil and Gas Company who were held to be liable for income tax on the value of the stock they received in a new pipeline company the parent company created to separate its pipeline business from its oil and gas operations.[29] In short, the realization doctrine has often functioned in practice not so much to deny that unrealized gains are truly gains as to determine the appropriate time or occasion for taking account of them for tax purposes. The chief exceptions are that transfers of property at death or by *inter vivos* gifts are not regarded as occasioning realization of capital gains or losses.

9 CORPORATE REORGANIZATIONS AND THE REALIZATION DOCTRINE

Even the realization doctrine, as applied by the Court, led to the creation of income tax liabilities sooner, in many instances, than Congress deemed wise or appropriate. These instances occurred mainly in connection with corporate mergers, consolidations, recapitalizations, and reorganizations. The stock- and bondholders of corporations participating in such readjustments commonly received new securities in exchange for their old ones. Before the Revenue Act of 1921 such exchanges were in some cases held to be the equivalent of sales, requiring the participants to report as a realized gain or loss any difference in value between the securities received and the cost or other basis of the securities surrendered.

Two objections were forcefully voiced against recognizing gain or loss for tax purposes on exchanges of this character. First, many

[27] *U. S. v. Phellis,* 257 U. S. 156, 42 Sup. Ct. 63 (1921); *Rockefeller v. U. S.,* 257 U. S. 176, 42 Sup. Ct. 68 (1921); *Cullinan v. Walker,* 262 U. S. 134, 43 Sup. Ct. 495 (1923); *Weiss v. Stearn,* 265 U. S. 242, 44 Sup. Ct. 490 (1924); and *Marr v. U. S.,* 268 U. S. 536, 45 Sup. Ct. 575 (1925). See Magill, *op. cit.,* for a brief account of these cases.

[28] James Parker Hall, Exchange of Securities in Corporate Reorganization as Income, 20 *Illinois Law Review* 601 (1926).

[29] *Rockefeller v. U. S.,* 257 U. S. 176, 42 Sup. Ct. 68 (1921).

corporate readjustments that involve the issuance of new securities for old do not interrupt the continuity of the taxpayer's investment or alter its essential character. The investor does not receive any money; the new securities merely replace the old ones. To require him to pay a tax on the paper profit imputed in such a transaction may force him to sell a portion of the securities and to make the sale at an unfavorable time as well. He is in essentially the same position as an investor with an unrealized gain.

Second, when all or many such exchanges are treated as occasioning a realization of gain or loss, corporate officials and securities owners hesitate to make various normal and useful readjustments in capital structures and intercorporate relations for fear of incurring immediate tax liabilities. During the Congressional hearings on the Revenue Act of 1921 it was contended that many corporate reorganizations the depression of 1920-21 had made desirable were being impeded by this fear.[30]

In response to these considerations, Congress specified in the Revenue Act of 1921 that no gain or loss shall be recognized in connection with certain classes of exchanges even if the property received in exchange has a realizable market value. The aim was not permanently to exclude these gains and losses from the income tax but to postpone recognition until a more appropriate occasion, i.e., sale. Wide openings for tax avoidance through the so-called reorganization provisions were soon discovered, however. Successive attempts to close the loopholes were made in the Revenue Acts of 1923, 1924, 1926, 1928, 1932, 1934 and, in minor ways, since. Under present law, which in the main embodies the elaborately contrived revisions enacted in 1934, 6 kinds of reorganization are defined in connection with which exchanges of property may take place without the recognition of gain or loss:

1) A statutory merger or consolidation by which one corporation absorbs another, or two or more corporations unite to form a new one.

2) The acquisition by one corporation, in exchange solely for all or a part of its voting stock, of at least 80 percent of the voting stock and at least 80 percent of all other classes of stock of another corporation.

3) The acquisition by one corporation, in exchange solely for all

---

[30] See *Hearings on Revenue Revision,* Ways and Means Committee, 66th Cong., 3d Sess.; *Report of the Ways and Means Committee,* 67th Cong., 1st Sess. (House Report 350); Seidman, *op. cit.,* p. 790.

or a part of its voting stock, of substantially all the properties of another corporation.

4) A transfer by a corporation of all or a part of its assets to another corporation if, immediately after the transfer, the transferor or its shareholders or both are in control of the corporation to which the assets are transferred.

5) A recapitalization.

6) A mere change in identity, form, or place of organization.

In addition, the *Internal Revenue Code,* Section 112 (b) (5) specifies: "No gain or loss shall be recognized if property is transferred to a corporation by one or more persons solely in exchange for stock or securities in such corporation, and immediately after the exchange such person or persons are in control of the corporation; but in the case of an exchange by two or more persons this paragraph shall apply only if the amount of stock or securities received by each is substantially in proportion to his interest in the property prior to the exchange. . . ." (Control is defined as ownership of stock possessing at least 80 percent of the total combined voting power of all classes of stock entitled to vote and at least 80 percent of the total number of shares of all other classes of stock.)

In seeking to confine the taxpayer's advantage from the nonrecognition provisions to postponement of, rather than exemption from, tax liability, Section 113 (a) (6), requires him to measure the gain on any subsequent sale of the property he receives by a basis determined by the original cost of the property given for it, minus any money received and plus any gain recognized. When a corporation issues its own stock as a consideration for property, the basis of the property acquired is the cost to the transferor, increased by the amount of any gain or decreased by the amount of any loss recognized by the latter in the transfer (Sec. 113 (a) (7)). In these ways, the law endeavors to take account eventually of the appreciation or depreciation occurring up to the time a piece of property is transferred in a tax-free exchange.

Specific as the reorganization provisions appear to have become, they still leave considerable room for judicial interpretation. The question of the distinction between an outright sale and a reorganization has arisen repeatedly. In *Pinellas Ice and Coal Storage Company v. Commissioner,* 287 U. S. 469 (1933), the assets of two companies were transferred to another company for cash and short term notes. The Court held that this was not a reorganization, observing that to rule otherwise "would make evasion of taxation very easy". In a series of decisions the Court appears to have arrived at the broad rule that, as respects the consideration received in what purports to be a tax-free reorganization rather than a sale, "common and preferred stock in sufficient proportion passes the test, while bonds do not".[31] The Court has indicated that a continuity of proprietary interest in the reorganized company must be maintained by the shareholders in the predecessor company.[32] It has excluded various tax-avoidance schemes by requiring that the exchange of assets by one corporation with another in a tax-free reorganization must have a business purpose, not merely the purpose of avoiding taxes.[33] It has held that the earnings of the predecessor companies participating in a tax-free reorganization are the earnings of the successor too, and therefore constitute taxable dividends when distributed to the shareholders. It thus prevented the use of reorganizations for the purpose of effecting tax-free distributions of accumulated corporate earnings. In all these respects it has generally insisted that the spirit as well as the letter of the law be observed. To be tax-free the exchanges must be "required by business exigencies" and must "effect only a readjustment of continuing interest in property under modified corporate forms".[34] The consequence has been to narrow the opportunities for tax-avoidance. Taking its language in part from the decisions of the Court, Congress amended the Internal Revenue Code in 1943 (Sec. 129) to provide that persons who obtained control of a corporation on or after October 8, 1940 and corporations that acquired the property of others the basis of which is also transferred, for the principal purpose of evading or avoiding income or excess profit taxes, are denied the deductions, credits, or other allowances requisite to attaining that end.

10 CONGRESS POSSESSES WIDE LATITUDE IN THE TAX TREATMENT OF CAPITAL GAINS AND LOSSES

In the light of these judicial decisions, Congress possesses wide constitutional powers respecting the tax treatment of capital gains and losses. It may tax realized capital gains in full as ordinary income, as it did under the income tax laws of 1913 through 1920. It may subject them to lower rates of tax or exempt varying proportions,

[31] Randolph E. Paul, *Studies in Federal Taxation,* 3d Series (Harvard University Press, 1940), p. 104.

[32] *Ibid.,* pp. 104-21, and Magill, *op. cit.,* pp. 153-62.

[33] *Gregory v. Helvering,* 293 U. S. 465 (1935); and *Lea v. Commissioner,* 96 F (2nd) 55 (1938).

[34] Treas. *Reg.* 103, Sec. 19, 112 (g)-1.

as it has done in one fashion or another at different times since 1921. There is no reason to believe that it lacks the power to exempt them altogether from ordinary income taxes. Its power to allow or to disallow deductions for losses to any extent it deems desirable is beyond dispute. Only the power to tax unrealized gains has been denied by the Supreme Court. Even here, there is a strong possibility that the Court might uphold at least the optional inventorying of securities and other capital assets on the basis of market value, if Congress saw fit to extend this privilege. Dealers in securities are at present permitted to inventory their holdings on the basis of market value if they choose. (Ordinary business concerns are usually required to account for their inventories on the basis of cost, or the lower of cost or market value, or on a 'last-in first-out' basis.[35]) If the law so permitted, the investor who elected to inventory his securities on a market value basis would, in effect, acquire the right to deductions for unrealized capital losses in exchange for agreeing to subject his unrealized profits to taxation. In the opinion of Professor Magill, the decision of the Supreme Court in *Helvering v. Independent Life Insurance Company* indicates that an optional provision of this kind would be valid.[36]

That the Court would uphold the *compulsory* inventorying of capital assets on a market value basis as a part of a general method of accounting and reporting for income tax purposes is doubtful, though not inconceivable. Although the issue is by no means clear, Professor Magill has pointed to several recent decisions indicating that such a plan might be upheld.[37] Whether Congress could constitutionally treat as income unrealized capital gains embodied in property transferred by *inter vivos* gift or at death is a major unsettled question.

Within these relatively moderate constitutional barriers Congressional policy is free to respond, in framing the tax treatment of capital gains and losses, to considerations of equity, economic effects, and administrative convenience. In beginning our discussion of these considerations, we turn first to the economic nature and sources of capital gains and losses.

[35] *Ibid., Reg.* 111, Sec. 29.22, (c)-5 and (c)-2; Sec. 22 (d).

[36] 292 U. S. 371, 54 Sup. Ct. 758 (1934); Magill, *op. cit.,* p. 121.

[37] *Op. cit.,* pp. 119-20. Magill cites *Helvering v. Bruun,* 309 U. S. 461, 60 Sup. Ct. 631 (1940); *Helvering v. Midland Mutual Life Insurance Company,* 300 U. S. 216, 57 Sup. Ct. 423 (1937).

Chapter 3

The Economic Nature of Capital Gains and Losses

Just how capital gains and losses differ from ordinary income in an economic sense is not often analyzed closely, and somewhat varied concepts have been used in different connections.

1 FROM THE STANDPOINT OF GENERAL ECONOMIC THEORY

From the standpoint of general economic theory the essential element in a capital gain or loss is its unexpected character. An expected rise in the price of *any* asset is ordinary income; an unexpected rise, a capital gain.[1]

The general economic theorist is broadly interested in the motivation, rewards, and behavior of business enterprises and consumers, and in the allocation of scarce resources among competing uses. Expected advances in prices and expected excesses of receipts over expenditures may reasonably be regarded as ordinary income because, like other kinds of income, they serve to attract and allocate our energies and resources. Moreover, we may spend an equal amount without reducing our capital. Unexpected gains, on the contrary, cannot serve as motives and guides to conduct and, not being known in advance, cannot be regarded as available for spending in the period in which they arise. They become a part of our capital without passing through our foreseen income. Similarly, expected losses, such as can be provided for systematically by insurance premiums or reserves for bad debts, fire, the wear and tear of machinery, are viewed as deductions from ordinary income, while unexpected losses, such as those from earthquakes, war, legislation, are regarded as capital losses, not chargeable against current income. Differences between the amounts of expected and actually realized

[1] Cf. J. R. Hicks, *Value and Capital* (Oxford University Press, 1939), Ch. XIV; Gunnar Myrdal, *Monetary Equilibrium* (Hodge, Glasgow, 1939), pp. 59-62; A. C. Pigou, *Public Finance*, pp. 102-3; J. M. Keynes, *General Theory of Employment, Interest and Money*, pp. 52-61; *A Treatise on Money* (Macmillan, London, 1929, 1936, and 1930 respectively), pp. 124-6.

income — between income *ex ante* and *ex post* (to borrow expressions introduced by the Swedish economists) are often called 'windfall gains and losses'. While not always so recognized, they are identical in principle with capital gains and losses as defined above.

2 THE CONVENTIONAL AND LEGAL CONCEPTS

The conventional view of capital gains and losses, which is the basis of the legal concept, appears at first sight to be entirely different. Here the emphasis is not nominally upon the presence or absence of surprise but upon the special character of capital assets. Assets used for capital purposes are quasi-permanent holdings acquired and owned for the incomes to be derived from them, not for selling at a profit. The capital investment consists of the physical asset, not its value. A rise in the value of a capital asset does not alter the real position of the owner; he has the same asset as before. Even if he sells it at a profit he is no better off the day after selling it than he was the day before. He will need the entire proceeds of the sale to repurchase the same asset or to buy another as good. Hence, whether or not realized by sale, a change in the value of a capital asset is not an addition to or subtraction from true income. In this view, which clearly descends from the physical, as against the value, concept of capital, a capital gain or loss occurs only in connection with a 'capital' asset.

The practical difference between the two views shrinks, however, when we inquire more closely into what is meant by a capital asset. For many purposes, capital may be regarded as wealth devoted to further production. For a country as a whole, excluding property rights in assets abroad, it is embodied in specific tangible goods such as roads, residential and factory buildings, machines, and inventories of various kinds. But for any individual or firm, capital includes also the value of intangible rights or claims held against others, such as bank deposits, leases, corporate securities, and government bonds — claims that are canceled by the corresponding liabilities of the others when the wealth or capital of a country as a whole is measured. The capital of an individual or firm therefore includes the value of all its property rights in both physical assets and securities. Yet conventionally, not all the items entering into a man's capital are regarded as capital assets. Excluded are goods acquired for early resale or for speedy transformation into goods to be offered for sale. The designation 'capital assets' is conventionally reserved for more or less 'fixed' assets the owner expects to hold for the income they yield in money or services, not to use up quickly or to sell soon. The distinction between capital assets and other property is not primarily in the character of the asset but in the owner's intention. The same machine that constitutes a capital asset for the factory owner who buys it is merely ordinary merchandise in the hands of its manufacturer and in those of the dealer who carries it in stock for sale to customers.

The conventional and legal distinction between an ordinary good and a capital asset rests, therefore, upon the presumed intention of the owner; and, to the degree that the presumption is valid, the resulting distinction between a capital gain and ordinary income closely approximates that made by economists. Profits on sales of merchandise constituting a part of a firm's stock-in-trade are presumed to be expected, although unforeseen changes in prices often vitiate the presumption. The usual rise in the value of a machine as it passes through the hands of a dealer is only an expected reimbursement for the dealer's costs and compensation for his services. Because it is expected, it is ordinary income. On the other hand, one does not usually sell one's capital assets. Hence the profits realized on sales of such assets are presumed to be unexpected and to constitute capital gains rather than ordinary income. For the *dealer* in real estate, securities, and similar property the profits are presumed to be expected and are recognized as ordinary income, not capital gains. The law cannot inquire closely into the intentions of each owner; it must be satisfied, for administrative reasons, with categorical presumptions.

The underlying kinship of the theoretical and the conventional view of capital gains and losses is further reflected by the attitude of business men toward expected and unexpected events. Expected losses are treated as items of operating expense or negative income, not capital loss, even when they are on capital assets. Deductions from gross earnings for reserves against loss by fire (by firms not insured by others) and the exceptionally rapid amortization of the costs of wartime plant additions are examples. The profits and losses due to unforeseen changes in the wholesale value of inventories are widely viewed as capital gains and losses rather than ordinary income, even though the law does not recognize these as such, and, for this and other reasons, the accounts seldom reflect this view.

3 FROM THE STANDPOINT OF NATIONAL INCOME ANALYSIS

Students of national income too have encountered, among many other problems, that of defining and dealing with capital gains and

losses in a manner suitable for their purposes. Conceivably, they
might have defined national income as the sum of the value of goods
and services consumed during a year plus the value of the net addition to the stock of wealth, with the value figures adjusted as well
as possible for changes in the value of money by the application of
price indexes. For the most part, however, they have conceived of
national income as the current product of *deliberate* economic
activity, of the nation's economic *effort*. They exclude extraordinary
additions to or subtractions from a nation's wealth during a year,
such as those caused by discoveries of new mineral resources on the
one hand, and destruction by war or earthquake, on the other, calling these capital gains and losses. Although conceding that these and
other 'accidental changes' affect the value of wealth at the disposal
of the inhabitants of the country, Simon Kuznets, for example,
declares that they are not the "results of productive activity broadly
defined. . . ."[2] It will be observed that this treatment is similar to the
exclusion of unexpected gains and losses from the concept of income
adopted by many general economic theorists for analyzing individual
behavior.

Also termed capital gains and losses by Kuznets and other students of national income are those arising from changes in the prices
of previously existing assets. No formal distinction is made between
'expected' and 'unexpected' changes, and none between merely nominal gains and losses — in which the rise or fall in price is only proportional to a shift in the general price level — and relative price
changes — those that result when the change in price is disproportionate to or different in direction from that in the general price
level. The gains and losses from all such changes in price are regarded as transfers of wealth or income rather than new additions
or reductions. They are viewed as different from income on the
ground that they are not the product of effort, cost, or input, and
because, in Kuznets' words, "they are not increments to or drafts
upon the heap of goods produced by the economic system for consumption or for stock destined for future use".[3]

[2] *National Income and its Composition,* 1919-38 (NBER, 1941), pp. 13-4.
[3] *Ibid.,* p. 12. For a criticism of the underlying logic of aggregating pecuniary
values to measure national income, see Lionel Robbins, *The Nature and
Significance of Economic Science* (London, Macmillan, 2d ed., 1935), p. 57;
and for a criticism of the concept of income as a quasi-physical collection of
goods and services, see H. C. Simons in *Studies in Income and Wealth, Volume Two* (NBER, 1938), pp. 255-9.

A concept or definition of national income framed to measure the current output of deliberate economic activity is not necessarily best for all purposes. Hicks, for example, holds that total realized income, including unexpected elements, is more appropriate for measuring economic progress.[4] Some economists who object in principle to excluding some or any capital gains from national income nevertheless concede that, as a practical matter, because of difficulties in evaluating capital gains and losses and in assigning them to any particular year, it is wise to set up a concept of national income that excludes them.[5]

The same and other economists insist that for some purposes, however, it is essential to include them in national income. These purposes are chiefly taxation, the distribution of income by income groups, the division of family incomes between the amounts saved and spent, and estimating expenditures for different types of commodities and services.[6]

One consequence of excluding from national income all 'extraordinary' gains resulting from discoveries and the like, and all created by changes in the prices of capital assets, is that inadequate account is taken of the fruits of much deliberate economic activity. The man who makes a so-called capital gain on a piece of land by erecting a building on a part of it to enhance the value of the rest performs a deliberate and effort-taking productive service. A firm that makes a business of exploring promising territory for oil, then realizes capital gains by selling the oil-bearing acreage it finds for more than its total cost is likewise engaged in deliberate productive activity. In these and many other types of cases, what pass for capital gains in ordinary parlance and in the income tax figures are the more or less expected fruits of deliberate economic activity, identical with or closely akin to ordinary business profits. This subject is discussed in some detail below.

4 CAPITAL GAINS AND CHANGES IN THE PRICE LEVEL

Many persons loosely assume that all or most capital gains and losses merely reflect changes in the general price level, in the value

---

[4] *Op. cit.*, p. 179.

[5] See M. A. Copeland and E. M. Martin in *Studies in Income and Wealth, Volume Two*, p. 242.

[6] *Ibid.*; see also the remarks of Roy Blough, W. W. Hewett, and Harold Groves in the same volume; Clark Warburton in *Studies in Income and Wealth, Volume One*, pp. 97-101; Carl S. Shoup, *Principles of National Income Analysis* (Houghton Mifflin, 1947), pp. 116-9.

of money. Doubtless many capital gains and losses are of this character. But large amounts are not. While all capital gains and losses are occasioned by changes in price, it is essential for clear understanding to distinguish between those that arise from a change in the price of one asset relative to others and those that merely reflect a change in the general price level. The latter are nominal or unreal in the same sense that a rise in wages may be said to be unreal if it merely equals a rise in the general price level. Such capital gains and losses might well be called illusory or spurious in contradistinction to those that change the recipient's real command over the world's goods and services. No rise in the general price level is needed to create a capital gain for the owner of common stock in a concern that patents a highly profitable product or that builds up a popular following for its branded unpatented goods. Many downtown business sites in our larger cities appreciated greatly in value during the long period of declining commodity prices in the last quarter of the 19th century. Strictly speaking, a capital gain or loss arising from a change in the price of a capital asset refers to one caused by a change in its *relative* price.

In practice, real and illusory capital gains and losses are seldom distinguished. They cannot be separated in the aggregate figures reported in *Statistics of Income* because detailed tabulations by length of ownership of the assets sold are not made. The fact that the same dollar amount of capital gains or losses may represent a 'real' change in his command over goods and services for one investor and a wholly illusory change for another creates one of the difficulties of framing a satisfactory tax treatment for capital gains and losses.

5 CONSUMPTION AS INCOME

In addition to the preceding views of capital gains as such, one broad definition of income, most thoroughly elaborated by Irving Fisher, has special application to capital gains: income consists only of services consumed and excludes all additions to or subtractions from one's wealth.[7] An increase in the value of a man's property, whether from ordinary savings or from a capital gain, represents, in this view, merely an increase in the value of the prospective future incomes to be obtained from his property, not an addition to his current income. To count such an increase as a part of his current

[7] Income, *Encyclopaedia of the Social Sciences,* and *Nature of Capital and Income* (Macmillan, 1932 and 1906 respectively), pp. 249-54; H. W. Fisher, co-author, *Constructive Income Taxation* (Harper, 1942), Ch. 7.

income and then also to count as income the receipts (when they are later received and consumed) previously discounted by the rise in value is to count the same thing twice, Fisher argued. By the same reasoning the consumption of capital is regarded as adding to current income.

Wisely or not, the world has not adopted this concept of income. Generally speaking, additions to a man's capital through savings are treated as a part of his income for tax and other purposes. The arguments for and against treating capital gains and losses in the same way are reviewed in Chapter 5.

6 PURE CAPITAL GAINS ARE WINDFALLS

Although the view that a capital gain is an unexpected increase in the value of a person's property seems to have wide acceptance among economists today, it is rarely expounded explicitly. For this reason and in order to point out some of its practical limitations, we examine it in some detail. We start with what might be called the pure theory of capital gains and losses and a naive concept of expectation. Subsequently we subject this concept to critical scrutiny and bring out the kinship of capital gains with various kinds of business profits.

In the purest sense, then, capital gains are windfall additions to the value of a man's property. That is, in the economic, in contrast to the conventional or legal sense, they are best regarded as unforeseen increases in the real value of a man's previously existing property, not directly attributable to his efforts, intelligence, capital, or risk-taking.[8] The investor may indeed have exerted himself intelligently, and doubtless he committed his capital and incurred risks. But the rewards he seeks or receives for these services are, as most economists see them, wages, interest, and 'ordinary' profits. He obtains a pure capital gain only to the extent that an unsought, uncalculated, unexpected, fortuitous rise takes place in the value of one of his previously existing assets.

Such a rise is different from the normal expected increase in the price of a good as it passes along any part of the route from mine or farm to manufacturer, wholesaler, jobber, retailer, and consumer.

[8] Cf. Pigou's definition of windfall gains in his *Public Finance,* p. 180; see also Roy Blough and W. W. Hewett, Capital Gains in Income Theory and Taxation Policy, *Studies in Income and Wealth, Volume Two,* pp. 191-216, and W. W. Hewett, *Definition of Income and Its Application in Federal Taxation* (*University of Pennsylvania,* 1925), pp. 1-91, as well as the other works cited in note 1.

A good alters its character, becomes a different product, as it moves along this route, for various cost-entailing services are added to it, such as transportation, packaging, and storage, and it faces new conditions of demand and supply. A pure capital gain, in contrast, is an unexpected rise in the value of the *same* good. It differs from the gain sought by a speculator in that it is not sought, foreseen, or expected.

Analogously, pure capital losses may be said to consist of unforeseen, unallowed for, windfall declines in the value of a piece of property, such as in the value of a portfolio of gilt-edged bonds by reason of an unexpected rise in interest rates.

Pure capital gains in this sense are due in the last analysis to our inability to foresee the future with accuracy and certainty. Most capital assets consist of more or less specialized and durable properties. To construct or otherwise acquire and own them requires a commitment of resources for a more or less long period. Although one investor may often recover his capital quickly by selling out to another, the aggregate capital devoted to a specialized use cannot usually be recovered from it except in the course of months or years. Meanwhile unexpected changes may alter the value of the asset, giving rise to a capital gain or loss.

Three main kinds of change create pure capital gains and losses: changes in expectations regarding the net receipts to be obtained from a capital asset, unexpected changes in interest rates, and changes in the disposition of investors to face uncertainties.

7 CHANGES IN EXPECTED NET RECEIPTS

When investors revise their expectations concerning the future income and recovery of principal to be received from an existing asset, the value of the latter tends to rise or fall in immediate reflection of the changed expectations. This is true because the value of a capital asset is in principle a reflection of the bundle of the net receipts, whether of services or of money, expected to be derived from it. Logically, the present value of these future receipts is calculated by discounting them by the rate of interest and by a rate reflecting the reluctance or desire of investors to assume the pattern of risks and uncertainties involved.

The incomes and capital recovery investors expect are subject to varying degrees of uncertainty. On gilt-edged bonds, best illustrated by United States government bonds, definite money amounts of income and principal payments are for practical purposes assured.

But some uncertainties remain even in this case: the risk that the purchasing power of the interest and principal payments will decline by reason of a rising price level and that the bonds will fall in market value by reason of a rise in interest rates. For most assets, such as real estate, corporate stocks, and business partnerships, the investor faces also a considerable range of divergent possibilities respecting the money amounts to be received. Some of these possibilities are calculable only vaguely if at all, and perhaps none can be estimated precisely. Nevertheless, the investor must reach a working expectation. Conceivably he might do this by explicitly weighting each major possibility by the best estimate he can make of its degree of probability. In effect, he may subject each possible receipt to a discount reflecting his estimate of the mathematical chance that he will not receive it. For example, in reaching a final estimate that the long run average earnings of a given common stock are likely to approximate $4.60 a share he might calculate that there is a 10 percent chance that they will average $10 a share, a 10 percent chance of $8, a 20 percent chance of $6, a 30 percent chance of $4, a 20 percent chance of $2, and a 10 percent chance of zero. He might reasonably combine these possibilities into a weighted average estimate of earning power of $4.60. While few investors

EARNING POWER ESTIMATE

Expected earning power	$10.00	$8.00	$6.00	$4.00	$2.00	$0
Estimated degree of probability (%)	10	10	20	30	20	10
Weighted expectation of earning power	$1.00	$.80	$1.20	$1.20	$.40	$0
Weighted average estimate of earning power	$4.60 (sum of weighted expectations on preceding line)					

make these calculations in detail, some such weighting and combining of divergent possibilities, however crude and unrecognized the process, is implicit in all appraisals of uncertain future receipts. One set of prospects as embodied in one security sells for a higher price than another, not haphazardly, but because investors can compare and measure the prospects sufficiently for their purposes. Usually the investor has various guides to assist him: the current level of earnings of the same or similar assets, the experience of owners of similar assets, and the current costs of reproducing the assets. His judgment of the range and character of the uncertainty present is aided and sharpened by comparing different investments. However vaguely some of the contingencies can be foreseen and however much all are subject to error in appraisal, investors are constantly engaged in appraising them. Rights to uncertain future incomes are bought and sold every day, and their prices are just as definite as those of any other goods.

The weighted average expectation is not the only significant consideration for most investors: the range and distribution of the various possibilities are also important. After all, even if the investor estimates the chances perfectly, the mathematical expectation represents merely the net result he would realize from an infinite number of commitments. The result of any single investment can be anywhere within the entire range of possibilities. Since an individual investor in practice can make only relatively few commitments of a given kind, he cannot avoid the possibility of actual results anywhere within this range. Conservative investors, such as insurance companies, banks, and trustees, as well as numerous individuals, usually try to avoid investments open to more than moderate possibilities of loss even though the weighted mathematical expectation of receipts of income and principal are high relative to the market price. On the other hand, patterns of uncertainty that include the possibility of very large gains have such great psychological attraction for many persons that assets embodying them often command disproportionately high prices relative to the mathematical expectation of gain. An investment that may conceivably return 100 for 1, but will probably result in a loss, for example, is likely to command a better price than one having a somewhat better mathematical expectation but no chance of yielding more than a small gain. This topic is discussed further below.

Most significant in the present connection is the fact that expectations representing a wide range of uncertain prospects are likely to be unstable. As Keynes emphasized, we have only an extremely precarious basis in knowledge for our estimate of prospective yields.[9] Our information about the present is far from complete, and what we can predict about the future is largely based upon conjecture. In consequence, the known facts about any capital asset exert a disproportionate influence in forming our long term expectations concerning it. Unexpected developments are common and produce large shifts in expectations.

In the case of common stocks and real estate there is a strong tendency on the part of many investors to approach the valuation by projecting indefinitely into the future either the current annual earnings or an average of the amounts expected to be reached in

[9] *General Theory of Employment, Interest and Money*, p. 149.

the future; that is, by capitalizing average earnings. A share of stock that displays a current annual earning power of $3 and offers no clear ground for belief that its life will be short or that its earnings will change markedly will be appraised, superficially, as if it offered a perpetual income of $3 a year. A share that has no present earning power may be appraised by estimating its future average earning power on the basis of the earnings of similar enterprises or on more fundamental studies of markets and costs.

Then, to take account of the estimated chances that the actual or prospective rate of earnings will not be indefinitely maintained, and usually, of the compensation needed to induce investors to assume the uncertainties and risks involved, the rate at which the market appears to capitalize the current earnings will be raised above the prevailing rate of interest on high grade bonds.[10] Also reflected in the rate at which the expected future earnings will be discounted or current earning power capitalized are such factors as the marketability of the asset, the care and supervision it requires, and the extent to which the earnings will be available in cash for the separate use of the investor. Because of differences in all these factors the common stock of an electric light and power company may be appraised by investors at 15 times current earnings, or the current earnings capitalized at 6⅔ percent, while the stock of a coal company is appraised at only 8 times current earnings.[11]

Each change in current or prospective earnings tends to produce a multiplied change in the asset's market value, the multiplier being the rate at which investors are capitalizing its earning power. A rise of $1 in the annual earnings of a stock normally selling at 10 times earnings will tend to cause its price to rise $10, for example. For this reason the market value of a common stock frequently rises sharply in response to the announcement of important new products, the acquisition of competing enterprises, or a rising trend of sales, and declines sharply in response to unfavorable news. An individual

[10] It may be reduced below the high grade bond rate if the pattern of possibilities is sufficiently attractive psychologically.

[11] An older and slightly different approach with the same effect is one in which the prospective earnings of an investment asset are appraised in terms of the number of years the investor is justified in waiting before the prospective payments will return to him the amount of his investment, leaving all further payments, if any, as profits. In view of the uncertainties, degree of supervision, and loss of liquidity involved, one asset may be valued at '10 years' purchase' and another at '20 years' purchase'. Such appraisals are identical with 10 and 20 times earnings, respectively.

security, other things being equal, tends to rise in price as it becomes more 'seasoned', that is, more familiar to investors, and therefore to some degree less attended by incalculable uncertainties. It tends to rise, also, as senior obligations are retired, and after a succession of stable earnings reports, because such developments are likely to raise the mathematical expectation of income as well as to reduce the compensation exacted by investors for facing the remaining risks.

Finally, expectations based upon a wide range of uncertainty are likely to be highly sensitive also to the changing psychological moods of investors. The same body of objective data may lead investors to make higher weighted estimates of income when they feel optimistic, and lower ones when they feel pessimistic. For all these reasons investors are continually revising their expectations of the net receipts to be obtained from capital assets. The resulting changes in the prices of the latter are always giving rise to pure capital gains and losses.

Contributing to the price movements of capital assets and to capital gains and losses are the attempts of speculators to forecast and to profit by prospective changes. Speculation on the general direction of such price movements, regardless of their underlying sources, often assumes a prominent role in the determination of asset prices and capital gains and losses in the short run. The influence of speculative activity is discussed in more detail in Section 12.

Reproduction cost limits the value and sustained yield of capital assets

In the case of a readily producible capital asset, one that can be obtained promptly in the desired quantities, such as a common machine, the cost of producing or otherwise obtaining it sets an upper limit upon its value. No matter how high its immediate yield, no one will value it at more than it can be purchased for. But its prospective yield over any long period could not be expected to remain above the going rate of return on other assets of equal cost and risk because a higher yield would attract more and more such machines into use until the differential disappeared. Hence the reproduction cost of readily producible assets tends to set an upper limit on their value and, together with the prevailing rate of return on such commitments, on the incomes they yield. Cost does not set a lower limit, however, on the yield or capital value of existing producible assets. If the present value of the prospective receipts from a machine declines below its cost of reproduction, new machines of this kind will not be made and no one will pay as much as its reproduction cost for an old machine. Its value will decline to the discounted sum of the net receipts expected from it.

Large amounts of capital assets consist of properties that are neither unique and fixed in supply nor instantly and abundantly reproducible. Business enterprises are notably of this character. Most of them can be duplicated by new firms in some degree. The newcomers need not be exact replicas of the existing ones. Even if they face higher costs and lower profits, their actual or potential competition tends to limit or impair the earning power of established firms. The value of the shares of ownership in a successful enterprise, therefore, cannot be determined in complete disregard of the cost of establishing a competing enterprise; for in the long run, this cost, together with the rate of return expected to prevail in similar industries, will tend to determine the net incomes to be expected.

On the other hand, successful established business enterprises are not quickly, easily, or perhaps ever fully reproducible. They already possess sizeable capital resources that the would-be newcomer still has to raise. Their presence increases his risks, and therefore his difficulty in raising adequate capital. Many would-be entrants may be deterred for this reason alone. The successful established enterprise commonly embodies other advantages the newcomer can acquire only with difficulty, cost, and delay, if at all. It often possesses favorable locations. It has built up smoothly functioning business relations with customers and suppliers. The goodwill acquired in this way has perhaps been supplemented by long continued advertising and by the branding or special packaging of its products. Its executives and workers have acquired special knowledge and skills based upon experience and perhaps research, including the composite skill derived from working together. The established concern has often come by these advantages without extra cost, as a mere by-product of its ordinary operations during many years. That is, outlays regularly made for their current usefulness in operating the business have had the incidental effect of building up various organizational advantages. The latter are usually hidden assets, not reflected in the firm's balance sheet, unless a price was paid for them in acquiring another enterprise. But the would-be newcomer can obtain them, if at all, only by extra capital outlay or effort.[12] The successful established concern may reasonably be expected, there-

---

[12] Some costs, such as those of educating consumers to demand products previously made popular by older firms, may be less for the new firm.

fore, to continue for long periods or indefinitely to earn a rate of
return on its own investment higher than that available to newcomers in its field. Investors will capitalize the extra earning power
due to its continuing advantages. They will capitalize also, but for
a shorter period, the additional extra earning power it possesses by
reason of the delays and difficulties obstructing the effective entrance
of competitors.

These considerations explain why, although business enterprises
and such related types of capital assets as hotels, office buildings,
and apartment houses are valued by investors primarily by discounting their expected earnings, the cost of supplying competing properties, including an allowance for unavoidable delays and the costs
of building up an equal goodwill, tends in the long run to set an
upper limit on this earning power and on its market value.

8 UNEXPECTED CHANGES IN INTEREST RATES

As we have noted, the value of a capital asset represents in principle a bundle of future net receipts. Some will not become available
for many years, others are expected in the near future, and some
may be much larger than others. The time-shape of the series of
receipts, that is, their distribution through time, will vary with dif-
fent assets. Generally speaking, investors will value more distant
receipts less highly than near ones. In calculating its present worth,
they will discount each future receipt for the expected period of
delay by the prevailing rate of interest. For this reason, a rise in
interest rates, by reducing the present value of the prospective
receipts, tends to reduce the value of capital assets, and a fall in
interest rates, to increase their value.

The prices of gilt-edged bonds sometimes move widely in response
to changes in interest rates. The prices of Liberty Bonds issued at
par during World War I declined as much as 18 percent in 1918-21.
During the sharp and prolonged fall in interest rates that began in
1933, numerous noncallable bonds of business corporations rose
far above the prices at which they had been issued. Several bonds
of the Pennsylvania Railroad, for example, had by March 1946
risen more than 30 percent above par. Two and one-half percent
British consols approximately doubled in market price between the
end of 1920 and the end of 1935.

The effects of changes in pure interest rates upon capital values
are by no means confined to fixed-income obligations. They extend
throughout the entire field of capital assets, including real estate and

common stocks. Nevertheless, their effects upon the market prices of equity interests in business enterprises and real estate are frequently obscured and offset in varying degree because of opposite changes in earnings prospects. Falling interest rates have often coincided with periods of low or declining business activity, when the favorable effects of lower interest rates upon the prices of capital assets have in many cases been more than offset by the unfavorable influence of the shrinking earnings prospects. Similarly, a rise in interest rates during prosperity has often had to compete for influence with the improving earnings prospects characteristic of such periods.

9 CHANGES IN THE DISPOSITION TO FACE UNCERTAINTIES

Logically, even after discounting prospective receipts by rates reflecting his estimates of the chance that they will not be received, and after discounting the remaining expectations by the pure rate of interest, the investor may be expected to demand additional compensation to induce him to face the uncertainties and risks. This compensation, widely regarded among economists as the most distinctive component of profits, takes the form of a third discount, which is usually combined with the rate of interest in the mind of the investor to form the total effective rate of return he seeks. If the investor did not allow for this extra compensation, and his receipts turned out to equal his weighted expectation exactly, he would be no better off upon the final liquidation of his investment than other investors who had assumed much smaller uncertainties and risks. If, therefore, he finds uncertainty irksome, he will not assume it unless he is compensated.

The popularity of gambling and of sports in which uncertainty plays a large role is evidence that, in suitable patterns and doses, risk-taking is by no means unpleasant. In fact, patterns of uncertainty that offer a small chance of a very large gain are widely popular even when the participants know the odds are against them. Governments, philanthropic organizations, and others frequently exploit this popularity by holding lotteries, such as the Irish Sweepstakes, in which the chances are sold for more than their mathematical values. If, for example, 200,000 tickets were offered at $1 each — the holder of the winning ticket, chosen by lot, to receive a purse of $100,000 — the lottery would be highly attractive to many even though the chances were sold at twice their actuarial value. The same propensity doubtlessly enables certain types of business enterprise,

such as gold-exploring or 'wild cat' oil-drilling, to obtain a portion
of or all their capital funds on terms that allow nothing or less than
nothing for the supposed reluctance of investors to assume risks.
But the sums that most of us will readily risk in extreme speculations
are only small fractions of our resources and are not enough to
finance all risky ventures. We are apt to be more cautious with the
main body of our capital. And the rewards offered by most investments that seem safe enough for large fractions of our resources are
likely to be of more modest proportions. They require risking say
$10,000 for the chance of getting an annual income of $500 or perhaps $1,000, or a capital profit of perhaps $1,000 or $2,000. The
investor knows, moreover, that even relatively safe investments entail
some only vaguely calculable risks of large loss. To reduce his risks
by widely diversifying his investments frequently requires greater
resources or a larger number of attractive investment opportunities
than he possesses. The resulting uncertainty and risk are commonly
believed to be sufficiently irksome over the field of investment as a
whole to command a price.

But the attitude of investors toward uncertainty is not fixed. Youth
proverbially regards risks lightly and age shrinks from them. The
moods of investors as a group likewise vary markedly from time to
time. The general optimism that usually characterizes a period of
expanding business activity is reflected not only in more generous
appraisals of future earnings but in a readier disposition to assume
risks. The less calculable uncertainties inhering in all investments
press less heavily upon investors at such times, leading them to exact
a smaller price for assuming risks. The opposite is true when a mood
of pessimism seizes the markets, perhaps after or accompanying a
period of declining business. Then safety seems to be prized above
all else. The number and resources of investors willing to buy or
hold the riskier assets at the old prices sharply shrink. The prospective rate of return needed to induce men to buy or hold such assets
rises, leading to bigger discounts of expected future incomes. These
bigger discounts, superimposed upon the concurrent reductions in
expectations, induce drastic declines in capital values.

10 SPECIAL CASES

While changes in expected receipts, unexpected changes in interest
rates, and changes in the disposition to face uncertainties comprise
the primary sources of 'pure' capital gains and losses, three special
cases deserve separate mention.

New discoveries and inventions, and catastrophic losses: This source is a special case of increases or decreases in expected receipts. New discoveries of natural resources, as when oil is found on a farm or valuable new bodies of ore are uncovered, frequently bring big additions to capital values. Unlocking a whole series of future incomes each such discovery may enormously enhance the capital value of the land on which it is found or the lease of drilling or other mineral rights. Not different in principle are various more or less fortuitous inventions which, with the aid of the patent laws, become the sources of a series of future incomes. The market value of the common stock of a Chicago clock manufacturing company suddenly rose several-fold a few years ago when its president in the course of his employment devised and patented a small electric organ that produced the sounds and volume of a large pipe-organ. On the other hand, unforseeable subtractions from capital values are frequently wrought by catastrophes against which no insurance was carried, such as fire, flood, and earthquakes; and, less dramatically, by technological obsolescence.

Change in inventory value: This too is a special case of increases or decreases in expected receipts. The cost of replacing stocks of goods on hand occasionally changes substantially and, to many, unexpectedly. An individual's or a firm's previously accumulated inventories become worth more or less than their original cost. The difference, provided it was not foreseen and does not reflect merely a change in the general price level, is in principle a pure capital gain or loss. An increase in the price of copper at the smelter, for example, will raise the cost of producing all products into which copper enters. The prices of these products will therefore rise. A wholesale firm or manufacturer with a large inventory of copper tubing acquired at a lower price will be able to charge the new price for it and will therefore obtain a capital gain in addition to its usual margin of profit. In practice, such capital gains and losses are usually combined in the accounts of the enterprise with ordinary operating results, but business men commonly recognize their special character and occasionally credit the gains to special reserve accounts against future inventory losses.

Windfall operating profits: Strictly speaking, the excess of the net earnings actually experienced in any year over those that had been expected also constitutes a capital gain. This type of capital gain is emphasized by certain British economists who would count as income only the expected part of the actually experienced results.[13] By this test, much of the exceptionally high wartime earnings of business enterprises would be designated capital gains, not income; and all unexpected operating losses would be regarded as capital losses. Logically, whenever the earnings of a period fall short of the expected amount, the difference would be accounted a capital loss. We discuss this type of gain and loss further in Section 15.

The foregoing three primary sources of 'pure' capital gains and losses and their special cases refer to 'real' gains and losses, not to price changes that merely reflect proportionate alterations in the value of money as shown by movements in the general level of prices. We shall give attention in Chapter 4 to pseudo capital gains and losses attributable to changes in the general purchasing power of money.

11 PERFECT APPRAISAL OF CHANCES CONSISTENT WITH WIDELY DIVERGENT RESULTS BY DIFFERENT INVESTORS

As noted, the weighted average of the probabilities of a given investment is only the net result that can be expected from a very large number of such investments. If the range of possible results is at all wide, as it usually is with equity investments, the gain on any individual commitment may fall far short of or greatly exceed the average expectation, however accurately appraised. A perfectly balanced coin is as likely to fall 'heads' as 'tails'; yet if two men each risk a dollar on whether it falls one way or the other, one is bound to double his money, and the other, to lose his. In the same way, different investors operating in the same field, each with one or a few commitments, and each assessing the probabilities accurately, are almost bound to experience different results. Since the motivation for many kinds of investment lies precisely in the possibilities of gain in excess of the mean expectation, a serious question arises as to the precise meaning to attach to 'expected' and 'unexpected' — a question we shall discuss presently in some detail.

12 SPECULATION

The combination of the foregoing influences is ample cause for wide and frequent changes in the prices of capital assets. The compounding of changes in expectations of earnings with opposite changes in the discounts that will induce investors to assume risks is mainly responsible for the wide fluctuations in the prices of capital assets

[13] See Hicks, *op cit.*, pp. 172-79; Keynes, *A Treatise on Money*, p. 124, and *General Theory of Employment, Interest and Money*, p. 57.

between prosperity and depression. When the estimated annual earning power of a share of stock rises from $3 to $5 while the rate at which investors capitalize these earnings drops from 20 to 10 percent, the effect is to raise the market price of the stock from $15 to $50; and when the opposite changes take place, to reduce the market value from $50 to $15. The price movements of the common stocks of some leading American iron and steel manufacturing companies in 1933-46 (see tabulation) illustrate how wide these swings

COMMON STOCKS OF SOME LEADING IRON AND STEEL COMPANIES
MARKET PRICES, APRIL 15, 1933, 1937, 1942, 1946

	CLOSING MARKET PRICE PER SHARE			
	1933	1937	1942	1946
American Rolling Mill Co.	$ 9.50	$ 38.13	$10.38	$ 32.75
Bethlehem Steel Corp.	17.13	91.75	56.25	105.38
Byers (A. M.) Co.	13.25	27.50	7.00ᵃ	29.00
Colorado Fuel & Iron Corp.	11.25	41.38ᵃ	14.25	17.88
Crucible Steel Co. of America	13.13	70.00	28.50	47.50
Inland Steel Co.	19.50	114.00	59.00	119.50
National Steel Corp.	21.50	88.25	47.75	89.00
Republic Steel Corp.	6.88	42.13	15.88	33.75
United States Pipe & Foundry Co.	9.50	61.00	23.38	59.00
United States Steel Corp.	32.50	112.63	47.50	83.38
Youngstown Sheet & Tube Co.	12.75	88.50	32.50	72.50

	PERCENTAGE CHANGE PER SHARE		
	1933-37	1937-42	1942-46
American Rolling Mill Co.	+301.37	−72.77	+215.51
Bethlehem Steel Corp.	+435.61	−38.70	+87.34
Byers (A. M.) Co.	+107.55	−74.55	+314.29
Colorado Fuel & Iron Corp.	+267.82	−65.56	+25.47
Crucible Steel Co. of America	+433.13	−59.29	+66.67
Inland Steel Co.	+484.62	−48.25	+102.54
National Steel Corp.	+310.47	−45.89	+86.39
Republic Steel Corp.	+512.35	−62.31	+112.53
United States Pipe & Foundry Co.	+542.11	−61.67	+152.35
United States Steel Corp.	+246.55	−57.83	+75.54
Youngstown Sheet & Tube Co.	+594.12	−62.15	+123.08

All iron and steel companies included in Standard and Poor's Corporation Averages.
ᵃ Mean of bid and asked prices.

can be even in the case of long established companies. United States Steel Corporation common stock, for example, more than tripled in price between April 1933 and 1937, then declined 58 percent by April 1942; during the next four years it rose 76 percent.[14] Eight of the 11 stocks quadrupled or more in 1933-37, and the smallest increase exceeded 100 percent. In the next 5 years all declined

[14] The Department of Labor wholesale price index (1926:100) averaged 65.9 in 1933, 86.3 in 1937, 98.8 in 1942, and 121.1 in 1946.

substantially, only 3 by less than 50 percent. In the succeeding 4 years 6 of the 11 stocks more than doubled, and none increased less than a fourth.

The frequency with which quoted capital values change and the practical significance of capital gains as a source of individual wealth have been immeasurably increased by the growth of stock exchanges and of active local markets for real estate. News affecting the various stocks and bonds is widely disseminated daily by financial news agencies and quickly reflected in market prices. To some extent the broader market substitutes frequent smaller fluctuations for infrequent major ones, and reduces discrepancies in market values as between different industries and localities. The constant flow of publicity promotes continuous comparisons and readjustments of the relative values of securities. The easy accessibility of would-be buyers and sellers through professional brokers gives the investor a ready power to transform rights to future earnings into a present capital sum, and an equally ready power to do the reverse. In consequence, many transactions are encouraged that would otherwise be postponed or never undertaken. The 'realization' of capital gains and losses through actual sale, once rare, now assumes large proportions.

In an economy where large, irregular changes continuously occur, it is natural that their probability will be widely taken into account, and that their frequency will create a fertile field for persons who specialize in dealing with changes. They seek income not primarily from the dividend, interest, or rental payments offered by the assets they buy, but from changes in their prices. The professional speculator hopes to foresee price movements and to profit by buying in advance of a rise and selling in advance of a fall.

But professional speculators are not the only ones who seek to forecast changes in the prices of capital assets. Most investors, including those who are interested primarily in obtaining a regular income from their holdings, nowadays take serious account of the possibility of substantial changes, upward or downward, in the market value of a contemplated investment.

Changes in the market value of capital assets had far less practical significance in older times when private wealth consisted mainly of land, title to which commonly passed by inheritance within family groups. Tradition or actual restriction in law or bequest, as when estates were entailed, discouraged its sale. Today the ownership of capital assets is far more mobile. Marketability is highly valued by investors. Although business corporations are usually chartered for long periods, even perpetuity, few of their stockholders think of themselves as irretrievably committing their funds for the life of the enterprise. They look to the market to supply a means of recovering their capital if a change in the prospects of the enterprise or in their personal circumstances makes this seem desirable. Similarly, few bondholders, save perhaps the larger life insurance companies, are willing to rely solely upon the scheduled redemption of their holdings at maturity as a means of recovering their capital. They too count on the ability to sell their bonds as a means of exit for their capital. As far as sale in the market at some time is contemplated as a possibility, all investors are interested in the probable price movements of their assets. In some degree like professional speculators, they try to take future price movements into account in the prices at which they buy and sell.

13 CONVENTIONAL CAPITAL GAINS ARE MIXTURES THAT INCLUDE ORDINARY INCOME

Consequently, not all changes in capital values are wholly unforeseen. On the contrary, many, perhaps most, are expected in some degree. As far as the possibility of a rise or fall in the capital value of an asset is foreseen by the investor, it enters into his calculation of the total compensation he is likely to receive for his personal services, the services of his capital, and his risk-taking in connection with the investment. In other words, what passes for a capital gain contains elements of ordinary income — wages, interest, rent, and profits.

Consider, for example, an investor who is debating the purchase and retention for a year or two of a certain common stock which, he estimates, can be expected during the coming year both to yield $5 a share in dividends (the rate it has paid for some years) and, because of improving earnings, to rise $10 a share in market value. His reasons for purchasing the stock properly include the total expected gain of $15, not merely the $5 of expected dividends. Both the expected dividends and the expected rise in market price are uncertain, of course. But uncertainty does not justify ignoring reasonable possibilities. It only demands that the possibilities be given values in accordance with the degrees of probability estimated to attach to them, and that the total probable yield include compensation for the reluctance of investors to assume the particular pattern of uncertainties presented by the investment. In his final estimates

DIVIDEND ESTIMATE

Expected dividend	$7.00	$6.00	$5.00	$4.00	$1.00
Estimated degree of probability (%)	10	10	65	10	5
Weighted expectation of dividend	$.70	$.60	$3.25	$.40	$.05

Weighted average estimate
of dividend $5.00   (sum of weighted expectations on preceding line)

PRICE APPRECIATION ESTIMATE

Expected increase in price	$30.00	$20.00	$15.00	$10.00	$0	−$10.00	−$20.00
Estimated degree of probability (%)	10	10	20	40	5	10	5
Weighted expectation of price increase	$3.00	$2.00	$3.00	$4.00	$0	−$1.00	−$1.00

Weighted av. estimate
of price increase $10.00   (sum of weighted expectations on preceding line)

of the probable dividend and price appreciation the investor might reasonably have combined various possibilities.[15]

In deciding whether to purchase the stock the investor might calculate that the mere use of his funds should entitle him to a basic return of, say, 3 percent on the ground that a high grade bond would yield this rate. He might hold also that for his personal effort and skill in choosing and timing the commitment he should receive an additional 3 percent, the rate of compensation for his personal services he thinks he could get in other activities or by managing other investments. He might hold further that he is entitled to an additional return of 6 percent annually for assuming the uncertainties of the return from the projected investment and the related risks, especially the risk, even though small, that part of or all his capital may be wiped out. The 6 percent would measure either the compensation he requires to overcome his subjective reluctance to assume such risks or, if his reluctance is less, the compensation he could obtain for assuming similar uncertainties in other investments — the disposition and ability to assume such uncertainties being scarce enough to command this rate. The 'expected' rate the investor will insist upon for these services in any given case will be strongly influenced by his psychological attitude toward the whole pattern of uncertainties presented by the particular investment. In the present case these uncertainties include a 10 percent chance that the rise in market value may be as much as $30 a share, and a 40 percent chance that it will be $15 or more. These chances not only affect the mathe-

[15] If we assume that the amount of the expected dividend and of the expected appreciation are statistically independent, an assumption that may be entirely reasonable for a short period.

matical expectation but may enhance the psychological attractiveness of the investment, and lead the investor to base his commitment on a lower 'expected' rate of return than would otherwise be necessary. The total of the required rates of return in the present case is 12 percent. The investor might conclude that the stock would be attractive whenever it could be bought for less than $125 a share, the price at which the total expected yield would be 12 percent. If he actually purchased the stock at $125 a share and realized his expectations perfectly by receiving $5 in dividends and by selling the stock a year later for $10 a share more than it cost him, ignoring commissions and taxes, the entire $10 would conventionally be regarded as a capital gain yet would consist essentially of interest, wages, and profits.

It is of course usually difficult to distinguish sharply if at all between the part of any conventional capital gain that was not 'expected', and is therefore pure, and the part that was correctly expected as compensation for labor, capital, and risk-taking, and is therefore more properly regarded as ordinary income. Sometimes, however, the distinction is quite clear. Bonds bearing coupon rates below the prevailing rate of interest on similar securities sell at a discount from par. The investor counts on the difference between the market price and the par amount to be received at maturity to supplement the low current interest return and in this way to bring up the total yield to the prevailing level for such securities at the time of purchase. The ostensible capital gain to be realized when his bond is redeemed is wholly expected and constitutes part of his true interest income. The same situation obtains in the case of the nominal capital loss an investor suffers when a high coupon bond he had bought at a premium is redeemed at par. This loss, fully expected at the time of purchase, merely reflects the excessive nominal interest payments, representing a partial return of capital, received before maturity.

Similarly, though less certainly, expected compensation for personal services may make up the bulk of an ostensible capital gain. The chief element in one investor's gain might be his studied selection of undervalued investments. Field surveys or intensive analysis of published materials might lead him to discover well in advance of the general market new developments favorable to the earning power of certain securities. A second may owe much of his gain to his skillful exploitation of seasonal or cyclical fluctuations in the market prices of certain common stocks whose typical behavior he has carefully followed. A third may largely create his own capital gains by inducing others to erect costly apartment houses or other buildings on land contiguous to his, thereby raising its value. A fourth may contribute largely to his capital gains by negotiating a profitable long term contract for a corporation in which he owns a large stock interest. A fifth may achieve the same result by acquiring successive small blocks of stock or parcels of land which, when aggregated in a large block, may be sold for a higher price per unit. A sixth, knowing that a certain individual is seeking to acquire control of a corporation, might persuade other minority stockholders to join with him until the members of his group own enough shares for effective control. Thereupon he and his associates, by offering their block of stock as a whole, might well be in a position to exact a substantially higher price per share from the individual seeking control. The gain in this case may be the expected result of tactics similar to those employed in games, when two or more players combine against others.[16] And so on.

All these increases in value which, when realized by sale, are conventionally regarded as capital gains, are in large part attributable to personal skill, exertion, and foresight for which many investors could command salaries, fees, or commissions if they employed their talents on behalf of others. In point of fact, this is precisely what managements of investment trusts and their professional staffs try to do. In return for their services, they receive salaries and fees that are often paid from the gross capital gains of the shareholders, though their compensation is usually payable even in the absence of capital gains.

Changes in interest rates and the resulting changes in bond prices are likewise anticipated by investors in greater or lesser degree. Some of the larger banks and bond dealers employ specialists who devote much of their time to forecasting interest rates. In response to forecasts, the size and maturity composition of their bond portfolios are sometimes altered substantially. Prospective levels of interest rates, moreover, affect prevailing rates. The present rate of interest for 10-year loans, for example, is influenced by the market's expectations of the rates likely to prevail for shorter term loans during this period. No one would lend money for 10 years at the same rate of interest as for 5 years if he believed the market rate would be materially higher during the second half of the decade. If, on the other

---

[16] See *Theory of Games and Economic Behavior,* John von Neumann and Oskar Morgenstern (Princeton University Press, 1944).

hand, interest rates were expected to decline, longer term loans would tend to command lower interest rates than shorter term. Other things being equal, the prevailing rate for a 10-year loan would tend to be the same as that for a 5-year loan only if interest rates were not expected to change materially. David Durand gives examples of each of these relationships between the yields of shorter and longer term investments in *Basic Yields of Corporate Bonds, 1900-1942* (NBER *Technical Papers 3* and *6,* June 1942 and 1947, respectively). Thus the rate of interest prevailing at any time for each type and maturity of investment itself reflects a forecast of future interest rates.

Changes in the disposition of investors to face uncertainties, especially between different phases of a business cycle, similarly invite forecasting and speculation. The professional speculator preeminently, and nearly all investors in some degree, are aware of the profound influence shifts in sentiment have upon capital values and are constantly trying to forecast them. Thus all three primary sources of pure capital gains are also the subjects of more or less informed, intelligent, and continuous attention by investors.

A pure capital gain is functionless. It serves neither to overcome the reluctance of investors to take risks nor to allocate this scarce and valuable disposition, and the other resources associated with it, among the fields competing for them. The considerations reviewed, however, lead to the conclusion that a significant fraction of what are conventionally regarded as capital gains are really in the nature of ordinary income. They are expected and they serve like ordinary income, particularly profits, as a stimulus and guide for eliciting and allocating labor, capital, and entrepreneurial services in connection with projects offering uncertain rewards.

14 CREATION OF EARNING POWER WITHOUT COMMENSURATE CAPITAL INVESTMENT

A major source of conventional capital gains is the planned creation of earning power in business enterprises without a commensurate investment of capital. A common reason for launching a new enterprise or expanding investment in an old one is the prospect that the rate of return will be higher than that prevailing in the market. The promoters may contemplate taking their profits in either of two ways: retain their ownership and enjoy an income that would otherwise be obtainable only from a larger capital investment or sell the venture, once it is established, for a price that discounts the relatively large prospective earnings, thereby realizing a capital gain equal to the difference between the capitalized value of the prospective earnings and the cost of the investment. If knowledge were complete and resources perfectly mobile competition would keep both kinds of profit very small. Competitors would quickly enter the field and, by offering the goods at lower prices, force a leveling down of the unusually high prospective rate of return. But the practical obstructions to the free flow of knowledge and resources are great. Opportunities for unusually profitable investment can rarely be recognized and exploited without specialized types of information, special skills, and established business connections. Further, to conceive, plan, assemble, and float a new enterprise require degrees of imagination, courage, and energy that are scarce. Many more investors are ready to purchase an interest in a business that is already organized, or in a piece of property such as an apartment building that is already constructed, than are willing or able to plan and organize such ventures themselves. Hence an entrepreneur may often purchase and assemble the components of a business enterprise or of a physical capital asset at a smaller cost than the components will be worth as an assembled entity. From an economic standpoint, the difference represents the profits of promotion; legally, it constitutes a capital gain if the asset is sold. If errors in judgment are made or if adverse changes occur in the industry, the property, when assembled, may promise a smaller rate of return on its cost than that prevailing in the market, and a capital loss will result.

Capital gains from the organization and launching of new business enterprises have been a powerful shortcut to wealth for many men of outstanding business ability and their associates. During the era of American railroad expansion, for example, huge gains sometimes went to promoters and bankers who brought about the consolidation of short lines into integrated systems. The rise in the earning power of the consolidated companies, as appraised by investors and speculators, led to sharp advances in the market value of their securities. A $1 million increase in annual earning power, for instance, could easily lead to an addition of $10 million or more to the market value of the company's common stock. The successful promoters and bankers benefited outstandingly both because they had received substantial amounts of stock in compensation for their services and because they had purchased additional amounts. Similar gains have been conspicuous in connection with the successful promotions and consolidations of various large public utility, industrial, and merchandising corporations.

The creation of disproportionately large earning power is by no means confined to the promotion and launching stages of a firm's existence. It is often more characteristic of subsequent stages. A business man or investor may reasonably contemplate that as his firm becomes progressively better established, its continued relations with dealers and consumers will increase their receptiveness to its products and diminish the selling costs per unit of sales. Its own experience and that of its suppliers will teach it how to buy more advantageously. An expanding volume of business will enable it to utilize its plants and personnel more fully, and to enjoy the economies of larger scale buying and selling. Often it will benefit from an increasingly efficient exploitation of patent rights, from monopolistic agreements with competitors, and from its own research.

After some years the wages and salaries a firm has paid to employees for their current labor services will be found to have purchased also an articulation of relationships among them, an organization, that a newcomer could not duplicate quickly merely by hiring an equal number of the various classes of workers. The employees will have acquired plant or company skills that in many cases are more valuable than trade skills. Its long operating experience and, perhaps, its organized research, will have produced a fund of knowledge, techniques, and potential new products that may be more valuable than its physical plants. Independent of patent rights or monopolistic agreements, a measure of monopoly position for the firm's products will have been acquired through long continued branding and advertising and the growth of an effective distributing organization. In all these ways a successful concern tends to develop an earning power that is disproportionately large relative to its capital investment.

But what explains its continuing ability to earn a rate of return on its invested capital higher than the prevailing one? Why do competitors not eventually enter the field, force a leveling down of the unusually high rate of return on the invested capital, and so prevent the emergence of large capital gains?

As we have indicated, this possibility materializes in many instances and does in fact tend to limit actual and prospective earnings and, therefore, capital gains. But to a significant degree, the earning power of a successful enterprise reflects more than the yield of readily reproducible assets. It embodies also what are essentially

rents received for various scarce intangible resources created by the
enterprise, and these rental elements may persist for long periods.
As we have indicated also, every successful firm tends to build up
a manufacturing and selling organization that is in some degree
unique. It can be reproduced only imperfectly, and with much difficulty, delay, and cost. In effect, this organization, including the
knowledge and skills of its personnel, and the established reputation
of the firm and its products, constitutes an intangible plant. Although
often more important to the earnings of the firm than the tangible
assets, neither the cost nor the value of the intangible plant is usually
recognized on the books. The wages and salaries, advertising expenditures, research appropriations, and other outlays through which
these intangible assets have been built up have, as a rule, all been

BOOK AND MARKET VALUES OF SELECTED COMMON STOCKS

	Book Value 1945[a]	Market Price Dec. 31, 1945	Ratio
Air Reduction	$17.68	$ 54.50	0.3
American Tobacco 'B'	26.64	90.38	0.3
Coca-Cola Co.	16.63	181.75[b]	0.1
Columbia Broadcasting[c]	12.62	45.25	0.3
Cream of Wheat	6.48	32.50[b]	0.2
DuPont (E. I.)	53.78	186.25	0.3
Homestake Mining	10.81	53.00	0.2
Lambert Co.	12.11	45.00	0.3
Monsanto Chemical	38.35	117.00	0.3
Penney (J. C.)	38.43	148.88	0.3
Pepsi-Cola	3.14	35.75	0.1
Radio Corp. of America	0.68	17.75	0.04
American Car & Foundry	93.09	64.00	1.5
American Woolen	57.42	31.38	1.8
Armour	26.90	13.13	2.0
Atlantic Refining	71.30	39.50	1.8
Bethlehem Steel	162.21	96.00	1.7
Consolidated Vultee	42.08	33.25	1.3
Cudahy Packing	61.19	44.50	1.4
Sloss-Sheffield Steel	40.23	20.62	2.0
Socony-Vacuum	26.48	17.25	1.5
Standard Oil of Indiana	53.63	40.50	1.3
Swift	47.92	38.50	1.2
U. S. Steel	141.90	81.13	1.7

These stocks were selected solely as examples of discrepancies between book
values and market prices at a particular time. They are not the most extreme
examples, nor is any of them represented as typical.

[a] As of December 31, 1945, except as follows: American Car & Foundry,
April 30, 1946; Armour, Cudahy Packing, and Swift, October 27, 1945; Con-
solidated Vultee, November 30, 1945. Book value figures as reported by
Standard & Poor's Corporation.

[b] Mean of bid and asked prices.

[c] Book value is for combined 'A' and 'B' stock. Market price is for 'B' stock
only.

charged off as current expenses as they were incurred. Unless a firm purchases the goodwill of another, no value is usually assigned to these intangibles on the firm's balance sheet. That investors appraise these intangible assets no less highly than the tangible is evidenced by the relation between the book and market values of the common stocks of companies that are believed by investors to have unusual prospective earning power — whether by reason of heavy outlays for research, advertising expenditures, patent rights, ownership of rich ores, or other factors. In the table on page 74, 12 well-known common stocks are listed whose book values at the end of 1945 were in no case more than 35 percent of their market prices.

Capital losses may arise in the opposite manner: through the creation of inadequate earning power relative to the capital investment. An enterprise that succeeds in achieving a net excess of operating profits over operating losses during a period of years may nevertheless fail to earn a rate of return equal to the going rate on the capital originally and subsequently committed to it. If its future looks no more promising, and its resources are too specialized to be shifted to other uses or to be liquidated without loss, or if those in effective control oppose liquidation, the market value of its common stock may fall substantially below the capital invested per share. The common stocks of many railroad, steel, oil, and other companies frequently sell at market prices substantially below their book values. W. E. Hutton & Company, a New York Stock Exchange house, issued on March 24, 1949 a list of 100 companies whose common stocks were selling at prices below even the *net working capital* per share, no value whatever being allowed for the fixed assets. The bottom half of the table gives 12 examples of well known stocks that were selling for substantially less than their book values at the end of 1945.

The capital gains expected from the organization and expansion of business enterprises constitute perhaps the major incentives and rewards for entrepreneurial activity. Are they truly capital gains or are they profits?

15 CAPITAL GAINS AND PROFITS

Various of the foregoing considerations compel us both to narrow and to blunt the concept of pure capital gains advanced at the beginning of this chapter. We said there that a pure capital gain is an unforeseen, uncalculated, fortuitous, or windfall addition to the value of a man's property. But just what shall we mean by these adjectives? Shall we apply them only to gains that were utterly unforeseen, in the sense that they were not even contemplated as outside possibilities? Or shall we apply them also to gains which, though they entered into the investor's calculations as possibilities, exceed his weighted expectations?

Consider the investor we discussed a few pages back, who bought a certain common stock at $125 a share because he 'expected' a total yield of $15 a year from it, $5 from dividends and $10 from a rise in the stock's market value. The investor had weighed the possibility that the stock might rise as much as $30 a share. This 10 percent possibility had entered into his calculation of the 'expected' gain, and was in fact responsible for $3 or 30 percent of the total weighted expectation of price appreciation. It may have influenced his attitude toward the whole pattern of contingencies presented by the stock, and induced him to make the commitment at a lower 'expected' rate of return than he would otherwise have required. Let us suppose the stock actually rises $35 a share by the end of one year and that the investor, having received his expected $5 in dividends, sells it. Besides the dividend, he receives $35 per share more than the stock cost him, $25 more per share than his weighted expectation of the rise, and $5 more per share than the maximum possibility he had contemplated. Which of these increments best qualifies as pure capital gain?

On the one hand, we might adhere closely to the mean 'expectation' and hold that a pure capital gain consists of the gain in excess of the weighted average expectation, the gain in excess of $10 in our illustration. This view seems quite reasonable at first blush, but involves several serious difficulties.

First, the mathematical expectation is only a weighted average of the results the investor can expect to realize if he makes an infinite number of investments of the same type. Even perfect estimation of the relative probabilities of different results does not ensure that the actual result in a single or a few investments will not depart widely from the mathematical expectation. A man who is betting that an evenly balanced coin will fall heads up knows perfectly well that the chances are one in two; that in any long series of tosses, the most probable result is an equal number of heads and tails. Nevertheless, if he bets on a single toss, he may double his money. This possibility is what motivates him to bet. In the same way, a considerable element of chance is inherent in all business investments. Even when their knowledge and experience give them a high degree of accuracy in estimating the probabilities, individual investors and business men cannot really look forward in most instances to results approximating the weighted average of the probabilities. They lack the financial resources and the personal energies, and they do not live long enough, to make an indefinitely large number of commitments of any given type. Their actual results may be anywhere within the entire range of possibilities, and most important, they are commonly motivated by the hope of realizing substantially more than the weighted average expectation.

Second, and related to the foregoing, is the fact, previously noted, that investors and business men are guided by the entire pattern of uncertainties presented by one investment as compared with another, rather than by the weighted expectation alone. The scatter of the chances of losing various fractions of one's capital and of making various percentage gains often receives far more attention than the mere average of these divergent possibilities. How much chance is there of losing one's entire capital? If the risk is slight, many investors will be attracted to the venture even though the mathematical expectation of gain is smaller than that offered by other commitments. The most significant expectation here is that respecting the safety of the capital, not the amount of appreciation. For others, however, investments believed to harbor possibilities of unusual gains exert an attraction that cannot be explained in terms of the mathematical expectation. Gold mining and other enterprises that offer this pattern attract the energies and funds of investors even when experience tells them their aggregate losses will probably exceed their aggregate gains. In more humdrum fields also, the outside possibility of being able after some years to sell out at a phenomenal profit attracts many investors. In these cases the mathematical expectation may be of relatively small practical importance. Can we usefully regard this outside possibility, given little weight in the mathematical average, as an unsought, unexpected reward that does not serve any economic function?

Third, the 'expected' gain is subjective. The same set of facts will be differently assessed by different individuals, even members of the same partnership and stockholders of the same corporation, and will result in different weighted expectations. Hence, if the gain in excess of the weighted average expectation were taxed differently from the rest of the gain, individuals receiving identical amounts of actual gain from similar or even joint investments would not be taxed alike.

And what would be the status of a realized gain that is less than the mathematical expectation? Strictly speaking, it should be regarded as not a gain at all. Instead, the amount by which it falls short of the expectation would have to be regarded as a capital loss.

To say that an individual's estimate of the weighted average of the probable results of a given investment is subjective is not to deny its usefulness to him in guiding his conduct. It may be the best guide available to him. The prudent disposition of irregular receipts from an investment, for example, how much to treat as current income and how much as a return of capital, may well be decided by applying as well as possible the weighted average of probabilities. And even if one investment has been completely liquidated with a sizeable gain, the investor may quite reasonably set aside some part of the gain, proportionate to the probabilities, as a reserve against a loss on his next commitment. Different business men and investors, however, will make different allowances of this kind, according to their varying expectations, and usually no records or objective tests of their varying expectations exist. But for purposes of income taxation, uniformity of treatment and objective tests and records are essential. Hence, if 'expected' and 'unexpected' gains are to be taxed differently, the mathematical concept of expectation does not appear to offer a practicable distinction for this purpose.

Finally, the whole concept of mathematical expectation can be applied to the risks and returns of business ventures only in a very loose and general fashion.[17] The grouping of investments into large homogeneous classes, which would be essential for any refined and reliable calculations of probabilities, is possible in practice to only a limited degree. The investor has neither an adequate statistical nor a clear *a priori* basis for such classification, except perhaps, and in only a broad way, for such broad groups as well protected mortgage bonds versus industrial common stocks, public utility versus industrial stocks, or various kinds of rented buildings and sites. Within each broad group of equity investments any adequate recognition of significant differences would require numerous subgroups containing only a few or even single enterprises. In the last analysis, after taking account of the factors he can measure in some degree and others he cannot measure, the investor arrives at a judgment or estimate. This will rarely be a calculated measure of the average probability, and will often be no more precise than that the commitment in question is likely to prove relatively profitable — say to yield more than 15 or

[17] For an excellent discussion of the fundamental limitations of applying probability calculations to business decisions see Frank H. Knight, *Risk, Uncertainty, and Profit* (Houghton Mifflin, 1921), especially Ch. VII.

20 percent and perhaps more than 100 percent — or that it is likely to prove at least moderately profitable and very unlikely to entail a loss. He commonly makes no clear line between expected and unexpected gains.

For one or more of the foregoing reasons, none or only the wholly uncontemplated gain, the last $5 in our example, is a true windfall or pure capital gain, in the minds of many. The rest is more or less definitely sought after, the object of purposeful activity. If we adopt the former view, capital gains and losses disappear into the category of profits; and even under the latter, the category of capital gains shrinks greatly. All the gains that enter into the calculations of investors as possibilities, even though greatly in excess of the weighted mathematical expectation, become ordinary profits. Doubtless some important cases of pure capital gains would remain, such as the discoveries and inventions mentioned earlier in our discussion of special cases. But a large part of what are conventionally regarded as capital gains would, in this view, be classified as ordinary profits. Similarly, since the possibilities of partial or complete loss are contemplated and weighed in connection with virtually all investments, most so-called capital losses would become ordinary losses. The subjective element that makes the concept of mathematical expectation difficult to apply would create difficulties also in determining what may reasonably be considered 'wholly uncontemplated', but the area of such difficulties would be very much smaller. Fairly arbitrary tests, such as those implicit in Sweden's restriction of the capital gains tax treatment to gains from real estate held 10 years or more or from securities or other property held 5 years or more, are probably the only ones possible.

Operating profits often include capital gains
The distinction between pure capital gains and ordinary income is blurred not only because a considerable proportion of all so-called capital gains are sought and expected in greater or less degree, but also because material amounts of so-called operating profits consist of more or less pure capital gains.

In the broad usage of the business world, realized capital gains, pure and otherwise, are a species of profits. Business men do not ordinarily make nice distinctions between various kinds or components of profits. They do not differentiate between 'pure' profits in the sense of the rate of return that constitutes the motive and necessary reward for risk-taking and profits in excess of this. Nor do they distinguish between either of these and the earnings properly attributable to the capital, labor, and other scarce resources provided by the owners of an enterprise, earnings the latter could largely command without going into business by hiring out these resources to others. The components of profits, as that term is ordinarily used, can be analyzed in greater or less detail; conspicuous in any classification would be:

1) Interest on the capital provided by the owners of the firm at a rate equal to what their capital as such could command elsewhere.

2) Wages for the time and trouble they devote to managing the business or to choosing men to manage it, measured by what they could earn as salaried employees performing similar services.

3) Rents received for scarce resources supplied by the owners including the special abilities and skills of the firm as an organized business enterprise, land and related physical resources, and various types of monopoly advantage.

4) Arbitrage gains arising from the exploitation of excessive discrepancies between the prices of the same or related goods in different markets, discrepancies larger than those justified by difference in costs. An unduly low price for a given type of raw material or labor may provide the occasion for such profits.

5) The rate of compensation needed to induce enterprisers to face the uncertainties and risks involved in their business.

6) Fortuitous gains, including the pure capital gains of the types discussed above.

The only common characteristic of these various components is that the return is contingent. The return a man receives on his government bonds is called interest rather than profits because the amount is fixed and guaranteed by contract; but the interest earned by a man's capital in his own business is regarded as a part of his profits because it is not guaranteed by anyone and its receipt is contingent upon earnings. Similarly, when the reward for personal services or land is not fixed but is contingent upon sales or earnings, it is regarded as a form of profit. Capital gains resemble other kinds of profit in that they too are uncertain and not fixed in advance by contract. Like operating profits, the conventional capital gain frequently represents expected compensation for personal services, interest on capital, and risk-taking. The area of wholly unexpected gains is much smaller, we found, than is often supposed.

The factors that create 'pure' capital gains and losses give rise also to unexpected increases or decreases in the reported operating profits of business enterprises. A part of the extraordinary profits of many American corporations in 1946 and 1947 was doubtless due to a more or less unexpected rise in the real value of their inventories as a result of the sudden release of demand that had been pent up during the war, and because wage disputes and shortages of certain critical materials severely impeded production. As these inventories were sold, the rise entered their books as operating profits. Another part was doubtless attributable to the rise in the general price level, which was reflected in a further increase in the money value of their inventories and in their reported profits. Still another part was due to the unusual scarcity of the equipment and organization possessed by many enterprises, a frequent source of unexpectedly large earnings during a short period. Because many types of business organization cannot be duplicated quickly, the established enterprises are able, in effect, to sell 1 to 2 years' use of their organizations at a higher price — profit — than they had expected. They will realize this unusual profit by charging higher prices for their products or by using their plants more fully than they had expected. Gains of this sort bulked large in 1942-49.

Or the unusual earnings may reflect lower costs than the enterprise had counted on. A lucky purchase of a major raw material may save it thousands of dollars. An unforeseen decline in interest rates may enable it to refund a large bond issue at a lower rate and thereby to reduce its annual interest costs for many years to come. Taxes may be cut unexpectedly. Conversely, the opposite of each of the foregoing occurrences may cause unexpected declines in earnings or increases in losses.

To the extent that these operating results are unexpected, they resemble pure capital gains: they do not guide or motivate conduct, they do not elicit or allocate resources.

To designate as capital gains and losses all unexpected profits and losses from operations raises the same questions with respect to the meaning of 'expected' discussed above. Does the 'expected' operating profit mean only the single most probable figure or does it include the entire range of expected possibilities, however remote some may be? As already noted, the investor or business man is usually interested in the whole pattern of possibilities rather than in their weighted average alone. If the 'expected' operating profit meant only the single most probable figure, actual operating earnings would clearly be different in nearly every case from the expected ones. Hence, if it were seriously proposed to apply this concept, a part of virtually all operating profits would have to be segregated as capital gains. Earnings less than the amount 'expected' would give rise to a capital loss equal to the deficiency. Operating losses in excess of operating profits over a reasonable period would become capital losses because investors would not ordinarily commit their funds if they 'expected' a loss. They would be apt to do this only in ventures offering the possibility of tremendous rewards relative to the amount risked.

The wisdom of attempting to separate windfall gains from ordinary income depends upon the purpose of the concept of income adopted and upon the kinds of records and information available. Those who distinguish unexpected gains from expected or ordinary income usually have in mind a concept of income that will serve an individual as a practical guide for prudent conduct. For purposes of taxation, however, as we saw, the distinction raises great difficulties. These difficulties have been obscured and disguised by the rough rule of thumb adopted by governments: gains and losses on capital assets are presumed to be unexpected, and other gains and losses, expected; and only the latter are regarded as ordinary income. Our discussion has revealed that the concept of pure capital gains becomes considerably blurred when analyzed, and that much overlapping exists between capital gains and ordinary income, and most especially between capital gains and profits. These results of our analysis of the underlying economic nature of capital gains and losses are surely significant for the question of their proper tax treatment, though not necessarily decisive by themselves. The concepts of income held by the public, differences of opinion respecting the equity of alternative tax treatments, and the practical consequences of the latter must also be considered. We turn to some of these in the next chapter.

Chapter 4

ARE CAPITAL GAINS APPROPRIATE ELEMENTS OF TAXABLE INCOME?

While in an economic sense ordinary income and even relatively pure capital gains overlap in considerable degree, the overlapping is by no means always complete. Different concepts of income, moreover, may be valid for different purposes. An individual may readily concede that a $100,000 legacy he received in 1951 increased his wealth by that amount, yet insist that to regard it as a part of his 1951 income would work an injustice on him and be misleading. Similar contentions have been made with respect to capital gains. The practical question faced by the lawmaker is: are the differences in practice between ordinary income and conventional capital gains and losses sufficient to warrant the exclusion of all or most of the latter from taxable income or, at any rate, to justify a special tax treatment for them?

Conflicts of opinion on this question are traceable to differences in the concepts of income we find useful for different purposes, in our attitudes toward different kinds of capital gains, in our tax objectives, and in our estimates of the practical economic effects of different tax treatments. Some of the chief considerations are examined in this and subsequent chapters.

1 DO CAPITAL GAINS REPRESENT LESS TAXPAYING CAPACITY?

As we have observed, capital gains, unlike wages, interests, rents, or ordinary profits, lack a continuing source such as a job, a farm, or a business enterprise. Instead, they arise out of discrete transactions that may occur only a few times in an individual's life. Hence they lack the relative stability and recurring character of ordinary income. For these reasons many believe that a capital gain represents less taxpaying capacity than ordinary income.

For the same reasons capital gains are usually excluded from what we might term the prudent consumption concept of income, a concept widely used to govern an individual's or a family's consumption expenditures. It distinguishes between sporadic and regularly recurring receipts on the ground that only the latter may prudently be spent. Sporadic gains are often followed by sporadic losses. A prudent man conserves much or all of the former to meet the latter. The implication is that he should not have to pay income taxes on receipts he cannot prudently spend.

These considerations obviously possess some merit. We illustrated them in Chapter 1 by comparing the position of a widow whose annual income of $18,000 comes from her ownership of $720,000 par value of 2½ percent Treasury bonds with that of her brother whose $3,000 of ordinary income is augmented in 1951 by a capital gain of $15,000 realized by the sale of a house he had owned 30 years. To tax the brother and sister alike as the recipients of $18,000 incomes in 1951 is to ignore a significant difference in quality between the two incomes. The bondholder will go on receiving her $18,000 a year indefinitely without significant risk, whereas her brother may never again receive an income in excess of $3,000. An income tax that does not distinguish between recurring and nonrecurring types of income might be said to ignore the fact that a man's capacity to pay taxes depends not only upon his income in any single year but upon the average income he has been receiving and to which he may reasonably look forward.

A contrary argument may also be advanced, however, and has often been used to support proposals for relatively heavy taxation of certain windfall receipts. The recipient of an unexpected gain can afford to pay more of it in taxes precisely because it is a windfall. He has not counted upon it for his ordinary expenditures. Since his gain was unsought, or at least was won without a commensurate service on his part, it is a fitting object for especially heavy taxation. The same reasons make it socially safe to impose such taxation, it is contended, for heavy taxes on unsought and unexpected receipts will not discourage effort and enterprise. Some proposals for special taxation of 'unearned increments', such as Henry George's proposal a few generations ago that increases in land values be taxed away, are based in part upon this view. The belief that relatively high rates of profits usually reflect windfall or unearned profits in large degree supplies much of the support for excess profits tax proposals.

But, as we have seen, conventional capital gains function in considerable measure like other profits in providing incentives for business men and investors and in guiding the allocation of our human and material economic resources; and we noted the practical impossibility of isolating the truly unsought and unearned elements in the total conventional capital gain. These considerations argue strongly against subjecting conventional capital gains to especially heavy taxation on the ground that they represent unearned windfall receipts.

On the other hand, when we examine more closely the prudent consumption concept of income and the related reasons for holding that capital gains represent less taxpaying capacity than ordinary income, we find that these require not so much the complete exclusion from taxable income of all sporadic receipts and losses as some effective provision for averaging them over the incomes of several years. Irregularity is not peculiar to capital gains. Some ordinary kinds of income, notably profits and commissions, are subject to substantial fluctuations, and even wages and salaries are far from stable in many industries. But capital gains and losses display this characteristic in extreme degree. The strong case that exists on equitable grounds for permitting variations in ordinary income to be averaged over a reasonable period to calculate taxable income becomes compelling when applied to capital gains and losses.

Effect of the progressive rate schedule

Not only are capital gains sporadic, but the amount technically realized in a given year may have actually emerged over many years. To impute an irregular or long emerging gain to a single year has serious practical consequences under a progressive scale of income tax rates because it pushes the gain into higher tax brackets than those into which it would fall if it were distributed among several years. A man whose ordinary net income was $10,000 a year in 1940-49 and who realized net capital gains totaling $50,000 in 1949 in securities purchased 10 years previously would be subject to additional income taxes approximating 42 percent of his capital gain if the latter were included in full as a part of his 1949 income whereas the additional taxes would have aggregated only 24 percent of the gain if the latter had been divided equally among the 10 annual tax returns and taxed as ordinary income at the 1949 rates.[1] Analogously, the tax reduction is smaller — barring changes in tax rates — if a long emerging capital loss or any sporadic loss is charged to the single year in which it is realized than if it is distributed over several years.

For administrative reasons primarily, though for other reasons

[1] Assuming taxpayer is married, does not have any dependents besides his wife, and filed a joint return in 1949.

as well, Congress has been reluctant to adopt direct averaging for either capital gains or ordinary income. One objection has been the resistance of taxpayers to having their tax liabilities increased in bad years by reason of their larger incomes in good years. The preferential tax rates applicable to capital gains during most of our income tax history have been an offset to the inequitable results of applying the progressive rate schedule to long emerging and other irregular capital gains, though different income groups have benefited from this offset in varying degree. In recent years Congress has established a partial measure of averaging by permitting net capital losses to be carried forward and applied against the net capital gains of the succeeding 5 years.

2 IS AN INCOME TAX ON CAPITAL GAINS REALLY A TAX ON CAPITAL?

One of the most persistent objections to taxing capital gains as income is the contention that it leads to the destruction of capital and to double taxation. This objection has been made with special force by those who emphasize the value to society of saving and capital accumulation. A rise in the value of a capital asset means merely an increase in the value of the future incomes expected from it, not in currently disposable income. If the rise is taxed, the owner's capital will be reduced, though by only a fraction of the rise in the value of his capital. For analogous reasons, it may be argued that capital losses should be excluded from the calculation of income. Great natural disasters such as earthquakes and floods, for example, produce losses primarily of future income or capital rather than of current income because the impact of the disaster is mainly on future earning power.

However, the tax cannot literally be paid out of the existing real capital of society as a whole, and therefore cannot directly reduce that capital, except in the limited and unusual case in which it absorbs funds needed to maintain the property and allow for its depreciation. The enhanced value of a piece of land, a mine, a building, or some shares of stock will not be cut by the tax, nor will the remaining capital of society be reduced in value in consequence of it. For society as a whole a capital gains tax, like any other tax, can be paid only from current income (with the limited exception already noted), and it can absorb capital only in the sense of reducing the amount of current income that would otherwise be saved.

For example, if the discovery of new ore veins arouses expectations that the future average net income from a given silver mine will be stepped up from $100,000 to $300,000 a year, and the going rate of return on such investments is 10 percent, the capital value of the mine will tend to rise to $3 million.[2] If the owners sell, they will realize a capital gain of $2 million. But the rise in capital value represents mainly silver still in the ground, most of which will not be available for some years. It represents future incomes. A tax levied on it cannot be paid this year from future income but must be paid from current funds which might otherwise be saved. This is true whether the funds for the tax come from the price paid by the purchasers or, if the latter pay in the form of promissory notes or other securities, from current savings made by or funds borrowed by the sellers.

There is ground for believing that taxes on capital gains tend to absorb potential current savings to a greater degree than taxes on ordinary components of income. Unusual, unexpected, sporadic, and lumped receipts are not often counted on to meet ordinary consumption needs, nor arc the consumption standards of the recipients likely to rise promptly to absorb them. Much of such receipts are apt to be treated as additions to capital, not available for consumption. In consequence, taxes on capital gains are more likely to be paid at the expense of savings than taxes on ordinary income.

The view that double taxation results when capital gains are taxed as income, which we examined in another connection in the preceding chapter, applies with equal force to the part of ordinary income that is saved and invested; and the most vigorous proponent of this view so applied it without distinguishing between the two (Ch. 3, note 7). Professor Fisher argued that to tax a man on wealth he acquires but does not consume, whether he obtains it through ordinary savings or through a rise in the value of his property, is to tax him for adding to the accumulated wealth of the nation.[3] Only a tax on consumption spending would approximate a true income tax in this view.[4] Under such a tax, consumption expenditures made from capital would be treated as income.

Saved income resembles capital gains further in that as soon as current savings from ordinary income are invested in durable goods,

[2] Assuming the mine may be regarded, for practical purposes, as having an infinite life and that it cost $1 million.

[3] Not all additions to an individual's wealth add to the wealth of society, however, as is brought out later.

[4] Strictly speaking, expenditures for durable consumption goods would have to be allocated over the life of the goods rather than counted as income of the year in which they were made.

they too become capital values representing future incomes. If a man invests $25,000 of his savings in a store building, he exchanges them for the future incomes expected from this building. If a tax is imposed both on the savings so invested and on the subsequent income he purchased with them, we have the same double taxation. The tax absorbs potential capital equally when it is levied on saved income as on capital gains, for in both cases it is paid from current income that might otherwise be saved. If the government spends the tax revenues for ordinary operating expenses, it might be said to consume potential capital (waiving the question of the availability of idle resources in the economy). If it spends them on capital improvements, it might be said to convert potential private capital into public capital. But the same statements may be made equally about taxes on saved income and on capital gains. In fact, all taxes absorb private income that might otherwise be saved by the taxpayers.

If, as is nowadays customary, we define income as consisting of consumption plus saving (positive or negative), no double taxation takes place when we tax both the saved part of current income and, subsequently, the income derived from the savings. The recipient has a choice of consuming his whole income or saving a part of it in order to increase his future income. With the same concept of income it may be argued that double taxation is similarly absent when realized capital gains are taxed as income. The investor need not reinvest his gains; he can increase his consumption by an equal amount without entrenching upon his capital. If the capital gain is not included in his income when realized, and the recipient consumes it, the gain would not be taxed even once. If he does reinvest the gain, and it is taxed as a part of his income, he is in the same position as one who saved an equal amount out of income from other sources: his reinvested gain is a part of his saved income, and any yield subsequently derived from it would be a part of his income in future years. Logically, the same argument can be extended to unrealized capital gains. These may be regarded as savings from current income which the investor could have chosen to realize and consume, but which he actually chose to reinvest. (Market quotations are not always a reliable measure of the sales value of large blocks of assets, which sometimes cannot be sold at prices per unit as high as those for smaller blocks and sometimes command higher prices.)

A possible distinction between capital gains and saved income is that the latter appears for a time to offer a wide range of choice with respect to the form the income may take, whereas the former is already embodied in a specialized form. This distinction may be useful for some purposes of national income analysis. A nation engaged in war could conceivably divert all its productive resources for a time to the creation of goods and services for current consumption, and in this way transform all potential savings from ordinary income into consumed income. But, except by selling assets to foreigners, it could not arrange to have all its capital gains take a currently consumable form. The new silver ores mentioned a few pages back will be consumable only in the future. In effect, for society as a whole, capital gains behave like specialized savings that are automatically invested and cannot be converted at will into consumption goods.

But this distinction has only limited application for individuals. By selling the asset embodying a capital gain, a man may convert his gain into any kind of goods. Except for the trouble and expense of selling, his position is not significantly different from that of a man who has saved an equal amount. If the capital gain has just been realized and is in cash, it is indistinguishable from an equal amount of money saved from current income. If the capital gain has not been technically realized by the sale of the asset, it is indistinguishable from an equal amount of ordinary savings invested in such an asset.

For society as a whole, moreover, saving and investing must be virtually simultaneous. An individual may accumulate wealth in the form of money or other claims against other individuals, but society as a whole cannot, for the increase in the claims of some individuals will be canceled by the increase in the obligations of others. Society as a whole can save only by simultaneously investing the savings in specific ways. The savings must take specific forms day by day as they arise because the surplus productive capacity they represent will not 'keep' unless converted into specialized products. A man's labor unused today cannot be added to the labor available tomorrow; it is lost forever.[5] In practice, therefore, the country's savings must be invested in more or less specialized assets just about as soon as they arise if they are not to be dissipated in losses, and these assets, like unrealized capital gains, then derive their value from the future incomes expected from them.

Although a concept of income that identifies it with consump-

---

[5] Except, of course, to the extent that rest or recreation increases his future productivity.

tion is doubtless valid for some purposes, its application to income
taxes appears to have had relatively few proponents among either
economists or laymen. Why? Perhaps one reason is that people
do not behave as if final consumption is their sole motivation in
earning and using their money incomes. Wealth yields power, security, and other satisfactions even when it is not consumed. Another
reason is that a reduction of inequalities in the distribution of income
has been an objective of tax policy, and in the minds of lawmakers
and others this objective has apparently outweighed solicitude for
the growth of capital. A more general reason, discussed further
below, is that a broader concept of income than the amount used
for consumption alone — current accessions to our power to spend
for both consumption and investment — has been widely accepted
as more useful for most purposes.

Concern over the ill effects of tax policies in dissipating potential
private savings has been far less widespread and influential in recent
years than formerly. J. M. Keynes and his followers during the
Great Depression attacked the assumption once generally made that
private savings are always promptly invested and add commensurately to society's wealth. Instead, they asserted that investment outlets are often insufficient to absorb all the would-be savings, so that
a portion of the latter remains barren. The attempt to save what
is not currently invested actually does damage, moreover, by reducing the aggregate demand for output and, therefore, for labor and
other productive factors. Applied to taxation, one moral of these
teachings was that when the government absorbs and spends private
funds that would otherwise be saved, or creates and spends new
funds, the effect is not always or even usually to reduce private real
capital accumulation. In times of underemployment of productive
capacity and of inadequate investment outlets for savings, it only
prevents these would-be savings from going to waste and from
reducing output and employment.

The foregoing view obviously rests upon the assumption that
the demand for savings is usually deficient, that underutilization
of productive capacity is the normal situation. But even if the opposite were usually or temporarily true, and would-be savings could
be expected to become fully invested, it might be contended that
the resulting additions to the country's capital would not necessarily
include some forms deemed essential for public purposes. Given
substantially full employment, private spending for capital purposes
competes no less actively than private spending for consumption

purposes with the purposes for which the government is raising revenue. Whether a man spends his income on short lived consumption goods, or on factory buildings and machinery, or on consumption goods that last a long time, he is disposing of scarce labor, materials, and other resources that the government is seeking to command by means of its tax revenues. In levying an income tax, the government implicitly seeks to transfer buying power from private hands to its own. Another objective, as noted above, is to reduce inequalities in income and wealth. A concept of taxable income confined to consumption expenditures would appear to be too narrow for these purposes of the income tax. As far as capital gains resemble saved income, therefore, and apart from other considerations noted below, it may be contended that they are properly included in a concept of income designed to serve as a base for the equitable distribution of the costs of government among taxpayers, although various practical considerations may constrain us to give them special treatment and to leave unrealized gains untaxed.

3 SOME CAPITAL GAINS NOT A PART OF SOCIAL INCOME

In the preceding section we implicity assumed that the capital gains and losses of individuals represent also additions to or subtractions from the wealth of society as a whole. The point was made and discussed that such gains and losses represent changes in the value of prospective future incomes rather than in the present disposable income of society, and in this sense constitute changes in capital, not income. New discoveries of natural resources are outstanding examples of private capital gains that are also additions to the wealth of the nation. The man who discovers an oil pool or copper ores may reap a capital gain that represents no less an addition to the country's wealth than an equivalent amount of saved and invested income. Beyond this, a mere redistribution of titles to property through purchase and sale may put capital assets into more active hands or superior uses and so enhance their value.

But many capital gains of individuals do not add anything to either the present or future income of society as a whole. They are gains made by some individuals at the expense of others. For example, the common stockholders of a corporation may obtain large capital gains at the expense of the preferred stockholders as the result of a recapitalization in which arrearages of preferred stock dividends are wiped out and the regular rate of preferred dividends is reduced in exchange for small concessions in cash or stock granted to the holders of preferred stock. The current and prospective net operating income of the company may be wholly unaffected by the recapitalization, but the relative rights of the two classes of stockholders in the distribution of this income have been altered to the advantage of the common stockholders.[6] Similarly, a marked reduction in federal tax rates on corporate income, by increasing the prospective earnings available for common stockholders, may lead to substantial appreciation in the value of common stocks and substantial realized capital gains without any correlative increase in the wealth or income of the country as a whole. The increase in private incomes is matched by a decline in the government's income. Analogously, a rise in corporate tax rates, other things being equal, will tend to bring capital losses to individual stockholders even though society as a whole many not sustain any corresponding loss (though it may lose indirectly by discouraging subsequent investment in common stocks of new or growing enterprises). Patents, copyrights, and unauthorized monopolies may enable some concerns to charge prices for their products far above costs. Their continuing ability to obtain a high rate of profit will be capitalized by the market, enabling their stockholders to realize large capital gains by selling their holdings. These gains will not represent additions to the wealth of society as a whole, but only the power of one section of the public to exact higher prices from the rest of the public. The increasing scarcity of land in all densely populated areas leads to increases in the rental value of land and, therefore, in its capital value, without necessarily bringing a corresponding net gain to society as a whole.[7]

In all these cases it may be argued that there is no social income corresponding to the capital gains, and that taxes levied upon the gains are therefore not taxes on true income. The individual has obtained an increase in the commodities and services he can command, but at the expense of other individuals, not from a net addition to the total of goods and services. This point, like a somewhat similar one in the preceding section, may be significant for some purposes. In estimating national income with the object of calculating how much might be available for military expenditures in the event of war, for example, it would obviously be absurd to include

[6] On the other hand, the recapitalization may benefit the preferred stockholders as well as the common by facilitating a general improvement in the corporation's affairs. A new and more vigorous management may be attracted and the company's credit position bettered.

[7] Cf. M. A. Copeland, Problems in the Theory of National Income, *Journal of Political Economy*, Feb. 1932, pp. 12-3.

current increases in the scarcity values of urban land because the resulting estimate of national income would be misleading for the purpose for which it is designed.

But is the same concept of income the most appropriate for income tax purposes? In taxing individual incomes Congress does not inquire, in connection with receipts of salaries, commissions, profits, etc., whether corresponding additions have been made to aggregate social income. The gambler's gains, the racketeer's extortions, the monopolist's exactions are all taxable as income. A prevailing view holds that our object in taxing income is to apportion the costs of government among individuals in accordance with their relative capacity to bear them. Income serves as the base for measuring such relative capacity. The income that is appropriate for this purpose, it may be contended, comprises all increases during the year in an individual's economic power except those, such as gifts and inheritances and unrealized gains and losses in property values, that we choose to exclude on special grounds of policy or expediency. A man who obtains a capital gain by shrewd or lucky trading in titles to property may not thereby raise the national income but he surely adds to his own power to command goods and services from others and to contribute to the support of government. Similarly, to the extent that the income tax is designed to reduce inequalities in the distribution of income — and this is a conspicuous effect of the progressive rates at which the tax is levied — the same emphasis upon changes in their relative economic power, including capital gains and losses, would seem to be appropriate.

4 HOW REAL ARE CAPITAL GAINS AND LOSSES DUE TO CHANGES IN INTEREST RATES?

The implication of some of the preceding discussion has been that if, instead of asking 'What is income?' we ask 'What concept of income is most suitable for the income tax?', many, though not all, persons who might deny that capital gains constitute income for various other purposes might conclude that they should be so regarded for the purpose of the income tax. But all capital gains and losses are not alike. Two kinds, in particular, are regarded by many as less indicative of taxpaying capacity than ordinary income: capital gains and losses due to changes in interest rates; and capital gains and losses due to changes in the general price level.

Changes in the rates of interest prevailing in the investment markets may produce capital gains and losses for investors without altering the interest and dividend payments they receive from their investments. John Smith owns $100,000 principal amount of 4½ percent 50-year railroad bonds which he bought at par in 1929. They have 30 years to run, but Mr. Smith wishes to sell them in order to reinvest the proceeds in bonds with more diversified maturities he deems safer. The average yield to maturity on the current market value of his old bonds and on those he wishes to buy is now 3 percent. If he sells, he will realize a capital gain of nearly $30,000, but he will have to reinvest the entire capital gain along with his original principal if he is to maintain an undiminished income of $4,500 a year for 30 years from his bond portfolio. If a part of his capital gain is taxed away, the remaining proceeds of his bond sales, invested at 3 percent, will not bring him as much interest income as he received before. But if he does not alter his holdings, he will not pay any tax and will maintain his $4,500 income undiminished. Is this kind of capital gain, a gain due solely to a decline in interest rates, properly treated as ordinary income for income tax purposes? Does it reflect increased taxpaying capacity?

A rise in interest rates may create capital losses of a similar debatable character. Suppose Mr. Smith, because he wishes to avoid the tax, decides not to sell his bonds. Suppose, instead, he achieves the diversification he desires by buying with other resources an additional $100,000 of 30-year prime public utility bonds at par to yield an average of 2½ percent. Suppose that 2 years later, interest rates on such bonds rise to 3½ percent. Smith's new bonds consequently decline in market value to about $82,240. Smith's investment adviser may now say to him: "If you sell this second $100,000 worth of bonds at market prices, you will technically realize a loss of more than $18,000. But you can use the proceeds to replace the bonds you sell with an equal amount of other bonds just as good, for many other good bonds are available with the same yields as the bonds you own. By selling your bonds you will be able to use your loss to reduce your taxable income, thereby cutting your income taxes by perhaps $6,000. Since 1942, the law has been that you must take into your income tax account half of the capital gains and losses from assets held more than 6 months and the full amount from those held 6 months or less. Hence your loss would fully offset an equal amount of long term capital gains or half of short term capital gains. If your taxable capital gains this year are not enough to absorb your allowable loss in full, you will be permitted to offset $1,000 of the remainder against your ordinary income this year and in each of the next 5 years, as well as to offset the rest against taxable capital gains realized in any of the next 5 years. Hence you are pretty sure to make a handsome tax saving by taking this loss. Yet your bond income will not be reduced at all, for you will get just as much interest on the new bonds you buy as you have been getting from those I advise you to sell." The investment counsellor should have added, however, that the shift in holdings will reduce the investor's cost basis, and will therefore create a larger taxable gain or a smaller deductible loss if the new holdings are subsequently sold.

If we confined our attention to relatively uncomplicated cases of this kind, and assumed that the investor intended never to consume any of such capital gains or to alter his consumption outlays by reason of such capital losses, most persons would probably be inclined to exclude this type of gain and loss from taxable income. The increase in Mr. Smith's economic power when his portfolio rises in value from $100,000 to $120,000 will not seem real to them if Mr. Smith continues to receive the same dollar amount of interest as before. Their attitude would be analogous with respect to the losses arising from a rise in interest rates. Such an attitude is likely to be especially strong in countries and among groups where *rentier* incomes are important.

But in practice several complicating considerations arise. Mr. Smith may not always keep his capital gains inviolate. When interest rates fall markedly, he may sell a portion of his bonds at a substantial gain and use some of the gain for consumption purposes. He may have expected the decline in interest rates and sought the accompanying capital gain as a species of profits, more or less as any speculator seeks to profit from a change in prices. He may now believe that interest rates are likely to go up, and he may speculate on this possibility by keeping his funds withdrawn for a time from fixed interest investments. He may invest a part or all of his capital gain and original principal in common stocks with the aim of profiting from an advance in stock prices or of augmenting his annual investment income. If he exercises any of these or other options, his capital gain serves him precisely as would a profit of equal amount on a business transaction. In short, if we think of Mr. Smith's gain as consumable or even as available for new and different types of investment operations we become inclined to modify our initial position that such gains and losses are unreal.

Another and related disturbing consideration is introduced when we compare Mr. Smith's position with that of Mr. Jones, whose sole income is his salary. When a decline in the interest rate enables Mr. Smith to realize a capital gain of $30,000, has not his economic position improved relative to that of Mr. Jones, whose salary income has been unaffected by the fall in the interest rate? Here, again, the question appears to turn upon whether it is reasonable to emphasize that Mr. Smith is free to consume his capital gain and his original principal. If we emphasize this aspect, the thought stands out that he now has the power to command $30,000 more of the world's goods and services than before, whereas Mr. Jones can command only the same dollar amount as before. If we assume that Mr. Smith will merely reinvest the proceeds of his sales in other similar bonds, we point attention to the fact that his interest income has not increased any more than has Mr. Jones' salary.

Mr. Smith's position has improved also relative to that of an individual who desires to invest for the first time. Both face lower interest rates, but Mr. Smith has an offset in his capital gain.

In principle, capital gains and losses arising from changes in interest rates would not seem to be different from those resulting from changes in other prices. An interest yielding security is simply a contract, a property right. Changes in its value produce the same alterations in the relative position of its owner as against the rest of the community as changes in the prices of other assets. If a lender contracts to supply the services of his funds at 4 percent a year for 10 years, and the market rate falls to 3 percent, his position is not different in principle from that of a firm that makes a transferable contract to deliver 100,000 pounds of copper a year for 10 years at 15 cents a pound just before a drop in the market price to 10 cents a pound. The contracts of both the lender and the copper firm are marketable pieces of property that have appreciated in value.

These conflicting considerations create doubts respecting the perfect justice in all cases of either excluding from or including in taxable income capital gains arising from changes in interest rates. If we attempted to treat these capital gains and losses specially, however, we would encounter difficulties. Were there merely one rate of interest, it might be possible to arrive at a workable measure of changes in it and, possibly, of the resulting capital gains and losses. But in practice many interest rates appear to exist. The pure rate for gilt-edged notes and bonds of some maturities is different from that for other maturities.[8] The supply of loanable and investible

[8] See David Durand, Basic Yields of Corporate Bonds, 1900-1942, and David Durand and Willis J. Winn, Basic Yields of Bonds, 1926-1947 (NBER, *Technical Paper 3* and *6*, 1942 and 1947, respectively).

funds is not perfectly interchangeable among the different maturities. Some investors, notably commercial banks, are constrained by the nature of their business or by governmental authorities to confine many of their purchases to short term securities. Variations in the confidence of these and other investors respecting the economic and political outlook alter their preferences for shorter or longer maturities at different times and bring about changes in the relative rates of interest. Nor are capital funds equally available for all classes of investments. Some funds are earmarked for gilt-edged investments alone. Other funds, in search of higher yields or speculative gains, are attracted to medium or lower grades of bonds and to the various grades of preferred and common stocks. Hence interest rates may move differently in different parts of the capital markets. Other forces, often stronger, are simultaneously affecting the market values of corporate securities, real estate, and other capital assets. To differentiate the part of a capital gain or loss that is attributable to a change in interest rates from the part attributable to all other forces would inevitably involve a large degree of conjecture.

Finally, it is doubtful that Congress and the public would accept the full logical implications of a special tax treatment for capital gains and losses arising from changes in interest rates. Let us suppose, for example, that these gains and losses were to be excluded from taxable income and that the difficulties of measuring them were overcome. An investor who purchased a certain second grade 5 percent 29 year railroad bond at 80, or $800 per $1,000 bond, because he believed its quality would soon improve and entitle it to sell on the same 3 percent yield basis as prime quality bonds, finds, 3 years later, that his judgment was correct. Because of a general rise in interest rates, however, the bond does not go up to $136, which would reflect a 3 percent yield on a 26 year obligation, but only to $116, at which price it is selling on the same 4 percent yield basis as other long term railroad bonds of prime quality. This investor will realize a capital gain of $360 per $1,000 bond when he sells, but if the effect of the rise in interest rates were excluded, his taxable gain would be $560 per bond. Such a discrepancy between the actual and taxable capital gain would be unlikely to be intelligible to the general public. Analogously, if, by reason of a reduction in earnings and dividends, a certain common stock declines in market value from $100 to $50 a share, then rises to $75 by reason of a sharp decline in interest rates, shall the investor who bought the stock at $100 a share and who sells it at $75, realizing a net loss of $25

per share, be credited for tax purposes with a net loss of $50 per
share on the ground that this is the true amount of his capital loss
when the effects of the decline in interest rates are excluded? Not to
exclude the effects of changes in interest rates in such cases but to
exclude them in others would obviously be inconsistent and unfair.
Yet to depart in this way from measuring gains and losses by actual
results in money would be, aside from the question of technical feas-
ibility, extremely likely to create misunderstanding and dissatisfaction.

We are compelled to conclude that the isolation and measurement
of capital gains and losses due solely to changes in interest rates
does not seem feasible; and that while some reason for doubt exists
respecting the perfect justice of either excluding them from or
including them in taxable income, we must perforce treat them
like other kinds of capital gains and losses.

5 ILLUSORY CAPITAL GAINS AND LOSSES FROM CHANGES IN THE VALUE OF MONEY

Far more questionable than the capital gains and losses due to
changes in interest rates are those due to changes in the value of
money. Shifts in the general price level create capital gains or losses
that are partly or wholly illusory. During 1944-50 many families
sold their houses at substantial profits only to find that houses of
the same size and character in the same or another city would take
the full proceeds; and that even if they spent these proceeds on
other goods they would command little more than the goods originally purchasable with a sum equal to the cost of the house at the
time of its original purchase. Did they enjoy a real gain, a real
increase in economic power? Should such capital gains be included
in their taxable income? Does not their nominal gain only or mainly
reflect a decline in the purchasing power or value of the dollar?[9]

The same questions may be asked respecting the capital gains
realized by business firms and individual investors when prices are
rising. For example, a corporation sells one or more of its plants
after a substantial rise in the general price level, and with the proceeds buys or constructs other plants, better located or better
designed for its purposes. The very rise in prices that created the
apparent capital gain on its old plant will inflate the cost of its new
acquisition. Similarly, a man who realizes a capital gain during such

[9] If they had owed money on their houses, however, they enjoyed a real gain
at the expense of the lenders by paying off the debts with dollars of smaller
purchasing power.

a period from an investment in common stocks may not enjoy any net increase in his command over goods and services. If he sells his stocks for double what he paid for them, but the general average of prices of stocks and of goods entering into the cost of living has also doubled, is it fair to tax his apparent capital gain as income?

Analogously, is it reasonable to allow capital losses as deductions from taxable income when the losses merely reflect declines in the general price level rather than real losses in economic power? Various cases of this sort occurred in the early 1930's. For example, if a man purchased an apartment house for $150,000 in 1926, when the net income from it approximated $15,000 a year, and sold it for $100,000 in 1933, when the net income had dropped to $10,000 a year, he realized a capital loss of $50,000. But $100,000 was then sufficient to purchase other apartment houses just as good as the one he had sold, and the $10,000 a year income he could expect from investing his $100,000 in such assets would purchase nearly as many consumer goods and services as the $15,000 income bought in 1926. The general run of other equity investments, notably common stocks, had suffered larger percentage declines in market value than his apartment house.[10] Does his capital loss of $50,000 truly represent a commensurate decline in his economic power? Should it be deductible in calculating his taxable income?

The obvious implication of the foregoing examples is that capital gains and losses that merely reflect changes in the general price level are not 'real' and that injustices are inflicted if they are treated as elements of taxable income. This is doubtless true. But these examples do not tell the whole story. By reason of both different degrees of sensitivity to general price movements and offsetting or accentuating influences in individual cases flowing from ordinary changes in the relative values of assets, all assets do not participate equally in a change in the general price level. When the latter rises 50 percent, some prices double, others triple, still others increase only 25 percent, while some prices do not rise at all, and perhaps a few may actually decline. The common stocks of automobile companies may rise in value both because the dollar amounts of their

[10] Between 1926 and 1933 rent paid by wage earners and lower salaried workers in 34 large cities, as tabulated by the Department of Labor, declined from 150.7 to 100.7 percent of the 1935-39 average. The total decline in the cost of living as measured by the goods purchased by these workers was from 126.4 to 92.4 percent of the 1935-39 average. The Dow-Jones average of industrial stock prices declined from 153.08 in 1926 to 83.73 in 1933 (average of daily closing figures).

earnings, like those of companies in other industries, are mounting, and because the automobile industry is faring relatively better than other industries. In addition, the stocks of some automobile companies may rise more than those of others because the companies are getting a larger share of the total motor car business; and the stocks of some companies may decline because of a shrinkage in their business. Hence the owners of some assets will enjoy very large real gains in their relative economic power after full allowance for the rise in the general price level; some will have smaller gains; others will be able to sell their assets for as much as or more money than before, but not for enough more to compensate for the rise in other prices; while the real losses of those whose assets decline in price will greatly exceed the amount of the decline. One important class of prices in particular will tend to remain unchanged or to decline somewhat: the prices of high grade debt instruments of all kinds, such as gilt-edged bonds, some preferred stocks and lease contracts, insurance policies, and bank deposits. Their loss in real value will not be reflected in a commensurate decline in price because their dollar claims to income and principal are not reduced. Some may decline moderately in price because some investors may press them for sale in an effort to transfer funds into common stocks and other equities whose prices are expected to participate in the general price rise. Individuals and enterprises owing relatively large long term debts, contracted in order to purchase property, will be able to service and retire these debts with a smaller proportion of their output or income, and the debt will constitute a smaller fraction of the total value of the property. Debtors in this way enjoy special real gains at the expense of their creditors when prices rise, in addition to any other real gains that may come to them in the event that the price advances in their assets outdistance the general price rise. In short, a substantial rise in the general price level usually produces large real as well as nominal capital gains and losses. Analogously, a substantial decline in the general price level tends to be accompanied by substantial changes in the relative economic power of individuals.

In recognition of the nominal character of some gains and losses and of the importance of the accompanying real ones the thought naturally occurs that we might measure and eliminate the former by means of price indexes and include only the latter in calculating taxable income. This is possible, though not without difficulty. Disputes over the choice of an index of prices appropriate for this purpose would be heated. At bottom, price indexes are only averages of what may possibly be highly dissimilar behavior on the part of the prices of different classes of goods and services. On the ground that investors characteristically use the receipts from sales of capital assets to purchase other similar assets, some would argue in favor of an index based wholly on investment assets, or of several such indexes, one for each major class of assets. Others, contending that the ultimate test of the value of the dollar is its ability to command consumption goods, would hold that an index based upon the latter's prices should be applied. Still others would argue for an all inclusive index of all kinds of prices.

To be consistent and fair in excluding from taxable income capital gains and losses that reflect changes solely in the value of the dollar, the law would have to provide not only for substituting, for tax purposes, amounts of gains and losses different from the amounts actually realized in dollars but also for substituting taxable net gains in some circumstances for dollar losses actually experienced, and deductible net losses for some dollar net gains actually experienced. If the price level fell 30 percent, an investor who sold his bonds at a 10 percent loss would properly be required to include a 28 4/7 percent gain in his taxable income. If the price level rose 50 percent, the investor who sold his bonds at the price he paid for them would properly be regarded as having realized a loss of 33⅓ percent, etc. Obviously, unless confined to exceptional circumstances, such tax treatment could be expected to be difficult to administer and highly confusing to the public. Moreover, allowances for imputed losses of the character illustrated, while consistent and fair, would be likely to stimulate an enormous and unnecessary turnover of fixed income securities, for the purpose of technically realizing imputed losses whenever the official index of prices rose significantly. A man whose $100,000 of high grade bonds remained at par while the official price index rose 25 percent would be motivated to sell his portfolio (probably replacing his bonds with other issues of like character immediately) in order to realize an imputed capital loss of $20,000. On the other hand, by not selling, many investors could avoid tax liability on imputed gains due to a fall in prices.

Such difficulties may lead different persons to diametrically opposite conclusions. Some, impressed with the large volume of purely nominal gains and losses, would minimize unfairness by excluding all capital gains and losses from taxable income. Others, impressed with the large volume of real gains and losses occurring at all times, and often accentuated by changes in the general price level, would minimize unfairness and avoid the difficulties of distinguishing one type of capital gain or loss from another by including all in taxable income.

The latter group will be joined by those who contend that the possibilities of change in the value of the dollar are risks investors must expect to bear and for which they demand and receive compensation; that the tax laws should not be designed to protect investors from such risks; and that protection from the risks of unstable money must rather be sought in our monetary policies and machinery. They further contend that those likely to be hit hardest by the inclusion of fictitious capital gains in taxable income are also likely to be those who, as holders of equities in real estate and common stocks, tend to gain most at the expense of creditors from the depreciation in the value of money. Similarly, in periods of price decline, when the holders of bonds, mortgages, annuities, and other fixed income contracts improve their real economic position relative to others, they tend to benefit less from the tax allowance for nominal capital losses than holders of equities. Hence, it is argued that the practical effects of including these illusory gains and losses in taxable income are roughly equitable.[11] These contentions doubtless possess considerable merit, but they suffer from being applicable in highly unequal degrees to individual cases.

Granting that it is not feasible to isolate spurious from real capital gains and losses with anything like precision, the question remains whether even a crude and limited attempt to make special provision for the former may not produce a net improvement in equity. Occasionally, when the value of a currency depreciates drastically, the resulting fictitious capital gains may be so tremendous as to dictate special provisions for excluding the increase in value between specified dates from income tax, and for allowing depreciation deductions to be based on the new price level. Something of this sort was done in Belgium after World War I, when the gold value of the franc was stabilized at about 3 cents (the prewar value was 19.3 cents).[12] It was done again in both France and Belgium after World War II (see Ch. 10). Even a gradual rise in the price level, if long continued, raises serious questions respecting both the equity and the practical effects of taxing all capital gains in full as ordinary income. In general it can be argued that the preferential tax treatment of capital gains and the limited allowances for capital losses in force in the United States since the 1920's constitute one means,

[11] Simons, *Personal Income Taxation*, pp. 155 ff.
[12] D. M. Van Buuren, *Revenue Revision of 1942*, Hearings, Ways and Means Committee, 77th Cong., 2d Sess., p. 997.

however crude, of recognizing the illusory character of many capital gains and losses.

6 SPECIAL OBSTRUCTIVE EFFECTS OF TAXES ON CAPITAL GAINS

Many persons who are not greatly impressed by the distinctive characteristics of capital gains and losses as reviewed in the foregoing nevertheless favor preferential tax treatment for them on the practical grounds indicated in Chapter 1. They emphasize that an equitable distribution of governmental costs or a reduction of inequalities in the distribution of income are not the sole objectives of tax policy: encouragement to the *creation* of a larger national income and the avoidance of strong deterrents are also major objectives. Taxes on capital gains, at least when applied only to realized gains, impede the mobility of capital and enterprise. A man who is tempted to reduce his ordinary income tax by working less or by keeping a part of his capital idle is restrained by the consideration that he will lose the income at the same time that he escapes the tax on it. He cannot save the hours he does not work this year and use them next year. Hence, to discourage his exertions, the tax must be so high that the additional income left to him after the additional taxes is not worth the extra effort. But a much smaller tax on a capital gain may, if not applicable to unrealized gains, be enough to dissuade a taxpayer from selling property that he would otherwise sell. He does not necessarily lose the gain by postponing the sale and the tax liability. He may feel that the chances are as good that the property will rise further in value as that it will decline, while by not selling, he defers or avoids a tax. Meanwhile, as we have observed, he will enjoy most of the benefits of the rise in the market value of his property even though he does not sell.

When a man is trying to make up his mind whether to sell a property that has appreciated in value, even a moderate tax rate on capital gains, one substantially lower than that on ordinary income, may be decisive. Suppose his taxable income is $50,000 and his capital gain on the sale will be $100,000. If he is like most men he will not be absolutely certain, apart from the question of taxes, that it would be wise to sell. While some of his friends are urging him to take advantage of the high market to make sure of his gain, others are advising him to hold on in the expectation of a further advance in value. The latter perhaps point out that meanwhile the property will continue to give him an income equal to, say, 8 percent of its present market value. The former perhaps urge the merits of a competing investment. In the absence of personal circumstances exerting a strong contrary influence, the tax considerations loom large. For if the man sells, he will forfeit $25,000 of his gain to the federal government (under 1950 law). If he postpones selling, he retains the use of this $25,000 without cost. He is now getting $2,000 a year, before taxes, from the $25,000 he would pay in capital gains taxes. And if he never sells, his estate, before death taxes, will be $25,000 larger, other things being equal.

The impeding influence upon property transfers of any substantial tax on realized capital gains, when accompanied by the exemption of unrealized gains, is frequently encountered in connection with the rearrangement of property holdings investors desire to make from time to time as they grow older. A man past middle life may no longer be disposed to exploit vigorously his full powers of ownership in a business enterprise or in a piece of vacant or improved real estate, for example. He might prefer, if a tax cost were not involved, to sell his holdings at the market price and invest the proceeds in securities that do not require active management, such as United States government bonds. A familiar additional motive for selling is to reduce the degree in which an estate is concentrated in a single business enterprise or other property, and in this way to give the heirs the protection that comes from a diversification of risks. But these reasonable motives for selling conflict with the desire to avoid the capital gains tax; the consequence is, in many instances, that the sale is postponed until after the owner's death. When the owner is advanced in years or in feeble health, the tax saving offered for delay looms more important because it is more imminent and certain. Under such circumstances, few investment advisers are apt to counsel against delay when the unrealized capital gains are large.

The deterrent influence of the tax may be felt earlier in a man's life also. Men who have accumulated wealth in one or more highly successful ventures early in life, and who would be ready to realize their gains and to transfer their energies and funds to new ventures, are sometimes deterred by the certain immediate loss in their resources and income from the capital gains tax if they sell. As against this certain loss, the profits of a new venture are still conjectural.

In the opinion of some students impediments to transfers of property, though inconvenient and costly to individuals, do not produce seriously unfavorable social consequences. The investments have already been made. Whether they are owned by one person or another is not of much importance to society. In fact, a reduction in property transfers should be welcomed because of the accompanying reduction in the energies and resources devoted to speculation, and because of the more responsible character of ownership that is stable. H. M. Groves, for example, declared: "We can't be sure that some reduction in the amount of exchange, or the number of exchanges of investments, would be socially bad. It is often observed that this buying of securities for appreciation results in a very fleeting citizenship in American corporations. Stock owners often take very little responsibility and acquire very little information about the companies they own because their ownership is so highly transitory."[13]

Nevertheless, probably few persons would wish to go far in the direction of obstructing transfers of property. Generally speaking, the unimpeded movement of the various kinds of property holdings from those who are less able or willing to carry and manage them to others who value them more is not only in the interest of the individual but in that of society as a whole. It tends to place the ownership of the various types of assets in the hands of those who are disposed to make the best or most vigorous use of them. The tax on realized capital gains, by setting up an impediment to such transfers, may be charged, therefore, with preventing the optimum use of capital assets. Real estate firms in the larger cities occasionally encounter this impediment when they are attempting to assemble several parcels of real estate as a site for a new office building, department store, or apartment house. One or more of the desired sites is found to be owned by individuals who refuse to sell at prices reflecting even generous appraisals because they desire to avoid the resultant tax on their capital gains.[14] In consequence, a substantial improvement in the use to which the property is put may be prevented. Similarly, it may be argued that if there were no capital gains tax the control of various business enterprises would more readily pass from those whose interest in them has flagged by reason of age or competing opportunities to those who would exploit them more fully or wisely. In short, it may be charged that any substantial

[13] *Capital Gains Taxation, Panel Discussion* (Tax Institute, 1946), p. 19.
[14] To justify their conduct they must be convinced, of course, that the property will not depreciate in value significantly before their deaths, and that the sacrifice of income from the potential selling price, after adjustment for the income now received from the property and for both the capital gains tax and ordinary income taxes, will be more than made up by the combination of the saving in the capital gains tax and the possible further appreciation of the property.

tax on capital gains injures society as a whole by tending to keep the control of capital assets in the frail hands of the aged and inactive.

Strictly speaking, the adverse effects of a capital gains tax upon the mobility of property and enterprise do not arise from the tax as such, but from the fact that it is confined to *realized* gains. If an equal tax were annually imposed upon unrealized gains, the motive for retaining appreciated property in order to defer or avoid taxes would be removed. In other words, it may be said that it is the realization criterion for the taxability of capital gains rather than the tax itself that impedes transfers of property. Various proposals to include unrealized appreciation and depreciation in values in taxable income are reviewed in Chapter 11. We have mentioned some formidable objections to doing so (Ch. 2, Sec. 8): an actual market transaction or something approximating it is widely regarded as an essential criterion of the receipt of income; the legal content of income must approximate that of the intelligent layman for the successful administration of a statute requiring the cooperation of millions of individual and corporate taxpayers; an annual appraisal of every taxpayer's assets, including assets with markets so unorganized that any appraisal would be highly conjectural, would involve serious difficulties and a heavy administrative burden; where the assets are not easily divisable, or are saleable in part only at a sacrifice, and the taxpayer lacks adequate other resources, severe inequities would result from sales forced by a tax on unrealized appreciation; etc.

The allowance of realized capital losses as deductions from taxable income has the opposite effect of taxes on realized capital gains; the one stimulates property transfers, the other discourages them. A man who can reduce his income tax by selling an investment that has depreciated in value has a powerful motive to do so if he can find a substitute investment of equal attractiveness. (Theoretically, the new investment may be less attractive up to an amount equal to the value of the prospective saving in income taxes.) In many cases, he can do so without difficulty. He may sell his shares of stock in one steel company and buy shares in another; he may sell one list of high grade public utility and railroad bonds and buy a list of different but similar bonds; he may sell one building and buy another like it; etc. The taxpayer who contemplates rearranging his property holdings in recognition of his changed health or other circumstances has a positive tax saving motive to sell assets on which he can realize a loss.

The various restrictions that have been imposed from time to time in the United States upon the deductibility of capital losses have doubtless weakened this stimulus to property transfers, but they have far from eliminated it. Since 1916 capital losses have been allowed at least up to the amount of capital gains, except for losses from 'wash sales' of securities.[15] Various nontax influences operate, however, to bring about a fuller realization of potential capital losses than of potential capital gains (Ch. 5, Sec. 4). Hence, it would be difficult to contend that the stimulus of the allowance for capital losses completely offsets the brake of taxes on capital gains.

The deterrent effect of capital gains taxes upon transfers of property must be distinguished from their effects upon business initiative and new investment. To the degree that capital gains are truly 'pure', i.e., unexpected, a tax on them can hardly be said to discourage investment. For if a new investment is made without expectation of a capital gain, but solely in response to the prospects of ordinary income, the tax on capital gains does not enter into the investor's decision. To the degree that capital gains are such merely in form but really represent expected, though contingent, compensation for labor services, interest on capital, rent of scarce resources, or risk-taking, taxes on them will probably exert the same restrictive effects upon new investment and business initiative as equal rates of tax upon ordinary income. But in this connection the markedly preferential tax treatment of capital gains as compared with ordinary income in the United States since 1922 is significant. It can be said to have offered a special stimulus to all ventures and investments whose returns could be made to take the form of capital gains rather than ordinary income. Some case studies illustrating this influence were recently published by two members of the staff of Harvard's Graduate School of Business Administration. Summarizing their conclusion concerning the investment policies of the individual investors in the Lithomat Corporation, they declared: "During the first stage (prior to the time when commercial production became feasible) . . . personal income taxes reduced somewhat the *amount* of savings which interested individuals had available for investment in the project but did not significantly affect their *willingness* to invest in it. . . .

[15] That is, if a taxpayer sells securities at a loss but purchases other, substantially identical, securities within 30 days before or after his sale, the loss is not allowed; nor are losses deductible if they occur in connection with exchanges of property between members of a family.

At the second stage (when production was under way but had not yet become profitable) the personal income tax structure actually *increased* the availability of outside capital to Lithomat. The wide disparity between high individual income tax rates, especially on large incomes, and the relatively low rates on capital gains strongly stimulated the interest of venturesome investors in the Lithomat development. . . . This incentive entirely outweighed in importance the fact that capital gains on the Lithomat project, if successful, would have been fully taxable, whereas capital losses might not have been fully deductible if the project had failed.

In many respects the experience of Lithomat . . . is typical of many new developments offering possibilities of large capital gains. For instance, the interest of individuals actively participating in such developments is usually so intense that personal income taxes are not likely to affect seriously their willingness to invest in the project. Similarly, in so far as the participation of outside capital is concerned, the tax incentive provided by the favorable treatment of capital gains is so pronounced that it must have far-reaching effects on the attitude of investors generally."[16]

The objections examined in this chapter to treating capital gains and losses like ordinary income have been found to possess varying elements of merit and to be subject to qualifications of varying seriousness. Competing with these objections for the attention of the intelligent citizen and legislator are the equitable arguments urged by many and presented in Chapter 1 against any special tax treatment for capital gains and losses.

In a controversy so marked by conflicting qualitative considerations, questions of practical expediency are often decisive. How strong is the tendency of taxes on capital gains to impede transfers of property? Do the figures obtained from income tax returns during the last quarter century and more offer any evidence respecting the practical importance of different rates of tax in this respect? And can we get any light from these figures on certain other unfavorable practical effects that are sometimes attributed to the taxation of capital gains? Further, what evidence exists respecting the influence of the different tax treatments of capital losses we have tried? We turn to these questions in the next three chapters.

[16] J. Keith Butters and John Lintner, *Effect of Federal Taxes on Growing Enterprises* (Harvard University Press, 1945), pp. 24-6.

Chapter 5

CAPITAL GAINS AND LOSSES AND THEIR DISTRIBUTION, 1917-1946

1 NATURE AND SOURCES OF DATA

The data reviewed in this chapter consist largely of tabulations of figures individuals entered on their income tax returns. The net capital gains and losses thus reported year by year are far from perfectly comparable for the 30 years 1917-46, for they were affected by changing statutory provisions and by certain gaps and changes in the government's tabulations. To reduce the effects of these sources of heterogeneity, we made various adjustments and supplied estimates to fill some of the blanks in the published data. By these adjustments and estimates, described in detail in Appendix One, we obtained a continuous series of figures possessing a useful, though by no means close, approach to homogeneity.

In the discussion that follows, and in the tables, 'net capital gain' and 'net capital loss' refer to all net gains and losses from the sale of assets not part of the taxpayer's stock-in-trade, as reported on federal income tax returns, whether or not they were specifically defined as 'capital' gains and losses in the statutes applicable to particular years. That is, we ignored the statutory exclusion in 1922-23 of assets held 2 years or less from the category of 'capital' assets, the exclusion in 1938-41 of assets subject to an allowance for depreciation, etc. Our figures are the net capital gains and losses realized on sales or taxable exchanges of all such assets as tabulated from the returns and published in *Statistics of Income,* with the adjustments referred to. Despite our adjustments, the annual statistical series reflect variations in the statutory treatment. Consequently, for some purposes we treat separately the statistics for each of the 5 periods marked off by major statutory differences: 1917-21, 1922-33, 1934-37, 1938-41, and 1942-46.

2 LARGE AMOUNTS OF CAPITAL GAINS AND LOSSES EXCLUDED FROM THE DATA

A major effect of the statutes upon the statistics has been to exclude very large amounts of both 'realized' and 'unrealized' appreciation and depreciation in the market values of capital assets.

First, capital gains realized since but representing appreciation accruing before March 1, 1913, the effective date of the first revenue act under the 16th Amendment, have not been taxable or included in our figures, though the comparable losses have been treated and reported like any other capital losses. Section 113 (a) (14) of the Internal Revenue Code provides that if a gain is realized on property acquired before March 1, 1913 and the seller's cost or other basis is less than the fair market value of that date, the latter value shall be the basis for measuring the taxable gain. On the other hand, if the property is sold at a loss, the ordinary rules for measuring a loss apply, with no exclusion of that part of the loss that accrued before March 1, 1913. Consequently, substantial amounts of realized capital gains, but not of realized capital losses, have been excluded from our figures.

Second, the statutes do not take account of changes in the value of capital assets, however large, unless the change is converted into a 'realized' profit or loss by actual sale or taxable exchange. For example, the capital gain of about $29 million realized by the late Senator Couzens upon the sale of his stockholdings in the Ford Motor Company in 1919 got into the figures, but the larger 'unrealized' gains enjoyed by Henry Ford and his wife did not. Their gains will never get into the figures because they died without selling their holdings. As we noted, the unrealized capital gains and losses embodied in the value of the property transferred at death are not regarded by the statutes as thereby 'realized' by the decedent, his estate, or the individual heirs. For this reason, very large amounts of capital gains and losses incorporated in family property holdings have never gotten into the income tax figures.[1]

[1] Such avoidance of taxes on capital gains is in many, but not all, cases partly offset by increases in estate taxes. Other things being equal, the value of an estate will be higher by the amount of capital gains taxes avoided, and the estate will therefore be subject to larger taxes. The offset is only partial and may be wholly absent because (a) only a tax rate as high as 100 percent against the portion of the estate arising from the avoidance of capital gains taxes would be sufficient for a full offset, whereas the actual rates have of course been less; (b) estates equal to or less in value than the exempted amount are not taxed at all, regardless of the unrealized capital gains they may include;

Much of the appreciation and depreciation from cost in the values of properties transferred by gift (*inter vivos*) has likewise been excluded by the statutes. The transfer of property by gift is not regarded by the law as occasioning realization of gain or loss by the donor. The donee, in turn, does not report a gain or loss as long as he retains the property, and he never reports any if he holds the property until his death. If he sells the property he must, under the existing statute, include on his income tax return as a gain or loss the difference between the amount he realizes by sale and the donor's cost.[2] Previous statutes have differed in their treatment of gifts, with the result that varying proportions of the actual appreciation or depreciation in market value of properties transferred by gift were excluded from income tax returns. Even when realized by sale, no appreciation is recognized for tax purposes if the donee is a tax-exempt institution.

The provisions of the successive income tax statutes with respect to tax-free exchanges and reorganizations have also had the effect of excluding considerable amounts of appreciation and depreciation in capital assets from the reported figures because the relevant gains and losses have not been regarded as technically 'realized'. For example, a man who builds up a chain of grocery stores, then sells the chain to a larger chain-grocery enterprise, at a big profit, but arranges the transaction in the form of a tax-free reorganization and takes payment in the latter's shares of stock, is not regarded as 'realizing' a capital gain unless and until he sells this stock. If he dies without selling the stock, and his heirs sell it later, no gain is ever reported for the appreciation in the value of his investment that occurred up to his death.

Finally, the figures reported for income tax purposes naturally do not include the capital gains and losses realized by individuals who were not required to file returns under the different statutes because they received net or gross incomes smaller than various specified amounts. Because individuals reporting net incomes under $5,000 generally accounted for sizeable proportions of aggregate

---

(c) instead of increasing his taxable estate by the amount of the tax avoided, the decedent may have increased his spending by a part or all of it.

[2] Except that the market value of the property at the time of the gift, if less than the donor's cost, must be substituted for the latter in measuring a loss. For example, if Smith gives his son securities having a market value of $10,000, for which Smith originally paid $20,000, and the son sells them for $5,000, the latter's allowable loss is $5,000, not $15,000.

net capital gains and losses, it seems probable that those not required to file returns also realized substantial amounts. For the years before 1928 the gains and losses of individuals who reported no net income are excluded because the relevant data were not compiled for them, and no data are available on the excess of short term losses over short term gains in 1938-41, for these were not allowed as deductible items by the statutes during this period and the amounts were not tabulated.[3]

3 NET GAINS EXCEEDED NET LOSSES ONLY MODERATELY DURING
THE PERIOD AS A WHOLE

Net capital gains realized during the 30 years by individuals filing income tax returns and reporting net incomes, including taxable fiduciaries' returns, totaled approximately $50 billion, and for returns reporting no net income about $0.7 billion (Table 1). The tabulated total of net capital losses was approximately $23 billion for individuals reporting net incomes and $9 billion for those reporting no net income. (These are the sums of the annual net balances of gains over losses or losses over gains for each taxpayer reporting transactions in capital assets, not the totals of gross capital gains or losses.) As will be recalled, the net losses incurred by individuals who reported no net income for years before 1928 and the excesses of short term losses over short term gains in 1938-41 are excluded because the amounts have not been tabulated or published and because we could not devise satisfactory means of estimating them in detail. If they were included, the total net losses would probably reach or exceed $35 billion. In short, about 69 percent of the net capital gains realized by individuals and taxable fiduciaries during these 30 years seem to have been offset by their net capital losses, and the excess of gains would appear to have been only about $16 billion.

4 UNREALIZED GAINS MAY HAVE GREATLY EXCEEDED UNREALIZED
LOSSES

It might seem that the net result of all the 'sound and fury' of capital gains transactions during these 30 years, involving many hundred billions of dollars in purchases and sales, was relatively small. Some persons might be inclined to infer that capital gain and loss transactions are of minor importance and that it makes little difference how they are treated by the tax laws. No such inferences would be justi-

[3] For further discussion of the deficiencies in the comparability of the data for the various subperiods, see Appendix One, Part I, Sections D and E.

fied. For one thing, there are reasons to suspect that the 'unrealized' capital gains excluded from the figures because the technical legal criteria of realization were not met exceeded the net losses similarly excluded. Second, even if capital gains and losses actually canceled in the aggregate, the evidence suggests that such a balance was not achieved either for most individuals or even for the main large groups of persons engaging in capital transactions.

Comprehensive quantitative evidence to confirm the suspicion that aggregate unrealized capital gains exceeded unrealized losses does not exist; a study of the gains and losses embodied in a large number of estates upon the deaths of the owners would be one way of obtaining quantitative evidence on this point. In its absence certain qualitative considerations supporting the suspicion cannot be ignored.

First, as noted above, realized capital gains representing appreciation accrued before March 1, 1913 have not been recognized for tax purposes or included in our figures, though the comparable capital losses have been treated and included as ordinary capital losses.

Second, we know that the timing of the realization of capital gains is more subject to choice than the timing of the realization of losses. Defaults, bankruptcies, margin calls, and the desire or necessity to stop a loss from growing frequently compel the technical realization of losses at specific times, whereas analogous situations that compel the technical realization of capital gains at unwanted times are less common. Thus, capital losses were notably heavy in the crisis and depression years 1920-21 and 1929-33. Approximately half of the net capital losses of individuals reporting no net income in 1928-46 was concentrated in the 3 years 1930-32. For many taxpayers much of the net loss did not reduce their income taxes because they did not have enough taxable income to use up their deductible net losses. Nevertheless, they were forced to realize their losses. This difference tends to cause a larger proportion of potential losses than of gains to be 'realized'.

Further, as far as the timing of realization has been at the taxpayer's discretion, tax considerations have offered a greater inducement to postpone or avoid the realization of gains than of losses. When realized, the gains have been subject to tax while the losses have been allowed as deductions from taxable income only in varying and usually limited degree. In some years between 1917 and 1946 the deductibility of capital losses was restricted to the amount of realized gains, or to realized gains plus $1,000 or $2,000. Such restrictions doubtless caused individuals to try to defer the realization of losses in years when they were not realizing gains, and to speed the realization of gains to the extent that losses were being realized in any given year. But this type of provision tended also to speed the realization of losses, when possible, to the extent that gains were being realized. And it left intact the influential considerations that as long as the realization of net capital gains (gains in excess of deductible losses) was deferred, the taxpayer retained the use of funds that would otherwise go to the government in taxes, and that if the postponement lasted until death, the capital gains tax would be avoided forever; whereas postponing the realization of losses could yield a tax advantage only if the losses were subsequently realized in a year when offsetting gains also were realized or when the statute permitted a more liberal deduction of losses.

The privilege open to individuals in earlier years of making *inter vivos* gifts to children and others free from gift and estate taxes and in the later years of making them at lower rates of tax than those applicable to bequests, together with the lower income taxes payable when the income from a given amount of property was shared by several members of a family than when received by a single member, strongly promoted the distribution of wealth within families. But since a tax was payable on gains realized upon the sale of property even if the proceeds were transferred as gifts, whereas no tax was payable either by the donor or donee on capital gains embodied in gifts of the property itself as long as the donee retained possession, gifts 'in kind', on which the capital gains remained 'unrealized', were favored over gifts in cash. No such considerations impeded the realization of capital losses. Indeed, reverse considerations were influential, for taxes could usually be reduced by realizing losses.

The use of tax-free exchanges and reorganizations, so-called, as a means of converting properties, heavy with unrealized capital gains but lacking good marketability, into listed securities with excellent marketability was conspicuous during many of these 30 years; and this practice also, as noted above, had the effect of avoiding the technical realization of capital gains.

In some cases the realization of large capital gains and losses was indefinitely deferred or forever avoided for reasons unconnected with tax considerations: the desire to keep a controlling interest in a business enterprise — because of family tradition or the salaries, power, and other perquisites of control — or the desire to transmit specific income-yielding properties to heirs. But properties retained for these reasons were also much more likely to embody capital gains than losses.

The effects of two motives for postponing the realization of capital losses, as far as the timing was discretionary with the investor, should also be weighed: (a) The varying limitations on the deductibility of *net* losses doubtless caused some deferring of final realization pending a year in which the losses could be used in full to offset capital gains. (b) Many persons are reluctant to make the final acknowledgment of error implicit in 'taking' a loss. As long as the loss is not actually realized, no bookkeeping confession is necessary, and the possibility of a happy reversal in prices may continue to be cherished.

On net balance, the foregoing considerations lead us to believe it highly probable that total unrealized capital gains significantly exceeded total unrealized capital losses during these 30 years.

5 MODERATE EXCESS OF TOTAL GAINS OVER LOSSES CONCEALS WIDE VARIATIONS IN INVESTORS' EXPERIENCES

Unfortunately, we cannot show conclusively to what extent the moderate excess of capital net gains over losses 'realized' in 1917-46 hides significant differences in the experience of individuals and groups of investors because the statistics aggregate the experience of large and varying numbers of individuals classified in each year by the amount of their income. Except for special groups, the figures do not trace the experience of identical individuals for a long period. Consequently, we have to be content with three pieces of fragmentary evidence which, as far as they go, corroborate the general impression that capital gains and losses do not cancel for individuals or for most groups.

First, taxpayers with larger statutory net incomes, i.e., including net capital gains and losses, generally reported a more favorable ratio between their capital gains and losses than those with smaller incomes (Chart 5 and Table 4). In 1929, for example, individuals with statutory net incomes under $5,000 reported net capital gains only eight-tenths as large, in the aggregate, as their net capital losses, whereas those with net incomes of $25,000-50,000 reported net capital gains 5.4 times their net capital losses, the $300,000-500,000 group, 10 times, and the $1 million and over group, 15.3 times. The same general pattern, with only occasional irregularities, is found in the other years since 1926.

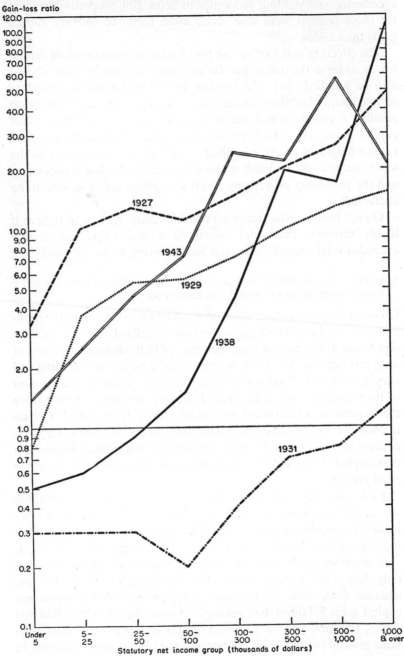

Chart 5
Net Capital Gain-Loss Ratio by Statutory Net Income Groups

Gain-loss ratio

120.0
100.0
90.0
80.0
70.0
60.0
50.0
40.0

30.0

20.0

1927

10.0
9.0
8.0
7.0
6.0
5.0

1943

1929

4.0

3.0

1938

2.0

1.0
0.9
0.8
0.7
0.6
0.5

1931

0.4

0.3

0.2

0.1
Under | 5- | 25- | 50- | 100- | 300- | 500- | 1,000
5 | 25 | 50 | 100 | 300 | 500 | 1,000 | & over

Statutory net income group (thousands of dollars)

Ratio scale

The fact that substantial capital gains by themselves lifted many individuals into higher brackets of statutory net income, thereby giving the higher income groups the benefit, statistically, of these gains, severely diminishes the value of the figures for this purpose. As respects losses the figures are better for our present purpose because in 1924-33 net capital losses segregated for tax credit were not deducted in determining the net income classification, and in subsequent years statutory limitations on the deductibility of net capital losses prevented any substantial downward shift in the income classification of the losers.

The second piece of evidence is the distribution of net capital gains and losses by the 'other income' of the recipient, i.e., income excluding net capital gains and losses, in the only year for which data have been tabulated, 1936. In that year, one of rising stock prices and of a considerable excess of capital gains over losses, the ratio between capital gains and losses was more favorable for persons with fairly high incomes, over $30,000, than for those with smaller incomes (Table 68). As we do not have any reason to believe this relationship was peculiar to 1936 we suspect that over a long period, such as the 30 years 1917-46, when total realized capital gains only moderately exceeded realized capital losses, individuals in the higher brackets of 'other income' made considerable net capital gains as a group while those in the other income brackets, in the aggregate, either made only small gains or suffered losses.

The third, and in some respects most pertinent, fragment of information is supplied by the net capital gains and losses in 1917-33 of 45 individuals, each of whom had a statutory net income of $1 million or more in 1924. Data respecting their experience became available through a study made by the staff of the Joint Committee on Internal Revenue Taxation in 1938.[4] Since these 45 individuals are all those among the 75 reporting incomes of $1 million or more in 1924 whose returns for all 17 years were available, the selection is unbiased except that unusual capital gains in 1924 may have led to the inclusion of some individuals who did not have a very substantial income from other sources in either that or other years. For the entire 17 years the 45 individuals had net capital gains of $187 million; if unreported losses in 1932 and 1933 were taken into account, the figure might be somewhat reduced, though in all likelihood not below $150 million. What is more significant, as may be seen in Chart 6 and Table 84, is that the total net gain is by no

[4] *Million Dollar Incomes* (Government Printing Office, 1938).

Chart 6

45 Persons with Million Dollar and Over Incomes in 1924
Net Capital Gains and Losses as Percentages
of Total Incomes, 1917-1933

To avoid the possibility of revealing the identity of anyone, yet indicate their
varying fortunes, the 45 taxpayers are divided into 8 groups on the basis
of the proportions their net gain or loss bore to their total income for the
17 years. Each horizontal line represents one taxpayer; its length, the
average percentage net gain or loss of his group.

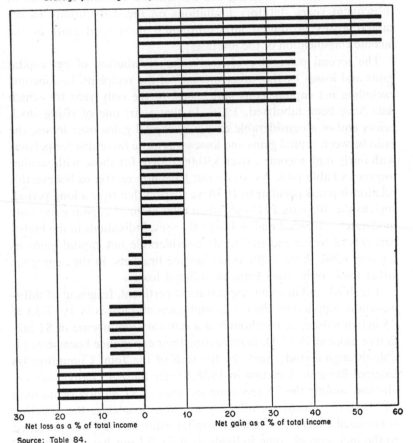

30   20   10   0   10   20   30   40   50   60
Net loss as a % of total income   Net gain as a % of total income

Source: Table 84.

means evenly distributed among the 45 individuals and that there
is little tendency for net gains in one year to be offset by net losses
in another year. As a result, 27 individuals had a net gain for the
entire period aggregating $253 million, while 18 showed an excess
of losses of $66 million. The net gains of the 27 ranged from less
than 5 to more than 50 percent of their total incomes (before negative and deduction items) for the 17 years, while the net losses of

the 18 ranged from less than 5 to 25 percent of their total incomes.

In addition to these fragments of direct evidence, a more general piece of statistical evidence to the same effect is the great irregularity from year to year in the relative amounts of aggregate net capital gains and losses. The 'twenties were favorable for making capital gains; the early 'thirties, unfavorable. Those who retired from speculative and investment activities or who died during the prosperous 'twenties did not get a chance to suffer offsetting losses during the depressed early 'thirties; and many who incurred severe losses in the latter period — as from investments in bonds that subsequently went into default — had not shared significantly in the large capital gains of the 'twenties.

6 ANNUAL CAPITAL GAINS AND LOSSES FLUCTUATE WIDELY

Net gains and losses fluctuated widely during the 30 years (Chart 7 and Table 1). Net gains rose to peaks of $4.8-4.9 billion in 1928, 1929, and 1945, and to $7.3 billion in 1946; in 1932 they fell to $184 million. The peak years for net losses were 1931 and 1932, when $3.2 and $2.9 billion respectively, were reported.

In Chart 2 and Table 5 net gains and losses are expressed as percentages of the net income reported on all returns with net incomes. For individuals with net income, net gains were 19.1 percent of their net income in 1928 and 18.9 percent in 1929; then the percentage dropped sharply. In 1932 it was only 1.4, and the net losses of net income reporting individuals constituted 15.6 percent of their net income.

7 TOTAL GAINS AND LOSSES FOLLOW STOCK MARKET MOVEMENTS

Since security transactions account for the major portion of capital gains and losses (Sec. 10), and since the stock market also reflects changes in the prevailing attitude toward capital assets in general, it is not surprising to find a general, though far from perfect, correspondence between fluctuations in capital gain and loss realization during the 30 years and the movements of security prices on the New York Stock Exchange (Tables 1 and 15). During the boom years 1924-29, when capital gains reached high levels and losses were relatively small, stock market prices were moving steadily upward. During the depression years 1930-32, when gains and losses showed the opposite picture, the trend in stock market prices was markedly downward. In the next 5 years, net gains, like the stock price index, rose in 1933, fell in 1934, rose in 1935 and 1936, and fell again in

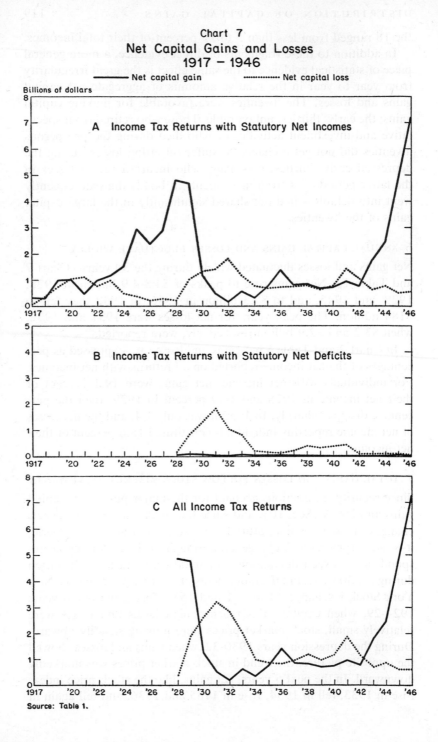

Chart 7
Net Capital Gains and Losses
1917 – 1946

——— Net capital gain ··········· Net capital loss

A   Income Tax Returns with Statutory Net Incomes

B   Income Tax Returns with Statutory Net Deficits

C   All Income Tax Returns

Billions of dollars

Source: Table 1.

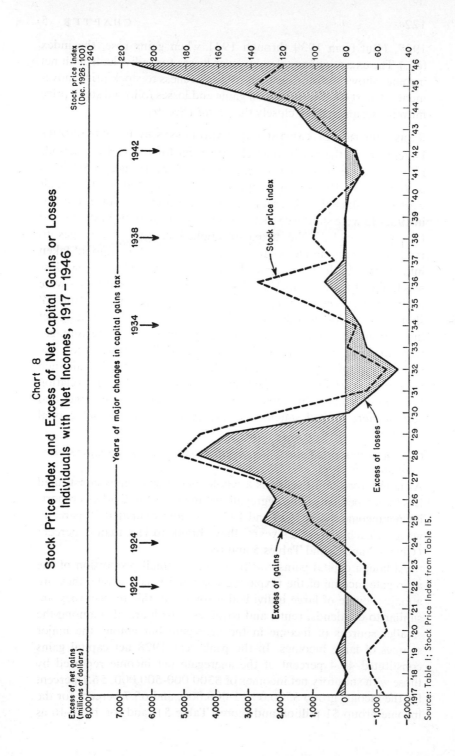

Chart 8

Stock Price Index and Excess of Net Capital Gains or Losses
Individuals with Net Incomes, 1917–1946

Source: Table 1; Stock Price Index from Table 15.

1937. (But from 1939 through 1941 when gains rose, the index fell.) The excess of capital gains over losses for individuals with net incomes shows the same general responsiveness to stock price movements (Chart 8). *Short term* net gains and losses followed stock price movements much more closely than *total* (Sec. 9).

8 DISTRIBUTION OF CAPITAL GAINS AND LOSSES BY INCOME GROUPS
Differences in the net income classification for the various periods rule out precise income level comparisons of annual data in *Statistics of Income*. In 1924-33 net capital losses segregated for tax credit were not deducted in determining the net income classification; nor in 1932-33 were short term net losses from transactions in stocks and bonds; in 1934-37 the taxpayer applied certain percentages to realized net gains and losses to determine the statutory amount taken into account in the net income classification, and deductible net loss was limited to $2,000; in 1938-41 realized net gains and losses were again reduced by applying certain statutory percentages, and all short term net loss was disallowed as a deduction in determining net income; and in 1942-46, somewhat different statutory percentages were in force as well as somewhat altered limitations upon the deductibility of net losses. Nevertheless, after allowing for all such variations, certain generalizations with respect to the relation between differences in income levels and capital gains emerge, and certain more limited statements may even be made about capital losses.

Capital gains a small part of aggregate net income but a major source of large incomes
As noted, for the 30 years as a whole, net capital gains constituted less than 5 percent of the aggregate net income of individuals reporting net income but in 1928 and 1929 they approximated 19 percent, while in each of 6 other years, they shrank to less than 2 percent (Charts 2 and 3; and Tables 5 and 6).

Although capital gains constitute only a small proportion of the aggregate income of the taxpaying community as a whole, they are a major source of large individual incomes. In this respect they are similar to dividends, rents, and royalties, which are also among the smaller sources of income in the aggregate but among the major sources of large incomes. In the peak year 1928 net capital gains constituted 49.4 percent of the aggregate net income reported by those with statutory net incomes of $300,000-500,000, 56.1 percent for the income group $500,000-1,000,000, and 65.7 percent for the income group $1 million and more (Table 5); and for 1917-46 as a whole, as noted, they accounted for nearly a third of the aggregate net income of individuals with statutory net incomes of $100,000 or more, and half of the total for those with $1 million or more (Chart 3 and Table 6).

The relatively greater importance of capital gains as a source of income at high than at low net income levels is illustrated for 5 years in Chart 9 and Table 5. Although the 5 years differed radically with respect to the tax rate on capital gains and total net gains realized, capital gains were a bigger source of larger than of smaller incomes in all. This was most pronounced in 1928, when the stock market boom was in full swing and net capital gains reached a new peak. The progressive importance of capital gains as we ascend the income

Chart 9

Net Capital Gains as Percentages of Net Income by Statutory Net Income Groups

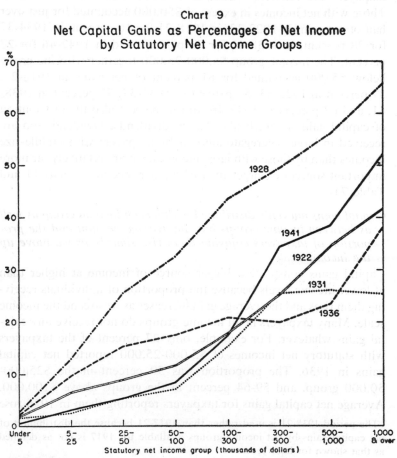

Source: Table 5.

scale is even more marked when short term gains are excluded, for, in contrast to long term gains, short term gains did not tend to increase as a proportion of net income above the income level $50,000-100,000 (Table 12).

Greater part of capital gains realized by taxpayers in other than the highest income groups

Although capital gains are far more important as sources of larger than of smaller incomes, the greater part of net capital gains in the aggregate is usually realized by individuals in the middle income groups. How net capital gains were shared by the different income groups in each of the 5 periods 1918-21,[5] 1922-33, 1934-37, 1938-41, and 1942-46 is shown in Chart 10 and Table 3. Higher income taxpayers did relatively better in 1922-33 than before or since. Those with net incomes in excess of $50,000 accounted for just over half of net gains in 1922-33; in 1918-21 for 10 percent, in 1934-37 for 28 percent, in 1938-41 for 38 percent, and in 1942-46 for 27 percent. The income group $5,000-25,000 together with the group below $5,000 accounted for 81 percent of net gains in 1918-21, 37 percent in 1922-33, 58 percent in 1934-37, 52 percent in 1938-41, and 62 percent in 1942-46. In this respect also the distribution of capital gains is much like that of dividends. Dividends too are received in larger aggregate amount by taxpayers with middle-size incomes than by those with large incomes, yet are relatively far more important sources of larger than of smaller incomes (Chart 11 and Table 7).

Capital gains unevenly distributed within each income group as well as between income groups but the average amount and the proportion of taxpayers enjoying them rise sharply as we move up the income scale

Capital gains constitute a bigger source of income at higher than at lower income levels because the proportion of individuals receiving them rises and the average gain increases as we ascend the income scale. Many taxpayers in all income groups do not receive any capital gains whatever. For example, only 27 percent of the taxpayers with statutory net incomes of $5,000-25,000 reported net capital gains in 1936. The proportion was 50 percent in the $25,000-50,000 group, and 59-64 percent in the groups above $100,000. Average net capital gains for taxpayers reporting them in 1936 rose

[5] The period 1918-21 is used rather than 1917-21 because the distribution of net capital gains by net income groups available for 1917 is not as detailed as that shown for later years.

sharply from about $3,000 in the $5,000-25,000 net income group to $10,000 in the $25,000-50,000 group, $55,000 in the $100,000-300,000 group, $126,000 in the $300,000-500,000 group, $282,000 in the $500,000-1,000,000 group, and to about $1.5 million in the $1 million or more group (Chart 12 and Table 79). Gains-realizing taxpayers in this highest income group reported net gains more than 400 times as large, on the average, as those with net incomes of $5,000-25,000.

Many individuals reach higher income levels mainly because of capital gains

Many taxpayers reach the higher levels solely or mainly because of

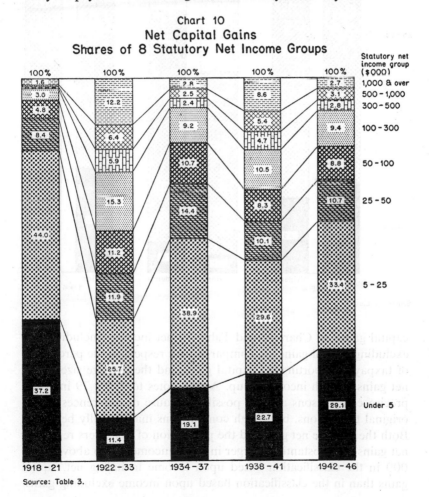

Chart 10
Net Capital Gains
Shares of 8 Statutory Net Income Groups

Source: Table 3.

Chart 11
Capital Gains and Dividends
Shares of 8 Statutory Net Income Groups

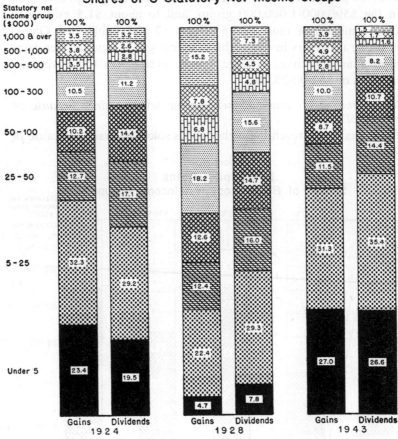

Statutory net income group ($000)

| | 1,000 & over | 500-1,000 | 300-500 | 100-300 | 50-100 | 25-50 | 5-25 | Under 5 |

Source: Table 7.

capital gains. In Chart 12 and Table 79 net incomes including and excluding capital gains are compared with respect to the percentage of taxpayers reporting net capital gains and the average size of the net gains in each income group. As the notes to Table 79 indicate, precise comparisons are not possible because of differences in the original tabulations, but rough comparisons may usefully be made. Both the average net gain and the proportion of taxpayers reporting net gains are substantially larger in every income group above $50,-000 in the classification based upon income including net capital gains than in the classification based upon income excluding gains.

Chart 12
**Average Net Capital Gain by Statutory Net Income Groups
Including and Excluding Statutory Net Capital
Gains and Losses, 1936**

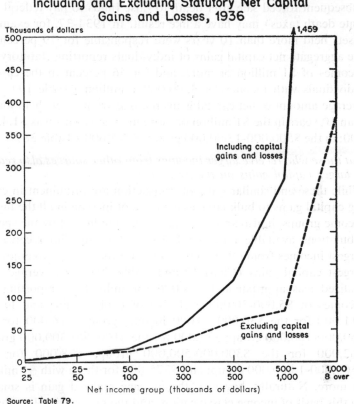

Source: Table 79.

In other words, net capital gains are important in pushing people up into the higher income groups.

Very substantial capital gains relative to 'other' income characteristically, though doubtless with many exceptions, arise from appreciation that has occurred over a long period but is realized legally in the single year the assets are sold. This is especially marked in the very highest income groups. A not uncommon occasion for a taxpayer's realization of an extremely large gain in a single year is the sale to the public, with the aid of investment bankers, of a large interest in what had previously been a family enterprise or similar closely held business corporation. The capital gain so realized forces the taxpayer into a higher income group than his usual one. The sale by a large stockholder of a substantial block of

stock in a widely owned business corporation (the motive of the
sale sometimes being to diversify investment holdings or avoid a
subsequent forced sale after death to raise funds to pay federal and
state death taxes) may have a like result. In 1934-37, for example,
assets held more than 10 years were responsible for 79 percent of
the aggregate net capital gains of individuals reporting statutory net
incomes of $1 million or more, and for 56 percent in the case of
individuals with incomes of $500,000-1 million (Table 19). The
average amount of net capital gains realized from assets held longer
than 10 years in the $1 million or more income groups was $1,459,-
500; in the $500,000-1,000,000 group, $315,600 (Table 38).

*But those who receive larger incomes from other sources also realize
    larger capital gains on the average*
While these and similar types of transaction are prominent in causing capital gains to bulk large as a source of income in all the higher
income groups, it also appears to be true, as indicated by the special
tabulations available only for 1936, that those who receive the
largest incomes from other sources tend on the average to enjoy the
largest capital gains (Chart 12 and Table 79). The average gain
realized was approximately $4,000 for individuals reporting net
incomes of $5,000-30,000 exclusive of capital gains and losses;
$11,000 for the $30,000-50,000 income group; $16,000 for the
$50,000-100,000 group; $32,000 for the $100,000-300,000 group;
$62,000 for the $300,000-500,000 group; $78,000 for the
$500,000-1,000,000 group; and $375,000 for those with $1 million
or more. Naturally, however, the average realized gain is smaller
on this basis of income classification, and the progression less sharp,
because taxpayers for whom large capital gains constitute the main
source of income are no longer automatically in the top income
groups but tend to be scattered among the various groups. The
average realized gain on assets held more than 10 years in the 3
uppermost income groups in Table 80 is roughly 2½ to 3 times as
large when income including capital gains and losses is the basis of
classification as when capital gains and losses are excluded.

*Some evidence that the largest net losses in relation to total income
    are sustained neither by the top nor the bottom group filing
    income tax returns*
Net capital losses segregated for tax credit were not deducted in
determining the net income classification in 1924-33, as noted
above, and varying amounts of net losses were not taken into account
in determining the net income classifications for subsequent years.

For these reasons, comparisons of the relative importance of net capital losses at different income levels over a period of years are considerably blurred. Despite this limitation, there seems to have been some regularity in pattern when net losses are expressed as a percentage of the net income reported on the returns for each income group. From 1926 through 1931 this percentage increased as net income (based on the statutory definition, i.e., without regard to segregated net losses) rose up to about the $100,000-300,000 level, then declined as net income rose (Chart 13 and Table 5). The pat-

Chart 13

Net Capital Losses as Percentages of Net Income by Statutory Net Income Groups, 1926-1931

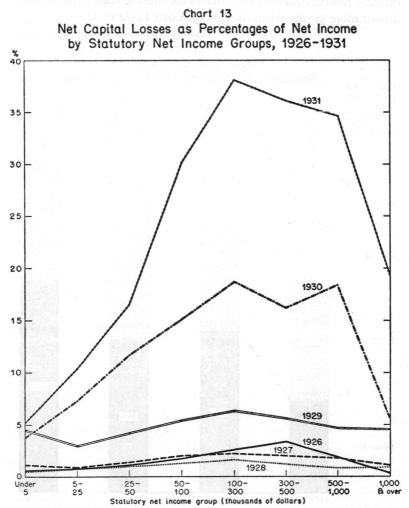

Source: Table 5.

tern is similar in 1934-37 and 1938-40 though the high point was reached at somewhat lower net income levels.

The same type of variation is shown for 1936 when the returns are classified by size of net income excluding net capital gains and losses. The ratio of net loss to other income in 1936 was lowest for individuals with net incomes from 'other' sources under $5,000, and highest for those with such net incomes of $5,000-30,000. On the other hand, if we confine our attention to returns with net capital losses, we find that the ratio of net loss to the other income reported on these returns declines as we ascend the income scale to the $1 million or more group, when the ratio jumps (Table 68).

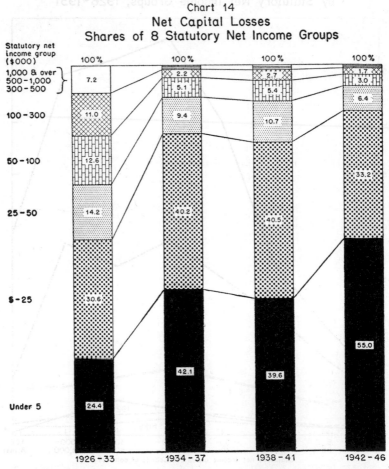

Chart 14
Net Capital Losses
Shares of 8 Statutory Net Income Groups

Source: Table 3.

Net losses more heavily concentrated than net gains in middle and lower income groups

As indicated above, taxpayers with larger net incomes generally experienced a more favorable ratio, as groups, between net capital gains and losses than those with smaller incomes (Chart 5 shows this for illustrative years, and annual figures 1926-46 are presented in Table 4). This was true in 1936 even when incomes were grouped by size excluding net capital gains and losses (Table 68). Subject to the reservations previously cited with respect to income classifications based on statutory net income, Chart 14 and Table 3 show how the net capital losses of taxpayers with net incomes were distributed among the various income groups in each of the 4 periods of markedly different tax treatment.

Taxpayers with net incomes of less than $5,000 accounted for 24 percent of the total net capital loss in 1926-33, 42 percent in 1934-37, 40 percent in 1938-41, and 55 percent in 1942-46. Taxpayers with net incomes of $5,000-50,000 accounted for an additional 45, 50, 51, and 40 percent respectively of the net losses in the 4 periods.

The concentration of net losses in the income groups below $50,000 is very much more marked than the concentration of net gains (Chart 15 and Table 3). Part, though not all, of the greater concentration occurs because net capital losses, to the extent they were deductible, shifted taxpayers into lower income groups; but this influence upon the income classification was not great because segregated losses (long term net losses of upper income individuals) were not taken into account in determining the income classification in 1924-33, and the deductibility of net losses was severely restricted in the subsequent years.

9 LONG VERSUS SHORT TERM GAINS AND LOSSES

Reasons for differentiating

Except for incidental references, our analysis and discussion so far have not differentiated between gains and losses from sales of assets held only a short period and those held a long time. Such a distinction is of interest for several reasons. First, some persons put them in different economic categories, asserting that short term capital gains are not, properly speaking, capital gains at all, but a species of speculative profit that constitutes a part of ordinary current income. If capital gains and losses are to be given special tax treatment, such persons would confine the special treatment to so-called

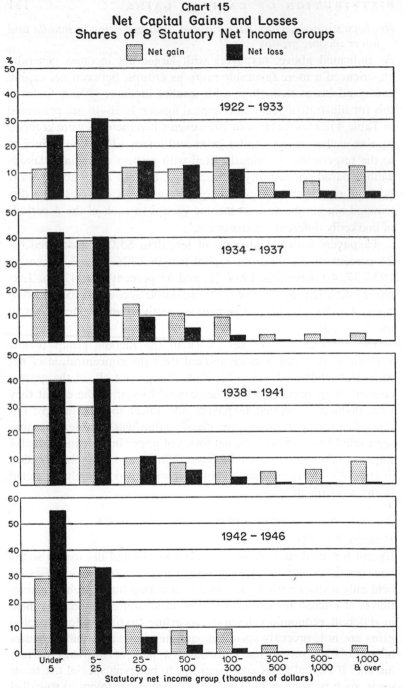

Chart 15
Net Capital Gains and Losses
Shares of 8 Statutory Net Income Groups

☐ Net gain   ■ Net loss

1922 – 1933

1934 – 1937

1938 – 1941

1942 – 1946

Statutory net income group (thousands of dollars)

Under 5 | 5–25 | 25–50 | 50–100 | 100–300 | 300–500 | 500–1,000 | 1,000 & over

Source: Table 3.

long term gains and losses, i.e., gains and losses on long-held assets.

Second, the equitable argument commonly advanced in favor of preferentially low tax rates on capital gains and restricted allowances for capital losses is relevant only for transactions extending over more than a year. Based upon the progressive rates at which income taxes are imposed, the argument is that if longer term gains and losses are treated as components of a single year's income, the gains become subject to higher rates and the losses cause larger tax reductions than if merely a *pro rata* part were regarded as emerging each year the asset was held. But this argument is obviously not relevant to gains and losses realized on assets held only 1 year or less.

Third, the effect of alternative tax treatments of short and long term capital gains and losses upon the timing and volume of capital transactions and upon the government's tax revenues has been the subject of considerable discussion and conjecture among legislators and others.

Finally, the various income groups differ with respect to the interval they have characteristically held their assets before realizing on them.

In response to the first 3 factors, the federal income tax statutes, beginning in 1922, have drawn a distinction, though a varying one, between long and short term transactions in capital assets. From 1922 through 1933 net gains from sales of assets held more than 2 years, called long term, were allowed to be segregated from other gains and from ordinary income and taxed at the flat rate of 12½ percent regardless of their amount or the taxpayer's other income, whenever the taxpayer's tax would thereby be reduced.[6] In 1924-33 net losses from assets held more than 2 years had to be segregated from other losses and from ordinary income for a flat tax credit of 12½ percent if the taxpayer's tax would thereby be increased. From 1934 through 1937, it will be recalled, the statutes divided capital gains and losses into 5 classes according to the interval the assets had been held, and recognized declining proportions of the gain or loss, as the duration of ownership increased, as components of income for tax purposes. In 1938-41 the periods were reduced to three: 18 months or less, 18-24 months, and longer than 24 months. Also, assets subject to allowance for depreciation were excluded

[6] In 1922 and 1923, however, this privilege was limited by a provision that the total tax, including that on capital gains, be at least 12½ percent of the net income.

from 'capital' assets for tax purposes. In 1942-46 only 2 periods were recognized: 6 months or less for short term, and over 6 months for long term.

Because of these differences in law, only general observations on the differential tax treatment of short and long term gains and losses are possible for 1922-46 as a whole: the several periods must be studied separately for more detailed observations. And for nearly all years the data on net capital losses are less adequate and reliable than those on net gains.[7]

*Importance of short term gains and losses has declined relative to
    long term in recent years*

Short term gains and losses appear to have declined markedly in relative importance during 1922-46 as a whole, although good figures are not available for the first half of the period and those for various parts of the remainder are not perfectly comparable.

An asset had to be held for 2 years in 1922-33, 18 months in 1938-41, and only 6 months in 1942-46 (as at present) to qualify the gain or loss as long term. Hence, if all other things had remained the same, the proportions that short term gains and losses constituted of the total would have fallen over the period 1922-46 as a whole merely by reason of the changing statutory definitions. But the figures within periods of similar tax treatment suggest that the decline was due to other factors as well.

From 1922 through 1933 long term gains, on assets held more than 2 years, were reported as such only by taxpayers who found it more profitable to exercise the option to subject these gains to a flat tax of 12½ percent than to treat them, together with short term gains, as ordinary income. As few taxpayers with incomes less than a figure that ranged from about $16,000 to $32,000 a year found it

[7] The amounts of net losses other than those segregated for tax credit at 12½ percent have not been published for years before 1926 and the published figures are incomplete for 1932 and 1933. Our estimates of net losses for 1917-25 and for 1932 and 1933, based in part on sample data, are less reliable than the tabulated data available for other years. *Statistics of Income* figures for 1926-28 understate unsegregated capital losses because many taxpayers listed them under 'general deductions', and not until 1929 did the Bureau of Internal Revenue begin to include capital losses so listed in its tabulations of capital losses. Segregated long term net losses in 1924-33, like segregated net gains, do not cover all transactions in assets held more than 2 years because most taxpayers with net incomes of less than about $16,000-32,000, since they were not required to segregate them, treated them as short term lossses for income tax purposes.

profitable, our figures for aggregate short term gains in 1922-33 include the long term gains of all except the higher income groups. The percentages these impure figures constituted of the total net

Chart 16

Short Term Net Capital Gains and Losses as Percentages of Total Individuals with Net Incomes, 1922-1943

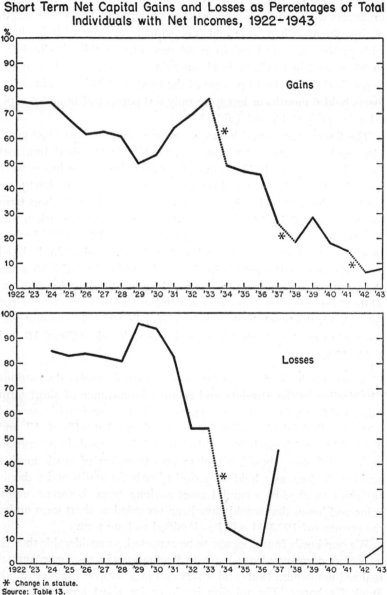

* Change in statute.
Source: Table 13.

gains of individuals reporting net incomes tended to decline during the 'twenties, then rose in the first 4 years of the 'thirties (Chart 16 and Table 13).

We have good figures for gains on assets held 2 years or less during 1934-37, and 18 months or less during 1938-41 because *all* taxpayers were required to report their gains according to the length of time the asset had been held. The short term gains of individuals with net incomes declined from 49 percent of total gains in 1934 to 26 percent in 1937. In 1941 net gains on assets held 18 months or less had shrunk to 15 percent of the total. In 1943 net gains from assets held 6 months or less were only 8.0 percent of total net capital gains (Chart 16 and Table 13).

The figures for capital losses, as previously noted, are less complete and satisfactory. No figures are available for short term net losses in 1922 and 1923 because long and short term losses were treated alike by the law; and no figures are available for short term net losses for 1938-41. The amounts and proportions of short term losses increased in 1929 and 1930 when the stock market was sharply declining, shrank very substantially in 1932 and 1933 when short term trading was on a much reduced scale, and again declined markedly during the upturn in the stock market in 1934-36 when short term losses amounted to only 7-14 percent of total net losses, while short term net gains accounted for almost half of total net gains. With the break in the stock market in 1937 the amount and proportion of short term losses again rose sharply (Chart 16 and Table 13).

Short term gains and losses closely reflect stock market fluctuations
The decline in the absolute and relative importance of short term gains and losses in most recent years has been associated in general with the diminished trading in the stock market (Chart 17 and Table 15), and is probably subject to quick reversal if any combination of factors should stimulate an expansion of stock market activity. As long as a holding period of only 6 months and a day is sufficient to classify a capital asset as long term, however, many gains and losses that would have been regarded as short term under the statutes of 1922-41 will be classified as long term.

We previously found, as was to be expected, a considerable though imperfect correspondence between fluctuations in aggregate annual realized net capital gains and losses and in prices on the New York Stock Exchange. The relation is closer for short term gains and losses alone (Chart 18). The correspondence in 1939-41, in particular, was more pronounced than for total net gains. In general, the

Chart 17

Shares Traded, New York Stock Exchange, and Arithmetic Sum of Short Term Net Capital Gains and Losses 1924 – 1946

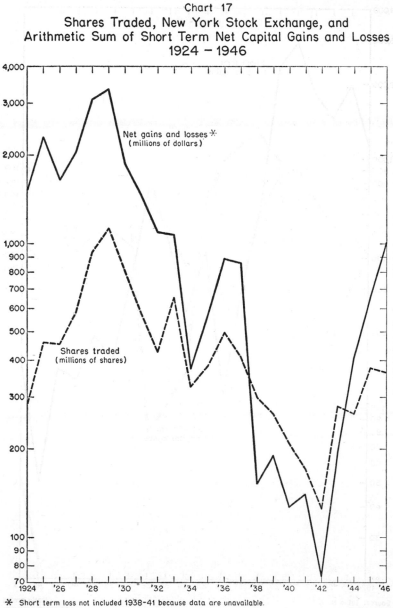

* Short term loss not included 1938–41 because data are unavailable.
Source: Table 15.   Ratio scale

Chart 18

Stock Price Index and Short Term Net Capital Gains and Losses
1924 – 1943

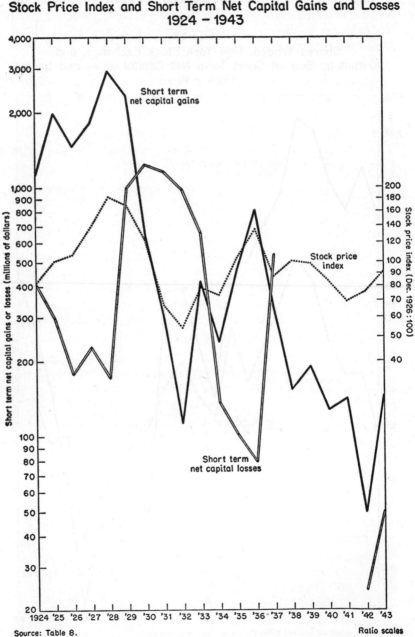

Source: Table 8.   Ratio scales

movements of net losses were the reverse of those of gains. The steep rise in losses recorded in 1929 is somewhat exaggerated because capital losses that were improperly classified were omitted from the tabulations in the preceding 3 years but were included beginning in 1929 (see note 7).

The securities and certain commodity markets are the only ones in which large short term transactions in capital assets are regularly feasible. When short term transactions are undertaken in real estate, they are commonly executed mainly by individuals and firms regularly engaged in the business, so that the resulting gains and losses are accounted components of current income rather than capital gains and losses.

Long term gains account for an increasing proportion of total net gains as we ascend the income scale

With remarkable consistency long term gains account for an increasing proportion of the total as we go up the income scale (Chart 19 and Table 13). In 1924, for example, they constituted 54 percent of the total net gains of taxpayers with net incomes of $50,000-100,000, 75 percent in the $100,000-300,000 group, 87 percent in the $300,000-500,000 group, 94 percent in the $500,000-1,000,000 group, and 95 percent for those with $1 million or more.

Tabulations for income groups below $50,000 are not available before 1933 because these taxpayers did not find it profitable under the varying provisions pertaining to personal exemptions, credits, and rates consistently to segregate their long from their short term gains in their income tax returns. The 1933 figures, however, in part estimated by us on the basis of sample data, show the same pattern for these income groups (Table 10). Long term net gains accounted for 13 percent of the total net gains of taxpayers with net incomes under $5,000, 22 percent for those in the $5,000-25,000 group, and 27 percent for those in the $25,000-50,000 group. The detailed data available for 1934-46, while reflecting a general diminution in the relative importance of short term gains, likewise display this pattern (Table 13). In 1934-37, for example, long term net gains accounted for 55 percent of the total net gains of taxpayers with net incomes under $5,000, 56 percent for those with incomes of $25,000-50,000, and 80 percent for those with incomes of $300,000-500,000.

A special illustration of the same general tendency is supplied by the figures for 1934-37 showing the importance of assets held more

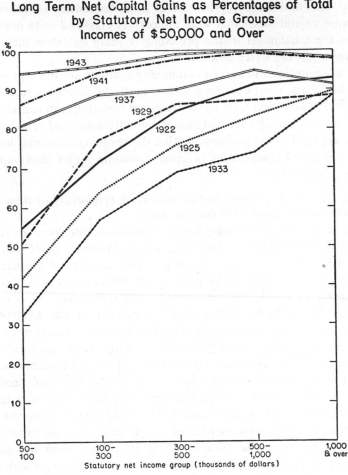

Chart 19

**Long Term Net Capital Gains as Percentages of Total
by Statutory Net Income Groups
Incomes of $50,000 and Over**

Source: Table 13.

than 10 years as a source of net capital gains in the different income groups (Chart 20 and Table 19). Assets held more than 10 years accounted for about a fifth of the net gains of taxpayers with net incomes under $25,000, for about a quarter of those in the $25,000-100,000 group, for about half of those in the $100,000-1,000,000 group, and for almost 80 percent of those in the $1 million or more group.

Short term losses constitute a large fraction of the total losses of the upper income groups

While long term net gains quite regularly constitute an increasing

Chart 20

Net Capital Gains from Assets Held more than 10 Years
as Percentages of Total by Statutory Net Income Groups
1934 – 1937

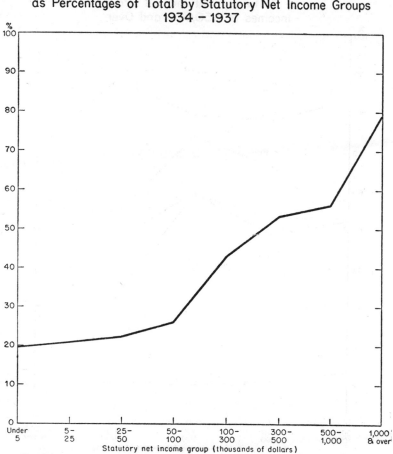

Source: Table 19.

fraction of total gains as we ascend the income scale, and short term
gains play a diminishing role, the like cannot be said of losses. Short
term losses often account for a large and sometimes a rising fraction
of total losses as we move up the income scale (Chart 21 and Table
13). One possible explanation is that taxpayers with large incomes
tend to be no more successful in their short term speculations than
those with smaller incomes, though distinctly more successful in
their longer term ventures. Another is that they tend to wind up
their losing ventures quickly, throwing a large part of their losses
into the short term category, while they hold their profitable invest-

Chart 21

Short Term Net Capital Losses as Percentages of Total
by Statutory Net Income Groups
Incomes of $50,000 and Over

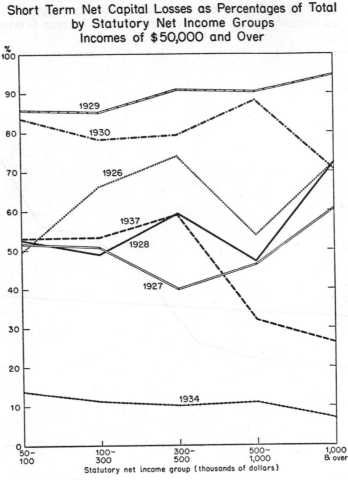

Statutory net income group (thousands of dollars)

Source: Table 13.

ments longer. In other words, they may follow the old adage of the stock market: 'Cut your losses short but let your profits run.' By allowing short term losses to be offset in full against income of all kinds and limiting the tax rate on long term gains to 12½ percent the tax laws offered a distinct incentive to follow this policy in 1922-31.

Average gains larger the longer the asset is held and the larger the net income

For both long and short term transactions in 1934-37 average gains were larger the longer the asset was held and the larger the net

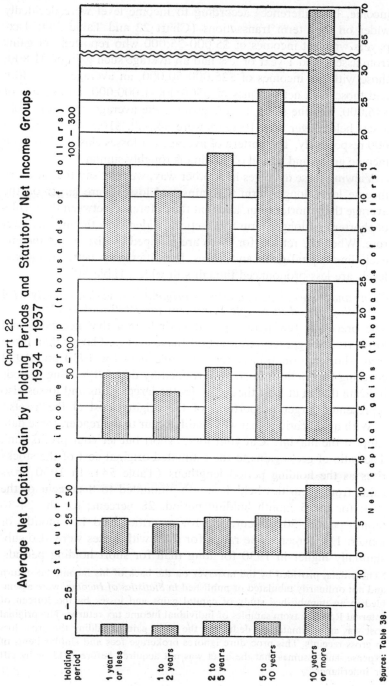

Chart 22

Average Net Capital Gain by Holding Periods and Statutory Net Income Groups
1934 – 1937

Statutory net income group (thousands of dollars)

5 – 25   25 – 50   50 – 100   100 – 300

Holding period

1 year or less

1 to 2 years

2 to 5 years

5 to 10 years

10 years or more

Net capital gains (thousands of dollars)

Source: Table 38.

income, but differences according to income level were decidedly
wider on long term transactions (Chart 22 and Table 38). Taxpayers with net incomes of $5,000-25,000 who reported net gains
from assets held 1 year or less had an average such gain of $1,800;
those with net incomes of $25,000-50,000, an average of $5,400;
and those with net incomes of $500,000-1,000,000, an average of
$46,000. For the same income groups, the average net gains from
assets held longer than 10 years were $4,600, $10,800, and $315,-
600 respectively. The pattern of average net losses classified by both
income group and period of holding is roughly similar.

Viewing these averages in another way, we may say that at every
income level, longer term net gains and losses were larger on the
average than shorter term, and that the difference between the results
of shorter and longer term transactions widened as the income level
rose. When the returns for 1936 are grouped by size of net income
excluding capital gains and losses, the differences between income
levels are less pronounced though still wide (Table 80).

*Gains and losses as percentages of original cost varied directly with
holding period in sample of returns for 1930 and 1932*
The preceding few paragraphs have indicated that net gains and
losses from longer term transactions have averaged larger than those
from shorter term transactions. Sample data for 1930 and 1932
covering transactions in stocks grouped by detailed holding periods
indicate that in at least these 2 years the larger gains and losses also
represented larger proportions of the original cost of the assets.[8]

With qualifications that will readily occur to the reader, these data
support the maxim: 'Cut your losses short but let your profits run'.
The ratio of gross gains to the estimated original cost of the stocks
rises as the holding period lengthens (Table 54). In 1930 gross
gains from securities held 1 month amounted to 8 percent of the
cost; for the 5 month holding period, 28 percent; for the 24-36
month period, 50 percent; and for securities held 120 months or
longer, 110 percent. The ratios for sales with losses were also substantially higher in 1930 for long than for short holding periods.

[8] These data, provided by the taxpayer on the back of his income tax return
and not ordinarily tabulated or published in *Statistics of Income,* were assembled in an unpublished study of capital gains and losses by the Bureau of
Internal Revenue from samples of individual income tax returns. The original
cost was approximated by deducting the gross gain or adding the gross loss
to gross receipts. This procedure ignores brokerage fees and similar items of
expense, and assumes that the asset was not acquired before 1913 or by gift
or inheritance.

In 1932 they rose from 8 percent for sales of stock held less than 1 month to 73 percent for the 36-48 month holding period, then declined for longer periods. The relative size of the ratios in the several periods reflects, of course, the level of stock prices in 1930 and 1932 as compared with the level at the time of purchase.

10 RELATIVE IMPORTANCE OF SECURITIES, REAL ESTATE, AND OTHER ASSETS AS SOURCES OF CAPITAL GAINS AND LOSSES

Common stocks the chief source of capital gains and losses
The great bulk of capital gains and losses is derived from transactions in securities, mainly from the common stocks of business corporations. In 1936, the only year for which comprehensive data are available, 79 percent of the total net gain and 68 percent of the total net loss were reported as derived from stocks and bonds (Table 69). The actual proportions were doubtless larger because a substantial fraction of the total gain and loss, approximating 15 percent in New York State, was attributed to 'unclassified assets'. Of all taxpayers reporting transactions in capital assets 73 percent reported sales of securities. While the figures do not distinguish between common and preferred stocks, the preponderance of the former is indicated by the much larger amounts outstanding and by their greater activity in the investment and speculative markets.

For New York, Pennsylvania, and Illinois, figures have been tabulated showing the relative importance of 9 types of assets as sources of capital gains and losses in 1936 (Table 74). In New York 82 percent of net gains and 74 percent of net losses were realized from sales of securities (an additional 15 percent of the gains and 14 percent of the losses were unclassified). Real estate and improvements were largest among the other assets but accounted for less than 2 percent of total gains and 9 percent of losses. In Illinois real estate was somewhat more important, especially as a source of loss; otherwise, the distribution in both Illinois and Pennsylvania was similar to that in New York.

Real estate losses exceed gains in 1936
If we approximate original cost by deducting the net gain from, or adding the net loss to, the gross receipts from sales of assets,[9] we find that the aggregate excess of gains over losses from transactions in securities reported on federal income tax returns from New York

[9] We thereby ignore brokers' fees and similar expenses, as well as any adjustments that might be required to make more accurate allowance for depreciation, cost of improvements, etc.

State in 1936 amounted to 3 percent of the estimated cost, whereas all other assets showed a loss amounting to 10 percent of their aggregate estimated cost (Table 75). Stocks were the biggest source of gain and loss for all income groups (Table 76). The highest loss ratios were for mortgages and loans, 31 percent, and for real estate and improvements, 18 percent. Real estate constituted a bigger source of loss than of gain for every income group, with one exception, as well as for all income groups combined.

Some reasons why real estate is a smaller direct source of capital gains and losses than it is a constituent of total private wealth
The subordinate importance of real estate as a source of capital gains and losses is in sharp contrast to its outstanding position as a constitutent of total private wealth. The Federal Trade Commission estimated that taxable real estate constituted about 53 percent of the total wealth of the United States in 1922; the National Industrial Conference Board placed the figure at 60 percent in 1938.[10] The values of the principal classes of real estate in the United States in 1930 have been estimated to be (in billions of dollars): residential nonfarm, 122.6; commercial, 57.0; farm, 47.9; industrial, 39.2; tax-exempt, 34.6; all other, 12.9; totaling, 314.2.[11] Price movements in real estate, moreover, are often substantial, giving rise to large possibilities of capital gains and losses. The value of American farm land nearly tripled between 1900 and 1920, rising from $24 billion to $66 billion. Thereafter it declined, falling $17.1 billion by 1925 and $14.5 billion more by 1940.[12] Similarly, the value of nonfarm real estate, after large advances, is estimated to have declined from $266 billion in 1930 to $172 billion in 1934.[13]

One reason for the disproportionately small role of real estate as a direct source of capital gains and losses reported on individual income tax returns is that the title to much of the country's more valuable real estate, e.g., the land and buildings that constitute much of the fixed plant of large industrial and merchandising enterprises and the more valuable office and store buildings and apartment houses in urban areas, is held by business corporations, not indi-

[10] *National Wealth and Income*, 69th Cong., 1st Sess., Senate Document 126, pp. 28, 30, and 34; *Economic Almanac, 1942-43*, p. 375.

[11] David L. Wickens, *Residential Real Estate* (NBER, 1941), pp. 2 and 3.

[12] *Census of Agriculture, 1940* (Department of Agriculture).

[13] Wickens, *op. cit.*, pp. 2 and 3. Estimates of the aggregate value of nonfarm land for Census years 1880-1922 are presented in Kuznets, *National Product since 1869* (NBER, 1946), p. 201.

viduals. When corporations sell real estate at a profit, the capital gains do not appear as such in the incomes of the individual stockholders. If and when the gains are distributed, they reach the stockholder as dividends; if retained by the corporation, they may enhance the market value of the stock and lead to capital gains from securities.

Nor are capital gains and losses from real estate fully reported as such by corporations. Many transactions that would result in statutory capital gains or losses if undertaken by the individual stockholders give rise to ordinary income when undertaken by a corporation formed by these stockholders to conduct their real estate operations: the corporation becomes a real estate dealer, not an investor entitled to special tax treatment. The statutory provisions and judicial decisions holding that gains and losses shall not be recognized for tax purposes in connection with various types of corporate mergers, acquisitions, and exchanges have also reduced the recognized amounts of capital gains and losses from real estate for both corporations and individuals.

Apart from the influence of legal form, real property in fact probably changes hands much less frequently than securities; consequently, a larger proportion of the appreciation and depreciation in value remains unrealized in a legal sense by the owners. Various factors make real estate a slow-moving asset as a rule. It is immobile. It must commonly be sold in relatively large units, in contrast to the remarkable divisibility of wealth in the form of securities. Each parcel has a unique location. An elaborate legal procedure must be gone through to assure a clear title. The real property owned by industrial and merchandising enterprises rarely comes on the market because it constitutes an important part of their fixed plants and is not commonly sold separately from the business itself. Some $65 billion, or more than half of the total value of nonfarm residential real estate in 1930, consisted of the value of houses occupied by their owners. An impulse to sell to realize a profit or avoid a loss is subject to restraining considerations of family and neighborhood ties, children's playmates and schools, habit, sentiment, etc., which are present far less commonly in connection with securities. The case is similiar with farms, most of which are occupied by their owners. An impulse to sell is often overcome by the thought that a home as well as an investment and a means of livelihood will be given up.

Nevertheless, though shifts in the ownership of real estate are probably less frequent than in securities, they are more frequent than the preceding considerations might suggest. The mobility of individuals and business enterprises in the United States doubtless counteracts these influences to some extent. A study of the duration of ownership of real property in New York State, made in 1930 under the direction of Robert M. Haig for the New York State Commission for the Revision of the Tax Laws, indicated that 56.5 percent of the urban properties comprising the sample had been sold at least once in the preceding 11 years, and 72.5 percent, in the preceding 21 years.[14] The turnover was slower in rural areas, 35.8 percent of the properties in the sample having been sold in the preceding 11 years, and 54.8 percent in the preceding 21 years. For all areas together, from half to three-fourths of the properties in the sample had been acquired by their 1930 owners within the preceding 21 years.

Considerable amounts of capital gains and losses from real estate go unreported because they are embodied in transfers of title at death instead of being realized through sale.

In a survey we made of the length of ownership of real properties in Manhattan by 41 individuals and estates known for the continuity of their ownership, including such famous family names as Astor, Adrian, Beekman, Bradley, Gerry, Goelet, Rhinelander, Rockefeller, Ruppert, and Stuyvesant, we found that one property had remained unsold for 97 years, another for 136 years, and 43 others for periods so long that the deeds did not bear any date. Of the 922 properties, comprising all those in Manhattan held in the names of

LENGTH OF OWNERSHIP OF
REAL ESTATE IN MANHATTAN BY 41 WEALTHY INDIVIDUALS AND ESTATES

YEARS HELD ON 12/31/1942	NUMBER OF PROPERTIES	PERCENTAGE OF TOTAL
10 or less	204	22.1
10 to 20	131	14.2
20 to 30	72	7.8
30 to 40	257	27.9
Over 40	258	28.0
Total	922	100.0

The last date of sale of all the real properties in Manhattan in the names of the 41 individuals and estates at the end of 1942 was obtained from the *Real Estate Directory of Manhattan.* Properties of the 41 owners outside Manhattan or legal title to which was vested in other names were not included.

[14] Edwin H. Spengler, *Turnover of Title to Real Property in New York,* New York State Commission for the Revision of Tax Laws, 1932.

these 41 individuals and estates at the end of 1942, fewer than half had been held less than 30 years.

Because of the foregoing factors, the reported amounts of capital gains and losses realized from real estate doubtless understate the power of increases and decreases in the value of real property to enrich or impoverish individuals.

Capital gains and losses from real estate are unlikely to cancel for most investors because diversification of risks is difficult

A considerable degree of diversification of risks is possible by investment in the securities of large corporations because such enterprises commonly do business on a nationwide scale and because the investment of even a moderate sum can readily be distributed among several corporations. Real estate is much different in these respects. The practicable unit of investment is relatively large: not more than 1 or 2 improved properties can usually be purchased for $15,000, for example. The properties chosen will of necessity be in only 1 or 2 areas and their value will be highly responsive to purely local developments. For these reasons few investors can widely diversify their risks. Hence, in the case of real estate even more than in that of securities, varying excesses of gains on the part of some investors and of losses on the part of others are more likely than a canceling of gains and losses.

The significance of this probability for tax purposes is that equal treatment of capital gains and losses may lead to wide disparities in the tax treatment of different individuals. Equal limitations on the proportions of gains and losses recognized for income tax, for example, will reduce the allowance for net losses for numerous investors who will get little or no benefit from the corresponding reduction in the taxation of capital gains. In short, the effect of such equal treatment is to accentuate both the gains of the winners and the losses of the losers.

Some examples of highly divergent movements in urban land values, taken from a survey we made of tax assessment values in Cleveland and in the borough of Manhattan in New York City, are shown as noted previously in Chart 1 and Table 91.[15]

[15] For Manhattan we obtained the 'unit values' of the land in the blocks in several areas, including many blocks on the four principal avenues, Fifth, Sixth, Seventh, and Eighth, from land value maps maintained by the Surveyor's Bureau of New York City's Tax Department. The 'unit value' in Manhattan, defined as the value per front foot of a lot 100 feet deep of "normal size and on a level with the grade of the street," is computed by capitalizing at

Cleveland

The tax assessment value of the land in Cuyahoga County, which contains the City of Cleveland, more than quadrupled between 1910 and 1924, rising from $295 million to $1,256 million. An ensuing decline, rapid at first and then gradual, left the total at $520 million in 1942, or 41 percent of the 1924 value and 176 percent of the 1910 value. Those who died or sold out before 1924 participated only in the upswing; those who bought after 1924, only in the downswing. Five lots, all on or adjacent to Euclid Avenue, illustrate the divergent experience of individual ground sites. Between 1910 and 1924 these 5 lots rose, respectively, 152, 569, 300, 700, and 33 percent in value. (Their locations were, respectively, Euclid Avenue near Third, 40th, 65th, and 105th Streets, and East 55th Street near Euclid.) They declined between 1924 and 1942 respectively 21, 86, 87, 45, and 73 percent. Three lots were worth less in 1942 than in 1910, while 2 remained far above their 1910 values (Chart 1 and Table 91).

------

6 percent the estimated income the site would yield if put to its highest economic use under current conditions. From it, the worth of the lots in the block is derived, after allowances for differences in shape, depth, and position from the standard unit. Corner lots and those next to corners, because of their greater accessibility and prominence, are appraised at higher values than those nearer the middle.

For Cleveland we obtained from John A. Zangerle, Auditor of Cuyahoga County, the assessed values of standard lots with 50 feet frontage and 150 feet depth at widely separated points on or near Cleveland's main thoroughfare, except that the figures supplied for one lot, that on East 55th Street near Euclid, were the actual sales prices.

Tax assessment values are not accurate measures of market values; but they are useful for our present purposes because we are primarily interested in the *relative* changes in the values of different sites, and in wide swings in value. Estimated in terms of the representative or unit lot, the assessor's figure for a particular property may depart substantially from its market value at a given time. Moreover, assessment values tend to lag behind movements in market values in both directions, but particularly on the downside, when pressure against reduced assessments is exerted by the debt limit of a city, which is usually based on the total assessed valuation, and by the desire to avoid an increase in the nominal tax rate. Different assessing areas assess property at different fractions of the estimated market value. These deficiencies are serious when assessed values are used for close measures of market values, but are much less so when used, as is done here, as measures of *relative* movements in the market values of different sites and as rough measures of very wide swings in market values.

Manhattan

The assessed value of the land in Manhattan increased from $3 billion in 1920 to a peak of $5.5 billion in 1931, then declined to $3.7 billion in 1942.[16] Both the $2.5 billion appreciation in the earlier period and the $1.8 billion depreciation in the later created opportunities for large capital gains and losses, but here too the movements of individual properties diverged markedly from the average and from one another.

In contrast to the wide movement of the assessed value of Manhattan land as a whole, relatively little change took place in parts of the financial district where land values have been highest. The block occupied by the Equitable Building, between Pine and Cedar Streets, was assessed on the Broadway side at $18,000 a front foot in 1909, $24,000 in 1929, and $21,000 in 1942.

On the other hand, the assessed value on Seventh Avenue near 34th Street (block number 786) was $2,400 per front foot in 1909, $3,400 in 1920-22, $5,000 in 1924, $8,400 in 1929, $9,400 in 1930-32, and $7,800 in 1940-42.

In the neighborhood of Grand Central Station, on 42nd Street from Fifth to Park Avenues, the unit values ranged from $4,200 to $5,000 per front foot in 1909, rose to $8,000 per front foot by 1913, and to peak values ranging from $19,700 to $22,000 a front foot in 1930, then declined to $16,000-18,000 per front foot by 1942.

We obtained from the assessment records the unit values between 1909 and 1942 of every other block on the east side of Fifth Avenue from Washington Square to 74th Street. The assessed values were lower in 1942 than in 1909 for some parts of the Avenue, higher for others. But on Seventh Avenue all the blocks were substantially higher in 1942 than in 1909.

In summary, in 1909-31 changes in the assessed value of units in the Manhattan blocks included in Chart 1 and Table 91 ranged from a 49 percent decline to a 633 percent increase; in 1931-42 from an 8 percent increase to a 51 percent decrease; and for the entire period 1909-42, from a net decline of 75 percent to a net increase of 467 percent.

[16] Annual Reports of the Tax Department and Tax Commission, New York City.

11 SPECIAL STUDIES OF CONTINUING GROUPS OF INDIVIDUALS WITH
    LARGE INCOMES

*Aggregate figures not necessarily representative of particular indi-
    viduals or groups*

From the statistical materials so far discussed, presenting various
aspects of gain and loss realization for aggregates of individuals filing
income tax returns during the 30 years 1917-46, we cannot follow
the experience of any one individual or of any small group and determine whether the over-all picture hides significant diversities in the
experience of different groups of taxpayers. Have gains and losses
canceled to a significantly lesser degree for certain groups than for
income taxpayers as a whole? Our analysis of the distribution of
gains and losses by income groups is deficient as a source of information in this respect because some of the individuals comprising each
income group in one year shifted into other groups in other years.

For this reason it is useful and interesting to supplement the foregoing discussion by analyzing a small body of materials pertaining
to the realized gains and losses of continuing groups of individuals
for a period of years. In its *Source Book of Statistics of Income* the
Bureau of Internal Revenue has a series of tabulations showing the
sources of income and the deduction items in 1917-36 for the 75
taxpayers who reported net incomes of $1 million or more in 1924.
Data for some of the individuals are incomplete; for 45 data are
complete from 1917 through 1933.

*45 individuals with 1924 net incomes of $1 million or more showed
    continuing high concentration in upper income groups*

The first thing to be noted about this group of individuals is that
the net incomes of the great majority remained at fairly high levels
throughout the period. Not more than 6 of the 45 reported net
incomes under $50,000 or net deficits in any year between 1917
and 1930, and well over half reported incomes in excess of $100,000
in the worst year of the period, 1932 (Table 83).

*Annual fluctuations in their gains and losses more accentuated than
    in those of all taxpayers*

The relation between the net gains and losses of these individuals
as a group 1922-33 and the movement of stock prices (Chart 23
and Table 85) is similar in a general way to that for all taxpayers
but the annual fluctuations are much more marked. Whereas the net
gains of all individuals with net incomes were about 30 times as large
in 1928 and 1929 as in 1932, those for the 45 individuals were more
than 100 times as great.

Chart 23
45 Persons with Million Dollar and Over Incomes in 1924
Net Capital Gains and Losses and Stock Price Index
1917 − 1933

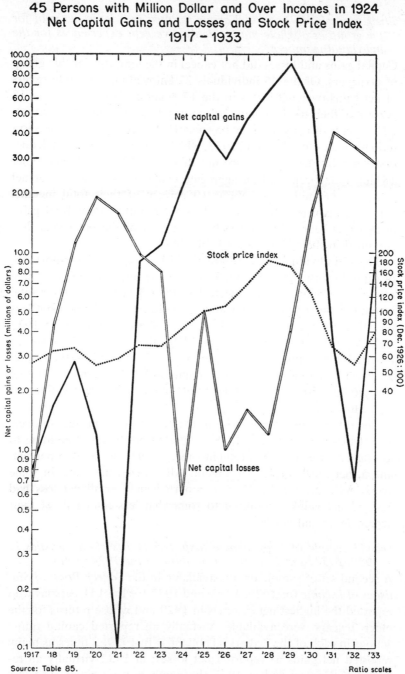

Source: Table 85.   Ratio scales

Their transactions in capital assets resulted in a large net gain for the group as a whole but in highly divergent experiences for the individual members

Capital gains and losses did not cancel in the long run for this group of taxpayers. Of the 45 individuals 27 enjoyed an aggregate excess of net gains over net losses in the 17 years of $253 million, or 18 percent of their total income (before negative and deduction items). (The excess of net gains may be somewhat overstated because short term net losses for 1932 and 1933, which were not allowed as deduction items by the statutes, are not taken into account.) The other 18 individuals reported an aggregate excess of net losses over net gains of $66 million, or about 10 percent of their total income. The 27 taxpayers with an over-all profit reported annual net gains aggregating four times as much as the sum of the net losses they sustained in their loss years (Table 84).

The 45 individuals differed greatly with respect to the importance of capital transactions as sources of income and deductions. Three reported net gains amounting to less than 5 percent of their total income in the 17 years, and may actually have realized a net loss on balance if account were taken of the short term losses in 1932 and 1933 that were not recognized by the statutes. Another 13 reported net gains ranging from 5 to 25 percent of their total incomes; 7, net gains of 25-50 percent, and 4, net gains amounting to more than 50 percent of their total incomes (before negative and deduction items).

The differences among those in the group that reported an over-all net loss were not as wide. Six reported net losses amounting to less than 5 percent of their total income, 7, net losses of 5-15 percent, and 5, net losses of 15-25 percent. All realized net gains in some years. As a group, the 18 who reported an over-all net loss had realized net gains amounting to somewhat less than half of their aggregate annual net losses.

Second sample of high income taxpayers shows characteristics in 1929, 1932, and 1937 similar to those of the 1924 group

A second set of sample data is available in the *Source Book of Statistics of Income* for 1929, 1932, and 1937 for the 141 persons who reported the highest net incomes in 1929 and whose returns for the other 2 years were available. Virtually all reported capital transactions in each of the 3 years (Table 86). In 1929, 3 times as many reported net gains as reported net losses; in 1932 virtually all reported net losses; and in 1937 the numbers were equal. The loss data for 1932 are incomplete because short term net loss from sales of securities was disallowed by statute as a deduction item.

The net gains realized by this group in 1937 were almost 3 times as large as the net losses, despite the stock market slump. On the whole, the group remained at relatively high income levels in 1937, only 7 reporting incomes below $100,000 or net deficits. The net incomes excluding capital gains and losses were above $100,000 in 1937 for all except 2. Even in 1932 more than half reported net incomes of $100,000 or more. Nearly all of those with net deficits in that year were in that category because of their capital losses (Table 86).

The chief inference to be drawn from these 2 sample studies is that aggregate figures for taxpayers as a whole or for large groups do in fact conceal significant differences in the capital gain and loss experience of various smaller groups and of individuals.

Chapter 6

Effects of the Changing Tax Treatment of Capital Gains upon Investors' Behavior

The most persistent and influential objection offered in Congress to any except very low taxes upon capital gains is that they obstruct and distort investment transactions. It is contended that:

1) They induce business men and investors to postpone many potential selling transactions for varying periods or indefinitely. The mobility of capital and enterprise is thereby impaired.

2) They seriously weaken the incentives to make risky though socially desirable investments: enterprise capital, the kind that is willing to forego a relatively safe and regular income in return for a chance for big gains, is deterred by the prospect that the tax collector will reduce the gains to moderate proportions if they are realized at all, and that he will make only niggardly concessions if losses are incurred.

3) They accentuate stock market booms and collapses by discouraging the liquidation of over-priced securities: such liquidation might check or moderate an unhealthy rise. If it does not take place, both the rise and the subsequent decline are accentuated.

4) They so cut down the volume of transactions that tax revenues are less than they would be were the rates lower.

Do the figures compiled from income tax returns provide clear-cut evidence respecting the validity and force of these contentions? And what light do they throw on the effects of specific changes in tax treatment? In examining these figures we must remember that they tell us directly, and inadequately, only *what* individuals did, not *why* they did it. Nor can the latter always be inferred. A whole complex of forces operates upon the motives and actions of investors. The tax treatment of capital gains and losses is only one of these, and its influence is usually inextricably interwoven with that of the others. In drawing inferences from the figures reviewed in this chapter a high degree of caution is therefore necessary.

1 ALTHOUGH IN 1917-21 EFFECTIVE TAX RATES ON LONG TERM
CAPITAL GAINS WERE THE HIGHEST IN OUR HISTORY, LARGE NET
GAINS WERE REALIZED

From 1913 through 1921 capital gains, both long and short term,
were subject in full to the ordinary income tax rates. These rates
were very low at first. In 1913-15 the maximum surtax rate was
only 6 percent, and in 1916 only 13 percent. But tax rates were
sharply raised during the war years 1917-18, and were lowered only
slightly in 1919-21. In 1918 the effective rate on an additional dollar of capital gains for a married individual with 2 dependents was
77 percent if his statutory net income would otherwise be $1 million;
64 percent, if $100,000; 36 percent, if $50,000; 23 percent, if
$25,000; 16 percent, if $10,000; and 7 percent, if $5,000. For long
term gains these rates were the highest in our history until 1942,
when they were exceeded for income levels below about $30,000
but not for those above (Chart 24 and Table 87).

Although capital gains were fully taxable, capital losses were not
at first fully deductible. In 1913-15 they were not deductible at all,

Chart 24
**Effective Tax Rate on an Additional Dollar of Long Term Capital Gains
Individuals at 6 Levels of Statutory Net Income, 1917-1950**

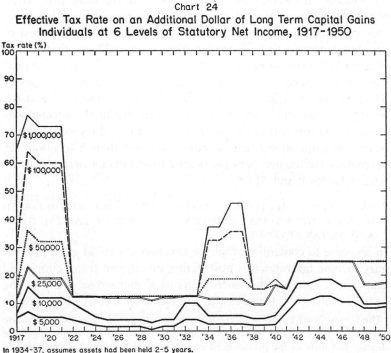

In 1934-37, assumes assets had been held 2-5 years.
In 1948-50, assumes a joint return.
Source: Table 87.

and in 1916-17 they were deductible only up to the amount of capital gains realized by the taxpayer. But in 1918-21 they were deductible against income of any kind.

The amounts of net capital gains and losses reported by individuals with net incomes under the 1917-21 tax treatment varied widely in the different years. Despite full taxability at the high regular income tax rates then in force, net capital gains in 1919 and again in 1920, doubtless reflecting the postwar boom, were among the 15 largest in 1917-46 (Table 1). Net gains reported for 1917, 1918, and 1921, on the other hand, were among the 5 lowest in the 30 years. Net capital losses were similarly irregular. The amounts in 1920 and 1921 were among the 9 largest in the 30 years, reflecting the crisis and depression of 1920-21, but in 1918, when net losses were just as fully deductible, the amount was among the 4 lowest.

In the uppermost income groups, however, there is evidence that the high tax rates discouraged the realization of capital gains. First, capital gains constituted a strikingly smaller proportion of incomes of $100,000 or more in 1917-21 than in any subsequent year (Table 5). Further, in 1917-21 they were only about the same proportion of the largest incomes as of all incomes, whereas in the other years they consistently accounted for a conspicuously bigger fraction of very large incomes than of smaller. Finally, in 1922, the first year in which a 12½ percent maximum tax was set on net long term capital gains, the aggregate amount realized by those with net incomes of $100,000 or more jumped very much more than the total realized by those in the other income groups. The rise in the former was about 2,400 percent; in the latter, 70 percent; and the contribution of capital gains to net income rose from less than 2 to about 25 percent for the former, but only from 2 to less than 4 percent for the latter (Tables 2 and 41).[1]

2 BIG CUTS IN EFFECTIVE TAX RATES IN 1922-33 WERE FOLLOWED
   BY BOTH THE FATTEST AND LEANEST YEARS OF CAPITAL GAINS
   AND OF TAX REVENUES

In response to contentions that the taxation of capital gains at ordinary income tax rates was obstructing investment transactions and that it was unfair to tax such gains as if they arose solely in the year of realization, Congress, in the Revenue Act of 1921, placed

[1] The comparisons between different years are not perfectly accurate because changes in the law and in tabulation practices affected the figures in some degree. But little of the pronounced contrasts cited here can be attributed to such changes.

an upper limit of 12½ percent upon tax rates applicable to net capital gains from assets held more than 2 years. This ceiling remained in force until the end of 1933.[2] During this period anyone whose long term gains would be subject to a higher rate if treated as ordinary income was permitted to pay a flat tax of 12½ percent on them in lieu of including them in his ordinary income tax computation. Those with net incomes of less than an amount that varied between about $16,000 and $32,000 in different years continued to be taxed at ordinary income tax rates on their long term net gains, and all taxpayers were so liable on gains from assets held 2 years or less.

Although the upper income groups alone benefited from the 12½ percent ceiling rate on long term capital gains, all taxpayers with capital gains benefited from the successive reductions in normal and surtax rates during the 'twenties. For the upper income groups these reductions lowered the effective rates on short term capital gains, and for other taxpayers, on both short and long term. For a married individual with two dependents and a statutory net income of $1 million, the effective rate on an additional dollar of short term capital gains was reduced from 73 percent in 1921 to 25 percent by 1925; if the statutory net income was $100,000, the reduction was from 60 to 25 percent; if the statutory net income was $50,000, from 32 to 18 percent; if the statutory net income was $25,000, from 19 to 12 percent. The rate for both short and long term gains was cut for those with smaller incomes: from 12 to 4 percent if the statutory net income was $10,000, and from 5 to 1.5 percent, if $5,000 (Chart 25 and Table 87).

Several years after the adoption of the 12½ percent ceiling rate on long term capital gains and after several successive reductions in normal and surtaxes, an unprecedented stock market boom developed in the United States, and the totals of net capital gains realized and of tax revenues from them rose to new heights. After a moderate rise from 94 in 1923 to 114 in 1924, the Dow Jones index of industrial stock prices jumped to 154 in 1925 (December average). The slight recession in 1926, to 149, merely interrupted the vigorous rise which brought the December 1927 average to 197.99 and the 1928 average to 281. Though the index fell to 247 in December 1929, the average for the year was 311. The movement of Standard

[2] For 1922 and 1923, but not for the subsequent years, the law provided that the total tax, including the tax on capital gains, of an individual electing the flat tax of 12½ percent in lieu of the normal and surtax rates, had to be at least 12½ percent of his total net income.

Chart 25
Effective Tax Rate on First Additional Dollar of Ordinary Income or Short Term Capital Gains Individuals at 6 Levels of Statutory Net Income, 1917-1950

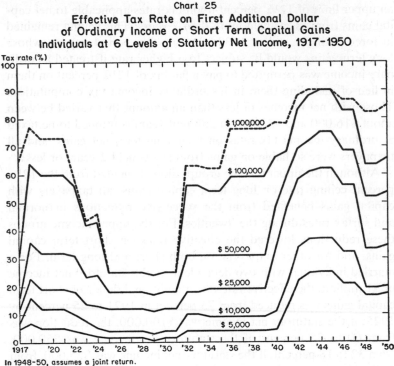

In 1948-50, assumes a joint return.
Source: Table 87.

and Poor's more comprehensive index of the prices of 90 industrial, railroad, and public utility company stocks, based upon 1926 prices was roughly similar. The December average in 1923 was 67.6; in 1924, 82.4; in 1925, 101.2; in 1926, 107.1; in 1927, 138.7; in 1928, 183.8; in 1929, 170.0; and the average for 1929 as a whole, 206.6. Considerable speculation in urban and suburban real estate and a large volume of speculative construction of houses, apartment and office buildings, and hotels accompanied the stock market boom.

From roughly $1,200 million in 1923 total net capital gains reported by taxpayers with net incomes, including both short and long term, rose to $1,500 million in 1924 and to $2,900 million in 1925 (Table 1). After a slight recession to $2,400 million in 1926 and a recovery to $2,900 million in 1927 they jumped to $4,800 million in 1928 and sagged a trifle to $4,700 million in 1929. In 1930 the total was again less than $1,200 million; in 1931 it was less than $500 million, or about half the amount reported under the very much higher tax rates of 1919 and 1920; in 1932 it was the lowest in the 30 years, $163 million; and in 1933, $553 million (Table 1).

The Treasury Department has estimated that its net revenues from capital gains and losses aggregated $1.5 billion in 1926-29,[3] or 41 percent of the total income tax liability of all individuals and taxable fiduciaries. This proportion was not approached in any other period for which figures are available (Table 90). In contrast, the Treasury has estimated that its net revenues in the next four years would have been some $168 million higher had capital gains and losses been excluded by statute from the determination of taxable income.

Did the tax treatment of capital gains and losses in the 'twenties contribute materially to the unprecedented amounts of net gains and of tax revenues from them?

3 MOST CAPITAL GAINS REPORTED IN 1922-33 WERE SUBJECT TO ORDINARY INCOME TAX RATES, WHICH REACHED THE LOWEST LEVELS SINCE 1917

We may note, first, that the greater part of capital gains reported in 1922-33 did not benefit from the 12½ percent ceiling rate because they were realized by taxpayers whose incomes from other sources were not large enough to subject them to a tax rate of more than 12½ percent if reported as ordinary income, or by upper income individuals who had held the assets 2 years or less. In 1922-33 approximately 98 percent of the aggregate net capital gains of taxpayers with net incomes under $50,000 was reported as ordinary income; slightly more than half of the net gains of those with net incomes between $50,000 and $100,000; and 62 percent of the aggregate net gains of all income groups (Table 13). In only one of the 12 years, 1929, did as much as half of the aggregate net gains of all income groups benefit from the 12½ percent ceiling rate (Table 13). In short, for the taxpayers who were responsible for about three-fifths of the total capital gains reported, the tax rates that counted in 1922-33 were those on ordinary income, not the special 12½ percent ceiling rate on capital gains.

Ordinary income tax rates were lower in 1925-31 than at any other time since 1917 (Chart 25 and Table 87). Consequently, the tax rates on short term capital gains were at their lowest. Those on long term gains were in no case higher than those on short term; moreover, they were specifically limited to a maximum of 12½ percent.

[3] *Revenue Revision of 1942*, Hearings, Ways and Means Committee, p. 1637.

In other words, the price, in taxes, of realizing net capital gains during the boom years of realization was the lowest in the history of our income tax except for 1913-16.

The tax provisions ruling in 1925-31 were especially favorable to short term capital transactions. Not only were short term net gains taxed at substantially lower rates than before or after, but short term net losses were fully deductible against income of any kind. For individuals with net incomes above a figure that varied between $16,000 and $32,000 in different years, the ceiling rate of 12½ percent on long term net capital gains was more favorable than the effective rates on short term gains, but this advantage was partly offset after 1923 by a corresponding limit of 12½ percent of the loss on the deductibility of long term net losses. In addition to making the 'tax cost' of realizing short term gains much lower than before or after, the tax provisions gave individuals with substantial incomes a special incentive to 'take' their losses while these were still short term, and to defer the realization of capital gains until the assets had been held more than 2 years.

4 NONTAX FACTORS WERE OF TRANSCENDENT IMPORTANCE IN THE BOOM OF THE 'TWENTIES

The outstandingly favorable tax laws offer such a tangible and readily intelligible explanation that the temptation is great to ascribe to them the major role in the capital gains boom of the 'twenties. But income tax figures and collateral data indicate that they accounted for only a part, and perhaps a small part, of the behavior of investors and speculators. We know that the boom did not begin as soon as tax rates were reduced, and that the favorable tax treatment did not prevent a drastic decline in capital gains in 1930-33.

Many factors contributed during the 'twenties to raise the prices of capital assets and to swell the volume of capital transactions and of realized capital gains. The period was one of enormous business expansion. The Federal Reserve Board index of industrial production rose from 67 in 1921 to 119 in 1929, or 78 percent. Bank deposits rose $18 billion, or about 50 percent. The underlying business situation received powerful support from such forces as house construction expenditures aggregating $34 billion (as against $8 billion in 1930-38); public utility and railroad construction of $20 billion (as against $11 billion in 1930-38); commercial and miscellaneous building of $20 billion (as against $13 billion in 1930-38); consumer credit expansion of $6 billion (as against a *contraction* of

$1 billion in 1930-38); and American loans to foreigners of $5 billion (as against $2 billion in 1930-38).[4]

The period was also one of rising corporate profits, numerous corporate mergers, and of generally declining interest rates. All three influences operated to raise the market values of capital assets: the first by increasing the income obtainable from corporate securities; the second by promising both a reduction in risks and an increase in income; and the third by giving each dollar of income a higher capital value. Corporate net income reported for income tax purposes rose from $4.3 billion in 1921 to $9.6 billion in 1925, $10.6 billion in 1928, and $11.7 billion in 1929. Moody's average of Aaa corporate bond yields was 5.97 percent in 1921, 4.88 percent in 1925, 4.55 percent in 1928, and 4.73 percent in 1929. And on top of the increases in value due directly to these influences, further increases occurred as speculators attempted to discount the continuation of the favorable trends. The middle 'twenties saw a widespread wave of speculation in urban real estate; the later 'twenties, unparalleled speculation in the stock market.

Unprecedented activity by speculative pools gave an extraordinary stimulus to stock speculation in the second half of the 'twenties. Unhampered by the restrictions imposed by the Securities and Exchange Commission legislation of 1933-34 many such pools were formed and conducted with the aid of corporate managements and of large holders of the stocks involved. Operating on a big scale, they provided organized leadership and attracted large followings. The market value of sponsored stocks not uncommonly rose 50 to 100 percent in a few months. New issues of securities, often of holding companies in the electric light and power industry, were frequently made the vehicles for spectacular speculative operations led by the sponsoring investment bankers. Many members of the upper income groups whose capital gains were usually derived from long term investments became participants in short term speculative operations through their relations with pool leaders and investment bankers.

Other influences also contributed to the rise. Attracted by the price behavior and the prospects of American securities, foreigners bought substantial amounts. More foreign funds supported the rise in American stocks by being lent in the call money market. Bank credit for stock speculation was abundant and margin requirements

[4] Lauchlin Currie, testimony before the Temporary National Economic Committee, Hearings, IX, 4010-11.

low, for besides foreign funds, the call loan market benefited from large amounts of the new capital raised through stock issues by domestic corporations and temporarily placed in the call market through New York banks.

And active throughout as both cause and effect in the tremendous rise of capital values during the middle and late 'twenties was the pervading speculative temper of the time.

That these nontax factors were at work does not prove that the low level of taxes on capital gains was of no influence in determining the amounts realized during the 'twenties; even the speculative temper doubtless owed something to the low taxes. The favorable tax situation may reasonably be supposed to have made some speculative and investment operations attractive that would not have been undertaken in the face of higher tax rates, and to have encouraged more realization than would otherwise have occurred. The favorable tax rates were doubtless most influential in the uppermost income groups. Those who had large incomes from other sources and those whose potential capital gains, if realized, were alone of sufficient size to place them in the topmost income groups would naturally be expected to be most sensitive to the character of the tax treatment of their capital gains. In 1922-29 capital gains contributed 62 percent of net income for individuals with net incomes of $1 million or more, 51 percent for those with net incomes of $500,000-1,000,000, 46 percent for those with net incomes of $300,000-500,000, 34 percent for those with net incomes of $100,000-300,000, and 11 percent for all income groups (Tables 2 and 41). While these figures reflect other and more fundamental forces as well as taxation, they show that the tax treatment in the 'twenties was sufficiently favorable to the upper income groups to be accompanied by the realization of gains on an enormous scale by members of these groups.

The low tax cost of short term gains at all income levels and the full deductibility of short term losses probably encouraged more short term trading than would otherwise have taken place. Other conditions also were peculiarly favorable to short term speculation, as we have seen, and, even in the face of materially higher taxes, these might well have produced a very large proportion of the speculative activity that actually occurred. Very much higher tax rates on both short and long term gains did not prevent net capital gains of a billion dollars a year in 1919 and 1920, when other conditions were favorable.

Despite the tax inducement to those with large incomes to convert their unrealized short term losses into realized ones as offsets against their taxable income, the figures do not indicate that this expedient was resorted to extensively — presumably for the very good reason that the trend of the market until 1929 was largely upward, making net gains more common than net losses.[5] From 1926 through 1929 individuals with net incomes of $50,000 or over reported aggregate long term net capital gains of $6.1 billion and aggregate short term net gains of $2.5 billion (Table 9). In contrast, their aggregate short term net losses, while nearly 3 times their long term net losses, were only $.4 billion, more than two-thirds of which was sustained in 1929, the year of the stock market crash (Table 9). Since the general run of long-held capital assets had appreciated markedly in value during the boom, short-held assets would naturally be expected to constitute the chief source of capital losses even if short and long term losses had been equally deductible for the income tax.

Nontax influences for the rising proportion of long term gains in total gains as we ascend the income scale may be reflected in the figures for 1925-31. The effective rate on additional short term gains, as on long, was exactly the same for all incomes of $100,000 or over. Hence, beginning at this income level those with bigger incomes had no more incentive, as far as the *rate* was concerned, to prefer long to short term gains than those with smaller incomes. Nevertheless, long term gains constituted a progressively larger proportion of the total in this period as in others as we go from incomes of $100,000-300,000 to $300,000-500,000, to $500,000-$1 million, and to $1 million or more (Table 13).

To the extent that those with bigger incomes tended to realize bigger average gains than those with smaller, however, the same tax *rate* would subject them to a larger absolute tax and might therefore deter them more than those with smaller incomes from realizing their potential gains: the same tax rate, 24 percent, on a short term capital gain and 12½ percent on a long, would take twice as many dollars out of a $200,000 gain as out of a $100,000.

5 DID THE 12½ PERCENT RATE ON LONG TERM GAINS OF THE UPPER INCOME GROUPS OBSTRUCT THE LIQUIDATION OF SECURITIES IN THE 1928-29 BOOM?

Curiously enough, the maximum rate of 12½ percent, inaugurated in 1922 as a stimulus to transfers of capital assets, was widely

[5] Since the tabulated figures are those of *net* gains and losses reported, they do not show losses that were less than the gains realized by a taxpayer.

charged in 1928 and 1929 with obstructing the liquidation of securities, and with thereby creating an artificial scarcity of stocks and artificially high stock prices. No doubt the rate seemed higher after 1925 than it had in 1921 because the rates on ordinary income had been so drastically reduced meanwhile: for a married individual with two dependents the maximum effective rate on an additional dollar of income had been cut from 73 percent in 1921 and 58 percent in 1922 to 25 percent by 1925. The ceiling tax rate for capital gains was therefore less of a 'bargain' rate after 1924 than it had been before. Nevertheless, it was only half the rate on additional ordinary income for individuals with net incomes of $100,000 or more (Table 87).

But for the many investors who lacked strong opinions respecting the probable trend of prices for one or more of their assets, even a moderate tax on capital gains could doubtless deter liquidation. Such an investor had to consider that if he sold, he not only gave up the chance of benefiting from a possible rise in the value of the asset but faced a certain loss of capital resources and earning power through paying the tax. If he contemplated shifting his funds to what seemed a more attractive investment, the tax on his accrued gains would rationally deter him unless the contemplated new commitment seemed sufficiently more attractive than the old to offset the *certain* loss of capital funds entailed by the transfer. To these influences must be added the consideration that although the 12½ percent ceiling rate on capital gains was only half the rate on ordinary income, it represented a considerable sum of money when gains were large. And this rate had to be compared not only with the rate on ordinary income but also with the zero rate open to those who kept their property until death or gave it to relatives and others who did not sell it.

Against the contention that the 12½ percent rate prevented a substantial amount of liquidation is the unprecedented volume of stock market sales in the boom years. Between January 1925 and July 1929 the average number of shares listed on the New York Stock Exchange more than doubled; yet the average number of shares sold monthly increased from 7.9 percent of the total in January 1926 to 8.7 and 14.2 percent respectively in January 1928 and 1929.[6] Such a volume of sales might be reconciled with a small volume of real liquidation if the sales represented primarily an enor-

[6] Based upon tables in the monthly issues of the *New York Stock Exchange Bulletin*.

mous turnover in a small fraction of the securities outstanding. But the evidence indicates that a very considerable diffusion of stock ownership took place. Berle and Means estimate that the number of stockholders in three of the largest American corporations, the American Telephone and Telegraph Company, the Pennsylvania Railroad, and the United States Steel Corporation, increased 237, 47, and 26 percent, respectively, between 1920 and 1929.[7] In a series of estimates of the number of stockholders of American corporations, excluding duplicate names, the midpoint of the estimates in 1927 is 5.5 million; in 1929, 8 million — an increase of 45 percent.[8] Total net gains realized by individuals with net incomes through the sale of securities and other capital assets during the 3 years 1927-29 exceeded the aggregate reported during the preceding decade.

Finally, the point needs emphasis that even if a lower rate or the complete tax exemption of long term capital gains might have led to substantially larger sales of stocks by certain individuals, these additional sales would not have exerted a moderating influence upon the general level of prices in the stock market unless the sellers had refrained from investing the proceeds in other stocks. Only if, in their judgment, the general outlook had become clouded or adverse would we expect a large number of sellers to liquidate particular securities without reinvesting in others. But if they thought the outlook had indeed become clouded or worse, the 12½ percent maximum rate on capital gains would not, rationally, act as a serious deterrent to selling. Since the tax applied to their *net gains* alone, not to the gross sales price, an expected decline of substantially less than 12½ percent in the market value of their stocks would more than justify the 'tax cost' of selling in the case of stockholders who were actually considering liquidation.

6 STRONG EVIDENCE THAT THE UNUSUALLY HIGH TAX RATES ON MEDIUM TERM GAINS OF UPPER BRACKET INCOMES AND THE LARGE DISCOUNTS OFFERED FOR CONTINUED HOLDING IN 1934-37 POSTPONED LIQUIDATION

The preferential tax treatment of capital gains took a new form in 1934. The flat 12½ percent ceiling rate on long term gains and losses, which had been effective for the upper income groups alone, was eliminated. Instead, for all taxpayers 70 percent of the capital

[7] *The Modern Corporation and Private Property* (Macmillan, 1933), p. 56.
[8] N. R. Danielian, *The Securities Markets* (Twentieth Century Fund, 1935), p. 50.

gains realized on assets held longer than 10 years was excluded from taxable income; 60 percent, if the assets had been held 5-10 years; 40 percent, if held 2-5 years; and 20 percent, if held 1-2 years. The remainder of the gains on assets held longer than 1 year, and the entire amount in the case of assets held 1 year or less, were made subject to the full scale of normal and surtax rates applicable to ordinary income. The same proportions of capital losses, similarly varying with the number of years the assets had been held, were excluded in calculating taxable income, except that a maximum of $2,000 net capital losses so computed was allowed as a deduction from ordinary income.

This new treatment caused the effective tax rates on capital gains to vary with the size of income throughout the income tax scale and with statutory changes in the exemptions, credits, and rates applicable to ordinary income. In general, the new treatment lowered the effective tax rates on the capital gains of individuals with small or moderately large incomes, but raised them on those with upper bracket incomes. The dividing line varied with the holding period. All income groups benefited from the treatment accorded gains from assets held 1-2 years because such gains had previously been taxed as ordinary income. On gains from assets held 2-5 years, the effective rates were raised for taxpayers whose surtax incomes, exclusive of the contemplated gains, exceeded about $22,000, and lowered for others; if the assets had been held 5-10 years, the dividing line was about $50,000; and if longer than 10 years, about $68,000.

The increases were especially sharp on gains from assets held 2-5 years realized by taxpayers with incomes approaching or exceeding $100,000, because the exclusion of 40 percent of the gain from taxation still left the effective rates in this part of the income scale far above the previous 12½ percent maximum. A taxpayer whose surtax net income from other sources was $50,000 in 1934 and who contemplated realizing a capital gain of $100,000 from an asset held 2-5 years faced a tax of $27,900, or 27.9 percent on his capital gain. If his surtax net income from other sources was $100,000, he faced an effective tax rate of 33.7 percent on his gain. (An upward adjustment in the surtax schedule raised these rates somewhat in 1936-37.) For all except the top income groups, the exclusion from taxable income of 60 and 70 percent of the gains from longer holding periods was enough to bring the effective rates either below or only moderately above those previously prevailing. If the $100,000 capital gain contemplated by the taxpayer in the last example was from an asset held more than 10 years instead of 2-5 years, the tax on the gain would be 16.8 instead of 33.7 percent.

The substantial tax cost of realizing a medium term capital gain when the addition to the taxpayer's ordinary income would put him in an upper income group can well be supposed to have dissuaded many persons from realizing such gains during this period. Accentuating the deterrent influence of the high tax rates were the direct incentives for postponement provided in the law. Prior to 1934-37 two years and a day was the only period of holding required to qualify a capital gain for the most preferential tax treatment. In 1934-37, however, the law offered the equivalent of a series of successively larger discounts from the tax rates on ordinary income for postponing realization of gains. In effect, those from assets held more than 10 years were given a discount of 70 percent and those from shorter periods of holding, discounts of 60, 40, or 20 percent, according as the asset had been held 5-10, 2-5, or 1-2 years, respectively.

Although these discounts were uniform for all income levels, their value was small at the lower levels because the ordinary income tax rates were low; and their value rose with income because of the progression of income tax rates. If a man with $5,000 income kept his asset more than 10 years instead of 1 year or less, he would reduce the effective tax rate on the first dollar of his gain only from 4 to 1.2 percent; but for a man with $100,000 income, the rate would be reduced from 54 to 16.2 percent, and for one with $1 million income, from 62 to 18.6 percent.[9] The stepdowns in the rates in the intervening periods were similarly progressive. The effective tax rate on the first dollar of capital gains was reduced by the following percentage points for the indicated amounts of income for holding an asset over 1 year, over 2 years, over 5 years, and over 10 years, respectively: for an income of $1 million, 12.4, 24.8, 37.2, and 43.4; for $100,000, 10.8, 21.6, 32.4, and 37.8; for $50,000, 6.2, 12.4, 18.6, and 21.7; for $25,000, 3.8, 7.6, 11.4, and 13.3; for $10,000, 1.8, 3.6, 5.4, and 6.3; for $5,000, .8, 1.6, 2.4, and 2.8.

The combined effect of the foregoing influences upon individuals with large incomes from ordinary sources or large amounts of medium term capital gains was a powerful inducement to defer realization for a longer period than under the two-year rule of 1921-33. And adding to this inducement was the hope that Congress might

[9] In 1934-35. The rates were somewhat higher and the margins slightly different in 1936-37; see Table 87.

be persuaded soon to reduce the effective rates on capital gains by reimposing a low ceiling rate or other means.

The operations and fortunes of investors are ordinarily the joint products of so many conflicting influences that clear evidence of the effects of tax factors upon their conduct cannot always be found in *Statistics of Income*. In the present instance, as in a few others, however, such evidence appears to exist. When a maximum tax of 15 percent on gains from assets held more than 2 years was substituted in 1938 for the rates prevailing in the preceding 4 years, the aggregate net capital gains of individuals with incomes of $100,000 or over jumped 144 percent — from $135 million in 1937 to $328 million in 1938 — even though the net gains of all other income groups *fell* $192 million, or 28 percent (Table 2).[10] The inference is reasonable that many selling transactions previously held up by the substantial tax rates imposed on the gains of upper bracket individuals were rushed through in 1938 when a ceiling rate of 15 percent was substituted.[11] This inference is supported by the behavior of net capital gains in the following year, when the amount reported by individuals with net incomes of $100,000 or over fell off nearly two-thirds, while the total reported by all other taxpayers increased somewhat.

The effect of the flat ceiling rate of 15 percent on gains from assets held more than 2 years and of the 20 percent maximum rate on gains from assets held 18-24 months does not appear to have been limited to 1938.[12] During the 4 years 1938-41 as a whole, the net gains of individuals with incomes of $100,000 and more increased $371 million, or about 67 percent, over those of 1934-37, in the face of a decline of $467 million, or about 17 percent, in the net gains reported by all other income groups (Table 2). Most of this increase

[10] The figures here cited only approximate the absolute and relative amounts involved because changes in the statutes and tabulations caused the classifications for 1938-41 to differ in certain respects from those for 1934-37. A less complete offsetting of losses against gains caused total net capital gains in 1938-41 to be somewhat overstated as compared with those in 1934-37, and the statutory net incomes included different percentages of capital gains and losses (see the statistical notes in Appendix One). But the movements here noted are so pronounced and of such character that their significance is not vitiated by these differences.

[11] The 15 percent maximum rate applied to gains from assets held more than 2 years; the ceiling was 20 percent on gains from assets held 18-24 months.

[12] A special Defense Tax of 10 percent of the total income tax liability as otherwise determined, imposed in 1940, raised the effective ceiling rates on capital gains 10 percent.

was accounted for by taxpayers with net incomes of $300,000 and over, whose aggregate net gains in 1938-41 were more than twice as large as in the preceding 4 years.

Several factors appear to account for the divergence between the experience of the uppermost income groups and that of other taxpayers in 1938-41 as compared with 1934-37. The conditions of 1938-41 were unfavorable for increases in capital values. The business recession, which had become marked in the latter part of 1937, deepened in 1938; and the shadow of World War II created grave uncertainties for investors well before its actual outbreak in September 1939. Partly because of military orders from abroad and from our own rearmament program, industrial production expanded sharply in 1940 and 1941, but capital values as measured by stock prices did not respond. In fact, the stock market was depressed throughout most of the 4 years. The December average of Standard and Poor's index of 90 stocks, which had been 135.5 in 1936 and 87.5 in 1937, was 100.7 in 1938; 98.2 in 1939; 83.7 in 1940; and 69.5 in 1941. Tax factors apart, a lower level of aggregate capital gains in 1938-41 than in 1934-37 was to be expected from the behavior of the stock market.

It seems reasonable to attribute the divergence of actual results from this expectation in the case of the uppermost income groups to the change in tax treatment, which encouraged the realization of accumulated capital gains previously dammed up by unfavorable tax treatment. On the other hand, because of the lower tax rates to which they had been subject, those who could realize capital gains in 1934-37 without moving their total taxable incomes close to or above the $100,000 level had been offered a much smaller incentive to postpone realization than those with larger incomes. In consequence, a relatively smaller amount of dammed-up realization was presumably released in these income groups by the tax treatment inaugurated in 1938.

Individuals with net incomes of less than $100,000 nevertheless continued to account for the greater part of aggregate net capital gains. Although their share fell from about 83 percent in 1934-37 to about 71 percent in 1938-41, it continued to dominate the totals (Table 3). Hence superficial inspection of the figures would show that the more favorable tax treatment of capital gains was accompanied by a reduction in the total realized. In reality, however, the income groups most affected by the changed treatment responded to it quite sharply in the face of adverse business conditions, while the other income groups, dominating the aggregate, did not respond, because the change for them was relatively small and was overshadowed by the other conditions affecting capital values.

Finally, the movement of some individuals into higher income groups through large-scale realization of capital gains doubtless contributed in some degree to the divergent changes in the amounts realized. Since the classification by incomes is based upon incomes including the statutory proportions of capital gains taxable as income, a taxpayer's decision to realize or postpone realizing any substantial amount in a particular year may be the primary influence in determining the income group in which he is counted in the published statistics for that year. The big increase in the capital gains reported by the uppermost income groups in 1938-41 was swelled by the gains of some taxpayers who reached a high income level in this period solely or primarily because they realized previously deferred capital gains. If, for example, a man with a surtax net income of $50,000 from ordinary sources in any of the years 1934-37 postponed realizing a capital gain of $300,000 on an asset held 2-5 years in order to avoid the substantial tax rates in force, then realized the gain in 1938, he would be in the $50,000 income group in 1934-37 and in the $200,000 income group in 1938 ($50,000 of ordinary income and 50 percent of the $300,000 capital gain).

7 SHARP ADVANCE IN TAX RATES SINCE 1942 ACCOMPANIED BY SUBSTANTIAL INCREASES IN REALIZED CAPITAL GAINS

The large expenditures for rearmament preceding our entrance into World War II led to sharp increases in income tax rates, and even sharper advances were made in the Revenue Act of 1942, following the United States declaration of war. Between 1939 and 1942 the exemption for a head of a family was reduced from $2,500 to $1,200 and that for a single individual from $1,000 to $500. The normal tax rate was raised from 4 to 6 percent, the initial surtax rate from 4 to 13 percent, the exemption from surtax of the first $4,000 of surtax net income was eliminated, other surtax rates were substantially advanced, and a new maximum surtax rate of 82 percent was made applicable to surtax net incomes over $200,000 instead of over $5 million. The combined effect of these changes is indicated by the rise in the effective tax rate on an additional dollar of income at various income levels. For a $5,000 a year married man with 2 children, the effective rate on an additional dollar of ordinary income rose from 4 to 22 percent; for one with $10,000 income, from 9 to

34 percent; $25,000, 19 to 58 percent; $50,000, 31 to 69 percent; $100,000, 59 to 83 percent; $1 million, 76 to 88 percent (Chart 25 and Table 87). For 1943 these rates were increased by the imposition of a special 5 percent Victory Tax with lower exemptions, credits, and deductions than usual, and were further increased in 1944 by several percentage points in most income brackets.

Because the maximum tax rates on capital gains remained unchanged in 1940, except for the Defense Tax cited in note 12, and 1941 in the face of the higher levies on ordinary income, the disparity of tax treatment for individuals with large incomes became wider than ever (Table 88). But the Revenue Act of 1942 imposed heavier taxes on capital gains and reduced the allowances for capital losses. The maximum effective rate on a long term capital gain, which had been 20 percent if the asset had been held 18-24 months, and 15 percent if held longer, was raised to 25 percent on all long term capital gains. In 1938-39 persons with surtax net incomes smaller than about $44,000 had been subject to rates lower than the 20 and 15 percent ceilings on long term gains; now, only those with surtax net incomes less than $18,000 were subject to effective tax rates on such gains lower than 25 percent. The special treatment of long term capital gains was achieved in substantially the same manner as previously: only half of such gains was included in taxable income, and the taxed half could be reported on a separate schedule subject to a flat 50 percent tax rate if inclusion in ordinary income would result in a rate higher than 50 percent.

For the previous unlimited deductibility of the statutory amounts of net long term capital losses from ordinary income there was substituted a maximum allowance of $1,000 in any one year, but the taxpayer was given the privilege of carrying forward the remainder of a net capital loss for 5 years, applying it to offset capital gains during this period to the full amount of the carry-over and to offset ordinary income up to $1,000 in each year.

These steps in the direction of more stringency were partly offset by a major concession respecting the holding period necessary to qualify a gain for preferential treatment. In response to strong representations that the realization of many bona fide capital gains is obstructed when a long holding period is required, Congress reduced this period to the shortest ever required, 6 months. A concession was made with respect to short term losses also. Previously these could be offset only against short term gains. Now they were combined with long term losses and could be used to offset short or long term gains, and to reduce other taxable income up to $1,000; and, as indicated above, the balance of any combined short and long term net loss could be carried forward for 5 years. Because only half of long term gains but the full amount of short term losses were taken into account, each dollar of short term loss offset the tax liability on $2 of long term gains.

Despite these concessions, the 1942 changes in tax treatment brought the effective tax rates on capital gains to the highest levels since 1921, with the exception, previously discussed, of a few categories of gains of the top income groups in 1934-37 (Chart 24 and Table 87). Nevertheless, the changes were followed by large increases in realized capital gains. The average annual amount in 1942-46 for returns with net incomes, $3.4 billion, was more than quadruple that of 1938-41, 1934-37, or 1917-21, and was about 71 percent in excess of 1922-33. Nor was the sharp rise in realized gains confined to the middle and lower income groups. Individuals with net incomes of $100,000 or over almost tripled their average annual capital gains over 1938-41.

These figures indicate that severer taxation did not prevent a considerable volume of gains-taking. On the other hand, they do not demonstrate that the higher taxes did not discourage some sales of capital assets. Obscuring the inhibiting effects of the higher rates, and perhaps offsetting them in part, was the stimulus to capital gains arising from the war-created expansion in business activity and in national income. As estimated by the Department of Commerce, national income rose from an average of $81.3 billion a year in 1938-41 to $170.7 billion in 1942-46. The amount of capital gains reported was also increased, it is probable, by the wider use of legal arrangements designed to convert ordinary income into capital gains. The extraordinarily high tax rates on ordinary income were a strong stimulus to many taxpayers to devise and use such expedients. One device, referred to later in this chapter, was the sale or liquidation of a corporation possessing large undistributed earnings rather than the distribution of these earnings in dividends. Another was the incorporation of a separate company for each of a series of ventures that would ordinarily be undertaken by a single enterprise, and the sale or liquidation of each company, after 6 months or more, as its separate venture was completed. These and other devices to convert ordinary income into capital gains will receive further attention in Chapter 9.

Also favoring the realization of capital gains was the reduction to 6 months and a day of the period an asset had to be held in order to qualify a gain from it as 'long term'. With so brief a period of ownership needed to obtain the benefit of tax rates only half or less of the rates applicable to ordinary income, many investors were doubtless induced to make some commitments they would not otherwise have made, and to take their gains sooner. We cannot measure the results of this influence, but the relatively narrow range of stock market fluctuations and the low to moderate volume of stock trading during most of this period suggest that they were not large. The number of shares traded on the New York Stock Exchange in 1946 was only about a third that of 1929. We have previously noted the close relation between short term gains and losses and fluctuations in stock prices, and between the former and the volume of stock trading (Charts 17 and 18; Tables 8 and 15).

Despite the substantial capital gains reported in 1942-46, it is probable that restraining influences were at work. The level and the recent rate of increase of national income favored larger amounts. Although national income in 1946 was more than twice that of 1929, net capital gains realized were only 1.5 times as large ($7.3 vs. $4.8 billion). Doubtless many factors conspired to produce this difference. Stock prices did not advance violently in 1942-46 as they had in 1927-29. Between January 1927 and September 1929 they jumped from 103.1 to 340.6 percent of 1926 prices, as measured by Standard and Poor's Corporation, while between 1942 and 1944 they rose only from 70.9 to 100.0, then to an average of 137.6 in December 1945 and to an average of 148.5 in May 1946. The uncertainties created by World War II, together with the increase in taxes on corporation income and the possibly adverse effects upon corporate earnings of renegotiations of war contracts, probably impeded the advance of capital values. And with memories of the Great Depression of the 'thirties still vivid, the whole tenor of the times was different from that of the late 'twenties. Among the many forces that restricted the realization of capital gains, the severer tax treatment probably played some part.

8 IS THE ABSOLUTE OR THE RELATIVE LEVEL OF CAPITAL GAINS
   TAXES MORE SIGNIFICANT?

In the opinion of some students the extraordinarily wide gap between the rates on capital gains and the rates on ordinary income in 1942-49 diminished the deterrent influence of the former, thereby tending to bring about more realization of gains.[13] As against the 25 percent ceiling on long term capital gains, the bracket rates on ordinary income reached as high as 94 percent for amounts in excess of $200,000. Though relatively to the latter, the capital gains rate seemed low, its absolute level was twice as high as the 12½ percent maximum prevailing during the stock market boom of the 1920's and that had been widely charged with contributing to the inflation of stock prices by deterring stockholders from selling their securities. The highest surtax rate during the late 'twenties, applicable to all surtax net income over $100,000, was 20 percent, in comparison with which the capital gains rate of 12½ percent doubtless seemed substantial. Could a capital gains tax rate twice as high, when coupled with very much higher rates on ordinary income, exert a smaller deterrent influence or a positively encouraging one upon sales of capital assets? We may note several ways in which this was possible:

First, there can be little doubt that the 25 percent capital gains tax now *looked* low relative to the rates on ordinary income. It was therefore a smaller psychological obstacle to sales than its absolute level might suggest. Because it was widely regarded as a 'bargain rate',[14] it probably gave some investors a positive stimulus to 'take' capital gains.

Second, the wide discrepancy speeded some sales of capital assets by creating the fear that Congress might soon reduce the degree of preference accorded capital gains or remove the preference altogether.[15]

Third, the very high rates on ordinary income made it prohibitively costly for wealthy individuals to receive previously accumulated corporate earnings in dividends from corporations they controlled, whereas the sale of their stock would enable them to obtain these previously accumulated earnings (to the extent that they were reflected in the price of the stock) plus any other capital gains subject only to the 25 percent rate. For example, suppose the owner of substantially all the capital stock of a textile mill, who was in the 80 percent tax bracket, desired to obtain for his personal disposition several hundred thousand dollars of the company's previously accumulated earnings. If he paid these earnings to himself in dividends he could keep only 20 percent of them after taxes. On the other hand,

[13] See remarks by George O. May, Thomas N. Tarleau, Eustace Seligman, Harry J. Rudick, and Lawrence H. Seltzer, in *Capital Gains Taxation,* pp. 54-8.
[14] Cf. J. K. Lasser, *Your Income Tax* (Simon and Schuster, 1944), p. 137.
[15] *Capital Gains Taxation,* p. 57.

if he seized a current opportunity to sell all or a part of his stock at a price per share equaling or exceeding the sum of his original cost and the reinvested earnings, he would have, after taxes, his original cost plus 75 percent of the reinvested earnings plus 75 percent of any additional payment made by the purchaser. Obviously this motive for selling would not exist if capital gains were subject to the same high tax rates as dividends. Even if they were taxable at moderately lower rates, the inducement to sell might well prove insufficient because the remaining advantage of the capital gains over the ordinary tax rate would have to be weighed against the disadvantages of relinquishing part or all of the ownership of the enterprise.

Fourth, the relative levels of the rates on ordinary income and on capital gains favored the sale by wealthy men of assets yielding large incomes but subject to heavy burdens of management or risk. Suppose, for example, the owner in the preceding example received a net income of $60,000 a year from his mill and net income from other sources of $40,000. At the 1944 rates, his total net income, $100,000, would be subject to a tax of $68,565.[16] If his income from the mill were eliminated, his tax would be cut to $19,545. Hence he might reasonably attribute $49,020 of his total tax to his income from the mill, leaving him only $10,980 from the latter after taxes. If he expected such high taxes to persist, he might reasonably decide to relieve himself of the managerial and risk burdens of his business even at the cost of a substantial reduction in his pre-tax income. By transferring his funds to safer and less exacting but lower yielding uses and by forfeiting part of his capital by paying the 25 percent tax on the capital gains he realizes in the transfer, he might sacrifice half of this part of his income. Most of the loss, however, would be borne by the government because of the accompanying reduction in his personal income tax. For example, assuming that the cost basis of the mill to him was $200,000 and that he sold it for $600,000, receiving $100,000 in cash and $500,000 in 6 percent mortgage bonds, he would have to pay a capital gains tax of $100,000, and his income from the mill would be cut in half, to $30,000. But the income tax on his total net income, $70,000, would now be only $42,645, a $25,920 reduction from the amount payable on $100,000 net income. In other words, the $30,000 decrease in his net income would cut his income taxes $25,920. After taxes, therefore, his net income would be reduced only $4,080 a year. He

[16] Assuming he was entitled to four exemptions (himself, his wife, and two dependent children).

might well consider such a reduction a small price to pay for his relief from the exertions and risks of owning and operating his business.

A capital gains tax rate of 25 percent should rationally exert a smaller deterrent influence upon the realization of gains when the effective tax rate on marginal amounts of ordinary income is 80 percent than when it is lower, say 50 percent, because the loss of principal through payment of the capital gains tax entails a smaller loss of income, after income taxes, in the former case than in the latter. If the effective ordinary rate was 80 percent, an investor whose unrealized capital gains of $100,000 are yielding him a pre-tax income of $10,000 and an after-tax income of $2,000 will lose only $500 a year in after-tax income by realizing his gains, paying 25 percent of them in taxes and reinvesting the balance at the same yield as before. With the same 25 percent capital gains tax rate, he would lose $1,250 a year in after-tax income if the effective rate on the relevant amounts of his ordinary income is 50 instead of 80 percent.[17]

On the other hand, if the wartime high levels of income tax rates were coupled with an effective tax rate on capital gains of 50 or 75 percent, shifts of investments that entailed the realization of large capital gains would doubtless be greatly discouraged. Even though high income investors could derive only a small yield, after income taxes, from their capital funds, they would be loath to pay capital gains taxes that made substantial inroads on their principal when they could avoid these taxes merely by not selling. As was the case in 1917-21, large numbers of them would postpone sales in the hope or expectation that tax rates on both ordinary incomes and on capital gains would not be held at high levels indefinitely, or in the expectation that their properties would be freed from all potential tax liability on the capital gains embodied in them by transfer at death. For these reasons, even the 25 percent rate probably deterred many sales in which large absolute amounts of gains would have been realized.

Finally, although the high tax rates on ordinary incomes rationally favored the realization of gains by some investors in connection with the shifting of their funds from more to less hazardous or exacting uses, they at the same time exerted an opposite influence. They discouraged transfers of funds, and the incidental realization of gains, in the search for higher yields. If a man in the 80 percent bracket

[17] Cf. Eustace Seligman's remarks in *Capital Gains Taxation,* pp. 57-8.

sees a chance to double his pre-tax yield of 10 percent by selling a property in which he has a large unrealized gain and buying another, he is confronted by the fact that the 10 percent differential in yield will be reduced to 2 percent by the income tax, and will be reduced further by the payment of the 25 percent capital gains tax. Under these circumstances the incentive to transfer funds from less to more remunerative employments, and the incidental realization of capital gains in the process, is greatly impaired.

On the whole, the figures for 1942-46 appear to be a reasonable reflection of the criss-cross influences operating upon investors during this period. Average annual capital gains were substantially higher than in any other period of uniform tax treatment. Although individuals with net incomes of $100,000 or over realized materially larger average annual capital gains than in the preceding period, the percentage increase in amount of gain was only somewhat more than half that of the other income groups. Their capital gains represented 33.9 percent of their total net income in 1942-46; they had been 27.6 percent in 1938-41, 18.2 percent in 1934-37, 41.8 percent in 1922-33, and 4.2 percent in 1917-21.

Summary

Some of the broader conclusions suggested by the evidence reviewed in this chapter are:

1) The disposition of the top income groups to realize or to defer taking capital gains has been clearly and markedly sensitive to the tax treatment.

2) The degree of responsiveness of the middle and lower income groups is less clearly revealed by the figures because the tax rates applicable to their long term gains have generally been substantially lower and have moved, for the most part, within a narrower absolute range (Table 87). The rate on the first dollar of long term capital gains for a $5,000 a year married man with two children, for example, was 7 percent in 1918, .5 percent in 1929, 2.4 percent in 1937,[18] and 11 percent in 1943; whereas the rate for a man with an income of $100,000 was 64 percent in 1918, 12.5 percent in 1929, 35.4 percent in 1937,[18] and 25 percent in 1943. Even after allowing for these differences in level and range, however, the responsiveness of the lower and middle income groups seems to have been less than that of the top income groups. Perhaps the smaller average gain and

---

[18] If the asset had been held 2-5 years.

the smaller absolute amount of capital gains taxes involved contributed, among other factors, to this result.

3) The figures for taxpayers as a whole have shown a much less consistent response to the changing tax treatments than those for the uppermost income groups because, among other reasons, they have most commonly been dominated by the lower and middle income groups. Individuals with net incomes under $25,000 accounted for 37 percent of aggregate net capital gains in 1922-33, 58 percent in 1934-37, 52 percent in 1938-41, and 62 percent in 1942-46; and those with net incomes under $50,000 accounted for 49, 72, 62 and 73 percent, respectively (Table 3).

4) The major influence upon aggregate capital gains realized annually has been neither the tax treatment nor the general level of prosperity as measured by national income. It has been, rather, the extent of changes in the prices and turnover of capital assets, notably common stocks. Total capital gains have varied widely in periods of uniform tax treatment and have not always responded even in direction to the influence of more or less leniency in tax treatment. Nor have they varied consistently even in direction with fluctuations in national income (for example, 1933-34, 1936-37, 1938-39, 1941-42). The much higher level of national income in 1942-46 as compared with that of 1929 was accompanied by a less than proportional increase in capital gains. Changes in taxation, not only on capital gains but also on individual and corporate income and on gifts and estates, and changes in national income are doubtless elements in the complex of forces that determine the price movements and trading in capital assets. But less tangible factors, such as the speculative temper of the times, the domestic and international political atmosphere, and governmental policies sometimes play more immediately important roles.

Chapter 7

EFFECTS OF THE CHANGING TREATMENT OF CAPITAL LOSSES AND OF SHORT TERM TRANSACTIONS

The character of the allowance for capital losses is in many respects an integral part of the tax treatment of capital gains. Any allowance for capital losses means that the government stands ready to bear a portion of the possible loss of a contemplated transaction, assuming that the loser has other taxable income or capital gains from which all or a portion of the loss may be deducted. The statutory loss allowance, no less than the tax rate on gains, therefore enters into the odds for any investor who can expect sufficient ordinary income or capital gains from which the loss allowance can be deducted. And the character of the loss allowance, like the effective tax rate, may influence the timing of the formal realization of capital gains and losses arising from investments previously made.

1 ALLOWANCES FOR CAPITAL LOSSES HAVE MODERATED THE DETERRENT INFLUENCES OF CAPITAL GAINS TAXES ON INCENTIVES TO MAKE NEW AND LIQUIDATE OLD COMMITMENTS

The preferential tax treatment of capital gains has usually been accompanied by a roughly corresponding or greater limitation upon the allowance for capital losses. Great Britain and other countries that exclude most types of capital gain from taxable income disallow also any deduction from taxable income for capital losses of the same types. In the United States since 1916 capital losses have invariably been allowed in full up to the amount of the capital gains of similar character or holding period, at least.[1] Limitations on deductibility have been confined to net losses, i.e., the excess of losses over gains. In 1918-21, when capital gains were fully taxable as ordinary income, capital losses were allowed in full against income of any kind. When, in 1922-33, the maximum effective tax rate on long term (over 2 years) capital gains was limited to 12½ percent,

[1] Despite the full taxability of capital gains as ordinary income in 1913-17, capital losses were completely disallowed in 1913-15, and were allowed only up to the amount of capital gains in 1916-17.

long term capital losses remained deductible in full at first, but in 1924-33 Congress limited the allowance to a maximum of a tax credit of 12½ percent of the loss, paralleling the preferential tax limit on long term capital gains. Short term capital losses meanwhile, 1922-33, were allowed in full against ordinary income, just as short term gains were fully taxed.[2] When in 1934-49 varying proportions of long term capital gains were exempted from taxation, the same proportions of long term losses were disallowed as deductions; and when in 1938-49 maximum tax rates on capital gains substantially lower than those on ordinary income were reestablished, the tax credits for long term net losses were restricted to similar percentages of the losses. Beyond such parallel treatment, however, the deductibility of *net* capital losses from taxable income has been arbitrarily limited at various times since 1934 to $2,000 or $1,000, or, in the case of *short term* net losses, has at times been eliminated altogether.

Reasons for parallel treatment of gains and losses

One reason for treating capital gains and losses in an at least roughly parallel manner is that the two possess some of the same peculiarities. Both commonly are from assets held longer than 1 year (or may be so defined for purposes of income taxation). If treated as arising solely in the year of realization and subjected to the regular progressive tax rate schedule, a long term capital gain is taxed more heavily, and a long term capital loss yields a smaller tax reduction, other things being equal, than if the gain and loss were divided among the years during which the asset was held. As far as this consideration justifies special tax treatment of capital gains, it justifies a corresponding special treatment of capital losses. Similarly, those who do not regard capital gains as adding commensurately, if at all, to the recipient's 'true' income or to his current taxpaying ability must, for the same reasons, regard capital losses as something less than full subtractions from 'true' income or current taxpaying ability.

Another view that has exerted considerable practical influence upon legislators regards those who report capital gains and losses as constituting a single group whose members both enjoy the gains and suffer the losses. In this view, the members of the group cannot justly ask that their gains be granted preferential tax treatment but

---

[2] In 1922-23 short term capital losses were not allowed against long term capital gains, though they were deductible in full against other income; and in 1932-33 short term losses on stocks and bonds were allowed only against short term gains from stocks and bonds.

their losses nevertheless be allowed without restriction. Equity demands equal treatment of gains and losses.

In practice the policy of balancing a preferential tax treatment of capital gains with a corresponding limitation upon the deductibility of capital losses has highly unequal effects upon individual investors. Those who lose their capital early are hurt immediately by limited loss allowance but may never benefit from the liberal treatment of gains. And all other investors whose losses exceed their gains can be expected to derive small consolation from the knowledge that the disallowance of part of their losses has been matched by the equal exemption from taxation of the net gains of their more fortunate fellow investors.

Nevertheless, before the investment is made, when the investor is calculating the odds, a parallel tax treatment of capital gains and losses tends to minimize the law's distortion of the odds and to be 'fair' or 'equal', in this sense, to each investor. If only half of any net capital gain or loss is recognized for tax purposes, for example, the risk of a disallowed loss is balanced against an equal chance for a tax-exempt gain.

2 EVEN LIMITED LOSS ALLOWANCE IS OF GREAT VALUE IN REDUCING DETERRENTS TO NEW COMMITMENTS AND TO REALIZATION

Under substantial tax rates the deductibility of capital losses is important in reducing risks even when it is limited to the amount of capital gains reported by the investor in the same year, i.e., even when *net* capital losses are completely disallowed.[3] To an investor who has already realized or can count upon subsequently realizing equal or bigger capital gains during the taxable year, a provision limiting the deductibility of a possible loss to the amount of gains would be of little practical importance. The loss, if realized, would be fully offset against gains otherwise taxable, and so qualify for complete deductibility. Professional short term traders and specula-

---

[3] In 1934-37, when the statutory or recognized gains and losses were varying fractions of the actual ones, a $2,000 limit on the excess of recognized losses over recognized gains was in force. In 1938-41 net short term losses were completely disallowed against ordinary income but could be carried forward to apply against short term gains of the succeeding year; there was no limit on the allowance for net long term losses. In 1942-50 the excess of recognized losses over recognized gains was deductible from ordinary income up to $1,000 or net income, whichever was smaller, and the balance could be carried forward and deducted unlimitedly against capital gains and up to $1,000 or net income, whichever was smaller, during each of the next 5 years.

tors are commonly in this position with respect to short term commitments, and many other investors are frequently in a similar position with respect to longer term investments, for they can choose when to sell various marketable assets in which they have unrealized profits. If a disallowed net capital loss is otherwise likely, an investor may choose to sell another asset on which he will realize an offsetting gain, thereby, in effect, being permitted to take this gain tax free. He may repurchase the asset the same day yet be considered to have realized his gain. Hence he can receive full allowance for his capital loss without jeopardizing his position in the other investment. The saving of taxes that would otherwise be payable at some time if he took the gain at all during his lifetime would be equivalent to a reduction of the loss on the losing transaction.

Besides encouraging new commitments by reducing risks, an allowance for capital losses encourages *realization* of gains and losses from old commitments. Whenever an investor with unrealized capital gains on other holdings incurs a capital loss he can realize his gains tax free to the extent of the loss allowance. He has, therefore, a motive for converting unrealized into realized gains. And whenever an investor with unrealized capital losses realizes a capital gain he has a motive to realize the former to the extent of his gain in order to avoid future taxes on the latter.

3 LARGE INVESTORS CAN TAKE BETTER ADVANTAGE OF LOSS ALLOW-
ANCES THAN SMALL BUT THE USUAL LIMITATIONS ARE HARDER
ON THE LATTER

The large investor is likely to benefit more than the small from the allowance for losses, whether or not the allowance is limited to the amount of capital gains. If the law permits deduction of capital losses from ordinary income, he is likely to have the advantage of a bigger ordinary income against which to offset losses. With unrestricted loss allowance, moreover, he may find it more feasible to reduce his current income taxes to the utmost by formally realizing his capital losses whenever they arise and postponing the realization of gains until his death, when his properties are inherited and become saleable without capital gains taxation.

Severe limitations on the allowance for net capital losses, nevertheless, are likely to be harder on small investors. When no deduction from other income is allowed for net capital losses, for example, the professional speculator and the investor who makes many commitments are favored over the small investor, other things being equal, because the laws of chance give them more probability of having some gains against which to offset losses. The small investor is more likely than the big to have his capital wiped out early by a succession of initial losses. The presumably wider variety of investments and the larger resources of the big investor give him more flexibility to choose, with an eye to the maximum tax advantage, the time to realize gains and losses. He is more likely to have other holdings that have appreciated in market value, and to be in a better position, therefore, to realize sufficient gains to give his losses full deductibility. In short, limitations on loss allowance paralleling the preferential treatment of capital gains are likely to be especially hard on the small investor.

4 CHIEF AIMS OF SEVERE LIMITATIONS ON LOSS ALLOWANCES IN RECENT YEARS: TO PREVENT EXCESSIVE TAX AVOIDANCE AND TO MAINTAIN REVENUES

Since 1922 Congress has consistently limited the allowance for capital losses more than it has granted preferences to capital gains. The chief motives have been to maintain revenues and to prevent excessive tax avoidance by individuals with big incomes through sales and exchanges deliberately undertaken to reduce taxes. Wide publicity was given in 1930-34 to cases in which wealthy individuals had established large net capital losses by selling securities to their wives, children, or close friends, from whom they repurchased the identical securities after 60 days.[4] Several eminent New York bankers testified before a Senate committee in 1933 that they had been able greatly to reduce or to wipe out their liabilities for income tax in this manner in 1929-30. Sales to controlled family corporations and family trusts also permitted legal recognition of loss even though an underlying continuity of ownership and control persisted. Coming at the same time as public revelations that many well-known financiers had avoided full payment of taxes on their capital gains during the booming 'twenties by using family corporations, trusts, and foreign corporations as vehicles for the receipt of their gains, this testimony aroused widespread resentment against the statutory weaknesses that permitted such tax avoidance.

Opportunities to establish losses by wash sales to relatives, friends, and family corporations were subsequently narrowed by new statutory restrictions. But Congress concluded that even in the absence

[4] Cf. Public Report 1455 (1934), 73d Cong., 2d Sess., Vol. 3, Ch. V, especially citations of testimony in Hearings on Stock Exchange Practices before the Committee on Banking and Currency.

of artificial arrangements large amounts of net capital losses were being realized deliberately to reduce income taxes, without correspondingly reducing the taxpayer's capacity to pay them. Opportunities for taking large capital losses without significantly altering the amount or character of the investor's holdings were abundant and nearly continuous during the long decline in the prices of securities and other capital assets in the 1930's. Suppose, for example, a man had invested $100,000 in a diversified list of stocks and bonds from which he received $4,000 a year in dividends and interest. If, as part of a general decline in the market, the market value of his portfolio shrank one-half, he could sell out, thereby establishing for tax purposes a capital loss of $50,000, and immediately use the proceeds to purchase a similar, though not identical, list of securities, also yielding an income of $4,000 a year. His investment position would be essentially the same, yet he would be able to claim a deduction from taxable income because of his $50,000 capital loss. If he waited 60 days after selling (now 30 days), he would have established his capital loss even if he bought back the identical securities.

The opposite situation, as we noted, has often been cited in support of proposals to exclude capital gains from taxable income. The capital gains of an investor who purchases for $80,000 a portfolio of securities yielding an annual income of $4,000 and, after a rise in the market, sells the portfolio for $100,000 and with these funds buys another but similar list of securities also yielding $4,000 a year, is not, the contention is, a true addition to income. The investor's dividend and interest income remains $4,000 a year, and his holdings of securities, though altered in detail, leave him in an essentially unchanged investment position.

The correspondence in principle between the character of the loss and of the gain in the examples just cited is clear, but Congress preferred to limit the allowance for losses and reduce the taxation of gains instead of excluding both gains and losses from the calculation of taxable income. On the one hand, it did not wish completely to exempt from taxes the large amounts of real as contrasted to nominal capital gains; that is, gains representing a true increase in the wealth or purchasing power of the investor rather than a mere reflection of a general rise in prices. When realized by sale, the increase in the value of a farm from $10,000 to $1 million after oil is discovered on it, and the increase in a stock's value from $40 to $75 a share because of the added earning power resulting from reinvested earnings or expected from new products or contracts, exemplify such real gains. On the other hand, Congress did not wish the government's revenues to be highly vulnerable to investors' shrewd exploitation of short run price declines and even to longer run declines. Although the initiative is in their hands, many investors find it convenient or necessary from time to time to realize gains that are nominal in some degree, thereby subjecting themselves to taxes on them. But whereas the taxation of gains discourages unnecessary realization of nominal gains, a full or liberal allowance for capital losses encourages the taking of what we have termed nominal losses. In other words, investors are given a tax incentive to minimize their realization of nominal gains but to maximize their realization of nominal losses.

In general, morever, the investor's discretionary control over the timing of the realization of gains and losses, together with the desire to maintain revenues, has probably been the most important factor in influencing Congress to limit the recognition of net losses. It has often permitted the investor to offset ordinary income and real capital gains with nominal losses due to temporary but general price movements in the security markets, and in other ways to whipsaw the government's efforts to tax him. Tax lawyers, accountants, and financial institutions encourage and aid the investor in such endeavors. Toward the close of each calendar year most persons known to possess sizeable security holdings are likely to receive reminders from brokers, banks, attorneys, or accountants that a worth while saving in taxes can be accomplished without risk or essential change in investment position by appropriate shifts of securities with a view to the realization of losses. It is less commonly pointed out that this advantage will be only temporary if the taxpayer subsequently sells the substitute investment. The cost or 'basis' of the latter will be less than that of the original asset by approximately the amount of loss previously reported. Hence the capital gain realized on the new asset will be larger, or the capital loss, smaller, by the same amount.

Even when the allowance for *net* losses is restricted, the investor's discretionary control over timing gives him a decided advantage. To a considerable degree, he can choose to avoid realizing his possible gains when these would be heavily taxed and to establish his losses in years when he would derive the largest tax advantage from them. That is, the investor can often choose to realize losses in years when his capital gains and other income are unusually large or when the treatment of losses, in his opinion, is unusually and only temporarily favorable, and to realize gains in years when his capital losses are large or his other income small or when the tax treatment of gains is regarded as unusually favorable. The taxpayer does not have any choice, however, with respect to losses from assets that become worthless. Unless they are reported for the year in which the worthlessness first becomes a fact they are not recognized.

While these reasons for limiting allowances for capital losses go far to explain Congressional policy in this regard, they do not necessarily justify it. The policy has doubtless had severely inequitable effects upon many investors whose timing of purchases and sales was not influenced by tax considerations. Further, by weighting the tax-odds against the risk-taker, its general effect is to discourage risky investment. The desire to maintain government revenues is not a sufficient justification for doing so at the expense of losers as against other taxpayers.

Capital losses, short and long term, were allowed in full in 1917-21. The sole limitation on the deductibility of capital losses in 1922-31 was on long term net losses, the maximum allowance for which was limited beginning in 1924 to 12½ percent.[5] This limitation corresponded with the ceiling tax rate of 12½ percent on long term net gains, and was effective only for individuals with substantial incomes. In 1932 and 1933, following large deductions for short term losses suffered in the stock market, Congress eliminated all allowance for net losses from stocks and bonds held 2 years or less, although short term gains from them remained fully taxable as ordinary income. In 1934-37 the law recognized the same proportions of capital losses as of gains, varying with the length of time the asset had been held, but imposed a limit of $2,000 on the amount of statutory net losses that could be deducted from other income. In 1938-41 this limit was removed, but all net losses on assets held 18 months or less were completely disallowed except that they could be carried forward and deducted up to the amount of the short term net gains in the succeeding year. Beginning in 1942 a flat limit on the deductibility of net capital losses in any one year was reimposed, this time at $1,000, but the balance of net losses could be carried forward for the following 5 years and used in each up to the amount of net capital gains plus $1,000.[6]

[5] Except that in 1922-23 net losses on assets held 2 years or less, while allowed in full against other income, were not allowed against long term capital gains.

[6] If the net income was less than $1,000 in the year the net loss was incurred or in any of the succeeding 5 years in which a balance of net loss was carried forward, the deductibility against ordinary income was limited to the amount of net income.

5 STATISTICS REVEAL NO CLOSE RELATION BETWEEN THE CHANGING
TAX TREATMENT OF CAPITAL LOSSES AND THE TOTALS REALIZED

Between 1917 and 1946, therefore, there were 5 periods of major
differences in the tax treatment of capital losses. The figures for the
5 periods when the various provisions were in effect cannot safely
be compared in detail because of variations in tabulating methods
and in statutory definitions. For taxpayers with net incomes the
annual average of total net capital losses varied moderately, amounting to $661 million in 1917-21, $837 million in 1922-33, $731
million in 1934-37, $911 million in 1938-41, and $705 million in
1942-46 (Table 1). The annual totals of net capital losses varied far
more within each period of uniform tax treatment except one than
did the averages for the different periods. The range in 1917-21 was
from $70 to $1,102 million; in 1922-33, from $213 to $1,815 million; in 1934-37, from $693 to $772 million; in 1938-41, from
$642 to $1,424 million; and in 1942-46, from $519 to $1,052 million. These figures indicate that the tax treatment of net capital losses
was not the major influence governing their amounts.

On the other hand, when the net capital losses of individuals
reporting statutory net deficits are added to the losses of those
reporting net incomes, the data, though too meagre for confident
inference, suggest that extreme limitations on the allowance for net
losses, such as were in force in 1934-37 and since 1942, may operate
to reduce loss realization. Figures on deficit returns are not available
before 1928. For the years since, the average annual net capital
losses of income and deficit returns combined were larger in the two
periods in which there was no absolute limit on the allowance,
1928-33 and 1938-41, than in the 2 periods in which the allowance
was rigidly limited, 1934-37 and 1942-46 (Table 1). Obscuring the
significance of this difference are the severe stock market declines in
the 2 periods when there was no ceiling on the allowance for losses.

Substantial net capital losses were nevertheless reported in
1934-37 and 1942-46, when their deductibility from other income
was stringently limited, and relatively small amounts were reported
in 1917-18 and 1922-23, when they were allowed in full. These facts
reflect the coercive force of nontax influences upon the timing of the
realization of capital losses. As already noted, investors on the
whole are likely to have less choice in timing the realization of their
capital losses than of their gains (Ch. 5, Sec. 4). Crises and depressions, such as occurred in 1920-21, 1929-33, and 1937-38, force the
technical realization of capital losses upon numerous taxpayers

through threatened and actual bankruptcies, margin calls, and other imperious demands for liquidation; periods of prosperity and boom do not equally coerce taxpayers to convert unrealized into realized gains.

In one major respect, all our revenue acts since 1916 have been similar: capital losses have been fully deductible up to the amount of a taxpayer's capital gains, at least.[7] In consequence, even when the taxpayer could use his discretion about timing a loss, he has had a strong motive to realize it as soon as he had offsetting gains or other income from which it could be deducted. Postponing realization could promise a larger tax advantage only if he was unable to report sufficient offsetting gains or other income or if he expected the statutory allowance for losses to be liberalized or believed the same loss allowance would save him more in taxes in a future year because effective tax rates on his gains and other income might be higher. Of such incentives to postponement, only two were likely to be strong enough to outweigh an immediate saving in taxes: the desire to avoid sacrificing a part of the tax-reducing value of a loss by 'taking' the latter in a year when offsetting gains, together with the allowable deduction from ordinary income, were less than the loss, and the desire to hold an available offset against an as yet unrealized large capital gain.

6 THE LAW TREATED LOSERS LESS LIBERALLY THAN GAINERS IN 1934-46, BUT THE NET RESULTS WERE FAVORABLE FOR UPPER INCOME GROUPS AND UNFAVORABLE FOR LOWER

As previously indicated, even a parallel special treatment of capital gains and losses may produce highly unequal results for different individuals. Taxpayers who realize net capital gains are sure to be taxed on them but those who incur net losses may not receive any allowance for them. Even the same individual may be taxed on his gains but not receive any allowance for his losses. Under the treatment in effect in 1924-31, for example, an investor with no other income who realized a net capital gain of $10,000 in all even-numbered years and a net capital loss of equal amount in all odd-numbered years, paid taxes on the gains of his good years and did not receive a tax reduction for the losses of his bad years. An unlimited power to carry forward the disallowed losses of one year to future years would greatly diminish, though not entirely remove,

[7] Except that short term net losses were at times not deductible from long term gains.

this source of inequality, but an unlimited carry-forward has never been in force.[8] When the law permits only a small fixed amount of capital losses to be deducted from other income, as in 1934-37 and since 1942, an otherwise parallel treatment of capital gains and losses is likely to have even more unequal effects for different individuals and for different classes of investors.

The tax treatment of capital gains and losses during 1934-37 resulted in excluding from tax somewhat more than a third of the net capital gains realized by individuals with net incomes but in disallowing more than three-fourths of their net losses. The excluded net gains amounted to $1.1 billion, the disallowed net losses to almost twice as much (Table 24). While the law required that identical percentages of gain and loss, varying with the number of years the asset had been held, be excluded in calculating the statutory amounts, the $2,000 limitation upon the deductibility of net capital losses imposed a special disadvantage upon those incurring such losses. (This disadvantage applied to *net* losses alone, not to capital losses that were offset by capital gains.)

For the top income groups, the advantage of having portions of their capital gains exempted from income tax strikingly outweighed the disadvantage of having the same portions of their losses disallowed, whereas the reverse was true for the other income groups. Taxpayers with net incomes of $100,000 or more had aggregate net gains about 5.9 times their aggregate net losses, whereas those with smaller incomes had larger aggregate net losses than gains. The exempted net gains of the former were about 3 times their disallowed net losses in 1934-37, whereas the disallowed net losses of the latter were about 2.6 times their exempted net gains (Table 24).

If the more complete figures available for 1936 are representative of the other years, the advantage of the upper income groups was not merely a reflection of the inclusion in this group of individuals with large capital gains. Taxpayers whose net incomes in 1936 from sources other than capital transactions amounted to $100,000 or over, like those with statutory net incomes of that size, had more of their capital gains than losses excluded from the tax base, whereas the opposite was the case for other taxpayers (Table 68).

[8] If the individual never again realized sufficient capital gains or other income from which the accumulated net loss could be deducted, the carry-forward would not benefit him. If the carry-forward were supplemented by a carry-back against the capital gains and other income of preceding years the more equal treatment of complete averaging of income would be approximated.

The $2,000 limit accounted for about a third of aggregate disal-
lowed net losses, and the statutory percentages, for two-thirds, in
1934-37

The statutory percentages accounted for the major part of the total disallowed loss reported on all returns with statutory net incomes in 1934-37: 64 percent in 1934, 70 percent in 1935, 77 percent in 1936, and 50 percent in 1937. In each year a moderate and irregular tendency existed for the $2,000 limit on the deductibility of net losses to be responsible for an increasing proportion of the total disallowed loss as we go up the income scale. In 1934, for example, the application of the percentages accounted for two-thirds of the disallowed loss of taxpayers with net incomes under $5,000, about one-half for taxpayers with net incomes of $100,000 or over except that the proportion for the group $300,000-500,000 was 66.7 percent (Table 25). In 1937 the $2,000 limit accounted for about 41 percent of the disallowed loss of returns with net incomes under $5,000, but was somewhat more important than the percentages in determining disallowed loss for the income groups above $25,000.

In a few instances at high income levels, the application of the percentages operated to *increase* the deductible net loss above the loss actually realized. This could occur with certain combinations of net gain on long term and net loss on short term transactions. For example, a taxpayer who realized a net gain of $1,000 from an asset held more than 10 years and a net loss of $1,500 from an asset held 1 year or less had a statutory net loss of $1,200 by the application of the statutory percentages, as compared with a realized net loss of $500. In 1937 the percentages operated in this way on net balance for all income groups between $100,000 and $500,000 (Table 25).

The $2,000 limit on the deductibility of net capital losses hurt lower
and middle income groups chiefly

While prevention of revenue loss and of inequity through tax avoidance by individuals with big incomes was a main reason for the adoption of the $2,000 limit on the allowance for net capital losses, the income tax data do not supply a good measure of the degree to which this objective was achieved. Of the $752 million of net capital losses disallowed in 1934-37 by reason of the $2,000 limit, 35 percent was disallowed taxpayers with net incomes under $5,000, and 76 percent was disallowed taxpayers with net incomes under $25,000 (Table 25). In contrast, only 6 percent of the total was accounted for by taxpayers with net incomes of $100,000 or over.

It would appear, therefore, that the middle and lower income groups were the main victims of the limitation. In the absence of any limit on deductibility, however, members of the top income groups might conceivably have chosen to realize additional losses by selling securities and other capital assets that had fallen in value below their book costs. Despite the statistical results, therefore, the limitation may have realized the objective of reducing opportunities for tax avoidance by those with large incomes. But a much more generous loss allowance, say $25,000, would have been of value primarily to taxpayers with lower incomes.

Even unrestricted deductibility, though it would have offered some major opportunities for tax saving for various individuals with large incomes from ordinary sources, would doubtless have been of most benefit in the aggregate to the middle and lower income groups. Under all the special statutory treatments of net capital losses, the medium and lower income groups have accounted for much the largest part of the aggregate losses reported by individuals with net incomes. Individuals with net incomes under $25,000 accounted for 55 percent of total net capital losses in 1926-33, 82.3 percent in 1934-37, 80.1 percent in 1938-41, and 88.2 percent in 1942-46. On the other hand, those with net incomes in excess of $100,000 accounted for only 18.2 percent in 1926-33, 3.2 percent in 1934-37, 4 percent in 1938-41, and 2.5 percent in 1942-46 (Table 3).

Because of their divergent investment experience, the top income groups continued to enjoy a net advantage, and the others, a net disadvantage, from the tax treatment of capital gains and losses in 1938-41

The allowance for long term net losses was greatly liberalized in 1938 by the removal of the $2,000 limit on their deductibility. On the other hand, net losses on assets held 18 months or less were disallowed completely except that they could be carried over to apply against short term gains of the succeeding year. At the same time, as already noted, a tax credit of 15 percent of net losses on assets held more than 24 months, and of 20 percent on those held 18-24 months, corresponding to the new ceiling rates on net capital gains, had to be substituted for the new allowance of 66⅔ percent of losses from assets held 18-24 months, and 50 percent of those from longer held assets, whenever this would increase the tax.

Because of the changes in the statute and consequent changes in tabulations, the figures for 1938-41 are not closely comparable with those for 1934-37 (Tables 22-4). Among other things, they understate the total realized and the disallowed net losses because they do not include net losses from assets held 18 months or less.

Largely reflecting the elimination of the $2,000 ceiling on the deductibility of net losses, the proportion of long term net losses disallowed was approximately the same as that of long term net gains excluded from the tax, about 50 percent for all taxpayers with net incomes. But the aggregate dollar amount of long term net losses disallowed was about 1.5 times the total net gains exempted, because total long term losses exceeded total long term gains by this proportion for all taxpayers with net incomes (Tables 8 and 20).

As in 1934-37, individuals with incomes of $100,000 or over and those with smaller incomes had quite different experiences, in the aggregate. The net gains of the former greatly exceeded their net losses,[9] $921 million vs. $143 million, whereas the net losses of the latter exceeded their net gains, $3,501 million vs. $2,223 million. In consequence, the partial disallowance of net capital losses and the corresponding exemption of equal percentages of net capital gains had the effect of accentuating the good fortune of the former and the misfortune of the latter, as groups. The disallowed long term net losses of taxpayers with net incomes under $100,000 were more than twice their exempted net gains, while the exempted net gains of those with net incomes of $100,000 or more were over 6 times their disallowed long term net losses (Table 24). These figures slightly understate the effective loss disallowance of the upper income groups in 1938-41 because they do not take account of the provision that the tax reduction resulting from a net capital loss could not exceed 15 percent of the loss from assets held longer than 24 months or 20 percent of that from assets held 18-24 months.

Heavy loss realization in 1938-41 does not seem to have been due primarily to removal of $2,000 limit

Net capital losses reported by individuals with net incomes in the 4 years after the removal of the $2,000 limit on loss allowance were substantially heavier than in the preceding 4 years. Their long and short term losses together amounted to $2,925 million in 1934-37, their long term losses alone to $3,494 million in 1938-41, exclusive of $149 million of losses on depreciable property used in the taxpayer's business as well as of short term losses which were completely disallowed.

The year 1941 was noteworthy because the total net capital losses

[9] Exclusive of short term net losses, which were completely disallowed in 1938-41 and therefore not tabulated in *Statistics of Income*.

reported, even though they excluded short term net losses, exceeded those of all years except 1929-33.

The behavior of the stock market, in conjunction with the growing expectation that the United States would enter the war, seems to be the primary explanation for the heavy loss realization of 1938-41. Between the end of 1934 and the end of 1936 stock prices rose markedly, Standard and Poor's index of 90 stocks (monthly average of daily prices) moving from 73.5 in December 1934 to 135.5 in December 1936. A sharp decline followed, the index sinking to 87.5 in December 1937. After small and short-lived recovery movements in 1938 and 1939, the down trend was resumed in 1940. A sharp increase in trading on the New York Stock Exchange accompanied an acceleration of the decline in the months immediately preceding and in the weeks following the Japanese attack on Pearl Harbor on December 7, 1941. The December 1941 index of 69.5 was lower than any monthly average since April 1935.

The removal of the $2,000 limit on loss allowance could be expected to stimulate loss realization but there is no decisive evidence that it was the major influence. The big increase in net losses occurred in 1941, the fourth year following the repeal of the limitation, rather than in 1938, 1939, or 1940 (Chart 7 and Table 1). Approximately 40 percent of the total net losses reported by those with net incomes and 36 percent of the total net losses reported for the 4 years were realized in 1941, while the losses reported for 1938, 1939, and 1940, even after allowing for the exclusion of short term losses, were either smaller or only moderately higher than those of the 3 years immediately preceding.

Nevertheless, a qualification of the foregoing observation is in order. As far as the timing of the realization of losses is in the discretion of the taxpayer, he can be expected not to take them in years when his ordinary income and capital gains are small, such as 1938-40. The removal of the $2,000 limit on loss allowance could be expected to become a stronger stimulus to loss realization after taxpayers' incomes from other sources had recovered, as happened in 1941.

A minor additional stimulus in 1938-41 was a further revision in the treatment of loss by which net losses realized on the sale, exchange, or involuntary conversion of buildings and other depreciable assets used in the taxpayer's trade or business were made fully deductible, whereas in 1934-37 they had been treated like any other capital losses. The rearmament program in 1940 and 1941 stimulated many transfers of such properties in which losses that had long before taken place in the market values of the properties were 'realized'. Of the $3,643 million of net losses realized by individuals with net incomes in 1938-41, $149 million was of this character.

The long term net losses of taxpayers with net incomes of $100,000 or over were about 50 percent larger in 1938-41 than their short and long term net losses together in 1934-37, while the percentage increase in the losses of other taxpayers was less than half as large. The omission from the 1938-41 figures of losses from assets held 18 months or less, which might have increased more for other taxpayers than for those with net incomes of $100,000 or over, impairs, but does not wholly invalidate, the basis for the inference that the removal of the $2,000 limit caused a relatively bigger increase in loss realization by upper than by lower income groups. In any event, the net losses of individuals with incomes of $100,000 and over constituted less than 4 percent of the total net losses of all individuals reporting net incomes in 1938-41.

5 year carryover of net capital losses since 1942 mitigates effect of $1,000 limit on annual deductibility from other income

The maximum allowance of $1,000 in any year for net capital losses, in force since 1942, is the smallest since 1917. But the fact that net capital losses not deducted in one year can be carried forward for the succeeding 5 years and used in full in any of them to offset net capital gains and up to $1,000 of other income removes much of the seeming harshness of the limitation. Indeed, in some respects the new treatment is more generous than any preceding one. Many who suffered large net capital losses in 1929-31 and 1938-41 enjoyed relatively little tax relief from the absence of a ceiling on the deductibility of net capital losses from ordinary income, for their net capital losses greatly exceeded their ordinary income and their unallowed losses could not be carried forward to future years. Under the new treatment taxpayers who sustain heavy capital losses relatively to their ordinary income can expect to obtain a fuller allowance for them because they can carry forward their disallowed losses for 5 years. Taxpayers who die soon after incurring large losses or lose substantially all their capital may suffer heavily from the small immediate allowance for losses yet derive no advantage from the carryforward provision. But for active speculators and investors the long period for which net losses can be carried forward improves their odds by making it more probable that the net capital losses sustained in any year will eventually be fully offset against the capital gains and ordinary income of other years.

Another respect in which the new treatment is more generous is that short term gains and losses may be used without restriction to offset statutory long term gains and losses, and vice versa, instead of being partly or wholly segregated. Half of realized gains and losses from capital assets held longer than 6 months and the full amounts of shorter term gains and losses are taken into account. The algebraic sum of the statutory amounts constitutes the statutory net capital gain or loss. After up to $1,000 of a statutory net capital loss has been deducted from ordinary income, the balance is carried forward as a short term net loss to the succeeding 5 years. Because $1 of short term capital losses offsets $2 of long term gains, a taxpayer may report a statutory net capital loss even when his transactions actually result in an excess of capital gains.

The new treatment went into force too recently for reliable comprehensive measures of its effects to be reflected in the income tax figures yet available. In 1943-46, $962 million of prior years' net capital loss was carried over on individual income tax returns. The entire amount did not result in current tax reductions mainly because some of it was reported on returns without enough offsetting capital gains. If the present provisions are continued, the aggregate loss carryover is likely in a few years to become very substantial. While it will doubtless operate to reduce tax revenues from capital gains in boom years, it will do so precisely because it will allow taxpayers to offset their gains in such years by losses incurred in the preceding 5 years.

7 EFFECTS OF THE TAX TREATMENT OF SHORT TERM GAINS

During the Congressional committee hearings on the Revenue Revision of 1942 opponents of heavy taxation of capital gains concentrated their attack chiefly upon the tax treatment of short term gains. This was understandable, for gains from assets held 18 months or less were then taxed in full as ordinary income, whereas half the gain from assets held more than 2 years was exempt or, at the option of the taxpayer, the whole was taxed a flat 15 percent, however large his other income.[10]

It was argued that only the lower income groups could afford to 'take' short term gains under the prevailing treatment, and that

---

[10] Of gains from assets held 18-24 months, a third was excluded from tax or, at the option of the taxpayer, the whole was taxed a flat 20 percent.

short term trading and tax revenues would increase tremendously if Congress would abolish the distinction between short and long term gains, disallow net capital losses completely, and segregate all capital gains from other income and tax them at a low flat rate such as 10 percent.[11] In support of these contentions reference was made to the extremely small volume to which stock market trading had fallen and to the small or negative revenues obtained by the Treasury from the tax treatment of capital gains and losses in recent years: a net revenue loss from this source was estimated to have been experienced in 1940 and 1941 (Table 90). What is the evidence?

The income tax statistics clearly reveal that the progressive increases in tax rates in the 1930's and early '40's were accompanied, in a general way, by a pronounced decline in the relative importance of short term gains at all the main income levels (Table 13). For example, short term gains (capital gains from assets held 2 years or less) averaged 51 percent of the total capital gains of individuals with net incomes of $50,000-100,000 in 1926-29, 41 percent in 1930-33, and slightly under 40 percent in 1934-37. In 1938-41 and in 1942-46, the average proportion fell to 15 and 4 percent, respectively, reflecting, in part, the reduction of the short term period first to 18 months, then to 6 months.

The bare statement of the effective tax rates on short term gains after 1931, particularly for individuals with large incomes, creates a strong presumption that they exercised a restraining influence upon short term trading (Table 87). By 1941 the rates were such that a married man with 2 children paid 48 percent of the next dollar of short term gains if his net income was otherwise $25,000, 59 percent if $50,000, 68 percent if $100,000, and 78 percent if $1 million.

In the face of such rates — they were advanced further in 1942-44 — one might wonder that any material amount of short term gains continued to be realized at all by individuals with sizeable incomes. Yet the Treasury Department, in opposing the contention that high tax rates were responsible for the relatively small importance of short term gains taken by upper income groups, showed that individuals with net incomes over $25,000 accounted for more than twice as large a fraction of the total short term gains as of total net income in each of the 3 years 1938-40.[12]

Outstanding importance of stock market activity
While the rising tax rates doubtless contributed to the declining

[11] *Revenue Revision of 1942,* Hearings, Ways and Means Committee, pp. 910, 922, 928, 983, 1656.
[12] *Ibid.,* p. 1638.

importance of short term capital gains in 1934-46, other forces, notably the movements of the stock market, exerted a strong and perhaps the dominant influence. A large fraction of the total decline took place between 1936 and 1937 when the stock market fell violently but tax rates remained constant (Table 8). In fact, tax rates were not raised for incomes under $50,000 until 1940, and the only advance between 1934 and 1940 for incomes above $50,000 occurred in 1936 when short term gains not only maintained their relative importance but their absolute amount rose to the highest level since 1929. We have already called attention (Ch. 5, Sec. 7, Chart 18, Table 8) to the close relation between fluctuations in stock prices and in short term net capital gains and losses.

The continued contraction in 1938-46 in the relative importance of short term gains at nearly all income levels would appear to be attributable largely to the declining trend of stock prices and the small volume of trading during much of the period and to the reduction of the holding period by changes in the statute, first to 18 months, then to 6 months. From early 1937 until 1943 no recovery that lasted as long as a year or that approached the high prices of 1936 occurred in the average of industrial stock prices. With stock market advances relatively limited in duration and extent, the opportunities for short term capital gains were fewer.[13]

On the other hand, the Treasury's testimony that individuals with net incomes above $25,000 accounted for more than twice as large a fraction of total short term gains as of total net income in 1938-40 does not prove that the high tax rates were not discouraging upper income individuals from short term transactions. The figures cited may be explained in considerable measure by the operations of professional short term traders and speculators, including both those legally designated as dealers and others not so classified. Their transactions account for a considerable proportion of total short term trading in securities. Data made available in recent years by the Securities and Exchange Commission indicate that stock exchange members alone, among such professionals, are commonly responsible for about a fourth of all the shares traded on the New York Stock and Curb Exchanges. Most transactions that stock exchange members conduct for their own account are generally believed to be short term. In addition to members of exchanges, many persons

[13] Short selling during periods of decline can in theory yield gains as large as from buying during periods of advance, but in practice, short selling is undertaken to a much smaller extent, even among professionals and semi-professionals.

devote all or a part of their time to short term speculation and may be properly classified as part- or full-time professionals.

Professional speculators are less likely than casual traders and investors to be deterred from short term commitments by high but nondiscriminatory taxes on their gains. They are practicing a profession or exercising a personal skill, primarily, rather than investing their capital. For this reason their gains are commonly taxed as ordinary income even by countries, such as Great Britain, that exempt similar profits when realized by ordinary investors. Their skill in discounting and otherwise exploiting short term movements in prices constitutes their intellectual capital, so to speak, and can yield them a return only if used. If they diverted their energies to other fields — in which, presumably, they would be less qualified — they would face equally high tax rates. Despite the higher tax costs of short term than of longer term trading, their funds are more profitably employed in numerous very short transactions, such as those characteristic of some floor traders on the New York Stock Exchange who close out each day's commitments before the end of the day's trading.

The deductibility of short term losses from short term gains, even in the absence of more generous allowances for losses, greatly lessens the deterrent influence of high tax rates upon the disposition of professionals to take the risks involved in their operations. Their superior knowledge of the market and the large number of their transactions make it reasonable for them to expect a net balance of gains over losses on their trading as a whole. The high tax rate on the possible gain from any single contemplated transaction is offset in considerable degree by the equally high tax-reducing power of the possible loss, for a loss will be fully deductible from the taxable gains of previous and future transactions within the taxable year. For the professional a 50 percent tax rate, for example, means that the government will not only take half of the possible gain from a contemplated transaction but also stands ready to absorb half the possible loss.[14]

Some short and medium term transactions are adversely affected The foregoing offsets to the restraining influence of high tax rates upon short term capital transactions apply with much less force to occasional traders and speculators. Those who enter into short term

[14] The practical effects of the tax treatment of capital losses is discussed further in the next chapter.

transactions only infrequently are likely to be more sensitive to high tax rates than professionals for two reasons:

First, they usually lack a backlog of short term gains realized during the taxable year from which a short term loss on a contemplated transaction would be deductible; nor, as previously pointed out, can they be as confident as professionals that they will realize capital gains in future years against which they can offset an excess of losses carried forward from the current year. Short term capital losses have not been deductible from ordinary income to more than an extremely small extent since 1931 (see note 3). Unlike the professional, therefore, they are not likely to be in the position in which the government, by reducing the income taxes otherwise payable on their gains, stands ready to absorb substantially the same fraction of the possible loss on a contemplated transaction as of the possible gain. In consequence, high tax rates may well dissuade the occasional short term trader or speculator from a particular transaction because the prospective gain after taxes docs not appear to compensate fully for the risk of capital loss.

Second, such investors, because their skill and information are less specialized for exploiting short term changes, are likely to be more attracted than professionals by the possibilities of reducing their taxes by delaying liquidation if the statute discriminates substantially in favor of longer term gains.

Large capital gains arise from short and medium term promotion efforts, such as the assembling of the constituent members of a merger, of adjoining parcels of real estate that are saleable at a higher figure under common than under separate ownership, and the organization of new enterprises with the deliberate intention of seeking buyers for them as soon as they are well launched. Sometimes the men who launch such ventures have little choice when to 'take' their gains; at other times they have considerable flexibility. If delay in selling significantly enhances the risks, as when large sums must be tied up and the outcome is sensitive to changes in business conditions, or when options to purchase the needed properties can be had only for short periods and the promoters lack the resources to take up the options unless they can sell the properties simultaneously, the possibility of reducing taxes by delaying liquidation will be of little influence. In such situations high tax rates on short term gains will doubtless prevent some transactions that would take place under lower rates, because the prospective gain after taxes does not seem to compensate fully for the risk of loss. But if a moderate delay in completing the transaction will not increase risk or expense much, a significant difference between the rates applicable to shorter and longer term gains will give investors a strong motive to postpone realization.

In the Revenue Acts of 1942-49 Congress was more responsive to these considerations than it had ever been before. In extending the preferential tax treatment of capital gains to those from assets held less than a year, Congress departed from one of the most widely accepted equitable grounds for differentiating between capital gains and ordinary income: the ground that under a steeply graduated system of tax rates it is unfair to tax a capital gain arising over several years as the income of the single year in which it is realized. The reduction to 6 months doubtless diminished the artificial incentive that had operated under previous Acts to delay some sales a year or more and to inhibit some purchases. Nevertheless the new provision encouraged many who had formerly been resigned to the ordinary tax rates on their short term gains to face the merely moderate delay now required in the technical consummation of such transactions to make their gains eligible for the large concession in tax rates.

The short period of required holding also stimulated the use of various artificial expedients for extending legal ownership of an asset beyond the 6 months even though the substantial equivalent of a sale had been made. For example, a man who wanted to sell 1,000 shares of United States Steel Corporation common stock at $70 a share after buying them only a month before at $65 a share, and yet to treat his $5,000 profit as a long term capital gain, would retain his own shares, for the time being, and sell another 1,000 shares he did not own, directing his broker to borrow the latter from some holder and deliver them to the purchaser. When the 6 months holding period had elapsed, he would close out his short position by delivering his original shares. A provision designed to close the short sale loophole was included in the Revenue Act of 1950. In real estate substantially similar results can be achieved, though with more risk. A seller postpones actual sale but gives an option, for which he exacts a heavy advance payment, exercisable on the day following the expiration of his 6 month ownership. Also used with the same effect is the device of entering into a sales contract but fixing the date for the actual transfer of title beyond the 6 month period.[15] When the required holding period for a long term capital gain was 1 or 2 years, such expedients were riskier and less attractive.

[15] J. K. Lasser, *Your Income Tax, 1948,* p. 118.

Chapter 8

EFFECTS OF THE CHANGING TAX TREATMENT UPON FEDERAL REVENUES

1 REVENUES HIGHLY ERRATIC

The federal government's net revenues from its tax treatment of capital gains and losses have been highly erratic. Individuals with net incomes paid more than $1.5 billion in such taxes in the 4 years of the stock boom, 1926-29; in the next 5 years their tax reductions because of the allowances for capital losses exceeded the taxes paid on their gains by $151 million. This figure does not measure the full revenue loss from this source during the 5 years because it does not include the taxes saved on their ordinary income by persons who, because of net capital losses, were enabled to report no taxable income. Their returns were excluded from the Treasury's estimates of net tax receipts from capital transactions before 1935, though they have been included for subsequent years. Capital gains and losses of individuals again returned negative revenues in 1940 and 1941, and the net positive yield for 1935-41, including deficit returns, averaged only $30 million a year. But after a modest recovery, to $68 million in 1942, the net receipts from this source soared to roughly $2.2 billion in the 4 years 1943-46, or 44 percent more than in 1926-29, and preliminary estimates indicated $500 million in 1947.[1]

[1] Table 90. In estimating net revenues from the tax treatment of capital gains and losses for 1926-34 the Treasury's method was as follows: To the surtax net income in each net income group, the statutory amounts of the net capital losses were added back and the statutory amounts of the net capital gains were subtracted, yielding a figure for statutory net income other than capital gains and losses. To this figure the Treasury applied the average tax rate for each net income group; the product is the estimate of tax revenues on income exclusive of capital gains and losses.

There was no attempt to weight the estimate for each income group by the dispersion around the average, and no allowance was made for the revenue losses occasioned when individuals with net incomes from other sources were enabled to report net deficits on their operations as a whole because of net

203

The proportion of total individual income tax receipts attributable to capital gains taxes has also varied greatly. In 1928 such taxes accounted for nearly half of the total, and the proportion exceeded 40 percent in the 4 years 1926-29 as a whole. This situation changed abruptly with the onset of the depression. In 1930-32, and again in 1940-41, as noted above, tax reductions resulting from the allowances for capital losses exceeded tax receipts from capital gains. In the other years between 1933 and 1942 the proportion of total individual income tax revenues contributed by capital gains and losses ranged from 14.1 percent in 1936 to less than .5 percent in 1939. With the tremendous rise of incomes and income tax rates during the war and early postwar years, even the large capital gains revenues of 1943-47 constituted only 1.8 to 5.2 percent of the annual individual income tax receipts.

Those who regard stability of yield as an essential characteristic of a satisfactory revenue source will obviously find that capital gains have been badly wanting in this respect. Congress has gone far since 1933 to reduce one cause of the instability by severely restricting the deductibility of net capital losses from other income. In consequence, even though taxpayers in the aggregate reported more capital losses than gains in all except 1 of the 10 years 1933-42, and reported an aggregate loss excess of $3,961 million for the decade as a whole, the Treasury obtained a positive net revenue from its tax treatment of these items.

The present restrictions ensure that the net revenues will rarely if ever be negative for taxpayers as a whole and that, at worst, an occasional negative yield will be held to a very small figure. By limiting the deductibility of a taxpayer's net capital loss from other income to $1,000 in any one year and by permitting his excess of capital losses to be offset against his capital gains of the succeeding 5 years, the treatment in force since 1942 makes for a more stable flow of revenue. This carryforward provision makes for a significant degree of averaging losses against gains. Not only are net losses prevented from making serious inroads on the tax revenues of the year in which they occur; in addition, the taxes otherwise payable on the

---

capital losses. Both these deficiencies in the Treasury's estimates for 1926-34 were severely criticized in an unpublished study, Capital Gains Tax, made for the New York Stock Exchange in 1947 by L. Robert Driver. For the years since 1935, the Treasury has used more refined procedures and included deficit returns. Consequently the estimated net revenues for 1926-34 in Table 90 are higher than they would be if made on the same basis as those for subsequent years.

net gains of prosperous years are reduced by the allowance for losses carried over from preceding years.

But this partial averaging is open only to those who first incur net capital losses and in subsequent years realize net gains. It does nothing to even out the taxable incomes of those whose years of net gains precede their years of net losses, or of those whose net gains vary widely from year to year. In the absence of more complete averaging, the possibilities of which are discussed in Chapter 11, continuing great irregularity in the tax receipts from capital transactions seems inevitable.

Instability of yield in a source of revenue has traditionally been regarded as a serious defect because it makes budget balancing difficult and may therefore endanger the government's credit. Since the depression of the 1930's, however, the desirability of stable revenues for a central government has been seriously and widely questioned. Indeed, many have urged a compensatory instability to offset opposite fluctuations in the private sector of the economy. A central government that insists upon collecting substantially the same amount of tax revenues in years of bad business as in good will, it is argued, accentuate the economy's difficulties in bad years by absorbing a larger proportion of the reduced private incomes, and exaggerate the prosperity of good years by taking a smaller proportion of the enlarged private incomes. Many persons who strongly oppose the view that a central government can usefully or safely incur a prolonged succession of budgetary deficits nevertheless favor seeking a balanced budget only for a business cycle rather than for each and every year. They would have the government deliberately incur deficits by reducing tax collections or spending more in bad years and collecting exceptionally large revenues or sharply reducing expenditures in good years.

And among those who share this general viewpoint a large number see certain advantages in varying tax receipts rather than public expenditures as far as possible: the former better protects the private sector of the economy from encroachment by the government; through a heavy use of taxes that are highly responsive in yield to changes in national income, such as graduated income taxes, it lends itself to automatic operation in considerable degree; and adjustments in either direction can be made with less delay, administrative cost, and political controversy, it is contended, than are involved in government spending programs. For those who hold any variant of the view that a central government's taxing policy should attempt to compensate for fluctuations in private spending, the instability of yield of capital gains taxation may appear benign, for a large excess of net capital gains tends to be realized in good years and smaller gains or net losses in bad, with the result that private incomes are reduced in prosperity and better maintained in depression.

It is doubtful, however, that capital gains will ever again contribute as big a proportion of total income tax revenues as they did in 1926-29. Although another stock market boom of the same or greater intensity and duration may well occur, our changed tax structure will alter its revenue significance. In 1926-29 personal exemptions and credits for dependents were so generous that only a few hundred thousand persons paid income taxes, and the individual income tax, including taxes on capital gains, yielded only slightly more than $1 billion in the best year. Taxes on ordinary income did not reach $600 million in any year.

In 1948, in contrast, more than 36 million individuals and fiduciaries filed taxable returns and their aggregate income tax liability approximated $16 billion. The amount of capital gains tax revenues that constituted nearly half of total individual income tax receipts in 1928 constituted less than 4 percent in 1948. In 1947 the actual proportion was about 2.7 percent. This percentage was raised somewhat under the Revenue Act of 1948 which, for individuals with sizeable incomes, reduced the effective tax rates on ordinary income much more sharply than on capital gains. The bracket rates on ordinary incomes were cut, and division of income between husband and wife was permitted, but the ceiling tax rate of 25 percent on long term capital gains was not altered. The rearmament program that was set in motion by the invasion of South Korea in June 1950 substituted the certainty of early and heavy tax increases for any possibility of further tax reductions. Some of these were made late in 1950, and additional tax revenues of $16.5 billion were requested by the President for the fiscal year beginning July 1, 1952. Hence, though taxes on capital gains may be expected to produce substantial absolute amounts of receipts in good years and small sums in bad years, the fluctuations are likely to have a relatively minor impact upon total federal revenues. For this reason the fluctuating character of capital gains tax revenues is now quantitatively unimportant, whether regarded as a defect or virtue.

2 WOULD A LOW TAX RATE INCREASE THE REVENUE YIELD?

The contention has been frequently advanced before Congressional committees that the revenue from capital transactions would be vastly increased if capital gains, both short and long term, were subject only to a uniform low flat rate of about 10 percent, and all allowances for net capital losses against ordinary income eliminated. In 1942 one witness presented calculations purporting to show that such a treatment might be expected to produce annual revenues of $200-600 million, as against the actual average annual yield of about $30 million in 1931-40.[2]

Such estimates are based upon two assumptions: that the volume of transactions and of realized gains is extremely sensitive to tax rates and that any significant allowance for net losses must drastically reduce revenue.

The first assumption is not supported by the data reviewed in Chapters 6 and 7. We found that although the changing tax treatment doubtless influenced the amounts of gains and losses realized, other forces, such as the trend and level of stock prices, have been of greater aggregate significance and have commonly swamped the influence of tax changes. The practical effect of these other forces is to reduce the responsiveness of capital gains and losses to tax changes: because of them, reductions in tax rates have a smaller stimulating effect and increases a smaller depressing effect upon the gains realized. The tax treatment was unchanged in 1926-31, yet the revenue yield ranged from $576 million in 1928 to a revenue loss of $89 million in 1931 (Table 90). In the face of increases in tax rates in 1936 over 1935, the realized net gains of individuals with net incomes nearly doubled. The reduction to 15 percent in the maximum tax rate in 1938-41 on gains from assets held more than 18 months produced no semblance of the huge revenues derived from long term gains during the late 1920's, when a 12.5 percent maximum rate was in force. Under a 25 percent maximum rate in 1945 and 1946, net capital gains exceeded the high levels of the late 1920's and net revenues from transactions in capital assets were higher than in any preceding year. Although total net capital gains in 1945 for individuals with net incomes were about equal to those in 1928, the tax revenue from them was about 25 percent larger.

The long run revenue cost of the present allowance for net capital losses cannot be estimated with confidence until we have had more experience with it. Its chief impact upon revenues is likely to come from the full deductibility of such losses against the capital gains

---

[2] Elisha M. Friedman, *Revenue Revision of 1942,* Hearings, Ways and Means Committee, p. 1656. The $30 million average yield cited by Mr. Friedman is reduced to $16 million by later Treasury estimates.

of the succeeding 5 years, rather than from the $1,000 allowance against ordinary income in the current and each of the succeeding 5 years. The 5-year carryforward can accumulate to a huge sum during a series of bad years. The net capital losses reported by individuals in 1930-34, for example, totaled $11.7 billion, while net gains were only $2.9 billion. In every year 1918-45 except 1927-29 net capital gains were less than the aggregate net capital losses of the preceding 5 years, but in 1946 net capital gains exceeded the aggregate net capital losses of the preceding 5 years.

But these figures do not mean that taxable capital gains would have been extinguished if the present carryforward had been in force. They pool the results of the divergent experiences of different persons, while taxes are assessed on an individual basis. Many taxpayers who had incurred heavy losses in 1930 or 1931 did not share in the capital gains subsequently enjoyed by some individuals, while not all the latter had previously sustained capital losses. The credit for losses carried forward by the one would not have reduced the tax liabilities of the other. Death, as well as ill-fortune in speculation, may remove the tax-reducing power of a taxpayer's loss carryforward. For these reasons, ready and precise inferences about the revenue results cannot be drawn from the totals of gains and losses of taxpayers as a whole. Nevertheless, these aggregates indicate that very substantial remissions of taxes in good years are likely from the credits for losses carried forward.

The reduction in revenue resulting from a taxpayer's actual use of such credits will, in a sense, merely prevent an overpayment of taxes. It will only reflect the use of a period longer than 1 year in which to measure the net gain from his transactions in capital assets, provided his losses precede his gains. And because the remission in taxes otherwise payable is confined to those who have actually incurred previous losses, the net loss carryforward is a more selective provision than alternative proposals that would deal with capital losses categorically without discriminating among taxpayers, such as completely disallowing capital losses.

The net revenues from the tax treatment of capital gains and losses reflect not only the volume of capital transactions and tax rates but also the opportunities for tax avoidance and the extent to which they are used. The technical realization of artificial losses and the technical avoidance of realizing gains by various legal devices, some of which are noted in the next chapter, as well as the taxpayer's ability to time many transactions with an eye to tax advantage, all take their toll of possible tax revenues. What is probably the largest single source of revenue loss in connection with capital gains is the elimination, by the owner's death of all tax liability for previous unrealized increases in the value of his property. And, as we have noted, the opportunity to avoid completely the capital gains tax by leaving the sale of appreciated property to one's heirs doubtless inhibits many transactions. Even a capital gains tax of only 10 or 15 percent, while low relative to income tax rates, appears costly to many investors when compared with the zero rate of tax on the gains embodied in property transferred at death.

3 REVENUES FROM CAPITAL GAINS AND THEIR ADMINISTRATIVE COST

Although revenues were large in some years, the average annual net tax revenues from capital gains and losses in the entire period 1917-47 have been small, and may even have been negative. The Treasury's estimates, we have noted, do not cover years before 1926, and do not include deficit returns for years before 1935. Capital losses were heavy in 1920 and 1921, when they were fully deductible from ordinary income and when the latter was taxed at high rates; and no absolute limit existed on the deductibility, at a maximum rate of 12½ percent of the loss, of the huge long term net capital losses reported in 1929-33. Even if we disregard deficit returns before 1935, the average annual net revenue from capital gains and losses in 1926-47 was only about $200 million. While tax rates on capital gains are now much higher, they do not ensure larger average revenues for a long period because of the possibility that the revenues otherwise arising from the gains of good years may now be largely offset by net losses carried forward from the preceding 5 years.

In view of the small, uncertain, and fluctuating revenues derived from capital gains and losses, the question has repeatedly been asked whether they are worth their administrative and legal costs. Driver (see note 1) has charged that no other sections of the Internal Revenue Code are so difficult to interpret and enforce, and that these sections deter or distort numerous business transactions, including various kinds of corporate reorganizations and exchanges. The conclusion is usually drawn that if capital gains and losses were excluded from the calculation of taxable income, these frictions and wastes would be greatly reduced or eliminated.

In the main this conclusion is fallacious. Some difficulties of taxpayer compliance and administrative costs and litigation might well be reduced. But the chief source of controversy and of tax-motivated legal expedients on the part of taxpayers and their lawyers would remain. The present elaborate enforcement efforts and controversies in this connection arise, for the most part, precisely because capital gains are taxed at lower rates than ordinary income. It is this preferential treatment that necessitates a nice distinction on the part of taxpayers, tax administrators, and the courts between capital gains and ordinary income. To exempt capital gains from income taxes would mean to put a zero rate of tax on them as compared with the substantial rates on ordinary income. Such a change would *increase,* not diminish, the inducement offered taxpayers to attempt to make their ordinary income take the form of capital gains as far as possible.

The same considerations apply to capital losses. At present, when capital losses are allowed only in part, the taxpayer has a motive to cause capital losses to assume the form of ordinary losses, and to contend that all borderline cases are cases of ordinary rather than capital losses. But the exclusion of capital losses from taxable income would not remove this motive. On the contrary, to deny all allowance for capital losses would give taxpayers a stronger motive than ever for contending that all losses are ordinary losses.

It may well be argued, therefore, that the mere enforcement of the graduated taxes on ordinary income would require careful definition of capital gains and losses, and administrative scrutiny of the transactions from which they are reported to arise. To the extent that the administrative costs incurred in connection with the capital gains tax provisions are essential to minimize avoidance and evasion of the ordinary income tax, they are properly chargeable to the latter.

In short, the exclusion of capital gains and losses from taxable income would not remove the main source of administrative and compliance difficulties because it would still be necessary for both the taxpayer and the Treasury to distinguish sharply between ordinary gains and losses and capital gains and losses. Indeed, if the elimination of such difficulties were our primary objective, it would be logical to move in the opposite direction: to reduce, rather than to increase, differences in the tax treatment of ordinary income and of capital gains and losses. The obliteration of all distinctions, for example, would eliminate these difficulties, though it would be open to objections of other kinds already noted.

Chapter 9

TAX AVOIDANCE THROUGH CAPITAL GAINS

As noted in Chapter 1, the markedly lower tax rates on capital gains have given many taxpayers a strong incentive both to choose investments likely to yield this type of reward and to contrive to have ordinary income take on its appearance. In an economic sense, as we saw in Chapter 4, a pure capital gain is best conceived as an unforeseen, unexpected increase in the value of a piece of property; ordinary income consists of more or less expected gains. We found this distinction difficult to apply in more than a general way because it becomes blurred when pressed far: 'expected' gains differ from 'unexpected' only in degree; most incomes are varying mixtures of expected and unexpected elements. The law nevertheless attempts to approximate this distinction by taxing as ordinary income the net receipts from a trade or profession, operating a business, or owning property, and by treating as capital gains those obtained from the sale of capital assets, i.e., assets not a part of the taxpayer's stock-in-trade. The former may be said to be expected because they tend to be recurring; the latter unexpected because they do not. But the law necessarily relies primarily upon the *form* of a transaction rather than its substance. It is not surprising, therefore, that in addition to the underlying difficulties of distinguishing sharply between economically overlapping types of income, difficulties arise from the application of the law itself. Particularly with the aid of the corporate form of business organization and property ownership, but through other means as well, many taxpayers have found it possible to convert into technical capital gains various amounts of more or less expected income actually representing personal services, profits, interest, or rents.

Congress and the Bureau of Internal Revenue have tried to meet the more obvious attempts to make ordinary income look like capital gains as a means of avoiding taxes by withholding preferential tax treatment from gains realized on capital assets owned less than a stipulated period, by successive technical refinements in the law, and by closer administrative scrutiny of questionable and borderline transactions. Nevertheless, the precise position of the dividing line between capital gains and ordinary income has been difficult to determine in certain types of case, and in others the established division has clearly permitted tax avoidance.

In the broad sense in which the expression 'tax avoidance' is used in this book, no unethical, immoral, or illegal intent on the part of the taxpayer is implied. The distinction between tax evasion, which connotes an illegal attempt to evade taxes, and lawful tax avoidance is often difficult to draw but is suggested by an analogy the late Senator Pat Harrison, then Chairman of the Senate Finance Committee, used in a conversation with the author: a traveller who goes over a toll bridge without paying the toll is guilty of unlawful evasion; but he may lawfully avoid the toll by going over a free bridge nearby.

If the law offers two forms for conducting a given transaction and levies higher taxes in connection with one than with the other, the taxpayer cannot be blamed for adopting the form that lessens his taxes. If, further, the tax-favored form is open only to some classes of transaction, not to others, though no real difference exists in the character of the income from each, different groups of taxpayers are treated unequally, and the favored group might be said to avoid taxes. Finally, the tax treatment may be unequal not because some taxpayers deliberately choose legal forms that give their incomes the guise of capital gains, but because the law itself gives this designation to some types of income that do not differ fundamentally from those taxed at regular rates.

In the discussion that follows, we use 'tax avoidance' in a loose sense to cover all cases in which essentially ordinary income is taxed as capital gains.

1 UNCERTAIN BORDER BETWEEN INVESTORS AND DEALERS

All purchases and sales of investments entail some personal effort by the investor or his agent. In some instances a man's talents and exertions may repeatedly enable him to acquire properties at bargain prices or, by judicious timing or adroit selection of buyers, to sell them at unusually high prices. His personal services, rather than the capital funds with which he works, may be responsible for most of his gains. In other instances the larger part of the investor's income may come from rents, interest, or dividends, but a sizeable proportion may nevertheless be obtained more or less regularly by profiting from informed judgment in timing the purchase and sale of investments. How much and what kinds of effort in buying and selling any type of property are enough to make a man a dealer in it rather than an investor? If classified as the former, his profits are taxed as ordinary income; otherwise, as capital gains. These questions are not answered specifically in the law. They raise difficulties for tax administrators and the indefiniteness of the answers creates opportunities for some taxpayers to convert the fruits of personal talent and exertions, even when regularly applied, into capital gains.

The chief considerations usually taken into account by the Bureau of Internal Revenue and the courts to distinguish the ordinary profits of a dealer from the capital gains of a trader or investor are the intention of the taxpayer (did he buy the property primarily for resale?), the proportion of his time devoted to the transactions, and, most important, the extent to which the purchases and sales actually require him to seek sellers and customers in the markets. The distinction does not turn on the type of good sold. A householder may realize a capital gain on an electric refrigerator or other consumer good, while a dealer in factory machinery is subject to ordinary income taxes on his profits from the sale of this class of capital goods. In the language of the Internal Revenue Code, Sec. 117 (a) (1): " 'Capital assets' means property held by the taxpayer (whether or not connected with his trade or business), but does not include stock in trade of the taxpayer or other property of a kind which would properly be included in the inventory of the taxpayer if on hand at the close of the taxable year, or property held by the taxpayer primarily for sale to customers in the ordinary course of his trade or business, or property, used in the trade or business, of a character which is subject to the allowance for depreciation provided in Section 23(1)...."

If an individual were to engage extensively in the purchase and sale of a narrow class of goods, motor trucks, for example, he would doubtless be termed a dealer under the foregoing definition. If he made a few purchases and sales a year, wholly apart from his regular business, the circumstances and his intentions would have to be examined to determine the character of his gains. But if his transactions covered a broad variety of properties, and did not entail the maintenance of inventories or a regular place of business, he would be permitted, in most cases, to treat his profits as capital gains. Finally, a taxpayer may buy and sell listed securities on the stock exchange in any amount and with any frequency without being called a dealer. He may acquire a big block of stock through the equivalent of a wholesale purchase, and dispose of it through several thousand separate sales of 100 shares each during a year, yet treat his profits as capital gains. Even professional traders and speculators who devote all their time to buying and selling securities for their own account are not regarded as dealers unless they hold securities "primarily for sale to cusomers" in the ordinary course of their trade or business. Hence, their profits are currently subject to the capital gain and loss tax provisions, rather than to those governing ordinary income.

British practice appears to differ from American in this respect, the British being readier to say that a series of similar transactions involving personal effort reflects a regular calling or business. A resident of Great Britain who can be shown to devote much or all of his time to stock market speculation, for example, is likely to be classified as a dealer and to have his profits taxed as ordinary income.[1] In the United States, even taxpayers whose entire incomes are from stock market speculation and investment are eligible for the preferential capital gains tax rates on their profits, provided they hold their securities longer than 6 months. Since the British exclude capital gains entirely from the income tax base, they have more reason to scrutinize hybrid and borderline transactions carefully.

Short term traders and speculators, however, do not benefit from the American treatment, since the effective tax rates on gains from capital assets held 6 months or less are the same as those on ordinary income. In fact, traders, because of the restricted deductibility of their net capital losses from other income, suffer a disadvantage when the net result of their short term operations is a capital loss.[2]

Dealings in real estate and in securities regarded differently
The situation of long term speculators and investors in real estate is different from that of those in corporate securities. A man who frequently buys and sells shares of stock in the leading steel companies is not usually thought of as engaging in the steel business,

[1] See R. M. Haig, Taxation of Capital Gains, *Wall Street Journal,* March 25 and 29, 1937.
[2] Until 1934, when Congress imposed a limit of $2,000 upon the deductibility of net capital losses, professional traders in securities were treated as dealers. Had they continued to be classified as dealers, their short term net losses on securities would have remained fully deductible. Congress avoided this result by excluding from the category of dealers, traders and others who do not hold securities "primarily for sale to customers."

because it is the steel companies, not their stockholders, who are viewed as engaged in that business. But a man who frequently buys and sells real estate is more readily regarded as a dealer. Both the Bureau of Internal Revenue and the courts have been inclined to regard even a moderate number of real estate transactions a year, if they involve the purchase and sale of similar properties such as houses or the disposition of a single large property in many small pieces, as sufficient to classify a man as a dealer even though he also practices law or medicine, or has some other occupation or business.

Anyone who subdivides his land for sale, regardless how long he previously owned it, is likely to have his profits taxed as ordinary income rather than as capital gains (Weil, TC memo op., Dec. 13, 973M). Even a man without previous transactions in real estate who acquires his land by inheritance but finds that he can dispose of it to good advantage only by selling it in several separate pieces through an agent is likely to be held to be engaged in trade as far as concerns the taxability of his profits from those sales (*Ehrman v. Com.*, 120 F (2d) 607, 314 U.S. 668). The presumption apparently is that frequent purchases and sales of real estate indicate resale at a profit as the primary purpose of the acquisitions, and that the transactions demand a sufficient search for customers on the part of the investor to constitute a business.

Even in real estate, however, a man may make a livelihood and a career from a series of similar transactions without being treated as a dealer for tax purposes. For example, if he made a practice of erecting a block of retail stores once every year or two, selling the block as a whole when the building was completed and the stores rented, the profit on each transaction would probably be taxed as a capital gain. But if he built 20 separate stores each year and sold them to 20 purchasers, it is likely, though far from certain, that his profits would be taxed as ordinary income, for then it would be easy to regard him as conducting a regular business. The former transactions appear to be discrete. They are not seen to constitute a more or less regular means of livelihood until looked at from the perspective of some years later. Similarly, many individuals enjoy the benefits of capital gains tax rates on their incomes from a more or less organized pursuit of profits through constructing or otherwise acquiring and selling a succession of apartment houses, theatres, hotels, etc.

2 PROMOTERS AND ORGANIZERS

The example just given of a man who makes a living and a career from a succession of separate construction projects is also representative of a wider class of situations in which the fruits of personal talent and effort take the form of capital gains. As noted in Chapter 4, some men make a life's work of promoting and organizing a succession of business enterprises, such as jewelry or furniture stores, or chains of them, and receive much of their compensation in the form of capital gains.

Promotion and organizing talents and services lend themselves peculiarly to compensation in the form of capital gains because their products can be embodied and sold in the form of the goodwill of a new or modified business enterprise. The assembling of a chain of 30 retail drug stores in a big city, for example, may create larger aggregate earnings on the invested capital by reason of quantity discounts on purchases and other advantages; and compensation for the promoter's services (and, in part, for his risks and capital investment) may readily take the form of a capital gain that represents the difference between the selling price of the chain based on a capitalization of its expanded earning power and the smaller aggregate of the purchase prices of the individual stores. Few other kinds of personal service can be sold in such a fashion. Professional men can sell their personal services only directly to an employer or to a number of individual clients, and the services are usually too personal to be readily transferable to others. Hence the relation between the professional man and his client is not usually saleable. Successful physicians, lawyers, accountants, and other professional men, and salaried corporate officials frequently complain that they do not share the recurring opportunities enjoyed by their friends among the independent business men to obtain compensation in the form of the preferentially taxed capital gains.[3] The promoter or organizer of a business firm differs by creating an organization that continues to function after his personal services have been withdrawn. To the degree that this organization yields an income in excess of the going rate of return on an amount equal to its original cost, it possesses a saleable goodwill.

Even among professional men capital gains are open to those who create continuing organizations; e.g., some physicians and others who have built up stable clienteles sell their practices. While these

[3] Some often get clues to profitable investments or actual participation in them in connection with their services to promoters, however.

capital gains are seldom large, there are noteworthy exceptions: organizing talent and a diminished emphasis upon the personal relationship in the reputation for superior services have enabled certain eminent physicians, engineers, accountants, advertising experts, and other professional men to build up continuing organizations possessing a valuable goodwill that persisted after their personal services had been withdrawn.

Although speculative talent may be employed in quest of capital gains without promotion effort, as in much stock market speculation, the two are often combined. The man who assembles a dozen parcels of land with an eye to the peculiar value of the assembled site for a particular use, then finds a buyer to exploit it, is an example. Somewhat similar is the case of a man who seeks a large capital gain by buying a promising piece of land, then contributing to the increase in its value by persuading others to build on contiguous sites.

In such ways the same personal qualities and exertions that enable one man to command a fully taxable salary of $100,000 a year from a large corporation may be used by another, with the aid of often trifling amounts of capital, to obtain rewards in the form of lower-taxed capital gains.

3 TRANSFORMING CURRENT INVESTMENT INCOME INTO CAPITAL GAINS THROUGH THE PERSONAL HOLDING COMPANY

The preceding discussion has been confined to individuals acting in their own names, and mainly to rewards for personal services. When the corporate form of conducting a business is used, the possibilities of transforming all kinds of ordinary income into capital gains are greatly facilitated and extended. The underlying reason is that the law conceives a corporation to be an entity distinct from its stockholders. A corporation's profits are therefore not regarded as the income of its stockholders unless and until distributed to them in dividends, and a stockholder may have buying and selling transactions with a corporation whose entire stock he owns.

An extreme use of this legal concept to convert dividends, interest, rents, and other income into capital gains took place in the 1920's and early 'thirties through the personal holding company: a corporation that is called a 'holding company' because its income is derived primarily from the ownership of securities rather than from the direct operation of a business, and 'personal' because it is owned by only one or a few persons. By forming such a company and transferring to it a portion or all of his stocks, bonds, and other securities in exchange for its capital stock, the investor could substitute the corporation for himself as the legal recipient of his dividends, interest, and other income. Although his ownership gave him control over its income, the investor was subject to individual income tax only on the part of its earnings that he caused to be paid in dividends to himself. The holding company's income from its dividend receipts was exempt from the corporation income tax,[4] and the tax rate applicable to the taxable portion of its income, chiefly interest, was usually lower than the upper surtax rates on personal incomes. By having his holding company retain and re-invest a part of or all its income, the investor could add to his wealth without having to pay personal income taxes on the increase; and when he chose, he could liquidate the company and treat as a capital gain the increase in its value derived from the accumulations of ordinary income.

The personal holding company offered other tax advantages also. Even if the taxpayer planned ultimately to have his personal holding company pay out in dividends all the income it received, he could arrange to have the distributions made in years when his taxes on them would be smallest, e.g., in a year when his income from other sources was small or negative. He could avoid subjecting an unusually large profit from a contemplated transaction to the upper surtax rates by having his personal holding company realize the gain, pay the corporation income tax on it, and either reinvest it or pay it to him in installments. He could form more than one personal holding company and arrange tax-saving transactions between them or between one of them and himself. He could retain his underlying ownership of an asset that had fallen in value, yet obtain the tax advantage of realizing a loss, by selling the asset to one of his personal holding companies, or by having one of them, if it was the legal owner, sell it to another or to himself.[5] By handling the transaction as a loan rather than a dividend distribution, he could even pocket and consume the income received by his personal holding company,

---

[4] Beginning in 1936, 15 percent of dividends received by corporations was included in taxable income for the purpose of the normal corporation income tax, corporate surtax, and declared-value excess profits tax, and the whole amount was included for determining distributable income for the purpose of the surtax on undistributed profits under the Acts of 1936 and 1938.

[5] The asset would acquire a lower 'basis' in the hands of its new legal owner, however, thereby increasing the taxable capital gain or reducing the allowable capital loss from a subsequent sale.

yet not pay any personal income tax on it. One individual who reported a large net loss on his personal return for 1936 was found to own a personal holding company, organized in Canada, that had an income in 1936 of over $1,500,000 from dividends of United States corporations; and a considerable part of his reported loss arose from a deduction he claimed for interest on a loan made to him by his personal holding company.[6] Some personal holding companies were able to offset taxable income from dividends and interest on securities or from capital gains by the losses they reported from renting yachts, summer houses, etc., to the sole or principal owner of their common stock.

So conspicuous were these and other tax advantages of the personal holding company that lawyers came to advise nearly everyone with substantial holdings of property to resort to its use. Until 1934 the only means available to the Treasury Department of preventing tax avoidance through this device was a provision (now Section 102 of the Internal Revenue Code) authorizing the Commissioner of Internal Revenue to impose a penalty tax on corporations formed or used for the purpose of avoiding the imposition of income taxes on their shareholders. This provision proved to be exceedingly difficult to apply because proof that retention of earnings was motivated by improper purposes was almost impossible to establish in the face of statements by the corporation's officers of the actual or intended uses for the funds. To eliminate the necessity of such proof when personal holding companies were employed, Congress, in the Revenue Act of 1934, levied graduated surtaxes of 30 and 40 percent on the undistributed earnings (after various allowable retentions) of *all* personal holding companies as defined in the Act. The range of these surtaxes was made 20-60 percent in the Revenue Act of 1935, and 8-48 percent in that of 1936. But this treatment was apparently inadequate. The Secretary of the Treasury reported in a letter to the President, dated May 29, 1937, that the single stockholder of one large domestic personal holding company "saved himself $322,000 by causing his company to distribute none of its income to him"; and that in another case, "a man and his wife saved $791,000 through the use of personal holding companies in 1936".

Compounding the difficulties of the tax administrators were the attempts of persons to avoid the surtax on personal holding companies by incorporating them in the Bahamas, Panama, Newfound-

[6] Hearings, Joint Committee on Tax Evasion and Avoidance, 75th Cong., 1st Sess. (1937), Part 1, p. 3.

land, and other places. The Secretary of the Treasury reported that 64 such companies were organized by Americans in the Bahamas alone in 1935. In some instances the formation of foreign personal holding companies was motivated by the desire to avoid the capital gains tax on profits about to be realized. A case of this sort was described by the Secretary as follows: "Perhaps the most flagrant case of this character is that of a retired American Army officer with a large income from valuable American securities which he desires to sell at a very large profit. To escape our income and inheritance tax laws, he used the device of becoming a naturalized Canadian citizen, and 6 days later organized four Bahamas corporations to hold his securities. He and his lawyers apparently think that he can now sell his securities free from any taxes on his profits, since there are no income taxes in the Bahamas, and that he has adroitly escaped American taxes."

The foreign personal holding companies offered special difficulties because they were frequently organized through foreign lawyers, with dummy incorporators and directors. The names of the real parties in interest were not evident, and the laws of the countries where the companies were established did not require that they be disclosed.

Following a special Presidential message on tax avoidance and evasion, and hearings before a joint Congressional committee, Congress greatly reduced the tax avoidance possibilities of personal holding companies in the Revenue Act of 1937, and further changes in this direction have since been made. A personal holding company is now defined in the statute as one that received at least 80 percent of its gross income for the taxable year from royalties, dividends, interest, annuities, compensation for personal services, and, if they constituted less than half of the gross income, rents; provided half or more in value of the company's common stock was owned directly or indirectly at any time during the second half of the year by not more than five individuals. An individual, for this purpose, is considered to own the stock owned directly or indirectly by or for his family or partner, and the family of an individual includes his brothers and sisters, spouse, ancestors, and lineal descendants. Only 70 instead of 80 percent of the gross income for the taxable year need be derived from the sources cited if, with certain exceptions, the company had been classified as a personal holding company for any preceding taxable year beginning after December 31, 1936. Besides being subject to the same rates of income tax as other corporations, statutory personal holding companies are subject to a surtax of 75 percent on the first $2,000 of their undistributed net income, after certain allowances, and to a surtax of 85 percent on the amount in excess of $2,000. The result has been that substantially all the net income of such companies, after the amounts permitted by statute to be retained, is now distributed to their stockholders and subjected to the individual income tax.[7] American shareholders of foreign personal holding companies, as defined in the statute, are required to report as a part of their personal incomes their shares of the latter's undistributed net incomes, after specified deductions.

While the foregoing provisions have been extremely effective against companies that come under the strict definition of the statute, they do not cover all companies that use the corporate form to enable their stockholders to convert ordinary income into capital gains or numerous other cases in which this result is achieved without being deliberately sought.

4 TRANSFORMING CORPORATE PROFITS INTO CAPITAL GAINS BY REINVESTING THEM

Probably the most important way in which current income — interest, rents, profits, and wages — is converted into capital gains is through the direct reinvestment of profits by ordinary business corporations. Between 1923 and 1929 more than 45 percent of the compiled net profits, after income and excess profits taxes, of all corporations reporting net incomes was retained by the corporations, and was therefore not subject to the individual income taxes applicable to their stockholders. When the figures for corporations reporting net deficits, for which their stockholders did not receive any allowance, are combined with the former, approximately 27 percent of the aggregate compiled net profits of *all* corporations, after income and excess profits taxes, was withheld (*Statistics of Income,* 1923-29). In the early 'thirties operating losses and large writedowns of plants, equipment, and intangible assets wiped out the surplus accumulations of many, though not all corporations. An aggregate net deficit of $11.5 billion was reported to the Bureau of Internal Revenue by corporations as a whole for the 3 years 1931-33. Individual differences, however, were marked. While most corpora-

---

[7] A personal holding company may retain all its net long term capital gains without becoming subject to surtaxes on them. Such retention does not result in avoidance of individual income taxes by the shareholders because the gains would be taxed at only 25 percent if realized by them directly.

tions were incurring net deficits totaling $20.3 billion, others earned net income totaling $8.8 billion.

The reinvested earnings of the 'twenties were also drawn upon to pay dividends in excess of current earnings during the early 'thirties. Here too, however, it is desirable to distinguish between the aggregate for all corporations and its components. According to *Statistics of Income,* 65 percent of the cash dividends disbursed in 1931-33 came from corporations that remained profitable, and their dividend distributions in the aggregate were less than their compiled net profits after income tax.

Individual case studies reveal more sharply than group statistics the importance of reinvested earnings in the growth of many enterprises. In a study of 72 major manufacturing and mercantile corporations for 1922-33, O. J. Curry found that 27 had increased their assets from reinvested earnings more than 50 percent.[8]

Among larger corporations the desire of the common stockholders for liberal dividends and that of the management to retain earnings is often compromised by the payment of a portion of the dividends in the form of additional common stock. Such stock dividends, though they capitalize current or previous retained earnings, are not taxable as income in the hands of the recipients. Yet the latter may realize cash from them by selling them. If the sale is at a price higher than the stockholder's cost per share, as adjusted for the larger number of shares, the excess is taxed as a capital gain. The shareholder enjoys the further advantage of being able to choose when to sell his stock dividend. By selling a portion of his holdings, the stockholder may achieve substantially the same result without a stock dividend. In both cases, however, the sale of stock reduces his proportionate interest in the corporation.

Doubtless most withholding of corporate earnings is motivated by legitimate business considerations. It takes place because it offers corporate managements a flexible and convenient means of securing new capital funds for additional inventories, plant capacity, and similar assets, or for liquid reserves against adverse contingencies. Nevertheless, on the earnings withheld, the stockholders avoid current personal income taxes. If the retained earnings are profitably employed, the market value of the common stock can be expected to rise in reflection of the resulting growth in the corporation's resources and earning power, though not in any fixed relation to the

[8] *Utilization of Corporate Profits in Prosperity and Depression* (Michigan Business Studies, IX, No. 4, University of Michigan, 1941), p. 40.

earnings reinvested. In such instances the stockholders can look forward to receiving a varying and uncertain proportion of the withheld earnings in the form of a rise in the earning power and market value of their holdings, or in the form of a capital gain, taxable at the preferentially low rate, if they sell their stock. As we noted also, even the capital gains tax will be avoided if the stockholders leave their unrealized gains to their heirs.

An extreme example is provided by the Ford Motor Company. Between the middle of 1903 and the end of 1926 the market value of the Ford Motor Company rose from about $100,000, the original investment including intangibles, to about $1 billion, the price offered by Hornblower and Weeks, an investment banking firm.[9] The vast expansion in the company's earning power was doubtless the immediate cause of the increase in its market value, but was itself due, in considerable measure, to the capital resources added through reinvestment of corporate profits. No other additional investment was made by the stockholders. The earnings directly reinvested by the company in its business during this period amounted to $714,802,288. The remainder of the increase in value was attributable to the creation of goodwill.

John W. Anderson and Horace H. Rackham, who had each invested $5,000 in the Ford enterprise in 1903, sold out to Henry Ford in 1919 for $12,500,000 each. The book value of the stock held by each had increased approximately $10,000,000 through the direct reinvestment of corporate earnings during their ownership; in addition, each had received cash dividends of $4,935,750.[10] It might be said, therefore, that $10,000,000 of ordinary income was converted, through corporate reinvestment of earnings, into a capital gain for each. As the law did not distinguish between capital gains and ordinary income in 1919, Anderson and Rackham did not enjoy preferential rates on their share of the corporate profits reinvested on their behalf. On the contrary, the concentration of so much realized income in a single year, as well as the rise in the whole level and progression of the income tax scale, caused them to pay larger taxes than they would have paid if they had received the same aggregate amount in installments during the entire period.

On the other hand, Henry Ford's son, Edsel, who had acquired 42 percent of the company's stock by 1920, presumedly through

[9] Lawrence H. Seltzer, *A Financial History of the American Automobile Industry* (Houghton Mifflin, 1928), p. 133.
[10] *Ibid.*, pp. 112, 128.

gifts from his father, and Henry Ford himself completely avoided both capital gains and ordinary personal income taxes on their shares of the company's reinvested profits because they did not sell any of the stock. In the hands of their heirs, the 'basis' of the stock for measuring gains and losses became the value on the day of death, not the original cost to the Fords.

Some evidence in support of the *a priori* presumption that reinvested earnings tend to raise the market value of a corporation's shares is to be found in *Common-Stock Indexes, 1871-1937*. Alfred Cowles and his associates portray the average experience of those investing in common stocks 1871-1937 by noting what would have happened to an investor's funds, ignoring brokerage charges and taxes, "if he had bought at the beginning of 1871 all stocks quoted on the New York Stock Exchange, allocating his purchases among the individual issues in proportion to their total monetary value, and each month up to 1937 had by the same criterion redistributed his holdings among all quoted stocks" (p. 2). For the 67 years as a whole, the average earnings annually retained by the listed corporations was 2.5 percent of the market value of their common stocks, and the stocks advanced in price at the rate of 1.8 percent a year (pp. 42-3). In short, on the average, for every $2.50 of earnings retained by a corporation the market value of its stock rose $1.80.

The absence of any close and consistent relation between the amount of earnings a corporation retains and the market value of its common stock is often conspicuous in the short run, and is not uncommon for longer periods also. The prospective earning power of different enterprises is affected in highly unequal degree by equal additions to their invested capital from profits. A rapidly expanding and unusually profitable company may be expected to raise its earning power more than a slowly growing or declining one by the use of a given amount of additional funds; hence the former's stock may well rise more than the amount of earnings retained, and the latter's, perhaps less. Sometimes, moreover, the reinvestment of a large proportion of its current earnings merely permits a concern to maintain its previous earning power. In other instances it may serve merely to retard a decline in earning power. In such situations the reinvestment of profits may operate mainly to prevent or moderate a decline in the price of the stock. When the common stock equity is relatively small, as in many railroad companies, the reinvestment of $4 or $5 a share in a particular year may affect the price of the common stock little if investors expect that the retained earnings will not appreciably improve the prospects of dividends for the common stock in the foreseeable future, but will be used only for increasing the margin of protection of the senior securities. If a corporate management decides to retain earnings to protect or expand the enterprise at a time when many of the stockholders would prefer to spend or invest the funds in other ways, the market may well add less to the value of the stock than the amount of earnings retained. These, among other, reasons help explain why the market prices of the common stocks of many well-known railroad, steel, oil, rubber, and other companies, through much of the decade of the 'forties, advanced less than the current additions to their book values from reinvested profits.

The deliberate retention of corporate earnings as a device for avoiding personal income taxes is doubtless much less prevalent than is sometimes charged, particularly among the larger corporations listed on national stock exchanges. When stock ownership in a corporation is widely diffused, as it is in most large corporations, the management is usually subject to strong and steady pressure by the numerous small stockholders to make the dividend payments as large as possible. And, in such cases, liberal dividend payments are often favored by the management as a means of enhancing the attractiveness of the stock to investors in the event of future stock financing. Some retention of earnings, sometimes substantial, may be essential to supplement the allowable deductions under the income tax for depreciation and obsolescence, as we have noted. Further, the mere maintenance of a firm's earning power may recurringly call for new investment in excess of the conventional depreciation charges against current operations because of changes in customer preferences with respect to products, in distribution practices, manufacturing techniques, and other factors. Beyond these requirements, the funds needed for a gradual expansion of the business can usually be secured more conveniently and economically through the direct reinvestment of earnings than through frequent offerings of relatively small amounts of new capital securities. Among smaller or closely held corporations the reinvestment of corporate earnings often affords the only practicable means of getting the capital funds needed for expansion.

Nevertheless, many persons have long been concerned that even the most justifiable retention and reinvestment of profits by corporations, beyond the amounts that are really supplementary depreciation allowances, impairs the effectiveness of the graduated rate schedule of the personal income tax by tending to substitute lower-taxed capital gains for dividend income for stockholders who sell, and by relieving those who do not sell from any personal income tax on their shares of reinvested corporate profits. As early as 1916, Thomas S. Adams of Yale University, who served as a consultant for the Treasury and the Congressional committees during the formative period of the federal income tax, in discussing the proposed Revenue Act of 1917, declared: "This question of taxing undistributed earnings carries us to the very heart of the difficult subject of business taxation. . . .

Should not the sole trader and partnership enjoy the same privilege as the corporation? Unfortunately, we cannot answer this question lightly in the affirmative. To say to every business man that the income tax is to apply only to amounts withdrawn from his business would seriously impair the productivity of the income tax. Moreover, if the corporation, partnership, and the active business men are to be taxed only on the sums withdrawn for consumption, we should be logically compelled to exempt all salaries and other personal income which is reinvested or saved. And we could not stop here. Much of our consumption is productive. We could not consistently exempt profits reinvested in the saloon business and tax the average citizen upon the savings which he invests in the education of his children.

. . . In short, the undivided profits of a corporation should be taxed at the rates which would apply if such profits were distributed to the shareholders. . . ."[11]

Professor Adams later changed his views concerning the correct method of achieving equality of treatment for reinvested corporate earnings and other saved income. In an address before the National Tax Association in 1923 he argued that the high level of income tax rates made it extremely desirable to exempt all saved income, personal and corporate, from the income tax.[12]

In one respect the capital gains attributable to the retention of corporate profits may be regarded as deserving a lower rate of tax than other capital gains or than most forms of ordinary personal income. Heavy income taxes have been paid by the corporation on

[11] *American Economic Review,* Vol. 8, No. 1, Supplement, March 1918, Dec. 1917, pp. 25-6.
[12] Evolution versus Revolution in Federal Tax Reform, *Proceedings, Sixteenth Annual Conference,* p. 306.

the reinvested earnings. For many stockholders the corporate rate alone is substantially higher than the rates they would pay if their share of a corporation's undistributed as well as distributed earnings were taxed as parts of their personal income. For some others, the sum of the corporate and the special capital gains taxes is larger than they would pay as individuals if their share of the corporation's total profits were included in their personal income. In short, if we regard the corporation income tax as a personal tax levied on the stockholders, rather than as an impersonal tax levied on the privilege of using the corporate form, capital gains attributable to the reinvestment of corporate profits have already been taxed through the corporate income tax.

However, as long as the corporation income tax is levied equally upon distributed and undistributed profits, the shareholder in a corporation that retains its earnings will enjoy a tax advantage over the shareholder in one that distributes its earnings, provided the former is able to obtain the equivalent of the reinvested earnings in the form of capital gains taxable at a preferential rate. Another difficulty is that not all capital gains from common stocks are attributable to reinvested corporate profits.

5 THE UNDISTRIBUTED PROFITS TAX

Congress has attempted to meet this problem at different times in one or more of three ways: (a) By ignoring the separate existence of the corporation and treating its earnings as those of the stockholders. This was done under the Civil War income tax acts, and is done at present, as noted several pages back, in the case of American shareholders of foreign personal holding companies. (b) By imposing corporation taxes designed to yield substitute revenues for the personal income taxes avoided through withholding corporate profits. The traditional corporation income tax, which involves a double tax on distributed corporate income, is regarded by some in this light. But the corporation income tax does not allow for differences in the dividend policies of corporations or in the amounts of personal income stockholders receive from other sources. (c) By imposing such severe taxes on undistributed earnings as to force their distribution — the present policy with respect to personal holding companies.

When the Senate Finance Committee first reported the bill that became the Revenue Act of 1917, it included a provision for a 15 percent tax, in addition to the regular corporate income tax, on undivided earnings exceeding 20 percent of the total net income. In the Act as finally passed, the 20 percent exemption was eliminated and the rate of additional tax was cut to 10 percent, applicable to the portion of the total net income, after federal income taxes, remaining undistributed 6 months after the end of the calendar or fiscal year, but the tax was rendered ineffective by a broad new exemption: "The tax imposed by this subdivision shall not apply to that portion of such undistributed net income which is actually invested and employed in the business, or is retained for employment in the reasonable requirements of the business, or is invested in obligations of the United States issued after September 1, 1917." The broad character of the permission to retain earnings without tax liability if such earnings are employed "in the reasonable requirements of the business" made it extremely difficult to prove tax liability; and the entire provision was repealed by the Revenue Act of 1918.

Further action in this direction was proposed in 1924, when the Senate approved the Jones amendment to the revenue bill then under consideration, providing for a schedule of tax rates on undistributed corporate earnings in addition to the ordinary corporation income taxes, but the House failed to pass the amendment. In 1927 a committee of the National Tax Association, reporting on 'Simplification of the Income Tax', declared: "One method might be to place a reasonable tax on the corporation on that portion of the income which it does not actually distribute. It is impossible to make this amount even roughly approximate the revenue which would be collected, if complete distribution were made, as the conditions vary in each and every corporation. It should therefore rather be considered as a premium tax paid by the corporation for its stockholders, in exchange for retaining the earnings in the business and thereby postponing the normal and surtax until a future day. For that purpose a tax of 10 percent on that amount of its net income which exceeds the dividends paid out in any year would be a reasonable tax.

Argument has been made that this form of tax is uneconomic, because it creates an incentive to pay out dividends instead of plowing the profits back into the business. One answer might be the question, 'Why should the Government permit corporations to accumulate partly tax-paid surplus to plow back into the business, where it insists on the full tax on surpluses of partnerships and individuals, even though they are plowed back into the business? The argument of an individual that he should receive an exemption from tax on that part of his year's earnings which goes back into his business would receive short shrift.'

In his message to Congress on March 3, 1936 President Roosevelt proposed a radical solution of the problem: the complete repeal of the corporation income, capital stock, and declared-value excess profits taxes and the substitution of graduated taxes on *undistributed* corporate profits only. The rates were to be high enough to encourage the current distribution of most corporate earnings, thereby subjecting them, when received by the shareholders, to the individual income tax rate schedule, and to compensate the Treasury for revenues lost through nondistribution. After extended committee hearings, Congress adopted the President's recommendations in part in the Revenue Act of 1936 by imposing graduated taxes on undistributed corporate earnings, but refused to remove the ordinary corporation income, capital stock, and declared-value excess profits taxes. The tax rates imposed on undistributed corporate earnings were 7 percent on the first 10 percent, and 12 percent on the next 10 percent, 17 and 22 percent respectively on each of the next two 20 percent segments of income retained, and 27 percent on the remainder. Banks, insurance and mutual investment companies, and corporations in receivership were exempted, and special relief provisions were included for corporations under contract to restrict payment of dividends or to use a stipulated portion of earnings to discharge debts, and for corporations with net incomes of less than $50,000.

The new law stimulated the distribution of dividends in 1936 and 1937, years of relatively good business and large profits. But with the recession that became evident in the second half of 1937, corporate officials increasingly demanded the repeal of the undistributed profits tax.

Certain features of the law were harsh. No allowance was made for the fact that the net income reported for any single year is essentially an estimate for which a margin of error, in the form of some retention of earnings tax-free, might well be allowed. Inadequate relief was provided for corporations that, because of deficits in their capital structures, could not pay dividends without violating state laws. The tax was hard on corporations that had incurred debts on the assumption that these could be retired out of earnings without penalty taxation. No retention of ordinary income tax-free was permitted to offset disallowed net capital losses (capital losses were deductible only to the extent of capital gains plus $2,000). Many business men objected that a varying fraction of a corporation's earnings is often not available in the form of cash, but is embodied in inventories, receivables, and the like, which cannot be paid to stockholders. But the harshest feature of all was the failure to allow generous carry-overs of losses. Without such an allowance, a corporation with alternate years of profit and loss would be unable to replenish its losses from the earnings of good years except by paying extra taxes.[13]

Corporations could avoid the surtaxes on retained earnings by paying dividends in the form of notes, bonds, and such stocks as constituted taxable income in the hands of the shareholders,[14] and some did meet the problem in this way; but many others shied away from the prospect of an endless increase in their capital securities. Beyond such specific objections as these, the managements of large widely held corporations disliked the added coercion to distribute more in dividends than they deemed wise, and the managements of smaller corporations objected to the penalty imposed on the use of a convenient and economic means of financing growth.

Despite the vigorous opposition of President Roosevelt, who, for a number of reasons, allowed the measure to become law without his signature, Congress in the Revenue Act of 1938 retained only a remnant of the tax on undistributed profits for 1938 and 1939 and provided for its complete elimination as of December 31, 1939.

As a partial offset to the repeal, Congress sought to strengthen the long existing provision (Sec. 102) for the imposition of a penalty tax upon corporations that retained earnings primarily for the purpose of enabling their stockholders to avoid individual income taxes on them. As previously noted, the older versions of this provision placed the burden of proof on the Commissioner and had never been very effective. In the Revenue Act of 1938, however, the statute was altered to shift the burden of proof to the corporation, and this change has been retained in subsequent revenue measures. Since 1939 Revenue agents have been instructed to make a definite affirmative or negative recommendation with respect to the application of

---

[13] For the history of this tax see George E. Lent, *The Impact of the Undistributed Profits Tax, 1936-1937* (Columbia University Press, 1948).

[14] In *Koshland v. Helvering*, 297 U.S. 702 (1936), the Supreme Court held that dividends paid in stock were taxable as income if they altered the proportionate interests of the shareholders, as when dividends in common stock are paid to holders of preferred stock.

Section 102 in every instance in which a corporation distributes less than 70 percent of its earnings in dividends. Corporations unable to prove, on request of the Commissioner, that the withheld current earnings have been retained for purposes other than the avoidance of surtaxes by their stockholders are subject to a surtax of 27½ percent on the first $100,000 of the undistributed net income and 38½ percent on the remainder. An appeal from the findings of the Commissioner may be made to the courts.

6 CLOSELY HELD OPERATING CORPORATIONS

This change in Section 102 of the Internal Revenue Code has doubtless been influential in restraining the more flagrant abuses of withheld corporate earnings on the part of operating companies. How effective it can be in borderline cases, where earnings are retained for mixed motives, both to avoid current personal income taxes and to expand the business, remains to be demonstrated. A group of corporations for which it seems specially applicable is that of closely held operating companies.

The tax-saving possibilities of such corporations to their shareholders resemble some of those previously possessed by personal holding companies. Even though a corporation is owned by only one individual, it escapes the statutory classification of a personal holding company if as little as 21 percent of its gross income is from the operation of a business as contrasted with returns from investments or personal services. A well-to-do individual owning and operating an incorporated business enterprise may turn over to it a portion of his income-yielding investments, including real estate, in return for some of its common stock, and have the corporation use its investment income in expanding its business. As in the case of the personal holding company, the owner would avoid current personal income taxes on the income from the transferred investments, and would substitute a contingent liability for a capital gains tax on the resulting increase in the corporation's value, if any, a tax that would be assessed only if and when he realized the gain through selling his stock.

Such a corporation can be used also to convert personal compensation into capital gains. A leading official of a major automobile manufacturing company, in an interview with the author, complained that this opportunity was robbing his company of some of its best executives. Under the 1948-49 income tax rates, an executive receiving a salary of $50,000 a year and filing a separate return with

4 exemptions, would add less than $15,000 to his income after income taxes if his employer doubled his salary to induce him to stay. But if he secured an automobile dealership, incorporated the enterprise, and gave it his full energies and talents while paying himself only a small salary, he would avoid a current individual income tax on most of the earnings attributable to his services, leaving these, after corporation income taxes, to be reinvested by his company as a part of its undistributed profits. In this way he would be converting personal compensation into potential capital gains. He could avoid current individual income taxes on the interest and profits earned by the capital he invested in the business also, leaving these current earnings to be reinvested by the corporation. He might enjoy other tax advantages by charging off as corporate expenses various outlays made on his behalf for more or less personal consumption, such as the cost of an automobile, perhaps with chauffeur, and a portion of the cost of travel and entertainment. If, after a time, he decided to sell out, the increase in the value of his holdings would be subject only to the capital gains tax, and he and his heirs would escape this tax too if his holdings were passed on to his heirs as a part of his estate.

The extent to which a closely held corporation can be used effectively to save taxes for its owners varies with the relative levels of corporation and personal income taxes, with the surtax brackets of the shareholders, with the applicability of Section 102 to the retained earnings and the extent to which it is enforced. Under the high income and excess profits taxes imposed on corporations during World War II, many business men with moderate incomes found it more economical from a tax standpoint to transform their corporations into partnerships. For many with large incomes, on the other hand, personal income tax rates have been so high in recent years that the conversion of the fruits of personal efforts and capital into unrealized capital gains through closely held corporations in the manner just described has offered a tax saving, especially in years when an excess profits tax was not in effect.

Viewed as penalties designed to discourage deliberate tax evasion, the surtax rates imposed for "improper accumulation of corporate surplus" may be too low to be fully effective. In his *Business Tax Guide for 1947*, J. K. Lasser advised his readers (p. 29): "Penalty tax rates on corporations are often considered relatively low. Sometimes, it may pay you to risk the tax. The rate is only 27½ percent on the first $100,000 of undistributed earnings. Stockholders who have incomes over $6,000 pay income taxes of over 27½ percent. Hence, they may lose nothing if they do not distribute all the earnings. *Caution:* If you distribute these dividends in the future the stockholders will have to pay the tax. But if these earnings are to be retained for long periods by the corporation, you should consider the whole problem with an eye as to how you may be benefited. Often a partial distribution is indicated."

It is probable, however, that the penalty rates themselves would be high enough to discourage most attempts to avoid taxes through retaining corporate earnings if they were reasonably certain to be imposed. The real difficulty is that the wide range of acknowledged legitimate reasons for retaining earnings not only protects corporations clearly motivated by business needs or contractual agreements, but makes the application of the tax to others highly uncertain, and hence invites attempts at avoidance.

7 DISTRIBUTING CORPORATE EARNINGS BY REDEEMING SECURITIES
If the organizers of a closely held corporation arrange to take the company's notes or bonds *pro rata* in exchange for a part of their capital contributions, they may subsequently receive distributions of its earnings in the form of a return of their capital through partial or complete redemption of the obligations. If the amount of earnings and of dividends distributed were the same, the latter would be taxable as ordinary income in the hands of the recipients; when received in redemption of bonds, the distributions are not taxable income.

The same principle was formerly applied also to preferred and common stocks. Instead of distributing taxable dividends, some corporations used equivalent amounts of earnings to make *pro rata* redemptions of their preferred stocks or *pro rata* purchases of common stock from their own stockholders. By an amendment to the Internal Revenue Code, Section 115 (g), Congress attempted to stop this form of tax avoidance, providing that when a corporation redeems its stock in such a manner as to make the redemption essentially equivalent to a taxable dividend, the distribution shall be treated as a dividend to the extent that it represents a distribution of earnings or profits.

Some corporations got around this provision by having a subsidiary buy a portion of their outstanding capital stock from their stockholders.[15] If the price paid was no more than the stockholder's
_____
[15] A practice that was held outside the scope of Section 115 (g) in *Commissioner v. Wanamaker* (178 Fed. (2d) 10).

cost, he did not report any taxable income from the transaction; if it was more, he reported a capital gain equal to the difference. Meanwhile, if the redemptions were *pro rata,* he retained as large a proportional interest in the enterprise as before. The net effect was a tax free distribution of earnings or the partial conversion of what would ordinarily be dividend income into capital gains.

In the Revenue Act of 1950 Congress amended Section 115 (g) to make it cover the indirect redemption of shares in a parent company through purchases by its subsidiary, but the Senate refused to accept a further extension proposed by the House to have the Section cover cases in which both the issuing corporation and the acquiring corporation, though not related as parent and subsidiary, are controlled directly or indirectly by the same interests.

8 COLLAPSIBLE CORPORATIONS

A device that not only transforms corporate profits and personal compensation into capital gains but also avoids the corporation income tax and all danger of penalty for "improper accumulation of surplus" is the collapsible or so-called Hollywood corporation. Section 115(c) of the Internal Revenue Code provides that if a corporation is liquidated completely through the distribution of its cash and its assets in kind, the latter are to be valued at the fair market value as of the date of liquidation, and the total amounts received by the stockholders are to be treated as full payment in exchange for the stock of the corporation. In consequence, for a person who has held his shares more than 6 months, any gain resulting from the liquidation qualifies as a long term capital gain under the provisions of Section 117(a) (4). Hence, whatever the source of the increase in value of the corporation's assets during its lifetime, the entire increase is transformed into a capital gain in the hands of the shareholders. And by liquidating the corporation soon after it has developed its assets to a point where they are about to yield large revenues, the owners will avoid the corporation income tax on the latter.

The commonest form of this tax-saving device is one that has been used extensively in the motion picture industry by independent producers, actors, story writers, directors, and others. While the procedure varies in detail, its general character is as follows: The principal interested parties in a contemplated film create a corporation with nominal capital, usually about $2,000. They subscribe to the stock in proportions previously agreed upon for the division of the profits. The picture may take from 6 months to a year to produce, and its cost may exceed a million dollars. The independent producer will frequently provide for about 40 percent of the total cost by entering into an agreement with one of the larger producing and distributing companies for both production and distribution. About half of the cost will be borrowed from a bank, and the remaining 10 percent provided by the independent producer in the form of his services.

As soon as the picture has been completed, and usually before its release, the producing company is dissolved and liquidated. At that time its principal asset is the completed picture, which may yield an income for some years. Each stockholder receives an undivided interest in the film, after allowance for prior claims, equal to the percentage of outstanding stock he had owned. Stockholders will value the film on their books at an amount equal to its total estimated earnings, minus indebtedness and prior charges against profits, including the estimated future distribution costs. They will report for income tax purposes as a long term capital gain the entire difference between this value and the nominal original cost of the stock, paying a 25 percent tax as a maximum on the difference. No further taxes, as a rule, will be paid by the former stockholders on their receipts from the production because these serve merely to amortize the value they had placed on the assets received in liquidation. If revenues from the distribution of the picture are found to have been overestimated, the stockholders will report the difference as an ordinary loss; if underestimated, as ordinary income. The Bureau of Internal Revenue has attacked the validity of these arrangements in some cases on the ground that they are merely subterfuges for avoiding ordinary income tax rates on salaries and profits, but no attack has been sustained on the broad principle that stockholders may transform their potential corporate and individual income into capital gains by dissolving a corporation at an opportune time.

A similar device is common in the building and construction industry. A special corporation is organized for each construction project and is liquidated upon completion of the project but before the buildings are sold. In the hands of the corporation or in those of individuals operating in their own names, the assets of the corporation would constitute "property of a kind which would properly be included in the inventory of the taxpayer if on hand at the close of the taxable year, or property held by the taxpayer primarily for

sale to customers in the ordinary course of his trade or business".
As such they would not qualify as capital assets under Section 117
of the Internal Revenue Code. The difference between the amount
received for the units comprising the construction project and the
cost of construction, minus expenses, would be taxable as ordinary
income if the corporation itself sold the units, and dividends distributed from these earnings would be taxable as ordinary income in
the hands of the stockholders. Dissolving the corporation as soon as
construction is completed or 6 months after the stock was issued,
whichever date is later, eliminates these taxes. The stockholders
report as a long term capital gain the difference between the market
value of the assets they receive and the cost basis of their stock. As
they sell the assets, they treat the proceeds as amortization of the
gain and cost they had previously reported, except that differences
between the estimated value and the actual receipts are reported as
ordinary gains or losses.

Taxes may similarly be saved by liquidating an old corporation
and distributing its assets in kind. For example, the owners of a
closely held corporation possessing inventories that can be sold at
an abnormally large profit liquidate it. The stockholders will then be
subject only to a capital gains tax on the difference between the current market value of the assets they receive and the cost of their
stockholdings; and they may continue the business as a partnership.
Or, if a closely held corporation owns valuable patents or leaseholds
it had acquired at a relatively low cost, and for which, therefore, its
allowance for depreciation or amortization is small as compared
with the income, a substantial tax saving can be accomplished by
liquidating it. The stockholders would acquire the patents or leaseholds at their current high market value, pay the 25 percent capital
gains tax, and transfer the assets at current value to a partnership
organized for the purpose of carrying on the business. In this way,
the partnership will acquire the patents or leaseholds at a value permitting a larger allowance for depreciation or amortization. The
bigger deduction may result in a net over-all tax saving for the
owners.

In the Revenue Act of 1950 Congress made a partial attack upon
the problem of tax avoidance through collapsible corporations by
enacting Section 117 (m): the gain realized from the sale or exchange (whether in liquidation or otherwise) of stock in a collapsible
corporation is to be treated as ordinary income for stockholders who,
with their close relatives, own 10 percent or more of the corpora-

tion's stock, if the gain realized during the year is more than 70 percent attributable to property produced by the corporation, and the gain is realized within 3 years following the completion of the manufacture, construction, or production of the property. A collapsible corporation is defined as one formed or availed of principally with a view to (a) the sale or exchange of stock by its shareholders or a distribution to its shareholders before the realization of a substantial part of the net income to be derived from the property produced or stock held, and (b) the realization by the shareholders of gain attributable to such property.

Other opportunities for tax avoidance through corporate liquidations could be reduced if the statute were modified to provide that the basis of property received by the shareholder in exchange for his stock upon the complete liquidation of a corporation that distributes its assets in kind shall be the same as the shareholder's basis for the stock. The effect of such a rule would be to tax the shareholder, when he sells the property, upon any appreciation in its value. If the assets he receives are capital assets in his hands, the gain would be treated as a capital gain; otherwise, as ordinary income. Another possibility is to amend the law to specify that a corporation that completely liquidates and distributes its assets in kind realizes taxable income or deductible loss in the amount of the difference between its cost or other basis and the fair market value of its assets at the time of the distribution. A more extreme possibility is to treat the excess of the value of the assets received by the stockholder over his cost as an ordinary dividend.

9 PARTNERSHIP LIQUIDATIONS

Selling an interest in a partnership too may offer an opportunity to avoid taxes. If the underlying assets contain substantial unrealized ordinary income, perhaps in the form of appreciated inventories, the withdrawing partner can treat his profit as a capital gain if he sells his interest as a whole. On the other hand, if the partnership's assets are worth less than they cost, liquidation of the assets by the partnership will establish a loss that is fully deductible from the net incomes of the partners from other sources.

10 STOCK PURCHASE OPTIONS AS PERSONAL COMPENSATION

Many corporations, including some very large ones with widely distributed ownership, have succeeded in compensating their executives partly through capital gains arising from stock purchase options granted them. The options are commonly contracts permitting the

recipient to purchase from the corporation, or from certain designated stockholders, stated amounts of the common stock during a
stipulated period of years at a price below, equal to, or slightly above
the market price at the time the option is granted. In this way the
recipients are enabled to benefit from increases in the market value
of shares without prior capital investment, and without subjecting
the gain, it has usually been hoped, to ordinary income tax rates, but
rather to the capital gains tax rates.

D. F. Zanuck, President of the Twentieth Century-Fox Film Corporation, received an option in 1940 good for 12 years to buy up to
100,000 shares of common stock from the corporation at $13 a
share.[16] The closing price of this stock on the New York Stock
Exchange at the end of June 1946 was just over $55 a share. The
aggregate market value on that date of the 100,000 shares optioned
to Mr. Zanuck was more than $4,200,000 greater than the amount
Mr. Zanuck was required to pay for this stock, whenever he chose to
take it up, under his option. Similarly, in May 1944 Harry F. Sinclair,
President of the Sinclair Oil Corporation, received a 3-year option
from the corporation to buy 150,000 shares of its stock at $13.25 a
share, about 50 cents above the market price. *Time* commented as
follows (May 29, 1944, p. 79): "Wall Streeters viewed Sinco's latest
fast financial footwork as a slick scheme to get a big raise in salary,
while avoiding the enormous top-bracket taxes. By the stock deal he
can increase his long term capital gains, which are taxable at only 25
percent. . . .

Many a solemn proponent of the free enterprise system, knowing
how difficult it is to build up an adequate capital position for executives, in order to make good corporate management worthwhile,
pondered and argued with the question: How can U. S. business pay
its top men the salaries they are really worth? But while slow-moving conservatives pondered, fast-moving Harry Sinclair might well
smile."

The decision of the Supreme Court in *Commissioner v. Smith,*
decided February 26, 1945 (324 U. S. 177), greatly circumscribed
the possibilities of using stock options to transmute personal compensation into capital gains. The Court held that when a stock option
is granted as compensation for services, its mere exercise when the
market price is higher than the option price gives rise to ordinary
taxable income equal to the difference, even if the market price was
only equal to or even below the option price when the option was

[16] Standard and Poor's Corporation, *The Outlook,* Feb. 19, 1945, p. 920.

granted. The income is recognized upon the exercise of the option even though the recipient does not actually realize a profit by selling the stock. The Court declared that in some circumstances the option itself, unexercised, might be found to constitute compensation for services rendered.

The Smith decision dealt with a stock option clearly granted as compensation for services. In several cases the lower courts had previously ruled that various stock options given employees were *not* intended to constitute additional compensation.[17] The gains realized in connection with them qualified as long term capital gains if the stock had been owned the required period. In these decisions the courts drew a distinction between stock options granted as compensation for services and those granted to employees "in order to benefit the company by making the employees more interested in the welfare of the company . . ." (*Charles E. Adams v. Commissioner*). The Treasury Department interpreted the Smith decision as overruling this distinction, and on April 12, 1946 the Bureau of Internal Revenue issued an amended regulation (T. D. 5507), providing that all capital stock obtained by employees through stock options granted after February 25, 1945 be regarded as compensation for services in the year the stock is received in the amount the fair market value exceeds the option price.

Congress apparently decided that this policy was too stringent, for in the Revenue Act of 1950, Section 218, the Internal Revenue Code was amended to provide for nonrecognition of income from the grant or exercise of certain kinds of employee stock options, called "restricted stock options," and for capital gains tax treatment of profits resulting from the sale of stock acquired under them; and the new rules were made retroactive to options granted, modified, extended, or renewed after February 25, 1945 and exercised after December 31, 1949.

Roughly, a restricted stock option is defined as an option granted by an employer corporation or its subsidiary or parent corporation to an employee in connection with his employment to buy stock in any of such corporations, provided the option price is at least 85 percent of the fair market value of the stock when the option is granted, the option is not transferable except at death, and the employee receiving the option does not at that time own more than 10 percent of the combined voting power of all classes of stock of the

[17] *Delbert B. Geeseman*, 38 B. T. A. 258, *Herbert H. Springford*, 41 B. T. A. 1,001, *Gordon M. Evans*, 38 B. T. A. 1,406.

corporation, including the holdings of close relatives and his proportionate share of stock owned by a partnership, estate, trust, or
corporation in which he has an interest.

If the option price is 95 percent or more of the fair market value
of the stock when the option is granted, the entire profit realized on
the sale of the stock is taxed as a capital gain, provided certain other
requirements are met. If the option price is less than 95 percent but
85 percent or more of the fair market value of the stock when the
option is granted, the difference between the option price and the fair
market value when the option is granted or when the stock is disposed
of, whichever is lower, is taxed as ordinary income when the stock
is disposed of, and the balance is taxed as a capital gain. To qualify
for such treatment, the stock must not be sold within 2 years of the
grant of the option or within 6 months of the purchase of stock under
the option, and the holder of the option must exercise it while an
employee, or within 3 months after he ceases to be an employee, of
the granting corporation or its parent or subsidiary.

Other devices have been used to afford the possibility of capital
gains as a means to attract, stimulate, and reward personal talent and
effort. Stock has been sold to valued employees in exchange for their
promissory notes, the notes containing a clause limiting the recourse
of the creditor to the seizure of the stock itself in the event of non-
payment. Like the stock option, this device puts the employee in a
position to benefit from an enhancement in the value of the stock
without prior capital investment and without risk. Another expedient
was employed by Paramount Pictures, Inc., which privately sold
$2,000,000 of 2¾ percent convertible debenture notes to its presi-
dent, Barney Balaban, in December 1944. The notes were convertible at the rate of $500,000 a year into common stock of the
corporation at $25 a share. The board of directors, in a letter to the
stockholders dated June 9, 1944, clearly stated that the purpose of
the arrangement was to give Mr. Balaban an adequate incentive to
remain with the enterprise: "Your directors have been trying for the
past few years to find a way to give Mr. Balaban a strong incentive
to remain as President of the Company for many years to come. They
offered Mr. Balaban options on common stock of the Company, but
Mr. Balaban was personally opposed to straight options; he felt that
he should give something to the Company therefor, above and beyond
serving it.

After long and serious study, your directors finally proposed to
Mr. Balaban that he purchase a $2,000,000 convertible note of your

Company on the terms set forth in the Proxy Statement. In this way, Mr. Balaban would be tied to the Company with a $2,000,000 investment on which he would make no profit unless your Company's stock rose above the conversion price and unless he remained with the Company long enough to exercise the options.

While your Company does not need to borrow $2,000,000 from Mr. Balaban this sale of the note is considered more advantageous to the Company than the granting of straight options, for it immediately provides the Company with $2,000,000 in cash out of which it may purchase Paramount stock in the open market. *To the extent of such purchases dilution of your Company's stock will be prevented."*

The market price of the stock rose above $80 a share in the spring of 1946, before the shares were split up 2 for 1. The convertible privilege of Mr. Balaban's debentures contained a clause adjusting the conversion price to offset the effects of such increases in the number of shares.

In view of the Smith decision and subsequent rulings of the Bureau of Internal Revenue, this and similar devices may be challenged in the courts. But other means of converting personal compensation into capital gains have received express statutory authority in connection with profit-sharing, stock-bonus, and pension plans, discussed in the next section.

11 DEFERRED COMPENSATION, PENSION, STOCK-BONUS, AND PROFIT-SHARING PLANS

Liberal retirement allowances to attract, retain, and compensate leading salaried officials of business corporations have expanded rapidly in recent years. An employer's current contributions to an employee's future retirement or separation benefits are not currently taxable as part of the latter's income, even if nonforfeitable, when made under a formal pension, profit-sharing, or stock bonus plan conforming to statutory requirements. The employee becomes taxable on his deferred compensation and the accumulated income on it only when and as they are received. Hence such arrangements usually reduce the individual income taxes of the recipients by deferring a portion of their effective compensation from the years it is earned and in which it would be taxed at higher bracket rates to years in which their other income and effective tax rates will presumably be less. Moreover, if the benefits are paid in a lump sum after separation from service, they are taxed as a long term capital gain.

On the other hand, the employer may deduct currently from his taxable income the full actuarial cost or other definite and reasonable appropriations for valid pension, profit-sharing, and stock bonus plans established for the exclusive benefit of employees and their beneficiaries. The trusts created under such plans are also tax exempt. This favorable tax treatment became more pronounced under the high corporate and personal income tax rates of the war and post-war periods. Consequently, the movement toward a wider adoption of corporate pension plans, which owed much to an increasing sense of responsibility on the part of corporations for their employees generally, as well as to motives cited above, was greatly stimulated.[18]

To prevent the tax advantages of these plans from being exploited primarily for the benefit of a few managerial employees or the stockholders, and to prevent corporations from using the plans to reduce corporate taxes unduly in years of large earnings through extraordinary deductions for this purpose, Congress enacted various restrictions, which it greatly altered and elaborated in the Revenue Act of 1942 (Internal Revenue Code, Secs. 23 and 165), and the Bureau of Internal Revenue has since issued an increasing number of regulations (R 111). In general, plans that qualify under the Act for current deductibility of the employer's contribution, tax-exemption of the trust set up for employee benefits, and deferment of the employee's tax liability on the employer's contribution on his behalf must be formal and definite, made known to employees, cover a large proportion of employees, be nondiscriminatory and nondiscretionary, and render impossible the diversion of the funds for any purpose except the exclusive benefit of the employees and their beneficiaries.

An employer's contributions to employees under a plan that does not conform to the requirements of Section 165 must be included in his gross income for the year in which the contributions are made if the employees' beneficial interest in them is nonforfeitable.

Presumably to avoid the restrictions governing the preferential tax status of qualified plans, several large corporations have recently entered into individual employment contracts with their chief officials calling for stated retirement allowances, stock bonuses, or profit-sharing rights. If the employee's benefits under these contracts are specifically subject to significant contingencies, such as the completion of a minimum term of future employment, or if they

[18] The Bureau of Internal Revenue found in a survey that of more than 9,000 pension, deferred profit-sharing, and stock bonus plans adopted by American business enterprises by August 31, 1946, covering more than 3.5 million employees, only 659 had been established before 1940.

become void if he enters the employ of a competitor, the corporation's contributions to his pension reserves or other deferred benefits presumably cannot be taxed as his current income. He acquires a nonforfeitable right to the contractual benefits only after conforming to the prescribed conditions.

Substantial retirement allowances have been adopted for leading corporate officials in many supplementary pension plans or individual employment contracts since 1944, and in many instances no contribution is required from the employee. The main provisions of some of these are to be found in data supplied to the SEC. Under a supplemental noncontributory retirement plan adopted in 1947 by a large can manufacturing enterprise, the three highest paid executives are entitled upon retirement to noncontributory annuities of $69,467, $48,344, and $36,139 respectively, in addition to pensions arising from the company's general pension plan to which employees contribute a part of the cost. The values of these annuities at age 65 are approximately $750,000, $500,000, and $300,000 respectively. A well-known producer of proprietary medicines and packaged foods has an employment contract with its leading official by which it agrees to pay him upon the termination of his employment, or to his heirs, $15,000 a year for as many years as the official shall have been employed after May 1, 1935. If he should continue with the company in his present capacity until he is 65 he will have accumulated the right to annual payments of $15,000 for 26 years, in addition to his rights under the company's general retirement plan. The noncontributory pension plan of an important steel producer provides annual retirement benefits ranging from $32,892 to $74,453 for 9 of the leading officials. Another steel company has entered into an employment contract with its chief executive officer calling for a life annuity, after 6 years of employment, when the official will be 61 years old, of $25,000, with payment for 8 years certain. The value of such an annuity will then be approximately $425,000. A major rubber producer has an employment contract with its president stipulating that it will pay deferred contingent compensation in annual instalments for 14 years unless he engages in a competing business within 3 years after he leaves it. A New York department store has similar contracts with 9 of its executives calling for deferred contingent compensation for 15 years after they leave it.

In the case of qualified pension, profit-sharing, and stock bonus plans ordinary income is converted into formal capital gains when the benefits are paid in a lump sum after separation from service

[Sec. 165, (b)]. Some plans specify the right to a lump sum settlement. Even when they do not, a corporation that carries its own pension reserves may be quite willing to commute the right into a capital sum at the annuitant's request. Some annuitants might well desire to sell their rights, particularly if they terminate at death, in order to add to their estates, or to obtain the advantage of the lower capital gains tax rate and invest the remaining proceeds in tax-exempt securities. Similarly, when an accumulation of stock bonuses is paid to a retiring employee, it is taxed as a capital gain though it represents compensation for personal services. Whether lump sum settlements of retirement allowances under nonqualified plans and individual employment contracts will also be accorded capital gains tax treatment under current law has yet to be determined.

In effect, the deferred compensation arrangements that qualify under the statute, and perhaps some that do not, permit an employee to accumulate savings and build up an estate free from the individual income tax during the period of accumulation. If, upon separation from service, he takes all his benefits in a lump sum, no tax is levied on the part that represents his own direct contributions, and only the preferential capital gains tax rate is applied on the remainder. If he takes his accumulations in the form of annual payments, no tax is levied on their capitalized value, even though the payments are scheduled to continue long after his death and are equal in value to a large capital sum, though ordinary income tax rates will apply to the part of the annual benefits that exceeds the allocated amount of his own direct contribution.

While qualified pension, profit-sharing, and stock bonus plans entail preferential tax treatment for some kinds of personal compensation, Congress has decided that it is good public policy to encourage retirement allowances and profit-sharing in this way.[19] Besides supplementing the Federal Social Security System for ordinary employees, they enable corporations and their executives to offset in some measure the effects of heavy personal income taxes in preventing highly-paid officials from accumulating an estate sufficient to provide income in retirement comparable with their incomes during their working lives; salaried positions are thereby made more attractive. The principle of retirement allowances as such is less commonly criticized than the absence of similar preferential tax treatment for the savings of professional men, partners, and other individuals who

[19] Report of Ways and Means Sub-Committee, 75th Cong., 3d Sess., Jan. 14, 1938, p. 48.

must accumulate resources for their old age outside of qualified pension systems.[20]

12 OTHER RIGHTS TO FUTURE INCOME

The whole question of when rights to future income should be deemed to constitute capital assets for tax purposes raises difficult practical problems. In some instances taxpayers can convert into capital gains their rights to future ordinary income from patents, copyrights, oil and gas leaseholds, annuity and insurance contracts, and life interests in trust estates. In other instances the net gains from sales of rights to future income have been held to constitute ordinary income.

From an economic standpoint it is impossible to draw a clear line between a capital asset and rights to future income precisely because the value of a capital asset is derived from and consists of the value of the future incomes that are expected from it. On the other hand, when the future incomes are fairly definite in amount, the sale may represent, in effect, only an advance collection of ordinary income. If the net proceeds are spent on consumption, the seller derives a tax advantage if they are taxed as capital gains. If they are reinvested, however, this advantage may be reduced or more than offset by the additional taxes at ordinary rates on the income derived from the reinvested funds.

When rights to receive rents or dividends are sold, the proceeds are usually taxed as ordinary income. When the future payments consist in large part of a return of capital, as in the case of insurance and annuity contracts, the net proceeds are usually taxed as capital gains. When the rights are somewhat indefinite and are deemed not to constitute 'property held primarily for sale to customers in the ordinary course of trade or business', they are frequently regarded as capital assets whose sale gives rise to capital gain or loss. Before 1950 a nonprofessional author such as General Eisenhower could obtain capital gains tax treatment for the net proceeds from his book by selling exclusive rights to it. He did not need to receive the purchase price in a lump sum. The sales contract could provide that the price be paid in installments calculated in the same manner as royalties. The taxpayer then had the additional advantage of being able to

[20] See John R. Nicholson, Pensions for Partners: Tax Laws Are Unfair to Lawyers and Firms, *American Bar Association Journal,* April 1947; Harry J. Rudick, More About Pensions for Partners, *ibid.,* Oct. 1947; Harry Silverstein, A New Tax Proposal, *American Mercury,* March 1947.

report the gains over a series of years. The price itself did not need to be a fixed number of dollars. A publisher could contract to pay the author a nominal sum at the time of the sale of the exclusive publishing rights, plus a stated percentage of the receipts from the sales of the book. The same principle may still be applied in connection with the sale of exclusive rights under a patent. Professional authors and inventors, however, were and are still regarded as earning ordinary income through such sales because the property is said to be held by the taxpayer for sale in the ordinary course of his trade or business. By section 210 of the Revenue Act of 1950, amateur authors and artists but not amateur inventors were put in the same tax position as professionals: their gains from sales of the products of their personal efforts were made taxable as ordinary income.

In some circumstances the courts have decided that the net proceeds from the sale of other rights to future income must be taxed as ordinary income. A lump sum payment to a retiring partner who was entitled to a share of future fees (90F. (2d) 590) and the sum paid for a promise not to compete (82F. (2d) 268) have been held to be ordinary income. Royalties under an oil and gas lease are ordinary income, but the unlimited conveyance for cash of a lessor's reserved royalties under an oil and gas lease may be treated as a sale of a capital asset (G. C. M. 12118). A woman who sold her life interest in a trust estate was held to have incurred a deductible capital loss when the sales price was less than the value of her interest on the date of the decedent's death (157F. (2d) 235).

Widely reported in the press during the summer and fall of 1948 were the attempts of the owners of the Amos 'n Andy and Jack Benny radio shows to transform into capital gains the ordinary income they were receiving from them. The owners of the Amos 'n Andy program were reported to have sold their rights to the show to the Columbia Broadcasting System for a capital sum. The owners of the Jack Benny show did likewise, but the Bureau of Internal Revenue apparently decided to distinguish the latter case from the former on the ground that new actors could be substituted in the former program without material damage, giving it the character of a capital asset, whereas the personal services and reputation of Mr. Benny and his staff were decisive elements in the value of the latter program. These transactions aroused so many inquiries that the Commissioner of Internal Revenue was moved to issue a statement (S 952, Jan. 3, 1949): "The tax effect of any business transaction is determined by its realities.

Accordingly, proposals of radio artists and others to obtain compensation for personal services under the guise of sales of property cannot be regarded as coming within the capital gains provisions of the Internal Revenue Code. Such compensation is taxable at ordinary income tax rates."

13 CONVERTING INTEREST INTO CAPITAL GAINS

Purchasing obligations at a discount

Interest income is frequently transformed into a capital gain for tax purposes, although to a much lesser extent than appears to be technically possible under the law. The simplest case is the purchase of corporation bonds at a discount. Bonds that bear a lower contractual rate of interest than the effective yield the market demands naturally sell at a discount. The discount, supplementing the contractual interest payments, must be sufficient to raise the effective rate of return on the amount actually invested to the going market rate. But when the full principal amount is paid off at maturity or at an earlier call date, the investor is permitted to treat the difference between his cost and the amount received upon redemption as a capital gain.[21] From an economic standpoint, however, this so-called capital gain is a part of the true interest income. It does not arise because of a change in interest rates or credit standing, but merely because a part of the interest return is not expressly so designated and is not received until the obligation matures.

Utilizing this legal situation, a lender can obtain a direct tax advantage at no cost to the borrower by arranging to have the loan take the form of the purchase of the borrower's low interest obligations at a substantial discount. Thus, a lender who purchased a 10-year 2 percent note at a discount of 19.95 percent would really be getting an effective interest yield of 4.5 percent annually. For income tax purposes, however, nearly half of his true interest return would take the form of a capital gain upon maturity (the current interest payments would amount to approximately 2.5 percent on his actual investment). Similarly, a 20-year mortgage obligation bearing a nominal rate of interest of 2 percent would yield 4.5 percent if purchased at 67.77 cents on the dollar, but ordinary income taxes

[21] On the other hand, he is permitted to amortize a bond premium. On fully tax-exempt bonds, Section 125 requires purchasers to amortize premiums during the life of the bond; on partly tax-exempt bonds, only corporations are required to do so; and on fully taxable bonds, both individuals and corporate purchasers may choose whether or not to amortize.

would be assessed only on the current interest receipts, while the capital gains rate would be applied to the $32.23 of postponed interest payments received at maturity on each $100 of nominal principal. The tax advantage of the lender is not accompanied by a corresponding disadvantage to the borrower because the discount, amortized over the life of the obligation, is no less deductible for tax purposes than direct interest expense. And the borrower too may gain if competition permits him to force the lender to share his tax advantage in the form of a lower effective interest charge.

Raising the selling price in lieu of interest

J. K. Lasser, in his widely used guide to taxpayers, advises: "If you sell a long term asset at a profit and payment is to be made in instalments over a period of years, it may be to your advantage if the sales contract did not provide for interest on the subsequent payments, and in lieu thereof, the sales price was increased."[22] In *Commissioner v. Caulkins* the Sixth Circuit Court of Appeals went so far as to hold that a man who made 10 annual payments of $1,512 each for the purchase of an "accumulative investment certificate," entitling him to $20,000 at the end of the 10 years, was subject to capital gains rather than ordinary income taxes on the amount of the increment he received above cost, though the increment was identical in amount with interest at 5 percent compounded annually.[23]

Switching out of securities with high book yields

When market rates of interest fall, owners of government and other bonds who amortize premiums and discounts in reporting their interest can reduce their taxable interest by selling the bonds and immediately reinvesting most of the proceeds in the same or similar bonds at the higher market prices. Their profits will be bonafide long term capital gains and will be so taxed if the bonds have been held the required interval (more than 6 months at present). The newly purchased bonds will yield substantially the same gross income in dollars as the bonds sold (ignoring commissions), but more of this income will be charged off as a return of capital because of the higher prices paid, and hence will not be taxed. In consequence, a part of the former taxable interest income will have been converted into capital gains. This example differs from the preceding in that the capital gains are genuine, though it can be contended in some cases that they represent mainly the rewards of professional skill.

[22] *Your Income Tax* (1945 ed.), p. 122.
[23] July 24, 1944, 114 Fed. (2d) 482.

Banks and similar institutions have been moved by tax considerations to realize such capital gains on a large scale in recent years, though the possibility of their doing so was created by the marked and nearly continuous decline in interest rates. In *Taxes — The Tax Magazine,* March 1946, S. S. Lawrence, advised bankers: "Sell taxable government bonds held over six months which show a profit after amortization. Buy back the same issues immediately. Any dealer will put through this trade at a cost of not more than 1/32. A tax of twenty-five per cent is paid and the bonds are back on your books at the new higher cost. The ordinary income is thereafter reduced because the yield is lower.

For instance, if a bond bought a year ago at a yield of 1.50 percent is sold and repurchased at a yield of 1.30 percent, the taxable ordinary income hereafter is only $13.00 annually instead of $15.00. If the bond has five more years to go, the ordinary income will be $10.00 less than if it had not been rolled over. This $10.00 is not lost because it has been taken out at the time the bond was sold and repurchased, but is the profit on the sale and subject to a twenty-five percent tax rate rather than the higher rate applicable to current income.

No gross income is lost except the broker's commission of 31¼¢ or less per bond. The saving is the differential between the ordinary rate and the long term capital gain rate, less 31¼¢. On the basis of thirty-five percent average tax on ordinary income for the next few years and twenty-five percent on long term gains, the saving effected in this case would be $1.00 less 31¼¢ or 68¾¢ per bond. On $100,-000 par value of bonds, the saving or, as we could describe it, the extra tax-free income, would be $68.75; on ten million dollars, $6,875.00.

. . . The writer takes a keen pleasure in converting income taxable at thirty-eight percent (fifty-three percent for Class II banks) into the same amount of income taxable at twenty-five percent. . . ."

14 RENTS

The chief method of converting current rental payments into capital gains appears to be that of making excessive deductions for depreciation from the gross income of apartment houses, office buildings, hotels, and similar structures. The Bureau of Internal Revenue allows the owners of such buildings to depreciate them at the rate of 2-3 percent a year. This often causes the owner's cost basis to decline more rapidly than the economic life or market value of the property.

When the owner sells, the difference between his reduced cost basis and the sales price is taxed as a capital gain. The part of the gross rental income that had been unnecessarily treated as an allowance for depreciation is in this way converted into a capital gain. This frequent possibility, together with the convenience of being able to reduce their annual taxable incomes by a non-cash expense (depreciation), has made the ownership of income-producing improved real estate attractive to many wealthy investors. The purchaser of a building is not required to adopt the depreciated basis of the seller as the basis for his depreciation allowances. A building that has been depreciated from $200,000 to $50,000 in the hands of one owner may acquire a basis of $150,000 in the hands of the purchaser.

In the oil and gas industry, the cash sales of rights to future leasal incomes of oil are converting ordinary income into profits taxable at capital gains rates. A corporation owning a leasehold in oil and gas lands on which producing wells have just been completed estimates the gross income for the next 12 months after deduction of gross production and severance taxes and without regard to development and operating expenses. The corporation then sells to a bank, at a discount representing interest, an in-oil payment right (a right to receipts of oil) for the expected gross income. On the ground that the in-oil payment right constitutes real property held more than 6 months and used in its trade or business, the corporation reports the gain on the sale as one taxable at a maximum rate of 25 percent under Section 117(j). If it had sold the oil or gas as it was produced, its receipts, minus expenses and other allowable deductions, would have been taxable as ordinary income.

15 CONVERTING CAPITAL LOSSES INTO ORDINARY LOSSES

Since 1942 the Internal Revenue Code has provided that depreciable property and real property used in trade or business are not capital assets, but gains on them shall nevertheless be treated as long term capital gains if the assets have been held more than 6 months, while losses on them shall be treated as ordinary losses.[24] These provisions have been used, especially in years of exceptionally high corporate taxes, to shift to the government large real estate losses not incidental to ordinary business operations or not due to wartime or other involuntary conversions. A department store, for example, whose land

[24] Sections 117(a)(1) and (j). The net loss or gain reported must cover the net results of transactions in these assets and of involuntary conversions of such property as well as transactions in long term capital assets.

and buildings had depreciated $5,000,000 over many years, may deduct the entire amount from the income of the year the loss is technically realized. If that year happens to be a year like 1944, when corporation income and excess profits taxes were high and corporate incomes large, the corporation might easily save in taxes nearly the entire amount of its reported loss. At the same time, by leasing back the property from the purchaser as a part of the selling arrangement, it may retain the use of the property. Numerous transactions of this type have been reported to the Bureau of Internal Revenue in recent years.

16 DEVICES TO POSTPONE OR AVOID TECHNICAL REALIZATION OF CAPITAL GAINS

Since a capital gain is not taxable as such until it is realized in a technical legal sense by sale or taxable exchange, investors and their lawyers have sought various devices to avoid technical realization while nevertheless achieving its approximate equivalent. The whole complex body of law relating to corporate reorganizations and to other tax-free versus taxable exchanges of property has largely grown out of the desire of Congress to permit the postponement of tax liability income in various cases where the continuity of ownership is essentially uninterrupted, and out of legislative action and court decisions restricting the types of transaction in which this is possible.

Tax-free exchanges of property are of two kinds: those in which the courts have held the investor obtains no separable profit or other income; and those Congress has expressly declared to be tax-free. In theory a tax-free exchange of either kind merely postpones recognition of the gain for tax purposes. The basis of the cost on which the investor will calculate his gain upon ultimate sale is not changed. As noted in Chapter 2, Congress was moved to provide for the nonrecognition of a taxable gain or loss in connection with certain types of exchange by the desire to avoid obstructing various common transactions in capital assets, notably between corporations and between corporations and their stockholders.

When mere postponement of tax liability is the sole result, no significant tax avoidance takes place. A taxpayer with such an unrealized capital gain may of course choose to realize it in a year when he suffers an offsetting capital loss, and in this way escape the tax on it entirely. As long as the offsetting is real, however, it only extends the opportunities already offered in the tax system for averaging capital gains and losses over a period longer than a year, an extension that has much to commend it from an equitable standpoint. But in many other cases the real effect of tax-free exchanges is to eliminate the taxation of capital gains altogether. The investor is enabled without tax payment to convert his gains into property more suitable for leaving to his heirs. With his death the contingent tax liability on his capital gains is eliminated. His heirs do not inherit the cost basis of his holdings, but place them on their books at their values on the date of his death. If unrealized capital gains embodied in property transferred at death were taxable as such, the ultimate tax avoidance now possible by postponing technical realization of capital gains would be largely eliminated.

A common example of tax avoidance of this kind is a corporate reorganization whereby the owners of a smaller or more localized or otherwise more specialized enterprise sell it at a profit to a large, more diversified corporation in exchange for some of the latter's common stock. By so doing, they achieve the same result as if they had sold their holdings for cash and invested the money in the stock of the larger corporation, except that a capital gains tax would be payable in the latter case and is not payable in the former. The stock they acquire may be highly marketable, may constitute excellent security for loans, and may enable them to transmit wealth to their heirs in a form they deem more desirable than their preceding hold-ings or even cash itself. Perhaps the most extreme example would be the exchange of ownership in a mercantile or industrial enterprise at a profit for shares of stock in an investment trust company. The proceeds would perhaps be in precisely the form in which the sellers would have invested the fruits of a cash sale, yet no taxable gain or loss would presumably be recognized unless and until they sold the stock received.

As implied in the preceding paragraph, a man with a very large unrealized capital gain may sometimes enjoy its substance without incurring a tax liability on it by borrowing a large fraction of its value, using the proceeds of his loan for consumption or new invest-ment, and retaining title to the property embodying his gain until his death. Suppose, for example, he owns a piece of city real estate that cost him $60,000 and is now yielding a net rental income of $40,000 a year from a long term lease and is worth $500,000. If he sells, he will be subject to a tax of $110,000. If he borrows $400,000 on the property, perhaps with his liability limited to the loss of the property, he will obtain in cash more than would be left to him after taxes from an outright sale; and he will still own a 20 percent residual equity in it which he can pass on to his heirs free from the capital gains tax.

We do not know how much revenue is lost to the government through the various methods whereby ordinary income is made to assume the form of capital gains. Such methods have doubtless been used far less extensively than their tax-saving possibilities would lead one to expect. Ignorance of these possibilities has probably been an important factor restricting their adoption. But as knowledge of them becomes more widespread, especially through professional tax advisers and published discussions of clarifying court decisions, they are likely to become increasingly exploited.

Chapter 10

THE TAX TREATMENT OF CAPITAL GAINS AND LOSSES IN OTHER COUNTRIES

Great variety exists in the tax treatment of capital gains and losses in other countries. At one extreme, in Great Britain and other members of the Commonwealth — Canada, Australia, South Africa, and New Zealand — the general rule is to exclude them from the taxable incomes of both individuals and corporations unless they have been incurred in the course of 'trade'. At the other extreme, in Greece and some other areas, they are treated as ordinary elements of income for both individuals and corporations. Most of the countries we have studied have policies between these extremes. France, which formerly excluded them from the taxable income of individuals except when realized in the course of business, now subjects half of the gains from casual sales of common stocks and similar investments to the individual surtaxes, though exempting them from normal tax, and includes them in full in the taxable incomes of corporations and of business firms. In Belgium and the Netherlands, capital gains and losses are included in the computation of taxable income when realized by individuals or firms in the course of business or by corporations in any event, but excluded when realized by individuals outside the course of their business. In Switzerland the federal income tax treats capital gains and losses in roughly the same way as Belgium and the Netherlands do, but the Swiss cantons and communes, which collect more tax revenues in the aggregate than the federal government, include several that tax all capital gains as ordinary income.

In some instances where the nominal rule is to exclude capital gains from taxable income, the exceptions are broad enough to subject a substantial proportion of them to income tax. In Sweden, for example, where capital gains of both corporations and individuals are exempt in principle, real estate must have been held 10 years or more, and securities, 5, for gains from them to be excluded from income tax. Zurich cantonal taxes include capital gains in taxable

254

income if derived from property held less than 10 years. In Norway, despite a general rule excluding capital gains of both corporations and individuals, ordinary income tax rates apply to gains from real estate held less than 10 years, and to all gains from the sale of patents, copyrights, property used in business, and property purchased with the intention of reselling.

Unrealized appreciation or depreciation is usually, though not invariably, disregarded in tax accounting. Czechoslovakia before World War II recognized unrealized gains and losses from securities for purposes of the income tax if the securities were owned by individuals or firms in business but were not being used in business operations or as a guaranty of contractual performance. Sweden until recently taxed the unrealized capital gains of individuals to a limited extent under the income tax by requiring that 1 percent of the taxpayer's net worth be added to his taxable income each year to form the base of the income tax. The tax on net worth is no longer a part of the income tax, but is the subject of a special graduated capital tax levied on individual net worth in excess of Kr. 30,000 at rates ranging from .6 to 1.8 percent. Since property values for this purpose are obtained from market quotations, assessment rolls, and the like, both the previous and the present Swedish capital tax take account of unrealized appreciation and depreciation. Unrealized capital gains and losses similarly enter into the annual net worth, net yield, or net worth increment taxes levied in Germany, Hungary, Austria, Norway, Denmark, Switzerland, France, Italy, Spain, Finland, and Luxembourg.

Because the effective tax laws of every country comprise a large and intricate body of statutes, court decisions, and administrative regulations and practices, the tax treatments of capital gains and losses in various countries can be only broadly outlined here.[1]

---

[1] The countries surveyed are those for which published information was readily accessible. Monographs on the tax laws and practices of most of them as of about 1935-36, prepared by officials of the various countries, are contained in *Das Internationale Steuerrecht des Erdballs* (Richard Rosendorff and Joseph Henggeler, ed. Zurich-Leipzig, 1936-37).

Through the cooperation of Percival Brundage, a partner in Price, Waterhouse & Co., and the foreign offices and correspondents of this firm, we were able to bring our discussion through 1948 for Great Britain, Canada, Australia, New Zealand, South Africa, the Netherlands, Belgium, France, Sweden, Norway, and Switzerland. We are grateful also for the aid of various consular officials and other experts in interpreting the laws and practices of these and other countries.

1 GREAT BRITAIN

In principle, capital gains are not taxable under the British income tax law and capital losses are not deductible. The statute does not expressly define them, but their exclusion rests upon the interpretation of Schedule D, which alone of the 5 schedules of the British income tax law covers gains and losses from the sale of property. The British income tax law does not apply to all income as such but only to the kinds specified in the 5 schedules. Schedule D provides for the taxation of "the annual profits or gains arising or accruing — (i) to any person residing in the United Kingdom from any kind of property whatever, whether situate in the United Kingdom or elsewhere; and (ii) to any person residing in the United Kingdom from any trade, profession, employment or vocation. . . ."

Trade is defined as including every "trade, manufacture, adventure or concern in the nature of trade".

As was brought out in Chapter 2, the concept of taxable income in Great Britain, as in other European countries, was greatly influenced by a long agricultural tradition in which income was regarded as derived from more or less permanent sources, such as land or a vocation, while casual and irregular receipts were viewed as of a different character. The language of the present law, which stresses the word 'annual', and which has remained essentially unchanged from the Income Tax Act of 1842, reflects this tradition. As a consequence, all "casual, non-recurring or occasional profits arising from transactions that do not form part of the ordinary business of the person who makes them" were excluded from taxable income until well after World War I.[2] The Royal Commission on the Income Tax recommended in 1920 (pars. 90 and 91) that the income tax be applied to gains from all transactions entered into with a view to making profit, though not to profits arising from ordinary changes of investment unless they are a regular source of profit. Although this recommendation was not embodied in legislation, it led the Board of Inland Revenue to reinterpret 'annual' in such a manner as to permit taxation of the profits of single transactions of a trading nature, and of a series of transactions that, individually considered, might not be regarded as ventures in trade but that viewed collectively could be so considered.[3]

[2] *Report of the Royal Commission on the Income Tax* (London, H. M. Stationery Office, 1920), Section VIII, p. 85.
[3] George O. May, The British Treatment of Capital Gains, *Journal of Accountancy,* June 1942.

The courts upheld this broadened application of the income tax. In *Martin v. Lowry* (11 T. C. 297, 1927) a dealer in agricultural machinery who made a single purchase of a large quantity of linen with the expectation of reselling it to certain linen manufacturers, but who was forced to embark on an extensive advertising and selling campaign to dispose of it, was held to have engaged in the linen trade. In *Rutledge v. C.A.R.* (14 T. C. 490) the court went further, holding that even a single purchase and resale was sufficient in this case to make the profit taxable as ordinary income. Mr. Rutledge, while in Germany on business in connection with his film company, had availed himself of an opportunity to purchase very cheaply a large quantity of paper, all of which he resold in England to a single customer at a large profit. Before 1920 such a gain would have escaped the income tax on the ground that it was 'casual'.

With the word 'annual' stripped of practical significance in this way, the distinction between capital gains and ordinary income came to turn on the interpretation of 'trade'. If a person devoted the greater part of his time to the purchase and sale of securities or other capital assets, he could be regarded as engaged in the trade of dealing or speculating in them, and his gains could be taxed as ordinary income. The assets that he owned from time to time in this trade were not a part of his fixed capital, such as his furniture and fixtures, but only circulating capital. A gain that he made by selling a part of his fixed capital, however, was not taxable.

In consequence of the agricultural tradition in England and other European countries, which early led to the concept of fixed capital assets as physical entities rather than amounts of pecuniary value, increases or losses in their value, whether realized or not, were regarded as quite distinct from the recurring incomes derived from them. A man who sold a portion of his fixed capital, even at a gain, received only its money's worth, not income. In line with this view, not only are gains and losses from the sale of capital assets excluded from the income tax, but the taxpayer is not given an allowance for depletion when his income is derived from wasting natural resources in the British Isles, or for the partial return of his capital if the income is derived from an annuity, or for depreciation if the income is from the rent of residential or commercial buildings.

No disposition has been evident on the part of income tax administrators, the courts, or Parliament in recent years to abandon the

general principle of exempting capital gains from income taxes.[4]
The practical problem has been to determine whether particular
profits are actually 'capital' in nature or incurred in the course of
trade. This is a question of fact, to be determined initially by one or
more of the 725 bodies of Commissioners for the General Purposes
of the Income Tax. B. Lachs (Income Tax on Capital Profits, *Modern Law Review,* April 1943, VI, 3), summarized the principle:
"The accretion of capital becomes taxable profit if it results from
trade. 'The circumstance that the profit is due to an accretion in the
value of the article does not negative the application of income tax,
because the accretion of value to the article may have been the very
thing that a trade within Case I (any trade not contained in any other
schedule) was established to secure' (per Rowlatt, J. in *Rees Roturbo
Development Syndicate v. Ducker*—13 T. C. 366). But this qualification needs further qualification. Not every capital profit in the
hands of a trader is taxable trading profit. It must be profit arising or
accruing from a trade, not just profit arising or accruing to a trade, or
to put it in more technical terms, the source of the taxable income is
the profit arising from the exercise of a trading activity, not the profit
from capital as such. It is obvious that a trading concern may have
capital which is not directly employed in the carrying on of its trade,
e. g., business premises, office furniture, investments, etc. and any
profit from an appreciation of value of such assets would not be taxable income. To put it in the shortest possible way: in the case of a
trader we have to distinguish between the assets with which he trades,
and those in which he trades."

Lachs then refers to, and cites judicial sanction for, the distinction
between "fixed capital", that embodied in plant, and "circulating
capital", that turned over in the course of business, saying that an
accretion to "fixed capital" is not taxable income, but that an accretion to "circulating capital" is. He finds, however, that the application
of this distinction is complicated by the fact that the same asset may
at one time represent fixed, and at another, circulating capital, for
either type may be converted into the other. A business may make
such a conversion of its assets as a whole or in part.

"A good example of a partial withdrawal of circulating capital is

---

[4] Some taxation of capital gains as income was introduced in the Income Tax
Act of 1945. Patents were made depreciable, but gains from casual sales of
them, previously exempt, were made taxable. Similarly, sales of machinery,
etc., for more than their depreciated basis now occasion a taxable gain up to
the amount of depreciation previously allowed.

afforded by the case of *Beams v. Weardale Steel, Coal, and Coke* — 21 T.C. 204. Here a company originally trading as colliery owners and steel manufacturers had acquired and added to slag heaps while carrying on business as steel manufacturers. After they had ceased to trade as steel manufacturers, but while they were carrying on the trade of colliery owners, they sold the slag heaps. The Commissioners found that the receipt from this sale was a capital receipt, and not trading income, and therefore not subject to income tax, and they were upheld. It appears that the particular asset, the slag heaps, which had been circulating capital as long as the company had been trading as steel manufacturers, was converted into fixed capital as soon as this trade ceased."

The determination of fact is difficult in borderline cases. The intention of the taxpayer, the number of his transactions in the asset, and other circumstances must be considered. The question of fact often arises because it involves the question of degree.[5] In *Tebrau (Johore) Rubber Syndicate Ltd. v. Farmer* (5 T.C. 658, 1910) the House of Lords held that a company incorporated to acquire rubber estates in the Malay Peninsula, to carry on the rubber business, and to sell the whole or any part of its property realized an exempt capital gain when it sold its entire property at a profit. Similarly, profits from the recurring sales of land by the Hudson's Bay Company, Ltd. (T.L.R. 709, 5 Tax Cas. 424, 438; C.A., 1909), were held to be nontaxable. On the other hand, in *Com'rs. v. Koren, Ltd.* (3, K.B. 258, 12 Tax, Cas. 181, 1921), a company incorporated to acquire mines, etc., and "to turn them into account" was held to be taxable on the profits from leasing one of its concessions.

Attempts by taxpayers to convert ordinary income into capital gains in order to escape taxation have been no less conspicuous in Great Britain than in the United States, and have led there as well as here to counteracting legislation. Neville Chamberlain, then Chancellor of the Exchequer, in his budget speech on April 20, 1937 called particular attention to one of the devices employed for this purpose and made recommendations for remedial legislation:

"The first one concerns the operation which is, no doubt, well known to most honorable members under the term 'bondwashing', the owner of securities sells them at a price that covers accrued dividend and buys them back again, after the dividend has been paid at a lower price. The result of these transactions, which are technically

[5] This difficulty is well illustrated in the case discussed by Magill, *op. cit.,* pp. 86-102.

of a capital character, is to deprive the Exchequer of a tax, which otherwise it would have received if the owner had retained the securities and drawn the dividends upon them."[6]

Such transactions on the part of individuals were facilitated by the readiness of various corporations dealing in securities to cooperate by serving as temporary purchasers. Since these corporations were engaged 'in trade', the taxable income from the dividend was offset by the allowance for the loss they sustained upon the sale of the security ex-dividend; and they were protected against loss through price declines from other causes by agreements of the original sellers to repurchase the securities. The remedial legislation (Finance Act of 1937, Part II, Sec. 12) provides that when the owner of securities agrees to sell or transfer them, then to reacquire the same or similar securities, any interest or dividend received by the purchaser shall be charged for income tax purposes to the original owner. It was estimated that the provision would add £1,000,000 of revenue a year.

The retention of earnings by closely held corporations in order to avoid current surtaxes on their stockholders, and the subsequent conversion of the accumulated earnings by the stockholders into capital gains through the sale of the stock led to legislation similar in intent to Section 102 of the U. S. Internal Revenue Code. Beginnings in this direction had been made in the Finance Act of 1922. In 1937, by Section 14(2)(b), additional powers were given the Special Commissioners to tax the owners of companies that did not distribute a reasonable proportion of their profits on the entire profit earned.

The widely publicized efforts of many Americans during the 1920's and '30's to avoid surtaxes on dividend and interest income by transferring securities to controlled foreign holding companies and trusts, which could convert the accumulated earnings into capital gains for their owners by subsequent liquidation and dissolution, had their counterpart in Great Britain. Even when the owners desired to receive income currently they could avoid a tax on it by arranging to have their receipts take the form of a loan from the foreign company or of a repayment of capital. This type of scheme led to the enactment of Section 18 in the Finance Act of 1936 which, as subsequently refined in Section 28 by the 1938 Act, provides that a British resident who transfers assets abroad into the hands of a foreign person but retains control of the income obtained by the latter shall

[6] *Parliamentary Debates, Commons, 1936-1937* (London, H. M. Stationery Office), Vol. 322, p. 1610.

be taxed as if he had actually received the income unless it can be shown that the transfer of assets was not made for the purpose of avoiding taxation.

In 1943 the Chancellor of the Exchequer set up a Departmental Committee to consider postwar fiscal policy, with particular regard to income taxation. The Institute of Chartered Accountants and other bodies of accountants in Great Britain were invited to make representations to the Committee. In urging that deductions from taxable income for depreciation should be allowed in connection with all fixed and wasting assets used for the carrying on of a trade, the memorandum of the joint accountancy bodies declared:

"The structure of our present income-tax law was designed almost exactly a century ago. The basic Act is still the Income Tax Act of 1842. Not until 1878 was any allowance given for depreciation (then limited to wear and tear of plant and machinery) and only in 1918 was loss due to obsolescence recognised (when the allowance given was limited by the requisite of replacement of the asset concerned). There is still no allowance in respect of forms of depreciation other than wear and tear of plant and machinery, and only a small and illogically calculated allowance in the case of certain buildings such as mills, factories, etc. It is not unreasonable to suggest that taxing machinery designed a hundred years ago, developed piecemeal by successive amendments in a long series of Finance Acts, with judicial interpretation spread over more than twenty large volumes of Reports, may need basic reconsideration in view of the unprecedented situation likely to arise at the end of the war. . . .

It follows that full allowance should be made for amortization of fixed and wasting assets of all types, spread over their estimated life. . . .

In applying the principles above set forth to the ascertainment of profits for the purposes of income-tax, it is necessary to remember that Schedule D taxes only the profits of the trade. Hence profits or losses from causes extraneous to the carrying on of the trade should be rigidly excluded in all cases."

Partly as the result of these and similar representations, the Income Tax Act of 1945 permitted deductions for the first time for the amortization of the cost of patents. The allowances for depreciation of plant and machinery were liberalized somewhat, but depreciation allowances continued to be withheld from ordinary commercial and residential buildings and similar non-industrial assets. In 1949 the depreciation allowances of the 1945 Act were extended to capital expenditures by British residents in mines, oil wells, and similar wasting assets outside the United Kingdom, but not inside.

The new provisions were accompanied by two related changes that newly subjected to income taxation two types of gain that were generally regarded as capital gains in principle. In accepting the view that patent rights should henceforth be subject to allowance for depreciation, the Chancellor of the Exchequer insisted in return that the gain made by an investor from the sale of a patent or patent rights, even though he was not a dealer in patents, must become subject to income tax. And in instituting a system of 'balancing allowances' to permit the deduction of losses sustained when plant or machinery not yet obsolete is scrapped without replacement, the Act provided (Sec. 17) that if a gain is realized from the sale of the scrapped asset, it should be taxed as ordinary income. These two violations of the long established British tradition that capital gains do not properly constitute taxable income were enacted over the vigorous opposition of the accountancy bodies.

Far more sweeping is the legislative authority contained in the Town and Country Planning Act of 1947 for the appropriation by the government of all increases in land values arising from the development or improvement of any land, urban or rural in England, Wales, or Scotland. Part VII empowers the Central Land Board to appropriate such increases in value by levying equivalent charges on the landowners. The Board and the landowner may contract to have the levy paid by a single capital sum, a series of capital payments, or a series of combined capital and interest payments. This legislation, which went into effect in July 1948, is designed to eliminate the private enjoyment of capital gains, realized and unrealized, from the ownership of land.[7]

2 CANADA

Canada follows British practice in most respects in the tax treatment of capital gains and losses. Unless the assets are of the nature of stock-in-trade in the hands of the seller, land, buildings, patents, securities, or other property, whether previously used in business or held for investment, may be sold by individuals or corporations without recognition of any resulting gain or loss for income tax purposes.

[7] Press Notice, The Ministry of Town and Country Planning, Jan. 8, 1947. See also statements by Lewis Silkin in *Parliamentary Debates,* Jan. 29, 1947, and in the *New York Times,* Jan. 8, 1947.

As in Great Britain, questions of fact arise concerning whether particular sales are made 'in trade'. The decisions of English as well as Canadian courts are used as precedents. If securities or real estate are dealt in casually apart from the business of the taxpayer, gains and losses are not recognized. But if an individual or corporation deals in them frequently, he may be deemed to be carrying on a trade even if he is also engaged in another business. The Minister of National Revenue has full power, subject to judicial review, to determine the taxable status of such transactions.

Until 1945, as in England to this day, Canada taxed both the capital and the interest components of annuity payments as ordinary income, but the capital element has been exempt since 1945.

Since capital gains are exempt from tax, taxpayers are naturally tempted so to frame transactions as to cause ordinary income to take their guise. Legislative and administrative attempts have been made to frustrate the various schemes employed. If the Minister of National Revenue is of the opinion that the undistributed profits of a corporation exceed the accumulation reasonably required, he may tax the excess as a dividend to the stockholders. Unlike the situation in the United States, stock dividends are taxed as income in the hands of the recipients. Their value for this purpose is fixed by the taxing authorities. Typically it is the amount of profits capitalized by the new stock, but the authorities may consider also the market value of the stock.

When principal and interest are commingled in a single payment, the Minister of National Revenue has power to separate them for the purpose of designating the interest as taxable income. Thus, if a bond or a share of preferred or common stock is redeemed at a sizeable premium, the premium may be taxed if it may reasonably be regarded as a payment of interest or a distribution of profits. It will not be taxed if it is viewed as only reasonable compensation for the cancellation of the investment.

Distributions to stockholders upon the liquidation of a corporation, or for the redemption of any of its common stock, and stock dividends capitalizing undistributed income are fully taxable as stockholders' income up to the amount of undistributed profits so disposed of (Income Tax Act of January 1, 1949, Sec. 8 and 9).

Unlike Great Britain, Canada under its new law, does not confine depreciation allowances to a narrow category of plant and equipment, but extends them to all depreciating assets, and permits deductions for depletion and obsolescence as well. Canada shifted in 1949 from the straight-line to the diminishing balance method of calculating depreciation, and the new law provides, in effect, for taxing previous excessive depreciation allowances when an asset is sold at a price exceeding its written-down value at the end of 1948, minus depreciation allowed after that date. In consequence capital gains realized from the sale of such assets are subject to tax up to the amount of the previously allowed depreciation.

3 AUSTRALIA

In Australia capital gains and losses except those of a bona fide prospector from the sale of rights or claims for gold-mining, are treated essentially as in Great Britain, with the statutory modification that the assessable income of persons and corporations includes profits arising: "(1) from the sale by the taxpayer of any property acquired by him for the purpose of profit-making by sale, or (2) from the carrying on or carrying out of any profit-making undertaking or scheme."[8] The corresponding losses may be deducted from assessable income received in the same year.

Whether particular gains and losses are truly 'capital' in character is a frequent source of argument between taxpayers and the federal revenue department. The contention that losses from the sale of property were deductible because the property had been acquired for profit-making by sale was made so often that Section 52 of the Federal Income Tax was amended in 1941 to specify:

"Provided that, in respect of property acquired by the taxpayer after the date of the commencement of this proviso (31st December, 1941), no deduction shall be allowable under this section (except where the Commissioner, being satisfied that the property was acquired by the taxpayer for the purpose of profit-making by sale or for the carrying on or carrying out of any profit-making undertaking or scheme, otherwise directs) unless the taxpayer, not later than the date upon which he lodges his first return under this Act after having acquired the property, notifies the Commissioner that the property has been acquired by him for the purpose of profit-making by sale or for the carrying on or carrying out of any profit-making undertaking or scheme."

The omission of this declaration is not conclusive against the taxpayer, for the Commissioner is empowered to direct that the loss

[8] Section 26 (a) of the Australian income tax law. See Ratcliffe, McGrath, and Hughes, *The Law of Income Tax* (Law Book Co., Australasia Printing Ltd., Sidney, 1938).

be allowed if he is satisfied that the property was acquired with the purpose of selling it or for the carrying on or carrying out of any profit-seeking undertaking. Similarly, if a taxpayer who realizes a gain has not given the notice specified under Section 52, his gain will not necessarily avoid taxation, for the Commissioner may determine that the property had been acquired with the idea of selling or for carrying on a profit-seeking enterprise.

In determining whether a profit from the sale of property is taxable, the Australian courts consider whether the intention of the seller was to make a nonbusiness use of the property. *Wright v. Deputy Commissioner* (So. Aust. S. R. 212, 1927) dealt with the taxability of a large profit on the sale of land purchased a short time previously for residence purposes. The taxpayer had been in the habit of purchasing land which he would work for a few years, then sell. Nevertheless, the court held that he was not taxable on the profit from the sale of his residence because at the time of purchase he had not intended to resell it.[9]

4 NEW ZEALAND

New Zealand also follows the general principle of excluding capital gains and losses from the calculation of income for tax purposes. Profit or loss from the sale of property is a part of taxable income if the business of the seller specifically includes buying, selling, or dealing in the property, or if the property was acquired for the purpose of reselling or otherwise disposing of it at a profit.[10]

The Wellington Steam Ferries Company was organized for various functions, including the operation of a steam ferry and of hotels and boarding houses; the acquisition of land; the development of recreation centers; the supplying of electricity, water and gas; and finally the buying, selling, leasing, or dealing in land. Following the closing out of its ferry business, the company sold some of its holdings of land at a profit. This gain was held taxable on the ground that the company had been granted by charter the power to buy and to sell land (*Wellington Steam Ferries Company v. Commissioner of Taxes,* 29 N. Z. L. R. 1028-1029).

But for a profit from this source to be taxable, the power to deal in land must be an important function of the company making the sale, or the intention to sell at a profit must have motivated the pur-

[9] Magill, *op. cit.,* p. 87, note.
[10] James H. Gilbert, *The Tax Systems of Australasia* (University of Oregon, 1943), pp. 108-10.

chase. The Marainanga Estates Ltd., organized to operate a sheep farm, bought a large estate and had power to purchase and to sell other properties. Following the sale of the estate, the taxability of the large profit realized was litigated. The court held that this gain was nontaxable because the main business of the company was not dealing in land, and the gain was not income from business. "The dominant object was the sheep-farming business; other operations were incidental or auxiliary thereto."[11]

New Zealand does not directly tax dividends received by stockholders as a part of the personal income, but includes all dividends, stock as well as cash, in the income base of the shareholders for the purpose of determining the rate of tax payable on taxable income. The Land and Income Tax Amendment Act of 1939 defines dividends to cover the value of any shares allotted by a corporation to its shareholders.

5 SOUTH AFRICA

The Union Income Tax Act of 1941 (Ch. II, Sec. 7 and 11) expressly excludes from the gross income of individuals and corporations "receipts or accruals of a capital nature", and disallows as deductions "expenses and losses of a capital nature". Profits and losses from the sale of fixed assets are therefore excluded. But any amounts previously allowed by the revenue authorities for depreciation of such assets are taxed if they are recovered in the sales price.

South Africa follows British practice more closely than the other Dominions in withholding depreciation allowances from 'buildings or works of a permanent nature', confining the allowances largely to machines and equipment; but unlike Great Britain, permits domestic mining companies to recover their capital investment free from tax through regular deductions over the estimated life of the mine.

Two provisions of the South African tax system cause reinvested corporate earnings to be a less important source of capital gains than in other countries. 'Public companies', defined as those whose shares of all classes are listed on a recognized stock exchange or are held in substantial amounts by the public, are subject not only to a normal tax of 20 percent of taxable income but also to a graduated undistributed profits tax on 'distributable income' not paid out in dividends. The basic rate of the latter tax, 20 percent, is reduced 2½ percentage points for each one-eighth of the distributable income

[11] *Marainanga Estates Co. Ltd. v. Commissioner of Taxes* (30 N. Z. L. R. 417).

paid out. 'Distributable income' is 80 percent of the company's taxable income plus dividends received, minus taxes and the amounts paid to redeem bonded debt.

Companies other than 'public' are termed private companies. The latter's taxable income, distributed and undistributed, is allocated among the stockholders in accordance with their shareholdings and is treated as a part of their individual incomes for the purpose of the normal tax, supertax, and provincial income taxes.[12]

6 FRANCE

Until 1949 capital gains and losses were excluded from the taxable incomes of individuals, but included in those of commercial or industrial enterprises, the liberal professions, and agriculture. Accordingly, an individual's profits from sales of real estate or securities were not taxable unless he habitually speculated in them or unless the property formed a part of the assets of his business. In 1949, however, along with substituting a uniform normal tax for the variety of normal tax rates previously applicable to different types of income, France adopted the recent American practice of subjecting to the graduated income surtaxes, but without the American ceiling rate, half of the capital gains realized by individuals from the sale of common stocks and similar investments. The gains are exempt if they do not exceed 100,000 francs, and they are exempt in any event from the proportional or normal tax. Capital gains of business firms are still taxed in full.

An individual owning a business establishment is not thereby precluded from making personal as distinguished from business dealings in property. But the two accounts must be kept separately, transfers between them must be at market prices, and, when assets are transferred from a firm to the owner, any gain or loss enters into the calculation of its taxable income. Thus an individual cannot avoid full taxation of the capital gain on an asset owned by his firm by having it transferred to him for sale. Commercial and industrial enterprises are required to register with a government agency and to cite the registration on their letterheads. The books of business enterprises are, in practice, examined every 3 years by a representative of the revenue administration.

The division between ordinary taxable income and formerly exempt and still half-exempt capital gains offers an inducement for the

[12] From information supplied by W. A. Horrocks, Commercial Secretary of the Embassy of the Union of South Africa, Washington, D. C.

conversion of income into capital gains. A favorite method formerly practiced on a large scale was selling French government loans, mainly *rentes,* just before the interest payment became due, when the market price reflected the accrued interest, then repurchasing them immediately after the price had fallen in reflection of the interest payment. This device has lost much of its attraction in recent years because the pronounced inflationary movements of commodity prices and the accompanying fears of further declines in the purchasing power of the franc led to erratic changes in the price of *rentes* and made their future prices, even for short periods, highly uncertain. Stocks are sometimes sold and repurchased, respectively, just before and after the dividend payment date, with the same object, but this practice is not common. Since *rentes* are ordinarily more stable in price, they are a better medium for operations of this kind.

As in the United States and other countries, tax avoidance also takes place through the reinvestment of corporate earnings and the subsequent realization of the accumulations by stockholders in the form of capital gains through sale of their stock. This method of tax avoidance has been somewhat restricted for owners of closely held corporations by a recent statutory provision that any profit on a sale of shares is fully subject to income tax if the vendor or a member of his family has been a director of the company for at least 5 years and the share of the family in the profits of the company exceeds 25 percent.

The capital gains and losses of business undertakings, whether carried on by an individual, a partnership, or a company, are included in the definition of taxable profit: ". . . the net profit, determined on the basis of the aggregate result of all the operations of any nature carried out by the enterprise, including the sale of any assets, whether in the course of, or on the termination of, the business." A ruling in 1941 defines net profit as the increment in net assets during the accounting year.

The taxation of capital gains of business enterprises has been modified in various ways during the last 10 years both to encourage reinvestment of such gains in the business and to allow for the depreciation of the French franc. The chief modifications are:
1) Capital gains on sales of real or intangible assets, including securities under certain circumstances, are not taxable if an amount equal to the proceeds is invested by the enterprise within the 3 succeeding calendar years in assets of a similar nature; in such case, however, the capital gain must be applied to reduce the cost of the new assets

so acquired, leaving only the balance of cost to be amortized from future earnings or to be taken into account when computing the taxable profit on the sale of these new assets. The taxation of the capital gain is therefore not waived, but the payment is deferred, perhaps for a considerable time.

2) No tax is payable on capital gains by the shareholders of a merged company on the transfer of the assets to the acquiring company, or on those arising when the business of an individual is transferred to members of his family or to his heirs. In all such instances, the tax is merely postponed, as the new owners must adopt as their cost for tax purposes the figures at which the assets were recorded before the transfer.

3) In May 1948 the normal rate of the profits tax, i.e., 24 or 28 percent, was reduced 50 percent for capital gains made on the termination or sale of a business.

4) Reflecting the reduced purchasing power of the franc, the law of May 13 and decree of May 15, 1948 greatly increased the authority granted business enterprises under previous measures to raise the book values of capital assets for purposes of calculating depreciation and capital gains. Book values can be increased up to certain multiples of the cost of the asset, but not above its present value. Assets acquired in or before 1914 may be revalued at up to 60 times their cost; those purchased in 1915, 42 times; 1916, 32; 1917, 22; 1918, 18; 1919, 17.4; 1920, 12; 1921, 18; 1922, 19.4; 1923, 15; 1924, 12.8; 1925, 11.4; 1926, 8.8; 1927, 9.6; 1928, 9.6; 1929, 9.8; 1930, 11; 1931, 12; 1932, 14; 1933, 15.4; 1934, 16; 1935, 18; 1936, 15; 1937, 10.6; 1938, 9.4; 1939, 9; 1940, 7.2; 1941, 6.6; 1942, 6; 1943, 4.4; 1944, 4; 1945, 2; 1946, 1.3; 1947, 1. Accrued depreciation to 1946 must be increased by the same multiples.

The excess of net book value after the revalorization must be credited to a special reserve account and will not be taxable as profit unless it is transferred for a purpose other than offsetting a deficit or conversion into share capital, when a 6 percent tax is imposed. Amounts set aside for cash dividends will be subject to the commercial profits tax of 28 percent, and the dividends tax of 30 percent. Taxable gains on future sales of the assets will be computed by taking the difference between the sale price and the revalorized net book value at the time of the sale. Depreciation is allowed on the basis of the revalorized net book values.

Persons and corporations who avail themselves of the revalorization privilege are subject to the profits tax at the 28 percent instead of the normal rate, 24 percent, and are required to reinvest in productive installations or equipment, within periods to be announced by decree, amounts equal to the enlarged depreciation allowances; if they do not, the depreciation allowance will be subject to the profits tax. Roughly similar provision was made for the permissible revaluation of securities and accounts receivable in foreign currencies.

7 BELGIUM

Corporations, and persons registered as 'in trade', include all gains from the sale of domestic property, whatever its description or use, with ordinary income for purposes of taxation. The corresponding losses are fully deductible from taxable income. They determine their taxable income or loss by comparing their balance sheets at the beginning and end of the tax year, after adjusting for distributions of earnings, changes in capital, etc. Their capital gains from investments abroad, however, are taxed at the same preferential rate as all other profits earned abroad, viz., at a quarter of the normal rate. Capital losses sustained in business from foreign investments are allowed in full.

Persons not registered as 'in trade' do not include in their reports of taxable income capital gains from sales of property, whether foreign or domestic, nor are their losses from this source deductible. These rules hold irrespective of the kind or use of the property.

Individuals who habitually perform acts designated in the Code of Commerce as those of trade are legally engaged in trade, and, like corporations, are required to register and to prepare balance sheets in a prescribed form (Art. 1 and 2). Trading activities comprise chiefly buying with the purpose of reselling, manufacturing, acting as a contractor or commission agent, transportation, banking. An individual who is in fact in trade but has not registered as such is not permitted to deduct capital losses. In practice, professional speculators register.

The Belgian franc, like the French franc, suffered a severe, and, with relatively brief interruptions, an almost continuous decline in purchasing power between 1918 and 1948. In consequence, the same problem arose as in France with respect to the measurement of taxable income and taxable capital gains in such manner as would permit adequate allowance for the cost of replacing capital assets worn out or sold.

The problem was met in much the same way as in France. Measures were enacted from time to time to permit industrial enterprises to revalue their properties within certain limits for the purpose of computing appropriate depreciation charges, the limits being set by lists of published coefficients, based upon the price level and related to the year of purchase, by which cost values and previously accrued depreciation allowances could be raised. The latest permissible revaluation was made as of December 31, 1945. When the surplus arising from such a revaluation is credited to the capital or capital reserves account, it is not taxable. If it is subsequently credited to income or used to pay dividends, it becomes subject to the income tax at the rate then in force. Further, the law of August 20, 1947 permits the use of the coefficients for raising the cost basis of property sold by a business concern in order to determine the taxable capital gain. This gain also becomes exempted from tax if it is credited to capital or capital reserve accounts. When the application of the coefficient yields a value higher than the sales price, the theoretical loss is not deductible.

Individual investors not 'in trade' are not affected by these measures because their capital gains and losses are not recognized for income tax purposes.

8 THE NETHERLANDS

For corporations, limited partnerships, and other business firms capital gains are included in taxable profits, and capital losses are deductible in full. As in Belgium, the taxable profit is measured by the difference between the net worth at the beginning and end of the fiscal year corrected for withdrawals or additions of capital, dividend disbursements, and income taxes paid. A capital increment levy at the rate of 50 percent of the increase in net worth between May 1, 1940 and December 31, 1945 of business firms, and at graduated rates of 50 to 70 percent on that of individuals, was imposed as a single levy, but an annual capital tax based on net worth was abolished as of January 1, 1947.

The capital gains of individuals are taxable as ordinary income if they arise from sales of real estate held less than 2 years or from marketable securities or goods held less than 1 year. Capital gains from assets held longer are not taxable unless they occur in connection with a man's business or the stock in a corporation of which an individual together with his wife and next of kin owns 25 percent or more. In the latter case, gains from the sale of any of the shares are taxed as income, though losses are not allowed. Nonbusiness capital losses are deductible from taxable capital gains realized in the same tax period, but are not allowed to offset ordinary income.

Unlike the United States, where the reinvestment of corporate earnings in the business instead of their distribution in dividends is subject to tax penalties unless the retention can be demonstrated to be motivated by a valid business purpose, the Netherlands government imposes severe tax penalties upon large corporations that distribute dividends in excess of 9 percent annually of their paid-up capital. In general, corporations with a nominal paid-up capital of 500,000 florins or more are required to restrict their dividends to the same percentage of the paid-up capital as they distributed in the last year before 1941; but beginning with the tax year 1946, a dividend up to 9 percent (earlier the exemption was 6 percent) is allowed without tax penalty. If more is paid out, a Super-Dividend Tax is levied at sharply rising rates ranging from 50 to 400 percent of dividends in excess of 9 percent. The maximum rate of tax is applicable to dividends of 14 percent or more, the rate applying to the entire amount of the dividend in excess of 9 percent. Since these taxes on liberal dividends are prohibitive, the benefits of unusual earnings come to stockholders mainly in the form of tax-free capital gains, though the effective ceiling on dividend distributions doubtless retards advances in the prices of equity securities commensurate with increases in earnings.

9 SWEDEN

Annual direct taxes upon individuals in Sweden are of 4 kinds: local income tax, local real property tax, national income tax, and national tax on capital owned. Except for differences in exemptions and allowances, taxable income is determined in the same way for both local and national taxes. All local income taxes are proportional. The rates vary as between localities, but average about 10 percent of taxable income.[13] The national income tax is levied at progressive rates ranging from 10 to 70 percent of the different brackets of taxable income, being 10 percent on amounts less than Kr. 1,000 and 70 percent on amounts in excess of Kr. 200,000 (the Swedish Krona is worth about 28 U. S. cents). The local real property tax is also an income tax in effect. It is levied on the income from the property, except that the income is assumed to be at least 5 percent of the assessed value.

Individuals who, jointly with their wives and minor children, own property with a market value exceeding Kr. 30,000 at the end of the calendar year are subject to an annual capital tax at bracket rates

[13] *Key to Swedish Taxes,* Skattebetalarnas Förening (Stockholm, 1948).

ranging from .6 to 1.8 percent of the value. The .6 percent rate applies to amounts between Kr. 30,000 and 100,000; 1 percent on the next Kr. 50,000; 1.2 percent on the next Kr. 50,000; 1.5 percent on the next Kr. 100,000; and 1.8 percent on amounts in excess of Kr. 300,000. The value of all property other than household furnishings, minus debts, constitutes the base of the annual capital tax.

Gains from the sale of real estate held less than 10 years, and from the sale of securities and other property held less than 5 years, are treated as ordinary taxable income for both the local and national income tax applicable to individuals. They are so treated also for the purpose of the local and national income taxes on corporations. Losses from such transactions are deductible only from the gains from them, except in the case of dealers. Corporations pay the same rates of local income and property taxes as individuals, but their national income tax rate is 40 percent.

Gains and losses from property held longer are not recognized for the national or local income taxes proper but are fully reflected in the annual capital tax. In fact, this tax by its nature takes into account unrealized as well as realized gains and losses. Despite a provision that limits the sum of the capital tax and national and local income taxes to not more than 80 percent of the taxpayer's net income, the joint effect of the income and capital taxes may cause an individual's net yield from investment to be negative after taxes. For example, a person with an earned income of Kr. 40,000, and an investment income of Kr. 20,000 from bonds or other property yielding 3 percent, would pay Kr. 20,275 of additional taxes by reason of his investment income and its capital value, or Kr. 275 more than his entire yield from his investment assets.

The gains and losses of dealers from sales of property are treated as elements of ordinary income regardless how long the property has been owned, but the distinction between dealers and nondealers is sharp. A dealer must actually possess a stock of the property from the turnover of which his income is derived. A real estate operator who buys land and holds or develops it to resell, and an investment banker who holds securities for sale, are dealers. But professional speculators, whether in real estate, stocks, commodities, or other property, are not dealers however frequent their purchases and sales.

10 NORWAY

Norway, like Sweden, imposes both national and local income taxes. The national income tax is levied at progressive rates upon the income of individuals, but at a flat rate upon corporate incomes. Gains and losses from the sale of capital assets used in business by an individual or corporation are elements of ordinary income under both national and local income taxes. Capital gains and losses on the sale of non-business assets are also treated as components of ordinary income if derived from the sale of building sites, patents, or copyrights. Gains and losses from the sale of real estate other than building sites are also included in calculating taxable income if the property has been held less than 10 years.

Other gains and losses from the sale of capital assets not used in business are excluded from both national and local income taxes. Thus profits from transactions in securities are usually taxable only if the buying and selling of securities is a business activity. Similarly, the gains and losses of individuals from the sale of furniture, jewelry, or other belongings are not recognized for the income tax. A blanket rule, however, provides for the full recognition of gains and losses from the sale of property purchased with the intention of reselling.

Both realized and unrealized capital gains and losses are embodied in the base for the annual tax on net worth, which is levied at progressive rates upon individuals and at a flat rate upon corporations.

11 DENMARK

The Danish statutes effect a partial integration of the income tax, from which most capital gains and losses are excluded, with the annual net worth tax, under which both unrealized and realized capital gains and losses form a part of the tax base.

Profits from sales of property are not taxed as income unless the sales constitute a part of the customary activities of the taxpayer or unless the property has been acquired with speculative intent. A presumption of speculative intent, subject to rebuttal, exists if the sale takes place within 2 years after purchase.

For the purpose of the annual tax on net worth which, like the income tax, is levied at progressive rates, property holdings are valued at market prices or, in the case of real estate, at assessment values. If the taxpayer's net income is less than various proportions of his net worth, he becomes entitled to varying rebates of the tax on the latter, the tax being reduced 80 percent if the taxpayer's income is zero or negative.[14]

---

[14] Hiort-Lorenzen and Pinholt, in *Das Internationale Steuerrecht des Erdballs*, I, 39-79.

12 FINLAND

In Finland taxable income includes capital gains from the customary business activities of the taxpayer, and in addition, all other capital gains realized through the sale of real property held less than 10 years and other property held less than 5 years. Capital losses are deductible from capital gains.

Net capital gains and losses of both individuals and corporate entities are included in the base for the annual tax on net worth, but the value of patents and copyrights is excluded if the taxpayer is the inventor or author.[15]

13 SWITZERLAND

The tax treatment of capital gains and losses in Switzerland differs as between the federal government and the cantonal and communal governments and also among the latter. The differences are significant because the burden of cantonal and communal income taxes is generally heavier than that of the federal government.

Under the Swiss Federal Defense Tax (as extended to 1949), business concerns, including individuals engaged in a business of a kind for which they are bound by law to keep a set of books, are required to treat capital gains and losses realized from business operations, including profits from the sale of real estate, securities, and from the sale or liquidation of a business, as taxable income (Art. 21, 1-d, and Art. 49, 1). They are required also to include unrealized capital gains and losses if these are recorded in their books.

Individuals in their private capacities are not subject to income tax on capital gains, realized or unrealized, and are not allowed to deduct capital losses. Under the annual capital or net fortune tax, however, both realized and unrealized capital gains and losses are reflected in the tax.

In Zurich canton realized capital gains of individuals are added to taxable income if they reflect increases in value during the 10 years preceding the sale; but no deductions are allowed for capital losses, realized or unrealized (Law of Oct. 29, 1944, as amended, Art. 77, 9a, and Art. 87).

In Basle the cantonal law requires that individuals treat as elements of ordinary income all realized capital gains and such unrealized ones as become apparent when computing their net fortune for purposes of the capital tax (Law of April 6, 1922, as amended, Art.

[15] See Aarre Linturi, *ibid.*, 563-96.

17, 1-4). They may deduct from capital gains realized capital losses and 'permanent' though unrealized decreases in values. Such capital losses or decreases in values may not be carried forward to be deducted from capital gains of future years (Art. 17a, 1 and 2).

In Geneva (Law of March 24, 1923, as amended) the treatment is substantially the same.

14 GERMANY

Detailed information on recent tax legislation in the two main zones into which Germany is now divided (1950) is difficult to obtain, and would be of dubious significance for our purposes if obtainable, because of the presumably tentative character of any recent changes. In the Western zone income taxes on individuals and corporations are of the same general character as before the war, though rates in general are higher.

Immediately before World War II, gains from speculative transactions, which were defined with reference to both the kind of assets sold and the period of ownership, were specifically included in the taxable incomes of both individuals and corporations. Profits from real estate held 2 years or less, from corporation shares or other property held 1 year or less, and from short sales regardless of the time held, were labeled speculative. On the other hand, gains from the sale of preferred stock of German railroads, bonds (unless they possessed convertible privileges), and other registered claims were exempt. Capital losses from speculative transactions could be deducted only from gains of like origin realized in the same calendar year.

A portion of certain other capital gains also was subject to income taxes. Profits from the sale in whole or in part of a farm, forest, or other business enterprise were regarded as 'extraordinary income', and, on petition of the taxpayer and approval of the authorities, could be excluded in part from income taxes. The taxed fraction commonly ranged from 10 to 25 percent for married persons and from 15 to 35 percent for single. The same practice was followed with respect to profits from the sale of shares of stock constituting more than 1 percent of the paid-in-capital of a corporation, by the individual owner of a 'substantial interest'. Such an interest existed if the seller or his relatives controlled 25 percent of the outstanding stock within 5 years preceding the sale.[16] Losses from the sale of an

[16] *Reichsgesetzblatt,* 1934, I, 1032, par. 6. See also Pfundtner-Neubert, *Das Neue Deutsche Reichsrecht,* V, Vermoegensteuer, Einkommensteuer.

enterprise, but not from the sale of the shares of stock, could be used to offset gains from similar sources.[17]

A striking extension of taxable income to embrace all realized capital gains was enacted in Germany in 1920, but was replaced by a quite different statute before it could take effect. The still-born law taxed any capital gain in full, but avoided the application of the full surtax rate by dividing the realized gain by the number of years, up to 5, that the asset had been held; calculating the average rate of tax on the taxpayer's other income plus this quotient; then applying this rate to the entire capital gain as well as to the remainder of his income. Losses were treated similarly.

Professor Haig has noted that the provisions finally adopted, calling for the taxation of speculative gains and the exemption of gains from investment transactions, stimulated taxpayers to adopt various expedients in arranging their transactions so as to avoid taxation.[18]

Capital gains and losses, realized and unrealized, form a part of the base of the annual tax on net worth.

15 CZECHOSLOVAKIA

At the outbreak of World War II the tax system of Czechoslovakia provided for the inclusion of some realized and unrealized capital gains as components of ordinary income, the taxation of others at special rates, and the complete exemption of still others.

Gains from the sale of real estate, whether used for personal or business purposes, were subject to a special tax at rates ranging from 5 to 50 percent, depending on both the amount of the gain and the period the property had been owned. Such gains were taxable again under the ordinary income tax if they had been realized by individuals or business enterprises in the course of a business operation or in a transaction undertaken with a speculative purpose.

Since business operations for profit were assumed to be conducted only by regular or established firms, most individuals selling real estate were subject to ordinary income tax on their gains only if the transaction was deemed speculative in intent. A speculative purpose was presumed if the property had been held not more than 2 years, but this presumption was subject to rebuttal. A loss from real estate sold in the course of business was fully deductible from ordinary income, but a loss from a speculative transaction in real estate could be deducted only from speculative gains realized in the same year.

[17] Income Tax Law of 1934, Sec. 5, par. 17.
[18] *Wall Street Journal*, April 13, 1937.

Business enterprises, whether conducted by individuals, partnerships, or corporations, were required to treat as taxable income not only realized capital gains and losses from securities and other movable property but also any unrealized gains or losses accruing during the year on securities held for purposes other than as a guaranty for the performance of some act or for use as part of the capital employed in operations. The accrued unrealized gains or losses were determined by the difference between the previous values and the market values at the year-end. Gains from the purchase by a corporation of its own stock below par, however, were exempt.

Gains realized by individuals from the sale of securities and other personal property held for nonbusiness purposes were exempt from income tax unless the property had not been held longer than 3 months. In the latter event, the gains were presumed to be speculative profits, taxable as ordinary income, unless the presumption of speculative intent was rebutted. Similarly, capital losses realized by individuals from the sale of personal property were disregarded for the purpose of the income tax unless incurred in speculative transactions similarly defined, in which case the losses were deductible only from speculative gains realized in the same year.

16 HUNGARY

In Hungary, just before World War II, individuals paid both a graduated tax on total net income, minus personal allowances, and a separate additional graduated tax, levied at higher rates, on net income from business. The latter tax applied to capital gains from the sale of securities and other movable property, whether the gains were casual or recurring or derived from business or from personal possessions. It applied also to dividends, interest, rents, entrepreneurial profits, and compensation received for services rendered irregularly, such as the fees of lawyers, doctors, and other independent practitioners. Capital losses of individuals from securities and other personal property were fully deductible from business income.

If a capital gain or loss had accrued over a period of years, the amount taxable or deductible in the year of realization was, within limits, proportionate to the period of holding, and the tax returns for preceding years were reopened to determine the change in tax liability due to including in them the *pro rata* shares of the gain or loss. The tax liability for income received in a single year for services performed over several years was also subject to this adjustment.

Capital gains of corporations realized from the sale of movable property were similarly treated. They were added to the other net income of corporations for taxation at progressive rates, and capital losses from movable property were fully deductible from taxable income. As for individuals, gains and losses that had accrued over a period of years were prorated, within limits, among the years of accrual.

Neither individuals nor corporations had to include gains from the sale of real estate in their taxable income, but both had to pay a graduated tax on the resulting increase in their capital. Corporations or individuals engaged in business could deduct the amount of this tax paid on business real estate from profits subject to income taxes.

Capital gains, realized and unrealized, were fully reflected in the base for the annual tax on net worth, which was levied at progressive rates.

17 GREECE

Greece taxes the income of individuals in 2 ways: once under various net yield imposts and a second time under a general or composition income tax. Capital gains realized from the sale of business or personal property, including securities and real estate, are embraced in the net yield levies, and capital losses are deductible from taxable net yields in the same year. Any excess of capital gains over losses, or losses over gains, is included with other components of income for taxation at the progressive rates of the general income tax.

Capital gains realized by corporations are taxed only under the net yield imposts; and only their undistributed net profits are taxed under the corporation income tax.

No general conclusion can confidently be drawn from the divergent practices of the countries covered in the foregoing review, except that the place of capital gains and losses in taxable income appears nearly everywhere to be subject to modification. Taxable income itself is a relatively new concept and is still being evolved. The early European income taxes were not conceived as personal taxes, but as levies upon certain kinds of income, usually those from more or less traditional sources, such as land, professions, business enterprises, and securities. Different rates of tax were often, and in some instances still are, applied to the different categories of income. As general or global income taxes came into use, they tended at first to be merely super-

imposed upon the total of 'schedular' incomes (the total of the different categories), which did not usually embrace capital gains or
losses. With increased acceptance of the view that the income tax is
a personal tax, the previous exclusion of capital gains and losses has
tended to be modified in different degrees in various countries. Short
term gains of individuals, sometimes defined as those from assets
held as long as 5 or 10 years, are in several countries now taxable in
full. The peculiar character of long-emerging capital gains and losses,
together with tradition, remains the ground for treating long term
gains in a special way or excluding them altogether in some countries.
Outside the British Commonwealth, the capital gains of corporations
are usually treated as ordinary income. Severe restrictions upon the
recognition of net capital losses of individuals, or their complete
exclusion, appears to be the rule everywhere.

Chapter 11

COMPETING PROPOSALS FOR THE TAX
TREATMENT OF CAPITAL GAINS AND LOSSES

The wide variety and still changing tax treatment of capital gains and losses in other countries and the repeated shifts in the American treatment clearly demonstrate that a single policy has not been universally accepted. Our analysis has brought out the major reasons. The proper treatment remains a problem everywhere because it presents various unresolved conflicts — in and between concepts of income, equitable considerations, revenue yield, administrative requirements, the desire to avoid harmful effects upon the markets for capital assets and upon investment incentives, and other objectives of tax policy.

In sharp contrast to British practice, the United States taxed capital gains in full as ordinary income at the beginning of its present series of income tax laws (under the 16th Amendment to the Constitution). After 9 years of such taxation and 4 of allowing capital losses in full, Congress responded to strong complaints that this treatment was seriously impeding the sale of assets on which individuals would realize gains and unduly stimulating the sale of those on which they could realize losses. Beginning with the Revenue Act of 1921 (applicable to 1922), a series of compromise measures was enacted. In each, capital gains continued to be classified as income, but the application of the rate schedule, the allowance for capital losses, the definition of capital assets, and other provisions were successively modified in different ways in an endeavor more adequately to satisfy one or more competing objectives. Since each new set of provisions was an *ad hoc* compromise, differences of opinion persisted. Current proposals for modification run the gamut from complete nonrecognition for income tax purposes to full inclusion of unrealized as well as realized changes in market values.

We may best preface a survey of the chief proposals by restating

281

in summary fashion the major considerations, discussed at length in preceding chapters, for and against excluding capital gains and losses from taxable income or treating them differently.

1 GENERAL CASE FOR EXCLUDING CAPITAL GAINS AND LOSSES FROM
TAXABLE INCOME OR TREATING THEM DIFFERENTLY

With the impressive support of prevailing practice in the United Kingdom and its dominions, complete exclusion has been urged upon Congress at various times since the adoption of the 16th Amendment. Essentially the same arguments have been offered from time to time for separating capital gains and losses from other taxable income and subjecting the net gains to a small flat rate, such as 5 or 10 percent, while disallowing net losses entirely, or for otherwise severely limiting the application of the income tax to capital gains and losses. The main reasons advanced for these positions are:

1) Capital gains and losses are not valid elements of true income as that term is widely used. The traditional concept of income includes only more or less regular and recurring or in any event, more or less expected receipts. An occasional sporadic gain or loss, especially if unexpected and unsought, does not function like income in guiding conduct or in determining the allocation of economic resources. For this reason many economists, for their general analytical purposes, though not specifically for those of taxation, confine the concept of income to more or less expected or recurring receipts. Similarly, the accountant usually separates capital gains and losses, if substantial, from ordinary income.

2) It is urged that when appreciation in the value of a capital asset is treated as income, it is really capital that is being taxed, for the appreciation usually represents merely an increase in the present value of expected future incomes to be derived from the asset, not an addition to current disposable income. In many instances, capital gains represent merely changes in the values of titles to some of the wealth of the country, not additions to it. Such gains do not constitute disposable income for the country as a whole. Even when capital gains represent real additions to the country's wealth, as when mines or oil resources are discovered, they are not currently disposable income for society as a whole.

To tax them as income, then, puts a double tax on the recipient — first on the capital value of future incomes, then on the incomes themselves as they are received. A man who reinvests a capital gain of $50,000 will be subject to income tax on his future income from the gain. To tax him also on the principal value of the gain itself is to tax him twice. Similarly, there is a double allowance for capital losses when taxable income is reduced by both the capital value of the loss and the subsequent decline in annual income.

3) The exclusion of capital gains and losses from taxable income avoids the unjust and otherwise harmful effects of taxing as income the spurious capital gains that merely reflect a rise in the general price level — a depreciation in the value of the monetary unit. Many home-owners experienced this type of illusory gain during and after World War II, when all the money profit they realized by selling a house in one city or neighborhood was commonly needed to help pay for a similar house elsewhere. It likewise avoids inappropriate allowances for the illusory capital losses that merely reflect a decline in the general price level or a rise in the purchasing power of money.

4) Similarly, capital gains and losses due to changes in interest rates, when realized incidentally to a shift of investments, may leave the investor's actual income unchanged. For example, the income from an investor's securities will remain $4,500 a year if he sells, at a $20,000 profit, $100,000 par value of 16 year 4½ percent bonds he purchased at par and reinvests the entire proceeds in approximately $120,000 of 3¾ percent similar bonds at par. When interest rates rise, the resulting fall in the market value of his securities, whether or not realized by sale, will similarly leave his interest income unchanged, because their smaller capital value, invested at the higher rates, will produce the same income as before.

5) Under the graduated rate schedule of the income tax, the imposition of the standard rates upon capital gains realized in a single year but emerging over a longer period is inequitable because it usually subjects the gain to a higher effective tax rate than would be applicable if the gain had been allocated among the years during which it arose. In the same way long emerging capital losses, if concentrated in the year of realization, have less tax-reducing value.

6) Overshadowing the foregoing economic and equitable considerations has been the emphasis, in statements before Congressional committees and elsewhere, upon various undesirable practical consequences said to flow from treating capital gains and losses as ordinary components of taxable income. A taxpayer usually cannot avoid taxes on ordinary income except by foregoing the income itself. But he can avoid the tax on a possible capital gain by refraining from realizing it, yet enjoy many of the advantages of the gain in the form

of an increase in his wealth and in the increased earning power, dividends, interest, or rent the unrealized gain commonly reflects. Since the investor commonly possesses a wide and often unlimited range of choice whether and when to realize his gains in a legal sense, any substantial tax acts as a deterrent to selling property yielding capital gains. The effect is to impose a heavy tax on transfers of such capital assets. In consequence, it is argued that society does not get the benefit of highly fluid markets for capital assets, and of their easy and continuous redistribution among those most anxious to own and use them. Individuals are deterred from making otherwise desirable shifts in the composition of their assets as their needs change. A conspicuous contention is that price movements in both directions are exaggerated in the markets for common stocks and other equities by the reluctance of owners to sell when prices are rising in the face of an avoidable tax on their gains, and their added disposition to sell when prices are declining in order to benefit from a deductible capital loss. The accentuated fluctuations reduce the attractiveness of equity investments. Further, since venturesome investment depends in considerable degree upon the prospect of exceptional returns, which are often possible only in the form of capital gains, heavy taxes on the latter may discourage the assumption of unusual risks.

Another point made is that the net revenues from any substantial taxation of capital gains and reasonably related allowances for capital losses are negligible over a long period because of the tendency for gains and losses to cancel and because the realization of losses is encouraged while that of gains is discouraged. In this event, excluding capital gains and losses would improve the stability of the yield from the personal income tax without seriously reducing its average amount. Under existing treatment, the freedom of taxpayers to choose whether and when to realize gains and losses enables them to time their transactions so as to minimize their tax liabilities. Well advised taxpayers are fairly certain to avail themselves of the tax benefits from realizing their losses when they have offsetting income, and to minimize taxes on their gains by realizing them mainly when they have offsetting losses or by not taking them at all, leaving them to pass untaxed (as far as the income, but not the estate, tax is concerned) to their heirs. A low flat rate on capital gains without allowance for capital losses has been urged as a means of increasing revenues by encouraging larger transfers of assets embodying capital gains. Finally, it is argued that estate and gift taxes provide rough offsets to the avoidance of income taxes on capital gains.

2 GENERAL CASE AGAINST EXCLUDING CAPITAL GAINS AND LOSSES OR TREATING THEM DIFFERENTLY

The main opposing arguments are:

1) Although different concepts of income may well be valid for other purposes, the proper measure of income for tax purposes is to be found in the actual *ex post* results of economic activity, not in subjective expectations or presumptions. Taxable income, it is urged, should measure the relative capacity of individuals to pay taxes, as indicated by the net annual additions to their wealth from economic activity plus their consumption. Capital gains supply an individual with the same additions as any other kind of personal income to his power to buy consumption goods or investments, and to provide for his family's future. To exclude profits of this kind from income tax or to grant them markedly preferential treatment seriously conflicts with the purposes of a graduated income tax. Capital gains constitute a major source of income for many individuals. Both the average capital gain per taxpayer and the proportion of taxpayers who report capital gains rise sharply from lower to higher incomes. In some years capital gains have exceeded dividends as a source of income for taxpayers reporting incomes above $100,000. And the unequal distribution of capital gains among taxpayers in each income group accentuates the inequity of excluding them from income tax or of giving them unduly preferential rates.

In economic character capital gains differ only in varying degree from other forms of personal income. They are often deliberately sought as a species of profits. They are rarely wholly 'unexpected' but, like ordinary business profits, represent varying mixtures of expected and unexpected elements. In fact, if capital gains did not so commonly constitute a sought reward for exertion and risk, it could be contended that they should be taxed more heavily than ordinary income because they would then not serve any function in spurring initiative and exertion or in allocating economic resources. In practice, capital gains embody large elements of personal compensation, interest, profits, and rents, and often constitute a thinly veiled disguise for these ordinary kinds of income. A conspicuous example occurs when the retention of earnings by a corporation over a period of years causes its stock to rise, enabling its stockholders to obtain a varying proportion of these reinvested earnings in the form of a capital gain by selling the shares, and even to avoid a personal income tax on these earnings by leaving their stock to their heirs.

The difficulty of distinguishing clearly, on economic grounds, between capital gains and other income creates serious administrative difficulties when the gains receive preferential tax treatment, and stimulates efforts on the part of taxpayers and their lawyers to convert ordinary income into this form. It is contended by some that the tax preference and the associated tax avoidance adversely affect the morale of the general body of taxpayers, whose cooperation is essential for the American system of a self-assessed income tax.

The sporadic and lumpy character of capital gains and losses is true also in varying degree of other kinds of income, notably business profits. Moreover, higher rather than lower taxes on long emerging capital gains can be justified as an interest charge: the taxpayer has enjoyed the free use of funds otherwise payable in taxes during the period he has postponed realizing his gain. The logical method of achieving equitable tax treatment of fluctuating incomes under a graduated rate schedule is to adopt some system of averaging, not exclude them.

2) The allegation that taxation is double when both a capital gain and its subsequent annual yield are taxed, and the related contention that this practice reduces the country's stock of capital, are not relevant, it is argued, for a personal income tax. Individuals are free to consume or to reinvest their realized capital gains. They are in the same position as those who have accumulated savings from other current income. The latter are subject to tax on the saved portion of their income and will pay taxes also on the yield subsequently derived from investing these savings. In both cases the income inclusive of current savings and capital gains measures the addition to the taxpayer's power to command and direct economic resources into channels of his own choosing. Income taxes are designed, among other purposes, to divert a fraction of this total power to the government. Were taxable income confined to consumed income, a sizeable proportion of total personal income would be exempt. Conceivably, this exclusion might be desirable under some circumstances, but the case for it would not apply peculiarly to capital gains.

All taxes impinge in some degree upon the capacity of taxpayers to save and to accumulate capital. One purpose of the income tax, as of estate and gift taxes, is to reduce inequalities in the distribution of income and wealth, even if this entails some reduction in private capital or in current additions to it. Whether the aggregate capital of the country is lessened by the same amounts depends upon what the government does with the tax proceeds; public roads, school buildings, and the like are also capital goods.

3) To the extent that capital gains and losses are offset by an opposite change in the purchasing power of money, they are doubtless fictitious in the sense that they do not measure a change in the economic status of the recipient. In the event of a rapid and substantial rise in the price level, such as occurred in various European countries during and after the two World Wars, special measures may well be warranted to exclude the illusory capital gains from income taxes. These could take the form, in inflation, of raising the cost basis of capital assets by stipulated percentages, as has been done recently in France and Belgium. Existing provisions protect holders of business assets in part by permitting them to postpone recognition of capital gains realized when the proceeds are invested in similar property; and a similar rule could be adopted for houses or even for all nonbusiness assets. If prices fell drastically, parallel treatment would call for deflating capital values by the use of indexes or to impose restrictions on the deductibility of capital losses.

Serious administrative and other difficulties would be involved in isolating and providing special treatment for capital gains and losses that reflect changes only in the general price level. Hence it is recognized that such a procedure, if adopted at all, is likely to be confined in practice to periods in which the price level fluctuates violently within a relatively short time. But a gradual price movement, if prolonged, may become sizeable in the aggregate, giving rise to substantial fictitious capital gains and losses. Some would ignore these effects of moderate or gradual changes in price levels. Others would not make any special provision for any illusory capital gains and losses on the ground that the only proper avenue of attack upon unstable price levels is through the broad instruments of monetary and fiscal policy. Still others would treat this problem by according a preferential tax treatment to all capital gains and imposing restrictions on the deductibility of all capital losses — the general manner in which long term capital gains and losses have been treated in the United States since 1921.

4) Capital gains and losses caused solely by changes in interest rates are not really illusory. An investor who realizes a $20,000 profit by selling his bonds after interest rates have fallen can command $20,000 more of the world's real goods. Relative to other individuals, he has gained in net worth, even though his interest income may remain the same.

5) It is argued that the alleged adverse effects upon the capital markets of including capital gains and losses in taxable income are greatly

exaggerated. Empirical evidence indicates that realized gains and losses have fluctuated mainly with stock prices rather than with changes in tax treatment. Much of the actual impediment to transfers of capital assets said to be created by substantial taxes on capital gains is really due to the possibility of avoiding such taxes completely by holding appreciated assets until death and by using them as gifts without incurring tax liability (the donee will incur such liability if he sells). The proper attack upon these impediments, it is urged, is to remove all possibility of avoiding the tax by making every transfer of property, during life or at death, an occasion for recognizing a capital gain or loss, and, possibly, by periodically recognizing accrued but unrealized gains and losses. Because gift and estate taxes are payable also by individuals who do not enjoy capital gains and by those who have paid income taxes on realized gains, they do not offset the inequity of taxing capital gains at lower rates or exempting them.

The point is made that the problem of inducing enough venturesome investment cannot be met equitably or adequately by the preferential tax treatment of capital gains, because the greater part of the rewards of risk-taking are often, perhaps usually, obtained from ordinary business profits, dividends, and rents. As far as we design the tax system to foster this type of investment, we should do so broadly, covering all the rewards for exceptional effort and risk, rather than a single and often spurious form of such rewards.

6) Even though capital gains and losses may conceivably cancel out in the long run for taxpayers as a whole, they do not do so for individuals. Just as we do not allow the aggregate net losses of deficit corporations and individuals to offset the taxable income of others, the net capital losses of some taxpayers do not, it is contended, justify complete tax exemption or preferential rates for the capital gains of others. Our taxation of capital gains, despite preferential rates, has actually yielded substantial revenues, only a portion of which can be attributed to the restricted deductibility of net capital losses. The irregularity of the revenues is not a solid reason for relinquishing them. Business profits too are notoriously unstable as a source of tax revenue. Reduction of the public debt is an excellent use for the surplus revenues of good years, and a revenue source that automatically yields less in bad years has the virtue of reducing the adverse effects of federal tax collections upon private spending in depressions.

The conflict of considerations barely summarized above and elaborated in preceding chapters is the 'problem' of capital gains and
losses: to devise a tax treatment that will most nearly satisfy the
demands of equity — of giving equal treatment to similarly circumstanced individuals — and at the same time avoid unduly impeding
useful transfers of capital assets. The major proposals for meeting
this problem fall into two broad groups. One group seeks the full
inclusion of capital gains and losses in taxable income while mini-
mizing the undesirable effects by averaging them or by averaging
total income over a number of years, or by including unrealized as
well as realized changes in market values of capital assets. The other
group would compromise the conflicts of equitable and practical
considerations by various *ad hoc* measures of the same general character as those employed in the United States since 1922, but with
more or less recognition of capital gains and losses as components
of taxable income. Common to both groups is the question whether
and to what extent unrealized appreciation and depreciation should
be recognized, particularly upon transfers of property by gift or at
death.

We begin with the more extreme proposals because they best
clarify the major issues.

3 FULL ANNUAL RECOGNITION OF BOTH ACCRUED AND REALIZED GAINS AND LOSSES

One line of attack proposed by some students to minimize the inequities and undesired practical effects of full recognition of sporadic
capital gains and losses *as realized,* while treating changes in capital
values as elements of taxable income, is to include all such changes,
whether or not realized by sale, in the income base.[1] Each taxpayer
would report on his income tax return the value of all his assets at the
beginning of the year, plus the cost of those acquired during the year
(legacies and gifts being entered at their value when received), and
their value at the end of the year. A net increase, including capital
gains realized during the year, would be added to his ordinary income, and a net decrease, including realized capital losses, would be
deducted. All special provisions for capital gains and losses, such as

[1] See National Tax Association, *Proceedings, Ninth Annual Conference*
(1915), p. 303, which presents a report of a committee of the Association;
Committee on Taxation of the Twentieth Century Fund, *Facing the Tax
Problem* (1937), p. 490; and *Capital Gains Taxation*, pp. 26-8, 95, which
presents a panel discussion.

preferential rates, percentage exclusion, holding periods, maximum alternative rates, and loss limitations would be eliminated.

The advantages claimed for this proposal are:

1) It would achieve a higher degree of uniformity of tax treatment of personal incomes than appears to be possible under any alternative proposal. Individuals who added to their wealth by capital gains would be taxed as fully as those whose additions came from other kinds of income. Deferring the realization of gains until death would no longer permit avoidance of the income tax on them, and postponing them would no longer give the holder the free use of tax money.

2) It would supply a means of subjecting stockholders to personal income tax on their *pro rata* shares of reinvested corporate profits, to the extent that the latter actually added to the market values of the shares. In this degree individuals whose saved income takes the form of corporate earnings reinvested in their behalf would be taxed at the same rates as those whose current savings are invested in other ways. The taxation of only realized capital gains, in contrast, allows large amounts of earnings accumulated through corporations to escape personal income taxes entirely by transfer of the stocks at death, and permits even the realized accumulations to be taxed at preferential rates under existing law.

3) Full recognition of unrealized gains would eliminate the present tax impediments to transfers of property. No additional tax liability would be incurred upon the sale of an appreciated investment, for the tax on the increase in value would be payable even if the asset was not sold. Indeed, the latter tax liability would serve as a spur to the taxpayer to sell any property he did not positively desire to hold. Hence when prices were rising, investors with large unrealized capital gains would no longer be 'frozen' in their assets by their desire to avoid capital gains taxes, and when prices were falling, the decline would not be accentuated by the desire of those with unrealized losses to obtain a tax deduction by selling.

4) Full recognition would probably cause a substantial increase in tax revenue. Some reduction might occur in the net yield from short term gains and losses because the realized gains are taxed in full under present law while the existing severe restriction on the allowance for net short term losses would be removed. But short term gains and losses constitute only a small proportion of the total. The main sources of additional revenue would be the sharply increased tax rates on realized long term gains, the taxability of these gains in full instead of at half their amount, and the inclusion in taxable

income of much appreciation that now escapes the income tax through the transfer of the property at death. The tax rate on capital gains, now limited to a maximum of 25 percent, would become equal to the top surtax bracket rates plus the normal tax rate for the various income groups under the ordinary income tax schedule, and would rise as high as 82.1 percent.

Partly offsetting the larger revenue from net long term capital gains would be the removal of the present limitations on the allowances for realized net capital losses and the full recognition of unrealized losses. In periods of declining values these allowances would wipe out the tax liability on other income for many taxpayers. In 1932, for example, the aggregate market value of the securities listed on the New York Stock Exchange alone declined about $30 billion. Some persons would therefore contend that a limitation on the allowance for capital losses is necessary for practical reasons. Others would welcome such a wholesale automatic reduction of tax liabilities in bad times, as well as the large increase in good times, as a valuable counter-cyclical influence.

Other effects and difficulties

The annual accrual method would be likely to cause alterations in the relative market values of different kinds of assets and shifts in the portfolios of various investors. To the extent that individuals chose their investments primarily because of the preferential tax treatment of capital gains, they would have a motive to shift out of these holdings. In addition, many investors who are content to own assets yielding a small or no current income when they do not incur any immediate tax liability for the price appreciation constituting a part of the total expected return would be unwilling or unable to hold such assets if the unrealized appreciation was taxed as current income. In consequence, assets that promise to yield most of their total return in the form of capital gains would tend to become relatively less attractive, other things being equal, than assets yielding most of their return in the form of current income. Corresponding changes would tend to occur in their relative market values. To the degree that unusually venturesome investments are of the former type, the tax incentive offered them under the present treatment would be removed. On the other hand, the introduction of unrestricted allowances for capital losses would stimulate this type of investment.

Various practical difficulties of the annual accrual proposal may be quickly noted. One is that annual changes in the market values of capital assets do not correspond closely with changes in the actual ability of their owners to obtain the cash required for income tax payments. This difficulty is not serious in the case of ordinary property taxes, as a rule, because they are levied at low rates, rarely exceeding 2-4 percent of the total valuation, and because assessment values and rates do not ordinarily fluctuate sharply. Nor is it serious for most listed securities if the taxpayer holds them in small blocks, for he may sell a portion, if necessary, to raise the tax money. Even in this instance, the selling induced by the tax may be sufficient in the aggregate to depress prices severely. But many kinds of property, such as improved real estate, are not easily divisible or readily saleable, and some assets that appear to be saleable in small portions must be retained in full by their owners for reasons of control, impairment of value by partial sale, etc. While many owners of such properties would doubtless pay the tax out of their other income, others in all except the lowest income groups, because of the high rates applicable on both their unrealized capital gains and their other income, would be compelled to borrow, retrench in personal expenditures, or sell other assets. Peculiarly difficult problems would be raised for trustees, life-tenants, and holders of other interests in property held in trust.

Large numbers of taxpayers would deem the inclusion of unrealized appreciation grossly unfair. Householders who did not intend to sell their homes, and long term investors in common stocks who had not consciously participated in a speculative boom, could be expected to complain strenuously if told that they must include increases in the paper values of their holdings in their taxable incomes. Taxpayers who might otherwise take little notice of the market value of their securities and other assets would be put on their guard to heed such changes. The practical effects of speculative changes in the market values of capital assets would be greatly increased. A pronounced rise in the general level of prices would, under this proposal, have much of the effect of a capital levy.

Since good markets with readily ascertainable prices do not exist for all the lands, buildings, contracts, rights, and equities that constitute capital assets, the annual appraisals of all such property would present formidable difficulties in countless cases.[2] The difficulties would be both those of compliance on the part of the taxpayer and

[2] George O. May stated the valuation difficulties well in a letter published in the *New York Times*, May 9, 1937.

of surveillance by the tax administrators. On small orders, market quotations for many unlisted securities fluctuate widely; sales of larger blocks, on the other hand, are often negotiated at prices materially higher or lower than market quotations. Several European countries, to be sure, have braved these difficulties in connection with annual personal taxes on net worth. The problems of valuation might be manageable for an income tax if close precision were not necessary to achieve rough justice. This would be the situation, however, only if the rate structure of the income tax and the ordinary income of the taxpayer remained relatively stable from year to year. Considerable latitude could then be permitted in the appraisal of assets whose market values were not readily ascertainable. Book values or rough approximations to market values could be accepted because intentional or unintentional errors would be subject to automatic and tolerably equitable adjustment upon actual realization of gain or loss or upon death. The progressive rate structure of the income tax would cause some disparity in the treatment of gains and losses even for a taxpayer with stable ordinary income and under an unchanging rate schedule. For example, under the 1949 rate schedule, a single person with ordinary net income of $20,000 would have his tax increased $2,512 if a $5,000 rise in the value of his capital assets was taxed as income, while a $5,000 decline would reduce his tax liability only $2,195. This discrepancy would be substantial only when the capital gain or loss exceeded the width of several surtax brackets.[3]

But with changing tax rates and fluctuating individual incomes, both of which are more likely, the progressive rate schedule could cause much larger discrepancies. A taxpayer's property might increase $10,000 in value in a year when tax rates were raised and his other income was large, but lose all this gain in one or more following years when, because of a reduction in tax rates or in his other income, the allowance for the decline in value would reduce his taxes by an amount materially smaller than had previously been added to them by the equal appreciation. Further, this defect of the

[3] Under the Revenue Act of 1948 the surtax brackets are $2,000 wide for net incomes of $2,000-22,000; the next $4,000 of income constitutes a single bracket; the brackets are $6,000 wide thereafter up to $50,000 net income; $10,000 wide for incomes of $50,000-100,000; and $50,000 wide for the next $100,000, at which point, $200,000, graduation ceases. For married persons filing joint returns, the surtax brackets are twice as wide, in effect, because additional segments of income are divided between the spouses for the purpose of determining the effective tax rates.

annual accrual method would be magnified by the tendency of capital losses to be larger in years of smaller than average ordinary incomes, and of capital gains to occur more largely in years of higher incomes. In addition, for many taxpayers the severe depreciation of capital values in bad times would exceed their ordinary incomes and would to this extent lose all tax-reducing value unless such unused net losses could be carried back or forward for long periods, or the accrual method was supplemented by an averaging device.

The failure of the annual accrual method to create a perfectly symmetrical tax treatment of capital gains and losses would give considerable importance to the allocation of estimated accruals of unrealized gains and losses as between one year and another. Wide latitude in annual appraisals, necessary for administrative reasons, would therefore create opportunities for tax avoidance and material for litigation. These difficulties would be reduced, however, if the annual accrual method was combined with averaging income for several years to determine each year's taxable income, or with a generous carryback or carryforward of net capital losses against ordinary income.

Constitutional difficulties of taxing unrealized appreciation
Whether the annual taxation of unrealized capital gains as income would be held constitutional under the 16th Amendment is debatable. In the Macomber case (1920), in which ordinary stock dividends were held not to constitute taxable income, the Supreme Court explicitly declared: "enrichment through increase in value of capital investment is not income in any proper meaning of the term"; and it strongly emphasized that a gain must be realized and "separated from capital" to be taxable as income (252 U. S. at 214 and 207). While some students think the Court might now reverse this decision,[4] few appear to believe that it would do so by abandoning the realization requirement, which is strongly rooted in American jurisprudence.

Nevertheless, competent authorities have expressed contrary views. Professor Isaacs contended that the Macomber case does not foreclose inquiry into the possible constitutional basis of an annual accrual plan of capital gains taxation.[5] As noted in Chapter 2, Mr. Justice Douglas, speaking for a minority of three justices in *Helver-*

[4] Rottschaefer, Present Taxable Status of Stock Dividends in Federal Tax Law, 28 *Minnesota Law Review,* 163 (1944).
[5] 46 *Harvard Law Review,* 776, 791 (1933).

ing v. Griffiths (318 U. S. 371, 1943), declared that he did not see any reason why Congress could not treat as income increases in the wealth of stockholders due to the reinvestment of corporate earnings; "the notion that there can be no 'income' to the shareholders in such a case within the meaning of the Sixteenth Amendment unless the gain is 'severed from' capital and made available to the recipient for his 'separate use, benefit and disposal' will not stand analysis. . . ."

The escape of reinvested corporate profits from personal income taxes levied upon shareholders unless the latter realize them in the form of capital gains, as well as the preferential rate at which the earnings are now taxed in the latter event, is perhaps the strongest reason motivating those who urge the taxation of accrued as well as of realized capital gains. Reinvested corporate profits, however, constitute only one source of capital gains, and a special treatment might conceivably be devised for them. It is possible to contend, as well as to deny, that such earnings are truly current income to the stockholders, whereas mere appreciation in land values, for example, is not. The conspicuous role of reinvested corporate profits in the thinking of those who propose changes in the current tax treatment of capital gains and losses is reflected at several other points in this chapter.

As a practical matter, it cannot be said that any strong and widespread demand appears to exist for the annual taxation as income of all unrealized appreciation in capital assets, and strong objections would doubtless be made to full annual allowance for all unrealized capital losses. In the light of this fact, of the constitutional doubts, and of the practical difficulties of requiring and checking annual valuations of capital assets, it seems unlikely that the annual accrual proposal will receive serious consideration by Congress in the near future.

4 CUMULATIVE AVERAGING OF INCOMES AND TAX LIABILITIES

A less familiar radical solution recently proposed for the full inclusion in taxable income of realized gains and losses calls for the cumulative averaging of taxable incomes and tax liabilities from year to year. The taxable income of any year would be defined as the taxpayer's average income over a period of years, including realized gains and losses, and his tax liability would be adjusted annually, for all previous over- or underpayments by reason of the reporting in preceding years of taxable incomes differing from his average income. Such an averaging device, first worked out by William

Vickrey,[6] would leave the aggregate tax burden on an individual unchanged by any shifts in the allocation of his income among the various years included in the averaging period. The scheme is designed to tax equitably all fluctuations in income as well as irregular capital gains and losses. It would not only eliminate the influence of fluctuations in income upon the effective tax rates under a graduated rate schedule but also avoid penalizing taxpayers whose larger incomes happened to be received in years when the entire rate schedule was high, and unduly favoring those whose larger incomes were received when the rate schedule was lower. By taking unrealized capital gains and losses into account only at the end of the averaging period, say every 10 years, or only upon the transfer of property at death or by gift, the device would avoid the need for annual appraisals of capital assets.

The procedure would be as follows: The taxpayer would report an initial valuation of his capital assets, perhaps at cost or on a compromise transition basis, at the beginning of the year in which the system went into effect or in which he entered the system. For the first year the income and calculation of tax liability would be as at present, except that realized capital gains and losses would be taken into account in full (unrealized changes in value would be disregarded). At the end of the second year the taxpayer would add that year's income to the first, and divide by 2 to arrive at his average annual income. From tables prepared by the Treasury Department, which would show the net effect on his average income of the tax rates in force in the preceding as well as in the current year, he would determine his total tax liability for the 2 years on the assumption that the average income had been received in each, and remit to or receive from the Treasury the difference between the aggregate tax due for the 2 years and the amount paid the first year. His return for the third year would contain the cumulated total of taxable income and of taxes paid for the preceding 2 years. He would add the income for the third year to the previous cumulated income, divide by 3 to arrive at the average income, consult the tax tables to determine the total tax liability for the 3 years, and subtract the cumulated sum paid earlier to determine his current tax payment; and so on until the end of the tenth year.

At that time, if this was the end of the averaging period, and if unrealized changes in capital values were then to be accounted for,

[6] *Journal of Political Economy*, June 1939, p. 379; and *Agenda for Progressive Taxation* (Ronald Press, 1947), Ch. 6.

he would present a current valuation of his property, supported in a manner prescribed by regulations. Any changes in the value since the end of the preceding averaging period or since the dates of subsequent purchases, other than those arising from gifts and inheritances, realized capital gains and losses, and other sources previously included in taxable income, would be added to or subtracted from the income of the tenth year; after which that year's income would be added to the cumulated total of the preceding nine years, then divided by 10 to arrive at the average annual income for the 10 years. The aggregate tax liability for this income over the 10 years would be determined by reference to the Treasury's tax tables. From this sum would be deducted total taxes previously paid. The remainder would be the payment due in the tenth year. Conceivably the averaging period could extend from the taxpayer's first income tax return or his majority until his death.

Cumulative averaging would not require the reopening of preceding years' tax returns, for only the number of years elapsed in the averaging period, the cumulated total of taxable income, and the sum of the taxes previously paid would be needed, and these figures could be carried forward from the tax return of each preceding year.

A separate table of effective tax rates would be prepared by the Treasury Department for each span of years covered by different taxpayers during an averaging period: some individuals, more recently become of age or for other reasons more recently entered into the averaging system, might be submitting income tax returns for only the third or fourth time while others were submitting them for the seventh or eighth. If the averaging period was 10 years, the Treasury would have to prepare 10 sets of tax tables, but each taxpayer would have to refer to only one each year. Since cumulative averaging, other things being equal, would reduce tax liabilities for those with fluctuating incomes without raising them for those with stable incomes, a somewhat higher level of tax rates would be needed to raise a given revenue.

With unrealized gains and losses accounted for only every 10 years, or possibly only at death or at the time a gift is made, the valuation problem would become more manageable. Taxpayers would be kept abreast of their tax liabilities, except for the final reconciliation for unrealized gains and losses at the end of the averaging period. With such advance notice, it could be assumed that they will have had ample opportunity to raise the sums required for taxes on unrealized gains. At the same time, the knowledge that unrealized capital gains and losses must be accounted for on these occasions, though on an average basis, might well reduce the influence of tax considerations upon the timing of realizations of gain and loss. Voluntary inclusion of appreciation in capital assets at any time during the averaging period could also be permitted.

For stricter equity and to reduce the incentive offered by the free use of tax funds to defer the realization of capital gains and other income, it has been suggested that an interest adjustment might be incorporated in the cumulative averaging of incomes. Taxpayers would be credited each year with a stipulated rate of interest on the cumulated taxes they had paid during the averaging period, and the same amount of interest would be added to their cumulated incomes. Those who deferred the realization of income would obtain smaller interest credits. This adjustment, however, is not an essential part of the device.

The cumulative averaging method would not avoid a heavy concentration of tax liability or tax credit in the year of realization. Taxpayers would have their preceding years' taxable incomes raised by current realizations of gains and lowered by current losses, and would be required at these times to make up deficiencies in earlier tax payments or to receive credits for previous overpayments. In consequence, an incentive would remain to defer the realization of gains and to speed that of losses. If unrealized gains and losses were to be accounted for at the end of each averaging period, the markets for capital assets would probably be subjected to a large volume of tax-motivated transactions as the end of the period approached. Such transactions would be distributed over time if, instead of uniform dates, the averaging periods of large groups of taxpayers were made to end in different years.

If, on the other hand, unrealized changes in capital values were to be recognized only at death or upon transfer of property by gift, there would be a strong inducement to postpone realizing gains until after the end of the averaging period. The fact that the action of one Congress may be amended or repealed would lead many investors to defer realization in the hope of favorable changes in the law. The treatment of unrealized changes in capital values as income at the end of each averaging period or upon transfer of property by gift or at death would raise the same questions of constitutional validity as under the annual accrual proposal.

As with annual accrual of unrealized changes in capital values, cumulative averaging would accentuate cyclical fluctuations in tax receipts. While taxable incomes would be raised in depression years by being averaged with larger preceding incomes, the average income itself would be smaller and this would create tax credits for preceding years that would tend to reduce the current year tax liabilities. Conversely, in prosperous periods the large incomes would be averaged downward when combined with the lower incomes of preceding years but the cumulated average would rise, thereby increasing current tax liabilities for the underreporting of average income in the preceding years. Nothing in the scheme would prevent raising tax rates in good years and lowering them in bad years to accentuate this effect. Those who favor a strong use of fiscal policy to reduce cyclical fluctuations in private incomes would welcome such sizeable and partly automatic responses in tax receipts to offset movements in national income; others would doubtless be alarmed.

Although cumulative averaging seems to possess many attractive possibilities, particularly in the direction of giving more equitable tax treatment to individuals whose incomes, including capital gains and losses, vary widely, the concept is novel and unfamiliar. It has never been considered by Congress, nor has it yet received any significant public attention. Its merits appear to justify serious study, but it seems unlikely to command legislative attention in the near future.

5 UNREALIZED CAPITAL GAINS AND LOSSES EMBODIED IN PROPERTY TRANSFERRED BY GIFT OR AT DEATH

Many persons who would oppose the inclusion of unrealized capital gains and losses in taxable income under the annual accrual proposal, or at the end of relatively brief averaging periods, favor such a treatment of gains and losses embodied in property transferred by gift or at death. Under any method of taxing only *realized* capital gains, including all devices hitherto tried in the United States, a broad avenue for tax avoidance is created by the exclusion of unrealized capital gains embodied in such transfers. Estate and gift taxes provide only a partial offset. They are payable also on estates that owe nothing to unrealized appreciation in capital assets and on those that have been reduced by income taxes previously paid on realized gains. Although, other things being equal, the taxable estate is increased, and often the marginal tax rate raised, when an estate contains unrealized capital gains, the increase in the estate tax ordinarily constitutes merely a small fraction of the income tax avoided on the capital gains.

To begin with, no addition to a taxable estate takes place when a man consumes during his lifetime the tax saved by not realizing his gains. Even when he consumes none of it, the addition to his estate tax cannot equal the saving in his income tax as long as the effective rate of the former is less than 100 percent. For most estates the effective rate on additions is far below the present top bracket rate, 77 percent, on amounts in excess of $10,000,000 (for the tentative estate tax, which is reduced by the allowable credit for inheritance or estate taxes paid to states). In an estate of half a million dollars, of which $400,000 represents unrealized appreciation, the total federal estate tax under the Revenue Act of 1948 would be $45,300 if half the estate was left to the decedent's widow and half to his children (after the maximum allowable credit for inheritance and estate taxes paid to states). Had the decedent realized the capital gains in the same amount before death and paid the maximum 25 percent rate on them, he would have paid $100,000 more in income taxes while reducing his estate tax only $13,800. The difference, $86,200, represents the net taxes avoided by holding his appreciated assets until death. The increase in the estate tax is a bigger offset in larger estates, but in no case approaches closely the amount of capital gains tax avoided.

Transfers of appreciated property by gifts *inter vivos* usually involve a smaller ultimate tax avoidance and sometimes even a net increase in taxes, because the donee, upon sale of the property, becomes subject to a capital gains tax on the difference between the proceeds and the donor's costs, and because a gift tax is payable by the donor on the value of the gift itself. Nevertheless, transfers by gift without recognition of accrued appreciation make possible extremely long postponement of the capital gains tax, conceivably for several generations; and the effective tax rates on gifts are generally much lower than on estates. Moreover, the present transfer of 'basis' from the donor to the donee is not consistent with the personal character of the income tax, for it permits appreciation accruing during ownership by a donor with a large income to be taxed, if the property is subsequently sold, at the lower rates applicable to donees with smaller incomes.

Gifts of appreciated property for recognized charitable and scientific purposes pose a special anomaly. By permitting the donor to deduct the full current market value of the donated property from his taxable income, up to 15 percent of the taxpayer's adjusted gross income, while not requiring him to include in his income the increase in its value occurring during his ownership, the law, in effect, recognizes the accrued appreciation as a deduction, but not as income. In consequence, taxpayers in high surtax brackets may often make charitable gifts in the form of appreciated assets at little net cost to themselves. In extreme cases, the saving in the donor's taxes is larger than the amount he could realize, net of taxes, by selling the property.[7]

The estate and gift taxes do not provide any offset to the avoidance of capital gains taxes (or the disallowance of unrealized capital losses) whenever the amounts of property transferred are smaller than the substantial exemptions and exclusions under the former. Under the property-splitting provisions of the Revenue Act of 1948, the amount that may be transferred tax-free was greatly increased. For these various reasons, the estate and gift taxes provide relatively small offsets in the aggregate to the capital gains taxes avoided through transfers of appreciated assets at death and by gift.

A major consideration urged in favor of recognizing unrealized capital gains and losses embodied in such transfers as components of income is that this treatment logically complements the use at all other times of the realization principle. To postpone recognition for tax purposes of a capital gain or loss until it is realized by sale or other transfer has many practical advantages over proposed treatments that require annual tax accounting for changes in the market value of capital assets, and is supported by long tradition and business usage. Unless capital gains and losses are finally accounted for at death, however, mere postponement of income tax liability or credit may become transformed into complete avoidance or disallowance. If transfers at death were made occasions for taxing accrued gains, postponement of realization during life would still have the advantage of a free use of funds otherwise currently payable in taxes, but would lose the more powerful advantage of full income tax exemption. Such a change would take most of the force from proposals to tax accrued gains.

[7] Under the 1948-49 rate schedule a single taxpayer with surtax net income of more than $200,000 or a married couple with a joint income of more than $400,000, after deduction of the maximum allowable charitable contribution, would be money ahead if, instead of selling assets that had appreciated approximately 71.5 percent or more, they gave them to charity. The reduction in income tax, 82.1275 percent of the value of the donated assets, plus the avoidance of the 25 percent tax on the appreciation, would exceed the value of the asset. If the taxpayer kept the asset, however, the capital gains tax would not apply. Hence donating it would be more profitable than selling it but not than keeping it.

This change has been urged also as perhaps the simplest and least disrupting means of ensuring that stockholders will ultimately be subjected to personal income tax on their *pro rata* shares of rein-vested corporate profits. Such profits now escape the personal income tax unless subsequently received in dividends or through realized capital gains. Though offset in uneven degree for different stockholders by the corporate income tax, this type of tax avoidance is regarded by many as the most serious inequity of the personal income tax.[8]

Apart from the question of equity, the fluidity of the market for capital assets is affected. Even a moderate tax on realized capital gains may be expected to discourage the sale of appreciated assets by aged individuals if gains may pass tax-free at death. This influence is enhanced by the fact that the equivalent of all or much of the gains may nevertheless be enjoyed during life by borrowing against the appreciated assets.

The valuation difficulties that would attend a general inclusion of unrealized capital gains and losses in taxable income would be much smaller if such treatment was confined to property passing at death or transferred by gift. Valuations are already required for estates large enough to be subject to federal or state estate and inheritance taxes, and for gifts subject to the gift tax. Many more valuations would be needed, however, to cover the assets of smaller estates and gifts, and special difficulties would be faced in connection with property held in trust.

The constitutional basis for taxing unrealized capital gains embodied in property transferred at death or by gift may be stronger than that for taxing other unrealized appreciation. It has been suggested that such transfers of property can be legally regarded as occasioning 'constructive realization' of capital gain or loss.[9] Even if this doctrine did not win judicial sanction, the same result might be achieved by imposing an excise tax on the accrued gains at the same rates and in combination with the taxes on ordinary income. Gift and death have been held to constitute appropriate occasions for a federal excise tax on property transfers. The constitutionality of applying an excise tax at graduated rates to only the part of each gift or be-

[8] See, for example, Simons, *Personal Income Taxation*, pp. 164-5.
[9] See remarks of Eustace Seligman and S. S. Surrey in *Capital Gains Taxation*, p. 41; H. M. Groves, *Production, Jobs and Taxes* (McGraw-Hill, 1944), p. 75, and *Postwar Taxation and Economic Progress* (1946), p. 219; Committee for Economic Development, *A Postwar Federal Tax Plan for High Employment* (Aug. 1944), p. 31; Vickrey, *Agenda for Progressive Taxation*, pp. 140-1 and 396.

quest that represents appreciation in the hands of the donor or decedent would appear to turn on whether such a classification is reasonable for the purpose of the tax.

Although the constructive realization proposal has been most commonly made in conjunction with programs for the full inclusion of capital gains and losses in ordinary income, it could be applied also to existing and similar preferential tax treatments of capital gains and limitations on the deductibility of capital losses as a means of reducing tax avoidance and postponement.

Transfer of basis

An alternative method of treating unrealized capital gains transferred at death appears to avoid the constitutional question involved in the doctrine of constructive realization. Bequests of appreciated property would be treated in the same way as gifts of such assets are now treated: the recipient would be required, when he sold the property, to calculate his taxable gain, if any, by the difference between the proceeds and the cost of the property to the decedent, rather than, as at present, by the difference between the proceeds and the value of the property on the date of death.[10] Such a method is open to the objection that, by transferring the 'basis' of one individual to another whose income may be in a much different tax bracket, it departs from the principle of a personal income tax. But Congress has not found this objection decisive in the case of gains embodied in gifts *inter vivos*.

Whether a decedent should be permitted to transfer unrealized capital losses raises a similar question. Much of the value of some bequests would then arise from their power to reduce the tax liability of the recipient, and testators could maximize the tax value of their unrealized losses by bequeathing properties embodying the largest losses to heirs with the largest taxable incomes. Congress shut off these possibilities in the case of gifts *inter vivos* by requiring the donee, upon sale of the property, to use market value on the date of transfer, if this was less than the cost to the donor, as the basis for calculating the capital loss. Congress would probably adopt a similar rule to limit the loss allowance if inheritors of property were required to adopt the basis of the decedent for calculating capital gains and losses.

The objections raised against taxing as income unrealized capital

[10] *Capital Gains Taxation*, p. 37, and Vickrey, *Agenda for Progressive Taxation*, p. 141.

gains embodied in property transferred at death are identical in part with those made against applying income taxes to any capital gains, and, more particularly, against unrealized capital gains. The latter are further removed from the traditional concept of income than realized capital gains. No market transaction has been completed by the decedent to mark the receipt of income represented by the unrealized capital gain. Federal and state death taxes already make up for some of the taxes that would be separately paid if a decedent's unrealized gains were taxed, and the rest would have the practical result of raising the effective rates of tax on estates. In many instances where unrealized gains constituted a large fraction of a sizeable estate, the difficulties already experienced by many executors in liquidating property to raise cash to pay the death taxes would be seriously increased.

6 AVERAGING DEVICES

The characteristically sporadic realization of capital gains and losses has been a main reason for according them special treatment under a graduated income tax. Otherwise they become subject to larger taxes or to smaller allowances than if the same amounts were distributed among the taxable incomes of the years in which they were emerging. The annual accrual proposal would avoid the bunching of tax recognition in the year of realization, but would not meet the problem of fluctuations in the annual accruals themselves. Appreciations in capital values would still tend to be bunched for most individuals in years of rising business activity, when the tax liabilities on them would be increased by the inclusion of the gains with enlarged ordinary incomes, the sum of which would be subject to the progressive rate schedule. For capital losses the tendencies would be opposite. The treatment of death and gift transfers as occasioning realization of gain or loss would, in the absence of countervailing measures, accentuate the tax consequences of concentrated realizations. Cumulative averaging of all incomes would meet this problem, as well as that of changing tax rates, but would be a radical departure from practice.

The special treatments of capital gains and losses under American income tax laws since 1921 have in no case closely approached those of allocating capital gains and losses among the years in which they arose. They have included, among other things, arbitrary narrow limits on the deductibility of net capital losses from other income and on the privilege of carrying forward unallowed net capital losses to future years. Such treatment of losses has been based in part on the assumption, often untrue, that the same taxpayers realize both gains and losses, and partly on the practical view that taxpayers have the initiative in realizing gains and losses, with the result that a more liberal allowance for losses would be likely to motivate wealthy taxpayers in particular to realize their losses but to leave their gains unrealized.

In an attempt to reach a better solution, various devices for averaging capital gains and losses have been proposed from time to time. In recent years the averaging idea has been extended by some to cover all highly fluctuating incomes and, as in the instance of cumulative averaging, even all incomes.[11] The object is to avoid imposing a higher tax upon individuals with variable incomes than upon those with the same aggregate of stable incomes.

Most of the recent averaging proposals contemplate the full inclusion of the averaged capital gains and losses in taxable income, but would restrict it to the realized amounts, except that property transfers at death or by gift would be regarded as occasioning constructive realization. Averaging realized gains and losses is urged as more manageable than the annual accrual proposal, though it too may be combined with the periodic recognition of unrealized capital gains and losses at longer intervals, say every 5 or 10 years. It may be combined also with preferential tax rates on gains and limitation upon the allowances for losses.

All averaging proposals that contemplate the full inclusion of capital gains and losses in taxable income entail sharp increases in the present effective tax rates on gains and in the allowances for capital losses. The equitable and practical effects of such increases, already discussed, should be differentiated, as far as possible, from the relative merits of different averaging devices, for, among other reasons, the latter may be combined with a varying degree of preferential treatment of capital gains and of limitations on the allowances for capital losses. Assuming a given degree of taxation, the relative merits of different averaging schemes turn mainly upon how well they offset the inequitable effects of a graduated rate schedule upon bunched realization of gains and losses, on how they affect the ability and disposition of taxpayers to time transactions with an eye to tax consequences, and their administrative complexity.

In addition to the cumulative averaging proposal discussed, three

[11] Simons, *op. cit.;* Vickrey, *Journal of Political Economy,* June 1939, and *Agenda for Progressive Taxation,* p. 166; Roy Blough, Averaging of Income for Tax Purposes, *Accounting Review,* Jan. 1945, p. 86.

other types of averaging devices may be distinguished: optional
periodic averaging of capital gains and losses, their proration over
a period of years, and carrybacks and carryforwards.

7 OPTIONAL PERIODIC AVERAGING OF CAPITAL GAINS AND LOSSES
A relatively simple method of providing relief to taxpayers whose
annual incomes fluctuate materially was proposed by Henry C.
Simons and has been supported by others.[12] A taxpayer would have
the option of averaging his income for the preceding 5 years, and of
computing his aggregate tax liability as if his annual income, including capital gains and losses, had been the average amount. He could
then apply for a refund of the difference between the total tax liability so computed and the taxes he actually paid. To avoid excessive
administrative costs when amounts are small, a moderate flat charge
of perhaps $20 plus 1 percent or less of the readjusted tax liability,
might be made.[13] If this device were applied only to capital gains and
losses rather than to all taxable income the administrative burden
would be much lighter because fewer returns would be averaged.

Apart from the difficulties of reopening past returns, it has been
objected that taxpayers would have to engage in a guessing game as
to which of the various 5-year periods available to them should be
averaged to give them the biggest refund. Many persons would not
receive the relief open to them because of ignorance or faulty choice
of the averaging period. Vickrey points out that the plan does not do
anything to correct the unduly favorable treatment of taxpayers
whose years of high income happen to coincide with years of reduced
rates. Such discriminations might become more significant if rates
were changed frequently as part of a policy of counter-cyclical ma-
nipulation of tax revenues.

Nevertheless, the relative simplicity of the proposal, its effect of
permitting a wide offsetting of capital gains against earlier capital
losses and vice versa, and the distribution of a gain or loss over 5
years, are highly attractive.

8 PRORATION OF CAPITAL GAINS AND LOSSES
Proration calls for evenly apportioning the amount of a capital gain
or loss among the years the asset was held, or over a fixed number
of years, such as 5. Five possible methods will be discussed in turn.

a) *Backward proration over a fixed number of years*
If a 5-year period were adopted, the taxpayer would divide the net

[12] *Op. cit.*, p. 154; H. M. Groves, *op. cit.*, pp. 85-6.
[13] Vickrey has suggested this type of charge, *Agenda for Progressive Taxation*,
pp. 171-2.

capital gain or loss realized in the current year into 5 equal parts and tentatively compute his tax for the current year, then recompute it for each of the preceding 4 years, on the assumption that one-fifth of his current year's capital gain or loss had been realized in each of the 5 years. The tax on or tax credit for the capital gain or loss would be the difference between the total tax liability for the 5 years and the taxes already paid.

b) *Backward proration over the number of years the asset was held*
If the period for prorating a realized capital gain or loss was the actual number of years the asset had been held, the computations would be much more complex. A gain or loss on an asset held 20 years would require reopening 19 annual tax returns; and a taxpayer who realized gains and losses in the same year from several assets held for varying periods would have to make a separate calculation, involving a different number of previous tax rates, for each gain or loss.

Under both proration devices just described, the necessity of reopening tax returns would create administrative difficulties. The second would be far more cumbersome. Nevertheless, an analogous device is now prescribed in the Internal Revenue Code, Section 107, in connection with income from personal services and "artistic work or invention" requiring 36 months or more to complete. Such income, provided more than 80 percent is received in one taxable year, may be prorated back over the period during which it was earned if the taxpayer chooses. Back pay exceeding 15 percent of the taxpayer's gross income in the year of receipt may also be allocated back to the years in which it was earned. A similar apportionment of realized capital gains over the period during which the asset was held was embodied in a measure (H. R. 14198) passed by the House of Representatives in 1920, but was rejected by the Senate because of its administrative and compliance difficulties. Apportionment backward over a fixed number of years, such as 5 or 10, would be much simpler, but would also necessitate the reopening of past returns. Individuals realizing capital gains or losses each year, of course, vastly outnumber the relatively few who are affected by Section 107.

c) *Backward proration with tax or credit determined by current income and rates*
One proration method that avoids reopening returns would have the taxpayer (1) divide his realized net capital gain or loss (presumably on assets held more than 1 year) into a fixed number of equal parts,

say 5; (2) compute the difference in his tax liability before and after adding one-fifth of the capital gain or loss to his other income in the year of realization; and (3) multiply this difference by 5 to arrive at the full amount of the tax or tax credit for the total capital gain or loss. The effective tax rate or tax credit would be determined by the taxpayer's ordinary income and the prevailing rate schedule in the year of realization rather than by the ordinary income and rate schedules during the years the gain or loss actually or presumptively accrued. The results would be identical only if the taxpayer's ordinary net income and the effective tax rate remained constant during the period. The equity sacrificed by assuming constancy of ordinary income and effective tax rate must be weighed against the tremendous reduction in the difficulties of compliance and administration.

Under all three methods of backward proration the tax would be payable or the loss deductible in the year of realization. This has the advantage of synchronizing the tax liability on a gain with the presumable receipt of funds with which to pay it, and of synchronizing the loss allowance with a realized loss. It has the disadvantage of retaining or increasing much of the present influence of tax considerations upon the timing of sales of capital assets. Under the third method, taxpayers would have a motive for bunching realizations of gains in years of low tax rates and small ordinary income and for bunching loss realizations in years of high rates and large ordinary income. If the prescribed averaging period was the number of years the asset had been held, a strong motive would be offered to realize losses quickly but to defer the realization of gains as long as possible.

Were a uniform averaging period adopted (presumably for all gains and losses on assets held more than 1 year), and were the effective tax rates those of the preceding 5 or 10 years, the effect upon the timing of transactions would be somewhat more diffuse, but would still be responsive to calculations of the relative tax liabilities under the income and tax rates of the preceding 5 or 10 years as against those in prospect. Under all three methods, moreover, taxpayers would retain an incentive to defer the realization of capital gains in order to avoid the immediate loss of capital funds to meet the tax liability; and they would be encouraged to take losses quickly to obtain immediate tax reductions.

d) *Forward proration over a fixed number of years*

A fourth method, which would reduce these influences, is to prorate capital gains and losses over the succeeding instead of the preceding 5 or 10 years. The taxpayer would include in his current taxable income only one-fifth of a net realized gain or loss, for example, and would carry forward one-fifth to each of the next 4 years. His tax or tax deduction would be determined by his ordinary income and the prevailing tax schedules in the current and succeeding 4 years, instead of those of the years in which the gain or loss actually or presumptively accrued.

The smaller immediate tax liability could be expected to weaken the deterrent effect of the tax upon decisions to realize gains. An investor contemplating the sale of appreciated property would face an immediate reduction in his liquid funds or earning assets of only one-fifth of the tax liability on his gains, if a 5-year period was adopted, and the remainder would be distributed over the ensuing 4 years. Similarly, if only one-fifth of a loss was deductible in the year of realization, the tax incentive to take losses at particular times would be less pronounced. The effective tax rates and allowances on the gains and losses carried forward would be unknown because they would depend upon the future tax schedules and the taxpayer's future income.

e) *Forward proration with tax or credit determined by current income and rates*

Instead of the amounts of untaxed gains and unallowed losses, the carryforwards might be in the form of a fixed tax liability or tax credit, determined by the taxable income and rate schedule of the year of realization, and payable or deductible in equal annual instalments, such as one-fifth. This scheme would differ from the preceding in that the taxpayer would know the total tax cost or tax allowance of his gain or loss and in that only one year's tax return would have to be looked at to determine the amount.

Forward proration of profits from instalment sales, including capital gains, is now permitted under the Internal Revenue Code, Section 44, the taxes due each year being only in proportion to the payments received. The practical advantage of synchronizing the tax liability with the receipt of income, which is achieved in the instalment sales provision, would be absent under universal forward proration of capital gains and losses. Some loss of revenue could doubtless be expected owing to the inability of some taxpayers to pay the deferred taxes on gains previously realized.

Deferred tax charges and credits easier to administer but less equitable than direct offsetting of gains and losses

Whether or not full deductibility of capital losses from ordinary income is allowed, averaging methods that permit the forward or backward offsetting of capital gains and losses against each other are likely to be more advantageous to taxpayers than those that merely fix the tax rate or tax credit by prorating gains and losses, for a graduated rate schedule causes the tax-reducing value of capital losses to be less than the taxes on equal amounts of capital gains, assuming that other income is constant. The practical importance of the difference is increased by the tendency for larger amounts of capital gains to be realized in higher income periods, and of capital losses to be heavier when ordinary incomes are lower. The difference would be further increased if the federal government adopted a policy of raising and reducing tax rates with upward and downward movements, respectively, in national income.

However, the administrative consideration that the determination of the tax or tax credit by referring to a single year's return is much simpler favors the third and fifth proration methods.

Any variant of the proration technique could be introduced on either a voluntary or compulsory basis. Since the primary objective would be to redress unfairness suffered only by some taxpayers, and since it is desirable to keep the administrative burden as small as possible, a voluntary basis would seem adequate.

9 DESIRABLE LENGTH OF THE AVERAGING PERIOD

If capital gains alone are considered, the averaging period necessary to overcome tolerably well the inequitable consequences of applying graduated rates to bunched realizations is much shorter, in all but exceptional cases, than might be imagined. In effect, averaging multiplies each surtax bracket by the number of years in the averaging period. For example, if the averaging period was 5 years, the whole of a $10,000 capital gain would be taxed at the rate applicable to an addition of only $2,000 a year to the surtax income. The existing surtax brackets are narrowest and the graduation of rates sharpest in the lower part of the surtax schedule; the brackets become fairly wide and the progression of rates small in the upper part. For married persons filing joint returns under the Revenue Act of 1950, the effective surtax brackets were $4,000 wide at the lower end of the surtax scale and $100,000 at the top. With a 5-year averaging period, these surtax brackets would in effect range from $20,000 at the lower end of the scale to $500,000 at the top. For single persons and married persons filing separate returns, the brackets would be half as wide.

These figures suggest that an averaging period as short as 5 or even 3 years would be sufficient in most instances to eliminate any sizeable tax penalties otherwise created by a concentration of capital gains in a single year. If the sole object of the present preferential tax rates on capital gains is to offset the over-taxation of bunched gains under a graduated rate schedule, the offset is excessive. The present rates are materially lower than those that would prevail even under an averaging period as long as 20 years.

Only a relatively small difference in effective rates would be obtained under a 20-year, as compared with a 5-year averaging period, if we assume that ordinary income is constant. For example, for a married couple without dependents filing a joint return reporting a net income of $50,000, the difference in the effective tax rate on a capital gain of $50,000 fully prorated over 20 instead of 5 years would be less than 2 percentage points. It would shrink for smaller capital gains and for larger incomes.

The differences are somewhat more substantial, but not large, for incomes of $25,000 or less. On a joint return reporting ordinary income of $5,000, the difference in effective tax rate between a 5- and a 20-year averaging period, with capital gains fully included, would be 1.6 percentage points for a $5,000 capital gain, less than one point for a $10,000 or $25,000 capital gain, and 2.9 points for a $50,000 capital gain.

A similar comparison with respect to capital losses is presented in Table 89. Since this table shows only the tax value of the deductibility of capital losses from ordinary income, which is limited to $6,000 over a 5-year period under present law, it understates the existing loss allowance to the extent that taxpayers offset their capital losses against capital gains. The tax value of allowances for losses under any system of averaging would depend also in large degree upon the extent to which the taxpayer were permitted and able to utilize his capital losses to offset capital gains. The table clearly shows the small existing allowance against ordinary income for capital losses, and the large increases that would follow from full allowance under averaging. For example, a married couple filing a joint return with a constant ordinary net income of $10,000 and reporting a $10,000 net capital loss now receives a reduction in tax amounting to 11.1 percent of the capital loss over the 5-year carry-over period. If the loss was allowed in full and prorated evenly over 5 years, the tax reduction for the loss would be almost double, 20.8 percent.

The equitable treatment of capital losses that are large relative to ordinary income would appear to require either a longer averaging period than that for capital gains or a carryover of unused capital losses from one averaging period to the next. Otherwise a taxpayer's income during the period may be insufficient to permit him to offset his losses for tax purposes. Under a 5-year averaging period a married couple filing a joint return showing a constant ordinary income of $5,000, and realizing a net capital loss of $50,000 in one year, would obtain a total tax reduction equal to only 6.3 percent of the loss, as compared with 12.6 and 16.6 percent, respectively, for 10- and 20-year averaging periods.

10 CARRYING CAPITAL LOSSES BACK AND FORWARD SOLELY AGAINST CAPITAL GAINS

A considerable measure of averaging capital gains and losses could be achieved merely by permitting taxpayers to offset capital gains realized in any year by unallowed capital losses reported during the preceding few years, and by permitting capital losses realized in any year not only to be carried forward against future capital gains but to offset capital gains reported in several preceding years. For example, offsetting could be permitted for 3 years back, and unused losses carried forward 3 years.

The present 5-year carryforward of capital losses against future capital gains is defective in that it benefits only those who realize future capital gains. Losers not lucky enough to obtain offsetting gains receive relief only to the extent that their net capital losses are covered by the existing allowance of $1,000 against ordinary income in each of 6 successive years. If they were permitted to offset losses also against earlier capital gains and to receive an appropriate tax refund or credit, the treatment would be more balanced. The discrimination now suffered by persons whose capital gains precede their capital losses, as against those whose losses come first, would be eliminated.

This method could be combined with any of the proration devices and with restrictions on the deductibility of capital losses from ordinary income and on the proportion of capital gains subject to income tax.

This type of averaging would obviously be more limited in its effects than the more comprehensive methods previously discussed. It would, however, achieve one of the major objectives: a more equitable treatment of taxpayers who realize both capital gains and losses in different years. Many persons who object to the full deductibility of capital losses from ordinary income would support a proposal of this character.

11 CONTROLLING INFLUENCE OF MARKET EFFECTS UPON EVOLUTION OF CAPITAL GAINS TAX TREATMENT IN THE U. S.

The more radical proposed departures from present practice reviewed in the foregoing all place a much greater emphasis upon equitable as opposed to operational considerations than Congress has been disposed to do. Moreover, the desire to avoid undue administrative complexity has been a serious obstacle to their adoption. Other barriers have been the desire to maximize tax revenues and to offer a special tax incentive for venturesome investment. Most important of all has been the fear of unduly impeding transactions in capital assets. In recommending in 1921 the abandonment of the full inclusion of realized capital gains and losses in taxable income, the Ways and Means Committee declared:

"The sale of farms, mineral properties, and other capital assets is now seriously retarded by the fact that gains and profits earned over a series of years are under the present law taxed as a lump sum (and the amount of surtax greatly enhanced thereby) in the year in which the profit is realized. Many such sales, with their possible profit taking and consequent increase of the tax revenue, have been blocked by this feature of the present law."

Again in 1923, in commenting on the pre-1922 full recognition, the Committee declared:

"But of much greater importance was the decided interference with the normal course of business and commerce. With a maximum tax of 77 percent there was a severe artificial restraint on sales at a profit, and many transfers of property extremely desirable from the standpoint of economic development and general public welfare were not only retarded but actually prevented. In addition, there was a serious loss of revenue, in that the initiative, as is always the case, remained with the taxpayer, who refrained from taking a profit but who did not hesitate to take a loss which could be deducted in full from his taxable income." This consideration has remained a dominant influence in most subsequent revisions of the tax treatment of capital gains.

Had Congress been concerned solely with the effects upon the markets for capital assets, it could have disposed of the problem merely by excluding capital gains from taxable income or by imposing a flat rate. The latter proposal has been strongly urged at various

times, and was incorporated in the Boland Bill of 1942 (H. R. 6358).
But equitable considerations, in the sense of the equal tax treatment
of similarly circumstanced taxpayers, led most legislators to insist
upon some degree of integration between taxes on capital gains and
on ordinary income. Three aspects of equity have been prominent in
this connection: the relative treatment of (a) equal incomes derived
from ordinary sources and from capital gains; (b) different amounts
of capital gains realized by taxpayers with equal ordinary incomes;
and (c) stable ordinary incomes and the characteristically bunched
realizations of capital gains emerging over a period of more than
one year.

The Revenue Act of 1921 attempted to reconcile these aspects of
equity with the demands of practical expediency by the full inclusion
of capital gains and losses in taxable income for all individuals whose
effective tax rate on capital gains would be 12½ percent or less; and
by the separate taxation of the gains realized by others at a flat rate
of 12½ percent. Subsequently a parallel treatment for the allowance
of capital losses was adopted. These provisions withheld preferential
rates from the gains of taxpayers with smaller incomes.

In the early and middle 1930's problems of tax avoidance and of
achieving more equity and progressivity in the income tax structure
assumed a larger place in public discussions than the maintenance of
active securities markets. The desirable degree of preference in tax
rates to be accorded capital gains was now thought to turn more
largely on their lumpy character and the consequent inequity of taxing them in full under a system of graduated rates. Accordingly, in
the Revenue Act of 1934 Congress removed the ceiling on the effective tax rates applicable to capital gains, graduated the degree of
preferential treatment in 5 stages according to the length of time the
asset had been held by excluding progressively larger fractions of
the gains from taxable income, and extended this treatment to all
taxable incomes.

Many persons mistakenly believed that the percentage exclusion
treatment adopted would yield substantially the same results, with
less administrative complexity, as the proration of capital gains and
losses over the same periods. But the degree of tax preference needed
solely to offset the higher tax rates otherwise applicable to the
bunched realization of long-emerging capital gains is smaller than
is commonly believed, as previously noted, and varies with income.
Since the tax brackets widen considerably and the progression of
rates slackens as we go up the income scale, only such bunched gains

COMPETING PROPOSALS   315

as are large relative to ordinary income in the lower and middle surtax brackets tend to raise materially the effective rates under the
rate schedule then or now in force. Consequently, different rather
than uniform percentages of exclusion for different income levels
would be needed to achieve results approximating those of proration.

As noted in Chapter 6, the graduated fractional recognition
method of 1934-37, which did not stipulate any special maximum
rate for capital gains, noticeably discouraged the realization of gains
by the upper income groups both because of the sharply increased
tax rates and because of the substantial tax reductions offered for
continued holding of an appreciated asset beyond the end of each
successive holding period. The percentage allowances for capital
losses of different age groups created anomalies by stimulating taxpayers to choose the assets on which to realize losses in such ways
as to offset relatively large gains from long-held assets with smaller
losses from shorter-held ones. On the other hand, the rigid limitation
of $2,000 on the deductibility of statutory net capital losses from
ordinary income aroused widespread complaint.

When the Revenue Act of 1938 was in the early stages of its legislative history the House Bill sought to reduce the sharp stepdowns
in effective rates for capital gains and losses as the period of ownership lengthened. Instead of only 5 age classes it was proposed to
substitute 49, with a gently graduated downward movement of effective rates as ownership lengthened. But this provision, which was
subsequently eliminated because of its administrative complexity,
would have been of doubtful efficacy in reducing the tax incentive to
postpone realizations of gains. Under the 1934 Act an investor who
had held an appreciating asset for 2 years could not ordinarily obtain
a further tax advantage from continued retention unless he was prepared to hold it for at least 3 years more; but under the 1938 House
Bill, every additional few months of holding beyond 2 years would
confer a tax advantage.

With its eyes fixed once more on the capital markets, Congress
finally reduced to only 2 the holding periods entitled to preferential
treatment: 18-24, and over 24 months; and it reimposed ceiling
rates on capital gains: 15 percent on gains from assets held longer
than 2 years, and 20 percent on gains from assets held 18-24 months.
At the same time it removed the $2,000 limit on the deductibility of
statutory net capital losses from other income, except that net losses
on assets held 18 months or less could be carried forward and deducted only from short term gains realized in the succeeding year.

The drastic increases in effective tax rates on ordinary incomes in 1939-41, preceding the entrance of the United States into World War II, were not accompanied by a rise in the maximum rates on capital gains. When further advances in ordinary rates were in process of enactment in 1942, the disparity seemed excessive on both equitable and practical counts, and Congress raised the ceiling rate on capital gains to 25 percent. As contrasted with the new high rates on ordinary incomes, this rate was believed to offer sufficient tax preference to avoid severely impeding transactions in capital assets. At the same time Congress returned to a single holding period for qualifying capital gains for preferential treatment. It merely excluded from taxable income half of the gains from all assets held more than 6 months. The maximum rate, 25 percent of the total gain, applied only when the inclusion of half the gain in ordinary income would impose a higher effective rate. Impressed by the large loss realizations of 1938-41 under the unlimited deductibility of statutory net long term capital losses then in effect, Congress reimposed restrictions on such allowances though in a new manner as discussed in Chapter 7.

Exclusion of short term gains and losses from special treatment

The evolution of American practice with respect to the exclusion of short term gains and losses from special treatment reflects a similar emphasis upon market effects, qualified by equitable considerations and by a desire to withhold preferential treatment from speculative gains. The initial 2-year holding period requirement became a part of the Revenue Act of 1921 through an amendment offered on the floor of the Senate. The bill under consideration proposed to extend preferential treatment to all capital gains, but Senator Walsh of Massachusetts objected to the absence of a distinction between "increased value . . . extending over a long period of years and that sudden and speculative increase that develops within a short period of time". He proposed a 3-year holding period, but compromised on 2-years when a 1-year requirement was suggested to overcome his objection.[14]

The persistence of this attitude toward short term speculative gains is indicated in the report of a subcommittee of the House Ways and Means Committee in 1938:

"It has always been the settled policy of the Congress to tax speculative gains in general in the same manner and to the same extent as earned income and business profits. . . . Your subcommittee believes

[14] *Congressional Record*, 67th Cong., 1st Sess., Vol. 61, Part 7, pp. 6575-6.

that this policy is wise and should be adhered to. It would be against sound public policy to make any changes in the revenue law whose tendency would be affirmatively to encourage speculation by preferential taxation. . . . Your subcommittee recognizes that a classification based solely upon the period of holding is not an exact method for segregating speculative from investment transactions, but it appears to be the only practicable method and is believed to be a sufficiently fair criterion for practical purposes."

But the unwillingness to grant tax privileges to speculative gains conflicted with the desire to avoid impeding the ready transfer of capital assets. Even under the relatively low income tax rates in force in the latter part of 1922-31, the 2-year holding period was criticized on the ground that it retarded the realization of gains and speeded that of losses. The step-down scale of 1934-37 reduced the minimum required period to 1 year. The Revenue Act of 1938 raised it to 18 months.

During the Congressional hearings on the Revenue Act of 1942 strong representations were made that the 18-month requirement was seriously interfering with the free transfer of capital funds, and the Boland Bill, as already noted, proposed to abolish the holding period. A 1-year period was suggested by others as most consistent with the annual taxation of ordinary income. The 6-month period finally adopted was the most liberal since the holding period concept was first introduced.

The existing tax treatment of capital gains and losses is clearly the product of long legislative experimentation. It would be foolhardy to predict that it will not be modified further, perhaps radically. Nevertheless, barring major alterations in the general income tax structure, it is reasonable to expect that the same group of competing considerations that governed Congress in evolving the present treatment will continue to be coercive, though they will doubtless vary in relative strength from time to time. Consequently, changes that retain the essential form of the present treatment are more likely to receive near-term serious consideration than others.

From a longer range standpoint it is well to emphasize that the whole concept of taxable income is relatively new and still evolving. The acceptance of the income tax as a personal impost, the greater reliance of governments upon it as a major source of revenue, and the tremendous growth in the importance of large scale corporate enterprise have refined and made more complex the concept of taxable income. The prominence of capital gains as a source of private wealth in the United States, and the origin of considerable amounts of them, though far from all, in reinvested corporate profits, early led this country to treat them as ordinary constituents of income. Their peculiar characteristics under an annual income tax thereupon raised problems that have so far defied satisfactory solution. On the one hand, capital gains add to the economic power of individuals no less than ordinary kinds of income. On the other hand, to treat capital gains as such under a graduated income tax raises questions of equity and of adverse operational effects upon transactions in capital assets. In these connections, numerous conflicting contentions have been made. In presenting various aspects of the problem our object is to give the reader analyses and empirical materials on which he can base his own judgments, not to make recommendations.

I INCOME TAX RETURNS OF INDIVIDUALS AND TAXABLE FIDUCIARIES

A Sources

1) *Statistics of Income,* 1917-1946: annual reports compiled from federal income tax returns (U. S. Treasury Department, Bureau of Internal Revenue).

2) *Source Book of Statistics of Income,* unpublished tabulations on file in the Bureau of Internal Revenue: federal income tax returns for 1934, 1935, 1936, and 1937 showing realized net gains and losses and the number of returns with either realized net gain or loss in each of 5 holding periods, by net income groups: $100,000 or over in each year 1934-37, $5,000-100,000 in 1937, sample returns with net incomes under $100,000 or with net deficits in 1936, each by income groups.

3) *Source Book of Statistics of Income:* tabulations of federal income tax returns with net incomes under $100,000 by income groups, and with net deficits for 1934, similar to Source 2, prepared by the Division of Tax Research, Treasury Department, in cooperation with the Works Projects Administration.

4) *Statistics of Income Supplement for 1936,* Section IV, Capital Gains and Losses: compiled from federal income tax returns for 1936, Division of Tax Research, in cooperation with the Works Projects Administration, June 1940; supplemented by:

a) *Source Book of Statistics of Income for 1936:* tabulations for the United States not published in the *Statistics of Income Supplement.*

b) *Ibid:* special tabulations of federal income tax returns for New York, Pennsylvania, and Illinois, showing capital gains and losses by type of asset and by net income group.

c) *Statistics of Income Supplement for 1936,* Section III, Patterns of Income.

d) *Ibid.,* Section I, Distribution and Sources.

5) *Source Book of Statistics of Income:* tabulations of capital gains and losses in 1930, 1932, and 1933, based on sample studies of federal individual income tax returns by the Bureau of Internal Revenue, Income Tax Unit, Statistical Section.

6) Special studies of capital gains and losses of groups of individuals with large net incomes.

a) *Million Dollar Incomes,* Report to the Joint Committee on Internal Revenue Taxation, 1938: annual data on capital gains and losses as well as other income and deduction items 1917-36 for 38 of the 75 returns reporting net incomes of $1 million or over in 1924.

b) *Source Book of Statistics of Income:* unpublished tabulations showing sources of income and deduction items 1917-36 for the 75 returns reporting net incomes of $1 million or over in 1924. Data are complete for only 45 returns 1917-33.

c) *Hearings,* Senate Select Committee on Investigation of the Bureau of Internal Revenue, 68th Cong., 1st and 2d Sess., 1924-25, VII, 3558, 3559, 3576, 3584.

d) *Report to the Senate Select Committee on Investigation of the Bureau of Internal Revenue,* 69th Cong., 1st Sess., Senate Report 27, Part 2, pp. 1-19.

e) *Report of the Joint Committee on Internal Revenue Taxation,* 1928, Vol. 1, pp. 43, 44.

Sources 6c, d, and e present data by years on sources of income and deduction items in 1916-24 of 4,063 individuals with net incomes of $100,000 or over in 1916. Sources 6c and d give also net capital gains and losses by type of asset for the combined period 1917-22 for 400 returns with net incomes of $100,000 or over in 1916. Source 6e gives also net capital losses in 1917-25 of 75 individuals with net incomes of $1 million or over in 1924, as well as estimates made for the Joint Committee on Internal Revenue Taxation of the net losses from sales of assets for all individual and taxable fiduciary income tax returns 1917-25.

f) *Report to the Joint Committee on Internal Revenue Taxation,* 71st Cong., I, Part VII, Supplementary Report on Capital Gains and Losses, 1929.

g) *Source Book of Statistics of Income:* unpublished tabulations showing sources of income and deduction items in 1929, 1932, and 1933 for individuals reporting the highest net incomes in 1929. Individuals reporting the highest net incomes excluding capital gains and losses but including tax-exempt interest were included in the sample.

B *Differences in Returns Covered by Basic Tabulations*

For returns with net incomes (returns with adjusted gross incomes in 1944-46) the data from Sources 1 and 2 cover individual and taxable fiduciary income tax returns (filed on Forms 1040 and 1040A, 1917-36, on Forms 1040, 1040A, and 1041, 1937-43, and on

Forms 1040, W-2, and 1041, 1944-46);[1] the data for returns with net deficits cover only returns filed by individuals (on Form 1040).[2] Data based on Source 3 cover only returns filed on Form 1040. Data based on Sources 4, 4a, and b exclude all returns filed on Form 1040A as well as returns filed on Form 1040 that did not give adequate information on the back with respect to the type of capital asset and holding period. Data based on Source 4c include returns with net incomes filed on Forms 1040 and 1040A, and those from Source 4d include all returns filed on Forms 1040 and 1040A except returns with neither net income nor net deficit. All the tabulations from Sources 4 and 4a-d were based on the 'duplicate' copies of the return filed by taxpayers whereas in Source 1 the 'original' returns were tabulated. Other minor differences between the data from Sources 4 and 1 reflect the fact that the tabulations in Source 4 of 'returns with net incomes under $5,000' were based on all returns reporting net incomes in this group, whereas the data in Source 1 were based on a sample.[3] Data from Source 5 cover samples of individual income tax returns filed on Form 1040.

C Changes in Filing Requirements

Since the statistics on capital gains and losses are from income tax returns, they reflect changes in filing requirements during the 30 years. These changes affect primarily the year to year comparability of the data for the lower income groups, but since such groups account for a substantial fraction of capital gains and losses, the com-

[1] Except that Table 35 from Source 1 covers only individual income tax returns in 1938-41.

[2] Data for returns with net deficits are not available before 1928. Net deficit returns include returns with zero net incomes in 1937-43. In 1944-46 the deficit classification represents returns with no adjusted gross incomes instead of returns with net deficits. Of 229,234 returns with net deficits in 1944, 191,905 show no adjusted gross incomes and 37,329 show adjusted gross incomes of various amounts and itemized deductions that exceed gross income. In 1945 the corresponding figures are 216,745; 181,792; and 34,953; and in 1946, 250,181; 216,077; and 34,104. The first of these deficit sub-groups is included in our tables under 'returns with net deficit'; the second, under 'returns with net income' which, for 1944-46, represent 'returns with adjusted gross income'.

[3] In 1943-46 sampling in Source 1 was extended to income groups above $5,000. Estimates were based upon samples for net income groups under $20,000 in 1943, and for adjusted gross income groups under $25,000 in 1944-46.

parability of the year to year totals of capital gains and losses is also affected.

The major changes in filing requirements may be summarized as follows:[4] From 1917 through 1923 married persons living with spouse were required to file returns if their net incomes were $2,000 or more; single individuals (including fiduciaries and married persons not living with spouse) if their net incomes were $1,000 or more. Beginning in 1921 all individuals with gross incomes of $5,000 or more were required to file returns, regardless of the amount of their net incomes. The minimum net income required for filing in the case of married persons was raised to $2,500 in 1924, to $3,500 in 1925, and lowered to $2,500 in 1932. In the case of single individuals it was raised to $1,500 in 1925 and lowered to $1,000 in 1932.

In 1940 the gross income required for filing was lowered to $2,000 for married persons and to $800 for single, in 1941 it was reduced to $1,500 for married persons and to $750 for single, and in 1942 it was further reduced to $1,200 for married persons and to $500 for single. In 1943 a married person with a gross income of $624 was required to file a return. Filing was required also of anyone liable for income taxes for 1942 and anyone entitled to a tax refund because of excessive withholding or overpayment on the estimated declaration.[5] In 1944-46 any person, including a minor, who had a gross income of $500 or more was required to file a return; persons filing for tax refund are also included in the tabulations.

D Basic Data on Capital Gains and Losses for the Various Periods

Changes in the statutory treatment of capital gains and losses account for substantial differences in the figures for the various years. The following paragraphs describe the series for 5 periods 1917-21, 1922-33, 1934-37, 1938-41, and 1942-46 and call attention to various estimates we prepared to make the statistics for the 5 periods more comparable. Most of the estimates are based on additional data for selected years taken from the back of the tax returns.

[4] For details of the changes in filing requirements see *Statistics of Income for 1940,* Part I, pp. 242-3, and the similar discussions in the volumes for later years. For discussion of effects of changes in filing requirements on the comparability of statistics see Income Forecasting by the Use of Statistics of Income Data, by J. F. Ebersole, S. S. Burr, and G. M. Peterson, *Review of Economic Statistics,* Nov. 1929 and Feb. and May 1930.

[5] The discharge of individual income tax liability on a 'pay-as-you-go' basis was instituted in 1943.

1   *1917-1921*

During these 5 years net capital gains were taxed at the same rates as other income. Each individual with a net profit (an excess of gains over losses) from the sale of assets reported the net amount on his return.[6] Our figures on net gain for 1917-21 are from Source 1; data are not available for earlier years.[7]

In 1917 capital losses were deductible only to the extent of gains, but in 1918-21 they were allowed in full against income. Net capital losses, tabulated in Source 1 in combination with other deduction items, were estimated by the method outlined below in Section 2b.

2   *1922-1933*

Net capital gains from the sales of assets held more than 2 years were, at the option of the taxpayer, taxable at 12½ percent in lieu of normal and surtax rates; all other net gains from sales of assets were taxed as ordinary income. In 1922 and 1923 the segregation at the 12½ percent rate was permitted only if the resulting total tax was 12½ percent or more of the total net income; in 1924 this provision was discontinued.

Net capital losses were allowed in full as a deduction in computing net income in 1922 and 1923. From 1924 through 1933 net capital loss from sales of assets held more than 2 years had to be segregated from other income, and a tax credit taken amounting to 12½ percent of the loss if the segregation led to a higher total tax than if the loss was deducted from total income. If the segregation led to a lower tax, the 12½ percent tax credit was not permitted but the net loss itself was deducted in computing net income. Net loss from sales of assets held 2 years or less was allowed in full as a deduction in computing net income 1924-33, except that in 1932 and 1933 net loss from sales of stocks and bonds, except government bonds, held 2 years or less was not deductible. The loss data in our tables include disallowed loss in 1932 and 1933, estimated as outlined below in Section c.

Net capital gain and loss, as defined in the statutes, applied only to net gain and loss from sales of assets held more than 2 years in order to distinguish gains and losses eligible for segregation at the special rate. In our tables, however, except when otherwise specified,

---

[6] The taxpayer reported the net amount from sales of securities separately from sales of other assets, but the combined amounts alone were published.

[7] Data on net capital gains in 1917 are not available for returns with net incomes under $2,000.

the terms are used in the broader sense to cover all net gains and losses from sales of capital assets.[8]

The following component series for net gain 1922-33 and for net loss 1924-33 are available, by income level, from Source 1: (1) Net capital gain from sales of assets held more than 2 years and segregated for tax at 12½ percent, 1922-33.[9] (2) Tax credit on net capital loss from sales of assets held more than 2 years and segregated for tax credit at 12½ percent, 1924-33. For 1924-30 we derived net capital losses segregated for tax credit by capitalizing the amounts of tax credit published in Source 1. For 1931-33 the actual amount of net capital loss segregated for tax credit was published in *Statistics of Income*. We based its distribution among income levels on the capitalized value of the tax credit at each level.[10] (3) Other net gain from sales of assets, 1922-33. (4) Other net loss from sales of assets, 1926-33.

Our series on total net capital gain, 1922-33, is the sum of (1) and (3) above; that on total net capital loss, 1926-33, the sum of (2) and (4), adjusted to include disallowed losses in 1932 and 1933, derived as described below in Section c;[11] and that on total net capital loss before 1926 is derived as described in Section b.

[8] The tabulated series on statutory net capital gain in *Statistics of Income* does not always correspond exactly with the definition in the statutes. In certain years the latter was equal to net capital gain minus specified deductions for net loss in ordinary net income and for net loss carried over from preceding years, whereas the tabulated figure is the amount before these deductions.

[9] In 1925, unlike the other years in this period, net capital gain was not tabulated as such, but was derived in *Statistics of Income* by capitalizing the amount of the 12½ percent tax. As a result, the figures for 1925 are slightly understated since on certain returns the tax was computed on net capital gain reduced as indicated in the preceding note.

[10] The capitalized value of the credit, which we used for 1924-30, understates actual net loss because the punch cards used in tabulating the data for *Statistics of Income* included only the amount of tax credit required to reduce the tax liability to zero, so that some of the tax credit on returns with no tax liability was omitted. The capitalized value of the tax credit was 81 percent of the actual net capital loss segregated for tax credit in 1931, 69 percent in 1932, and 74 percent in 1933. The two series were probably in closer agreement in the earlier years of the period.

[11] Total net losses are understated somewhat because the basic tabulations exclude net losses from sales of capital assets held more than 2 years an individual listed on his return but, because he was nontaxable, neither segregated for tax credit at 12½ percent nor deducted from total income in computing his net income or deficit. In 1932 and 1933, however, the Bureau of Internal Revenue transferred such net losses reported by deficit returns to 'other net loss from sales of assets', thereby including them in the basic tabulations.

Series (3) includes two components which were not tabulated separately: (a) net gains from sales of assets held 2 years or less and (b) net gains from sales of assets held over 2 years not segregated for the tax at 12½ percent. Series (4), similarly, includes (c) net losses from sales of assets held 2 years or less and (d) net losses from sales of assets held over 2 years not segregated for tax credit at 12½ percent. For the upper income groups, however, the series represent items (a) and (c) only, since few taxpayers failed to take advantage of the tax saving possible by segregating their net long term gains and applying the 12½ percent rate, and the regulations required that they segregate their long term net losses. For the medium and lower income groups such tax saving on gains was not possible and segregation of losses was not required; hence for them 'long' and 'short' term gains or losses cannot be segregated.[12] This is the reason our tables on long and short term capital gains from series (1) and (3) above, and those on long and short term losses from series (2) and (4) above, carry warnings that an unknown proportion of long term gains and losses are included in the short term series for 1922-33.

The income tax return for 1933 differed from that used earlier in providing for three items of unsegregated net gain and two items of unsegregated net loss: net gains from sales of stocks and bonds except government bonds held 2 years or less; net gains or losses from sales of other assets held 2 years or less; and net gains or losses from sales of assets held more than 2 years except those segregated at 12½ percent (Table 10). Total net gain or loss other than that segregated at 12½ percent, as shown here and in *Statistics of Income* (the sum of the tabulated amounts of the three components of gain, two components of loss) is overstated in 1933 as compared with earlier years because the net gains in any one of its three components were not offset by the net losses in the other components realized by the same individual.

[12] *Statistics of Income* shows net gains segregated for the alternative 12½ percent tax beginning with the net income group $15,000-20,000 in 1922 and 1923, and segregated net gain and the tax credit on segregated net loss beginning with the net income groups $25,000-30,000 in 1924, $30,000-40,000 in 1925-31, and $15,000-20,000 in 1932 and 1933. In some instances returns with net incomes above these amounts did not segregate their gains or losses because with certain combinations of ordinary income and capital net gain or loss, the segregation for returns with net gain would have resulted in a higher tax, and for returns with net loss, in a lower tax, than if the gain or loss was treated as ordinary income.

The numbers of returns with segregated net gain or loss and with 'other' net gain or loss are from Source 1. The returns are distributed by size of gain or loss but not by size of net income. The total number with capital transactions is not available and cannot be derived by adding the component series because one individual may have had both long and short term gains and losses.

a) *Losses understated in 1926-28*
'Other net loss' is understated in 1926-28 as compared with the rest of the period because in these 3 years the BIR did not tabulate such net losses from sales of assets held more than 2 years as were taken as a deduction in computing net income if the taxpayer listed them on his return under the general heading 'other deductions'. The degree of understatement is impossible to estimate but may have been sizeable because the instructions did not indicate clearly under which item on the return losses of this kind were to be entered. Beginning in 1929 the BIR, for purposes of *Statistics of Income,* transferred losses of this kind to 'other net loss from the sale of assets' if they could be identified, and so included them in its tabulations.

b) *Estimated net loss before 1926*
In 1917-25 net losses, except segregated long term losses in 1924 and 1925, were combined in *Statistics of Income* with other deduction items. Our estimates of total net capital loss were derived as follows (see table).

Returns with net incomes of $100,000 or over
1) The percentage of total deductions accounted for by net losses from sales of assets each year 1917-25 was computed from a sample of 75 individuals with net incomes of $1 million or over in 1924 (Source 6e; total deductions reported on this group of returns are erroneously labeled 'losses on sale of assets' in Source 6e, p. 43). For 1924 and 1925 the sample data on losses and total deductions appear to include losses segregated for tax credit at 12½ percent.
2) Similar percentages were computed for each year 1917-24 from a sample of 4,063 returns with net incomes of $100,000 or over in 1916 (Source 6c-e; the percentages for 1920 and 1922-24, which differ from those in Source 6e, p. 43, were computed from total deductions and losses for this group of returns from Source 6d).
3) The two percentages for each year, weighted by total deductions as reported in the two samples for the year, were averaged. (These averages agree with the percentages in Source 6e, p. 44.)

ESTIMATED REALIZED NET CAPITAL LOSS

STATUTORY NET INCOME GROUP	1917	1918	1919	1920	1921	1922	1923	1924	1925
			NET CAPITAL LOSS (millions of dollars)						
1 $100,000 & over	12.9	62.3	122.7	135.9	79.5	70.7	77.5	57.0	64.7
2 Under $100,000	57.1	297.0	613.8	901.0	1,022.4	688.9	899.4	419.7	295.0
3 All returns with net incomes	70.0	359.3	736.6	1,037.0	1,102.0	759.6	976.8	476.8	359.7
			NET CAPITAL LOSS AS PERCENTAGE OF TOTAL DEDUCTIONS						
4 $100,000 & over	12.5	31.4	45.6	56.9	48.8	35.4	36.2	22.4	19.0
5 Under $100,000	7.3	18.3	26.6	33.2	28.5	20.6	21.1	11.2	9.5
6 All returns with net incomes	7.9	19.7	28.6	35.1	29.4	21.5	21.8	11.9	10.5

DERIVATION OF LINE 4

Sample Returns: Net Capital Loss as Percentage of Total Deductions

	1917	1918	1919	1920	1921	1922	1923	1924	1925
7 4,063 returns with net incomes of $1 million & over in 1916	13.4	32.4	45.9	56.5	48.8	33.0	35.8	22.3	19.0
8 75 returns with net incomes of $1 million & over in 1924	4.5	22.5	43.2	58.0	49.5	43.8	32.4	18.8	19.0
9 Weighted average	12.5	31.4	45.6	56.9	48.8	35.4	36.2	22.4	19.0

DERIVATION OF LINE 5 (see text)

All Returns: Net Capital Loss as Percentage of Total Deductions

	1926	1927	1928	1929	1930	1931	*Av.* 1926-31
	Including Loss Segregated at 12½%						
10 Net incomes under $100,000	5.1	6.8	4.8	18.0	27.6	32.6	
11 Net incomes of $100,000 & over	13.8	12.7	9.9	32.1	49.2	64.0	
	Excluding Loss Segregated at 12½%						
12 Net incomes under $100,000	4.6	6.2	4.4	17.7	27.0	30.6	
13 Net incomes of $100,000 & over	9.6	6.8	5.6	29.5	43.4	45.4	
Ratio (%)							
14 Line 10 ÷ Line 11	37.0	53.5	48.5	56.1	56.1	50.9	50.3
15 Line 12 ÷ Line 13	47.9	91.2	78.6	60.0	62.2	67.4	67.9

Lines 7 and 8 based on Source 6e; lines 10-13 on Source 1.

329

4) The average percentages were assumed to apply to all returns with net incomes of $100,000 or over. Accordingly, the percentage for each year 1917-23 from step 3 was applied to the total deductions reported by all returns with net incomes of $100,000 or over in the corresponding year (Source 1) to determine the annual aggregate net loss from sales of assets. For 1924 and 1925 the percentage was applied to the sum of total deductions and net losses segregated for tax credit at 12½ percent reported by returns in this income group because we were estimating total net losses, both segregated and unsegregated.

Returns with net incomes under $100,000
Sample data were not available for these income groups in 1917-25. Some individuals included in the samples used in steps 1 and 2 actually had net incomes of less than $100,000 in some of these years but they could not be regarded as representative of such income groups with respect to capital losses in relation to total deductions.

5) For each year 1926-31 the percentage of total deductions accounted for by net losses from sales of assets was calculated for (a) all returns with net incomes under $100,000 and (b) all returns with net incomes of $100,000 or more (Source 1); net capital losses segregated for tax credit at 12½ percent were excluded.

6) For each year 1926-31 the ratio of percentage (a) to percentage (b) was calculated, then the ratios for the 6 years were averaged. The average showed that the percentage of total deductions accounted for by net losses from sales of assets was about two-thirds as large for returns with net incomes under $100,000 as for returns with net incomes of $100,000 or more (the annual ratios are shown in the preceding table).

7) Percentages and ratios for 1926-31 were calculated similar to those described in steps 5 and 6 except that net capital losses segregated for tax credit at 12½ percent were included in both losses and deductions. The average ratio indicated that the percentage for returns with net incomes under $100,000 was approximately half that for returns with net incomes of $100,000 or more.

8) We assumed for each year 1917-23 for returns with net incomes under $100,000 that the percentage of total deductions accounted for by net losses from sales of assets was seven-twelfths (an average of two-thirds from step 6 and one-half from step 7) as large as the corresponding percentage (from step 3) for returns with net incomes of $100,000 or more. For 1924 and 1925 we used one-half (step 7)

rather than seven-twelfths because we were estimating net losses including those segregated for tax credit at 12½ percent.

9) The aggregate net loss from sales of assets was derived in each year 1917-23 by applying the appropriate percentage (from step 8) to the total deductions reported on all returns with net incomes under $100,000 in the corresponding year (Source 1), and in 1924-25 to the sum of total deductions and net loss segregated for tax credit at 12½ percent reported on all returns in this income group (Source 1).

Total net losses are the sum of the estimates for the under and over $100,000 groups.[13] For 1924-25 long term net losses segregated for tax credit at 12½ percent are the capitalized values of the tax credits (Source 1), and short term net losses are the difference between estimated total net losses and long term segregated net losses.

c) *Estimated disallowed net loss in 1932 and 1933*
1) The ratios of disallowed to statutory net loss in 1932 and 1933 were calculated by income groups from the sample data in Source 5. The statutory amount excluded net loss segregated for tax credit at 12½ percent.

2) Each annual ratio was applied to the total statutory net loss, excluding net loss segregated for tax credit at 12½ percent, reported on all returns in the corresponding income group and year (Source 1). Total disallowed net loss for each year is the sum of the estimates for the various income groups.[14]

3) Total net loss other than that segregated for special tax treatment, for 1932 and 1933, is the sum of estimated disallowed net loss from step 2 and statutory net loss, other than that segregated for tax credit at 12½ percent, from Source 1 (the actual computations are shown in Tables 48 and 49). This sum is overstated slightly as compared with the corresponding series for earlier years because the sample data from Source 5, and hence our estimates of disallowed and total net loss, include some disallowed loss reported by individuals with over-all net capital gains. On the other hand, our estimates may be too low because they assume that disallowed

[13] These estimates are lower than those in Source 6e. In its estimates the Joint Committee on Internal Revenue Taxation assumed that the two samples mentioned in steps (1) and (2) above were representative of all net income groups.

[14] A second, lower, estimate was based on the ratio of disallowed loss to statutory net loss, including in the latter net loss segregated for tax credit. We used the first estimate because the second assumed that the sample correctly represented the proportions of segregated and unsegregated statutory net loss.

losses were reported in full on the back of the sample returns from Source 5. Though taxpayers in the sample did give detailed information on transactions resulting in short term net losses, even though disallowed, there may nevertheless be some understatement. The fact that the sample for 1932 and 1933 included only persons who had at least 5 sales of capital assets in either those years or 1930 may have led to some bias. For a description of the sample from Source 5, see Section F1.

3   *1934-1937*

The statutes provided that certain specified percentages, varying with the length of the period the asset had been held, were to be applied to realized capital gains and losses to determine the statutory amounts subject to tax: 100 percent for assets held 1 year or less, 80 percent for assets held 1-2 years, 60 percent for assets held 2-5 years, 40 percent for assets held 5-10 years, and 30 percent for assets held longer than 10 years. Moreover, net capital loss, after the application of these percentages, was not to exceed $2,000, except for a joint return, on which a net loss up to $4,000 was allowed. Statutory net capital gains and losses, i.e., gains and losses *after* the application of the percentages listed above and *after* the $2,000 limitation on net losses, in *Statistics of Income* for this period are the sum of the net figures reported on the face of returns. Each taxpayer with capital transactions reported only one figure on the face of his return.

We present estimates of total realized net gains and losses, i.e., net gain and loss *before* the application of the statutory percentages and *before* the $2,000 limitation on net losses, as well as the statutory amounts. Unless *statutory* net gains and losses are specified, the amounts in our tables are *realized*.

The taxpayer reported his realized net gains and net losses on the back of his return separately under each of 5 holding period groups before the application of the statutory percentages and before the loss limitation. These amounts were available in Sources 2 and 3 for the following net income groups: $100,000 or over in each year 1934-37; $5,000-100,000 in 1937; under $100,000 or net deficits in 1934 and for a sample of returns in 1936, each by income group.

Our estimate of total realized net gain in each year is the sum, for returns with statutory net gains, of the net gains reported in the 5 holding periods minus the sum, for the same groups of returns, of the net losses in those holding periods (Sources 2 and 3). Total realized net loss is the sum, for returns with statutory net losses, of the net losses reported in the 5 holding periods minus the sum of the net gains. Realized long term net gain (loss) is the sum, for all returns with capital transactions, of the net gains (losses) in the 3 long term holding periods (2-5, 5-10, over 10 years), and realized short term net gain (loss) is the sum, for all returns with capital transactions, of the net gains (losses) in the 2 short term holding periods (under 1, 1-2 years, plus a third category — 'not stated'). The sum of our series on long and short term gains (losses) for these years does not equal our estimates of total realized net gain (loss) because of the difference in the returns covered: total realized net gain covers returns with statutory net gain only (realized losses on such returns having been offset against realized gains), while long and short term gains cover all returns with capital transactions, that is, returns with both statutory net gain and loss. Similarly, total realized net loss covers returns with statutory net loss only, while long and short term losses cover all returns with capital transactions (see Sec. E2).

The estimates of long, short, and total realized gains and losses were taken directly from Sources 2 and 3, except as noted below, and except when the statutory net gain or loss for a given income group from these Sources differed slightly from the figure in Source 1. In the latter event, we adjusted realized net gains and losses so that they would correspond with statutory net gains and losses as published in Source 1.[15]

For income groups not covered by Sources 2 and 3 — returns with net incomes under $100,000 or with net deficits in 1935, and returns with net incomes under $5,000 or with net deficits in 1937 — our estimates of realized amounts were based on the statutory amounts in Source 1 and the relation between the statutory and realized amounts for the income group in the preceding or following year (Tables 16-9). For 1935 we estimated total realized net gain and loss for returns with net incomes under $100,000, by income group, and for returns with net deficits by assuming that the ratio of statutory to total realized net gain (loss) for each income group in 1935

[15] The ratio of total realized net gain (loss) to statutory net gain (loss) at each income level from the tabulation in Source 2 or 3 was applied to statutory net gain (loss) in Source 1 for that income level. This was the method used also in estimating total realized net gain and loss in 1936 for net incomes under $100,000 and for the net deficit group from the sample data. The distributions of these totals by holding period were based upon the corresponding percentage distributions from the sample.

equaled the average of the corresponding ratios for 1934 and 1936. The distribution of total realized net gain (loss) by holding period in 1935 for each income group was assumed to be the same as the percentage distribution for the average of 1934 and 1936. For 1937 total realized net gain and loss for returns with net deficits was based upon similar ratios for 1936; that for returns with net incomes under $5,000 upon the ratios for returns with net incomes of $5,000-10,000 in 1937, adjusted to take into account the variation in the ratios in 1936 between the 'under $5,000' and the $5,000-10,000 income groups. The distributions of estimated total realized net gain and loss by holding period for net deficit returns in 1937 were based on the corresponding percentage distributions by holding period in 1936, and those for returns with net incomes of under $5,000 in 1937 upon the percentage distributions for the $5,000-10,000 group in 1937. The estimates for these income groups in 1935 and 1937 are therefore extremely tentative and were derived only in order to complete the holding period picture for the four years 1934-37.

The number of returns with statutory net gain or loss is from Source 1. The number of returns with realized net gain or loss in each holding period (Table 34) and average realized net gain or loss by holding period (Table 38) were derived from Sources 2 and 3. As we did not attempt to estimate the number of returns with realized net gains and losses in the several holding periods for returns with net incomes under $100,000 or with net deficits in 1935, or for returns with net incomes under $5,000 or with net deficits in 1937, these groups, which are not covered in Sources 2 and 3, do not appear in Tables 34 and 38. Estimates for 'holding period not stated' in all 4 years are omitted from both tables. For returns with net incomes under $100,000 or with net deficits in 1936, the number of returns with realized net gains and losses in the various holding periods was derived by dividing the average realized net gain or loss in each holding period and income group from sample data into the corresponding aggregate estimated as described in footnote 15 above.

See Section F2 for description of special tabulations for 1936.

4 *1938-1941*

As in 1934-37, the law excluded from statutory net gain and loss various proportions of the amounts actually realized. The entire gain or loss from capital assets held 18 months or less (short term) was included; 66⅔ percent from capital assets held 18-24 months and

50 percent from capital assets held more than 24 months (long term).

Instead of the $2,000 limitation on net capital loss as in 1934-37, the statute allowed all long term net capital losses as deductions in computing net income but disallowed all short term, i.e., short term net loss was not taken into account in computing net income. However, short term net loss not exceeding the net income in the year it was sustained could be carried over to the next taxable year and used to offset the net short term capital gain in that year but only to the extent of the short term net gain.

The definition of capital assets differed from that in 1934-37 by excluding "property used in trade or business of a character which is subject to allowances for depreciation". In our tables, however, net gains and losses from the sale of depreciable property are included in order to make the figures more nearly comparable with those for earlier years.[16]

The years 1938-41 also differed from the preceding period in that receipts from long and short term transactions could not be offset. The taxpayer computed separately two items of 'capital' net gain or loss — from assets held more than 18 months and 18 months or less — and a third item, net gain or loss from sales of depreciable assets (excluded from the statutory definition of capital assets). Three corresponding series on net gains are tabulated in Source 1: statutory long term net gain (from assets held more than 18 months), statutory short term net gain (from assets held 18 months or less), and net gain from sales of depreciable assets. Two series are available for net losses from Source 1: statutory long term net capital loss and net loss from sales of depreciable assets. Short term net loss disallowed by the statutes as a current deduction is not available. Net loss carryover from the preceding year is tabulated in Source 1 for 1939-41.

Realized long term gains and losses in 1938-41 were estimated by capitalizing statutory long term net gains and losses on the basis of the statutory provisions for different percentage reductions for assets

[16] Net gain and loss from sales of depreciable property are tabulated in Source 1 under 'Net gain (loss) from sales of property other than capital assets'. Beginning in 1941 the category 'property other than capital assets' was extended to include 'obligations of the United States or any of its possessions, a State or Territory or any political subdivision thereof, or the District of Columbia, issued on or after March 1, 1941, on a discount basis and payable without interest at a fixed maturity date not exceeding one year from date of issue'.

held 18-24 months and 24 months or over.[17] Estimates of realized long term net gain are for returns with statutory long term net gain only; those of realized long term net loss are for returns with statutory long term net loss only.

Short term net gains are from Source 1; our series is not reduced by short term net loss carried over from the preceding year,[18] shown separately in Table 27. Net gain and loss from sales of depreciable assets are also taken directly from Source 1.

Total realized net gain in 1938-41 is the sum of realized long term net gain, short term net gain unreduced by prior year loss carryover, and net gain from sales of depreciable assets. Total realized net loss is the sum of realized long term net loss and net loss from sales of depreciable assets. As explained below, short term net losses are not included in our estimates of total realized net loss in this period.

Gains and losses from sales of depreciable assets, included in our estimates of total realized net gain and loss, are not included in the long and short term series because it was impossible to classify them by holding period. For this reason, the sum of long and short term net gains (losses) does not equal total net gain (loss).

Statutory net gain in 1938-41 is the sum of 3 components: statutory long term net gain, short term net gain, and net gain from sales of depreciable assets. To present the data on a current basis, and to increase comparability with earlier years, statutory net gains in 1939-41 were adjusted to exclude loss carried over from the preceding year.[19] Statutory net loss is the sum of statutory long term net loss and net loss from sales of depreciable assets. As in the preceding period, unless *statutory* net gains and losses are specified, the amounts in our tables are *realized*.

a) *Understatement of losses, 1938-1941*
Our estimates of total realized and of disallowed net loss understate the actual amounts because we could not estimate disallowed short

[17] It was assumed that the proportion of long term net gain from assets held more than 18 months realized in the 18-24 months period decreased from 5 to 1 percent as net income increased, whereas for net loss, the corresponding proportion was assumed to be 12 percent at all income levels.

[18] That is, our figures on short term net gains represent current year transactions, and are larger than the statutory amounts in Source 1 where prior year loss carryovers have been offset against short term net gains of the current year.

[19] That is, our series is higher than the statutory amounts in Source 1 where the loss carryover has been offset against current year short term net gains.

term net loss in this period (rough estimates for 1938 are shown in Table 28). The published data on net loss carryover are minimum figures because the carryover was limited by the short term net gain of the year to which it was carried and by the net income of the preceding year. Moreover, returns with such carryover may have appeared at very different income levels in the year the disallowed loss was incurred and in the year to which it was carried.

5   *1942-1946*

In 1942-46 the statutes again distinguished between long and short term gains and losses. Short term were defined as gains and losses from sales of assets held 6 months or less; long term as those from sales of assets held more than 6 months. Half of the realized long term was taken into account in computing net gain or loss from sales of capital assets. Short term net gain and loss were counted in full.

Gains and losses from long and short term transactions in 1942-46, unlike 1938-41, were offset against each other by the taxpayer in computing his over-all net gain or loss. Deductible net capital loss, however, was limited to $1,000, or to the net income computed without regard to gains and losses from capital assets, whichever was smaller. The balance of the net loss — disallowed net loss — could be carried forward as a short term net loss in any of the succeeding 5 years to the extent that it exceeded the net gain from sales of capital assets plus net income computed without regard to capital gains or losses, or $1,000, whichever was smaller, in any one of the 5 years. In 1942 short term net loss carried over from 1941 could be applied against current year short term net capital gain.

Beginning in 1942 the categories of property excluded from the statutory definition of capital assets were extended to 'real property used in trade or business'. Sales of such property, together with sales of business property on which depreciation was allowed and sales of certain government obligations are tabulated in Source 1 under 'gain (loss) from sales of property other than capital assets'. In our tables these amounts are shown under 'gains (losses) from sales of depreciable assets'. As in 1938-41, they are included in our estimates of total realized capital gain and loss.

Although depreciable business property and real property used in trade or business were excluded from the statutory definition of capital assets, net gains from selling them if derived from property held more than 6 months could be counted as long term capital gains.

Hence, only half were counted in computing net income. Net losses from transactions in these assets were treated as ordinary net losses and were fully deductible.

Data published by income level in Source 1 include (1) statutory long term net capital gain, (2) statutory long term net capital loss, (3) short term net capital gain, (4) short term net capital loss, (5) net gain from sales of property other than capital assets, (6) net loss from sales of property other than capital assets, (7) statutory net capital gain, and (8) statutory net capital loss. The first four of these series are shown separately for returns with statutory net capital gains and losses. Loss series (2) and (4) are the amounts before the limitation on deductible net loss described above was applied, whereas loss series (8) is after the limitation. Loss carryover is included in various of these series as indicated in Section a below. Source 1 also has separate tabulations of loss carryover for returns with statutory net capital gains and losses, by income level.

We estimated realized long term net capital gain (loss) by capitalizing statutory long term net gain from series 1 (loss from series 2) reported on *all returns* with capital transactions, i.e., returns with statutory net capital gains and losses. Realized short term net gain (loss) represents series 3 (4) for all returns with capital transactions, adjusted for loss carryover as described in Section a below.

We estimated total realized net gain by capitalizing the statutory amounts of long term net gain and loss reported on *returns with statutory net capital gains,* then combining these capitalized figures with the short term net gains and losses reported on the same group of returns, i.e., total realized net gain equals the sum of realized long and short term gains — series (1) capitalized plus series (3) — for returns with statutory net gains, minus the sum of realized long and short term losses — series (2) capitalized plus series (4) — for returns with statutory net gains. The series in our tables are the sum of these amounts and net gains from sales of depreciable assets, series (5). The same procedure was followed for *returns with statutory net capital losses* in estimating total realized net loss. For discussion of the adjustments for loss carryover in deriving these estimates, and for derivation of our statutory capital gain and loss series see Section a below.

The sum of long and short term gains (losses) does not equal total realized net gain (loss) because (a) long and short term gains (losses) cover all returns with capital transactions whereas total gain (loss) covers returns with statutory net gains (losses); (b) gains (losses) from sales of depreciable assets are not included in the long and short term series; and (c) adjustments for loss carryover in 1944-46 differ (Sec. a). As in the earlier periods, unless *statutory net gains and losses* are specified, the amounts in our tables are *realized*.

In 1944-46 the basis of income classification, unlike that in preceding years, was adjusted gross income, not net income. When our estimates of capital gains and losses are headed 'returns with statutory net income' and 'returns with statutory net incomes of $5,000 or over' they cover for 1944-46 'returns with adjusted gross income of $1 or over' and 'returns with adjusted gross income of $5,000 or over', and when headed 'returns with net deficits' the 1944-46 gain and loss series cover 'returns with no adjusted gross income' (Sec. G).

a) *Loss carryover*

Loss carried over from preceding years is excluded from our series on total realized net gain and loss for 1942-46 and from our series on short term gain and loss for 1942-43 but not for 1944-46. In 1942, as in 1939-41, loss carryover was deductible only to the extent of current year short term net gain. We increased the short term net gain in Source 1 by the amount of prior year loss carryover the taxpayer had subtracted from it, and included this adjusted amount in total realized gain and loss. In 1943-46 net loss carryover could be used either to reduce short term net gains or to increase short term net losses. Both short term and total realized gains and losses in 1943 are based upon a special tabulation in Source 1 of short term net gain and loss before the loss carryover was included. In 1944-46 similar tabulations were not available. The short term series in 1944-46 could not be adjusted to exclude loss carryover because the division of carryover between the amount subtracted from short term net gains and the amount added to short term net losses could not be ascertained. However, we excluded carryover from total realized net gain and loss for 1944-46 as follows. Total net gain, that realized on returns with statutory net capital gains, was increased by the amount of loss carryover reported on this group of returns, i.e., the amount of loss carryover that had been subtracted was added back; and total net loss was decreased by the amount of loss carryover reported on returns with statutory net capital losses. Because we could not adjust the short term gain and loss series in 1944-46 to remove the loss carryover, our series on short term gain understates, and that on short term loss overstates, the actual annual amounts realized during 1944-46.

The loss carryover series in 1942-46 (Tables 20 and 27) represents the amount filers reported on their returns and took into account in determining series 3 and 4 in Source 1. It overstates the amount actually deducted from current year's income. The filer reported the *full* amount of prior years' disallowed net capital loss as a carryover on the back of his return (with a limitation in 1942 alone) whereas, owing to the statutory capital loss limitation, only a *portion* of the carryover reported on some returns with statutory net capital losses actually increased the amount of statutory net capital loss allowed as a deduction. For example, a taxpayer with a loss carryover of $50,000 from 1943 reported the entire amount on his 1944 return, and all is included in the loss carryover series and is taken into account in the short term series in Source 1, even though only $1,000 is included in the statutory loss series if the taxpayer had no capital transactions in 1944. The same kind of overstatement in the loss carryover series could occur in 1942, as well as in later years, even though loss carryover from 1941 was limited to 1942 short term net gains. For example, in 1942 a return with a current year short term net gain of $5,000, a net loss carryover from 1941 of $5,000, and a statutory long term net loss of $5,500 (half of $11,000), would show a statutory net loss of only $1,000 because of the $1,000 limitation on net capital loss. If loss carryover were excluded, the statutory net loss would be $500. Therefore, owing to the $1,000 loss limitation, the $5,000 carryover increased the current year's statutory net loss only $500. Because the loss carryover reported in 1942 was limited by the size of the current year net short term capital gain the overstatement in the tabulated series was smaller than in 1943-46.

Another type of overstatement occurs in the loss carryover series for 1944-46 (Tables 20 and 27) in that it includes portions of the carryover already reported and included in the carryover figures for preceding years. For example, in 1943 the taxpayer reported as a carryover the amount of net capital loss disallowed in 1942. Since the loss could be carried forward to the succeeding 5 years, the amount disallowed in 1942 was again reported as a carryover in 1944, 1945, and 1946 to the extent that it was again disallowed as a deduction in 1943, 1944, and 1945.

We derived statutory net capital gain by adjusting the figures in Source 1 to exclude net loss carried over from preceding years, i.e., by adding to series 7 the loss carryover reported on returns with statutory net capital gains (Source 1). Statutory loss data could not be adjusted similarly because the proportion of tabulated carryover (Tables 20 and 27) actually included in statutory net loss is unknown. As already noted, owing to the $1,000 limitation on deductible net capital loss, loss carryover in 1942-46 increased statutory net loss by only a portion of the tabulated amount. This is the reason statutory losses excluding carryover are not shown in Tables 20, 22, and 23. Our series on statutory net gains and losses, like total realized gains and losses, include amounts on sales of depreciable assets.[20]

The inclusion in Source 1 of net loss carried over from preceding years in statutory net capital gain and loss distorts, to an unknown degree, the distribution of data between returns with statutory net gain and loss. Because loss carryover is included, some returns that would have shown a statutory net gain on a current basis are classified as returns with a statutory net loss. For example, in 1943 a return with a $1,000 current year net gain after a statutory percentage reduction, and a $2,000 net loss carryover, would be tabulated as a return with a $1,000 statutory net loss, although on a current basis (without carryover) it would have a $1,000 statutory gain.[21] Our estimates of total realized gain and loss are adjusted to exclude loss carryover but not to take account of the errors in classification due to the carryover. As indicated earlier, estimates of total realized net gain and loss are for returns with statutory net gains and losses respectively. Consequently, the current year net gains of returns that show statutory net losses only because of loss carryover reduce our estimate of total realized net loss. Concomitantly, total realized net gain is understated by the amount of the current year net gains on those returns. Such errors of classification noticeably affect the data in 1945-46. In 1945 returns with statutory

[20] However, Tables 29, 31, 36, and 37 exclude returns with net gains or losses from sales of depreciable assets in 1942-46.

[21] In 1942, although loss carryover was limited to the current year short term net gains, it could still produce a statutory net loss for a return that would have shown a statutory net gain on a current basis; e.g., a return with a $1,000 statutory long term loss, after percentage reduction, a $2,000 current year short term gain, and a $2,000 loss carryover would have shown a $1,000 statutory loss. If carryover were excluded, the return would have shown a $1,000 statutory gain. The loss carryover probably affected the classification of fewer returns in 1942 than in 1943-46, because permissible amounts of carryover were more severely limited.

net capital losses in the adjusted gross income group $300,000-
500,000 show an estimated realized net loss of $2,324,000 when loss
carryover is included. If it is subtracted, the current year net loss is
only $7,000. Moreover, if net losses from sales of depreciable assets
are excluded, deduction of loss carryover results in an over-all net
gain of $593,000 for returns with statutory net capital losses in
this income group. In 1946 returns in the adjusted gross income
group of $1,000,000 and over show an estimated aggregate net loss
of $1,335,000 when loss carryover is included. Exclusion of loss
carryover reduces the net loss to $654,000. If net losses from sales
of depreciable assets are likewise excluded, the result is an over-all
net gain of $198,000 for returns with statutory net loss in this
income group.

E Differences in the Estimates of Realized Capital Gains and Losses for the Various Periods

Despite the adjustments made in an effort to get a continuous series
on net capital gains and losses, the figures for the 30 years are far
from homogeneous. In this section we summarize the major differences in the estimates for various periods.

1 Total Realized Net Capital Gains and Losses

Changes in the requirements for filing income tax returns, described
in Section C, are a major source of differences in the basic data. The
omission for years before 1928 of returns with net deficits also impairs the comparability of the series, particularly for losses. The
understatement in the loss series for 1926-28 and 1938-41, and the
nature of the estimates of losses for 1917-25, 1932, and 1933 were
described above.

In all years the data are for realized amounts alone; i.e., differences in the relative size of unrealized gains and losses in various
years are not reflected.

The effect of many other factors causing disparity in the annual
data could not be measured. Among the chief are changes in the
statutory basis for computing gains and losses from assets acquired
before 1913 and from assets acquired as gifts, in the treatment of
gains and losses realized by partnerships and fiduciaries, and certain
changes in the statutory definition of capital assets such as occurred
in connection with 'worthless' stock. Nor was it possible to adjust
the statistics, which are based on unaudited returns, to take account of deliberate or other errors in taxpayers' reports, such as
those due to the understatement of realized gains or the reporting

of the same loss in successive years with a view to its eventual approval by the auditor as a deduction.

Differences in the 'netness' of gains and losses in the various periods should also be stressed. Total net capital gain 1922-33 and total net capital loss 1926-33 are overstated as compared with similar series for 1917-21, 1934-37, and 1942-46. Whereas in 1917-21 a taxpayer could offset his entire gain and loss against each other, except that he had to report security transactions separately, in 1922-33 he might report both a long term net gain segregated for tax at 12½ percent and a short term net loss, or, in 1924-33 both a long term net loss segregated for tax credit at 12½ percent and a short term net gain. An individual with a $3,000 net gain from sales of assets held more than 2 years and a $1,000 net loss from sales of assets held less than 2 years, for example, would report both figures (if his net income was large enough to make it profitable for him to segregate his gain) whereas in 1917-21 he would have reported only a $2,000 net gain.[22]

In our estimates for 1934-37 we offset an individual's entire gain and loss against each other.

Total realized net gain is overstated again in 1938-41 because, unlike 1934-37 and 1942-46, series are not available for returns with over-all statutory net capital gains and losses. We estimate total

[22] The overstatement from this factor can be estimated for 1933 alone, when, as indicated above, it was even larger than in other years of the period because the return had spaces for 3 amounts of 'net gain other than that segregated for the special tax', and the tabulated amount in *Statistics of Income for 1933* was derived by adding the 3 items. Table 65 shows estimates, based on a sample of returns, of the degree of overstatement in 1933, i.e., the relation between total realized net gain derived by adding the various tabulated series on net gain and by adding the net amounts on returns that reported a realized net gain from all capital transactions combined. Lines 10 and 22 show the overstatement in unsegregated net gain and loss, and lines 8 and 20 the overstatement in total net gain and loss. Lines 12 and 24 show the overstatement in total net gain and loss that would have occurred if 'other net gain' and 'other net loss' had been tabulated in 1933 as they were in earlier years. The realized net gain derived as the sum of tabulated net gains from sales of assets segregated at 12½ percent and tabulated amounts of other net gains from sales of assets was 38 percent higher than the realized net gain from sales of all assets. The corresponding proportion for net loss was 10 percent. However, since this overstatement arises only when substantial net gains in one series and substantial net losses in another were reported on many returns, it was undoubtedly much larger in 1933 than in the earlier boom period. In 1933, as Table 57, Section C, indicates, substantial short term gains were reported on returns with over-all net losses.

net gains as the sum of three items: statutory short term net gains, realized long term net gains, and net gains from sales of depreciable assets. A taxpayer might report a net gain under one of the three headings and a net loss under either the second or third. The total is overstated as compared with the totals for the preceding period, therefore, because for any group of returns the net gain in any one of the three items has not been reduced by the net loss in the others. The overstatement in total realized net loss in 1938-41, the sum of realized long term net losses and net losses from sales of depreciable assets, is, of course, more than outweighed by the understatement due to the omission of short term net capital losses.

In 1942-46 the entire capital gain and loss as defined by the statutes were offset against each other on the individual's return, and hence, in our estimates. However, the statutes excluded net gains and losses from sales of depreciable assets from the definition of capital assets. These amounts were added to our gain and loss series, thereby overstating them somewhat because, for any group of returns, net losses (gains) from sales of capital assets have not been reduced by net gains (losses) from sales of depreciable assets. This overstatement is reduced in the gain series by the statutory provision whereby long term net gains from sales of certain categories of depreciable assets could be included in long term capital gains.

Another, though less important, reason our total net gain and loss in 1934-37 and 1942-46 does not correspond with the series for earlier years is that total realized net gain is the estimated total for returns with statutory net gains, and total realized net loss, the estimated total for returns with statutory net losses. For years prior to 1934 the figures are total net gain and loss on all returns.[23]

Some taxpayers reporting statutory net gains may have realized net losses and some reporting statutory net losses may have realized net gains. For example, because of the application of the statutory percentages in 1934-37, a taxpayer with a realized gain of $5,000 on an asset held more than 10 years and a realized loss of $3,000 on an asset held 1 month was allowed a statutory net loss of $1,500 (30 percent of $5,000 minus $3,000) despite his total realized net gain of $2,000. In 1942-46 he would report a statutory net loss of $500 (half of $5,000 minus $3,000). Before 1934, his total realized net gain, $2,000, would appear as such in our series on net capital gain, provided his income did not justify segregation of long term gain at

[23] See, however, the preceding discussion of the effect of the segregation of capital gains and losses on the figures for 1922-33.

12½ percent. In our tables for 1934-37 and 1942-46 the $2,000 is excluded from total realized net gain because his return is classified as having a statutory net loss; moreover, total realized net losses (on returns with statutory net losses) has been reduced by this $2,000 net gain. For a discussion of the effect of loss carryover on the classification of returns in 1942-46 see Section D5. The degree of this type of understatement in the figures for 1934-37 and 1942-46 as compared with the series for earlier years could not be measured because the basic division in the tabulations is between returns with statutory rather than total realized net gains and losses.

For a discussion of why, beginning in 1934, total net gains and losses do not equal the sum of our long and short term series see Section 2 below.

a) *Capital gains and losses through partnerships and fiduciaries*
Our basic tables for all years include the net capital gains and losses reported on both individual and taxable fiduciary income tax returns. However, the several periods differ with respect to the method used by a beneficiary of fiduciary income or a partner to report on his individual income tax return the capital gains and losses realized by the fiduciary or partnership (or on a taxable fiduciary return in the case of one fiduciary reporting capital gains and losses received through another or through a partnership). When such capital gains and losses were reported on the individual or taxable fiduciary return under the heading 'capital gains and losses' they are included in our series, but when they were reported as 'fiduciary' or as 'partnership' income they are excluded. Hence, in 1922-33 our net capital gain and loss exclude amounts received through partnerships and fiduciaries, except long term amounts segregated for special tax treatment at 12½ percent which were reported together with other segregated amounts. In 1934-37 all net capital gain and loss received through partnerships or fiduciaries are excluded because they were reported as partnership profit and as income from fiduciaries respectively. In 1938-46 our series exclude net capital gain and loss received through fiduciaries except common trust funds but include amounts received through partnerships and common trust funds because they were reported together with other net capital gains and losses.

2 Long and Short Term Net Capital Gains and Losses
In 1922-33 long term net gains and losses cannot be separated from short except for the upper income groups, because they were not reported separately except when segregated for special tax or tax

credit. For 1933, however, we could estimate total long term net gains (Table 10) because the income tax return required more detail than in other years of the period.

For 1934-37 we set the dividing line between long and short term at 2 years to match the dividing line for the preceding period. The long term figures are overstated as compared with those for the preceding period because we added the realized amounts reported by the taxpayer for 3 holding periods: 2-5 years, 5-10, and over 10 years. The same type of overstatement appears in the short term series for 1934-37, where we added the amounts reported in the holding periods 1-2 years, under 1 year, and holding period not stated.

The difficulty arises because if the same taxpayer had a net gain from transactions in one holding period and a net loss in other periods, he reported, and our figures include, both. For example, if taxpayer A reported a $500 net gain from sales of assets held less than 1 year and a $300 net loss from sales of assets held 1-2 years, whereas B reported a $100 net gain in the first period and an $800 net loss in the second, the over-all realized net gain in the combined under 2 year period should be $200 (taxpayer A) and the over-all net loss, $700 (taxpayer B). These figures would be more nearly comparable with the corresponding series for 1922-33. The sums of the figures for the 2 holding periods combined, however, $600 for net gains and $1,100 for net losses, are the figures that appear in our series; hence both gains and losses are overstated. Similarly, the sum of the data for the 3 holding periods covering assets held longer than 2 years overstates both the net gains and net losses from transactions in assets held more than 2 years.

Since we do not know whether the overstatement is larger for transactions in assets held less or more than 2 years, the proportions of 'long' and 'short' term gains and losses in 1934-37 and 1922-33 should be compared with caution. In 1922-33 at net income levels where gains and losses were segregated for tax or tax credit at 12½ percent, the net gains or losses from transactions in assets held 2 years or less were calculated for each return by offsetting all losses against all gains; the net gains or losses from assets held more than 2 years were derived similarly.

In 1934-37 our series for long and short term realized net gains and losses and those for the total are not directly comparable. The long and short term series cover transactions reported on all returns with sales of capital assets, whereas total net gains represent the net gains (realized net gains minus net losses in the 5 holding periods) reported on returns with statutory net gains, and total net losses represent the net losses reported on returns with statutory net losses. Consequently, the sum of long and short term gains (losses) does not equal total net gain (loss); but the sum of long and short term gains minus the sum of long and short term losses does equal the excess of total net gain over total net loss. (Long and short term net gains and losses are shown separately for returns with statutory net gains and losses in Tables 16 and 18.)

The above procedure was adopted in order to make our series as comparable as possible with those for preceding and following years. Long term net gains in 1922-33 cover 'all' returns, i.e., all returns segregating such gains for tax at 12½ percent, regardless whether the return showed a total (long plus short) net gain or loss on balance. Accordingly, our long term net gain series for 1934-37 is the sum of the net gains reported on all returns in the 3 long term holding periods: 2-5 years, 5-10, and over 10 years. This seemed preferable to confining our series to amounts reported on returns with statutory net gains, thus excluding net gains in these holding periods reported on returns with statutory net losses. Similarly, long term net losses and short term net gains and losses cover transactions reported on all returns.

Total realized net gains and losses in 1934-37, on the other hand, represent the net amounts reported on returns with statutory net gains and losses, respectively. An alternative procedure would be to define total realized net gain (loss) as the sum of our estimates of realized long and short term net gain (loss) (Tables 8 and 9). However, it would overstate total net gain because net loss would not be offset against net gain for an individual who had a net gain in one holding period, a net loss in another, and a gain on balance. Similarly, it would overstate total net losses for individuals reporting a loss on balance. It seemed preferable therefore to confine the estimate of total realized net gain to returns reporting statutory net gains, and that for total realized net loss to returns reporting statutory net losses. The estimates would be better had the returns been classified as having a gain or loss on balance on the basis of *total realized* instead of *statutory* amounts, but this kind of classification was not available except in certain special tabulations for 1936 (Sec. F2).

Because of the difference in coverage, the percentage relation between long or short term net gains (losses) and total net gains (losses) in 1934-37 in Table 13 cannot be derived by dividing the one series by the other (Table 9 by Table 2); instead, we computed the percentages by dividing our long and short term series by the sum of the net gains (losses) reported in all 5 holding periods by all returns with capital transactions (Table 18).

In 1938-41 the dividing line between long and short term gains and losses was moved from 2 years to 18 months. Short term net loss was disallowed as a deduction and does not appear at all in our series, but could be carried over to the next taxable year and applied against short term net gains. To increase comparability with earlier years, our short term net gains are adjusted to exclude the reductions due to loss carryover.

Another source of incomparability with earlier years is the segregation of gains and losses on depreciable assets from capital gains and losses, 1938-41. Although these segregated amounts are included in our total net gain and loss series, they are not in our long and short term series because we do not have any information on the length of the holding period for depreciable assets. As a result, total net gain in 1938-41 is somewhat more than the sum of long and short term net gains.

In 1942-46 the statutory definition of long and short term gains and losses was further revised by moving the dividing line to 6 months. Net gains from sales of certain types of business property ordinarily excluded from the statutory definition of capital assets were treated as long term if derived from property held more than 6 months. Thus they are included in our long term gains. Other net gains and all net loss from sales of depreciable assets are excluded from the data classified by holding period.[24]

As in 1934-37, the long and short term series for 1942-46 cover all returns with capital transactions, and are to be distinguished from total realized net gain, which covers returns with statutory net gains only, and total realized net loss, which covers returns with statutory net losses only. This treatment was followed for the reasons explained above in the discussion of the similar problem in 1934-37. Because of this difference in coverage and also because gains and losses on

[24] Net gains from sales of business property subject to allowance for depreciation and from real property used in trade or business, if derived from assets held more than 6 months, could be counted as long term capital gains. The amounts under 'net gains from sales of depreciable assets' in our series (under 'net gains from sales of property other than capital assets' in Source 1) consist of short term gains from sales of such assets, and long and short term gains from sales of specified types of government obligations.

sales of depreciable assets are excluded from the long and short term series, the sum of long and short term gain (loss) does not equal total net gain (loss). In 1942 and 1943 loss carried over from preceding years is excluded from our series. However, in 1944-46, since we could not determine how much of the carryover was offset against short term net capital gains and how much added to short term net capital losses, short term losses are overstated and short term gains understated as compared with the short term series for earlier years, and with the total realized net gain and loss series for 1944-46 where we excluded the loss carryover.

The percentages in Table 13 for 1942-46 are similar to those for 1934-37 in that the denominator used in deriving them was not the total net capital gain (loss) series in our tables, which covers returns with statutory net capital gains (losses) only, but the sum of the realized long and short term net gains (losses), which cover all returns with capital transactions.

F Supplementary Series on Capital Gains and Losses

1 Sample Data for 1930, 1932, and 1933

In addition to the basic data for 1922-33 discussed above, we present Tables 42-65 for 1930, 1932, and 1933 based on sample studies of capital gains and losses from Source 5. These samples were confined, except as noted below, to returns filed by individuals who reported at least 5 sales of capital assets with the dates of purchase and sale. In choosing the samples care was taken to have all areas represented but special attention was focused on places near active stock markets, such as New York and Illinois. The samples were drawn from all net income and deficit groups. However, a comparison of the income distributions of the net gains and losses reported in the samples with those from Source 1 (Table 2, Sec. C, and Table 42) indicates that the higher income levels are overweighted in the sample study. In 1932, for example, less than a quarter of the excess of capital loss over gain reported in the sample on returns with net incomes was in statutory net income groups under $25,000 (Table 42, Sec. B) though for all returns a half was found (Table 2, Sec. C). Part of the reason may be the exclusion of returns reporting fewer than 5 sales.

For 1930 the sample included 1,904 returns. For 1932 and 1933 it had 2 components: 'matched' and 'new', the former comprising all the individuals in the 1930 sample whose returns for 1932 and 1933 were available and who reported some capital transactions.

The restriction that the return must report at least 5 sales did not apply to the 'matched' group in 1932 and 1933. In 1932, 1,211 'matched' and 2,193 'new' returns were included, and in 1933, 1,192 'matched' and 2,164 'new' returns.

Since data for each sale of assets, as reported on the back of the return, were tabulated, we know the gross amount received, gross gains on sales with gain, and gross losses on sales with loss, classified by the month of sale, by the number of months the asset was held, and by the type of asset sold, as well as the percentage relation in 1932 and 1933 between disallowed losses from securities held 2 years or less and other losses. Most taxpayers apparently listed their losses on the back of the return even though they could not deduct them in calculating their net income. Total disallowed net losses in the 2 years were estimated from these data (Sec. D2). The overweighting of the higher income levels in the sample, mentioned above, was not reflected in our estimates of total disallowed net loss, which were based on the income level distributions from Source 1 instead of from the sample (see Tables 48 and 49).

For each return in the sample, information was transcribed for each sale on the type of security (stock, bond), dates of purchase and sale, gross amount received (selling price), and capital gain or loss.[25] Sales of securities subject to disallowance, i.e., stocks and bonds (except government) held 2 years or less, were distinguished from other sales in 1932 and 1933, and sales of assets where the gain or loss was segregated for special tax treatment were transcribed separately in all 3 years. Sales of assets other than securities were also available but since the items were relatively few and extremely heterogeneous and since the samples were not designed to measure the relative magnitude of sales other than securities, these sales were excluded from most of our tables.[26]

[25] In 1933 some returns with gains equal to losses are excluded from our tables, and in 1930 and 1932 some sales with no gain or loss.

[26] Fewer than 200 of the returns in the samples for 1930 and 1932 reported sales of assets other than securities. Such sales were transcribed under two headings: 'Sales except stocks and bonds', including sales of real estate, commodities, stock exchange seats, etc.; and 'other items', including transactions not properly classified as sales in the current year, such as security sales in a preceding year, brokerage fees that could not be allocated to each sale, syndicate interest, options expired, mortgage foreclosures.

In a few instances the tabulations were for all assets combined (securities plus other assets); e.g., tabulations of gross receipts from sales in 1930 and 1932 when classified by income level. Our hand tabulations of the sample for 1933 included all sales of assets, since the exclusion of assets other than securities would have increased the work substantially.

'Market traders' were arbitrarily distinguished from others on the basis of gross receipts from all sales of assets. In 1930 they comprised the returns reporting gross receipts of $500,000 or over, and in 1932 and 1933, of $300,000 or over. Various subgroups of market traders were also distinguished by the holding period of the major portion of the securities sold (day to day, short cycle, long term traders, and traders with miscellaneous accounts) but separate data for these groups are not presented here.

For 1930 and 1932 our tables are summaries of the most significant BIR tabulations. For 1933, on the other hand, the Bureau of Internal Revenue did not complete the tabulations, and our tables are based on summary data we took from its transcript cards. The most significant tabulations for 1930 and 1932 are those showing gains and losses by month of sale and by holding period, determined from the transcribed dates of purchase and sale. '0 months' include assets held less than 15 days; '1 month', assets held 0.5-1.5 months, etc.

2 Special Tabulations for 1936

In Tables 66-81 we present detailed information on capital gains and losses in 1936 based on special tabulations of federal income tax returns (Source 4). These tabulations differ from the figures in Source 1 because they are based on 'duplicate' instead of 'original' returns, and because they exclude all returns filed on Form 1040A and also returns filed on Form 1040 that were incomplete with respect to information on capital gains and losses (Sec. B).

Data on realized gains and losses from Source 4 differ from those from Sources 1 and 2 in that (a) the basic distinction is between returns with total realized net gain or loss in Source 4, and statutory net gain or loss in Sources 1 and 2; (b) different net income classifications are used, statutory net income excluding statutory net capital gain or loss in Source 4, and statutory net income in Sources 1 and 2. Another difference arises because our estimates of realized net gains and losses for income groups under $100,000 from Source 2 are based on a *sample* of the returns whereas the data from Source 4 were tabulated from *all* returns in those income groups.

Statutory net gains and losses from Source 4 are lower than the corresponding figures from Sources 1 and 2, reflecting its smaller coverage (Table 78). Realized net gain on returns with such gains from Source 4 is also lower than the comparable figure from Sources 1 and 2, i.e., excess of realized net gain over loss reported on returns with statutory net gains. The reverse relation would be expected

were it not for the smaller coverage of Source 4, because more realized net gains should be reported by the group with realized net
gains (in Source 4) than by the group with statutory net gains (in
Sources 1 and 2). The excess of realized gain over loss for all returns
agrees very closely in the two sources.

Net gain and loss for any combination of the 10 types of asset
shown in Tables 74-6, e.g., the 4 types of security, overstates the
actual net gain and loss from the combination, e.g., from all securities,
because the net gain from any one type of asset has not been reduced
by the net losses from other types. As in the similar case of the data
by holding period, this difficulty arises because the same individual
may have had a net gain from sales of one type of asset and net losses
from sales of other types. If an individual had an over-all net gain
from transactions in securities, his net losses from any one type
should properly be subtracted from his net gains to determine his
over-all net gain from securities.

The overstatement is more serious when numbers of returns with
net gains from the various types of asset are added. For example,
the sum of returns with net gains from each of the 4 types of security
overstates the actual number of returns with net gains from securities
because the same individual may have had a net gain from 2 or more
types and because some individuals with a net gain from one type
may have had a larger net loss from sales of another type.

'Other tangible' assets include such items as store fixtures and factory machinery; 'intangible assets' include royalties, patent rights,
goodwill, and copyrights.

Table 66 shows distributions for 1936 by size classes of net income
defined in 3 ways: 1) statutory net income; 2) net income excluding
statutory net capital gains and losses; and 3) net income including
realized but excluding statutory net capital gains and losses. Contrary to what has sometimes been assumed, the exclusion of statutory
capital gains and losses from net income does not reduce income
inequality — at least as measured by Lorenz curves for this particular
year. A Lorenz curve shows cumulated percentages of income accounted for by cumulated percentages of returns, starting with those
reporting the lowest incomes, i.e., the largest deficits. If curves are
drawn for returns with capital transactions using the 3 income definitions available for 1936 (by cumulating the various pertinent sets of
percentages in Table 66), those based on the first two definitions
are very similar. In fact, the 50 percent of returns with lowest statutory net incomes (or with statutory net deficits) accounted for 10.5

percent of total statutory net income (minus deficit) reported on all returns with capital transactions (definition 1), whereas the lowest half of returns when ranked by income excluding capital gains and losses accounted for only about 8.3 percent of total net income excluding gains and losses (definition 2). That is, the income inequality for returns with capital transactions is slightly greater when statutory capital gains and losses are removed from the distribution.

Unfortunately, it is not possible to determine whether this was true in other years because data comparable with those for 1936 are not available. However, for 1944 there is evidence that inequality was slightly higher when capital gains and losses were removed, except for returns at the very highest income levels (*Studies in Income and Wealth, Volume Thirteen,* Part VII). In this study capital gains and losses were removed from the 1944 distribution of tax returns on the basis of actual data from individual transcript cards for returns with incomes of $100,000 or over, and of partly estimated data for returns in lower income groups. Both 1936 and 1944 were years with a sizeable excess of statutory capital gains over losses.

When realized instead of statutory capital gains and losses are included in net income (definition 3), the Lorenz curve shows more inequality than under definition 1 or 2. The lowest 50 percent of returns when ranked by definition 3 accounted for about 4 percent of total net income including realized gains and losses (Table 66) — less than half the corresponding proportion received under definition 1 or 2.

G *Differences in Income Classification in the Various Periods*

In all tables showing distributions by net income groups, the classification corresponds to the definition in *Statistics of Income* unless otherwise stated. The income group 'under $5,000' includes only returns with positive net incomes; whenever data for net deficit returns are available, they are shown separately. The 'total' column in tables showing distributions by net income groups is a combination of the various income groups actually shown; it excludes net deficit returns unless otherwise indicated.

Differences in the net income distribution in the various periods reflect changes in filing requirements (Sec. C). Furthermore, changes in the net income classification arise from changes in the definition of statutory net capital gain and loss (Sec. D). They may be summarized as follows: From 1924 through 1933 net capital losses segregated for tax credit were not deducted in determining the net income classification;[27] in 1932 and 1933 short term net losses from transactions in stocks and bonds, except government bonds, were not taken into account. From 1934 through 1937 the taxpayer applied certain percentages to realized net gains and losses to determine the statutory amount taken into account in the net income classification, and deductible net loss was limited to $2,000. In 1938-1941, realized net gains and losses were again reduced by certain statutory percentages. As explained above, these percentages differed from those in effect in 1934-37. Moreover, in 1938-41 all short term net loss was disallowed in determining net income. The net income classification was further affected by the provisions allowing for carrying over certain amounts of short term net loss disallowed in the preceding taxable year. In 1942-46 percentage reductions were again applied to realized net gains and losses, although the percentages were not the same as in earlier years. Deductible net loss was limited to $1,000. As in 1938-41, certain amounts of carryover were permitted for disallowed loss, but the carryover provisions were more liberal in 1943-46 than in preceding years.

Further disparity is introduced in 1944-46 because returns were not tabulated by net income, but by adjusted gross income for individual returns (Forms W-2 and 1040) and total income for taxable fiduciaries (Form 1041). Adjusted gross income differs from net income in that it is not reduced by allowable personal deductions, such as contributions, medical expenses, taxes, interest, and casualty losses. Total income for fiduciaries is conceptually comparable with the adjusted gross income tabulated for individual returns for 1944-46. As in other years, data for individual and taxable fiduciary returns in 1944-46 are shown together in most of our tables.

Table headings 'returns with statutory net incomes', 'returns with statutory net incomes of $5,000 and over', and 'returns with net deficits' apply to all years except 1944-46 when the headings should read 'returns with adjusted gross incomes of $1 and over', 'returns with adjusted gross incomes of $5,000 and over', and 'returns with no adjusted gross incomes'.

Further differences in the net income classification during the 30 years arise because of factors not directly connected with capital gains and losses, e.g., changes in the statutory provisions for carrying over net operating business losses, and for including interest.

[27] The same problem does not arise in connection with net capital gain segregated for the 12½ percent tax, since this gain was included in determining the net income classification.

Although we could estimate realized as opposed to statutory net capital gains and losses, we did not attempt to make such estimates classified by size of income redefined to include gains and losses excluded by statute. Net gains and losses in 1934-37, 1938-41, and 1942-46 by net income groups are the realized net gains and losses reported on returns classified by statutory net income groups. Similarly, excluded gains and disallowed losses are the amounts at each statutory net income level. The series on long term net capital loss segregated for tax credit at 12½ percent for 1924-33 are for returns in the various size ranges of statutory net income determined without regard to such segregated losses.

To facilitate comparisons among the series, all tables are classified by broad net income groups. Most of the basic data from the sources listed above are available by more detailed net income and net deficit groups. *Statistics of Income for 1940,* for example, presents data on net capital gains and losses for 40 net income levels. For most purposes the broad groups are adequate to reveal differences among income levels and variations over time in the behavior of given income groups.

Some tables, mainly those based on Source 4, are classified by net income groups defined to exclude statutory net capital gain or loss. In tables utilizing income classifications other than statutory net income, except for 1944-46 for which the appropriate classifications are described just above, the headings indicate the definition of net income used.

Net income (Table 41) is statutory except in 1934-46 when it was adjusted to include realized net capital gain and loss, except that realized short term net loss was not taken into account in 1938-41.[28] Net income in Table 41 represents amounts reported on all individual and taxable fiduciary returns with net incomes, regardless whether any capital transactions were reported. Net income reported on returns with capital transactions is not available except in special tabulations for 1936 (Tables 66, 68).

In determining net income for Table 41, 4 percent of the gross

[28] For 1917 net income in Table 41, used as a base for percentages in Tables 5 and 6, is from *Statistics of Income for 1917,* and is not reduced by deductions for contributions. Revised net income data for 1917, including deductions for contributions, are available in *Statistics of Income for 1942.* The revised net income total for 1917 is $10,946.2 million; the unrevised total used in our tables, $11,191.2 million. Both revised and unrevised figures for 1917 exclude data for 1,640,758 returns with net incomes under $2,000, showing aggregate net income of $2,461.1 million (see footnote 7 above).

income reported on returns filed on Form 1040A in 1941, and 6 percent in 1942 and 1943, were excluded. In 1944-46 net income was tabulated in Source 1 for returns with itemized deductions only. Net income reported by filers who took advantage of the standard deduction allowed in these years was estimated in the following manner. For returns with adjusted gross income of less than $5,000, adjusted gross income was reduced 10 percent, approximately the standard deduction allowed. For returns with adjusted gross income of $5,000 and over, the allowable standard deduction, $500, was subtracted. The final net income is the sum of the estimated net income on returns with a standard deduction and the tabulated net income on returns with itemized deductions.

Net incomes for 1944-46 (Table 41) are classified by adjusted gross income instead of net income group. However, the amounts cover returns with net income only and exclude returns with adjusted gross income that showed a net deficit after itemized personal deductions had been subtracted. In 1944, 37,329 returns, in 1945, 34,953 returns, and in 1946, 34,104 with adjusted gross income of $1 or more showed net deficits. These returns, as well as returns reporting no adjusted gross income, are excluded from the net income series for 1944-46 in Table 41.

Percentages in Tables 5, 6, and 12 are slightly overstated in 1944-46 because the gain and loss series used as a numerator cover all returns with adjusted gross incomes of $1 or more, while the net income series used as a denominator covers returns with net income only. It was impossible to ascertain the capital gains and losses reported on returns with adjusted gross income of $1 or more that showed net deficits after personal deductions had been subtracted. However, the overstatement due to this factor is probably insignificant, since less than 0.1 percent of the total number of returns with adjusted gross income of $1 or more showed net deficits in 1944-46.

II Income Tax Returns of Corporations

Tables for corporations, based on Source 1, cover returns filed on Forms 1120 and 1120A by domestic and resident foreign corporations not exempt from tax under the Internal Revenue Code, Section 101, returns filed on Form 1120L by domestic life insurance companies and by foreign life insurance companies carrying on business within the United States, and returns filed on Form 1120M in 1942-47 by mutual insurance companies.

Comparability is reduced by changes in requirements for filing consolidated returns that affect the degree of 'intercompany elimination' in the figures for net capital gains and losses. In 1928 a consolidated return could be filed if one corporation owned at least 95 percent of the stock of another (except nonvoting stock, limited and preferred as to dividends), or if at least 95 percent of the voting stock of two or more corporations was owned by the same interests. Beginning in 1929 consolidated returns could be filed only when one or more chains of corporations were connected through stock ownership with a common parent corporation, which owned directly at least 95 percent of the stock of at least one of the other corporations, and at least 95 percent of the stock of each corporation, except the common parent, was owned directly by one or more of the other corporations. The Revenue Act of 1934, restricting the privilege of filing consolidated returns to affiliated groups of railroad corporations, was in force until 1940 except that beginning in 1936 the privilege was extended to urban and interurban electric railways.[29] In 1940 and 1941 the privilege was extended to Pan-American trade corporations, i.e., domestic corporations engaged solely in active trade or business in Central or South America. Beginning in 1942 the privilege of filing a consolidated return for normal tax and surtax was, with certain limited exceptions, extended to all affiliated corporations.

Comparability of data on the net income of corporations in Table 93 is affected by the fact that before 1936 dividends from domestic corporations were excluded from net income, whereas beginning in 1936, they were included. Other differences occur in some years because of differences with respect to the inclusion of interest from government obligations and of contributions.

We present statutory net capital gains and losses of corporations filing income tax returns. Total realized amounts could not be estimated for years when the statutory figures do not cover all gains and losses. Net gains are not available for corporations before 1928; net losses, before 1930. Tax treatment within 5 periods was fairly similar: 1928-31, 1932-33, 1934-39, 1940-41, 1942-47.[30]

[29] The Revenue Act of 1938 expanded the 1936 definition of 'railroad' to include a street or suburban trackless trolley system, or a street or suburban bus system operated as part of a street or suburban electric railway or trackless trolley system.

[30] Comparability of data in Table 96 is affected by differences in the tax treatment of capital gains in various years and by the fact that the classification by type of company in 1939 is not exactly comparable with that for later years. For differences in the industrial classification of financial corporations in 1939 and later years see *Statistics of Income for 1940*, Part II, pp. 310-1.

1928-1931

As all realized net gains and losses were taken into account in computing net income the statutory amounts in tables for corporations are realized net gains and losses.

1932-1933

Net loss from sales of stocks and bonds (except government) held 2 years or less was disallowed as a deduction except for banks and trust companies. Statutory net loss therefore understates realized losses, and statutory net gains overstate realized gains. It was impossible to estimate the disallowed net loss for corporations in these 2 years as was done for individuals and taxable fiduciaries.

1934-1939

Net gains were taken fully into account in determining net income so that statutory net gains are comparable in this respect with those for 1928-31. Since net losses allowed as a deduction were limited to $2,000 for each corporation, with certain exceptions in the case of banks and trust companies, the statutory figures understate realized losses. As in 1932-33, disallowed net loss could not be estimated for corporations to parallel those for individuals in 1934-37.

Beginning in 1938 net gain or loss from depreciable assets was reported and tabulated separately from net amounts from sales of other assets. Our tables include gains and losses from depreciable assets. Net gains and losses in our tables are overstated as compared with those for earlier years because net gains and losses from sales of depreciable and other assets reported by the same corporations are not offset against each other; net losses are overstated, further, as compared with earlier years because the $2,000 loss limitation did not apply to sales of depreciable assets.

1940-1941

Gains and losses from sales of capital assets were divided according to the period held: short term — from sales of assets held 18 months or less; long term — from sales of assets held more than 18 months. Short term net capital loss was disallowed as a deduction in the current year but (in an amount not in excess of the net income for the year the loss was sustained) could be carried forward and applied against short term net gains of the next taxable year. That is, beginning in 1941, net gains are reduced by the preceding year's short term net loss carryover. Long term net capital losses were allowed in full, except that for personal holding companies they were limited to $2,000.

As in 1938 and 1939, gains and losses from sales of depreciable assets are excluded from capital assets as defined in the statutes but are included in our series. Short term noninterest bearing government obligations issued on or after March 1, 1941 on a discount basis are treated similarly.

Net gain for 1940-41 is the sum of 2 components from Source 1: (a) net gain from sales of capital assets (tabulated in Source 1 as a single item but is the sum of long and short term net gains computed separately); (b) net gain from sales of other assets (net gain from sales of depreciable assets). Our net loss series is also the sum of 2 components in Source 1: (c) net loss from sales of capital assets (long term net loss only); (d) net loss from sales of other assets (net loss from sales of depreciable assets).

Gains for 1940-41 are overstated as compared with earlier years because receipts from long and short term transactions are not offset against each other; i.e., for any given return a long term net capital gain is not reduced by a short term net capital loss; a short term net capital gain is not reduced by a long term net capital loss. Moreover, as in 1938-39, receipts from sales of depreciable property are not offset against receipts from sales of property included in the statutory definition of capital assets. The latter deficiency affects also losses in 1940-41. However, the overstatement of net capital loss due to this factor is insignificant in comparison with the understatement due to the complete disallowance of short term net capital losses.

1942-1947

Capital assets were again divided according to holding period, but the dividing-line between long and short term transactions differed from that in the preceding period. Long term net gains and losses were defined as those from capital assets held longer than 6 months; short term as those from assets held 6 months or less. These both were offset against the other to derive the final figure on the tax return.

All net loss from sales of capital assets was disallowed as a deduction in the current year. It could be carried over and applied against capital gains in the succeeding 5 taxable years. Net gains were reported in full for tax purposes, except that those for the current year were reduced by preceding years' loss carryover as follows: In 1942 current year short term net gains were reduced by short term net loss carried over from 1941. Beginning in 1943 current year net gains (long and short combined) were reduced by prior years' loss carryover. The gains reduction resulting from loss carryovers is probably smaller in 1942 than in later years, because the loss carryover in 1942 was limited to the current year's short term net gains, whereas, beginning in 1943, loss carryovers could be applied against all current year net capital gains (long and short).

Depreciable and real property used in trade or business were excluded from the statutory definition of capital assets in 1942-47. However, net gains from their sale or exchange and from the involuntary conversion of such properties and of capital assets if held longer than 6 months were treated as long term capital gains; net losses were deductible as ordinary net losses.

Net capital gain in our tables for 1942-47 is the sum of net gains from sales of 'capital' assets and of other property (Source 1).[31] Net losses represent only losses on sales of property 'other than capital assets'. As noted above, all net losses from sales of 'capital' assets were disallowed as a current deduction.

[31] In 1944-47 net capital gain was tabulated as follows in Source 1: excess of long term net gain over short term net loss (which, beginning in 1942, could be segregated from other corporate net income and taxed at a flat 25 percent rate); excess of short term net gain over long term net loss. Our net gains series in 1944-47 is the sum of these amounts and amounts tabulated under 'net gain, sales other than capital assets'. The division of net capital gain into the 2 categories does not produce any overstatement as compared with 1942-43 because their sum is equivalent to the single item 'net capital gain' tabulated in the preceding 2 years.

Appendix Two

I Basic Data for 1917-1946

The basic data on capital gains and losses from federal income tax returns filed by individuals and taxable fiduciaries in 1917-46 are presented in Tables 1-41.

They are far from perfectly comparable for the 30 years, because of changing statutory provisions and gaps and changes in the government's tabulations. The amounts realized on the sale or taxable exchange of capital assets (ignoring the statutory exclusion between 1922 and 1933 of assets held 2 years or less from 'capital' assets, and between 1938 and 1946 of assets subject to an allowance for depreciation) are as published in *Statistics of Income,* with the following adjustments made in order to reduce their heterogeneity.

1) To fill an important gap in the published tabulations, we estimated for each year 1917-25 the net capital loss of individuals reporting net income on the basis of sample data for this period and of the relation between capital losses and total deductions in the following period.

2) We based short term net capital losses disallowed by statute in 1932 and 1933 on sample data.

3) We estimated the net capital gains and losses in 1934-37 and 1942-46, and the net capital gains in 1938-41 that were excluded from the determination of tax liability because of the statutory provision recognizing only declining fractions of capital gains and losses as the holding period was lengthened. For 1938-41, we estimated net capital losses from sales of assets held more than 18 months (excluded because of the aforesaid statutory provision), but because of the lack of basic data, not from those held 18 months or less, disallowed by the statutes.

Despite the adjustments, our annual series reflect various differences in the statutory treatment of capital gains and losses during the 30 years, which detract from the homogeneity of the statistics for the different periods, 1917-21, 1922-33, 1934-37, 1938-41, and

1942-46. The chief differences are due to changes in the requirements for filing income tax returns, omission for the years before 1928 of returns with net deficits, understatement in the capital loss series for 1938-41 and 1926-28, deficiencies in the estimates of capital losses for 1917-25 and 1932-33, differences in the 'netness' of the series for various periods, and changes in the definition of 'long' and 'short' term capital gains and losses. These and other factors making for lack of comparability in the data are described in Appendix One, Sections D and E.

Notes to Tables 1-41

[1] Data for all years except 1944-46 classified by statutory net income; 1944-46 data classified by adjusted gross income. For differences in definition of statutory net income in different years and for definition of adjusted gross income, see Appendix One, Section G. Where a 'total' is shown, it is a combination of the various statutory income groups in the table and excludes data for returns with statutory deficits. 'Returns with statutory net incomes', 'returns with statutory net deficits', and 'returns with net incomes of $5,000 and over' are applicable to all years except 1944-46, when they should read 'returns with adjusted gross incomes', 'returns with no adjusted gross incomes', and 'returns with adjusted gross incomes of $5,000 and over'.

[2] For method of deriving estimates of net capital losses, 1917-25, see Appendix One, Section D2b.

[3] In 1929-33 for returns with net incomes or deficits, net capital loss from assets held more than 2 years reported by the taxpayer as a deduction in computing net income or deficit is included in short term net loss and in total net loss. In 1926-28 it is not included in either short term or total net loss if the taxpayer listed the amount under 'other deductions' on his return. See Appendix One, Section D2a.

[4] In 1932-33 capital loss estimates represent statutory net loss plus estimated disallowed short term net loss from sales of stocks and bonds. For method of deriving loss estimates for 1932 and 1933, see Tables 48 and 49, and for limitations of the estimates, see Appendix One, Section D2c.

[5] In 1932 and 1933 for returns with net deficits, net capital loss from assets held more than 2 years not taken into account by the taxpayer in computing net deficit or segregated for tax credit at 12½ percent is included in short term net loss and in total net loss. It is not included in short term or in total net loss in 1928-31 for returns with net deficits, or in any year 1924-33 for returns with net incomes.

[6] In 1934-37 represents estimated realized net capital gain and loss before the application of statutory percentages and before the $2,000 limitation on net loss. The method of deriving estimates for 1934-37, and the limitations of the estimates for net income groups under $100,000 in 1935, under $5,000 in 1937, and for the net deficit groups in 1935 and 1937, are described in Appendix One, Section D3.

Total realized net capital gain in 1934-37 does not equal the sum of realized long and short term net capital gains because of the following difference in the returns covered. Total realized net capital gain covers returns with statutory net capital gains only (realized losses reported on such returns having been offset against realized gains), whereas long and short term net gains cover both returns with statutory net capital gains and returns with statutory net capital losses. Similarly, total realized net capital loss does not equal the sum of realized long and short term net capital losses. For discussion, see Appendix One, Section E2.

In tables for 1934-37 where data are not classified by holding period, total realized net capital gain is the sum of the realized net gains in the various holding periods reported on returns with statutory net capital gains minus the sum of the realized net losses in the various holding periods reported on such returns; realized net capital loss is the sum of the realized net losses in the various holding periods reported on returns with statutory net capital losses minus the sum of the realized net gains in the various holding periods reported on such returns. In tables where data are classified by 5 or 6 holding periods, realized net gain is the net gain in a given holding period (or periods) reported on the designated group of returns before offsetting against such gain the net loss in that holding period reported on other returns in the same group; realized net loss is defined similarly. For definition of realized long and short net gains and losses, see Appendix One, Section D3.

[7] In 1938-41 represents estimated realized net capital gain and loss before the application of statutory percentages. Capital loss covers long term net loss only. Net gains and losses from sales of depreciable assets are included in total net capital gains and losses but not in the long or short term series. Short term net gains and total net gains in 1939-41 are before deduction of prior year short term net loss carried over to the current year (Table 27, Sec. A). For method of deriving estimates for 1938-41, see Appendix One, Section D4. For estimate of short term net losses in 1938, see Table 28. For net gains and losses from sales of depreciable assets, see Table 26, Section A.

[8] In 1942-46 represents estimated realized net capital gain and loss before the application of statutory percentages and before the $1,000 limitation on net loss. Net gains and losses from depreciable assets are included in total net capital gains and losses (except in Tables 36-7) but not in the long or short term series. For derivation of estimates for 1942-46, see Appendix One, Section D5. For net gains and losses from sales of depreciable assets, see Table 26, Section B.

Total realized net capital gain in 1942-46 does not equal the sum of realized long and short term net capital gains because gains from sales of depreciable assets are excluded from the long and short term series and because of the following differences in the returns covered. Total realized net capital gain covers returns with statutory net capital gains only (realized losses reported on such returns having been offset against realized gains) whereas long and short term net gains cover both returns with statutory net capital gains and returns with statutory net capital losses. Similarly, total realized net capital loss does not equal the sum of realized long and short term net capital losses. For discussion, see Appendix One, Section E2.

Prior years' loss carryover is excluded from total realized net capital gain and loss in 1942-46 and from the short term series in 1942 and 1943. However, the figures for short term gains and losses in 1944-46, unlike those for 1942 and 1943, have not been adjusted to exclude capital loss carried over from preceding years because it was impossible to determine how much of the carryover was offset against current year short term net capital gains and how much added to current year short term net capital losses. As a result, short term capital losses on current year transactions are overstated by our figures for 1944-46, and short term capital gains on current year transactions are understated. For amount of capital loss carried over in 1942-46 see Table 27, Section B.

[9] Statutory net income, except for 1934-46 when statutory net income was adjusted to include realized net capital gain and loss instead of statutory (except that realized short term net loss was not taken into account in 1938-41). Net income represents amounts reported on all individual and taxable fiduciary income tax returns with net incomes, regardless whether any capital transactions were reported; net income reported on all returns with capital transactions is not available except for special tabulations for 1936 in Tables 66 and 68. For 1941-43 see note 25 below for the adjustment for returns filed on Form 1040A. For 1944-46 net income was estimated as explained in Appendix One, Section G.

[10] Long term net gain included in short term series in 1930-33.

[11] In 1934-37 short term net gain and loss include amounts from sales of assets when holding period is not stated.

[12] 11.1 percent of total net gain was reported with holding period not stated; included here in short term net gain.

[13] 20.3 percent of total net gain was reported with holding period not stated; included here in short term net gain.

[14] Represents statutory net loss and hence excludes disallowed short term net loss from sales of stocks and bonds (except government).

[15] Returns are classified as having statutory net capital gains if they reported a net gain (after the application of the statutory percentages) for all 5 holding periods combined.

[16] Returns are classified as having statutory net capital losses if they reported a net loss (after the application of the statutory percentages) for all 5 holding periods combined.

[17] This total, i.e., the sum of net gains in the various holding periods, overstates the over-all realized net gain from transactions in all holding periods combined because the net gain in any one holding period has not been reduced by net losses in other holding periods realized by the same individuals. A similar overstatement appears in the sum of net losses in the various holding periods, and the same difficulty arises when the net gains (or losses) from two or more holding periods are added. See Appendix One, Section E2.

[18] In 1938-41 statutory capital gains and losses include gains and losses from sales of depreciable assets. Short term net capital loss, disallowed in 1938-41,

is excluded from the statistics for these years. Capital gain is the amount reported before deducting the prior year short term net loss carried over to the current year.

In 1942-46 gains from sales of depreciable assets are included in statutory net capital gains, which were adjusted to exclude amounts of capital loss carried over. Statutory net capital loss excluding prior years' loss carryover is not shown for 1942-46 because it was impossible to adjust statutory capital loss data to exclude loss carried over. The loss carryover for returns with statutory net capital loss, as tabulated in Source 1, overstates the prior years' loss actually included in statutory net capital loss. It was impossible to determine the proportion of the tabulated loss carryover that actually served to increase the current year statutory net capital loss. For amount of capital loss carryover in 1942-46 see Table 27, Section B; for further discussion, see Appendix One, Section D5.

[19] For returns with net deficits, net gains from sales of depreciable assets in 1938-46 were (in millions of dollars) 1.5, 1.6, 2.4, 2.4, 0.8, 0.7, 2.2, 3.9, and 1.3 respectively, and net losses 21.4, 27.8, 33.1, 35.2, 40.1, 48.8, 56.4, 57.2, and 25.1. Net gains from sales of depreciable assets in the 9 years accounted for the following percentages of total net capital gains reported on returns with net deficits: 6.9, 7.8, 14.4, 15.5, 5.9, 3.1, 6.8, 5.7, and 2.7. In the 5 years 1942-46 net losses from sales of depreciable assets accounted for 43.0, 56.9, 62.9, 57.9, and 33.9 percent, respectively, of total net capital losses reported on returns with net deficits.

[20] Prior years' short term net loss carryover reported on returns with net deficits were (in millions of dollars) 0.4 in 1939, 0.3 in 1940, 6.0 in 1943, 3.5 in 1944, 7.2 in 1945, and 4.9 in 1946. No short term net loss carryover was reported on returns with net deficits in 1941 and 1942. It was reported on 292 returns with net deficits in 1939 and on 138 in 1940. The number of returns with net loss carryover is not available for 1942-46.

[21] 'Other net gain' and 'other net loss' include assets held 2 years or less (short term) plus assets held more than 2 years (long term) if not segregated for special tax treatment.

[22] In 1928, 126,343 returns with net incomes under $5,000 (Form 1040) reported 'other net gain', 4.1 percent of the total number filed in that income group. The returns were distributed among the 8 size-of-gain groups in Table 30, Section A as follows: 74,253; 48,070; 3,895; 93; 27; 5; 0; 0. The average 'other net gain' in the net income group under $5,000 was $1,346.

In 1942-46 excludes returns with gain or loss from sales of depreciable assets. For these 5 years the number of returns reporting statutory net capital gains in the net income group under $5,000 in 1942-43 and in the adjusted gross income group under $5,000 in 1944-46 were 245,432, 476,023, 710,802, 1,150,136, and 1,553,137, respectively, and the number reporting statutory net capital losses were 318,784, 270,042, 282,952, 263,944, and 301,931. Returns reporting gains constituted 0.7, 1.1, 1.6, 2.4, and 3.1 percent, respectively, of total returns filed in the income group; returns reporting losses constituted 0.9, 0.6, 0.6, 0.6, and 0.6 percent. Average realized net capital gains in the under $5,000 income group were $750 in 1942, $877 in 1943, $928 in

1944, $1,078 in 1945, and $1,404 in 1946; and average realized net capital losses were $1,502, $1,091, $1,472, $1,001, and $929, respectively.

[23] In 1938-41 long term net gain and loss refer to capital assets held more than 18 months. 'Short term' net gain refers to capital assets held 18 months or less. Short term net loss was disallowed as a deduction in the current year. Net gains and losses from sales of depreciable assets are not included in the long and short term series. Depreciable assets cover certain types of assets distinguished from capital assets in the statutes; see Appendix One, Section E2.

[24] The following amounts of statutory long term net capital gains and losses were reported on returns with net deficits in 1938-41, respectively (millions of dollars): statutory long term net capital gains: 6.4, 6.3, 4.6, 4.3; statutory long term net capital losses: 192.2, 151.0, 175.5, 203.2; statutory long term net capital losses segregated for tax credit: 6.8, 4.6, 9.5, 30.8.

[25] In the net income groups under $5,000, 4 percent of the gross income reported on returns filed on Form 1040A in 1941, and 6 percent in 1942 and 1943, were excluded. For 1944-46 net income was estimated as explained in Appendix One, Section G.

Table 1

Net Capital Gains and Losses: Annual Totals, 1917-1946 (millions of dollars)

	RETURNS WITH STATUTORY NET INCOMES[1]			RETURNS WITH STATUTORY NET DEFICITS[1]			ALL RETURNS		
	Net gain	Net loss	Excess of gain	Net gain	Net loss	Excess of gain	Net gain	Net loss	Excess of gain
1917-21[2]									
1917	318.2	70.0	248.2						
1918	291.2	359.3	−68.1						
1919	999.4	736.6	262.8						
1920	1,020.5	1,037.0	−16.5						
1921	462.9	1,102.0	−639.1						
1922-33									
1922[2]	991.4	759.6	231.8						
1923[2]	1,168.5	976.8	191.7						
1924[2]	1,513.7	476.8	1,036.9						
1925[2]	2,932.2	359.7	2,572.5						
1926	2,378.5	212.8	2,165.8						
1927	2,894.6	276.1	2,618.5						
1928	4,807.9	212.8	4,595.2	53.9	144.6	−90.7	4,861.8	357.4	4,504.4
1929[3]	4,682.6	1,037.7	3,644.9	86.7	839.0	−752.3	4,769.3	1,876.7	2,892.6
1930[3]	1,193.1	1,313.7	−120.6	68.1	1,307.1	−1,239.0	1,261.2	2,620.8	−1,359.6
1931[3]	471.6	1,400.6	−929.0	29.6	1,818.7	−1,789.1	501.2	3,219.3	−2,718.1
1932[3,4]	162.9	1,814.6	−1,651.7	20.6	1,051.0[5]	−1,030.4	183.5	2,865.6	−2,682.1
1933[3,4]	553.2	1,207.5	−654.3	67.5	816.5[5]	−749.0	620.7	2,024.0	−1,403.3
1934-37[6]									
1934	312.7	772.0	−459.3	27.4	197.6	−170.2	340.1	969.6	−629.6
1935	730.7	693.1	37.5	33.4	159.6	−126.3	764.0	852.8	−88.7
1936	1,377.6	716.4	661.3	39.2	111.7	−72.6	1,416.8	828.1	588.7
1937	818.6	743.0	75.6	29.3	209.8	−180.5	847.9	952.8	−104.9
1938-41[7,a]									
1938	820.4	789.6	30.8	22.1	394.3	−372.2	842.5	1,184.0	−341.5
1939	673.4	642.2	31.2	20.6	320.8	−300.2	694.0	963.0	−269.0
1940	707.6	787.3	−79.7	16.5	373.6	−357.2	724.0	1,161.0	−436.9
1941	942.2	1,424.2	−482.0	15.5	429.4	−413.9	957.7	1,853.6	−895.9
1942-46[8]									
1942	751.1	1,052.2	−301.1	13.9	92.9	−79.0	765.0	1,145.1	−380.1
1943	1,752.3	631.7	1,120.6	20.1	83.5	−63.3	1,772.4	715.1	1,057.3
1944	2,431.1	774.8	1,656.3	30.8	85.4	−54.6	2,461.9	860.2	1,601.7
1945	4,808.9	518.7	4,290.2	67.1	90.3	−23.2	4,876.0	609.0	4,267.0
1946	7,210.8	545.1	6,665.7	44.6	65.9	−21.3	7,255.4	611.0	6,644.4
Totals									
1917-46[a,b]	50,179.8	23,443.9	26,736.1	706.9	8,591.7	−7,885.0	50,886.5	32,035.8	18,850.9
1917-21[b]	3,092.2	3,304.9	−212.7				3,092.2	3,304.9	−212.7
1922-33	23,750.2	10,048.7	13,701.5	326.4	5,976.9	−5,650.5	24,076.6	16,025.6	8,051.1
1934-37	3,239.6	2,924.5	315.1	129.3	678.7	−549.6	3,368.8	3,603.2	−234.5
1938-41[a]	3,143.6	3,643.3	−499.7	74.7	1,518.1	−1,443.5	3,218.2	5,161.6	−1,943.3
1942-46	16,954.2	3,522.5	13,431.7	176.5	418.0	−241.4	17,130.7	3,940.4	13,190.3

Based on Source 1, supplemented in 1934-37 by Sources 2 and 3, and for losses in 1932-33 by Source 5. Losses in 1917-25 based in part on Sources 6c-e. For discussion of differences in the data for the various periods see Appendix One, Sections D and E.

a Excludes short term net losses in 1938-41.

b Totals for net deficit returns and for all returns exclude returns with net deficit for years prior to 1928.

For numbered notes see pp. 362-6.

Table 2

Aggregate Net Capital Gains and Losses by Statutory Net Income Groups, 1917-1946 (millions of dollars)

A GAINS

	TOTAL[1]	STATUTORY NET INCOME GROUP (thousands of dollars)[1]								
		Under 5	5-25	25-50	50-100	100-300	300-500	500-1,000	1,000 & over	Subtotal 50 & over
1917-21										
1917	318.2	100.2		165.1		29.5	8.2	5.8	9.3	
1918	291.2	103.8	129.3	24.8	13.9	11.4	1.7	4.0	2.4	33.4
1919	999.4	322.1	407.3	95.8	68.9	50.2	8.9	8.4	37.9	174.3
1920	1,020.5	396.5	495.5	73.0	32.4	14.2	2.8	1.6	4.6	55.6
1921	462.9	208.4	188.7	39.2	17.7	6.4	1.6	0.5	0.4	26.6
1922-33										
1922	991.4	251.3	318.6	107.6	93.7	94.5	29.4	37.2	59.0	313.8
1923	1,168.5	400.6	330.6	106.8	92.8	98.1	36.0	30.8	72.8	330.5
1924	1,513.7	354.5	488.8	192.5	154.2	159.6	52.9	57.6	53.6	477.9
1925	2,932.2	268.2	890.6	415.4	346.0	417.6	163.1	167.3	264.0	1,358.0
1926	2,378.5	241.3	673.7	294.5	263.1	343.7	143.5	134.7	283.9	1,168.9
1927	2,894.6	301.5	725.6	361.4	346.8	463.3	178.3	178.0	339.6	1,506.0
1928	4,807.9	227.6	1,075.4	593.9	603.9	874.0	327.8	376.5	728.8	2,911.0
1929	4,682.6	291.8	944.6	489.2	506.3	837.4	349.6	404.2	859.4	2,956.9
1930	1,193.1	109.1	326.8	130.3	130.6	194.6	72.4	82.4	147.0	627.0
1931	471.6	105.1	127.1	43.7	37.7	62.9	26.1	26.7	42.2	195.6
1932	162.9	41.2	51.0	19.3	16.8	18.3	5.8	10.6	*	51.5
1933	553.2	110.9	168.2	75.1	60.5	61.4	17.7	17.4	42.1	199.1
1934-37[6]										
1934	312.7	70.5	120.7	43.8	28.6	27.6	6.3	8.0	7.2	77.7
1935	730.7	147.9	284.1	104.5	76.9	51.5	16.5	32.9	16.4	194.2
1936	1,377.6	219.7	538.8	211.7	158.5	138.2	26.3	31.9	52.5	407.4
1937	818.6	179.7	314.0	106.5	83.9	80.0	29.4	9.2	15.9	218.4
1938-41[7]										
1938	820.4	146.1	208.4	75.2	62.6	83.5	43.1	59.6	141.9	390.7
1939	673.4	168.5	250.9	81.0	55.1	48.4	20.9	19.2	29.2	172.8
1940	707.6	172.4	231.4	72.7	59.7	77.5	26.9	38.1	28.9	231.1
1941	942.2	227.5	240.6	87.6	82.9	121.1	56.3	54.2	71.9	386.4

1942-46[8]										
1942	751.1	225.0	196.2	70.9	63.4	79.9	23.9	41.4	50.4	259.0
1943	1,752.3	472.8	549.0	201.2	152.4	175.8	48.2	85.2	67.8	529.3
1944	2,431.1	700.0	845.2	263.4	221.2	220.6	69.3	68.6	42.8	622.6
1945	4,808.9	1,276.4	1,634.4	570.9	469.0	480.3	152.5	129.4	95.9	1,327.1
1946	7,210.8	2,256.2	2,432.8	713.4	583.7	644.1	181.4	203.1	196.2	1,808.5
Totals										
1917-46	50,179.8	10,096.8	6,121.0	25,901.9	2,652.4	5,965.6	2,126.8	2,324.5	3,764.0	12,096.2
1917-21	3,092.2	1,131.0	1,257.6	1,751.6		111.7	23.2	20.3	54.6	
1922-33	23,750.2	2,703.1	931.3	2,829.7		3,625.4	1,402.6	1,523.4	2,892.4	
1934-37	3,239.6	617.8		466.5	347.9	297.3	78.5	82.0	92.0	897.7
1938-41	3,143.6	714.5		316.5	260.3	330.5	147.2	171.1	271.9	1,181.0
1942-46	16,954.2	4,930.4	5,657.6	1,819.8	1,489.7	1,600.7	475.3	527.7	453.1	4,546.5

B Losses

1917-21[2]									
1917	70.0			57.1			12.9		
1918	359.3			297.0			62.3		
1919	736.6			613.8			122.7		
1920	1,037.0			901.0			135.9		
1921	1,102.0			1,022.4			79.5		
1922-33									
1922[2]	759.6			688.9			70.7		
1923[2]	976.8			899.4			77.5		
1924[2]	476.8			419.7			57.0		
1925[2]	359.7			295.0			64.7		
1926	212.8	55.8	60.7	22.3	23.6	31.8	11.4		
1927	276.1	91.4	71.2	28.1	31.2	31.7	8.8		
1928	212.8	41.9	67.6	22.5	24.0	33.1	8.0		
1929[3]	1,037.7	362.0	255.5	91.2	89.7	117.1	34.9		
1930[3]	1,313.7	285.7	486.0	162.1	139.2	148.0	33.6		
1931[3]	1,400.6	347.3	498.5	135.5	159.0	155.7	36.9		
1932[3,4]	1,814.6	363.1	561.6	336.9	273.4	184.3		95.3	553.0
1933[3,4]	1,207.5	278.3	287.8	262.3	199.6	122.8		56.7	379.1

	TOTAL[1]	Under 5	5-25	25-50	50-100	100-300	300-500	500-1,000	1,000 & over	Subtotal 50 & over
1934-37[6]										
1934	772.0	322.4	327.0	69.4	29.6	16.1	3.1	2.6	1.9	53.3
1935	693.1	299.6	265.9	64.7	34.1	26.1	0.3	2.0	0.5	63.0
1936	716.4	297.9	262.5	76.5	55.0	13.2	4.7	1.7	4.9	79.5
1937	743.0	312.3	321.1	63.3	29.9	9.5	0.1	4.0	2.7	46.2
1938-41[7,a]										
1938	789.6	302.5	337.6	83.6	40.5	18.4	2.2	3.5	1.3	65.9
1939	642.2	251.8	262.0	71.0	33.2	15.4	2.1	1.4	5.4	57.5
1940	787.3	305.2	311.7	89.2	45.4	24.4	5.4	2.4	3.6	81.2
1941	1,424.2	581.5	563.3	145.9	76.6	39.5	7.0	4.0	6.5	133.6
1942-46[8]										
1942	1,052.2	532.6	366.9	84.3	38.8	23.2	2.3	1.8	2.4	68.4
1943	631.7	337.0	215.7	43.7	21.0	7.3	2.2	1.5	3.2	35.3
1944	774.8	458.0	237.3	40.7	21.7	13.1	1.0	1.6	1.4	38.7
1945	518.7	295.9	169.4	25.1	13.9	9.1	*	2.8	2.5	28.3
1946	545.1	313.4	179.6	31.3	10.2	6.1	0.5	3.3	0.7	20.7
Totals										
1926-33	7,475.8	1,825.5	2,288.9	1,060.9	939.7	824.5	536.3 (brace)		10.0	2,300.5
1934-37	2,924.5	1,232.2	1,176.5	273.9	148.6	64.9	8.2	10.3	16.8	242.0
1938-41[a]	3,643.3	1,441.0	1,474.6	389.7	195.7	97.7	16.7	11.3	10.2	338.2
1942-46	3,522.5	1,936.9	1,168.9	225.1	105.6	58.8	6.0	11.0	10.2	191.4

STATUTORY NET INCOME GROUP (thousands of dollars)[1]

C EXCESS OF GAINS OVER LOSSES

	TOTAL[1]	Under 5	300-500
1917-21[2]			
1917	248.2	208.2	39.9
1918	-68.1	-25.2	-42.8
1919	262.8	280.3	-17.3
1920	-16.5	96.4	-112.7
1921	-639.1	-568.4	-70.6

Year									
1922[2]		231.8	82.3				149.4		
1923[2]		191.7	31.4				160.2		
1924[2]		1,036.9	770.3				266.7		
1925[2]		2,572.5	1,625.2				947.3		
1926	185.5	2,165.8	613.0	272.2	239.5	311.9	132.1	128.9	282.7
1927	210.1	2,618.5	654.4	333.3	315.6	431.6	169.5	171.2	332.7
1928	185.7	4,595.2	1,007.8	571.4	579.9	840.8	319.8	371.0	718.7
1929[3]	−70.1	3,644.9	689.1	398.1	416.6	720.3	314.8	372.9	803.4
1930[3]	−176.6	−120.6	−159.3	−31.9	−8.6	46.6	38.9	43.5	126.8
1931[3]	−242.2	−929.0	−371.4	−91.7	−121.3	−92.8	−10.7	−8.9	9.9
1932[3,4]	−321.9	−1,651.7	−510.6	−317.6	−256.6	−166.0		−78.9	
1933[3,4]	−167.4	−654.3	−119.6	−187.2	−139.1	−61.4		20.5	
1934-37[6]									
1934	−251.9	−459.3	−206.3	−25.5	−1.1	11.6	3.2	5.4	5.3
1935	−151.6	37.5	18.1	39.8	42.9	25.4	16.2	31.0	15.8
1936	−78.2	661.3	276.4	135.3	103.5	125.0	21.5	30.2	47.7
1937	−132.6	75.6	−7.1	43.2	54.0	70.4	29.3	5.2	13.2
1938-41[7, a]									
1938	−156.4	30.8	−129.2	−8.4	22.1	65.1	40.9	56.1	140.6
1939	−83.3	31.2	−11.1	10.1	22.0	33.0	18.8	17.8	23.9
1940	−132.8	−79.7	−80.3	−16.5	14.4	53.1	21.4	35.6	25.3
1941	−354.0	−482.0	−322.7	−58.3	6.3	81.7	49.3	50.2	65.4
1942-46[8]									
1942	−307.6	−301.1	−170.7	−13.4	24.6	56.7	21.6	39.7	48.0
1943	135.9	1,120.6	333.3	157.4	131.3	158.6	45.9	83.6	64.5
1944	241.9	1,656.3	607.8	222.6	199.5	207.5	68.4	67.1	41.4
1945	980.5	4,290.2	1,465.0	545.9	455.2	471.1	152.5	126.6	93.4
1946	1,942.8	6,665.7	2,253.1	682.1	573.5	638.0	180.9	199.8	195.5
Totals									
1926-33	−396.9	9,668.8	1,803.4	946.6	1,026.0	2,031.0	70.2	4,258.8	82.0
1934-37	−614.3	315.1	81.1	192.8	199.3	232.4	130.4	71.8	255.2
1938-41[a]	−726.5	−499.7	−543.3	−73.1	64.8	232.9	469.3	159.7	442.8
1942-46	2,993.5	13,431.7	4,488.5	1,594.6	1,384.1	1,541.9		516.8	

See Table 1, source note.   ᵃ See Table 1, note a.   * Less than $50,000.   For numbered notes see pp. 362-6.

Table 3

Aggregate Net Capital Gains and Losses: Percentage Distribution by Statutory Net Income Groups, 1917-1946

	TOTAL[1]	STATUTORY NET INCOME GROUP (thousands of dollars)[1]							
		Under 5	5- 25	25- 50	50- 100	100- 300	300- 500	500- 1,000	1,000 & over
				A GAINS					
1917-21									
1917	100.0	31.5		51.9		9.3	2.6	1.8	2.9
1918	100.0	35.6	44.4	8.5	4.8	3.9	0.6	1.4	0.8
1919	100.0	32.2	40.8	9.6	6.9	5.0	0.9	0.8	3.8
1920	100.0	38.9	48.6	7.2	3.2	1.4	0.3	0.2	0.4
1921	100.0	45.0	40.8	8.5	3.8	1.4	0.3	0.1	0.1
1922-33									
1922	100.0	25.4	32.1	10.9	9.5	9.5	3.0	3.8	6.0
1923	100.0	34.3	28.3	9.1	7.9	8.4	3.1	2.6	6.2
1924	100.0	23.4	32.3	12.7	10.2	10.5	3.5	3.8	3.5
1925	100.0	9.1	30.4	14.2	11.8	14.2	5.6	5.7	9.0
1926	100.0	10.1	28.3	12.4	11.1	14.5	6.0	5.7	11.9
1927	100.0	10.4	25.1	12.5	12.0	16.0	6.2	6.2	11.7
1928	100.0	4.7	22.4	12.4	12.6	18.2	6.8	7.8	15.2
1929	100.0	6.2	20.2	10.4	10.8	17.9	7.5	8.6	18.4
1930	100.0	9.1	27.4	10.9	10.9	16.3	6.1	6.9	12.3
1931	100.0	22.3	27.0	9.3	8.0	13.3	5.5	5.7	8.9
1932	100.0	25.3	31.3	11.8	10.3	11.2	3.6	6.5	†
1933	100.0	20.0	30.4	13.6	10.9	11.1	3.2	3.1	7.6
1934-37[6]									
1934	100.0	22.5	38.6	14.0	9.1	8.8	2.0	2.6	2.3
1935	100.0	20.2	38.9	14.3	10.5	7.0	2.3	4.5	2.2
1936	100.0	15.9	39.1	15.4	11.5	10.0	1.9	2.3	3.8
1937	100.0	22.0	38.4	13.0	10.2	9.8	3.6	1.1	1.9
1938-41[7]									
1938	100.0	17.8	25.4	9.2	7.6	10.2	5.3	7.3	17.3
1939	100.0	25.0	37.3	12.0	8.2	7.2	3.1	2.9	4.3
1940	100.0	24.4	32.7	10.3	8.4	11.0	3.8	5.4	4.1
1941	100.0	24.2	25.5	9.3	8.8	12.9	6.0	5.8	7.6
1942-46[8]									
1942	100.0	30.0	26.1	9.4	8.4	10.6	3.2	5.5	6.7
1943	100.0	27.0	31.3	11.5	8.7	10.0	2.8	4.9	3.9
1944	100.0	28.8	34.8	10.8	9.1	9.1	2.9	2.8	1.8
1945	100.0	26.5	34.0	11.9	9.8	10.0	3.2	2.7	2.0
1946	100.0	31.3	33.7	9.9	8.1	8.9	2.5	2.8	2.7
Totals									
1917-46	100.0	20.1		51.6		11.9	4.2	4.6	7.5
1917-21	100.0	36.6		56.5		3.6	0.8	0.7	1.8
1922-33	100.0	11.4	25.7	11.9	11.2	15.3	5.9	6.4	12.2
1934-37	100.0	19.1	38.9	14.4	10.7	9.2	2.4	2.5	2.8
1938-41	100.0	22.7	29.6	10.1	8.3	10.5	4.7	5.4	8.6
1942-46	100.0	29.1	33.4	10.7	8.8	9.4	2.8	3.1	2.7

		STATUTORY NET INCOME GROUP (thousands of dollars)[1]							
	TOTAL[1]	Under 5	5-25	25-50	50-100	100-300	300-500	500-1,000	1,000 & over

B L o s s e s

1917-21[2]									
1917	100.0			81.6				18.4	
1918	100.0			82.7				17.3	
1919	100.0			83.3				16.7	
1920	100.0			86.9				13.1	
1921	100.0			92.8				7.2	
1922-33									
1922[2]	100.0			90.7				9.3	
1923[2]	100.0			92.1				7.9	
1924[2]	100.0			88.0				12.0	
1925[2]	100.0			82.0				18.0	
1926	100.0	26.2	28.5	10.5	11.1	15.0	5.4	2.8	0.6
1927	100.0	33.1	25.8	10.2	11.3	11.5	3.2	2.5	2.5
1928	100.0	19.7	31.8	10.6	11.3	15.6	3.8	2.6	4.7
1929[3]	100.0	34.9	24.6	8.8	8.6	11.3	3.4	3.0	5.4
1930[3]	100.0	21.7	37.0	12.3	10.6	11.3	2.6	3.0	1.5
1931[3]	100.0	24.8	35.6	9.7	11.4	11.1	2.6	2.5	2.3
1932[3,4]	100.0	20.0	30.9	18.6	15.1	10.2		5.3	
1933[3,4]	100.0	23.0	23.8	21.7	16.5	10.2		4.7	
1934-37[6]									
1934	100.0	41.8	42.3	9.0	3.8	2.1	0.4	0.3	0.2
1935	100.0	43.2	38.4	9.3	4.9	3.8	†	0.3	0.1
1936	100.0	41.6	36.6	10.7	7.7	1.8	0.7	0.2	0.7
1937	100.0	42.0	43.2	8.5	4.0	1.3	†	0.5	0.4
1938-41[7,a]									
1938	100.0	38.3	42.8	10.6	5.1	2.3	0.3	0.4	0.2
1939	100.0	39.2	40.8	11.1	5.2	2.4	0.3	0.2	0.8
1940	100.0	38.8	39.6	11.3	5.8	3.1	0.7	0.3	0.5
1941	100.0	40.8	39.5	10.2	5.4	2.8	0.5	0.3	0.5
1942-46[8]									
1942	100.0	50.6	34.9	8.0	3.7	2.2	0.2	0.2	0.2
1943	100.0	53.3	34.2	6.9	3.3	1.1	0.4	0.2	0.5
1944	100.0	59.1	30.6	5.3	2.8	1.7	0.1	0.2	0.2
1945	100.0	57.1	32.7	4.8	2.7	1.8	†	0.5	0.5
1946	100.0	57.5	33.0	5.8	1.9	1.1	0.1	0.6	0.1
Totals									
1926-33[b]	100.0	24.4	30.6	14.2	12.6	11.0		7.2	
1934-37	100.0	42.1	40.2	9.4	5.1	2.2	0.3	0.4	0.3
1938-41[a]	100.0	39.6	40.5	10.7	5.4	2.7	0.5	0.3	0.5
1942-46	100.0	55.0	33.2	6.4	3.0	1.7	0.2	0.3	0.3

See Table 1, source note.

†Less than 0.05 percent.

ᵃ See Table 1, note a.

ᵇ These figures were used for the loss distribution in the top section of Chart 14, with the percentage in the $300,000 and over income group arbitrarily apportioned equally among the last 3 income groups.

For numbered notes see pp. 362-6.

Table 4

Net Capital Gain-Loss Ratio by Statutory Net Income Groups, 1926-1946

	STATUTORY	NET	INCOME	GROUP	(thousands of dollars)[1]		
	Under 5	5-25	25-50	50-100	100-300	300-500	500-1,000	1,000 & over
1926-33								
1926	4.3	11.1	13.2	11.1	10.8	12.6	22.8	218.4
1927	3.3	10.2	12.9	11.1	14.6	20.3	26.2	49.2
1928	5.4	15.9	26.4	25.2	26.4	41.0	68.5	72.2
1929[3]	0.8	3.7	5.4	5.6	7.2	10.0	12.9	15.3
1930[3]	0.4	0.7	0.8	0.9	1.3	2.2	2.1	7.3
1931[3]	0.3	0.3	0.3	0.2	0.4	0.7	0.8	1.3
1932[3,4]	0.1	0.1	0.1	0.1	0.1		0.2	
1933[3,4]	0.4	0.6	0.3	0.3	0.5		1.4	
1934-37[6]								
1934	0.2	0.4	0.6	1.0	1.7	2.0	3.1	3.8
1935	0.5	1.1	1.6	2.3	2.0	55.0	16.4	32.8
1936	0.7	2.1	2.8	2.9	10.5	5.6	18.8	10.7
1937	0.6	1.0	1.7	2.8	8.4	294.0	2.3	5.9
1938-41[7]								
1938	0.5	0.6	0.9	1.5	4.5	19.6	17.0	109.2
1939	0.7	1.0	1.1	1.7	3.1	10.0	13.7	5.4
1940	0.6	0.7	0.8	1.3	3.2	5.0	15.9	8.0
1941	0.4	0.4	0.6	1.1	3.1	8.0	13.6	11.1
1942-46[8]								
1942	0.4	0.5	0.8	1.6	3.4	10.4	23.0	21.0
1943	1.4	2.5	4.6	7.3	24.1	21.9	56.8	21.2
1944	1.5	3.6	6.5	10.2	16.8	69.3	42.9	30.6
1945	4.3	9.6	22.7	33.7	52.8	[a]	46.2	38.4
1946	7.2	13.5	22.8	57.2	105.6	362.8	61.5	280.3

See Table 1, source note.

[a] Current year net capital loss is less than $50,000. Current year net capital gain is $152.5 million. Since the computations are based upon data in millions of dollars, no ratio is shown for the income group. See Appendix One, Section D5 for discussion of the effect on aggregate net loss of carrying over loss from preceding years.

For numbered notes see pp. 362-6.

Table 5

Aggregate Net Capital Gains and Losses as Percentages of Net Income Reported on All Returns,[9] by Statutory Net Income Groups, 1917-1946

| | TOTAL[1] | STATUTORY NET INCOME GROUP (thousands of dollars)[1] | | | | | | | |
		Under 5	5-25	25-50	50-100	100-300	300-500	500-1,000	1,000 & over
				A **Gains**					
1917-21									
1917	2.8	2.4		3.1		3.4	3.9	2.7	3.0
1918	1.8	1.1	3.3	2.5	2.0	1.9	1.2	3.4	1.7
1919	5.0	2.9	7.6	7.5	7.7	6.9	5.6	6.5	24.8
1920	4.3	2.6	8.8	5.6	4.0	3.0	3.1	2.0	6.0
1921	2.4	1.6	4.4	4.0	3.0	2.1	2.6	1.2	0.8
1922-33									
1922	4.6	1.9	6.5	8.9	11.6	17.9	25.2	34.5	41.7
1923	4.7	2.4	6.4	7.9	11.1	18.1	28.9	32.4	47.9
1924	5.9	2.2	8.4	12.0	14.5	21.2	30.9	36.3	34.4
1925	13.4	2.9	12.7	20.4	24.4	34.0	48.0	51.1	62.5
1926	10.8	2.8	9.0	15.1	18.9	27.9	42.2	42.4	57.4
1927	12.8	3.6	9.5	17.6	22.6	32.6	41.4	47.1	56.5
1928	19.1	2.8	12.9	25.5	32.5	43.5	49.4	56.1	65.7
1929	18.9	3.6	11.1	22.5	30.8	45.1	55.7	60.3	70.9
1930	6.6	1.4	4.9	9.4	14.2	24.5	35.0	38.9	40.8
1931	3.5	1.6	2.6	5.3	7.1	15.4	25.5	26.1	25.4
1932	1.4	0.6	1.8	3.1	4.3	7.7	11.0	18.3	†
1933	5.0	1.6	6.3	11.9	15.1	22.9	32.4	30.7	48.4
1934-37[8]									
1934	2.5	0.9	3.7	6.6	7.3	10.7	14.4	13.0	11.9
1935	5.0	1.7	7.2	12.2	14.6	15.1	19.4	35.7	20.3
1936	7.2	2.2	9.7	15.3	17.5	20.8	19.9	23.5	38.0
1937	3.9	1.5	5.5	8.0	9.9	13.6	21.6	7.9	17.3
1938-41[7]									
1938	4.4	1.2	4.4	8.6	12.7	24.3	43.9	55.1	78.7
1939	2.9	1.1	4.5	7.5	8.8	12.2	23.3	23.3	31.2
1940	1.9	0.6	3.7	5.8	8.3	15.9	24.0	37.5	26.7
1941	1.6	0.5	3.1	5.3	8.3	17.4	34.4	38.5	52.1
1942-46[8]									
1942	1.0	0.4	2.1	3.3	4.8	9.5	14.3	27.3	45.4
1943	1.8	0.6	4.2	6.8	8.8	16.2	24.9	44.7	52.5
1944	2.3	0.9	4.8	8.1	11.8	20.0	35.6	40.6	36.1
1945	4.4	1.6	8.3	14.2	20.6	35.5	58.3	58.1	58.7
1946	5.9	2.6	9.8	14.6	21.6	39.0	57.2	65.1	69.2

375

	TOTAL[1]	Under 5	5-25	25-50	50-100	100-300	300-500	500-1,000	1,000 & over
				B LOSSES					
1917-21[2]									
1917	0.6			0.6				0.8	
1918	2.3			2.0				6.3	
1919	3.7			3.3				10.5	
1920	4.4			3.9				18.7	
1921	5.6			5.3				17.2	
1922-33									
1922[2]	3.6			3.4				7.9	
1923[2]	3.9			3.8				8.5	
1924[2]	1.9			1.7				4.6	
1925[2]	1.6			1.5				2.8	
1926	1.0	0.6	0.8	1.1	1.7	2.6	3.4	1.9	0.3
1927	1.2	1.1	0.9	1.4	2.0	2.2	2.0	1.8	1.1
1928	0.8	0.5	0.8	1.0	1.3	1.6	1.2	0.8	0.9
1929[3]	4.2	4.5	3.0	4.2	5.4	6.3	5.6	4.7	4.6
1930[3]	7.3	3.8	7.3	11.7	15.1	18.7	16.2	18.4	5.6
1931[3]	10.3	5.2	10.4	16.5	30.1	38.1	36.1	34.7	19.4
1932[3,4]	15.6	4.9	19.8	53.5	69.5	77.5		65.5	
1933[3,4]	11.0	4.1	10.9	41.6	49.8	45.8		28.6	
1934-37[5]									
1934	6.3	4.3	10.1	10.5	7.6	6.2	7.1	4.2	3.1
1935	4.8	3.5	6.7	7.6	6.5	7.6	0.4	2.2	0.6
1936	3.8	2.9	4.7	5.5	6.1	2.0	3.6	1.3	3.5
1937	3.5	2.5	5.6	4.8	3.5	1.6	0.1	3.4	2.9
1938-41[7,a]									
1938	4.2	2.5	7.1	9.6	8.2	5.4	2.2	3.2	0.7
1939	2.8	1.7	4.7	6.6	5.3	3.9	2.3	1.7	5.8
1940	2.2	1.1	4.9	7.2	6.3	5.0	4.8	2.4	3.3
1941	2.5	1.3	7.3	8.9	7.7	5.7	4.3	2.8	4.7
1942-46[8]									
1942	1.4	0.8	3.9	3.9	2.9	2.7	1.4	1.2	2.2
1943	0.6	0.4	1.6	1.5	1.2	0.7	1.1	0.8	2.5
1944	0.7	0.6	1.4	1.3	1.2	1.2	0.5	0.9	1.2
1945	0.5	0.4	0.9	0.6	0.6	0.7	†	1.3	1.5
1946	0.4	0.4	0.7	0.6	0.4	0.4	0.2	1.1	0.2

See Table 1, source note.
† Less than 0.05 percent.
ᵃ See Table 1, note a.
For numbered notes see pp. 362-6.

Table 6: Aggregate Net Capital Gains as Percentages of Net Income and of Property Income[a] Reported on All Returns: 3 Statutory Net Income Groups, Total for Period 1917-1946

STATUTORY NET INCOME GROUP[1]	NET INCOME[9] (millions of dollars)	GAINS[6,7,8] Amount	% of net income
All returns with net incomes	1,047,553.7	50,179.8	4.8
Returns with $100,000 & over	42,936.4	14,180.9	33.0
Returns with $1,000,000 & over	7,356.5	3,764.0	51.2
	PROPERTY INCOME[a]		% of property income
All returns with net incomes	444,518.2	50,179.8	11.3

See Table 1, source note.　　　　　　　　For numbered notes see pp. 362-6.

[a] Statutory total income from Source 1, exclusive of wages and salaries, adjusted in 1934-46 to include realized net capital gain instead of statutory.

Table 7: Aggregate Net Capital Gains and Dividends: Percentage Distribution by Statutory Net Income Groups and as Percentages of Net Income Reported on All Returns, 1924, 1928, 1941, and 1943

STATUTORY NET INCOME GROUP (thousands of dollars)[1]

	TOTAL[1]	Under 5	5- 25	25- 50	50- 100	100- 300	300- 500	500- 1,000	1,000 & over
		PERCENTAGE DISTRIBUTION							
Net capital gains									
1924	100.0	23.4	32.3	12.7	10.2	10.5	3.5	3.8	3.5
1928	100.0	4.7	22.4	12.4	12.6	18.2	6.8	7.8	15.2
1941[7]	100.0	24.2	25.5	9.3	8.8	12.9	6.0	5.8	7.6
1943[8]	100.0	27.0	31.3	11.5	8.7	10.0	2.8	4.9	3.9
Dividends									
1924	100.0	19.5	29.2	17.1	14.4	11.2	2.8	2.6	3.2
1928	100.0	7.8	29.3	16.0	14.7	15.6	4.8	4.5	7.3
1941	100.0	34.2	31.0	12.3	9.3	7.9	1.8	1.8	1.8
1943[a]	100.0	26.6	35.4	14.4	10.7	8.2	1.6	1.7	1.5
Net income[9]									
1924	100.0	62.0	22.8	6.2	4.2	2.9	0.7	0.6	0.6
1928	100.0	32.8	33.0	9.2	7.4	8.0	2.6	2.7	4.4
1941	100.0	80.2	13.3	2.8	1.7	1.2	0.3	0.2	0.2
1943	100.0	80.1	13.5	3.0	1.8	1.1	0.2	0.2	0.1
		PERCENTAGE OF NET INCOME REPORTED ON ALL RETURNS[9]							
Net capital gains									
1924	5.9	2.2	8.4	12.0	14.5	21.2	30.9	36.3	34.4
1928	19.1	2.8	12.9	25.5	32.5	43.5	49.4	56.1	65.7
1941	1.6	0.5	3.1	5.3	8.3	17.4	34.4	38.5	52.1
1943	1.8	0.6	4.2	6.8	8.8	16.2	24.9	44.7	52.5
Dividends									
1924	12.7	4.0	16.2	34.7	43.9	48.5	53.7	53.2	65.8
1928	17.2	4.1	15.3	29.8	34.5	33.9	31.3	29.4	28.5
1941	6.2	2.7	14.5	27.0	33.6	40.8	40.1	46.2	46.2
1943[a]	3.1	1.0	8.2	15.0	18.9	23.1	25.2	27.3	34.7

Based on Source 1. For period differences, see Appendix One, Sections D, E.

[a] Excludes dividends filed on Form 1040A in 1943.

For numbered notes see pp. 362-6.

Table 8

Long and Short Term Net Capital Gains and Losses: Annual Totals, 1922–1946 (millions of dollars)

| | RETURNS WITH STATUTORY NET INCOMES[1] | | | | RETURNS WITH STATUTORY NET DEFICITS[1] | | | | ALL RETURNS | | | |
| | Long Term | | Short Term | | Long Term | | Short Term | | Long Term | | Short Term | |
	Gain	Loss	Gain	Loss	Gain	Loss	Gain	Loss	Gain	Loss	Gain	Loss
1922–33												
1922[2]	249.2		742.1									
1923[2]	305.4		863.1									
1924[2]	389.1	72.3	1,124.6	404.5								
1925[2]	940.6	61.3	1,991.7	298.4								
1926	912.9	34.6	1,465.6	178.2								
1927	1,081.2	48.2	1,813.4	227.9								
1928	1,879.8	41.0	2,928.1	171.7	0.3		53.6	144.6				
1929[3]	2,346.7	43.0	2,335.9	994.7	1.4		85.3	839.0				
1930[3]	556.4	80.9	636.7	1,232.8	[10]		68.1[10]	1,307.1				
1931[3]	169.9	239.9	301.7	1,160.8	[10]		29.6[10]	1,818.7				
1932[3,4]	50.1	832.4	112.8	982.3	[10]		20.6[10]	1,051.0[5]				
1933[3,4]	133.6	553.8	419.6	653.7	[10]		67.5[10]	816.5[5]				
Long term includes assets held longer than 2 years if segregated for special tax treatment; short term includes assets held 2 years or less plus assets held longer than 2 years if not segregated for special tax treatment												
1934–37[6]												
1934	245.9	807.0	237.7	135.8	26.7	173.2	43.6	20.2	272.5	980.3	257.8	179.4
1935	534.3	863.8	468.5	101.5	34.6	157.5	27.3	24.0	568.8	1,021.3	492.6	128.9
1936	973.4	1,044.2	810.7	78.7	41.7	123.9	13.5	23.0	1,015.0	1,168.0	833.7	92.2
1937	926.9	640.0	323.9	535.0	38.0	223.3	24.9	29.7	964.8	863.5	353.6	559.9
Long term includes assets held longer than 2 years; short term includes assets held 2 years or less												

Long term includes assets held longer than 18 months; *short term* includes assets held 18 months or less

Long term includes assets held longer than 6 months; *short term* includes assets held 6 months or less

1938-41[7,a]												
1938	645.7	767.8	12.8	372.9	7.8			658.5	1,140.7	159.9		
1939	455.2	614.8	12.5	293.0	6.5			467.7	907.8	196.2		
1940	538.7	749.2	9.2	340.6	4.9			547.9	1,089.8	132.3		
1941	733.8	1,362.4	8.6	394.1	4.5			742.4	1,756.5	144.6		
1942-46[8]												
1942	662.9	969.0	49.5	24.1	12.7	52.3	0.6	0.7	675.6	1,021.3	50.1	24.9
1943	1,597.8	575.7	145.9	49.9	19.9	35.4	2.0	1.6	1,617.7	611.1	147.8	51.5
1944[b]	2,321.9	702.8	123.1	284.2	28.0	27.1	1.4	6.2	2,349.9	729.9	124.5	290.4
1945[b]	4,548.4	472.2	293.9	360.0	62.3	33.3	2.2	8.3	4,610.7	505.5	296.1	368.3
1946[b]	7,259.0	463.7	258.2	748.9	44.9	38.9	1.7	10.1	7,303.9	502.6	260.0	759.0
Totals												
1922-33	9,014.9	2,007.4[c]	14,735.3	[10]	6,305.0[e]		324.7[c,10]	5,976.9[e]				
1934-37	2,680.5	3,355.0	1,840.8	851.0[e]	677.9	96.9	109.3		2,821.1	4,033.1	1,937.7	960.4
1938-41	2,373.4	3,494.2	609.2	1,400.6	43.1	23.7			2,416.5	4,894.8	633.0	
1942-46	16,390.0	3,183.4	870.6	1,467.1	167.8	187.0	7.9	26.9	16,557.8	3,370.4	878.5	1,494.1

[e] For returns with statutory net income, long and short term loss cover 1924-33; for returns with statutory net deficit, long and short term loss cover 1928-33.

For numbered notes see pp. 362-6.

Based on Source 1, supplemented in 1934-37 by Sources 2 and 3, and for losses in 1932-33 by Source 5. 'Short term' losses in 1924-25 based in part on Sources 6c-e. For discussion of differences in the data for the various periods, see Appendix One, Sections D and E.

[a] See Table 1, note a.

[b] In 1944-46, understates current year short term gains and overstates current year short term losses because of inclusion of prior years' loss carryover. See Appendix One, Section D5.

379

Table 9

Long and Short Term Net Capital Gains and Losses by Statutory Net Income Groups, 1922-1946 (millions of dollars)

		STATUTORY NET INCOME GROUP (thousands of dollars)[1]								
	TOTAL[1]	Under 5	5-25	25-50	50-100	100-300	300-500	500-1,000	1,000 & over	Subtotal 50&over
A LONG TERM GAINS										
Assets held longer than 2 years if segregated for special tax treatment										
1922-33	9,014.9		2.7	280.2	1,302.6	2,549.7	1,109.9	1,255.3	2,514.7	8,732.2
1922	249.2			16.5	51.4	67.7	24.9	34.0	54.8	232.8
1923	305.4			22.3	61.8	85.4	34.3	29.1	72.5	283.1
1924	389.1			35.6	82.7	119.9	46.1	54.2	50.7	353.6
1925	940.6			29.0	145.2	266.5	124.0	139.4	236.5	911.6
1926	912.9			28.2	141.5	258.2	119.8	116.6	248.7	884.8
1927	1,081.2			32.4	169.5	312.1	131.8	137.9	297.5	1,048.8
1928	1,879.8			46.5	248.5	517.5	219.9	267.1	580.3	1,833.3
1929	2,346.7			28.5	257.9	646.0	301.4	352.5	760.3	2,318.1
1930	556.4			13.6	87.8	172.7	67.2	78.4	136.8	542.9
1931	169.9			4.3	25.0	53.4	23.2	24.6	39.3	165.5
1932	50.1		0.9	8.3	11.7	15.4	5.1	8.7	*	40.9
1933	133.6		1.8	15.0	19.6	34.9	12.2	12.8	37.3	116.8
Assets held longer than 2 years										
1934-37[6]	2,680.5	495.7	944.8	361.8	327.3	292.6	81.8	80.4	96.2	878.3
1934	245.9	47.9	85.8	36.3	25.0	29.5	4.5	8.1	8.7	75.8
1935	534.3	101.3	187.0	70.2	61.8	46.8	19.0	32.0	16.1	175.7
1936	973.4	157.4	348.3	124.8	128.2	110.9	23.9	26.6	53.4	343.0
1937	926.9	189.1	323.7	130.5	112.3	105.4	34.4	13.7	18.0	283.8
Assets held longer than 18 months										
1938-41[7]	2,373.4	423.9	602.7	241.3	220.2	308.9	140.9	166.0	269.7	1,105.7
1938	645.7	83.1	132.7	57.7	53.7	78.7	41.5	56.7	141.8	372.4
1939	455.2	96.8	150.6	56.3	42.7	43.0	18.6	18.1	29.1	151.5
1940	538.7	105.6	158.8	57.6	52.1	72.9	25.8	37.4	28.5	216.7
1941	733.8	138.4	160.6	69.7	71.7	114.3	55.0	53.8	70.3	365.1

Assets held longer than 6 months

Year										
1942-46[8]	16,390.0	4,530.8	5,400.9	1,838.0	1,523.9	1,628.5	479.6	530.9	457.5	4,620.3
1942	662.9	175.7	169.6	65.7	59.9	77.0	23.7	40.9	50.4	251.8
1943	1,597.8	394.4	489.9	191.5	149.5	172.9	48.1	85.0	66.5	522.0
1944	2,321.9	640.6	793.7	260.7	224.2	222.3	68.9	68.4	43.2	627.0
1945	4,548.4	1,176.7	1,500.5	554.2	462.1	478.4	152.3	128.5	95.6	1,317.0
1946	7,259.0	2,143.4	2,447.2	765.9	628.2	577.9	186.6	208.1	201.8	1,902.5

B SHORT TERM GAINS

Assets held 2 years or less plus assets held longer than 2 years if not segregated for special tax treatment — *Assets held 2 years or less if not segregated for special tax treatment*

Year										
1922-33	14,735.3	2,703.1	6,118.3	2,549.5	1,349.8	1,075.7	293.0	267.7	377.8	3,364.0
1922	742.1	251.3	318.6	91.0	42.4	26.7	4.6	3.2	4.2	81.1
1923	863.1	400.6	330.6	84.5	31.0	12.7	1.8	1.7	0.3	47.5
1924	1,124.6	354.5	488.8	156.9	71.6	39.7	6.8	3.3	3.0	124.4
1925	1,991.7	268.2	890.6	386.4	200.8	151.2	39.1	27.9	27.4	446.4
1926	1,465.6	241.3	673.7	266.4	121.6	35.5	23.7	18.1	35.3	284.2
1927	1,813.4	301.5	725.6	329.0	177.2	151.2	46.5	40.1	42.2	457.2
1928	2,928.1	227.6	1,075.4	547.4	355.4	356.5	107.9	109.4	148.5	1,077.7
1929	2,335.9	291.8	944.6	460.7	248.3	191.4	48.2	51.7	99.0	638.6
1930	636.7	109.1	326.8	116.7	42.8	21.9	5.3	4.0	10.2	84.2
1931	301.7	105.1	127.1	39.4	12.7	9.5	2.9	2.0	2.9	30.0
1932	112.8	41.2	50.1	11.0	5.1	2.9	0.7	1.8	*	10.5
1933	419.6	110.9	166.4	60.1	40.9	26.5	5.5	4.5	4.8	82.2

Assets held 2 years or less[11]

Year										
1934-37[6]	1,840.8	403.9	785.0	289.4	210.9	104.7	20.6	16.6	9.4	362.2
1934	237.7	56.7	104.5	35.3	22.5	12.1	2.6	2.9	1.0	41.1
1935	468.5	105.0	199.6	71.4	54.0	23.5	5.9	3.6	5.5	92.5
1936	810.7	149.1	337.6	141.2	108.1	55.7	8.2	9.4	1.2	182.6
1937	323.9	93.1	143.3	41.5	26.3	13.4	3.9	0.7	1.7	46.0

Assets held 18 months or less

Year										
1938-41[7]	609.2	197.7	270.8	69.3	37.2	20.7	6.2	5.1	2.3	71.5
1938	152.1	50.3	67.2	16.7	8.5	4.8	1.5	2.9	0.2	17.9
1939	189.6	56.7	88.8	23.4	12.0	5.3	2.3	1.1	0.1	20.8
1940	127.4	42.7	57.6	13.7	6.9	4.3	1.1	0.7	0.4	13.4
1941	140.1	48.0	57.2	15.5	9.8	6.3	1.3	0.4	1.6	19.4

	TOTAL[1]	Under 5	STATUTORY NET INCOME GROUP (thousands of dollars)[1]							Subtotal 50 & over
			5-25	25-50	50-100	100-300	300-500	500-1,000	1,000 & over	
Assets held 6 months or less										
1942-46[8]	870.6	286.8	409.0	91.1	45.3	28.4	4.0	4.0	2.2	83.7
1942	49.5	15.5	20.0	5.8	3.9	3.4	0.2	0.6	0.1	8.1
1943	145.9	40.7	69.7	18.0	8.5	6.9	0.6	0.2	1.3	17.5
1944[a]	123.1	34.0	61.2	14.3	7.4	4.5	0.9	0.9	0.1	13.7
1945[a]	293.9	82.7	145.7	34.3	17.5	9.7	1.9	1.4	0.6	31.2
1946[a]	258.2	113.9	112.4	18.7	8.0	3.9	0.4	0.9	0.1	13.2
C LONG TERM LOSSES										
Assets held longer than 2 years if segregated for special tax treatment										
1924	72.3			16.1	24.2	17.5	5.4	5.4	1.6	56.2
1925	61.3			7.6	14.4	22.4	5.6	5.4	5.8	53.6
1926-33	1,873.8		185.5	464.1	519.1	450.5	97.9	88.3	68.6	1,224.4
1926	34.6			5.8	11.9	10.8	3.0	2.7	0.4	28.8
1927	48.2			5.8	15.1	15.6	5.3	3.7	2.7	42.4
1928	41.0			3.6	11.4	17.0	3.3	2.9	2.8	37.4
1929	43.0			3.3	12.8	17.5	3.3	3.1	3.1	39.8
1930	80.9			7.9	23.0	32.5	7.0	4.7	5.9	73.1
1931	239.9			26.8	74.4	79.4	19.5	19.0	20.8	213.1
1932	832.4		116.1	241.1	219.1	169.9	29.3	41.8	15.1	475.2
1933	553.8		69.4	169.8	151.4	107.8	27.2	10.4	17.8	314.6
Assets held longer than 2 years										
1934-37[6]	3,355.0	1,216.5	1,314.9	365.7	264.0	127.0	25.0	21.0	21.0	458.0
1934	807.0	301.6	340.0	84.1	41.9	26.7	3.5	4.9	4.1	81.1
1935	863.8	319.2	330.0	92.0	63.8	41.2	7.8	4.2	5.6	122.6
1936	1,044.2	359.8	382.4	124.8	118.6	36.5	10.1	5.5	6.5	177.2
1937	640.0	235.9	262.5	64.8	39.7	22.6	3.6	6.4	4.8	77.1
Assets held longer than 18 months										
1938-41[7]	3,494.2	1,350.0	1,431.3	382.0	192.0	95.9	16.2	10.7	16.1	330.9
1938	767.8	290.2	330.8	82.3	40.1	18.2	2.1	3.2	1.0	64.6
1939	614.8	236.3	253.3	69.5	32.2	15.0	2.0	1.4	5.1	55.7
1940	749.2	281.8	300.9	87.0	44.5	23.9	5.2	2.3	3.6	79.5

1942-46[8]	3,183.4	1,675.2	1,090.2	224.5	110.5	60.0	6.2	10.1	6.6	193.7
1942	969.0	474.8	349.9	81.2	36.7	22.1	2.1	1.2	1.0	63.1
1943	575.7	290.6	205.6	43.7	21.4	7.9	2.3	1.4	2.7	35.8
1944	702.8	402.3	221.0	40.5	22.3	14.0	0.6	1.2	1.0	39.1
1945	472.2	252.9	161.3	27.3	16.1	9.6	0.6	2.5	1.8	30.7
1946	463.7	254.6	152.4	31.8	14.0	6.4	0.6	3.8	0.1	25.0

D Short Term Losses

Assets held 2 years or less plus assets held longer than 2 years if not segregated for special tax treatment

1924[2]	404.5		379.4					25.0		
1925[2]	298.4		273.0					25.5		
1926-33	5,602.1	1,825.5	2,103.4	596.7	420.9	374.1		281.3		1,076.3
1926	178.2	55.8	60.7	16.4	11.7	21.1	8.4	3.1	0.9	45.2
1927	227.9	91.4	71.2	22.3	16.1	16.1	3.5	3.2	4.2	43.1
1928	171.7	41.9	67.6	18.9	12.6	16.2	4.7	2.6	7.3	43.4
1929[3]	994.7	362.0	255.5	87.9	76.9	99.6	31.6	28.3	52.9	289.3
1930[3]	1,232.8	285.7	486.0	154.2	116.3	115.5	26.6	34.2	14.2	306.8
1931[3]	1,160.8	347.3	498.5	108.7	84.7	76.3	17.3	16.5	11.4	206.2
1932[3,4]	982.3	363.1	445.5	95.8	54.4	14.3		9.1		77.8
1933[3,4]	653.7	278.3	218.4	92.5	48.2	15.0		1.3		64.5

Assets held 2 years or less[11]

1934-37[6]	851.0	297.4	334.0	93.1	75.0	37.8	6.9	4.3	2.6	126.6
1934	135.8	54.9	56.6	13.0	6.7	3.4	0.4	0.6	0.3	11.4
1935	101.5	38.7	38.5	9.9	9.2	3.7	0.9	0.4	0.2	14.4
1936	78.7	24.9	27.1	6.2	14.3	5.0	0.4	0.3	0.4	20.4
1937	535.0	178.9	211.8	64.0	44.8	25.7	5.2	3.0	1.7	80.4

Assets held 6 months or less

1942-46[8]	1,467.1	437.5	566.1	207.9	130.9	88.0	13.4	10.6	13.0	255.6
1942	24.1	11.4	8.4	2.2	1.2	0.8	0.1	0.1	*	2.1
1943	49.9	21.6	18.4	5.0	3.0	1.7	0.1	0.1	*	4.9
1944[a]	284.2	98.3	104.2	38.2	23.6	13.7	2.2	1.7	2.4	43.5
1945[a]	360.0	110.1	137.6	52.7	30.9	20.9	3.5	1.7	2.6	59.6
1946[a]	748.9	196.1	297.5	109.8	72.2	50.9	7.5	7.0	8.0	145.5

See Table 8, source note. *Less than $50,000. [a] See Table 8, note b. For numbered notes see pp. 362-6.

Table 10

Long and Short Term Net Capital Gains and Losses by Statutory Net Income Groups, 1933

		STATUTORY NET INCOME GROUP (thousands of dollars)[1]							
	TOTAL[1]	Under 5	5-25	25-50	50-100	100-300	300-500	500-1,000	1,000 & over
				MILLIONS OF DOLLARS					
Gain from assets held:									
2 yrs. or less									
Securities	331.4	88.1	120.0	50.0	36.2	23.6	4.9	3.8	4.6
Other assets	34.0	8.0	11.9	4.9	4.7	2.9	0.6	0.7	0.3
Over 2 yrs.									
Incl. in total income	54.2	14.7	34.5	5.0					
Segregated at 12½%	133.6		1.8	15.0	19.6	34.9	12.2	12.8	37.3
Total	553.2	110.9	168.2	75.1	60.5	61.4	17.7	17.4	42.1
Loss from assets held:									
2 yrs. or less[4]	359.8	105.7	99.2	90.4	48.2	15.0		1.3	
Over 2 yrs.									
Deducted from total income	293.8	172.6	119.2	2.0					
Segregated at 12½%	553.8		69.4	169.8	151.4	107.8		55.4	
Total	1,207.5	278.3	287.8	262.3	199.6	122.8		56.7	
				PERCENTAGE DISTRIBUTION					
Gain from assets held:									
2 yrs. or less									
Securities	100.0	26.6	36.2	15.1	10.9	7.1	1.5	1.2	1.4
Other assets	100.0	23.6	35.1	14.4	13.9	8.4	1.7	1.9	0.8
Over 2 yrs.									
Incl. in total income	100.0	27.1	63.6	9.3					
Segregated at 12½%	100.0		1.4	11.3	14.7	26.1	9.1	9.6	27.9
Total	100.0	20.0	30.4	13.6	10.9	11.1	3.2	3.1	7.6

	PERCENTAGE OF TOTAL NET GAIN OR LOSS								
Loss from assets held:									
2 yrs. or less[4]	100.0	29.4	27.6	25.1	13.4	4.2	0.4		
Over 2 yrs.									
Deducted from total income	100.0	58.8	40.6	0.7					
Segregated at 12½%	100.0		12.5	30.7	27.3	19.5	10.0		
Total	100.0	23.0	23.8	21.7	16.5	10.2	4.7		
Gain from assets held:									
2 yrs. or less									
Securities	59.9	79.5	71.3	66.8	59.8	38.5	27.7	22.2	10.9
Other assets	6.1	7.2	7.1	6.5	7.8	4.7	3.3	3.8	0.6
Over 2 yrs.									
Incl. in total income	9.8	13.3	20.5	6.7					
Segregated at 12½%	24.2		1.1	20.0	32.4	56.8	69.0	74.0	88.5
Total	100.0	100.0	100.0	100.0	100.0	100.0	100.0	100.0	100.0
Loss from assets held:									
2 yrs. or less[4]	29.8	38.0	34.5	34.5	24.1	12.2	2.3		
Over 2 yrs.									
Deducted from total income	24.3	62.0	41.4	0.8	75.9	87.8	97.7		
Segregated at 12½%	45.9		24.1	64.7					
Total	100.0	100.0	100.0	100.0	100.0	100.0	100.0		

Total gains and losses and amounts segregated at 12½ percent based on Source 1; other lines based on unpublished data.
For numbered notes see pp. 362-6.

Table 11

Long and Short Term Net Capital Gains and Losses: Percentage Distribution by Statutory Net Income Groups, 1922-1946

	TOTAL[1]	Under 5	5- 25	25- 50	50- 100	100- 300	300- 500	500- 1,000	1,000 & over
			STATUTORY NET INCOME GROUP (thousands of dollars)[1]						

A LONG TERM GAINS
Assets held longer than 2 years if segregated for special tax treatment

	TOTAL[1]	Under 5	5-25	25-50	50-100	100-300	300-500	500-1,000	1,000 & over
1922-33									
1922	100.0			6.6	20.6	27.2	10.0	13.6	22.0
1923	100.0			7.3	20.2	28.0	11.2	9.5	23.7
1924	100.0			9.1	21.2	30.8	11.8	13.9	13.0
1925	100.0			3.1	15.4	28.3	13.2	14.8	25.1
1926	100.0			3.1	15.5	28.3	13.1	12.8	27.2
1927	100.0			3.0	15.7	28.9	12.2	12.8	27.5
1928	100.0			2.5	13.2	27.5	11.7	14.2	30.9
1929	100.0			1.2	11.0	27.5	12.8	15.0	32.4
1930	100.0			2.4	15.8	31.0	12.1	14.1	24.6
1931	100.0			2.6	14.7	31.4	13.7	14.5	23.2
1932	100.0		1.8	16.6	23.3	30.8	10.2	17.4	†
1933	100.0		1.4	11.3	14.7	26.1	9.1	9.6	27.9

Assets held longer than 2 years

	TOTAL[1]	Under 5	5-25	25-50	50-100	100-300	300-500	500-1,000	1,000 & over
1934-37[6]									
1934	100.0	19.5	34.9	14.8	10.2	12.0	1.8	3.3	3.5
1935	100.0	19.0	35.0	13.1	11.6	8.8	3.6	6.0	3.0
1936	100.0	16.2	35.8	12.8	13.2	11.4	2.5	2.7	5.5
1937	100.0	20.4	34.9	14.1	12.1	11.4	3.7	1.5	1.9

Assets held longer than 18 months

	TOTAL[1]	Under 5	5-25	25-50	50-100	100-300	300-500	500-1,000	1,000 & over
1938-41[7]									
1938	100.0	12.9	20.5	8.9	8.3	12.2	6.4	8.8	22.0
1939	100.0	21.3	33.1	12.4	9.4	9.4	4.1	4.0	6.4
1940	100.0	19.6	29.5	10.7	9.7	13.5	4.8	6.9	5.3
1941	100.0	18.9	21.9	9.5	9.8	15.6	7.5	7.3	9.6

Assets held longer than 6 months

	TOTAL[1]	Under 5	5-25	25-50	50-100	100-300	300-500	500-1,000	1,000 & over
1942-46[8]									
1942	100.0	26.5	25.6	9.9	9.0	11.6	3.6	6.2	7.6
1943	100.0	24.7	30.7	12.0	9.4	10.8	3.0	5.3	4.2
1944	100.0	27.6	34.2	11.2	9.7	9.6	3.0	2.9	1.9
1945	100.0	25.9	33.0	12.2	10.2	10.5	3.3	2.8	2.1
1946	100.0	29.5	33.7	10.6	8.7	9.3	2.6	2.9	2.8

	TOTAL[1]	Under 5	5-25	25-50	50-100	100-300	300-500	500-1,000	1,000 & over
Totals									
1922-33	100.0			†	3.1	14.4	28.3	12.3	13.9	27.9
1934-37	100.0	18.5	35.2	13.5	12.2	10.9	3.1	3.0	3.6
1938-41	100.0	17.9	25.4	10.2	9.3	13.0	5.9	7.0	11.4
1942-46	100.0	27.6	33.0	11.2	9.3	9.9	2.9	3.2	2.8

B SHORT TERM GAINS
Assets held 2 years or less plus assets held longer than 2 years if not segregated for special tax treatment

	TOTAL[1]	Under 5	5-25	25-50	50-100	100-300	300-500	500-1,000	1,000 & over
1922-33									
1922	100.0	33.9	42.9	12.3	5.7	3.6	0.6	0.4	0.6
1923	100.0	46.4	38.3	9.8	3.6	1.5	0.2	0.2	†
1924	100.0	31.5	43.5	14.0	6.4	3.5	0.6	0.3	0.3
1925	100.0	13.5	44.7	19.4	10.1	7.6	2.0	1.4	1.4
1926	100.0	16.5	46.0	18.2	8.3	5.8	1.6	1.2	2.4
1927	100.0	16.6	40.0	18.1	9.8	8.3	2.6	2.2	2.3

	TOTAL[1]	STATUTORY NET INCOME GROUP (thousands of dollars)[1]							
		Under 5	5- 25	25- 50	50- 100	100- 300	300- 500	500- 1,000	1,000 & over
1928	100.0	7.8	36.7	18.7	12.1	12.2	3.7	3.7	5.1
1929	100.0	12.5	40.4	19.7	10.6	8.2	2.1	2.2	4.2
1930	100.0	17.1	51.3	18.3	6.7	3.4	0.8	0.6	1.6
1931	100.0	34.8	42.1	13.1	4.2	3.1	1.0	0.7	0.9
1932	100.0	36.5	44.4	9.7	4.5	2.6	0.6	1.6	†
1933	100.0	26.4	39.6	14.3	9.8	6.3	1.3	1.1	1.2

Assets held 2 years or less[11]

1934-37[6]									
1934	100.0	23.9	44.0	14.9	9.5	5.1	1.1	1.2	0.4
1935	100.0	22.4	42.6	15.2	11.5	5.0	1.3	0.8	1.2
1936	100.0	18.4	41.6	17.4	13.3	6.9	1.0	1.2	0.1
1937	100.0	28.7	44.2	12.8	8.1	4.1	1.2	0.2	0.5

Assets held 18 months or less

1938-41[7]									
1938	100.0	33.1	44.2	11.0	5.6	3.1	1.0	1.9	0.1
1939	100.0	29.9	46.8	12.3	6.3	2.8	1.2	0.6	0.1
1940	100.0	33.5	45.2	10.8	5.4	3.4	0.9	0.5	0.3
1941	100.0	34.3	40.8	11.1	7.0	4.5	0.9	0.3	1.1

Assets held 6 months or less

1942-46[8]									
1942	100.0	31.3	40.5	11.8	7.9	6.8	0.4	1.3	0.1
1943	100.0	27.9	47.8	12.3	5.9	4.8	0.4	0.1	0.9
1944[a]	100.0	27.6	49.7	11.6	6.0	3.6	0.7	0.7	†
1945[a]	100.0	28.1	49.6	11.7	6.0	3.3	0.7	0.5	0.2
1946[a]	100.0	44.1	43.5	7.2	3.1	1.5	0.2	0.3	†

Totals									
1922-33	100.0	18.3	41.5	17.3	9.2	7.3	2.0	1.8	2.6
1934-37	100.0	21.9	42.6	15.7	11.5	5.7	1.1	0.9	0.5
1938-41	100.0	32.5	44.5	11.4	6.1	3.4	1.0	0.8	0.4
1942-46	100.0	32.9	47.0	10.5	5.2	3.3	0.5	0.5	0.3

C Long Term Losses

Assets held longer than 2 years if segregated for special tax treatment

1924-33									
1924	100.0			22.3	33.4	24.3	7.4	10.4	2.3
1925	100.0			12.5	23.6	36.5	9.2	8.9	9.4
1926	100.0			16.9	34.4	31.2	8.6	7.8	1.0
1927	100.0			12.0	31.3	32.4	10.9	7.6	5.7
1928	100.0			8.9	27.8	41.4	7.9	7.2	6.9
1929	100.0			7.7	29.8	40.7	7.6	7.1	7.2
1930	100.0			9.7	28.4	40.1	8.6	5.8	7.3
1931	100.0			11.2	31.0	33.1	8.1	7.9	8.7
1932	100.0		13.9	29.0	26.3	20.4	3.5	5.0	1.8
1933	100.0		12.5	30.7	27.3	19.5	4.9	1.9	3.2

Assets held longer than 2 years

1934-37[6]									
1934	100.0	37.4	42.1	10.4	5.2	3.3	0.4	0.6	0.5
1935	100.0	37.0	38.2	10.7	7.4	4.8	0.9	0.5	0.6
1936	100.0	34.5	36.6	12.0	11.4	3.5	1.0	0.5	0.6
1937	100.0	36.9	41.0	10.1	6.2	3.5	0.6	1.0	0.8

387

STATUTORY NET INCOME GROUP (thousands of dollars)[1]

	TOTAL[1]	Under 5	5-25	25-50	50-100	100-300	300-500	500-1,000	1,000 & over
				Assets held longer than 18 months					
1938-41[7]									
1938	100.0	37.8	43.1	10.7	5.2	2.4	0.3	0.4	0.1
1939	100.0	38.4	41.2	11.3	5.2	2.4	0.3	0.2	0.8
1940	100.0	37.6	40.2	11.6	5.9	3.2	0.7	0.3	0.5
1941	100.0	39.8	40.1	10.5	5.5	2.8	0.5	0.3	0.5
				Assets held longer than 6 months					
1942-46[8]									
1942	100.0	49.0	36.1	8.4	3.8	2.3	0.2	0.1	0.1
1943	100.0	50.5	35.7	7.6	3.7	1.4	0.4	0.2	0.5
1944	100.0	57.2	31.4	5.8	3.2	2.0	0.1	0.2	0.1
1945	100.0	53.6	34.2	5.8	3.4	2.0	0.1	0.5	0.4
1946	100.0	54.9	32.9	6.9	3.0	1.4	0.1	0.8	†
Totals									
1926-33	100.0		9.9	24.8	27.7	24.0	5.2	4.7	3.7
1934-37	100.0	36.3	39.2	10.9	7.9	3.8	0.7	0.6	0.6
1938-41	100.0	38.6	41.0	10.9	5.5	2.7	0.5	0.3	0.5
1942-46	100.0	52.6	34.2	7.1	3.5	1.9	0.2	0.3	0.2

D SHORT TERM LOSSES

Assets held 2 years or less plus assets held longer than 2 years if not segregated for special tax treatment

	TOTAL[1]	Under 5	5-25	25-50	50-100	100-300	300-500	500-1,000	1,000 & over
1924-33									
1924[2]	100.0			93.8				6.2	
1925[2]	100.0			91.5				8.5	
1926	100.0	31.3	34.1	9.2	6.5	11.8	4.7	1.8	0.5
1927	100.0	40.1	31.2	9.8	7.1	7.1	1.5	1.4	1.8
1928	100.0	24.4	39.3	11.0	7.4	9.4	2.8	1.5	4.2
1929[3]	100.0	36.4	25.7	8.8	7.7	10.0	3.2	2.8	5.3
1930[3]	100.0	23.2	39.4	12.5	9.4	9.4	2.2	2.8	1.2
1931[3]	100.0	29.9	42.9	9.4	7.3	6.6	1.5	1.4	1.0
1932[3,4]	100.0	37.0	45.3	9.8	5.5	1.5		0.9	
1933[3,4]	100.0	42.6	33.4	14.1	7.4	2.3		0.2	
				Assets held 2 years or less[11]					
1934-37[6]									
1934	100.0	40.4	41.7	9.6	5.0	2.5	0.3	0.4	0.2
1935	100.0	38.1	37.9	9.8	9.1	3.6	0.9	0.4	0.2
1936	100.0	31.6	34.4	7.9	18.2	6.4	0.1	†	0.1
1937	100.0	33.4	39.6	12.0	8.4	4.8	1.0	0.6	†
				Assets held 6 months or less					
1942-46[8]									
1942	100.0	47.4	34.8	9.2	5.0	3.2	0.2	0.3	†
1943	100.0	43.3	36.9	10.0	6.0	3.4	0.2	0.2	†
1944[a]	100.0	34.6	36.6	13.4	8.3	4.8	0.8	0.6	0.8
1945[a]	100.0	30.6	38.2	14.6	8.6	5.8	1.0	0.5	0.7
1946[a]	100.0	26.2	39.7	14.7	9.6	6.8	1.0	0.9	1.1
Totals									
1926-33	100.0	32.6	37.5	10.7	7.5	6.7		5.0	
1934-37	100.0	34.9	39.2	10.9	8.8	4.4	0.8	0.5	0.3
1942-46	100.0	29.8	38.6	14.1	8.9	6.0	0.9	0.7	0.9

See Table 8, source note. [a] See Table 8, note b. † Less than 0.05 percent.
For numbered notes see pp. 362-6.

Table 12

Long and Short Term Net Capital Gains and Losses as Percentages of Net Income Reported on All Returns,[9] by Statutory Net Income Groups, 1922-1946

	TOTAL[1]	Under 5	5- 25	25- 50	50- 100	100- 300	300- 500	500- 1,000	1,000 & over
			STATUTORY NET INCOME GROUP (thousands of dollars)[1]						

A LONG TERM GAINS

Assets held longer than 2 years if segregated for special tax treatment

1922-33

1922	1.2			1.4	6.4	12.8	21.3	31.6	38.8
1923	1.2			1.7	7.4	15.8	27.5	30.6	47.7
1924	1.5			2.2	7.8	15.9	26.9	34.2	32.5
1925	4.3			1.4	10.2	21.7	36.5	42.6	56.0
1926	4.2			1.4	10.2	21.0	35.2	36.7	50.3
1927	4.8			1.6	11.0	21.9	30.6	36.5	49.5
1928	7.5			2.0	13.4	25.8	33.1	39.8	52.3
1929	9.5			1.3	15.7	34.8	48.0	52.6	62.7
1930	3.1			1.0	9.6	21.8	32.4	37.0	38.0
1931	1.2			0.5	4.7	13.1	22.7	24.0	23.7
1932	0.4		†	1.3	3.0	6.5	9.7	15.0	†
1933	1.2		0.1	2.4	4.9	13.0	22.3	22.6	42.9

Assets held longer than 2 years

1934-37[6]

1934	2.0	0.6	2.6	5.5	6.4	11.4	10.3	13.1	14.4
1935	3.7	1.2	4.7	8.2	11.7	13.7	22.4	34.7	20.0
1936	5.1	1.5	6.3	9.0	14.2	16.7	18.1	19.6	38.6
1937	4.4	1.5	5.6	9.8	13.2	17.9	25.3	11.7	19.6

Assets held longer than 18 months

1938-41[7]

1938	3.4	0.7	2.8	6.6	10.9	22.9	42.3	52.5	78.6
1939	2.0	0.6	2.7	5.2	6.8	10.9	20.7	22.0	31.1
1940	1.5	0.4	2.5	4.6	7.3	15.0	23.0	36.8	26.4
1941	1.3	0.3	2.1	4.3	7.2	16.5	33.6	38.2	50.9

Assets held longer than 6 months

1942-46[8]

1942	0.9	0.3	1.8	3.0	4.5	9.1	14.2	27.0	45.4
1943	1.6	0.5	3.7	6.5	8.6	16.0	24.9	44.5	51.5
1944	2.2	0.8	4.5	8.0	12.0	20.2	35.4	40.5	36.4
1945	4.2	1.5	7.6	13.8	20.3	35.4	58.2	57.7	58.5
1946	5.9	2.4	9.8	15.6	23.2	41.0	58.9	66.7	71.1

B SHORT TERM GAINS

Assets held 2 years or less plus assets held longer than 2 years if not segregated for special tax treatment

1922-33

1922	3.5	1.9	6.5	7.5	5.3	5.1	3.9	3.0	3.0
1923	3.5	2.4	6.4	6.3	3.7	2.3	1.4	1.8	0.2
1924	4.4	2.2	8.4	9.8	6.7	5.3	4.0	2.1	1.9
1925	9.1	2.9	12.7	19.0	14.2	12.3	11.5	8.5	6.5
1926	6.7	2.8	9.0	13.6	8.8	6.9	7.0	5.7	7.1
1927	8.0	3.6	9.5	16.0	11.5	10.6	10.8	10.6	7.0
1928	11.6	2.8	12.9	23.5	19.1	17.8	16.3	16.3	13.4
1929	9.4	3.6	11.1	21.2	15.1	10.3	7.7	7.7	8.2
1930	3.5	1.4	4.9	8.4	4.7	2.8	2.6	1.9	2.8
1931	2.2	1.6	2.6	4.8	2.4	2.3	2.8	2.0	1.7
1932	1.0	0.6	1.8	1.7	1.3	1.2	1.3	3.1	†
1933	3.8	1.6	6.3	9.5	10.2	9.9	10.1	7.9	5.5

	TOTAL[1]	Under 5	5-25	25-50	50-100	100-300	300-500	500-1,000	1,000 & over
Assets held 2 years or less[11]									
1934-37[6]									
1934	2.0	0.7	3.2	5.3	5.8	4.7	5.9	4.7	1.6
1935	3.2	1.2	5.1	8.3	10.2	6.8	6.9	3.9	6.8
1936	4.2	2.5	6.1	10.2	11.9	8.4	6.2	6.9	0.9
1937	1.5	0.7	2.5	3.1	3.1	2.2	2.9	0.6	1.9
Assets held 18 months or less									
1938-41[7]									
1938	0.8	0.4	1.4	1.9	1.7	1.4	1.5	2.7	0.1
1939	0.8	0.4	1.6	2.2	1.9	1.3	2.6	2.3	0.1
1940	0.3	0.2	0.9	1.1	1.0	0.9	1.0	0.7	0.4
1941	0.2	0.1	0.7	0.9	1.0	0.9	0.8	0.3	1.2
Assets held 6 months or less									
1942-46[8]									
1942	0.1	†	0.2	0.3	0.3	0.4	0.1	0.4	0.1
1943	0.1	0.1	0.5	0.6	0.5	0.6	0.3	0.1	1.0
1944[a]	0.1	†	0.3	0.4	0.4	0.4	0.5	0.5	0.1
1945[a]	0.3	0.1	0.7	0.9	0.8	0.7	0.7	0.6	0.4
1946[a]	0.2	0.1	0.5	0.4	0.3	0.2	0.1	0.3	†

C LONG TERM LOSSES

Assets held longer than 2 years if segregated for special tax treatment

	TOTAL[1]	Under 5	5-25	25-50	50-100	100-300	300-500	500-1,000	1,000 & over
1924-33									
1924	0.3			1.0	2.3	2.3	3.2	4.7	1.0
1925	0.3			0.4	1.0	1.8	1.6	1.6	1.4
1926	0.2			0.3	0.9	0.9	0.9	0.8	0.1
1927	0.2			0.3	1.0	1.1	1.2	1.0	0.4
1928	0.2			0.2	0.6	0.8	0.5	0.4	0.3
1929	0.2			0.2	0.8	0.9	0.5	0.5	0.3
1930	0.4			0.6	2.5	4.1	3.4	2.2	1.6
1931	1.8			3.3	14.1	19.4	19.1	18.6	12.5
1932	7.1		4.1	38.3	55.7	71.4	55.8	72.2	42.9
1933	5.0		2.6	27.0	37.8	40.2	49.8	18.3	20.5
Assets held longer than 2 years									
1934-37[6]									
1934	6.6	4.0	10.5	12.7	10.8	10.4	8.0	8.0	6.8
1935	5.9	3.7	8.3	10.8	12.1	12.1	9.2	4.6	6.9
1936	5.5	3.5	6.9	9.1	13.1	5.5	7.6	4.1	4.7
1937	3.0	1.9	4.6	4.9	4.7	3.8	2.7	5.5	5.2
Assets held longer than 18 months									
1938-41[7]									
1938	4.1	2.4	7.0	9.4	8.1	5.3	2.1	3.0	0.6
1939	2.7	1.6	4.5	6.5	5.2	3.8	2.2	1.7	5.5
1940	2.1	1.0	4.8	7.0	6.2	4.9	4.6	2.3	3.3
1941	2.4	1.2	7.1	8.7	7.6	5.6	4.2	2.7	4.6
Assets held longer than 6 months									
1942-46[8]									
1942	1.3	0.8	3.7	3.7	2.8	2.6	1.3	0.8	0.9
1943	0.6	0.4	1.6	1.5	1.2	0.7	1.2	0.7	2.1
1944	0.7	0.5	1.3	1.2	1.2	1.3	0.3	0.7	0.8
1945	0.4	0.3	0.8	0.7	0.7	0.7	0.2	1.1	1.1
1946	0.4	0.3	0.6	0.6	0.5	0.4	0.2	1.2	†

D Short Term Losses

Assets held 2 years or less plus assets held longer than 2 years if not segregated for special tax treatment

1924-33

	TOTAL[1]	Under 5	5- 25	25- 50	50- 100	100- 300	300- 500	500- 1,000	1,000 & over
1924[2]	1.6			1.6				2.0	
1925[2]	1.4			1.4				1.1	
1926	0.8	0.6	0.8	0.8	0.8	1.7	2.5	1.0	0.2
1927	1.0	1.1	0.9	1.1	1.0	1.1	0.8	0.8	0.7
1928	0.7	0.5	0.8	0.8	0.7	0.8	0.7	0.4	0.7
1929[3]	4.0	4.5	3.0	4.0	4.7	5.4	5.0	4.2	4.4
1930[3]	6.8	3.8	7.3	11.1	12.7	14.6	12.8	16.2	3.9
1931[3]	8.5	5.2	10.4	13.2	16.0	18.7	16.9	16.1	6.9
1932[3,4]	8.4	4.9	15.7	15.2	13.8	6.0		6.2	
1933[3,4]	5.9	4.1	8.2	14.6	12.0	5.6		0.7	

Assets held 2 years or less[11]

1934-37[6]

	TOTAL[1]	Under 5	5- 25	25- 50	50- 100	100- 300	300- 500	500- 1,000	1,000 & over
1934	1.1	0.7	1.7	1.9	1.7	1.4	0.9	1.0	0.5
1935	0.7	0.4	1.0	1.2	1.7	1.1	1.1	0.4	0.2
1936	0.4	0.3	0.5	0.5	1.6	0.8	0.3	0.2	0.3
1937	2.5	1.5	3.7	4.8	5.3	4.3	3.9	2.6	1.8

Assets held 6 months or less

1942-46[8]

	TOTAL[1]	Under 5	5- 25	25- 50	50- 100	100- 300	300- 500	500- 1,000	1,000 & over
1942	†	†	0.1	0.1	0.1	0.1	0.1	0.1	†
1943	0.1	†	0.1	0.2	0.2	0.2	0.1	0.1	†
1944[a]	0.3	0.1	0.6	1.2	1.3	1.2	1.1	1.0	2.0
1945[a]	0.3	0.1	0.7	1.3	1.4	1.5	1.3	0.8	1.6
1946[a]	0.6	0.2	1.2	2.2	2.7	3.1	2.4	2.2	2.8

See Table 8, source note.

† Less than 0.05 percent.

[a] See Table 8, note b.

For numbered notes see pp. 362-6.

Table 13

Long and Short Term Net Capital Gains and Losses as Percentages of Total Gain and Loss Respectively by Statutory Net Income Groups, 1922-1946

STATUTORY NET INCOME GROUP (thousands of dollars)[1]

	TOTAL[1]	Under 5	5-25	25-50	50-100	100-300	300-500	500-1,000	1,000 & over	Subtotal 50 & over
A LONG TERM GAINS										
Assets held longer than 2 years if segregated for special tax treatment										
1922-33										
1922	25.1			15.4	54.8	71.7	84.5	91.3	92.8	74.2
1923	26.1			20.9	66.6	87.1	95.1	94.5	99.5	85.6
1924	25.7			18.5	53.6	75.1	87.2	94.2	94.5	74.0
1925	32.1			7.0	42.0	63.8	76.0	83.3	89.6	67.1
1926	38.4			9.6	53.8	75.1	83.5	86.5	87.6	75.7
1927	37.4			9.0	48.9	67.4	73.9	77.5	87.6	69.6
1928	39.1			7.8	41.1	59.2	67.1	70.9	79.6	63.0
1929	50.1			5.8	50.9	77.1	86.2	87.2	88.5	78.4
1930	46.6			10.4	67.2	88.7	92.7	95.1	93.1	86.6
1931	36.0			9.9	66.3	84.9	88.8	92.4	93.2	84.6
1932	30.7		1.8	43.0	69.7	84.2	87.5	82.5	80.0	79.6
1933	24.2		1.1	20.0	32.4	56.8	69.0	74.0	88.5	58.7
Assets held longer than 2 years										
1934-37[6]										
1934	50.8	45.8	45.1	50.8	52.6	70.9	63.6[12]	73.5	89.9	64.8
1935	53.3	49.1	48.4	49.6	53.4	66.5	76.2	90.0	74.5[13]	65.5
1936	54.6	51.4	50.7	46.9	54.3	66.6	74.4	73.8	97.7	65.2
1937	74.1	67.1	69.4	75.9	81.0	88.7	90.0	94.9	91.4	86.0
Assets held longer than 18 months										
1938-41[7]										
1938	78.7	56.9	63.7	76.7	85.8	94.2	96.2	95.1	99.9	95.3
1939	67.6	57.4	60.0	69.5	77.5	88.9	88.9	94.1	99.5	87.7
1940	76.1	61.2	68.7	79.2	87.3	94.1	95.9	98.2	98.7	93.8
1941	77.9	60.8	66.8	79.6	86.4	94.4	97.6	99.3	97.8	94.5
Assets held longer than 6 months										
1942-46[8]										
1942	85.5	75.7	82.0	88.5	92.2	95.3	99.1	98.5	99.9	96.3
1943	87.7	80.4	84.6	90.5	94.2	96.0	98.8	99.7	98.1	96.6
1944	92.5	89.6	90.5	94.2	96.6	97.9	98.1	98.7	99.9	97.7
1945	92.7	90.8	89.8	93.8	96.2	97.9	98.7	98.9	99.4	97.6
1946	95.0	91.9	94.0	97.2	98.5	99.4	99.7	99.5	100.0	99.2
Totals										
1922-33	38.0			†	9.9	49.1	70.3	79.1	82.4	86.9	72.2
1934-37	59.3	55.1	54.6	55.6	60.8	73.6	79.9	82.9	91.1	70.8
1938-41	75.5	59.3	64.7	76.2	84.6	93.5	95.7	97.0	99.2	93.6
1942-46	92.8	89.4	91.0	94.7	96.8	98.2	99.0	99.2	99.6	98.1

	TOTAL[1]	Under 5	5-25	25-50	50-100	100-300	300-500	500-1,000	1,000 &over	Sub-total 50 & over

B SHORT TERM GAINS

Assets held 2 years or less plus assets held longer than 2 years if not segregated for special tax treatment

1922-33

	TOTAL[1]	Under 5	5-25	25-50	50-100	100-300	300-500	500-1,000	1,000 &over	Sub-total 50 & over
1922	74.9	100.0	100.0	84.6	45.2	28.3	15.5	8.7	7.2	25.8
1923	73.9	100.0	100.0	79.1	33.4	12.9	4.9	5.5	0.5	14.4
1924	74.3	100.0	100.0	81.5	46.4	24.9	12.8	5.8	5.5	26.0
1925	67.9	100.0	100.0	93.0	58.0	36.2	24.0	16.7	10.4	32.9
1926	61.6	100.0	100.0	90.4	46.2	24.9	16.5	13.5	12.4	24.3
1927	62.6	100.0	100.0	91.0	51.1	32.6	26.1	22.5	12.4	30.4
1928	60.9	100.0	100.0	92.2	58.9	40.8	32.9	29.1	20.4	37.0
1929	49.9	100.0	100.0	94.2	49.1	22.9	13.8	12.8	11.5	21.6
1930	53.4	100.0	100.0	89.6	32.8	11.3	7.3	4.9	6.9	13.4
1931	64.0	100.0	100.0	90.1	33.7	15.1	11.2	7.6	6.8	15.3
1932	69.3	100.0	98.2	57.0	30.3	15.8	12.5	17.5	20.0	20.4
1933	75.8	100.0	98.9	80.0	67.6	43.2	31.0	26.0	11.5	41.3

Assets held 2 years or less[11]

1934-37[6]

	TOTAL[1]	Under 5	5-25	25-50	50-100	100-300	300-500	500-1,000	1,000 &over	Sub-total 50 & over
1934	49.2	54.2	54.9	49.1	47.4	29.2	36.5[12]	26.5	10.1	35.2
1935	46.8	50.9	51.6	50.5	46.7	33.5	23.8	9.9	25.5[13]	34.5
1936	45.5	48.7	49.2	53.2	45.7	33.4	25.6	26.2	2.4	34.7
1937	25.9	33.1	30.7	24.1	18.9	11.3	10.0	5.1	8.6	13.9

Assets held 18 months or less

1938-41[7]

	TOTAL[1]	Under 5	5-25	25-50	50-100	100-300	300-500	500-1,000	1,000 &over	Sub-total 50 & over
1938	18.5	34.4	30.3	22.2	13.6	5.7	3.6	4.9	0.1	4.6
1939	28.2	33.6	35.4	28.9	21.7	10.9	10.8	5.9	0.5	12.0
1940	18.0	24.8	24.9	18.9	11.6	5.5	4.1	1.8	1.3	5.8
1941	14.9	21.1	23.8	17.7	11.9	5.2	2.3	0.7	2.2	5.0

Assets held 6 months or less

1942-46[8]

	TOTAL[1]	Under 5	5-25	25-50	50-100	100-300	300-500	500-1,000	1,000 &over	Sub-total 50 & over
1942	6.4	6.7	9.7	7.9	6.0	4.2	0.7	1.5	0.1	3.1
1943	8.0	8.3	12.0	8.5	5.4	3.9	1.2	0.2	1.9	3.2
1944[a]	4.9	4.8	7.0	5.2	3.2	2.0	1.3	1.3	0.1	2.1
1945[a]	6.0	6.4	8.7	5.8	3.7	2.0	1.3	1.1	0.6	2.3
1946[a]	3.4	4.9	4.3	2.4	1.3	0.6	0.2	0.4	†	0.7

Totals

	TOTAL[1]	Under 5	5-25	25-50	50-100	100-300	300-500	500-1,000	1,000 &over	Sub-total 50 & over
1922-33	62.0	100.0	100.0	90.1	50.9	29.7	20.9	17.6	13.1	27.8
1934-37	40.7	44.9	45.4	44.4	39.2	26.4	20.1	17.1	8.9	29.2
1938-41	19.4	27.7	29.1	21.9	14.3	6.3	4.2	3.0	0.8	6.1
1942-46	4.9	5.7	6.9	4.7	2.9	1.7	0.8	0.7	0.5	1.8

C LONG TERM LOSSES

Assets held longer than 2 years if segregated for special tax treatment

1924-33

	TOTAL[1]	Under 5	5-25	25-50	50-100	100-300	300-500	500-1,000	1,000 &over	Sub-total 50 & over
1924	15.2		9.6				56.1			
1925	17.0		7.5				60.6			
1926	16.2			26.2	50.5	33.8	26.1	46.3	27.9	38.9
1927	17.5			20.6	48.4	49.3	60.1	53.8	39.6	49.6
1928	19.3			16.2	47.4	51.2	40.8	53.1	27.9	46.3
1929	4.1			3.6	14.3	14.9	9.3	9.8	5.5	12.1
1930	6.2			4.9	16.5	21.9	20.8	12.0	29.4	19.2
1931	17.1			19.8	46.8	51.0	53.0	53.5	64.6	50.8
1932	45.9		20.7	71.6	80.1	92.2		90.5		85.9
1933	45.9		24.1	64.7	75.9	87.8		97.7		83.0

STATUTORY NET INCOME GROUP (thousands of dollars)[1]

	TOTAL[1]	Under 5	5- 25	25- 50	50- 100	100- 300	300- 500	500- 1,000	1,000 &over	Sub- total 50 & over
			Assets held longer than 2 years							
1934-37[6]										
1934	85.6	84.6	85.6	86.6	86.2	88.8	89.9	89.1	93.2	87.7
1935	89.4	89.2	89.5	90.4	87.4	91.7	90.0	91.7	96.1	89.5
1936	93.0	93.6	93.4	95.3	89.3	88.0	95.6	96.0	93.0	89.7
1937	54.5	56.9	55.3	50.3	46.9	46.9	41.0	68.0	73.7	49.0
			Assets held longer than 6 months							
1942-46[8]										
1942	90.1	87.9	92.7	92.7	90.9	91.8	89.4	63.7	40.7	88.7
1943	82.2	82.0	83.7	80.6	78.5	68.3	86.1	86.5	84.0	77.0
1944	66.3	74.2	64.0	48.4	45.5	47.2	18.0	33.1	26.1	43.6
1945	52.3	64.1	49.9	31.7	31.9	28.7	12.6	52.6	34.7	31.0
1946	36.2	52.6	32.3	21.6	15.7	10.7	7.0	35.0	1.5	14.1
Totals										
1926-33	25.1		8.1	43.7	55.2	54.6		47.5		53.2
1934-37	79.8	80.4	79.7	79.7	77.9	77.1	78.4	83.0	89.0	78.3
1942-46	63.4	72.4	61.8	49.0	43.1	37.8	28.3	44.1	28.0	40.0

D SHORT TERM LOSSES

Assets held 2 years or less plus assets held longer than 2 years if not segregated for special tax treatment

	TOTAL[1]	Under 5	5- 25	25- 50	50- 100	100- 300	300- 500	500- 1,000	1,000 &over	Sub- total 50 & over
1924-33										
1924[2]	84.8		90.4				43.8			
1925[2]	83.0		92.5				39.4			
1926	83.8	100.0	100.0	73.8	49.5	66.2	73.9	53.7	72.1	61.1
1927	82.5	100.0	100.0	79.4	51.6	50.7	39.9	46.2	60.4	50.4
1928	80.7	100.0	100.0	83.8	52.6	48.8	59.2	46.9	72.1	53.7
1929[3]	95.9	100.0	100.0	96.4	85.7	85.1	90.7	90.2	94.5	87.9
1930[3]	93.8	100.0	100.0	95.1	83.5	78.1	79.2	88.0	70.6	80.8
1931[3]	82.9	100.0	100.0	80.2	53.2	49.0	47.0	46.5	35.4	49.2
1932[3,4]	54.1	100.0	79.3	28.4	19.9	7.8		9.5		14.1
1933[3,4]	54.1	100.0	75.9	35.3	24.1	12.2		2.3		17.0

Assets held 2 years or less[11]

	TOTAL[1]	Under 5	5- 25	25- 50	50- 100	100- 300	300- 500	500- 1,000	1,000 &over	Sub- total 50 & over
1934-37[6]										
1934	14.4	15.4	14.3	13.3	13.8	11.2	10.1	10.9	6.9	12.3
1935	10.5	10.7	10.4	9.7	12.6	8.4	10.1	8.4	3.9	10.5
1936	7.0	6.6	6.6	4.7	10.8	12.0	4.3	4.0	7.0	10.3
1937	45.5	43.2	44.7	49.6	53.0	53.1	59.0	32.0	26.2	51.0

Assets held 6 months or less

	TOTAL[1]	Under 5	5- 25	25- 50	50- 100	100- 300	300- 500	500- 1,000	1,000 &over	Sub- total 50 & over
1942-46[8]										
1942	2.2	2.1	2.2	2.5	3.0	3.2	2.4	3.4	0.1	2.9
1943	7.1	6.1	7.5	9.2	10.9	14.5	3.0	7.4	0.6	10.5
1944[a]	26.8	18.1	30.2	45.7	48.2	46.1	61.6	45.1	63.9	48.6
1945[a]	39.9	27.9	42.5	61.2	61.3	62.0	74.8	36.4	48.5	60.3
1946[a]	58.5	40.6	63.0	74.7	80.7	84.9	88.8	63.9	88.9	81.9
Totals										
1926-33	74.9	100.0	91.9	56.2	44.8	45.4		52.5		46.8
1934-37	20.2	19.6	20.3	20.3	22.1	22.9	21.6	7.0	11.0	21.7
1942-46	29.2	18.9	32.1	45.3	51.1	55.4	61.2	46.3	55.1	52.8

See Table 8, source note.   [a] See Table 8, note b.   † Less than 0.05 percent.
For numbered notes see pp. 362-6.

Table 14

Long and Short Term Net Capital Gains and Losses by Size, 1927-1933

Returns with net incomes of $5,000 and over

	TOTAL	NET CAPITAL GAIN GROUP (thousands of dollars)							
		Under 1	1-5	5-25	25-50	50-100	100-500	500-1,000	1,000 & over

A GAINS (millions of dollars)

Long term (assets held longer than 2 years if segregated for special tax treatment)

Year	TOTAL	Under 1	1-5	5-25	25-50	50-100	100-500	500-1,000	1,000 & over
1927	1,081.2	1.1	11.5	80.4	94.7	150.5	372.8	112.9	257.2
1928	1,879.8	1.3	13.9	111.4	148.0	238.5	637.7	254.4	474.7
1929	2,346.7	0.8	8.8	81.5	133.3	240.4	851.1	328.7	702.0
1930	556.4	0.6	4.8	29.2	37.1	72.5	204.7	71.7	135.9
1931	169.9	0.3	1.6	7.5	9.4	21.7	58.6	26.6	44.3
1932	50.1	0.2	1.0	5.5	8.1	9.5	18.9	6.9	
1933	133.6	0.4	2.1	10.1	13.8	18.0	43.2	15.0	31.1

Short term (assets held 2 years or less plus assets held longer than 2 years if not segregated for special tax treatment)

Year	TOTAL	Under 1	1-5	5-25	25-50	50-100	100-500	500-1,000	1,000 & over
1927	1,511.9	36.4	241.9	674.4	241.2	128.0	144.0	30.8	15.2
1928	2,700.6	40.3	324.9	1,062.1	444.7	290.5	365.8	79.2	93.1
1929	2,044.1	35.8	273.1	890.8	356.8	189.7	189.2	39.2	69.4
1930	527.7	22.9	102.9	255.6	76.8	31.6	27.6	3.5	6.8
1931	196.6	11.0	37.1	90.4	28.1	11.5	14.4	2.5	1.6
1932	71.6	5.7	16.8	32.4	7.4	3.1	4.4	1.8	
1933	308.7	13.6	62.5	126.4	43.7	30.0	25.4	1.8	5.3

B LOSSES (millions of dollars)

Long term (assets held longer than 2 years if segregated for special tax treatment)

Year	TOTAL	Under 1	1-5	5-25	25-50	50-100	100-500	500-1,000	1,000 & over
1929	43.0	0.3	2.5	10.6	6.8	7.9	11.7	0.7	2.4
1930	80.9	0.3	3.1	18.2	14.6	14.9	23.9	1.5	4.4
1931	239.9	0.2	2.7	25.5	34.5	45.0	78.3	15.1	38.6
1932	832.4	0.6	7.9	108.2	138.0	156.3	271.2	64.2	85.9
1933	553.8	0.6	8.5	79.3	99.7	105.2	176.5	35.3	48.8

Short term (assets held 2 years or less plus assets held longer than 2 years if not segregated for special tax treatment)

Year	TOTAL	Under 1	1-5	5-25	25-50	50-100	100-500	500-1,000	1,000 & over
1929	632.5	11.6	66.5	185.7	96.4	91.9	120.1	27.0	33.2
1930	947.1	14.5	97.8	306.8	157.3	134.3	171.5	36.1	28.8
1931	813.5	11.3	88.6	292.7	148.1	105.8	118.0	20.6	28.5
1932[14]	174.6	6.0	46.1	98.2	15.9	4.2	4.3		
1933[14]	153.0	7.5	46.6	83.0	11.1	2.7	2.1		

395

	TOTAL	Under 1	1-5	5-25	25-50	50-100	100-500	500-1,000	1,000 & over

C PERCENTAGE DISTRIBUTION OF GAINS

Long term

	TOTAL	Under 1	1-5	5-25	25-50	50-100	100-500	500-1,000	1,000 & over
1927	100.0	0.1	1.1	7.4	8.8	13.9	34.5	10.4	23.8
1928	100.0	0.1	0.7	5.9	7.9	12.7	33.9	13.5	25.3
1929	100.0	†	0.4	3.5	5.7	10.2	36.3	14.0	29.9
1930	100.0	0.1	0.9	5.2	6.7	13.0	36.8	12.9	24.4
1931	100.0	0.2	0.9	4.4	5.6	12.8	34.5	15.6	26.1
1932	100.0	0.4	1.9	10.9	16.1	19.0	37.8	13.8	
1933	100.0	0.3	1.6	7.6	10.3	13.5	32.3	11.2	23.3

Short term

	TOTAL	Under 1	1-5	5-25	25-50	50-100	100-500	500-1,000	1,000 & over
1927	100.0	2.4	16.0	44.6	16.0	8.5	9.5	2.0	1.0
1928	100.0	1.5	12.0	39.3	16.5	10.8	13.5	2.9	3.4
1929	100.0	1.8	13.4	43.6	17.5	9.3	9.3	1.9	3.4
1930	100.0	4.3	19.5	48.4	14.5	6.0	5.2	0.7	1.3
1931	100.0	5.6	18.8	46.0	14.3	5.8	7.3	1.3	0.8
1932	100.0	8.0	23.5	45.2	10.3	4.3	6.2	2.5	
1933	100.0	4.4	20.2	40.9	14.2	9.7	8.2	0.6	1.7

D PERCENTAGE DISTRIBUTION OF LOSSES

Long term

	TOTAL	Under 1	1-5	5-25	25-50	50-100	100-500	500-1,000	1,000 & over
1929	100.0	0.8	5.8	24.7	15.9	18.4	27.3	1.7	5.5
1930	100.0	0.4	3.9	22.5	18.1	18.4	29.5	1.8	5.4
1931	100.0	0.1	1.1	10.6	14.4	18.8	32.6	6.3	16.1
1932	100.0	0.1	0.9	13.0	16.6	18.8	32.6	7.7	10.3
1933	100.0	0.1	1.5	14.3	18.0	19.0	31.9	6.4	8.8

Short term

	TOTAL	Under 1	1-5	5-25	25-50	50-100	100-500	500-1,000	1,000 & over
1929	100.0	1.8	10.5	29.4	15.2	14.5	19.0	4.3	5.2
1930	100.0	1.5	10.3	32.4	16.6	14.2	18.1	3.8	3.0
1931	100.0	1.4	10.9	36.0	18.2	13.0	14.5	2.5	3.5
1932[14]	100.0	3.4	26.4	56.2	9.1	2.4	2.4		
1933[14]	100.0	4.9	30.4	54.3	7.2	1.8	1.4		

Based on Source 1.

† Less than 0.05 percent.

For numbered notes see pp. 362-6.

Table 15

Shares Traded, New York Stock Exchange, Stock Price Index, and Arithmetic Sum of Short Term Net Capital Gains and Losses, 1917-1946

	Shares Traded[a] (million)	Stock Price Index[b]	Gains & Losses[c] ($ mil.)
1917-21			
1917	184.6	55.3	
1918	143.3	63.8	
1919	318.3	66.0	
1920	227.6	53.7	
1921	172.8	58.0	
1922-33			
1922	260.9	68.2	
1923	236.5	67.6	
1924	284.0	82.4	1,529.1[2]
1925	459.7	101.2	2,290.1[2]
1926	451.9	107.1	1,643.8
1927	581.7	138.7	2,041.3
1928	930.9	183.8	3,099.8
1929	1,124.8	170.0	3,330.6[3]
1930	810.6	123.2	1,869.5[3]
1931	576.8	67.0	1,462.5[3]
1932	425.2	54.2	1,095.1[3,4]
1933	654.8	79.2	1,073.3[3,4]
1934-37			
1934	323.8	73.5	373.5[6]
1935	381.6	103.6	570.1[6]
1936	496.0	135.5	889.4[6]
1937	409.5	87.5	858.9[6]
1938-41			
1938	297.5	100.7	152.1[7]
1939	262.0	98.2	189.6[7]
1940	207.6	83.7	127.4[7]
1941	170.6	69.5	140.1[7]
1942-46			
1942	125.7	75.6	73.6[8]
1943	278.7	91.2	195.8[8]
1944	263.1	104.0	407.4[8]
1945	377.6	137.6	653.9[8]
1946	363.7	120.2	1,007.1[8]

[a] *New York Stock Exchange Yearbook, 1947.*

[b] Standard and Poor's December averages of the daily prices of 90 stocks (1926 average: 100).

[c] Reported on returns with statutory net incomes.[1] Includes net gains and losses on assets held 2 years or less 1924-37,[21] 18 months or less 1938-41, and 6 months or less 1942-46, except that the figures for 1924-33 include longer term gains and losses that were not segregated for preferential tax treatment, and the figures for 1938-41 do not include short term losses because the data are not available. See Table 8, source note.

For numbered notes see pp. 362-6.

Table 16: Net Capital Gains and Losses in 5 Holding Periods: Annual Totals, 1934-1937 (millions of dollars)

YEARS HELD	REALIZED NET GAIN[9] Returns with statutory net			REALIZED NET LOSS[9] Returns with statutory net			EXCESS OF GAIN OVER LOSS Returns with statutory net		
	Gains or losses	Gains[15]	Losses[16]	Gains or losses	Gains[15]	Losses[16]	Gains or losses	Gains[15]	Losses[16]
RETURNS WITH STATUTORY NET INCOMES OR DEFICITS									
1934									
1 or less	154.5	122.5	32.0	105.2	6.2	99.0	49.3	116.3	−67.0
1- 2	89.0	60.7	28.3	45.0	6.0	39.1	43.9	54.7	−10.8
2- 5	62.5	53.3	9.3	384.7	27.9	356.9	−322.2	25.4	−347.7
5-10	54.9	46.2	8.7	449.6	33.4	416.2	−394.7	12.9	−407.6
Over 10	155.1	124.4	30.7	146.0	6.9	139.1	9.1	117.5	−108.3
Not stated	14.3	13.6	0.7	29.2	0.3	28.9	−14.9	13.3	−28.1
Total[17]	530.4	420.7	109.6	1,159.8	80.7	1,079.1	−629.6	340.1	−969.6
1935									
1 or less	318.6	281.0	37.6	78.3	9.5	68.8	240.3	271.5	−31.2
1- 2	150.1	124.2	25.9	35.7	9.6	26.0	114.4	114.6	−0.2
2- 5	182.9	159.9	23.0	227.7	37.5	190.2	−44.7	122.4	−167.2
5-10	105.2	96.8	8.4	574.0	86.1	487.9	−468.8	10.7	−479.5
Over 10	280.7	244.5	36.2	219.6	21.9	197.7	61.1	222.6	−161.6
Not stated	23.9	23.0	0.9	15.0	0.8	14.1	9.0	22.2	−13.2
Total[17]	1,061.4	929.4	132.0	1,150.2	165.5	984.7	−88.7	764.0	−852.8
1936									
1 or less	582.4	531.1	51.3	63.4	11.2	52.2	519.9	519.9	−0.9
1- 2	241.2	211.0	30.1	22.5	6.9	15.6	218.7	204.1	14.6
2- 5	389.3	350.3	38.9	88.0	23.8	64.2	301.4	326.6	−25.3
5-10	196.0	187.5	8.6	763.5	176.0	587.5	−567.4	11.4	−578.9
Over 10	429.7	397.5	32.2	316.5	50.9	265.6	113.2	346.6	−233.4
Not stated	10.1	9.6	0.6	6.3	1.5	4.8	3.9	8.1	−4.2
Total[17]	1,848.7	1,686.9	161.8	1,260.1	270.2	990.0	588.7	1,416.8	−828.1
1937									
1 or less	167.1	138.3	28.8	427.0	57.8	369.2	−259.9	80.5	−340.4
1- 2	167.6	110.6	57.1	110.8	16.4	94.3	56.9	94.1	−37.3
2- 5	354.0	235.1	118.9	76.2	7.4	68.7	277.9	227.7	50.1
5-10	219.6	174.6	45.0	503.8	45.1	458.7	−284.2	129.5	−413.7
Over 10	391.2	316.1	75.1	283.5	16.9	266.6	107.7	299.2	−191.5
Not stated	18.9	18.0	1.0	22.1	1.1	21.0	−3.2	16.9	−20.1
Total[17]	1,318.5	992.6	325.8	1,423.3	144.7	1,278.6	−104.9	847.9	−952.8

1934

1 or less	142.0	113.6	28.4	80.3	5.7	74.7	61.7	107.9	−46.2
1- 2	82.6	57.0	25.5	37.6	5.7	31.9	45.0	51.3	−6.3
2- 5	55.7	47.5	8.2	317.8	25.1	292.7	−262.1	22.4	−284.5
5-10	48.9	41.2	7.7	376.0	30.8	345.3	−327.2	10.4	−337.5
Over 10	141.3	114.6	26.7	113.2	6.1	107.2	28.1	108.6	−80.5
Not stated[17]	13.1	12.4	0.6	17.9	0.2	17.7	−4.8	12.2	−17.0
Total[17]	483.5	386.3	97.2	942.9	73.6	869.3	−459.3	312.7	−772.0

1935

1 or less	304.4	272.0	32.4	60.7	9.0	51.6	243.8	262.9	−19.2
1- 2	141.1	120.4	20.7	31.1	9.4	21.7	110.0	111.0	−1.0
2- 5	173.3	152.7	20.5	193.4	35.4	158.0	−20.2	117.3	−137.5
5-10	97.5	90.3	7.2	495.4	81.9	413.5	−397.9	8.4	−406.2
Over 10	263.5	230.4	33.2	174.9	20.9	154.1	88.6	209.5	−120.9
Not stated[17]	23.0	−22.3	0.7	9.8	0.8	9.0	13.2	21.5	−8.3
Total[17]	1,002.9	888.1	114.8	965.3	157.5	807.9	37.5	730.7	−693.1

1936

1 or less	569.0	522.9	46.1	52.9	10.9	42.0	516.1	512.0	4.1
1- 2	231.8	207.4	24.4	20.4	6.9	13.5	211.5	200.5	11.0
2- 5	378.0	341.8	36.1	78.4	22.9	55.5	299.5	318.9	−19.5
5-10	186.9	179.5	7.5	693.5	169.9	523.6	−506.5	9.6	−516.1
Over 10	408.5	378.2	30.2	272.3	49.7	222.6	136.2	328.5	−192.4
Not stated[17]	9.9	9.5	0.3	5.4	1.5	4.0	4.4	8.0	−3.6
Total[17]	1,784.1	1,639.3	144.7	1,122.9	261.7	861.2	661.3	1,377.6	−716.4

1937

1 or less	151.2	132.1	19.1	407.6	57.5	350.0	−256.4	74.6	−331.0
1- 2	154.2	107.9	46.3	106.2	16.4	90.5	47.3	91.5	−44.2
2- 5	342.2	228.7	113.5	59.2	6.8	52.4	283.0	222.0	61.0
5-10	211.5	168.6	43.0	379.0	40.4	338.6	−167.5	128.1	−295.6
Over 10	373.2	301.7	71.5	201.8	16.1	185.7	171.3	285.6	−114.3
Not stated[17]	18.5	17.9	0.6	20.5	1.0	19.5	−2.0	16.9	−18.9
Total[17]	1,250.8	956.9	293.9	1,175.1	138.2	1,036.9	75.6	818.6	−743.0

Based on Sources 1, 2, and 3.

For numbered notes see pp. 362-6.

Table 17

Net Capital Gains and Losses in 5 Holding Periods: Percentage Distribution, 1934-1937

YEARS HELD	REALIZED NET GAIN[6] Returns with statutory net Gains or *losses*	Gains[15]	Losses[16]	REALIZED NET LOSS[6] Returns with statutory net Gains or losses	Gains[15]	Losses[16]
RETURNS WITH STATUTORY NET INCOMES OR DEFICITS						
1934						
1 or less	29.1	29.1	29.2	9.1	7.7	9.2
1- 2	16.9	14.4	25.8	3.9	7.4	3.6
2- 5	11.8	12.7	8.5	33.2	34.5	33.1
5-10	10.3	11.0	7.9	38.8	41.4	38.6
Over 10	29.2	29.6	28.0	12.6	8.6	12.9
Not stated	2.7	3.2	0.7	2.5	0.4	2.7
Total[17]	100.0	100.0	100.0	100.0	100.0	100.0
1935						
1 or less	30.0	30.2	28.5	6.8	5.7	7.0
1- 2	14.1	13.4	19.6	3.1	5.8	2.6
2- 5	17.2	17.2	17.4	19.8	22.7	19.3
5-10	9.9	10.4	6.4	49.9	52.1	49.5
Over 10	26.4	26.3	27.4	19.1	13.2	20.1
Not stated	2.3	2.5	0.7	1.3	0.5	1.4
Total[17]	100.0	100.0	100.0	100.0	100.0	100.0
1936						
1 or less	31.5	31.5	31.7	5.0	4.1	5.3
1- 2	13.0	12.5	18.7	1.8	2.6	1.6
2- 5	21.0	20.8	24.1	7.0	8.8	6.5
5-10	10.6	11.1	5.3	60.6	65.1	59.4
Over 10	23.2	23.6	19.9	25.1	18.8	26.8
Not stated	0.5	0.6	0.3	0.5	0.6	0.5
Total[17]	100.0	100.0	100.0	100.0	100.0	100.0
1937						
1 or less	12.7	13.9	8.8	30.0	39.9	28.9
1- 2	12.7	11.1	17.5	7.8	11.4	7.4
2- 5	26.9	23.7	36.5	5.4	5.1	5.4
5-10	16.7	17.6	13.8	35.4	31.1	35.9
Over 10	29.7	31.8	23.0	19.9	11.7	20.8
Not stated	1.4	1.8	0.3	1.6	0.7	1.6
Total[17]	100.0	100.0	100.0	100.0	100.0	100.0

YEARS HELD	REALIZED NET GAIN[8] *Returns with statutory net* losses	Gains[15]	Losses[16]	REALIZED NET LOSS[6] *Returns with statutory net* Gains or losses	Gains[15]	Losses[16]

RETURNS WITH STATUTORY NET INCOMES

1934

YEARS HELD	losses	Gains[15]	Losses[16]	Gains or losses	Gains[15]	Losses[16]
1 or less	29.4	29.4	29.3	8.5	7.7	8.6
1- 2	17.1	14.8	26.3	4.0	7.8	3.7
2- 5	11.5	12.3	8.4	33.7	34.1	33.7
5-10	10.1	10.7	7.9	39.9	41.8	39.7
Over 10	29.2	29.7	27.5	12.0	8.3	12.3
Not stated	2.7	3.2	0.6	1.9	0.3	2.0
Total[17]	100.0	100.0	100.0	100.0	100.0	100.0

1935

1 or less	30.4	30.6	28.2	6.3	5.7	6.4
1- 2	14.1	13.6	18.0	3.2	6.0	2.7
2- 5	17.3	17.2	17.9	20.0	22.5	19.6
5-10	9.7	10.2	6.3	51.3	52.0	51.2
Over 10	26.3	25.9	28.9	18.1	13.3	19.1
Not stated	2.3	2.5	0.6	1.0	0.5	1.1
Total[17]	100.0	100.0	100.0	100.0	100.0	100.0

1936

1 or less	31.9	31.9	31.9	4.7	4.2	4.9
1- 2	13.0	12.7	16.9	1.8	2.6	1.6
2- 5	21.2	20.8	24.9	7.0	8.8	6.4
5-10	10.5	10.9	5.2	61.8	64.9	60.8
Over 10	22.9	23.1	20.9	24.2	19.0	25.8
Not stated	0.6	0.6	0.3	0.5	0.6	0.5
Total[17]	100.0	100.0	100.0	100.0	100.0	100.0

1937

1 or less	12.1	13.8	6.5	34.7	41.6	33.8
1- 2	12.3	11.3	15.8	9.1	11.9	8.7
2- 5	27.4	23.9	38.6	5.0	4.9	5.1
5-10	16.9	17.6	14.6	32.3	29.2	32.7
Over 10	29.8	31.5	24.3	17.2	11.6	17.9
Not stated	1.5	1.9	0.2	1.7	0.8	1.9
Total[17]	100.0	100.0	100.0	100.0	100.0	100.0

Based on Sources 1, 2, and 3.
For numbered notes see pp. 362-6.

Table 18

Net Capital Gains and Losses in 5 Holding Periods by Statutory Net Income Groups, 1934-1937

YEARS HELD	TOTAL[1]	STATUTORY NET INCOME GROUP (thousands of dollars)[1]							
		Under 5	5-25	25-50	50-100	100-300	300-500	500-1,000	1,000 & over

A Annual Totals (millions of dollars)

1934

RETURNS WITH STATUTORY NET CAPITAL GAINS OR LOSSES[15,16]

Realized Net Capital Gain[6]

YEARS HELD	TOTAL[1]	Under 5	5-25	25-50	50-100	100-300	300-500	500-1,000	1,000 & over
1 or less	142.0	35.6	63.7	20.9	12.8	6.6	1.0	0.9	0.4
1- 2	82.6	17.1	36.0	12.7	8.6	4.9	0.8	2.0	0.5
2- 5	55.7	14.6	24.0	8.0	5.4	2.6	0.3	0.6	*
5-10	48.9	11.2	18.2	6.1	5.1	4.2	1.1	1.5	1.4
Over 10	141.3	22.1	43.6	22.2	14.5	22.7	3.1	6.0	7.3
Not stated	13.1	4.0	4.8	1.7	1.1	0.6	0.8	*	0.1
Total[17]	483.5	104.6	190.4	71.6	47.6	41.6	7.2	10.9	9.7

Realized Net Capital Loss[6]

YEARS HELD	TOTAL[1]	Under 5	5-25	25-50	50-100	100-300	300-500	500-1,000	1,000 & over
1 or less	80.3	33.0	34.0	7.1	3.9	1.7	0.3	0.3	0.1
1- 2	37.6	13.3	16.3	4.1	2.3	1.2	0.1	0.1	0.2
2- 5	317.8	117.2	132.6	34.0	16.0	13.5	0.5	2.6	1.3
5-10	376.0	139.2	162.8	39.1	19.4	10.6	0.4	2.1	2.3
Over 10	113.2	45.2	44.6	11.0	6.5	2.6	2.6	0.2	0.5
Not stated	17.9	8.6	6.3	1.8	0.5	0.5	*	0.2	*
Total[17]	942.9	356.5	396.6	97.1	48.6	30.1	4.0	5.5	4.4

Excess of Realized Gain over Loss

YEARS HELD	TOTAL[1]	Under 5	5-25	25-50	50-100	100-300	300-500	500-1,000	1,000 & over
1 or less	61.7	2.6	29.7	13.8	9.0	4.9	0.7	0.6	0.3
1- 2	45.0	3.8	19.7	8.6	6.3	3.7	0.7	1.9	0.3
2- 5	−262.1	−102.6	−108.6	−26.0	−10.6	−11.0	−0.2	−2.0	−1.2
5-10	−327.2	−128.0	−144.6	−33.0	−14.3	−6.5	0.7	−0.7	−0.9
Over 10	28.1	−23.2	−1.0	11.1	8.0	20.1	0.5	5.8	6.7
Not stated	−4.8	−4.6	−1.5	−0.1	0.5	0.2	0.8	−0.2	0.1
Total	−459.3	−251.9	−206.3	−25.5	−1.1	11.6	3.2	5.4	5.3

RETURNS WITH STATUTORY NET CAPITAL GAINS[15]

Realized Net Capital Gain[6]

YEARS HELD	TOTAL[1]	Under 5	5-25	25-50	50-100	100-300	300-500	500-1,000	1,000 & over
1 or less	113.6	28.3	50.9	16.7	10.3	5.4	0.9	0.6	0.4
1- 2	57.0	12.3	25.9	7.9	6.0	3.0	0.7	0.8	0.4
2- 5	47.5	12.7	20.5	6.8	4.4	2.1	0.3	0.5	*
5-10	41.2	9.6	15.5	5.2	4.4	2.7	1.1	1.5	1.1
Over 10	114.6	18.3	33.4	16.8	11.2	20.2	2.9	5.5	6.2
Not stated	12.4	3.7	4.6	1.6	1.0	0.6	0.8	*	0.1
Total[17]	386.3	85.1	150.8	54.9	37.5	34.0	6.7	9.0	8.3

Realized Net Capital Loss[6]

YEARS HELD	TOTAL[1]	Under 5	5-25	25-50	50-100	100-300	300-500	500-1,000	1,000 & over
1 or less	5.7	1.0	2.2	1.1	0.8	0.4	0.1	0.1	*
1- 2	5.7	1.1	2.3	0.8	0.7	0.4	0.1	0.1	0.1
2- 5	25.1	5.0	10.5	3.4	3.4	2.0	0.1	0.1	0.7
5-10	30.8	6.0	12.6	4.9	3.0	3.4	0.1	0.7	0.2
Over 10	6.1	1.4	2.5	0.8	1.0	0.3	*	0.1	*
Not stated	0.2	0.1	0.1	*	*	*	*	*	*
Total[17]	73.6	14.6	30.1	11.1	8.9	6.4	0.5	1.0	1.1

Excess of Realized Gain over Loss

YEARS HELD	TOTAL[1]	Under 5	5-25	25-50	50-100	100-300	300-500	500-1,000	1,000 & over
1 or less	107.9	27.3	48.7	15.6	9.5	5.0	0.8	0.5	0.4
1- 2	51.3	11.2	23.6	7.1	5.3	2.6	0.6	0.7	0.2
2- 5	22.4	7.8	10.1	3.4	1.0	0.1	0.2	0.5	−0.7
5-10	10.4	3.6	2.9	0.3	1.5	−0.7	1.0	0.8	0.9
Over 10	108.6	17.0	30.9	15.9	10.2	19.9	2.9	5.5	6.2
Not stated	12.2	3.6	4.5	1.6	1.0	0.6	0.8	*	0.1
Total	312.7	70.5	120.7	43.8	28.6	27.6	6.3	8.0	7.2

RETURNS WITH STATUTORY NET CAPITAL LOSSES[16]

Realized Net Capital Gain[6]

YEARS HELD	TOTAL[1]	Under 5	5-25	25-50	50-100	100-300	300-500	500-1,000	1,000 & over
1 or less	28.4	7.3	12.8	4.2	2.5	1.2	0.1	0.2	*
1- 2	25.5	4.7	10.1	4.8	2.7	1.9	0.1	1.2	0.1
2- 5	8.2	1.9	3.5	1.2	1.0	0.5	*	*	*
5-10	7.7	1.5	2.8	1.0	0.6	1.5	*	*	0.3
Over 10	26.7	3.7	10.1	5.4	3.3	2.5	0.2	0.4	1.0
Not stated	0.6	0.3	0.3	*	*	*	*		
Total[17]	97.2	19.5	39.5	16.7	10.1	7.6	0.4	1.9	1.4

YEARS HELD	TOTAL[1]	Under 5	5-25	25-50	50-100	100-300	300-500	500-1,000	1,000 & over

1934

Realized Net Capital Loss[6]

YEARS HELD	TOTAL[1]	Under 5	5-25	25-50	50-100	100-300	300-500	500-1,000	1,000 & over
1 or less	74.7	32.0	31.8	6.1	3.1	1.3	0.2	0.2	0.1
1- 2	31.9	12.2	14.0	3.3	1.6	0.8	*	*	*
2- 5	292.7	112.3	122.2	30.6	12.6	11.6	0.4	2.5	0.6
5-10	345.3	133.2	150.3	34.2	16.4	7.3	0.3	1.5	2.1
Over 10	107.2	43.9	42.1	10.2	5.5	2.3	2.6	0.1	0.5
Not stated	17.7	8.5	6.2	1.8	0.5	0.4	*	0.2	
Total[17]	869.3	342.0	366.5	86.1	39.7	23.7	3.5	4.5	3.3

Excess of Realized Gain over Loss

YEARS HELD	TOTAL[1]	Under 5	5-25	25-50	50-100	100-300	300-500	500-1,000	1,000 & over
1 or less	−46.2	−24.7	−19.0	−1.8	−0.6	−0.1	−0.1	0.1	−0.1
1- 2	−6.3	−7.4	−3.9	1.5	1.1	1.1	*	1.2	*
2- 5	−284.5	−110.4	−118.7	−29.4	−11.6	−11.1	−0.4	−2.5	−0.5
5-10	−337.5	−131.6	−147.5	−33.2	−15.8	−5.8	−0.3	−1.5	−1.8
Over 10	−80.5	−40.1	−31.9	−4.8	−2.2	0.2	−2.4	0.3	0.5
Not stated	−17.0	−8.2	−6.0	−1.7	−0.5	−0.4	*	−0.2	
Total	−772.0	−322.4	−327.0	−69.4	−29.6	−16.1	−3.1	−2.6	−1.9

1935

RETURNS WITH STATUTORY NET CAPITAL GAINS OR LOSSES[15,16]

Realized Net Capital Gain[6]

YEARS HELD	TOTAL[1]	Under 5	5-25	25-50	50-100	100-300	300-500	500-1,000	1,000 & over
1 or less	304.4	72.3	131.0	46.7	34.5	14.7	3.1	1.4	0.7
1- 2	141.1	28.4	62.3	22.6	18.0	6.6	0.8	1.9	0.4
2- 5	173.3	38.9	67.4	23.9	20.7	13.6	3.9	3.4	1.4
5-10	97.5	22.0	39.3	13.0	12.8	6.5	1.5	2.2	0.2
Over 10	263.5	40.4	80.3	33.3	28.3	26.7	13.6	26.4	14.5
Not stated	23.0	4.3	6.3	2.1	1.5	2.2	2.0	0.3	4.4
Total[17]	1,002.9	206.3	386.7	141.5	115.8	70.4	24.9	35.6	21.6

Realized Net Capital Loss[6]

YEARS HELD	TOTAL[1]	Under 5	5-25	25-50	50-100	100-300	300-500	500-1,000	1,000 & over
1 or less	60.7	23.7	23.5	5.2	6.7	1.0	0.4	0.1	*
1- 2	31.1	10.5	11.9	3.0	2.2	2.5	0.5	0.3	0.2
2- 5	193.4	73.0	74.5	20.6	13.8	5.3	4.4	0.4	1.5
5-10	495.4	176.7	188.3	47.1	41.5	31.8	3.0	3.3	3.6
Over 10	174.9	69.5	67.2	24.3	8.5	4.1	0.4	0.5	0.5
Not stated	9.8	4.5	3.1	1.7	0.3	0.2	*	*	*
Total[17]	965.3	357.9	368.6	101.8	73.0	45.0	8.7	4.6	5.8

Excess of Realized Gain over Loss

YEARS HELD	TOTAL[1]	Under 5	5-25	25-50	50-100	100-300	300-500	500-1,000	1,000 & over
1 or less	243.8	48.6	107.5	41.5	27.8	13.7	2.7	1.3	0.7
1- 2	110.0	17.9	50.4	19.7	15.8	4.1	0.3	1.6	0.2
2- 5	−20.2	−34.1	−7.1	3.3	6.9	8.2	−0.4	3.0	*
5-10	−397.9	−154.6	−149.0	−34.1	−28.7	−25.2	−1.6	−1.1	−3.4
Over 10	88.6	−29.1	13.1	9.0	19.8	22.6	13.2	26.0	14.0
Not stated	13.2	−0.2	3.2	0.4	1.2	2.0	2.0	0.3	4.4
Total	37.5	−151.6	18.1	39.8	42.9	25.4	16.2	31.0	15.8

RETURNS WITH STATUTORY NET CAPITAL GAINS[15]

Realized Net Capital Gain[6]

YEARS HELD	TOTAL[1]	Under 5	5-25	25-50	50-100	100-300	300-500	500-1,000	1,000 & over
1 or less	272.0	63.6	119.6	43.2	27.7	13.0	2.9	1.3	0.6
1- 2	120.4	24.1	53.2	19.3	15.1	5.9	0.7	1.9	0.4
2- 5	152.7	33.7	59.0	21.5	18.5	12.3	3.7	3.0	1.2
5-10	90.3	20.7	36.0	12.4	12.3	6.1	0.4	2.2	0.2
Over 10	230.4	36.6	71.1	29.0	24.3	24.4	9.2	25.7	10.2
Not stated	22.3	4.1	6.1	2.0	1.5	2.2	1.7	0.3	4.4
Total[17]	888.1	182.7	345.0	127.4	99.4	63.8	18.6	34.3	16.9

Realized Net Capital Loss[6]

YEARS HELD	TOTAL[1]	Under 5	5-25	25-50	50-100	100-300	300-500	500-1,000	1,000 & over
1 or less	9.0	1.5	3.4	1.5	1.9	0.5	0.1	*	*
1- 2	9.4	1.7	3.7	1.1	1.1	1.3	0.2	0.2	0.2
2- 5	35.4	7.1	14.6	4.7	5.8	2.1	0.6	0.3	0.2
5-10	81.9	19.2	32.0	12.1	10.0	7.1	0.9	0.5	0.2
Over 10	20.9	4.9	7.1	3.5	3.8	1.1	0.2	0.2	*
Not stated	0.8	0.3	0.3	*	*	0.1			
Total[17]	157.5	34.7	61.0	23.0	22.5	12.3	2.1	1.3	0.5

Excess of Realized Gain over Loss

YEARS HELD	TOTAL[1]	Under 5	5-25	25-50	50-100	100-300	300-500	500-1,000	1,000 & over
1 or less	262.9	62.1	116.3	41.7	25.8	12.5	2.7	1.3	0.6
1- 2	111.0	22.4	49.5	18.2	14.1	4.5	0.5	1.6	0.2
2- 5	117.3	26.6	44.4	16.8	12.7	10.1	3.1	2.7	1.0
5-10	8.4	1.5	4.1	0.3	2.3	−1.0	−0.6	1.7	*
Over 10	209.5	31.6	64.0	25.5	20.5	23.2	9.0	25.4	10.2
Not stated	21.5	3.8	5.8	2.0	1.4	2.1	1.7	0.3	4.4
Total	730.7	147.9	284.1	104.5	76.9	51.5	16.5	32.9	16.4

YEARS HELD	TOTAL[1]	STATUTORY NET INCOME GROUP (thousands of dollars)[1]							
		Under 5	5-25	25-50	50-100	100-300	300-500	500-1,000	1,000 & over

1935

RETURNS WITH STATUTORY NET CAPITAL LOSSES[16]

Realized Net Capital Gain[6]

YEARS HELD	TOTAL[1]	Under 5	5-25	25-50	50-100	100-300	300-500	500-1,000	1,000 & over
1 or less	32.4	8.7	11.4	3.5	6.8	1.7	0.2	0.1	0.1
1- 2	20.7	4.4	9.1	3.3	2.9	0.7	0.2	*	*
2- 5	20.5	5.2	8.5	2.4	2.2	1.3	0.3	0.4	0.3
5-10	7.2	1.3	3.3	0.6	0.5	0.4	1.1	*	
Over 10	33.2	3.8	9.3	4.3	4.0	2.3	4.4	0.8	4.3
Not stated	0.7	0.2	0.2	*	*	*	0.2	*	
Total[17]	114.8	23.6	41.7	14.1	16.4	6.6	6.4	1.3	4.7

Realized Net Capital Loss[6]

YEARS HELD	TOTAL[1]	Under 5	5-25	25-50	50-100	100-300	300-500	500-1,000	1,000 & over
1 or less	51.6	22.2	20.2	3.6	4.9	0.5	0.2	0.1	*
1- 2	21.7	8.9	8.3	1.9	1.1	1.2	0.3	0.1	*
2- 5	158.0	65.9	59.9	15.9	8.0	3.2	3.8	0.1	1.3
5-10	413.5	157.4	156.4	35.0	31.6	24.7	2.1	2.8	3.5
Over 10	154.1	64.6	60.2	20.8	4.7	3.0	0.2	0.3	0.5
Not stated	9.0	4.2	2.8	1.6	0.3	0.1	*	*	*
Total[17]	807.9	323.1	307.6	78.8	50.5	32.6	6.6	3.3	5.2

Excess of Realized Gain over Loss

YEARS HELD	TOTAL[1]	Under 5	5-25	25-50	50-100	100-300	300-500	500-1,000	1,000 & over
1 or less	-19.2	-13.5	-8.8	-0.1	1.9	1.2	*	*	0.1
1- 2	-1.0	-4.5	0.9	1.4	1.8	-0.5	-0.1	*	*
2- 5	-137.5	-60.7	-51.4	-13.5	-5.8	-1.9	-3.5	0.3	-1.0
5-10	-406.2	-156.1	-153.1	-34.5	-31.0	-24.2	-1.0	-2.8	-3.5
Over 10	-120.9	-60.8	-50.9	-16.5	-0.7	-0.6	4.2	0.5	3.8
Not stated	-8.3	-4.0	-2.6	-1.6	-0.3	*	0.2	*	*
Total	-693.1	-299.6	-265.9	-64.7	-34.1	-26.1	-0.3	-2.0	-0.5

1936

RETURNS WITH STATUTORY NET CAPITAL GAINS OR LOSSES[15,16]

Realized Net Capital Gain[6]

YEARS HELD	TOTAL[1]	Under 5	5-25	25-50	50-100	100-300	300-500	500-1,000	1,000 & over
1 or less	569.0	111.1	238.3	98.1	74.3	36.2	4.9	5.8	0.3
1- 2	231.8	37.3	96.2	42.7	33.6	15.7	2.9	3.0	0.3
2- 5	378.0	69.0	146.4	58.6	56.9	30.1	5.3	8.3	3.4
5-10	186.9	32.7	72.1	25.7	26.5	22.9	2.6	3.7	0.8
Over 10	408.5	55.7	129.8	40.5	44.8	57.9	16.0	14.6	49.2
Not stated	9.9	0.7	3.1	0.4	0.2	3.8	0.4	0.6	0.6
Total[17]	1,784.1	306.6	685.8	266.1	236.3	166.5	32.1	36.0	54.7

Realized Net Capital Loss[6]

YEARS HELD	TOTAL[1]	Under 5	5-25	25-50	50-100	100-300	300-500	500-1,000	1,000 & over
1 or less	52.9	16.0	17.2	2.9	13.3	2.8	0.1	0.2	0.4
1- 2	20.4	7.9	8.6	1.3	1.0	1.1	0.3	0.1	*
2- 5	78.4	33.0	28.7	6.2	7.3	2.2	0.3	0.2	0.4
5-10	693.5	228.4	253.0	70.5	96.2	26.1	9.4	4.4	5.6
Over 10	272.3	98.4	100.7	48.1	15.1	8.2	0.4	0.9	0.5
Not stated	5.4	1.0	1.3	2.0		1.1	*	*	*
Total[17]	1,122.9	384.7	409.5	130.9	132.9	41.5	10.6	5.8	7.0

Excess of Realized Gain over Loss

YEARS HELD	TOTAL[1]	Under 5	5-25	25-50	50-100	100-300	300-500	500-1,000	1,000 & over
1 or less	516.1	95.1	221.1	95.3	61.0	33.4	4.8	5.6	-0.1
1- 2	211.5	29.4	87.6	41.4	32.6	14.6	2.6	2.9	0.3
2- 5	299.5	35.9	117.7	52.4	49.6	27.9	5.0	8.1	3.0
5-10	-506.5	-195.7	-180.9	-44.7	-69.6	-3.2	-6.8	-0.7	-4.8
Over 10	136.2	-42.7	29.1	-7.6	29.7	49.7	15.6	13.7	48.7
Not stated	4.4	-0.3	1.7	-1.5	0.2	2.7	0.4	0.6	0.6
Total	661.3	-78.2	276.4	135.3	103.5	125.0	21.5	30.2	47.7

RETURNS WITH STATUTORY NET CAPITAL GAINS[15]

Realized Net Capital Gain[6]

YEARS HELD	TOTAL[1]	Under 5	5-25	25-50	50-100	100-300	300-500	500-1,000	1,000 & over
1 or less	522.9	100.7	226.0	94.6	57.0	34.2	4.7	5.5	0.3
1- 2	207.4	33.0	86.2	40.2	29.2	14.0	2.0	2.7	0.2
2- 5	341.8	60.6	132.3	54.3	51.6	27.7	4.9	7.3	3.0
5-10	179.5	31.5	67.8	25.4	26.0	21.8	2.6	3.6	0.8
Over 10	378.2	51.4	119.7	36.3	38.0	56.0	14.6	13.6	48.6
Not stated	9.5	0.5	2.9	0.4	0.2	3.8	0.4	0.6	0.6
Total[17]	1,639.3	277.6	634.9	251.2	201.9	157.5	29.2	33.4	53.5

Realized Net Capital Loss[6]

YEARS HELD	TOTAL[1]	Under 5	5-25	25-50	50-100	100-300	300-500	500-1,000	1,000 & over
1 or less	10.9	1.5	2.9	1.0	3.3	1.6	0.1	0.1	0.4
1- 2	6.9	1.5	3.5	0.5	0.4	0.8	0.2	*	
2- 5	22.9	5.8	8.5	2.4	4.9	0.9	0.2	*	0.2
5-10	169.9	38.3	64.8	25.4	24.7	12.8	2.4	1.2	0.3
Over 10	49.7	10.4	15.6	10.1	10.3	3.0	0.1	0.2	*
Not stated	1.5	0.5	0.8	*		0.1	*		
Total[17]	261.7	57.9	96.2	39.5	43.5	19.3	2.9	1.5	1.0

YEARS HELD	TOTAL[1]	Under 5	5-25	25-50	50-100	100-300	300-500	500-1,000	1,000 & over

1936

Excess of Realized Gain over Loss

YEARS HELD	TOTAL[1]	Under 5	5-25	25-50	50-100	100-300	300-500	500-1,000	1,000 & over
1 or less	512.0	99.2	223.1	93.6	53.7	32.6	4.6	5.4	−0.1
1- 2	200.5	31.5	82.7	39.7	28.8	13.2	1.8	2.7	0.2
2- 5	318.9	54.8	123.9	51.8	46.7	26.8	4.7	7.3	2.8
5-10	9.6	−6.8	3.0	*	1.3	9.0	0.2	2.5	0.5
Over 10	328.5	41.0	104.1	26.2	27.7	53.0	14.5	13.4	48.6
Not stated	8.0	*	2.0	0.4	0.2	3.7	0.4	0.6	0.6
Total	1,377.6	219.7	538.8	211.7	158.5	138.2	26.3	31.9	52.5

RETURNS WITH STATUTORY NET CAPITAL LOSSES[16]
Realized Net Capital Gain[6]

YEARS HELD	TOTAL[1]	Under 5	5-25	25-50	50-100	100-300	300-500	500-1,000	1,000 & over
1 or less	46.1	10.5	12.2	3.6	17.3	2.0	0.2	0.3	0.1
1- 2	24.4	4.4	10.0	2.5	4.4	1.7	1.0	0.3	0.2
2- 5	36.1	8.4	14.0	4.3	5.2	2.4	0.4	0.9	0.4
5-10	7.5	1.2	4.3	0.3	0.5	1.1	*	0.1	
Over 10	30.2	4.2	10.1	4.2	6.8	1.9	1.4	1.0	0.6
Not stated	0.3	0.2	0.1			*		*	
Total[17]	144.7	28.9	50.8	14.9	34.3	9.0	2.9	2.6	1.2

Realized Net Capital Loss[6]

YEARS HELD	TOTAL[1]	Under 5	5-25	25-50	50-100	100-300	300-500	500-1,000	1,000 & over
1 or less	42.0	14.6	14.3	1.9	10.0	1.2	*	*	*
1- 2	13.5	6.4	5.1	0.8	0.7	0.3	0.1	*	*
2- 5	55.5	27.3	20.1	3.8	2.4	1.3	0.2	0.2	0.2
5-10	523.6	190.0	188.2	45.1	71.5	13.3	7.0	3.3	5.3
Over 10	222.6	88.0	85.1	38.0	4.8	5.3	0.2	0.7	0.5
Not stated	4.0	0.6	0.5	2.0		0.9	*	*	*
Total[17]	861.2	326.8	313.3	91.5	89.4	22.2	7.6	4.3	6.0

Excess of Realized Gain over Loss

YEARS HELD	TOTAL[1]	Under 5	5-25	25-50	50-100	100-300	300-500	500-1,000	1,000 & over
1 or less	4.1	−4.1	−2.0	1.7	7.3	0.8	0.1	0.3	0.1
1- 2	11.0	−2.0	4.9	1.7	3.7	1.4	0.8	0.3	0.2
2- 5	−19.5	−18.9	−6.1	0.5	2.8	1.2	0.2	0.7	0.2
5-10	−516.1	−188.8	−183.9	−44.7	−70.9	−12.2	−7.0	−3.2	−5.3
Over 10	−192.4	−83.8	−75.0	−33.8	2.0	−3.4	1.1	0.3	0.1
Not stated	−3.6	−0.4	−0.4	−2.0		−0.9	*	*	*
Total	−716.4	−297.9	−262.5	−76.5	−55.0	−13.2	−4.7	−1.7	−4.9

1937

RETURNS WITH STATUTORY NET CAPITAL GAINS OR LOSSES[15,16]
Realized Net Capital Gain[6]

YEARS HELD	TOTAL[1]	Under 5	5-25	25-50	50-100	100-300	300-500	500-1,000	1,000 & over
1 or less	151.2	45.9	68.6	17.1	11.6	4.5	2.0	0.2	1.1
1- 2	154.2	42.2	66.9	22.4	13.5	6.7	1.5	0.5	0.6
2- 5	342.2	85.7	139.6	49.7	35.8	19.7	5.7	1.8	4.2
5-10	211.5	44.5	75.9	31.5	24.4	22.2	7.0	4.6	1.5
Over 10	373.2	58.9	108.2	49.3	52.1	63.5	21.7	7.3	12.3
Not stated	18.5	5.0	7.8	2.0	1.2	2.2	0.4	*	*
Total[17]	1,250.8	282.2	467.0	171.9	138.5	118.8	38.1	14.4	19.7

Realized Net Capital Loss[6]

YEARS HELD	TOTAL[1]	Under 5	5-25	25-50	50-100	100-300	300-500	500-1,000	1,000 & over
1 or less	407.6	136.3	160.7	48.6	34.0	20.7	3.8	1.9	1.6
1- 2	106.9	33.9	42.3	13.4	10.0	4.8	1.3	1.0	0.1
2- 5	59.2	20.9	23.3	5.8	4.5	2.9	1.2	0.4	0.3
5-10	379.0	138.4	155.2	39.7	23.0	13.6	1.6	5.2	2.3
Over 10	201.8	76.6	84.0	19.3	12.2	6.1	0.8	0.8	2.2
Not stated	20.5	8.7	8.8	2.0	0.8	0.2	0.1	0.1	*
Total[17]	1,175.1	414.8	474.1	128.7	84.6	48.4	8.8	9.2	6.5

Excess of Realized Gain over Loss

YEARS HELD	TOTAL[1]	Under 5	5-25	25-50	50-100	100-300	300-500	500-1,000	1,000 & over
1 or less	−256.4	−90.4	−91.9	−31.5	−22.3	−16.2	−1.9	−1.7	−0.4
1- 2	47.3	8.3	24.5	9.0	3.5	1.9	0.2	−0.5	0.5
2- 5	283.0	64.9	116.3	43.9	31.3	16.8	4.4	1.4	4.0
5-10	−167.5	−93.9	−79.1	−8.2	1.4	8.6	5.4	−0.6	−0.9
Over 10	171.3	−17.6	24.2	29.8	39.8	57.4	20.9	6.5	10.2
Not stated	−2.0	−3.7	−1.2		0.3	2.0	0.3	−0.1	*
Total	75.6	−132.6	−7.1	43.2	54.0	70.4	29.3	5.2	13.2

RETURNS WITH STATUTORY NET CAPITAL GAINS[15]
Realized Net Capital Gain[6]

YEARS HELD	TOTAL[1]	Under 5	5-25	25-50	50-100	100-300	300-500	500-1,000	1,000 & over
1 or less	132.1	39.6	61.4	14.6	9.6	3.7	1.9	0.1	1.1
1- 2	107.9	28.0	48.9	15.4	8.9	4.3	1.3	0.4	0.6
2- 5	228.7	56.0	99.1	31.7	22.1	10.7	4.1	1.0	4.0
5-10	168.6	34.1	62.4	24.4	19.0	17.2	6.0	4.1	1.5
Over 10	301.7	45.8	88.0	39.4	39.3	55.5	18.8	5.3	9.5
Not stated	17.9	4.8	7.6	1.8	1.1	2.2	0.4		*
Total[17]	956.9	208.3	367.4	127.3	100.1	93.5	32.5	11.1	16.6

YEARS HELD	TOTAL[1]	Under 5	5- 25	25- 50	50- 100	100- 300	300- 500	500- 1,000	1,000 & over

1937

Realized Net Capital Loss[6]

YEARS HELD	TOTAL[1]	Under 5	5- 25	25- 50	50- 100	100- 300	300- 500	500- 1,000	1,000 & over
1 or less	57.5	9.8	20.5	9.3	7.7	7.2	2.0	0.5	0.5
1- 2	16.4	2.9	6.1	2.7	2.6	1.1	0.5	0.4	0.1
2- 5	6.8	1.5	2.7	1.1	0.8	0.4	0.1	0.1	*
5-10	40.4	10.0	16.6	5.7	3.4	3.9	0.5	0.2	0.1
Over 10	16.1	4.0	7.2	2.0	1.4	0.9	0.1	0.5	*
Not stated	1.0	0.2	0.3	0.2	0.2	0.1		0.1	
Total[17]	138.2	28.6	53.4	20.8	16.2	13.5	3.1	1.9	0.7

Excess of Realized Gain over Loss

YEARS HELD	TOTAL[1]	Under 5	5- 25	25- 50	50- 100	100- 300	300- 500	500- 1,000	1,000 & over
1 or less	74.6	29.7	40.9	5.3	1.9	−3.5	−0.1	−0.4	0.6
1- 2	91.5	25.1	42.8	12.7	6.3	3.2	0.8		0.5
2- 5	222.0	54.4	96.4	30.6	21.3	10.3	4.0	0.9	4.0
5-10	128.1	24.0	45.8	18.7	15.6	13.3	5.5	3.9	1.4
Over 10	285.6	41.8	80.8	37.4	37.9	54.6	18.7	4.8	9.5
Not stated	16.9	4.6	7.1	1.6	0.9	2.1	0.4	−0.1	*
Total	818.6	179.7	314.0	106.5	83.9	80.0	29.4	9.2	15.9

RETURNS WITH STATUTORY NET CAPITAL LOSSES[16]

Realized Net Capital Gain[6]

YEARS HELD	TOTAL[1]	Under 5	5- 25	25- 50	50- 100	100- 300	300- 500	500- 1,000	1,000 & over
1 or less	19.1	6.3	7.3	2.5	2.1	0.8	*	0.1	*
1- 2	46.3	14.2	17.9	7.0	4.6	2.4	0.2	0.1	*
2- 5	113.5	29.8	40.5	18.0	13.7	9.0	1.5	0.7	0.3
5-10	43.0	10.4	13.6	7.1	5.4	5.0	1.0	0.5	*
Over 10	71.5	13.1	20.2	9.8	12.7	8.0	2.9	1.9	2.8
Not stated	0.6	0.1	0.2	0.2	*	*	*	*	
Total[17]	293.9	73.9	99.6	44.6	38.5	25.3	5.6	3.4	3.1

Realized Net Capital Loss[6]

YEARS HELD	TOTAL[1]	Under 5	5- 25	25- 50	50- 100	100- 300	300- 500	500- 1,000	1,000 & over
1 or less	350.0	126.5	140.1	39.3	26.3	13.5	1.9	1.4	1.0
1- 2	90.5	31.0	36.2	10.7	7.4	3.7	0.8	0.6	*
2- 5	52.4	19.3	20.6	4.7	3.7	2.6	1.2	0.2	0.3
5-10	338.6	128.4	138.5	34.0	19.6	9.7	1.1	5.0	2.3
Over 10	185.7	72.5	76.8	17.4	10.8	5.2	0.7	0.3	2.1
Not stated	19.5	8.5	8.5	1.8	0.6	0.1	*		*
Total[17]	1,036.9	386.2	420.7	107.9	68.4	34.8	5.7	7.4	5.8

Excess of Realized Gain over Loss

YEARS HELD	TOTAL[1]	Under 5	5- 25	25- 50	50- 100	100- 300	300- 500	500- 1,000	1,000 & over
1 or less	−331.0	−120.1	−132.8	−36.8	−24.2	−12.7	−1.9	−1.3	−1.0
1- 2	−44.2	−16.8	−18.3	−3.7	−2.8	−1.3	−0.6	−0.5	*
2- 5	61.0	10.4	19.9	13.3	10.0	6.4	0.3	0.5	
5-10	−295.6	−118.0	−124.9	−26.9	−14.2	−4.7	−0.1	−4.5	−2.3
Over 10	−114.3	−59.5	−56.6	−7.6	1.9	2.8	2.2	1.6	0.7
Not stated	−18.9	−8.3	−8.3	−1.6	−0.6	−0.1	*		*
Total	−743.0	−312.3	−321.1	−63.3	−29.9	−9.5	−0.1	−4.0	−2.7

1934

B PERCENTAGE DISTRIBUTION

RETURNS WITH STATUTORY NET CAPITAL GAINS OR LOSSES[15,16]

Realized Net Capital Gain[6]

YEARS HELD	TOTAL[1]	Under 5	5- 25	25- 50	50- 100	100- 300	300- 500	500- 1,000	1,000 & over
1 or less	29.4	34.1	33.5	29.2	27.0	15.9	13.9	8.1	4.3
1- 2	17.1	16.3	18.9	17.7	18.2	11.8	11.5	18.4	4.6
2- 5	11.5	14.0	12.6	11.2	11.5	6.2	4.8	5.4	0.5
5-10	10.1	10.7	9.6	8.6	10.7	10.1	15.9	13.4	14.8
Over 10	29.2	21.1	22.9	31.0	30.4	54.6	42.9	54.7	74.6
Not stated	2.7	3.8	2.5	2.2	2.2	1.5	11.1	†	1.2
Total[17]	100.0	100.0	100.0	100.0	100.0	100.0	100.0	100.0	100.0

Realized Net Capital Loss[6]

YEARS HELD	TOTAL[1]	Under 5	5- 25	25- 50	50- 100	100- 300	300- 500	500- 1,000	1,000 & over
1 or less	8.5	9.3	8.6	7.3	8.0	5.6	6.5	5.1	3.3
1- 2	4.0	3.7	4.1	4.2	4.7	4.1	3.5	1.9	3.6
2- 5	33.7	32.9	33.4	35.0	33.0	44.9	13.1	46.7	29.0
5-10	39.9	39.0	41.0	40.3	39.9	35.3	11.2	39.0	52.5
Over 10	12.0	12.7	11.2	11.3	13.3	8.6	65.6	3.4	11.7
Not stated	1.9	2.4	1.6	1.8	1.1	1.5	0.1	3.9	†
Total[17]	100.0	100.0	100.0	100.0	100.0	100.0	100.0	100.0	100.0

RETURNS WITH STATUTORY NET CAPITAL GAINS[15]

Realized Net Capital Gain[6]

YEARS HELD	TOTAL[1]	Under 5	5- 25	25- 50	50- 100	100- 300	300- 500	500- 1,000	1,000 & over
1 or less	29.4	33.3	33.8	30.3	27.6	15.9	13.1	7.1	4.8
1- 2	14.8	14.5	17.2	14.3	16.0	8.8	10.9	9.2	4.8
2- 5	12.3	14.9	13.6	12.4	11.8	6.2	4.8	6.1	0.1
5-10	10.7	11.3	10.3	9.4	11.8	8.0	16.7	16.2	13.7
Over 10	29.7	21.6	22.2	30.6	29.9	59.4	42.8	61.3	75.3
Not stated	3.2	4.4	3.0	3.0	2.8	1.7	11.8	0.1	1.4
Total[17]	100.0	100.0	100.0	100.0	100.0	100.0	100.0	100.0	100.0

* Less than $50,000.

YEARS HELD	TOTAL[1]	STATUTORY NET INCOME GROUP (thousands of dollars)[1]							
		Under 5	5- 25	25- 50	50- 100	100- 300	300- 500	500- 1,000	1,000 & over

1934

Realized Net Capital Loss[6]

YEARS HELD	TOTAL	Under 5	5-25	25-50	50-100	100-300	300-500	500-1,000	1,000 & over
1 or less	7.7	6.8	7.4	9.7	9.3	5.5	18.5	11.8	0.5
1- 2	7.8	7.6	7.7	7.3	8.2	6.3	21.6	10.2	13.7
2- 5	34.1	34.0	34.7	30.9	38.3	30.8	28.5	5.8	65.2
5-10	41.8	41.3	41.7	44.3	33.1	53.0	26.4	66.1	18.3
Over 10	8.3	9.4	8.3	7.6	11.0	4.3	5.0	6.0	2.2
Not stated	0.3	0.8	0.3	0.3	0.1	0.1		0.1	0.2
Total[17]	100.0	100.0	100.0	100.0	100.0	100.0	100.0	100.0	100.0

RETURNS WITH STATUTORY NET CAPITAL LOSSES[16]
Realized Net Capital Gain[6]

YEARS HELD	TOTAL	Under 5	5-25	25-50	50-100	100-300	300-500	500-1,000	1,000 & over
1 or less	29.3	37.5	32.3	25.5	24.8	16.0	26.3	12.4	1.7
1- 2	26.3	24.2	25.6	28.8	26.4	25.3	20.4	61.7	3.9
2- 5	8.4	9.9	8.7	7.4	10.0	6.1	5.7	2.1	2.4
5-10	7.9	7.9	7.0	5.8	6.4	19.2	3.6	0.5	21.5
Over 10	27.5	19.1	25.7	32.2	32.4	33.2	43.8	23.3	70.6
Not stated	0.6	1.5	0.6	0.3	0.1	0.3	0.2		
Total[17]	100.0	100.0	100.0	100.0	100.0	100.0	100.0	100.0	100.0

Realized Net Capital Loss[6]

YEARS HELD	TOTAL	Under 5	5-25	25-50	50-100	100-300	300-500	500-1,000	1,000 & over
1 or less	8.6	9.4	8.7	7.0	7.7	5.6	5.0	3.6	4.2
1- 2	3.7	3.6	3.8	3.8	4.0	3.4	1.2	†	0.2
2- 5	33.7	32.8	33.3	35.6	31.8	48.7	11.1	56.0	17.2
5-10	39.7	39.0	41.0	39.7	41.4	30.6	9.3	32.8	63.7
Over 10	12.3	12.8	11.5	11.8	13.8	9.8	73.5	2.9	14.8
Not stated	2.0	2.5	1.7	2.0	1.3	1.9	0.1	4.8	
Total[17]	100.0	100.0	100.0	100.0	100.0	100.0	100.0	100.0	100.0

1935

RETURNS WITH STATUTORY NET CAPITAL GAINS OR LOSSES[15,16]
Realized Net Capital Gain[6]

YEARS HELD	TOTAL	Under 5	5-25	25-50	50-100	100-300	300-500	500-1,000	1,000 & over
1 or less	30.4	35.0	33.9	33.0	29.8	20.9	12.5	3.9	3.3
1- 2	14.1	13.8	16.1	16.0	15.6	9.4	3.4	5.3	1.9
2- 5	17.3	18.8	17.4	16.9	17.9	19.3	15.8	9.5	6.6
5-10	9.7	10.7	10.2	9.2	11.1	9.3	5.8	6.1	0.9
Over 10	26.3	19.6	20.8	23.5	24.4	37.9	54.6	74.4	67.0
Not stated	2.3	2.1	1.6	1.5	1.3	3.2	7.9	0.7	20.3
Total[17]	100.0	100.0	100.0	100.0	100.0	100.0	100.0	100.0	100.0

Realized Net Capital Loss[6]

YEARS HELD	TOTAL	Under 5	5-25	25-50	50-100	100-300	300-500	500-1,000	1,000 & over
1 or less	6.3	6.6	6.4	5.1	9.2	2.2	4.4	2.6	0.3
1- 2	3.2	2.9	3.2	2.9	3.0	5.7	5.7	5.7	3.6
2- 5	20.0	20.4	20.2	20.2	18.9	11.9	50.3	9.0	25.3
5-10	51.3	49.4	51.1	46.3	56.9	70.7	34.6	72.1	62.7
Over 10	18.1	19.4	18.2	23.9	11.6	9.1	5.1	10.6	8.1
Not stated	1.0	1.2	0.8	1.7	0.4	0.5	†	0.1	†
Total[17]	100.0	100.0	100.0	100.0	100.0	100.0	100.0	100.0	100.0

RETURNS WITH STATUTORY NET CAPITAL GAINS[15]
Realized Net Capital Gain[6]

YEARS HELD	TOTAL	Under 5	5-25	25-50	50-100	100-300	300-500	500-1,000	1,000 & over
1 or less	30.6	34.8	34.7	33.9	27.9	20.4	15.5	3.9	3.6
1- 2	13.6	13.2	15.4	15.2	15.2	9.2	3.6	5.4	2.2
2- 5	17.2	18.5	17.1	16.9	18.6	19.2	19.8	8.7	6.9
5-10	10.2	11.3	10.4	9.8	12.3	9.6	2.1	6.3	1.2
Over 10	25.9	20.0	20.6	22.7	24.5	38.2	49.6	74.9	60.2
Not stated	2.5	2.2	1.8	1.6	1.5	3.5	9.4	0.7	26.0
Total[17]	100.0	100.0	100.0	100.0	100.0	100.0	100.0	100.0	100.0

Realized Net Capital Loss[6]

YEARS HELD	TOTAL	Under 5	5-25	25-50	50-100	100-300	300-500	500-1,000	1,000 & over
1 or less	5.7	4.4	5.5	6.7	8.4	4.1	6.9	3.6	1.1
1- 2	6.0	4.8	6.0	4.7	4.8	10.8	10.6	15.8	31.2
2- 5	22.5	20.5	23.9	20.4	25.7	17.2	28.2	24.9	37.2
5-10	52.0	55.3	52.4	52.7	44.2	57.5	45.1	38.1	28.3
Over 10	13.3	14.2	11.6	15.3	16.9	9.2	9.1	17.5	2.2
Not stated	0.5	0.8	0.5	0.2	0.1	1.2			
Total[17]	100.0	100.0	100.0	100.0	100.0	100.0	100.0	100.0	100.0

RETURNS WITH STATUTORY NET CAPITAL LOSSES[16]
Realized Net Capital Gain[6]

YEARS HELD	TOTAL	Under 5	5-25	25-50	50-100	100-300	300-500	500-1,000	1,000 & over
1 or less	28.2	36.8	27.3	24.7	41.4	25.9	3.1	6.0	2.3
1- 2	18.0	18.6	21.9	23.5	17.7	11.3	3.1	1.8	0.5
2- 5	17.9	21.8	20.3	17.2	13.4	20.4	4.7	30.4	5.7
5-10	6.3	5.6	7.9	4.0	3.3	6.8	17.2	2.1	
Over 10	28.9	16.2	22.2	30.4	24.3	35.2	68.8	59.3	91.5
Not stated	0.6	1.0	0.4	0.2	†	0.3	3.1	0.4	
Total[17]	100.0	100.0	100.0	100.0	100.0	100.0	100.0	100.0	100.0

		STATUTORY NET INCOME GROUP (thousands of dollars)[1]							
YEARS HELD	TOTAL[1]	Under 5	5-25	25-50	50-100	100-300	300-500	500-1,000	1,000 & over

1935

Realized Net Capital Loss[6]

1 or less	6.4	6.9	6.6	4.6	9.6	1.5	3.0	2.1	0.2
1- 2	2.7	2.7	2.7	2.4	2.2	3.7	4.5	1.6	0.7
2- 5	19.6	20.4	19.5	20.2	15.8	9.9	57.6	2.6	24.1
5-10	51.2	48.7	50.8	44.4	62.5	75.6	31.8	85.8	66.3
Over 10	19.1	20.0	19.6	26.3	9.2	9.1	3.0	7.8	8.7
Not stated	1.1	1.3	0.9	2.1	0.6	0.2	†	0.1	†
Total[17]	100.0	100.0	100.0	100.0	100.0	100.0	100.0	100.0	100.0

1936

RETURNS WITH STATUTORY NET CAPITAL GAINS OR LOSSES[15,16]
Realized Net Capital Gain[6]

1 or less	31.9	36.3	34.8	36.9	31.4	21.7	15.1	16.2	0.6
1- 2	13.0	12.2	14.0	16.1	14.2	9.4	9.2	8.4	0.6
2- 5	21.2	22.5	21.3	22.0	24.1	18.1	16.6	23.0	6.2
5-10	10.5	10.7	10.5	9.7	11.2	13.7	8.0	10.2	1.5
Over 10	22.9	18.2	18.9	15.2	19.0	34.8	49.8	40.6	90.0
Not stated	0.6	0.2	0.4	0.2	0.1	2.3	1.3	1.6	1.2
Total[17]	100.0	100.0	100.0	100.0	100.0	100.0	100.0	100.0	100.0

Realized Net Capital Loss[6]

1 or less	4.7	4.2	4.2	2.2	10.0	6.8	1.2	2.7	6.4
1- 2	1.8	2.1	2.1	1.0	0.8	2.6	2.8	1.3	0.5
2- 5	7.0	8.6	7.0	4.8	5.5	5.3	3.3	3.9	5.8
5-10	61.8	59.4	61.8	53.8	72.4	62.9	89.0	76.0	80.0
Over 10	24.2	25.6	24.6	36.7	11.4	19.8	3.3	16.1	7.2
Not stated	0.5	0.3	0.3	1.5		2.6	0.3	†	0.1
Total[17]	100.0	100.0	100.0	100.0	100.0	100.0	100.0	100.0	100.0

RETURNS WITH STATUTORY NET CAPITAL GAINS[15]
Realized Net Capital Gain[6]

1 or less	31.9	36.3	35.6	37.7	28.2	21.7	16.1	16.6	0.5
1- 2	12.7	11.9	13.6	16.0	14.4	8.9	6.7	8.1	0.3
2- 5	20.8	21.8	20.8	21.6	25.6	17.6	16.9	22.0	5.6
5-10	10.9	11.3	10.7	10.1	12.9	13.8	8.8	10.8	1.6
Over 10	23.1	18.5	18.9	14.5	18.8	35.5	50.1	40.7	90.9
Not stated	0.6	0.2	0.5	0.2	0.1	2.4	1.5	1.8	1.2
Total[17]	100.0	100.0	100.0	100.0	100.0	100.0	100.0	100.0	100.0

Realized Net Capital Loss[6]

1 or less	4.2	2.5	3.0	2.6	7.5	8.5	2.9	7.8	45.6
1- 2	2.6	2.6	3.7	1.2	0.8	4.2	5.1	1.9	
2- 5	8.8	10.0	8.9	6.2	11.3	4.8	6.1	1.2	17.0
5-10	64.9	66.1	67.4	64.2	56.8	66.5	80.5	75.6	34.8
Over 10	19.0	18.0	16.2	25.7	23.6	15.3	5.0	13.5	2.7
Not stated	0.6	0.8	0.9	0.1		0.7	0.4		
Total[17]	100.0	100.0	100.0	100.0	100.0	100.0	100.0	100.0	100.0

RETURNS WITH STATUTORY NET CAPITAL LOSSES[16]
Realized Net Capital Gain[6]

1 or less	31.9	36.2	24.2	23.8	50.4	21.9	5.3	11.0	5.2
1- 2	16.9	15.1	19.6	17.0	12.9	18.5	34.0	11.4	14.8
2- 5	24.9	29.1	27.4	29.2	15.3	26.1	13.6	36.3	31.0
5-10	5.2	4.2	8.5	1.7	1.6	12.0	0.2	2.2	
Over 10	20.9	14.7	19.9	28.2	19.8	21.2	47.0	39.0	49.0
Not stated	0.3	0.6	0.3			0.3		†	
Total[17]	100.0	100.0	100.0	100.0	100.0	100.0	100.0	100.0	100.0

Realized Net Capital Loss[6]

1 or less	4.9	4.5	4.6	2.1	11.2	5.4	0.5	0.8	†
1- 2	1.6	2.0	1.6	0.9	0.8	1.2	2.0	1.1	0.6
2- 5	6.4	8.3	6.4	4.2	2.7	5.8	2.2	4.9	4.0
5-10	60.8	58.1	60.1	49.3	80.0	59.7	92.3	76.2	87.3
Over 10	25.8	26.9	27.2	41.4	5.4	23.7	2.7	17.0	7.9
Not stated	0.5	0.2	0.2	2.1		4.2	0.3	†	†
Total[17]	100.0	100.0	100.0	100.0	100.0	100.0	100.0	100.0	100.0

1937

RETURNS WITH STATUTORY NET CAPITAL GAINS OR LOSSES[15,16]
Realized Net Capital Gain[6]

1 or less	12.1	16.3	14.7	9.9	8.4	3.8	5.3	1.5	5.6
1- 2	12.3	15.0	14.3	13.0	9.7	5.6	3.8	3.5	3.0
2- 5	27.4	30.4	29.9	28.9	25.8	16.6	14.9	12.4	21.4
5-10	16.9	15.8	16.3	18.3	17.6	18.7	18.3	32.0	7.7
Over 10	29.8	20.9	23.2	28.7	37.6	53.4	56.8	50.5	62.3
Not stated	1.5	1.8	1.7	1.2	0.8	1.9	0.9	0.1	†
Total[17]	100.0	100.0	100.0	100.0	100.0	100.0	100.0	100.0	100.0

YEARS HELD	TOTAL[1]	STATUTORY NET INCOME GROUP (thousands of dollars)[1]							
		Under 5	5-25	25-50	50-100	100-300	300-500	500-1,000	1,000 & over

1937

Realized Net Capital Loss[6]

1 or less	34.7	32.9	33.9	37.7	40.2	42.8	43.3	20.6	24.4
1- 2	9.1	8.2	8.9	10.4	11.8	10.0	15.0	10.7	1.8
2- 5	5.0	5.0	4.9	4.5	5.3	6.1	14.1	3.9	4.3
5-10	32.3	33.4	32.7	30.8	27.2	28.2	18.3	55.8	36.1
Over 10	17.2	18.5	17.7	15.0	14.4	12.6	8.6	8.3	33.3
Not stated	1.7	2.1	1.9	1.5	1.0	0.3	0.7	0.7	†
Total[17]	100.0	100.0	100.0	100.0	100.0	100.0	100.0	100.0	100.0

RETURNS WITH STATUTORY NET CAPITAL GAINS[15]

Realized Net Capital Gain[6]

1 or less	13.8	19.0	16.7	11.5	9.6	4.0	6.1	1.3	6.6
1- 2	11.3	13.5	13.3	12.1	8.9	4.6	3.9	3.7	3.5
2- 5	23.9	26.9	27.0	24.9	22.1	11.4	12.7	9.4	23.8
5-10	17.6	16.3	17.0	19.1	19.0	18.3	18.4	37.3	8.9
Over 10	31.5	22.0	24.0	31.0	39.3	59.3	57.8	48.3	57.1
Not stated	1.9	2.3	2.1	1.4	1.1	2.3	1.1		0.1
Total[17]	100.0	100.0	100.0	100.0	100.0	100.0	100.0	100.0	100.0

Realized Net Capital Loss[6]

1 or less	41.6	34.5	38.4	44.6	47.4	53.3	62.3	28.6	73.9
1- 2	11.9	10.3	11.4	12.8	16.2	8.3	15.6	23.2	9.9
2- 5	4.9	5.4	5.1	5.1	5.1	2.7	2.0	7.7	3.7
5-10	29.2	35.1	31.1	27.2	21.2	28.9	15.9	11.2	8.8
Over 10	11.6	14.0	13.5	9.5	8.8	6.3	3.4	25.9	3.7
Not stated	0.8	0.7	0.6	0.8	1.3	0.5	0.8	3.4	
Total[17]	100.0	100.0	100.0	100.0	100.0	100.0	100.0	100.0	100.0

RETURNS WITH STATUTORY NET CAPITAL LOSSES[16]

Realized Net Capital Gain[6]

1 or less	6.5	8.6	7.3	5.6	5.4	3.2	0.5	2.4	0.4
1- 2	15.8	19.2	18.0	15.6	11.8	9.4	3.3	2.8	0.5
2- 5	38.6	40.3	40.6	40.4	35.6	35.6	27.4	22.1	8.2
5-10	14.6	14.1	13.6	15.9	14.0	19.9	17.5	14.7	0.8
Over 10	24.3	17.7	20.3	22.1	33.1	31.7	51.3	57.6	90.2
Not stated	0.2	0.2	0.2	0.4	0.1	0.2	†	0.3	
Total[17]	100.0	100.0	100.0	100.0	100.0	100.0	100.0	100.0	100.0

Realized Net Capital Loss[6]

1 or less	33.8	32.7	33.3	36.4	38.5	38.7	32.8	18.6	18.1
1- 2	8.7	8.0	8.6	9.9	10.8	10.7	14.7	7.6	0.8
2- 5	5.1	5.0	4.9	4.4	5.3	7.3	20.8	3.0	4.4
5-10	32.7	33.2	32.9	31.5	28.7	27.9	19.6	67.0	39.5
Over 10	17.9	18.8	18.2	16.1	15.8	15.0	11.4	3.8	37.1
Not stated	1.9	2.2	2.0	1.7	0.9	0.3	0.7		†
Total[17]	100.0	100.0	100.0	100.0	100.0	100.0	100.0	100.0	100.0

Based on Sources 1, 2 and 3. † Less than 0.05 percent.
For numbered notes see pp. 362-6.

Table 19

Net Capital Gains from Assets Held Longer than 10 years[6] as Percentages of Total:[17] Returns with Statutory Net Capital Gains or Losses by Statutory Net Income Groups, 1934-1937

Statutory Net Income Group ($000)[1]	1934	1935	1936	1937	1934-37
Total[1]	29.2	26.3	22.9	29.8	26.3
Under 5	21.1	19.6	18.2	20.9	19.7
5- 25	22.9	20.8	18.9	23.2	20.9
25- 50	31.0	23.5	15.2	28.7	22.3
50- 100	30.4	24.4	19.0	37.6	26.0
100- 300	54.6	37.9	34.8	53.4	43.0
300- 500	42.9	54.6	49.8	56.8	53.1
500-1,000	54.7	74.4	40.6	50.5	56.0
1,000 & over	74.6	67.0	90.0	62.3	78.8

Based on Sources 1, 2, and 3. For numbered notes see pp. 362-6.

Table 20

Total Realized and Statutory Net Capital Gains and Losses, 1917-1946 Returns with Statutory Net Incomes[1] (millions of dollars)

	NET CAPITAL GAINS				NET CAPITAL LOSSES			
	Stat. long term seg. at 12½%	Other stat.	Total statutory	Total realized	Stat. long term seg. at 12½%	Other stat.	Total statutory	Total realized
1917-21								
1917[2]			318.2	318.2			n.a.	70.0
1918[2]			291.2	291.2			n.a.	359.3
1919[2]			999.4	999.4			n.a.	736.6
1920[2]			1,020.5	1,020.5			n.a.	1,037.0
1921[2]			462.9	462.9			n.a.	1,102.0
1922-33								
1922[2]	249.2	742.1	991.4	991.4			n.a.	759.6
1923[2]	305.4	863.1	1,168.5	1,168.5			n.a.	976.8
1924[2]	389.1	1,124.6	1,513.7	1,513.7	72.3	n.a.	n.a.	476.8
1925[2]	940.6	1,991.7	2,932.2	2,932.2	61.3	n.a.	n.a.	359.7
1926	912.9	1,465.6	2,378.5	2,378.5	34.6	178.2	212.8	212.8
1927	1,081.2	1,813.4	2,894.6	2,894.6	48.2	227.9	276.1	276.1
1928	1,879.8	2,928.1	4,807.9	4,807.9	41.0	171.7	212.8	212.8
1929[3]	2,346.7	2,335.9	4,682.6	4,682.6	43.0	994.7	1,037.7	1,037.7
1930[3]	556.4	636.7	1,193.1	1,193.1	80.9	1,232.8	1,313.7	1,313.7
1931[3]	169.9	301.7	471.6	471.6	239.9	1,160.8	1,400.6	1,400.6[4]
1932[3]	50.1	112.8	162.9	162.9	832.4	375.4	1,207.8	1,814.6[4]
1933[3]	133.6	419.6	553.2	553.2	553.8	365.8	919.6	1,207.5[4]
1934-37								
1934			211.3	312.7[8]			183.8	772.0[8]
1935			509.7	730.7[8]			145.7	693.1[8]
1936			973.8	1,377.6[8]			129.7	716.4[8]
1937			434.1	818.6[8]			264.2	743.0[8]

Based on Sources 1, 2, and 3. For numbered notes see pp. 362.

Statutory gains and losses based on Source 1. For total realized gains and losses see Table 8, source note.

n.a.: not available.

1938–41

Year	Stat. long term	Stat. short term loss after offsetting loss carryover	Loss carryover	Gain from depr. assets	Stat. incl. depr. assets but excl. loss carryover	Stat. capital loss incl. loss carryover	Stat. long term	Loss from depr. assets	Stat. incl. depr. assets	Stat. incl. depr. assets
1938	324.8	152.1		22.6	499.5[18]	820.4[7]	395.8	21.8	417.6[18]	789.6[7]
1939	229.5	168.4	21.2	28.5	447.6[18]	673.4[7]	316.9	27.3	344.3[18]	642.2[7]
1940	271.4	122.4	5.0	41.4	440.2[18]	707.6[7]	386.2	38.1	424.3[18]	787.3[7]
1941	369.4	136.1	4.0	68.3	577.8[18]	942.2[7]	702.3	61.8	764.1[18]	1,424.2[7]

1942–46

Year	Stat. capital gain after offsetting loss carryover	Loss carryover	Gain from depr. assets	Stat. incl. depr. assets but excl. loss carryover	Stat. capital loss incl. loss carryover	Stat. capital loss incl. loss carryover over	Loss carryover over	Loss from depr. assets	Stat. incl. depr. assets	Stat. incl. depr. assets
1942[18]	361.9	0.8[a]	62.6	425.3[18]	751.1[18]	244.4	2.0[a]	82.9	[18]	1,052.2[8]
1943[18]	882.4	18.9[a]	77.7	979.0[18]	1,752.3[18]	192.6	144.8[a]	75.1	[18]	631.7[8]
1944[18]	1,223.0	13.6[a]	65.6	1,302.2[18]	2,431.1[18]	215.0	192.9[a]	73.8	[18]	774.8[8]
1945[18]	2,475.5	32.1[a]	65.1	2,572.7[18]	4,808.9[18]	183.4	253.7[a]	70.8	[18]	518.7[8]
1946[18]	3,550.9	24.6[a]	123.3	3,698.9[18]	7,210.8[18]	235.5	281.3[a]	68.1	[18]	545.1[8]

[a] Loss carryovers as reported on current year tax returns. In 1942 represents amounts of short term net loss disallowed in 1941; the amounts that could be carried over in 1942 were limited both by the net income reported in 1941 and by the net short term gain in 1942. Loss carryovers reported in 1943-46, on the other hand, represent all net losses, long and short, that were disallowed beginning in 1942. In these years the full amount of loss carryover that filers reported on their returns is included in the 'loss carryover' series in our tables (and in Source 1) even though, as a result of the statutory loss limitation, only a portion of the carryover actually increased statutory net capital loss. In other words, carryovers on returns with statutory net capital losses each year 1942-46 overstate the deductions from current year income, i.e., overstate the carryovers included in the column headed 'Stat. capital loss incl. loss carryover'. Since carryovers reported in 1943-46 were less severely limited than in 1942, the overstatement was greater in the 4 later years; see Appendix One, Section D5.

For numbered notes see pp. 362-6.

Table 21

Disallowed, Statutory, and Total Realized Net Capital Losses by Statutory Net Income Groups, 1932 and 1933

	RETURNS WITH STAT. NET INCOMES	STATUTORY NET INCOME GROUP (thousands of dollars)[1]						RETURNS WITH STAT. NET DEFICITS	ALL RETURNS
		Under 5	5-25	25-50	50-100	100-300	300 & over		
			NET LOSS (millions of dollars)						
1932									
Not seg. at 12½%	982.3	363.1	445.5	95.8	54.4	14.3	9.1	1,051.0	2,033.3
Disallowed short term	606.8	162.3	289.3	88.0	49.6	10.8	6.8	215.8	822.6
Statutory	375.4	200.8	156.2	7.9	4.8	3.5	2.3	835.3	1,210.7
Segregated at 12½%	832.4		116.1	241.1	219.1	169.9	86.2		832.4
Total net loss	1,814.6	363.1	561.6	336.9	273.4	184.3	95.3	1,051.0	2,865.6
1933									
Not seg. at 12½%	653.7	278.3	218.4	92.5	48.2	15.0	1.3	816.5	1,470.2
Disallowed short term	287.9	65.5	79.6	85.6	45.0	12.1	0.1	42.6	330.5
Statutory	365.8	212.8	138.7	6.9	3.2	2.9	1.3	773.9	1,139.7
Segregated at 12½%	553.8		69.4	169.8	151.4	107.8	55.4		553.8
Total net loss	1,207.5	278.3	287.8	262.3	199.6	122.8	56.7	816.5	2,024.0
			PERCENTAGE DISTRIBUTION						
1932									
Disallowed short term	100.0	26.7	47.7	14.5	8.2	1.8	1.1		
Stat. not seg. at 12½%	100.0	53.5	41.6	2.1	1.3	0.9	0.7		
Segregated at 12½%	100.0		13.9	29.0	26.3	20.4	10.3		
1933									
Disallowed short term	100.0	22.7	27.7	29.7	15.6	4.2	†		
Stat. not seg. at 12½%	100.0	58.2	37.9	1.9	0.9	0.8	0.4		
Segregated at 12½%	100.0		12.5	30.7	27.3	19.5	10.0		

Based on Source 1; disallowed short term net loss, on Source 5.
For method of estimating disallowed net loss see Tables 48-9 and Appendix One, Section D2.

† Less than 0.05 percent.
For numbered notes see pp. 362-6.

Table 22

Disallowed, Statutory, and Total Realized Net Capital Gains and Losses
Annual Totals, 1934-1946 (dollar figures in millions)

A 1 9 3 4 - 1 9 3 7

	1934	1935	1936	1937
RETURNS WITH STATUTORY NET CAPITAL GAINS				
Returns with stat. net incomes[1]				
Realized gain[6]	312.7	730.7	1,377.6	818.6
Statutory gain	211.3	509.7	973.8	434.1
Excluded gain	101.4	221.0	403.9	384.5
% excluded	32.4	30.2	29.3	47.0
Returns with stat. net deficits[1]				
Realized gain[6]	27.4	33.4	39.2	29.3
Statutory gain	17.7	20.4	22.5	16.9
Excluded gain	9.6	13.0	16.7	12.4
% excluded	35.1	38.8	42.5	42.2
Returns with stat. net incomes or deficits				
Realized gain[6]	340.1	764.0	1,416.8	847.9
Statutory gain	229.1	530.1	996.3	451.1
Excluded gain	111.0	233.9	420.5	396.9
% excluded	32.6	30.6	29.7	46.8
RETURNS WITH STATUTORY NET CAPITAL LOSSES				
Returns with stat. net incomes[1]				
Realized loss[6]	772.0	693.1	716.4	743.0
Statutory loss	183.8	145.7	129.7	264.2
Disallowed loss	588.3	547.4	586.6	478.8
% disallowed	76.2	79.0	81.9	64.4
Returns with stat. net deficits[1]				
Realized loss[6]	197.6	159.6	111.7	209.8
Statutory loss	27.3	21.6	14.8	28.7
Disallowed loss	170.3	138.0	96.9	181.1
% disallowed	86.2	86.5	86.7	86.3
Returns with stat. net incomes or deficits				
Realized loss[6]	969.6	852.8	828.1	952.8
Statutory loss	211.0	167.3	144.6	292.9
Disallowed loss	758.6	685.4	683.5	659.9
% disallowed	78.2	80.4	82.5	69.3
RETURNS WITH STATUTORY NET CAPITAL GAINS OR LOSSES				
Returns with stat. net incomes[1]				
Realized gain or loss[6]	−459.3	37.5	661.3	75.6
Statutory gain or loss	27.6	364.0	844.1	169.9
Excluded gain or loss	−486.9	−326.4	−182.8	−94.3
% excluded	106.0	−869.5	−27.6	−124.6

413

A 1934-1937 (concl.)

	1934	1935	1936	1937
Returns with stat. net deficits[1]				
Realized gain or loss[6]	−170.2	−126.3	−72.6	−180.5
Statutory gain or loss	−9.5	−1.2	7.7	−11.7
Excluded gain or loss	−160.7	−125.1	−80.2	−168.8
% excluded	94.4	99.0	110.5	93.5
Returns with stat. net incomes or deficits				
Realized gain or loss[6]	−629.6	−88.7	588.7	−104.9
Statutory gain or loss	18.0	362.8	851.7	158.2
Excluded gain or loss	−647.6	−451.5	−263.0	−263.0
% excluded	102.9	508.9	−44.7	250.8

B 1938-1941

	1938	1939	1940	1941
RETURNS WITH STATUTORY NET CAPITAL GAINS				
Returns with stat. net incomes[1]				
Realized gain[7]	820.4	673.4	707.6	942.2
Statutory gain[18]	499.5	447.6	440.2	577.8
Excluded gain	320.9	225.8	267.3	364.4
% excluded	39.1	33.5	37.8	38.7
Returns with stat. net deficits[1]				
Realized gain[7]	22.1	20.6	16.5	15.5
Statutory gain[18]	15.8	14.4	11.9	11.3
Excluded gain	6.3	6.2	4.6	4.3
% excluded	28.7	30.1	27.8	27.5
Returns with stat. net incomes or deficits				
Realized gain[7]	842.5	694.0	724.0	957.7
Statutory gain[18]	515.3	462.0	452.1	589.0
Excluded gain	327.2	232.0	271.9	368.7
% excluded	38.8	33.4	37.6	38.5
RETURNS WITH STATUTORY NET CAPITAL LOSSES				
Returns with stat. net incomes[1]				
Realized loss[7]	789.6	642.2	787.3	1,424.2
Statutory loss[18]	417.6	344.3	424.3	764.1
Disallowed loss	372.0	297.9	363.0	660.1
% disallowed	47.1	46.4	46.1	46.3
Returns with stat. net deficits[1]				
Realized loss[7]	394.3	320.8	373.6	429.4
Statutory loss[18]	213.6	178.8	208.6	238.4
Disallowed loss	180.7	142.0	165.0	191.0
% disallowed	45.8	44.3	44.2	44.5
Returns with stat. net incomes or deficits				
Realized loss[7]	1,184.0	963.0	1,161.0	1,853.6
Statutory loss[18]	631.2	523.1	632.9	1,002.5
Disallowed loss	552.7	439.9	528.0	851.1
% disallowed	46.7	45.7	45.5	45.9

	1938	1939	1940	1941

RETURNS WITH STATUTORY NET CAPITAL GAINS OR LOSSES

Returns with stat. net incomes[1]

	1938	1939	1940	1941
Realized gain or loss[7]	30.8	31.2	−79.7	−482.0
Statutory gain or loss[18]	81.9	103.3	15.9	−186.3
Excluded gain or loss	−51.1	−72.1	−95.7	−295.7
% excluded	−166.1	−231.1	120.0	61.4

Returns with stat. net deficits[1]

Realized gain or loss[7]	−372.2	−300.2	−357.2	−413.9
Statutory gain or loss[18]	−197.9	−164.4	−196.7	−227.7
Excluded gain or loss	−174.3	−135.8	−160.4	−186.7
% excluded	46.8	77.3	58.6	45.1

Returns with stat. net incomes or deficits

Realized gain or loss[7]	−341.5	−269.0	−436.9	−895.9
Statutory gain or loss[18]	−116.0	−61.0	−180.8	−413.5
Excluded gain or loss	−225.5	−207.9	−256.1	−482.4
% excluded	66.0	45.2	44.9	53.8

C   1 9 4 2 - 1 9 4 6

	1942	1943	1944	1945	1946

RETURNS WITH STATUTORY NET CAPITAL GAINS

Returns with stat. net incomes[1]

	1942	1943	1944	1945	1946
Realized gain[8]	751.1	1,752.3	2,431.1	4,808.9	7,210.8
Statutory gain[18]	425.3	979.0	1,302.2	2,572.7	3,698.9
Excluded gain	325.8	773.3	1,128.9	2,236.2	3,511.9
% excluded	43.4	44.1	46.4	46.5	48.7

Returns with stat. net deficits[1]

Realized gain[8]	13.9	20.1	30.8	67.1	44.6
Statutory gain[18]	7.6	11.1	16.9	36.5	23.6
Excluded gain	6.3	9.1	13.8	30.6	20.9
% excluded	45.2	45.2	44.9	45.6	46.9

Returns with stat. net incomes or deficits

Realized gain[8]	765.0	1,772.4	2,461.9	4,876.0	7,255.4
Statutory gain[18]	432.9	990.0	1,319.1	2,609.2	3,722.5
Excluded gain	332.1	782.4	1,142.7	2,266.8	3,532.9
% excluded	43.4	44.1	46.4	46.5	48.7

Statutory amounts based on Source 1; realized amounts for 1934-37 based on Sources 1, 2, and 3, for 1938-41 and 1942-46 estimated from Source 1 as described in Appendix One, Sections D4 and 5.

For numbered notes see pp. 362-6.

Table 23

Disallowed, Statutory, and Total Realized Net Capital Gains and Losses by Statutory Net Income Groups, 1934-1946
(dollar figures in millions)

			STATUTORY NET INCOME GROUP (thousands of dollars)[1]						
	TOTAL[1]	Under 5	5- 25	25- 50	50- 100	100- 300	300- 500	500- 1,000	1,000 & over
			A 1934-1937						
1934	*Returns with Statutory Net Capital Gains*								
Real. gain[6]	312.7	70.5	120.7	43.8	28.6	27.6	6.3	8.0	7.2
Stat. gain	211.3	51.1	88.5	29.7	19.1	13.5	3.5	3.3	2.5
Excl. gain	101.4	19.4	32.2	14.1	9.5	14.1	2.8	4.6	4.7
% excluded	32.4	27.5	26.6	32.1	33.3	51.0	44.7	58.0	65.0
	Returns with Statutory Net Capital Losses								
Real. loss[6]	772.0	322.4	327.0	69.4	29.6	16.1	3.1	2.6	1.9
Stat. loss	183.8	92.8	76.2	10.1	3.4	1.1	0.1	0.1	*
Disal. loss	588.3	229.6	250.8	59.3	26.2	15.0	3.0	2.5	1.8
% disallowed	76.2	71.2	76.7	85.5	88.5	93.3	97.3	97.4	97.5
	Returns with Statutory Net Capital Gains or Losses								
Real. gain or loss[6]	−459.3	−251.9	−206.3	−25.5	−1.1	11.6	3.2	5.4	5.3
Stat. gain or loss	27.6	−41.7	12.3	19.7	15.7	12.5	3.4	3.3	2.5
Excl. gain or loss	−486.9	−210.2	−218.6	−45.2	−16.7	−0.9	−0.2	2.1	2.8
% excluded	106.0	83.4	106.0	177.0	1,582.2	−7.8	−6.3	39.2	53.5
	PERCENTAGE DISTRIBUTION								
	Returns with Statutory Net Capital Gains								
Real. gain[6]	100.0	22.5	38.6	14.0	9.1	8.8	2.0	2.6	2.3
Stat. gain	100.0	24.2	41.9	14.1	9.0	6.4	1.6	1.6	1.2
Excl. gain	100.0	19.1	31.7	13.9	9.4	13.9	2.8	4.6	4.6
	Returns with Statutory Net Capital Losses								
Real. loss[6]	100.0	41.8	42.3	9.0	3.8	2.1	0.4	0.3	0.2
Stat. loss	100.0	50.5	41.5	5.5	1.9	0.6	†	†	†
Disal. loss	100.0	39.0	42.6	10.1	4.5	2.6	0.5	0.4	0.3
1935	*Returns with Statutory Net Capital Gains*								
Real. gain[6]	730.7	147.9	284.1	104.5	76.9	51.5	16.5	32.9	16.4
Stat. gain	509.7	109.8	208.8	75.9	53.6	30.8	9.2	12.7	8.8
Excl. gain	221.0	38.1	75.2	28.5	23.3	20.7	7.3	20.2	7.6
% excluded	30.2	25.8	26.5	27.3	30.3	40.1	44.2	61.3	46.2
	Returns with Statutory Net Capital Losses								
Real. loss[6]	693.1	299.6	265.9	64.7	34.1	26.1	0.3	2.0	0.5
Stat. loss	145.7	76.7	56.9	8.0	3.0	1.0	0.1	0.1	*
Disal. loss	547.4	222.8	209.1	56.7	31.1	25.1	0.2	1.9	0.5
% disallowed	79.0	74.4	78.6	87.7	91.2	96.3	60.6	97.5	96.7
	Returns with Statutory Net Capital Gains or Losses								
Real. gain or loss[6]	37.5	−151.6	18.1	39.8	42.9	25.4	16.2	31.0	15.8
Stat. gain or loss	364.0	33.0	152.0	68.0	50.6	29.9	9.1	12.7	8.8
Excl. gain or loss	−326.4	−184.7	−133.8	−28.2	−7.7	−4.4	7.1	18.3	7.0
% excluded	−869.5	121.8	−738.6	−70.9	−18.1	−17.5	43.9	59.0	44.5
	PERCENTAGE DISTRIBUTION								
	Returns with Statutory Net Capital Gains								
Real. gain[6]	100.0	20.2	38.9	14.3	10.5	7.0	2.3	4.5	2.2
Stat. gain	100.0	21.5	41.0	14.9	10.5	6.1	1.8	2.5	1.7
Excl. gain	100.0	17.3	34.1	12.9	10.6	9.4	3.3	9.1	3.4
	Returns with Statutory Net Capital Losses								
Real. loss[6]	100.0	43.2	38.4	9.3	4.9	3.8	†	0.3	0.1
Stat. loss	100.0	52.7	39.0	5.5	2.0	0.7	0.1	†	†
Disal. loss	100.0	40.7	38.2	10.4	5.7	4.6	†	0.3	0.1
1936	*Returns with Statutory Net Capital Gains*								
Real. gain[6]	1,377.6	219.7	538.8	211.7	158.5	138.2	26.3	31.9	52.5
Stat. gain	973.8	166.9	396.9	164.1	115.1	82.4	13.8	17.6	17.1
Excl. gain	403.9	52.8	141.9	47.7	43.4	55.9	12.4	14.3	35.5
% excluded	29.3	24.0	26.3	22.5	27.4	40.4	47.4	44.8	67.5

416

	TOTAL[1]	Under 5	5-25	25-50	50-100	100-300	300-500	500-1,000	1,000 & over
Returns with Statutory Net Capital Losses									
Real. loss[6]	716.4	297.9	262.5	76.5	55.0	13.2	4.7	1.7	4.9
Stat. loss	129.7	66.9	50.3	7.8	3.3	1.2	0.1	0.1	*
Disal. loss	586.6	231.0	212.1	68.7	51.7	12.0	4.6	1.6	4.8
% disallowed	81.9	77.6	80.8	89.8	94.0	90.9	97.7	95.2	99.3
Returns with Statutory Net Capital Gains or Losses									
Real. gain or loss[6]	661.3	−78.2	276.4	135.3	103.5	125.0	21.5	30.2	47.7
Stat. gain or loss	844.1	100.0	346.6	156.3	111.8	81.2	13.7	17.5	17.0
Excl. gain or loss	−182.8	−178.2	−70.2	−21.0	−8.3	43.8	7.8	12.7	30.6
% excluded	−27.6	227.8	−25.4	−15.5	−8.0	35.1	36.3	42.0	64.3
PERCENTAGE DISTRIBUTION									
Returns with Statutory Net Capital Gains									
Real. gain[6]	100.0	15.9	39.1	15.4	11.5	10.0	1.9	2.3	3.8
Stat. gain	100.0	17.1	40.8	16.8	11.8	8.5	1.4	1.8	1.8
Excl. gain	100.0	13.1	35.1	11.8	10.7	13.8	3.1	3.5	8.8
Returns with Statutory Net Capital Losses									
Real. loss[6]	100.0	41.6	36.6	10.7	7.7	1.8	0.7	0.2	0.7
Stat. loss	100.0	51.6	38.8	6.0	2.5	0.9	0.1	0.1	†
Disal. loss	100.0	39.4	36.2	11.7	8.8	2.1	0.8	0.3	0.8

1937

	TOTAL[1]	Under 5	5-25	25-50	50-100	100-300	300-500	500-1,000	1,000 & over
Returns with Statutory Net Capital Gains									
Real. gain[6]	818.6	179.7	314.0	106.5	83.9	80.0	29.4	9.2	15.9
Stat. gain	434.1	108.8	182.3	54.4	38.5	29.0	11.2	3.1	6.7
Excl. gain	384.5	70.9	131.7	52.1	45.4	50.9	18.2	6.1	9.2
% excluded	47.0	39.4	41.9	48.9	54.1	63.7	61.8	66.4	57.6
Returns with Statutory Net Capital Losses									
Real. loss[6]	743.0	312.3	321.1	63.3	29.9	9.5	0.1	4.0	2.7
Stat. loss	264.2	124.4	108.9	19.5	8.1	2.8	0.2	0.1	*
Disal. loss	478.8	187.9	212.2	43.8	21.8	6.7	−0.1	3.9	2.7
% disallowed	64.4	60.2	66.1	69.2	72.8	70.2	a	96.4	98.7
Returns with Statutory Net Capital Gains or Losses									
Real. gain or loss[6]	75.6	−132.6	−7.1	43.2	54.0	70.4	29.3	5.2	13.2
Stat. gain or loss	169.9	−15.5	73.4	34.9	30.3	26.2	11.0	2.9	6.7
Excl. gain or loss	−94.3	−117.1	−80.5	8.3	23.7	44.2	18.3	2.2	6.5
% excluded	−124.6	88.3	1,133.6	19.2	43.8	62.8	62.5	43.1	49.3
PERCENTAGE DISTRIBUTION									
Returns with Statutory Net Capital Gains									
Real. gain[6]	100.0	22.0	38.4	13.0	10.2	9.8	3.6	1.1	1.9
Stat. gain	100.0	25.1	42.0	12.5	8.9	6.7	2.6	0.7	1.6
Excl. gain	100.0	18.4	34.3	13.6	11.8	13.2	4.7	1.6	2.4
Returns with Statutory Net Capital Losses									
Real. loss[6]	100.0	42.0	43.2	8.5	4.0	1.3	†	0.5	0.4
Stat. loss	100.0	47.1	41.2	7.4	3.1	1.1	0.1	0.1	†
Disal. loss	100.0	39.3	44.3	9.2	4.5	1.4	†	0.8	0.6

a Statutory net loss exceeds realized net loss.

B 1938-1941

1938

	TOTAL[1]	Under 5	5-25	25-50	50-100	100-300	300-500	500-1,000	1,000 & over
Returns with Statutory Net Capital Gains									
Real. gain[7]	820.4	146.1	208.4	75.2	62.6	83.5	43.1	59.6	141.9
Stat. gain[18]	499.5	105.0	142.8	46.6	35.9	44.3	22.4	31.4	71.2
Excl. gain	320.9	41.0	65.7	28.6	26.7	39.2	20.7	28.3	70.7
% excluded	39.1	28.1	31.5	38.0	42.7	47.0	48.0	47.4	49.8
Returns with Statutory Net Capital Losses									
Real. loss[7]	789.6	302.5	337.6	83.6	40.5	18.4	2.2	3.5	1.3
Stat. loss[18]	417.6	161.9	177.4	43.7	21.1	9.6	1.2	1.9	0.9
Disal. long term loss	372.0	140.6	160.3	39.9	19.4	8.8	1.0	1.6	0.5
% disallowed	47.1	46.5	47.5	47.7	48.0	47.8	46.1	44.7	35.7
Returns with Statutory Net Capital Gains or Losses									
Real. gain or loss[7]	30.8	−156.4	−129.2	−8.4	22.1	65.1	40.9	56.1	140.6
Stat. gain or loss[18]	81.9	−56.8	−34.6	2.9	14.8	34.7	21.2	29.4	70.4
Excl. gain or loss	−51.1	−99.6	−94.6	−11.3	7.3	30.4	19.7	26.7	70.2
% excluded	−166.1	63.7	73.2	134.8	33.0	46.8	48.1	47.6	49.9

	TOTAL[1]	Under 5	5-25	25-50	50-100	100-300	300-500	500-1,000	1,000 & over

PERCENTAGE DISTRIBUTION

Returns with Statutory Net Capital Gains

	TOTAL[1]	Under 5	5-25	25-50	50-100	100-300	300-500	500-1,000	1,000 & over
Real. gain[7]	100.0	17.8	25.4	9.2	7.6	10.2	5.3	7.3	17.3
Stat. gain[18]	100.0	21.0	28.6	9.3	7.2	8.9	4.5	6.3	14.3
Excl. gain	100.0	12.8	20.5	8.9	8.3	12.2	6.4	8.8	22.0

Returns with Statutory Net Capital Losses

	TOTAL[1]	Under 5	5-25	25-50	50-100	100-300	300-500	500-1,000	1,000 & over
Real. loss[7]	100.0	38.3	42.8	10.6	5.1	2.3	0.3	0.4	0.2
Stat. loss[18]	100.0	38.8	42.5	10.5	5.0	2.3	0.3	0.5	0.2
Disal. long term loss	100.0	37.8	43.1	10.7	5.2	2.4	0.3	0.4	0.1

1939

Returns with Statutory Net Capital Gains

	TOTAL[1]	Under 5	5-25	25-50	50-100	100-300	300-500	500-1,000	1,000 & over
Real. gain[7]	673.4	168.5	250.9	81.0	55.1	48.4	20.9	19.2	29.2
Stat. gain[18]	447.6	120.8	176.4	53.1	33.9	27.0	11.6	10.2	14.7
Excl. gain	225.8	47.8	74.5	28.0	21.3	21.4	9.3	9.0	14.5
% excluded	33.5	28.4	29.7	34.5	38.6	44.3	44.3	46.9	49.6

Returns with Statutory Net Capital Losses

	TOTAL[1]	Under 5	5-25	25-50	50-100	100-300	300-500	500-1,000	1,000 & over
Real. loss[7]	642.2	251.8	262.0	71.0	33.2	15.4	2.1	1.4	5.4
Stat. loss[18]	344.3	137.3	139.3	37.3	17.5	8.1	1.1	0.8	2.9
Disal. long term loss	297.9	114.5	122.7	33.7	15.6	7.2	1.0	0.7	2.5
% disallowed	46.4	45.5	46.8	47.5	47.1	47.2	47.7	46.9	45.6

Returns with Statutory Net Capital Gains or Losses

	TOTAL[1]	Under 5	5-25	25-50	50-100	100-300	300-500	500-1,000	1,000 & over
Real. gain or loss[7]	31.2	−83.3	−11.1	10.1	22.0	33.0	18.8	17.8	23.9
Stat. gain or loss[18]	103.3	−16.5	37.1	15.8	16.3	18.8	10.6	9.4	11.8
Excl. gain or loss	−72.1	−66.7	−48.2	−5.7	5.7	14.2	8.3	8.3	12.1
% excluded	−231.1	80.1	435.7	57.1	25.7	43.0	44.0	46.9	50.5

PERCENTAGE DISTRIBUTION

Returns with Statutory Net Capital Gains

	TOTAL[1]	Under 5	5-25	25-50	50-100	100-300	300-500	500-1,000	1,000 & over
Real. gain[7]	100.0	25.0	37.3	12.0	8.2	7.2	3.1	2.9	4.3
Stat. gain[18]	100.0	27.0	39.4	11.9	7.6	6.0	2.6	2.3	3.3
Excl. gain	100.0	21.2	33.0	12.4	9.4	9.5	4.1	4.0	6.4

Returns with Statutory Net Capital Losses

	TOTAL[1]	Under 5	5-25	25-50	50-100	100-300	300-500	500-1,000	1,000 & over
Real. loss[7]	100.0	39.2	40.8	11.1	5.2	2.4	0.3	0.2	0.8
Stat. loss[18]	100.0	39.9	40.4	10.8	5.1	2.4	0.3	0.2	0.8
Disal. long term loss	100.0	38.4	41.2	11.3	5.2	2.4	0.3	0.2	0.8

1940

Returns with Statutory Net Capital Gains

	TOTAL[1]	Under 5	5-25	25-50	50-100	100-300	300-500	500-1,000	1,000 & over
Real. gain[7]	707.6	172.4	231.4	72.7	59.7	77.5	26.9	38.1	28.9
Stat. gain[18]	440.2	120.3	152.8	44.1	33.8	41.1	14.0	19.4	14.7
Excl. gain	267.3	52.1	78.6	28.6	25.9	36.4	12.8	18.6	14.2
% excluded	37.8	30.2	34.0	39.3	43.4	46.9	47.8	49.0	49.2

Returns with Statutory Net Capital Losses

	TOTAL[1]	Under 5	5-25	25-50	50-100	100-300	300-500	500-1,000	1,000 & over
Real. loss[7]	787.3	305.2	311.7	89.2	45.4	24.4	5.4	2.4	3.6
Stat. loss[18]	424.3	168.7	165.9	47.1	23.8	12.8	2.9	1.3	1.8
Disal. long term loss	363.0	136.6	145.8	42.2	21.5	11.6	2.5	1.1	1.7
% disallowed	46.1	44.7	46.8	47.3	47.5	47.6	46.3	45.0	48.4

Returns with Statutory Net Capital Gains or Losses

	TOTAL[1]	Under 5	5-25	25-50	50-100	100-300	300-500	500-1,000	1,000 & over
Real. gain or loss[7]	−79.7	−132.8	−80.3	−16.5	14.4	53.1	21.4	35.6	25.3
Stat. gain or loss[18]	15.9	−48.3	−13.1	−2.9	10.0	28.4	11.1	18.1	12.8
Excl. gain or loss	−95.7	−84.4	−67.2	−13.6	4.4	24.8	10.3	17.5	12.5
% excluded	120.0	63.6	83.6	82.3	30.6	46.6	48.2	49.2	49.3

PERCENTAGE DISTRIBUTION

Returns with Statutory Net Capital Gains

	TOTAL[1]	Under 5	5-25	25-50	50-100	100-300	300-500	500-1,000	1,000 & over
Real. gain[7]	100.0	24.4	32.7	10.3	8.4	11.0	3.8	5.4	4.1
Stat. gain[18]	100.0	27.3	34.7	10.0	7.7	9.3	3.2	4.4	3.3
Excl. gain	100.0	19.5	29.4	10.7	9.7	13.6	4.8	7.0	5.3

Returns with Statutory Net Capital Losses

	TOTAL[1]	Under 5	5-25	25-50	50-100	100-300	300-500	500-1,000	1,000 & over
Real. loss[7]	100.0	38.8	39.6	11.3	5.8	3.1	0.7	0.3	0.5
Stat. loss[18]	100.0	39.7	39.1	11.1	5.6	3.0	0.7	0.3	0.4
Disal. long term loss	100.0	37.6	40.2	11.6	5.9	3.2	0.7	0.3	0.5

1941

Returns with Statutory Net Capital Gains

	TOTAL[1]	Under 5	5-25	25-50	50-100	100-300	300-500	500-1,000	1,000 & over
Real. gain[7]	942.2	227.5	240.6	87.6	82.9	121.1	56.3	54.2	71.9
Stat. gain[18]	577.8	159.2	161.1	53.0	47.3	64.1	28.9	27.4	36.8
Excl. gain	364.4	68.3	79.5	34.6	35.7	57.0	27.4	26.9	35.0
% excluded	38.7	30.0	33.0	39.5	43.0	47.1	48.7	49.5	48.8

Returns with Statutory Net Capital Losses

	TOTAL[1]	Under 5	5-25	25-50	50-100	100-300	300-500	500-1,000	1,000 & over
Real. loss[7]	1,424.2	581.5	563.3	145.9	76.6	39.5	7.0	4.0	6.5
Stat. loss[18]	764.1	319.0	298.6	76.5	40.2	20.7	3.7	2.2	3.4
Disal. long term loss	660.1	262.5	264.7	69.4	36.4	18.8	3.3	1.8	3.1
% disallowed	46.3	45.1	47.0	47.6	47.6	47.7	47.7	46.0	48.1

	TOTAL[1]	Under 5	5-25	25-50	50-100	100-300	300-500	500-1,000	1,000 & over
STATUTORY NET INCOME GROUP (thousands of dollars)[1]									

Returns with Statutory Net Capital Gains or Losses

	TOTAL[1]	Under 5	5-25	25-50	50-100	100-300	300-500	500-1,000	1,000 & over
Real. gain or loss[7]	−482.0	−354.0	−322.7	−58.3	6.3	81.7	49.3	50.2	65.4
Stat. gain or loss[18]	−186.3	−159.8	−137.5	−23.5	7.1	43.5	25.2	25.2	33.5
Excl. gain or loss	−295.7	−194.2	−185.2	−34.8	−0.8	38.2	24.1	25.0	31.9
% excluded	61.4	54.9	57.4	59.7	−12.5	46.8	48.8	49.8	48.8

PERCENTAGE DISTRIBUTION

Returns with Statutory Net Capital Gains

	TOTAL[1]	Under 5	5-25	25-50	50-100	100-300	300-500	500-1,000	1,000 & over
Real. gain[7]	100.0	24.2	25.5	9.3	8.8	12.9	6.0	5.8	7.6
Stat. gain[18]	100.0	27.6	27.9	9.2	8.2	11.1	5.0	4.7	6.4
Excl. gain	100.0	18.7	21.8	9.5	9.8	15.6	7.5	7.4	9.6

Returns with Statutory Net Capital Losses

	TOTAL[1]	Under 5	5-25	25-50	50-100	100-300	300-500	500-1,000	1,000 & over
Real.loss[7]	100.0	40.8	39.5	10.2	5.4	2.8	0.5	0.3	0.5
Stat. loss[18]	100.0	41.8	39.1	10.0	5.3	2.7	0.5	0.3	0.4
Disal. long term loss	100.0	39.8	40.1	10.5	5.5	2.8	0.5	0.3	0.5

C 1942-1946

Returns with Statutory Net Capital Gains

1942

	TOTAL[1]	Under 5	5-25	25-50	50-100	100-300	300-500	500-1,000	1,000 & over
Real. gain[8]	751.1	225.0	196.2	70.9	63.4	79.9	23.9	41.4	50.4
Stat. gain[18]	425.3	138.9	114.1	38.8	33.7	41.6	12.0	21.0	25.2
Excl. gain	325.8	86.1	82.2	32.1	29.7	38.3	11.9	20.4	25.2
% excluded	43.4	38.3	41.9	45.3	46.8	47.9	49.7	49.3	50.0

PERCENTAGE DISTRIBUTION

	TOTAL[1]	Under 5	5-25	25-50	50-100	100-300	300-500	500-1,000	1,000 & over
Real. gain[8]	100.0	30.0	26.1	9.4	8.4	10.6	3.2	5.5	6.7
Stat. gain[18]	100.0	32.7	26.8	9.1	7.9	9.8	2.8	4.9	5.9
Excl. gain	100.0	26.4	25.2	9.9	9.1	11.8	3.6	6.3	7.7

1943

	TOTAL[1]	Under 5	5-25	25-50	50-100	100-300	300-500	500-1,000	1,000 & over
Real. gain[8]	1,752.3	472.8	549.0	201.2	152.4	175.8	48.2	85.2	67.8
Stat. gain[18]	979.0	282.4	315.0	109.3	79.9	91.0	24.3	42.7	34.5
Excl. gain	773.3	190.5	234.1	91.9	72.5	84.8	23.9	42.5	33.3
% excluded	44.1	40.3	42.6	45.7	47.6	48.2	49.5	49.9	49.1

PERCENTAGE DISTRIBUTION

	TOTAL[1]	Under 5	5-25	25-50	50-100	100-300	300-500	500-1,000	1,000 & over
Real. gain[8]	100.0	27.0	31.3	11.5	8.7	10.0	2.8	4.9	3.9
Stat. gain[18]	100.0	28.8	32.2	11.2	8.2	9.3	2.5	4.4	3.5
Excl. gain	100.0	24.6	30.3	11.9	9.4	11.0	3.1	5.5	4.3

1944

	TOTAL[1]	Under 5	5-25	25-50	50-100	100-300	300-500	500-1,000	1,000 & over
Real gain[8]	2,431.1	700.0	845.2	263.4	221.2	220.6	69.3	68.6	42.8
Stat. gain[18]	1,302.2	386.1	461.3	138.9	113.0	111.8	35.1	34.7	21.2
Excl. gain	1,128.9	313.8	383.9	124.4	108.2	108.8	34.2	33.9	21.6
% excluded	46.4	44.8	45.4	47.2	48.9	49.3	49.3	49.4	50.4

PERCENTAGE DISTRIBUTION

	TOTAL[1]	Under 5	5-25	25-50	50-100	100-300	300-500	500-1,000	1,000 & over
Real. gain[8]	100.0	28.8	34.8	10.8	9.1	9.1	2.9	2.8	1.8
Stat. gain[18]	100.0	29.7	35.4	10.7	8.7	8.6	2.7	2.7	1.6
Excl. gain	100.0	27.8	34.0	11.0	9.6	9.6	3.0	3.0	1.9

1945

	TOTAL[1]	Under 5	5-25	25-50	50-100	100-300	300-500	500-1,000	1,000 & over
Real. gain[8]	4,808.9	1,276.4	1,634.4	570.9	469.0	480.3	152.5	129.4	95.9
Stat. gain[18]	2,572.7	695.9	899.4	301.3	242.0	243.6	77.0	65.2	48.2
Excl. gain	2,236.2	580.5	735.1	269.6	227.1	236.6	75.5	64.1	47.7
% excluded	46.5	45.5	45.0	47.2	48.4	49.3	49.5	49.6	49.7

PERCENTAGE DISTRIBUTION

	TOTAL[1]	Under 5	5-25	25-50	50-100	100-300	300-500	500-1,000	1,000 & over
Real. gain[8]	100.0	26.5	34.0	11.9	9.8	10.0	3.2	2.7	2.0
Stat. gain[18]	100.0	27.1	35.0	11.7	9.4	9.5	3.0	2.5	1.9
Excl. gain	100.0	26.0	32.9	12.1	10.2	10.6	3.4	2.9	2.1

1946

	TOTAL[1]	Under 5	5-25	25-50	50-100	100-300	300-500	500-1,000	1,000 & over
Real. gain[8]	7,210.8	2,256.2	2,432.8	713.4	583.7	644.0	181.4	203.1	196.2
Stat. gain[18]	3,698.9	1,209.1	1,261.7	350.5	282.4	311.4	88.6	99.6	95.6
Excl. gain	3,511.9	1,047.0	1,171.1	362.9	301.3	332.7	92.8	103.5	100.6
% excluded	48.7	46.4	48.1	50.9	51.6	51.6	51.2	51.0	51.3

PERCENTAGE DISTRIBUTION

	TOTAL[1]	Under 5	5-25	25-50	50-100	100-300	300-500	500-1,000	1,000 & over
Real. gain[8]	100.0	31.3	33.7	9.9	8.1	8.9	2.5	2.8	2.7
Stat. gain[18]	100.0	32.7	34.1	9.5	7.6	8.4	2.4	2.7	2.6
Excl. gain	100.0	29.8	33.3	10.3	8.6	9.5	2.6	2.9	2.9

See Table 22, source note.   * Less than $50,000.   † Less than 0.05 percent.
For numbered notes see pp. 362-6.

Table 24

Disallowed, Statutory, and Total Realized Net Capital Gains and Losses by Statutory Net Income Groups, Totals for 3 Periods, 1934-1946

| | ALL RETURNS WITH STAT. NET INCOMES[1] | | STATUTORY NET INCOME GROUP[1] | | | |
	$ mil.	%	$100,000 & over $ mil.	%	Under $100,000 $ mil.	%
A 1934-1937						
Returns with Statutory Net Capital Gains						
Realized gain[6]	3,239.6	100.0	549.8	100.0	2,689.8	100.0
Statutory gain	2,128.9	65.7	265.3	48.3	1,863.6	69.3
Excluded gain	1,110.8	34.3	284.5	51.7	826.3	30.7
Returns with Statutory Net Capital Losses						
Realized loss[6]	2,924.5	100.0	93.4	100.0	2,831.1	100.0
Statutory loss	723.4	24.7	7.1	7.6	716.3	25.3
Disallowed loss	2,201.1	75.3	86.2	92.3	2,114.9	74.7
Returns with Statutory Net Capital Gains or Losses						
Real. gain or loss[6]	315.1		456.5		−141.4	
Stat. gain or loss	1,405.6		258.3		1,147.3	
Excl. gain or loss	−1,090.4		198.3		−1,288.7	
B 1938-1941						
Returns with Statutory Net Capital Gains						
Realized gain[7]	3,143.6	100.0	920.7	100.0	2,222.6	100.0
Statutory gain[18]	1,965.1	62.5	479.2	52.0	1,486.1	66.9
Excluded gain	1,178.4	37.5	441.4	47.9	736.9	33.2
Returns with Statutory Net Capital Losses						
Realized loss[7]	3,643.3	100.0	142.5	100.0	3,501.0	100.0
Statutory loss[18]	1,950.3	53.5	75.3	52.8	1,875.3	53.6
Disallowed loss	1,693.0	46.5	67.2	47.2	1,625.8	46.4
Returns with Statutory Net Capital Gains or Losses						
Real. gain or loss[7]	−499.7	100.0	778.2	100.0	−1,278.1	100.0
Stat. gain or loss[18]	14.8	−3.0	404.1	51.9	−389.0	30.4
Excl. gain or loss	−514.6	103.0	374.2	48.1	−888.9	69.5
C 1942-1946						
Returns with Statutory Net Capital Gains						
Realized gain[8]	16,954.2	100.0	3,056.8	100.0	13,897.4	100.0
Statutory gain[18]	8,978.1	53.0	1,524.5	49.9	7,453.6	53.6
Excluded gain	7,976.1	47.0	1,532.5	50.1	6,443.6	46.4

See Table 22, source note.

For numbered notes see pp. 362-6.

Table 25

Disallowed Net Capital Loss due to Application of Statutory Percentages and to $2,000 Limitation,[a] by Statutory Net Income Groups, 1934-1937 (dollar figures in millions)

	TOTAL[1]	STATUTORY NET INCOME GROUP (thousands of dollars)[1]							
		Under 5	5- 25	25- 50	50- 100	100- 300	300- 500	500- 1,000	1,000 & over
1934									
Disallowed net capital loss due to									
Application of stat. %	373.7	152.7	159.1	34.8	15.4	7.5	2.0	1.4	0.9
$2,000 limitation	214.6	76.9	91.7	24.5	10.8	7.5	1.0	1.1	0.9
Total	588.3	229.6	250.8	59.3	26.2	15.0	3.0	2.5	1.8
$2,000 limitation as % of total	36.5	33.5	36.6	41.3	41.2	50.0	33.3	46.2	50.0
1935									
Disallowed net capital loss due to									
Application of stat. %	383.5	161.5	147.9	37.3	21.1	15.9	-1.1	1.2	-0.2
$2,000 limitation	163.9	61.3	61.2	19.4	10.0	9.2	1.3	0.7	0.7
Total	547.4	222.8	209.1	56.7	31.1	25.1	0.2	1.9	0.5
$2,000 limitation as % of total	29.9	27.5	29.3	34.2	32.2	36.7	[b]	36.8	140.0
1936									
Disallowed net capital loss due to									
Application of stat. %	449.7	179.9	164.3	49.8	39.2	8.9	3.1	1.4	3.1
$2,000 limitation	136.9	51.1	47.8	18.9	12.5	3.1	1.5	0.2	1.7
Total	586.6	231.0	212.1	68.7	51.7	12.0	4.6	1.6	4.8
$2,000 limitation as % of total	23.3	22.1	22.5	27.5	24.2	25.8	32.6	12.5	35.4
1937									
Disallowed net capital loss due to									
Application of stat. %	241.8	111.6	110.3	16.8	3.7	-1.5	-1.5	1.4	0.9
$2,000 limitation	237.0	76.3	101.9	27.0	18.1	8.2	1.4	2.5	1.8
Total	478.8	187.9	212.2	43.8	21.8	6.7	-.1	3.9	2.7
$2,000 limitation as % of total	49.5	40.6	48.0	61.6	83.0	122.4	[c]	64.1	66.7

Based on Sources 1, 2, and 3.

[a] For returns with statutory net capital losses.

[b] Application of statutory percentages increases statutory above the realized loss; all disallowed net loss due to $2,000 limitation.

[c] Statutory exceeds realized net loss.

For numbered notes see pp. 362-6.

Table 26

Net Capital Gains and Losses from Sales of Depreciable Assets by Statutory Net Income Groups, 1938-1946

	TOTAL[1,19]	STATUTORY NET INCOME GROUP (thousands of dollars)[1]							
		Under 5	5-25	25-50	50-100	100-300	300-500	500-1,000	1,000 &over

A 1 9 3 8 - 1 9 4 1   (MILLIONS OF DOLLARS)

Net gains

	TOTAL	Under 5	5-25	25-50	50-100	100-300	300-500	500-1,000	1,000 &over
1938	22.6	12.7	8.6	0.8	0.4	*	0.1		
1939	28.5	15.1	11.5	1.3	0.4	0.1	0.1	*	
1940	41.4	24.2	14.9	1.4	0.7	0.3	*	*	
1941	68.3	41.2	22.8	2.4	1.4	0.5	*	*	*

Net losses

	TOTAL	Under 5	5-25	25-50	50-100	100-300	300-500	500-1,000	1,000 &over
1938	21.8	12.3	6.9	1.3	0.4	0.2	0.1	0.3	0.3
1939	27.3	15.5	8.7	1.4	0.9	0.4	*	*	0.3
1940	38.1	23.4	10.8	2.2	0.9	0.4	0.2	0.2	*
1941	61.8	39.8	17.0	2.6	1.4	0.6	0.1	0.2	

Percentage Distribution

Net gains

	TOTAL	Under 5	5-25	25-50	50-100	100-300	300-500	500-1,000	1,000 &over
1938	100.0	56.0	38.0	3.7	1.8	0.2	0.4		
1939	100.0	52.9	40.4	4.6	1.5	0.4	0.2	†	
1940	100.0	58.3	36.0	3.3	1.6	0.8	†	†	
1941	100.0	60.2	33.4	3.5	2.0	0.8	0.1	†	†

Net losses

	TOTAL	Under 5	5-25	25-50	50-100	100-300	300-500	500-1,000	1,000 &over
1938	100.0	56.4	31.5	5.8	1.9	1.1	0.5	1.2	1.6
1939	100.0	56.6	31.8	5.2	3.5	1.5	0.1	0.2	1.1
1940	100.0	61.3	28.3	5.8	2.4	1.2	0.6	0.5	†
1941	100.0	64.4	27.5	4.3	2.2	1.0	0.2	0.3	0.1

NET GAINS FROM DEPRECIABLE ASSETS AS % OF TOTAL REALIZED NET GAINS

	TOTAL	Under 5	5-25	25-50	50-100	100-300	300-500	500-1,000	1,000 &over
1938	2.8	8.7	4.1	1.1	0.7	†	0.2		
1939	4.2	8.9	4.6	1.6	0.8	0.2	0.3	†	
1940	5.9	14.0	6.5	1.9	1.1	0.4	†	†	
1941	7.3	18.1	9.5	2.7	1.7	0.4	0.1		†

B 1 9 4 2 - 1 9 4 6   (MILLIONS OF DOLLARS)

Net gains

	TOTAL	Under 5	5-25	25-50	50-100	100-300	300-500	500-1,000	1,000 &over
1942	62.6	41.0	17.1	2.7	1.2	0.4	*	*	
1943	77.7	55.1	19.3	2.2	0.6	0.3	*	0.1	*
1944	65.6	40.6	22.0	1.7	0.6	0.2	0.4	*	
1945	65.1	36.6	25.3	2.1	0.8	0.4	*		
1946	123.3	75.2	42.7	3.4	1.3	0.5	0.1	0.1	*

Net losses

	TOTAL	Under 5	5-25	25-50	50-100	100-300	300-500	500-1,000	1,000 &over
1942	82.9	53.7	19.2	4.2	2.5	1.2	0.2	0.6	1.4
1943	75.1	42.3	21.6	5.5	2.9	2.0	0.3	0.1	0.5
1944	73.8	41.6	20.3	4.9	3.1	2.0	0.7	0.8	0.4
1945	70.8	31.6	24.5	6.1	3.4	3.1	0.6	0.5	0.9
1946	68.1	33.0	22.6	5.4	3.2	2.6	0.4	0.1	0.9

| | | STATUTORY NET INCOME GROUP (thousands of dollars)[1] | | | | | | | |
TOTAL[1,19]	Under 5	5-25	25-50	50-100	100-300	300-500	500-1,000	1,000 &over

Percentage Distribution

Net gains

1942	100.0	65.6	27.4	4.3	1.9	0.7	0.1	†	
1943	100.0	71.0	24.9	2.8	0.8	0.4	†	0.1	†
1944	100.0	61.8	33.6	2.7	0.9	0.3	0.7	†	
1945	100.0	56.3	38.8	3.2	1.2	0.6	†		
1946	100.0	61.0	34.6	2.8	1.1	0.4	0.1	0.1	†

Net losses

1942	100.0	64.7	23.1	5.0	3.0	1.4	0.2	0.7	1.7
1943	100.0	56.3	28.7	7.3	3.9	2.7	0.4	0.1	0.7
1944	100.0	56.4	27.5	6.7	4.1	2.7	1.0	1.1	0.5
1945	100.0	44.7	34.6	8.6	4.9	4.4	0.8	0.7	1.3
1946	100.0	48.4	33.1	8.0	4.7	3.8	0.5	0.2	1.3

NET GAINS FROM DEPRECIABLE ASSETS AS % OF TOTAL REALIZED NET GAINS

1942	8.1	17.7	8.3	3.6	1.9	0.5	0.2	†	
1943	4.3	11.3	3.3	1.0	0.4	0.2	†	0.1	†
1944	2.6	5.7	2.5	0.6	0.3	0.1	0.6	†	
1945	1.3	2.8	1.5	0.4	0.2	0.1	†		
1946	1.6	3.2	1.6	0.4	0.2	0.1	0.1	†	†

NET LOSSES FROM DEPRECIABLE ASSETS AS % OF TOTAL REALIZED NET LOSSES

1942	7.7	9.9	5.1	4.8	6.1	5.0	8.2	32.9	59.3
1943	10.7	11.9	8.8	10.1	10.6	17.3	11.0	6.1	15.4
1944	6.9	7.7	5.8	6.0	6.2	6.7	20.4	21.8	10.1
1945	7.8	8.0	7.6	7.0	6.8	9.3	12.6	11.1	16.8
1946	5.3	6.8	4.8	3.7	3.6	4.4	4.2	1.1	9.5

Based on Source 1. * Less than $50,000. † Less than 0.05 percent.
For numbered notes see pp. 362-6.

Table 27

Net Capital Loss Carryover by Statutory Net Income Groups, 1939-1946

| | | STATUTORY NET INCOME GROUP (thousands of dollars)[1] | | | | | | | |
TOTAL[1,20]	Under 5	5-25	25-50	50-100	100-300	300-500	500-1,000	1,000 &over

A 1939-1941

SHORT TERM NET LOSS CARRYOVER (millions of dollars)

1939	21.2	3.5	10.8	3.8	2.0	0.8	0.1	*	*
1940	5.0	1.4	2.2	0.8	0.4	0.2	*	*	*
1941	4.0	0.2	2.3	0.6	0.4	0.4	*	*	*

NO. OF RETURNS WITH NET INCOMES OF $5,000 OR MORE AND WITH SHORT TERM NET LOSS CARRYOVER

1939	10,305		7,958	1,501	579	237	14	12	4
1940	3,591		2,735	524	210	104	10	6	2
1941	2,740		1,931	426	215	144	14	7	3

	TOTAL[1,20]	Under 5	5-25	25-50	50-100	100-300	300-500	500-1,000	1,000 & over

B 1942-1946

SHORT TERM NET LOSS CARRYOVER[a] (millions of dollars)

Returns with Statutory Net Capital Gains or Losses

	TOTAL[1,20]	Under 5	5-25	25-50	50-100	100-300	300-500	500-1,000	1,000 & over
1942	2.8	0.7	1.2	0.4	0.3	0.1	*	*	
1943	163.7	43.6	74.4	22.4	11.9	9.3	1.2	0.5	0.3
1944	206.5	68.9	76.4	29.5	16.3	10.2	1.7	1.6	1.9
1945	285.7	79.0	116.9	41.4	25.2	16.3	3.0	1.4	2.5
1946	305.9	94.0	123.2	41.1	25.4	15.6	2.2	1.7	2.6

Returns with Statutory Net Capital Gains

	TOTAL	Under 5	5-25	25-50	50-100	100-300	300-500	500-1,000	1,000 & over
1942	0.8	0.2	0.4	0.1	*	*	*	*	
1943	18.9	3.2	8.2	3.5	2.1	1.4	0.3	0.2	0.1
1944	13.6	1.4	4.9	3.7	1.5	1.5	0.3	0.3	*
1945	32.1	4.3	12.4	5.8	4.7	3.8	0.6	0.4	0.1
1946	24.6	2.8	9.4	4.0	3.5	2.1	0.7	0.2	2.0

Returns with Statutory Net Capital Losses

	TOTAL	Under 5	5-25	25-50	50-100	100-300	300-500	500-1,000	1,000 & over
1942	2.0	0.5	0.8	0.3	0.3	0.1	*	*	
1943	144.8	40.4	66.2	18.9	9.8	8.0	1.0	0.3	0.2
1944	192.9	67.6	71.5	25.8	14.8	8.7	1.4	1.3	1.9
1945	253.7	74.7	104.5	35.7	20.5	12.5	2.3	1.1	2.4
1946	281.3	91.2	113.8	37.1	22.0	13.5	1.6	1.5	0.7

Source 1.   [a] See Table 20, note a.   * Less than $50,000.

For numbered notes see pp. 362-6.

Table 28

Disallowed Short Term and Total Realized Net Capital Loss by Statutory Net Income Groups, 1938

NET LOSS (millions of dollars)

	TOTAL[1]	Under 5	5-25	25-50	50-100	100-300	300-500	500-1,000	1,000 & over
Disallowed short term	165.2	74.8	67.5	12.4	5.5	2.8	0.3	1.2	0.8
Realized long term	767.8	290.2	330.8	82.3	40.1	18.2	2.1	3.2	1.0
From depreciable assets	21.8	12.3	6.9	1.3	0.4	0.2	0.1	0.3	0.3
Total	954.8	377.2	405.1	96.0	46.0	21.2	2.5	4.7	2.1

PERCENTAGE DISTRIBUTION

	TOTAL[1]	Under 5	5-25	25-50	50-100	100-300	300-500	500-1,000	1,000 & over
Disallowed short term	100.0	45.3	40.9	7.5	3.3	1.7	0.2	0.7	0.5
Realized long term	100.0	37.8	43.1	10.7	5.2	2.4	0.3	0.4	0.1
Total	100.0	39.5	42.4	10.1	4.8	2.2	0.3	0.5	0.2

Net loss from depreciable assets based on Source 1; other lines based on unpublished data.

For numbered notes see pp. 362-6.

Table 29: Number of Returns with Net Capital Gains or Losses: Annual Totals, 1927-1946
Returns with Net Incomes of $5,000 and Over[1]

1 9 2 7 - 1 9 3 3

| | | RETURNS WITH GAINS | | RETURNS WITH LOSSES | | RETURNS WITH GAINS OR LOSSES AS % OF TOTAL FILED | | | |
| | TOTAL RETURNS FILED | | | | | Returns with Gains | | Returns with Losses | |
		Long term seg. at 12½%	Other[21]	Long term seg. at 12½%	Other[21]	Long term seg. at 12½%	Other[21]	Long term seg. at 12½%	Other[21]
1927	913,597	20,235	265,838			2.2	29.1		
1928[22]	1,010,887	27,704	344,546			2.7	34.1		
1929	1,032,071	23,610	301,206	3,111	79,808	2.3	29.2	0.3	7.7
1930	810,431	8,862	140,379	4,318	110,220	1.1	17.3	0.5	13.6
1931	590,731	2,920	62,578	5,593	95,311	0.5	10.6	0.9	16.1
1932	356,442	2,030	31,032	19,578	43,462[24]	0.6	8.7	5.5	12.2[24]
1933	331,892	3,591	80,631	15,772	47,220[24]	1.1	24.3	4.8	14.2[24]

1 9 3 4 - 1 9 3 7

| | | RETURNS WITH GAINS | RETURNS WITH LOSSES | RETURNS WITH GAINS OR LOSSES AS % OF TOTAL FILED | |
| | TOTAL RETURNS FILED | Statutory gain | Statutory loss | Returns with Gains | Returns with Losses |
		Long term seg. at 12½%	Long term seg. at 12½%	Statutory gain	Statutory loss
1934	422,647	61,704	80,110	14.6	19.0
1935	500,115	117,617	68,953	23.5	13.8
1936	677,011	195,809	69,914	28.9	10.3
1937	705,033	127,070	126,583	18.0	18.0

1 9 3 8 - 1 9 4 1[23]

		RETURNS WITH GAINS			RETURNS WITH LOSSES		RETURNS WITH GAINS OR LOSSES AS % OF TOTAL FILED				
	TOTAL RETURNS FILED	Statutory			Statutory loss		Returns with Gains			Returns with Losses	
		Long term	Short term	Depreciable assets	Stat. long term	Depreciable assets	Statutory gain		Depreciable assets	Stat. long term	Depreciable assets
							Long term	Short term			
1938	592,446	53,459	65,940	6,711	87,948	6,290	9.0	11.1	1.1	14.8	1.1
1939	693,590	76,003	76,072	9,356	92,814	9,311	11.0	11.0	1.3	13.4	1.3
1940	779,929	75,374	64,508	11,822	101,936	10,878	9.7	8.3	1.5	13.1	1.4
1941	949,350	70,977	65,427	18,585	141,330	15,344	7.5	6.9	2.0	14.9	1.6

1 9 4 2 - 1 9 4 6[22]

| | | RETURNS WITH GAINS | RETURNS WITH LOSSES | RETURNS WITH GAINS OR LOSSES AS % OF TOTAL FILED | |
| | TOTAL RETURNS FILED | Statutory gain | Statutory loss | Returns with Gains | Returns with Losses |
		Short term	Long term	Statutory gain — Short term	Statutory loss
1942	1,177,100	91,307	143,476	7.8	12.2
1943	1,616,809	225,107	130,524	13.9	8.1
1944	2,495,106	360,240	143,514	14.4	5.8
1945	2,675,953	567,608	117,509	21.2	4.4
1946	3,314,161	736,996	182,384	22.2	5.5

425

Based on Source 1. For discussion of differences in the data for the various periods, see Appendix One, Sections D and E. For numbered notes see pp. 362-6.

Table 30

Number of Returns with Net Capital Gains or Losses by Size, 1927-1933

Returns with Net Incomes of $5,000 and Over

		SIZE OF NET GAIN OR LOSS (thousands of dollars)							
	TOTAL	Under 1	1- 5	5- 25	25- 50	50- 100	100- 500	500- 1,000	1,000 & over

A GAIN

With Long Term Net Gains Segregated at 12½%

1927	20,235	2,598	4,284	6,410	2,640	2,124	1,896	163	120
1928	27,704	2,752	5,114	8,578	4,123	3,375	3,200	358	204
1929	23,610	2,003	3,235	6,071	3,679	3,369	4,495	473	285
1930	8,862	1,498	1,859	2,292	1,022	1,035	1,007	102	47
1931	2,920	715	672	607	261	307	296	39	23
1932	2,030	749	390	424	225	133	99	10	
1933	3,591	1,017	863	822	383	255	214	21	16

With Other Statutory Net Gains[21]

1927	265,838	95,175	95,595	65,139	7,145	1,929	802	45	8
1928[22]	344,546	99,454	125,782	99,748	13,068	4,304	2,020	121	49
1929	301,206	92,769	107,227	86,432	10,699	2,906	1,069	63	41
1930	140,379	69,206	42,690	25,526	2,300	483	165	5	4
1931	62,578	36,938	15,600	8,953	844	172	66	4	1
1932	31,032	20,171	7,277	3,289	220	48	25	2	
1933	80,631	39,916	26,119	12,683	1,310	447	150	3	3

PERCENTAGE DISTRIBUTION

With Long Term Net Gains Segregated at 12½%

1927	100.0	12.8	21.2	31.7	13.0	10.5	9.4	0.8	0.6
1928	100.0	9.9	18.5	31.0	14.9	12.2	11.6	1.3	0.7
1929	100.0	8.5	13.7	25.7	15.6	14.3	19.0	2.0	1.2
1930	100.0	16.9	21.0	25.9	11.5	11.7	11.4	1.2	0.5
1931	100.0	24.5	23.0	20.8	8.9	10.5	10.1	1.3	0.8
1932	100.0	36.9	19.2	20.9	11.1	6.6	4.9	0.5	
1933	100.0	28.3	24.0	22.9	10.7	7.1	6.0	0.6	0.4

With Other Statutory Net Gains[21]

1927	100.0	35.8	36.0	24.5	2.7	0.7	0.3	†	†
1928	100.0	28.9	36.5	29.0	3.8	1.2	0.6	†	†
1929	100.0	30.8	35.6	28.7	3.6	1.0	0.4	†	†
1930	100.0	49.3	30.4	18.2	1.6	0.3	0.1	†	†
1931	100.0	59.0	24.9	14.3	1.3	0.3	0.1	†	†
1932	100.0	65.0	23.4	10.6	0.7	0.2	0.1	†	
1933	100.0	49.5	32.4	15.7	1.6	0.6	0.2	†	†

B LOSS

With Long Term Net Losses Segregated at 12½%

1929	3,111	844	973	920	191	112	69	1	1
1930	4,318	841	1,193	1,523	416	214	127	2	2
1931	5,593	569	960	1,980	969	641	437	20	17
1932	19,578	1,338	2,816	7,647	3,915	2,248	1,475	98	41
1933	15,772	1,480	3,057	5,869	2,830	1,525	938	54	19

With Other Statutory Net Losses[21]

1929	79,808	30,919	27,108	16,950	2,771	1,327	673	41	19
1930	110,220	35,864	38,926	27,859	4,586	1,967	949	53	16
1931	95,311	27,584	34,678	26,454	4,324	1,555	668	31	17
1932[14]	43,462	14,598	18,252	10,027	497	62	26		
1933[14]	47,220	19,178	18,944	8,706	339	40	13		

	TOTAL	Under 1	1- 5	5- 25	25- 50	50- 100	100- 500	500- 1,000	1,000 & over

PERCENTAGE DISTRIBUTION

With Long Term Net Losses Segregated at 12½%

1929	100.0	27.1	31.3	29.6	6.1	3.6	2.2	†	†
1930	100.0	19.5	27.6	35.3	9.6	5.0	2.9	†	†
1931	100.0	10.2	17.2	35.4	17.3	11.5	7.8	0.4	0.3
1932	100.0	6.8	14.4	39.1	20.0	11.5	7.5	0.5	0.2
1933	100.0	9.4	19.4	37.2	17.9	9.7	5.9	0.3	0.1

With Other Statutory Net Losses[21]

1929	100.0	38.7	34.0	21.2	3.5	1.7	0.8	0.1	†
1930	100.0	32.5	35.3	25.3	4.2	1.8	0.9	†	†
1931	100.0	28.9	36.4	27.8	4.5	1.6	0.7	†	†
1932[14]	100.0	33.6	42.0	23.1	1.1	0.1	0.1		
1933[14]	100.0	40.6	40.1	18.4	0.7	0.1	†		

Based on Source 1. † Less than 0.05 percent.
For numbered notes see pp. 362-6.

Table 31

Number of Returns with Net Capital Gains or Losses by Statutory Net Income Groups, 1934-1946
Returns with Net Incomes of $5,000 and Over[1]

	TOTAL[1]	STATUTORY NET INCOME GROUP (thousands of dollars)[1]						
		5- 25	25- 50	50- 100	100- 300	300- 500	500- 1,000	1,000 & over

A 1934-1937

Total returns filed

1934	422,647	393,716	20,931	6,093	1,672	116	86	33
1935	500,115	463,406	26,029	8,033	2,291	206	109	41
1936	677,011	617,535	41,137	13,620	4,150	330	178	61
1937	705,033	649,617	38,948	12,318	3,627	312	162	49

Returns with statutory net gains

1934	61,704	53,389	5,715	1,915	598	41	34	12
1935	117,617	101,446	10,969	3,846	1,166	108	60	22
1936	195,809	164,625	20,541	7,759	2,526	209	113	36
1937	127,070	110,941	10,957	3,842	1,148	104	58	20

Returns with statutory net losses

1934	80,110	69,832	7,160	2,334	685	50	37	12
1935	68,953	59,717	6,280	2,157	694	64	30	11
1936	69,914	59,505	6,814	2,569	885	74	48	19
1937	126,583	105,576	13,694	5,276	1,781	148	89	19

	TOTAL[1]	5-25	25-50	50-100	100-300	300-500	500-1,000	1,000 &over
		STATUTORY NET INCOME GROUP (thousands of dollars)[1]						
		PERCENTAGE DISTRIBUTION						
Total returns filed								
1934	100.0	93.2	5.0	1.4	0.4	†	†	†
1935	100.0	92.7	5.2	1.6	0.5	†	†	†
1936	100.0	91.2	6.1	2.0	0.6	†	†	†
1937	100.0	92.1	5.5	1.7	0.5	†	†	†
Returns with statutory net gains								
1934	100.0	86.5	9.3	3.1	1.0	0.1	0.1	†
1935	100.0	86.3	9.3	3.3	1.0	0.1	0.1	†
1936	100.0	84.1	10.5	4.0	1.3	0.1	0.1	†
1937	100.0	87.3	8.6	3.0	0.9	0.1	†	†
Returns with statutory net losses								
1934	100.0	87.2	8.9	2.9	0.9	0.1	†	†
1935	100.0	86.6	9.1	3.1	1.0	0.1	†	†
1936	100.0	85.1	9.7	3.7	1.3	0.1	0.1	†
1937	100.0	83.4	10.8	4.2	1.4	0.1	0.1	†
		B 1938-1941						
Total returns filed								
1938	592,446	556,377	26,336	7,259	2,092	207	118	57
1939	693,590	649,405	31,992	9,272	2,553	212	111	45
1940	779,929	728,450	37,264	10,673	3,095	267	128	52
1941	949,350	879,982	49,521	14,850	4,404	367	169	57
Returns with:[23]								
Statutory long term net gains								
1938	53,459	45,365	5,087	1,936	838	113	71	49
1939	76,003	64,971	7,317	2,615	921	97	58	24
1940	75,374	64,226	7,263	2,638	1,045	107	67	28
1941	70,977	59,521	7,004	2,907	1,262	166	88	29
Statutory short term net gains								
1938	65,940	58,094	5,569	1,628	526	57	47	19
1939	76,072	66,295	6,902	2,150	630	54	27	14
1940	64,508	55,550	6,207	1,997	641	67	35	11
1941	65,427	55,406	6,580	2,476	832	79	43	11
Net gains from depreciable assets								
1938	6,711	6,249	321	116	22	2	1	
1939	9,356	8,637	532	143	37	5	2	
1940	11,822	10,865	697	184	68	4	3	1
1941	18,585	16,839	1,229	359	139	12	2	5
Statutory long term net losses								
1938	87,948	76,207	8,326	2,603	716	56	35	5
1939	92,814	79,481	9,181	3,105	921	72	38	16
1940	101,936	86,011	10,873	3,694	1,191	113	37	17
1941	141,330	118,299	15,575	5,531	1,719	127	61	18
Net losses from depreciable assets								
1938	6,290	5,613	461	132	60	6	8	10
1939	9,311	8,288	691	244	69	6	6	7
1940	10,878	9,504	941	308	102	15	6	2
1941	15,344	13,518	1,221	397	174	23	8	3

	TOTAL[1]	5-25	25-50	50-100	100-300	300-500	500-1,000	1,000 & over
				PERCENTAGE DISTRIBUTION				
Total returns filed								
1938	100.0	93.9	4.4	1.2	0.4	†	†	†
1939	100.0	93.6	4.6	1.3	0.4	†	†	†
1940	100.0	93.4	4.8	1.4	0.4	†	†	†
1941	100.0	92.7	5.2	1.6	0.5	†	†	†
Returns with:[23]								
Statutory long term net gains								
1938	100.0	84.9	9.5	3.6	1.6	0.2	0.1	0.1
1939	100.0	85.5	9.6	3.4	1.2	0.1	0.1	†
1940	100.0	85.2	9.6	3.5	1.4	0.1	0.1	†
1941	100.0	83.9	9.9	4.1	1.8	0.2	0.1	†
Statutory short term net gains								
1938	100.0	88.1	8.4	2.5	0.8	0.1	0.1	†
1939	100.0	87.1	9.1	2.8	0.8	0.1	†	†
1940	100.0	86.1	9.6	3.1	1.0	0.1	0.1	†
1941	100.0	84.7	10.1	3.8	1.3	0.1	0.1	†
Net gains from depreciable assets								
1938	100.0	93.1	4.8	1.7	0.3	†	†	
1939	100.0	92.3	5.7	1.5	0.4	0.1	†	
1940	100.0	91.9	5.9	1.6	0.6	†	†	†
1941	100.0	90.6	6.6	1.9	0.7	0.1	†	†
Statutory long term net losses								
1938	100.0	86.7	9.5	3.0	0.8	0.1	†	†
1939	100.0	85.6	9.9	3.3	1.0	0.1	†	†
1940	100.0	84.4	10.7	3.6	1.2	0.1	†	†
1941	100.0	83.7	11.0	3.9	1.2	0.1	†	†
Net losses from depreciable assets								
1938	100.0	89.2	7.3	2.1	1.0	0.1	0.1	0.2
1939	100.0	89.0	7.4	2.6	0.7	0.1	0.1	0.1
1940	100.0	87.4	8.7	2.8	0.9	0.1	0.1	†
1941	100.0	88.1	8.0	2.6	1.1	0.1	0.1	†
				C 1942-1946				
Total returns filed								
1942	1,177,100	1,085,946	65,137	19,793	5,570	415	199	40
1943	1,616,809	1,497,615	86,203	25,362	6,896	456	222	55
1944	2,495,106	2,352,720	103,549	30,106	7,905	511	246	69
1945	2,675,953	2,506,782	124,229	35,006	8,974	585	294	83
1946	3,314,161	3,111,050	150,195	41,078	10,627	713	379	119
Returns with statutory net gains[22]								
1942	91,307	76,104	9,822	3,765	1,371	139	81	25
1943	225,107	188,939	24,327	8,537	2,909	228	127	40
1944	360,240	309,645	33,788	12,366	3,941	310	149	41
1945	567,608	487,131	54,533	19,258	5,931	466	225	64
1946	736,996	640,168	65,920	22,749	7,192	560	309	98
Returns with statutory net losses[22]								
1942	143,476	119,529	16,163	5,778	1,805	122	70	9
1943	130,524	109,010	14,559	5,198	1,567	122	57	11
1944	143,514	120,570	15,452	5,594	1,694	117	65	22
1945	117,509	99,120	12,723	4,287	1,244	71	48	16
1946	182,384	153,374	20,494	6,571	1,764	112	54	15

		STATUTORY NET INCOME GROUP (thousands of dollars)[1]						
	TOTAL[1]	5-25	25-50	50-100	100-300	300-500	500-1,000	1,000 & over

PERCENTAGE DISTRIBUTION

Total returns filed

1942	100.0	92.3	5.5	1.7	0.5	†	†	†
1943	100.0	92.6	5.3	1.6	0.4	†	†	†
1944	100.0	94.3	4.2	1.2	0.3	†	†	†
1945	100.0	93.7	4.6	1.3	0.3	†	†	†
1946	100.0	93.9	4.5	1.2	0.3	†	†	†

Returns with statutory net gains

1942	100.0	83.3	10.8	4.1	1.5	0.2	0.1	†
1943	100.0	83.9	10.8	3.8	1.3	0.1	0.1	†
1944	100.0	86.0	9.4	3.4	1.1	0.1	†	†
1945	100.0	85.8	9.6	3.4	1.0	0.1	†	†
1946	100.0	86.9	8.9	3.1	1.0	0.1	†	†

Returns with statutory net losses

1942	100.0	83.3	11.3	4.0	1.3	0.1	†	†
1943	100.0	83.5	11.2	4.0	1.2	0.1	†	†
1944	100.0	84.0	10.8	3.9	1.2	0.1	†	†
1945	100.0	84.4	10.8	3.6	1.1	0.1	†	†
1946	100.0	84.1	11.2	3.6	1.0	0.1	†	†

Based on Source 1.   †Less than 0.05 percent.

For numbered notes see pp. 362-6.

Table 32

Number of Returns with Net Capital Gains or Losses: Percentage of Total Returns Filed, by Statutory Net Income Groups, 1934-1946 Returns with Net Incomes of $5,000 and Over[1]

		STATUTORY NET INCOME GROUP[1] ($000)						
	TOTAL[1]	5-25	25-50	50-100	100-300	300-500	500-1,000	1,000 & over

A 1 9 3 4 - 1 9 3 7

RETURNS WITH

1934

Stat. gains	14.6	13.6	27.3	31.4	35.8	35.3	39.5	36.4
Stat. losses	19.0	17.7	34.2	38.3	41.0	43.1	43.0	36.4

1935

Stat. gains	23.5	21.9	42.1	47.9	50.9	52.4	55.0	53.7
Stat. losses	13.8	12.9	24.1	26.9	30.3	31.1	27.5	26.8

1936

Stat. gains	28.9	26.7	49.9	57.0	60.9	63.3	63.5	59.0
Stat. losses	10.3	9.6	16.6	18.9	21.3	22.4	27.0	31.1

1937

Stat. gains	18.0	17.1	28.1	31.2	31.7	33.3	35.8	40.8
Stat. losses	18.0	16.3	35.2	42.8	49.1	47.4	54.9	38.8

STATUTORY NET INCOME GROUP[1] ($000)

	TOTAL[1]	5-25	25-50	50-100	100-300	300-500	500-1,000	1,000 & over
B 1 9 3 8 - 1 9 4 1[23]								
1938								
Stat. long term gains	9.0	8.2	19.3	26.7	40.1	54.6	60.2	86.0
Stat. short term gains	11.1	10.4	21.1	22.4	25.1	27.5	39.8	33.3
Gains from depr. assets	1.1	1.1	1.2	1.6	1.1	1.0	0.8	
Stat. long term losses	14.8	13.7	31.6	35.9	34.2	27.1	29.7	8.8
Losses from depr. assets	1.1	1.0	1.8	1.8	2.9	2.9	6.8	17.5
1939								
Stat. long term gains	11.0	10.0	22.9	28.2	36.1	45.8	52.3	53.3
Stat. short term gains	11.0	10.2	21.6	23.2	24.7	25.5	24.3	31.1
Gains from depr. assets	1.3	1.3	1.7	1.5	1.4	2.4	1.8	
Stat. long term losses	13.4	12.2	28.7	33.5	36.1	34.0	34.2	35.6
Losses from depr. assets	1.3	1.3	2.2	2.6	2.7	2.8	5.4	15.6
1940								
Stat. long term gains	9.7	8.8	19.5	24.7	33.8	40.1	52.3	53.8
Stat. short term gains	8.3	7.6	16.7	18.7	20.7	25.1	27.3	21.2
Gains from depr. assets	1.5	1.5	1.9	1.7	2.2	1.5	2.3	1.9
Stat. long term losses	13.1	11.8	29.2	34.6	38.5	42.3	28.9	32.7
Losses from depr. assets	1.4	1.3	2.5	2.9	3.3	5.6	4.7	3.8
1941								
Stat. long term gains	7.5	6.8	14.1	19.6	28.7	45.2	52.1	50.9
Stat. short term gains	6.9	6.3	13.3	16.7	18.9	21.5	25.4	19.3
Gains from depr. assets	2.0	1.9	2.5	2.4	3.2	3.3	1.2	8.8
Stat. long term losses	14.9	13.4	31.5	37.2	39.0	34.6	36.1	31.6
Losses from depr. assets	1.6	1.5	2.5	2.7	4.0	6.3	4.7	5.3
C 1 9 4 2 -1 9 4 4[22]								
1942								
Stat. gains	7.8	7.0	15.1	19.0	24.6	33.5	40.7	62.5
Stat. losses	12.2	11.0	24.8	29.2	32.4	29.4	35.2	22.5
1943								
Stat. gains	13.9	12.6	28.2	33.7	42.2	50.0	57.2	72.7
Stat. losses	8.1	7.3	16.9	20.5	22.7	26.8	25.7	20.0
1944								
Stat. gains	14.4	13.2	32.6	41.1	49.9	60.7	60.6	59.4
Stat. losses	5.8	5.1	14.9	18.6	21.4	22.9	26.4	31.9
1945								
Stat. gains	21.2	19.4	43.9	55.0	66.1	79.7	76.5	77.1
Stat. losses	4.4	4.0	10.2	12.2	13.9	12.1	16.3	19.3
1946								
Stat. gains	22.2	20.6	43.9	55.4	67.7	78.5	81.5	82.4
Stat. losses	5.5	4.9	13.6	16.0	16.6	15.7	14.2	12.6

Based on Source 1.
For numbered notes see pp. 362-6.

Table 33

Number of Returns with Statutory Long Term Net Capital Gains or Losses and with Alternative Tax Treatment, by Statutory Net Income Groups, 1938-1946
Returns with Net Incomes of $5,000 and Over[1]

	TOTAL[1]	STATUTORY NET INCOME GROUP (thousands of dollars)[1]						
		5-25	25-50	50-100	100-300	300-500	500-1,000	1,000 &over

A 1938-1941
Returns with Statutory Long Term Net Gains[23]

Total

1938	53,459	45,365	5,087	1,936	838	113	71	49
1939	76,003	64,971	7,317	2,615	921	97	58	24
1940	75,374	64,226	7,263	2,638	1,045	107	67	28
1941	70,977	59,521	7,004	2,907	1,262	166	88	29

Returns with alternative tax

1938	2,630		133	1,441	828	108	71	49
1939	3,503		236	2,170	918	97	58	24
1940	9,462	343	5,383	2,489	1,045	107	67	28
1941	18,136	7,900	5,996	2,697	1,261	166	87	29

Percentage with alternative tax

1938	4.9		2.6	74.4	98.8	95.6	100.0	100.0
1939	4.6		3.2	83.0	99.7	100.0	100.0	100.0
1940	12.6	0.5	74.1	94.4	100.0	100.0	100.0	100.0
1941	25.6	13.3	85.6	92.8	99.9	100.0	98.9	100.0

Returns with Statutory Long Term Net Losses[23]

Total

1938	87,948	76,207	8,326	2,603	716	56	35	5
1939	92,814	79,481	9,181	3,105	921	72	38	16
1940	101,936	86,011	10,873	3,694	1,191	113	37	17
1941	141,330	118,299	15,575	5,531	1,719	127	61	18

Returns with alternative tax credit

1938	4,134	104	981	2,247	710	54	34	4
1939	4,843	44	959	2,793	921	72	38	16
1940	16,521	2,105	9,521	3,537	1,191	113	37	17
1941	51,214	30,079	13,990	5,220	1,719	127	61	18

Percentage with alternative tax credit

1938	4.7	0.1	11.8	86.3	99.2	96.4	97.1	80.0
1939	5.2	0.1	10.4	90.0	100.0	100.0	100.0	100.0
1940	16.2	2.4	87.6	95.7	100.0	100.0	100.0	100.0
1941	36.2	25.4	89.8	94.4	100.0	100.0	100.0	100.0

B 1942-1946
Returns with Statutory Net Gains

Total

1942	91,307	76,104	9,822	3,765	1,371	139	81	25
1943	225,107	188,939	24,327	8,537	2,909	228	127	40
1944	360,240	309,645	33,788	12,366	3,941	310	149	41
1945	567,608	487,131	54,533	19,258	5,931	466	225	64
1946	736,996	640,168	65,920	22,749	7,192	560	309	98

Returns with alternative tax

1942	12,946	2,517	6,184	2,862	1,164	119	76	24
1943	32,848	6,534	16,311	6,958	2,664	219	123	39
1944	53,327	13,796	24,975	10,442	3,645	296	134	39
1945	90,579	24,618	42,464	17,154	5,613	453	216	61
1946	86,167	10,971	47,468	20,023	6,778	541	293	93

Percentage with alternative tax

1942	14.2	3.3	63.0	76.0	84.9	85.6	93.8	96.0
1943	14.6	3.5	67.0	81.5	91.6	96.1	96.9	97.5
1944	14.8	4.5	73.9	84.4	92.5	95.5	89.9	95.1
1945	16.0	5.1	77.9	89.1	94.6	97.2	96.0	95.3
1946	11.7	1.7	72.0	88.0	94.2	96.6	94.8	94.9

Based on Source 1.   For numbered notes see pp. 362-6.

Table 34: Number of Returns with Net Capital Gains or Losses by 5 Holding Periods, 1934-1937

RETURNS WITH	RETURNS WITH REALIZED NET GAINS IN HOLDING PERIOD					RETURNS WITH REALIZED NET LOSSES IN HOLDING PERIOD				
	1 yr. or less	1-2	2-5	5-10	Over 10	1 yr. or less	1-2	2-5	5-10	Over 10
	Net Incomes of $5,000 and Over									
1934										
Stat. gains[15]	35,738	17,183	15,154	8,210	8,789	2,911	3,368	7,438	6,791	2,167
Stat. losses[16]	16,352	11,236	4,868	2,788	4,908	21,927	12,233	38,107	36,090	12,052
All	52,090	28,419	20,022	10,998	13,697	24,838	15,601	45,545	42,881	14,219
1936										
Stat. gains[15]	104,704	57,999	67,878	32,890	26,523	7,400	8,002	11,121	29,061	11,363
Stat. losses[16]	16,302	11,002	12,975	3,334	4,763	14,827	6,784	14,168	35,229	17,223
All	121,006	69,001	80,853	36,224	31,286	22,227	14,786	25,289	64,290	28,586
1937										
Stat. gains[15]	56,791	32,719	43,614	32,273	23,815	14,617	8,818	4,941	12,376	5,988
Stat. losses[16]	13,917	18,986	25,314	11,257	9,382	65,464	30,636	19,093	46,145	24,817
All	70,708	51,705	68,928	43,530	33,197	80,081	39,454	24,034	58,521	30,805
STATUTORY NET INCOME GROUP ($000) (Returns with stat. gains or losses)										
	Net Incomes of $100,000 and Over									
1934										
100- 300	550	393	239	170	313	277	214	508	501	207
300- 500	46	30	14	17	19	19	18	34	35	24
500-1,000	25	30	13	9	22	20	7	26	24	13
1,000 & over	10	6	7	5	10	6	5	12	9	3
1935										
100- 300	928	632	721	320	512	329	374	494	724	290
300- 500	83	57	73	32	62	33	40	53	75	27
500-1,000	42	25	39	11	39	22	16	21	38	15
1,000 & over	13	12	12	7	14	6	7	9	11	5
1936										
100- 300	1,957	1,404	1,674	786	869	465	331	477	1,227	665
300- 500	161	111	139	56	95	35	40	38	116	47
500-1,000	84	66	92	36	58	27	15	15	60	36
1,000 & over	18	13	21	6	19	7	6	7	18	14
1937										
100- 300	690	681	1,258	795	763	1,307	796	496	868	584
300- 500	63	61	106	83	87	117	69	54	85	55
500-1,000	30	23	69	44	53	71	45	32	47	38
1,000 & over	10	6	19	12	14	18	10	7	12	10

Based on Sources 1, 2, and 3.

For numbered notes see pp. 362-6.

433

Table 35

Number of Returns with Net Capital Gains or Losses by Size and by Statutory Net Income Groups, 1930 and 1935-1941
Returns with Net Incomes of $5,000 and Over

STATUTORY NET CAPITAL LOSS ($000)	TOTAL[1]	STATUTORY NET INCOME GROUP (thousands of dollars)[1]						
		5-25	25-50	50-100	100-300	300-500	500-1,000	1,000 & over
A 1930, RETURNS WITH LOSSES[a]								
Returns with Net Capital Losses from Sales of Assets Held Longer than 2 Years & Segregated for Tax Credit at 12½%								
Under 1	841		331	341	149	11	7	2
1- 5	1,193		482	507	175	16	10	3
5- 10	693		237	326	115	11	2	2
10- 25	830		188	418	196	20	5	3
25- 50	416		36	209	142	20	7	2
50-100	214		3	77	116	8	8	2
100-500	127		1	4	86	21	11	4
500 & over	4				1		1	2
Total	4,318		1,278	1,882	979	108	51	20
Returns with Other Net Capital Losses[21]								
Under 1	35,616	32,481	2,149	686	255	22	17	6
1- 5	38,746	34,109	3,272	1,022	304	21	15	3
5- 10	14,934	11,846	2,102	765	201	16	4	
10- 25	12,906	8,723	2,433	1,182	511	33	20	4
25- 50	4,584	2,424	1,020	675	392	49	19	5
50-100	1,966	754	447	356	323	53	20	13
100-500	948	210	130	181	276	80	49	22
500 & over	69	5	5	9	15	6	19	10
Total	109,769	90,552	11,558	4,876	2,277	280	163	63

STATUTORY NET CAPITAL GAIN OR LOSS ($000)	TOTAL[1]	5-25	25-50	50-100	100-300	300-500	500-1,000	1,000 & over
B 1935								
Returns with Statutory Net Capital Gains								
Under 0.5	45,104	41,695	2,520	696	173	11	8	1
0.5- 1	16,705	15,124	1,175	313	86	6	1	
1- 5	37,138	32,481	3,352	1,019	258	20	5	3
5- 10	10,578	8,529	1,430	462	144	7	5	1
10- 25	5,956	3,477	1,709	577	167	16	7	3
25- 50	1,475	121	738	478	121	8	8	1
50-100	483	18	37	285	128	11	3	1
100-500	157	1	7	16	89	29	9	6
500 & over	21		1				14	6
Total	117,617	101,446	10,969	3,846	1,166	108	60	22
Returns with Statutory Net Capital Losses								
Under 0.5	26,777	24,499	1,641	488	132	12	3	2
0.5-1	11,435	10,308	814	225	82	4	2	
1-2	12,533	10,678	1,301	423	120	4	5	2
2-4	18,208	14,232	2,524	1,021	360	44	20	7
Total	68,953	59,717	6,280	2,157	694	64	30	11

[a] Estimated from unpublished data for 1930. No attempt was made to adjust for minor differences between these figures and those in Tables 29 and 30.

STATUTORY NET CAPITAL GAIN OR LOSS ($000)	TOTAL[1]	STATUTORY NET INCOME GROUP (thousands of dollars)[1]						
		5- 25	25- 50	50- 100	100- 300	300- 500	500- 1,000	1,000 &over

C 1936
Returns with Statutory Net Capital Gains

Under 0.5	62,668	57,345	3,886	1,107	297	21	8	4
0.5- 1	26,558	23,911	1,898	586	148	12	3	
1- 5	67,442	58,953	5,958	1,951	516	41	18	5
5- 10	21,594	17,267	3,004	1,004	290	19	8	2
10- 25	12,874	6,916	4,085	1,429	395	28	17	4
25- 50	3,276	204	1,636	1,100	298	24	10	4
50-100	1,032	26	67	563	350	16	10	
100-500	344	3	7	18	230	47	30	9
500 & over	21			1	2	1	9	8
Total	195,809	164,625	20,541	7,759	2,526	209	113	36

Returns with Statutory Net Capital Losses

Under 0.5	30,598	27,582	2,140	652	206	14	3	1
0.5-1	11,824	10,400	1,032	297	84	5	4	2
1-2	12,275	10,078	1,391	580	201	15	8	2
2-4	15,217	11,445	2,251	1,040	394	40	33	14
Total	69,914	59,505	6,814	2,569	885	74	48	19

D 1937
Returns with Statutory Net Capital Gains

Under 0.5	58,246	53,371	3,550	1,029	261	22	10	3
0.5- 1	19,237	17,277	1,396	438	118	7	1	
1- 5	35,297	30,658	3,266	1,052	281	17	18	5
5- 10	8,410	6,793	1,087	397	110	12	9	2
10- 25	4,371	2,707	1,099	434	117	9	4	1
25- 50	1,013	116	523	285	78	8	3	
50-100	333	13	31	192	92	3	1	1
100-500	155	6	5	14	88	26	11	5
500 & over	8			1	3		1	3
Total	127,070	110,941	10,957	3,842	1,148	104	58	20

Returns with Statutory Net Capital Losses

Under 0.5	42,441	38,764	2,662	753	232	18	11	1
0.5-1	19,068	17,084	1,382	461	127	8	6	
1-2	26,200	21,338	3,259	1,194	364	34	9	2
2-4	38,874	28,390	6,391	2,868	1,058	88	63	16
Total	126,583	105,576	13,694	5,276	1,781	148	89	19

E 1938[b]
Returns with Statutory Short Term Net Capital Gains

Under 0.5	35,248	32,013	2,359	639	201	19	14	3
0.5- 1	10,585	9,477	815	219	60	7	5	2
1- 5	14,574	12,532	1,465	426	127	10	8	6
5- 10	2,182	1,705	316	114	40	4	1	2
10- 25	1,015	649	235	84	35	1	8	3
25- 50	175	40	94	29	10		1	
50-100	66	11	12	29	10	2	1	1
100-500	10	1		2	7			
Total	63,855	56,428	5,296	1,543	490	43	38	17

STATUTORY NET CAPITAL GAIN OR LOSS ($000)	STATUTORY NET INCOME GROUP (thousands of dollars)[1]							
	TOTAL[1]	5-25	25-50	50-100	100-300	300-500	500-1,000	1,000 &over

Returns with Statutory Long Term Net Capital Gains

Under 0.5	27,863	25,406	1,801	509	137	6	4	
0.5- 1	6,567	5,828	536	145	51	6	1	
1- 5	10,965	9,197	1,199	430	125	10	3	1
5- 10	2,702	1,994	468	165	64	10	1	
10- 25	1,681	809	526	248	88	5	4	1
25- 50	512	36	196	191	78	7	3	1
50-100	248	8	8	113	111	3	2	3
100-500	206	3	3	2	126	49	17	7
500 & over	57					2	25	30
Total	50,801	43,280	4,737	1,803	780	98	60	43

Returns with Statutory Long Term Net Capital Losses

Under 0.5	31,550	29,197	1,742	472	123	9	6	1
0.5- 1	14,276	12,936	1,026	259	47	7	1	
1- 5	29,209	24,981	3,130	881	205	6	6	
5- 10	6,850	5,180	1,134	423	102	8	3	
10- 25	3,859	2,502	882	347	118	8	2	
25- 50	894	469	220	128	64	6	6	1
50-100	215	97	45	37	25	4	6	1
100-500	48	11	8	12	10	2	4	1
500 & over	1			1				
Total	86,902	75,383	8,187	2,560	694	50	34	4

F 1939[b]

Returns with Statutory Short Term Net Capital Gains

Under 0.5	39,489	35,651	2,773	782	247	20	9	7
0.5- 1	11,969	10,547	1,023	312	78	6	2	1
1- 5	17,728	15,012	1,933	603	163	8	5	4
5- 10	2,643	2,005	418	169	45	4	1	1
10- 25	1,062	622	305	97	31	4	3	
25- 50	166	43	74	37	8	2	2	
50-100	47	1	6	24	12	2	1	1
100-500	8		1	2	4	1		
Total	73,112	63,881	6,533	2,026	588	47	23	14

Returns with Statutory Long Term Net Capital Gains

Under 0.5	42,228	38,296	2,883	803	225	12	8	1
0.5- 1	10,207	8,925	919	280	73	9	1	
1- 5	15,043	12,229	1,920	677	198	12	7	
5- 10	2,846	1,998	530	230	76	5	6	1
10- 25	1,556	640	526	266	109	8	6	1
25- 50	419	33	156	150	67	8	2	3
50-100	148	3	11	69	55	5	4	1
100-500	117			3	61	27	18	8
500 & over	10						1	9
Total	72,574	62,124	6,945	2,478	864	86	53	24

Returns with Statutory Long Term Net Capital Losses

Under 0.5	39,957	36,327	2,665	748	199	13	5	
0.5- 1	15,425	13,668	1,255	417	73	8	2	2
1- 5	27,534	22,859	3,268	1,063	316	16	9	3
5- 10	5,195	3,718	961	373	129	8	4	2
10- 25	2,727	577	683	325	118	13	7	4
25- 50	558	268	160	84	33	7	6	
50-100	142	45	38	32	21	4	2	
100-500	31	5	7	4	9	1	1	4
Total	91,569	78,467	9,037	3,046	898	70	36	15

STATUTORY NET CAPITAL GAIN OR LOSS ($000)	TOTAL[1]	STATUTORY NET INCOME GROUP (thousands of dollars)[1]						
		5- 25	25- 50	50- 100	100- 300	300- 500	500- 1,000	1,000 & over

G 1940[b]
Returns with Statutory Short Term Net Capital Gains

Under 0.5	38,046	33,789	2,997	942	270	27	18	3
0.5- 1	9,569	8,228	987	254	82	11	4	3
1- 5	11,876	9,766	1,457	484	149	12	7	1
5- 10	1,741	1,305	281	102	45	6	1	1
10- 25	737	458	168	80	26	3		2
25- 50	125	31	50	26	16	1	1	
50-100	29	3	5	10	9	1	1	
100-500	13			3	7	3		
Total	62,136	53,580	5,945	1,901	604	64	32	10

Returns with Statutory Long Term Net Capital Gains

Under 0.5	41,496	37,593	2,911	797	179	13	3	
0.5- 1	9,618	8,363	903	261	83	6	2	
1- 5	14,950	12,301	1,782	627	218	18	2	2
5- 10	3,215	2,306	576	233	89	6	2	3
10- 25	1,791	882	548	248	102	6	3	2
25- 50	534	28	179	238	74	6	7	2
50-100	234	4	7	88	125	7	2	1
100-500	172			6	104	34	22	6
500 & over	21						10	11
Total	72,031	61,477	6,906	2,498	974	96	53	27

Returns with Statutory Long Term Net Capital Losses

Under 0.5	41,988	37,990	2,916	834	229	13	4	2
0.5- 1	16,652	14,650	1,499	371	120	10	1	1
1- 5	30,819	25,272	3,849	1,302	355	31	9	1
5- 10	6,465	4,477	1,264	522	178	15	5	4
10- 25	3,590	2,072	905	423	164	19	5	2
25- 50	737	341	194	116	70	7	5	4
50-100	224	84	50	46	32	8	4	
100-500	55	8	8	13	14	7	4	1
500 & over	1							1
Total	100,531	84,894	10,685	3,627	1,162	110	37	16

H 1941[b]
Returns with Statutory Short Term Net Capital Gains

Under 0.5	39,551	34,502	3,440	1,178	383	33	14	1
0.5- 1	8,712	7,372	916	332	81	5	4	2
1- 5	11,418	9,216	1,394	557	216	19	12	4
5- 10	2,006	1,598	246	114	40	5	2	1
10- 25	876	535	206	87	39	7	2	
25- 50	189	32	82	53	15	1	5	1
50-100	39	2	7	15	12	2	1	
100-500	28		1	6	17	3		1
Total	62,819	53,257	6,292	2,342	803	75	40	10

Returns with Statutory Long Term Net Capital Gains

Under 0.5	37,940	34,046	2,757	865	242	18	12	
0.5- 1	8,391	7,315	727	263	75	8	3	
1- 5	14,165	11,778	1,564	611	189	15	6	2
5- 10	3,404	2,542	550	228	75	8	1	
10- 25	2,174	991	729	304	132	14	4	
25- 50	669	21	256	278	103	4	5	2
50-100	360	1	3	171	168	10	4	3
100-500	300	2	1	5	188	76	24	4
500 & over	31						17	14
Total	67,434	56,696	6,587	2,725	1,172	153	76	25

STATUTORY NET CAPITAL GAIN OR LOSS ($000)	STATUTORY NET INCOME GROUP (thousands of dollars)[1]							
	TOTAL[1]	5- 25	25- 50	50- 100	100- 300	300- 500	500- 1,000	1,000 & over

Returns with Statutory Long Term Net Capital Losses

Under 0.5	46,188	41,561	3,328	1,021	259	14	5	
0.5- 1	21,884	19,279	1,867	560	161	12	4	1
1- 5	50,167	41,649	5,994	1,976	511	22	15	
5- 10	12,443	9,148	2,209	829	235	16	5	1
10- 25	7,060	4,463	1,495	747	318	18	14	5
25- 50	1,316	613	327	228	120	20	5	3
50-100	322	118	63	64	54	15	6	2
100-500	84	15	16	18	20	7	6	2
500 & over	33							3
Total	139,467	116,846	15,299	5,443	1,678	124	60	17

Source 1.   [b] Fiduciary income tax returns excluded 1938-41.
For numbered notes see pp. 362-6.

Table 36

Net Capital Gain or Loss Per Return[a]: Annual Averages, 1927-1946 (dollars)

Returns with Net Incomes of $5,000 and Over[1]

	AVERAGE NET GAIN		AVERAGE NET LOSS	
	1927-1933			
	Long term seg. at 12½%	Other[21]	Long term seg. at 12½%	Other[21]
1927	53,431	5,687		
1928[22]	67,852	7,838		
1929	99,394	6,786	13,831	7,925
1930	62,784	3,759	18,734	8,593
1931	58,202	3,141	42,889	8,535
1932	24,667	2,309	42,515	4,018[14]
1933	37,209	3,829	35,114	3,239[14]

	1934-1937		
	Realized[6]		Realized[6]
1934	3,925		5,613
1935	4,955		5,708
1936	5,914		5,985
1937	5,028		3,402

	1938-1941[23]				
	Realized[7]		Depr. assets	Realized long term[7]	Depr. assets
	Long term	Short term			
1938	10,524	1,544	1,483	5,431	1,510
1939	4,716	1,748	1,434	4,078	1,274
1940	5,746	1,313	1,455	4,585	1,351
1941	8,389	1,407	1,462	5,807	1,434

	1942-1946[22]		
	Realized[8]		Realized[8]
1942	5,526		3,418
1943	5,584		2,006
1944	4,736		1,983
1945	6,173		1,562
1946	6,657		1,078

Based on Sources 1, 2, and 3.   For numbered notes see pp. 362-6.

[a] Net gain or loss of each type is an average per return with statutory net gain or loss of that type respectively.

Table 37

Average Net Capital Gain or Loss per Return[a] by Statutory Net Income Groups, 1934-1946 (dollars)
Returns with Net Incomes of $5,000 and Over[1]

	TOTAL[1]	STATUTORY NET INCOME GROUP (thousands of dollars)[1]						
		5-25	25-50	50-100	100-300	300-500	500-1,000	1,000 & over
A 1934-1937								
1934								
Realized gain[b]	3,925	2,260	7,669	14,928	46,216	153,415	234,618	599,917
Realized loss[b]	5,613	4,682	9,693	12,701	23,476	61,940	69,622	157,333
Statutory gain	2,597	1,658	5,205	9,957	22,627	84,854	98,471	209,917
Statutory loss	1,136	1,091	1,408	1,463	1,577	1,700	1,784	4,000
1935								
Realized gain[b]	4,955	2,800	9,526	20,001	44,174	152,343	548,917	743,727
Realized loss[b]	5,708	4,453	10,308	15,789	37,584	3,922	65,400	48,909
Statutory gain	3,400	2,059	6,923	13,933	26,452	85,019	212,233	400,091
Statutory loss	1,000	952	1,272	1,382	1,409	1,547	1,667	1,636
1936								
Realized gain[b]	5,914	3,273	10,309	20,430	54,725	125,656	281,929	1,458,944
Realized loss[b]	5,985	4,411	11,224	21,412	14,971	63,973	34,917	255,421
Statutory gain	4,121	2,411	7,987	14,839	32,606	66,110	155,531	473,750
Statutory loss	899	846	1,140	1,281	1,359	1,459	1,688	1,684
1937								
Realized gain[b]	5,028	2,830	9,720	21,834	69,671	282,673	158,466	795,700
Realized loss[b]	3,402	3,041	4,622	5,667	5,358	764	45,124	141,474
Statutory gain	2,560	1,643	4,963	10,011	25,302	108,029	53,276	337,350
Statutory loss	1,105	1,032	1,423	1,544	1,595	1,635	1,640	1,842

STATUTORY NET INCOME GROUP (thousands of dollars)[1]

B 1938-1941

Realized Net Gain or Loss[25,7]

	TOTAL[1]	5-25	25-50	50-100	100-300	300-500	500-1,000	1,000 & over
1938								
Long term gain	10,524	2,924	11,334	27,723	93,908	366,885	798,254	2,892,878
Short term gain	1,544	1,156	3,001	5,207	9,106	27,140	62,638	9,474
Gain from depr. assets	1,483	1,374	2,583	3,509	1,636	45,500	92,771	195,200
Long term loss	5,431	4,340	9,884	15,397	25,377	37,732	33,625	34,900
Loss from depr. assets	1,510	1,223	2,729	3,144	3,950	18,000		
1939								
Long term gain	4,716	2,318	7,700	16,345	46,689	191,670	311,500	1,213,042
Short term gain	1,748	1,340	3,388	5,560	8,375	41,926	41,889	9,643
Gain from depr. assets	1,434	1,333	2,455	2,979	3,243	10,600	1,500	
Long term loss	4,078	3,187	7,575	10,374	16,241	28,208	36,895	316,812
Loss from depr. assets	1,274	1,049	2,059	3,873	5,899	5,667	7,500	44,571
1940								
Long term gain	5,746	2,473	7,937	19,767	69,749	240,692	557,761	1,017,036
Short term gain	1,313	1,037	2,211	3,472	6,669	16,413	19,543	35,273
Gain from depr. assets	1,455	1,374	1,981	3,571	4,779	1,000	333	*
Long term loss	4,585	3,498	8,005	12,036	20,101	46,106	60,919	209,294
Loss from depr. assets	1,351	1,136	2,329	2,909	4,304	15,933	29,000	1,500
1941								
Long term gain	8,389	2,699	9,958	24,655	90,574	331,072	611,920	2,422,621
Short term gain	1,407	1,032	2,353	3,976	7,588	16,608	8,302	143,727
Gain from depr. assets	1,462	1,355	1,921	3,897	3,820	3,167	2,000	6,200
Long term loss	5,807	4,618	9,196	13,598	22,583	54,425	62,475	357,389
Loss from depr. assets	1,434	1,257	2,156	3,489	3,678	4,609	25,125	14,000

C 1942-1946

Realized Net Gain or Loss[8,22]

1942								
Gain	5,526	2,353	6,943	16,511	57,986	171,374	511,630	2,015,800
Loss	3,418	2,909	4,956	6,280	12,192	17,131	16,771	106,778
1943								
Gain	5,584	2,804	8,178	17,776	60,342	211,373	669,740	1,694,100
Loss	2,006	1,781	2,627	3,489	3,355	15,967	24,702	247,364
1944								
Gain	4,736	2,658	7,743	17,836	55,931	222,281	460,691	1,044,000
Loss	1,983	1,800	2,319	3,324	6,577	2,162	11,738	45,500
1945								
Gain	6,173	3,303	10,431	24,316	80,917	327,197	574,933	1,498,391
Loss	1,562	1,462	1,493	2,434	4,814	−8,352[b]	46,708	100,188
1946								
Gain	6,657	3,733	10,770	25,601	89,485	323,773	657,019	2,001,929
Loss	1,078	1,024	1,264	1,064	1,960	1,661	58,519	−13,200[b]

Statutory amounts based on Source 1; realized amounts on Sources 1, 2, and 3 for 1934-37, and on Source 1 for 1938-46.

* Less than $500.

a See Table 36, note a.

b Exclusion of loss carryover and of net loss from sales of depreciable assets results in a current year's realized net capital gain for this income group; see Appendix One, Section D5.

For numbered notes see pp. 362-6.

Table 38

Average Net Capital Gain or Loss per Return[a] by 5 Holding Periods, 1934-1937 (dollars)

STATUTORY NET INCOME GROUP ($000)	AVERAGE REALIZED NET GAIN[9]					AVERAGE REALIZED NET LOSS[9]				
	1 yr. or less	1-2	2-5	5-10	Over 10	1 yr. or less	1-2	2-5	5-10	Over 10

A   NET INCOMES OF $5,000 AND OVER

1934-1937[b]

Returns with Statutory Net Capital Gains or Losses

5- 25	1,800	1,600	2,300	2,300	4,600	2,000	1,200	2,300	4,200	3,900
25- 50	5,400	4,600	5,700	6,000	10,800	4,200	2,100	4,500	8,000	8,800
50- 100	10,200	7,300	11,200	11,800	24,700	7,900	3,500	6,600	19,000	9,200
100- 300	15,000	10,900	16,900	26,900	69,500	11,000	5,600	12,200	24,700	12,000
300- 500	31,100	23,400	46,000	64,500	206,600	22,500	13,500	36,300	46,600	27,300
500-1,000	46,000	51,400	66,000	119,400	315,600	17,600	17,300	37,900	89,000	23,300
1,000 & over	50,300	47,900	153,500	132,900	1,459,500	59,300	18,500	98,200	277,700	114,100

1934

Total	2,000	2,300	2,000	3,400	8,700	1,900	1,600	4,400	5,500	4,800
With stat. gains[15]	2,400	2,600	2,300	3,800	11,000	1,600	1,400	2,700	3,600	2,200
With stat. losses[16]	1,300	1,900	1,300	2,200	4,700	1,900	1,600	4,700	5,900	5,300

1936

Total	3,800	2,800	3,800	4,300	11,300	1,700	800	1,800	7,200	6,100
With stat. gains[15]	4,000	3,000	4,100	4,500	12,300	1,300	700	1,500	4,500	3,500
With stat. losses[16]	2,200	1,800	2,100	1,900	5,500	1,900	1,000	2,000	9,500	7,800

1937

Total	1,500	2,200	3,700	3,800	9,500	3,400	1,800	1,600	4,100	4,100
With stat. gains[15]	1,600	2,400	4,000	4,200	10,700	3,300	1,500	1,100	2,500	2,000
With stat. losses[16]	900	1,700	3,300	2,900	6,200	3,400	1,900	1,700	4,600	4,600

B NET INCOMES OF $100,000 AND OVER

Returns with Statutory Net Capital Gains or Losses

1934

100- 300	12,000	12,500	10,700	24,600	72,600	6,100	5,700	26,600	21,200	12,600
300- 500	21,700	27,500	24,700	67,100	162,200	13,700	7,800	15,400	12,800	109,200
500-1,000	35,100	66,700	45,100	162,600	270,700	13,900	15,000	98,600	89,100	14,500
1,000 & over	42,200	75,300	6,300	288,600	725,800	24,000	31,400	106,800	25,800	172,000

1935

100- 300	15,800	10,500	18,800	20,400	52,100	3,100	6,800	10,800	43,900	14,100
300- 500	37,400	14,600	53,900	45,400	219,600	11,500	12,400	82,700	40,200	16,400
500-1,000	33,300	75,200	87,000	198,800	678,100	5,400	16,300	19,700	87,200	32,300
1,000 & over	55,000	33,300	119,100	27,900	1,033,900	2,500	29,600	162,800	329,800	93,600

1936

100- 300	18,500	11,200	18,000	29,100	66,600	6,100	3,300	4,600	21,300	12,400
300- 500	30,200	26,500	38,300	45,800	168,200	3,600	7,500	9,200	81,000	7,500
500-1,000	69,400	45,600	90,100	102,200	251,900	5,800	5,100	15,100	73,800	26,000
1,000 & over	17,700	24,900	160,300	139,500	2,588,100	63,700	5,800	58,300	310,800	36,000

1937

100- 300	6,600	9,800	15,600	27,900	83,200	15,800	6,100	5,900	15,700	10,400
300- 500	31,900	24,000	53,500	83,900	248,900	32,700	19,200	23,100	19,000	13,800
500-1,000	7,400	22,100	25,900	104,900	137,300	26,900	22,000	11,300	109,700	20,100
1,000 & over	111,100	99,500	221,800	125,900	877,400	88,300	11,900	40,300	195,300	216,400

Based on Sources 1, 2, and 3.

a Average net gain or loss per return with realized net gain or loss respectively in the holding period.

b For income groups under $100,000, 1935 is excluded.

For numbered notes see pp. 362-6.

Table 39

Statutory Long Term Net Capital Gains and Losses: Total and Amount Segregated for Alternative Tax Treatment, by Statutory Net Income Groups, 1938-1941[24]

| | TOTAL[1] | STATUTORY NET INCOME GROUP (thousands of dollars)[1] | | | | | | | |
		Under 5	5- 25	25- 50	50- 100	100- 300	300- 500	500- 1,000	1,000 & over
			GAINS (millions of dollars)[23]						
Total									
1938	324.8	42.1	67.0	29.0	27.0	39.4	20.8	28.4	71.1
1939	229.5	49.0	76.0	28.4	21.5	21.6	9.3	9.1	14.6
1940	271.4	53.5	80.2	29.0	26.2	36.5	12.9	18.7	14.3
1941	369.4	70.1	81.1	35.1	36.0	57.3	27.5	27.0	35.2
Segregated									
1938	170.4			0.2	14.3	38.9	17.6	28.3	71.1
1939	66.7			0.2	12.7	20.8	9.3	9.1	14.6
1940	118.9		0.2	13.4	23.0	36.4	12.9	18.7	14.3
1941	229.1		14.9	32.7	34.9	57.3	27.5	26.5	35.2
% segregated									
1938	52.5			0.5	53.1	98.7	84.5	99.7	100.0
1939	29.1			0.8	59.2	96.6	100.0	100.0	100.0
1940	43.8		0.2	46.1	88.0	99.6	99.9	100.0	100.0
1941	62.0		18.4	93.1	96.9	100.0	100.0	98.0	100.0
			LOSSES (millions of dollars)[23]						
Total									
1938	395.8	149.6	170.5	42.4	20.7	9.4	1.1	1.7	0.5
1939	316.9	121.8	130.6	35.8	16.6	7.7	1.0	0.7	2.6
1940	386.2	145.3	155.1	44.9	22.9	12.3	2.7	1.2	1.8
1941	702.3	279.2	281.6	73.8	38.8	20.0	3.6	2.0	3.3
Segregated									
1938	51.7	1.0	4.9	13.9	19.3	9.3	1.1	1.7	0.5
1939	42.4	0.2	2.3	12.0	15.7	7.7	1.0	0.7	2.6
1940	109.2	1.6	24.3	42.7	22.6	12.3	2.7	1.2	1.8
1941	303.3	11.2	154.5	70.9	37.8	20.0	3.6	2.0	3.3
% segregated									
1938	13.1	0.7	2.9	32.8	93.7	99.8	99.7	100.0	99.8
1939	13.4	0.2	1.8	33.5	94.8	100.0	100.0	100.0	100.0
1940	28.3	1.1	15.6	95.2	98.6	100.0	100.0	100.0	100.0
1941	43.2	4.0	54.9	96.0	97.6	100.0	100.0	100.0	100.0

STATUTORY NET INCOME GROUP (thousands of dollars)[1]

	TOTAL[1]	Under 5	5-25	25-50	50-100	100-300	300-500	500-1,000	1,000 & over

PERCENTAGE DISTRIBUTION

GAINS[23]

Total

	TOTAL[1]	Under 5	5-25	25-50	50-100	100-300	300-500	500-1,000	1,000 & over
1938	100.0	13.0	20.6	8.9	8.3	12.1	6.4	8.7	21.9
1939	100.0	21.4	33.1	12.4	9.4	9.4	4.1	3.9	6.4
1940	100.0	19.7	29.6	10.7	9.7	13.5	4.8	6.9	5.3
1941	100.0	19.0	22.0	9.5	9.8	15.5	7.5	7.3	9.5

Segregated

	TOTAL[1]	Under 5	5-25	25-50	50-100	100-300	300-500	500-1,000	1,000 & over
1938	100.0			0.1	8.4	22.9	10.3	16.6	41.7
1939	100.0			0.3	19.1	31.2	14.0	13.6	21.9
1940	100.0		0.1	11.3	19.4	30.6	10.9	15.7	12.0
1941	100.0		6.5	14.3	15.2	25.0	12.0	11.5	15.4

LOSSES[23]

Total

	TOTAL[1]	Under 5	5-25	25-50	50-100	100-300	300-500	500-1,000	1,000 & over
1938	100.0	37.8	43.1	10.7	5.2	2.4	0.3	0.4	0.1
1939	100.0	38.4	41.2	11.3	5.2	2.4	0.3	0.2	0.8
1940	100.0	37.6	40.2	11.6	5.9	3.2	0.7	0.3	0.5
1941	100.0	39.8	40.1	10.5	5.5	2.8	0.5	0.3	0.5

Segregated

	TOTAL[1]	Under 5	5-25	25-50	50-100	100-300	300-500	500-1,000	1,000 & over
1938	100.0	1.9	9.4	26.9	37.4	18.1	2.1	3.2	1.0
1939	100.0	0.5	5.5	28.3	37.1	18.2	2.5	1.7	6.2
1940	100.0	1.5	22.2	39.1	20.7	11.3	2.5	1.1	1.7
1941	100.0	3.7	50.9	23.4	12.5	6.6	1.2	0.6	1.1

Based on Source 1.   For numbered notes see pp. 362-6.

Table 40

Excess of Statutory Long Term Gain Over Short Term Loss Segregated for Alternative Tax Treatment, by Statutory Net Income Groups, 1942-1946

STATUTORY NET INCOME GROUP (thousands of dollars)[1]

	TOTAL[1]	Under 5	5-25	25-50	50-100	100-300	300-500	500-1,000	1,000 & over

MILLIONS OF DOLLARS

	TOTAL[1]	Under 5	5-25	25-50	50-100	100-300	300-500	500-1,000	1,000 & over
1942	144.7	3.3	22.8	26.3	37.2	10.5	19.6	25.2	
1943	324.8	10.2	65.6	67.2	82.8	23.6	42.4	33.2	
1944	399.9	22.3	90.5	95.3	104.3	33.5	33.1	21.0	
1945	860.2	43.1	201.7	205.2	226.5	73.8	63.4	46.4	
1946	1,022.2	12.6	193.4	241.3	297.6	85.7	98.2	93.4	

PERCENTAGE DISTRIBUTION

	TOTAL[1]	Under 5	5-25	25-50	50-100	100-300	300-500	500-1,000	1,000 & over
1942	100.0	2.3	15.7	18.2	25.7	7.2	13.5	17.4	
1943	100.0	3.1	20.2	20.7	25.5	7.3	13.1	10.2	
1944	100.0	5.6	22.6	23.8	26.1	8.4	8.3	5.2	
1945	100.0	5.0	23.4	23.9	26.3	8.6	7.4	5.4	
1946	100.0	1.2	18.9	23.6	29.1	8.4	9.6	9.1	

Based on Source 1.   For numbered notes see pp. 362-6.

Table 41

Net Income Reported on All Income Tax Returns[9] by Statutory Net Income Groups, 1917-1946

	TOTAL[1]	STATUTORY NET INCOME GROUP (thousands of dollars)[1]							
		Under 5	5- 25	25- 50	50- 100	100- 300	300- 500	500- 1,000	1,000 & over
		MILLIONS OF DOLLARS							
1917-1921									
1917	11,191.2	4,180.8	3,514.7	1,042.3	846.9	875.1	209.9	214.6	306.8
1918	15,924.6	9,394.4	3,882.2	978.0	679.7	589.1	144.5	119.1	137.5
1919	19,859.5	11,149.7	5,366.4	1,277.4	896.5	729.5	159.1	128.3	152.6
1920	23,735.6	15,274.2	5,616.2	1,307.8	810.4	480.7	89.3	80.0	77.1
1921	19,577.2	13,215.4	4,336.9	979.6	582.2	309.5	61.3	42.8	49.4
1922-1933									
1922	21,336.2	13,532.2	4,897.8	1,208.3	805.2	527.0	116.7	107.7	141.4
1923	24,777.5	16,488.8	5,191.1	1,350.7	833.9	541.2	124.6	95.1	152.1
1924	25,656.2	15,905.0	5,846.6	1,599.8	1,066.8	752.3	171.2	158.5	156.0
1925	21,894.6	9,116.9	7,008.8	2,032.2	1,418.9	1,228.2	339.8	327.4	422.5
1926	21,958.5	8,730.8	7,499.6	1,954.7	1,389.3	1,231.6	340.2	317.9	494.4
1927	22,545.1	8,480.9	7,643.8	2,051.8	1,535.4	1,423.3	431.1	378.2	600.6
1928	25,226.3	8,270.4	8,320.4	2,326.5	1,857.9	2,007.6	663.9	670.9	1,108.9
1929	24,800.7	8,104.8	8,506.8	2,174.5	1,646.5	1,857.9	628.2	669.9	1,212.1
1930	18,118.6	7,597.5	6,646.5	1,383.6	919.0	793.2	207.1	211.7	359.9
1931	13,605.0	6,663.4	4,813.7	820.6	528.0	408.7	102.2	102.3	166.1
1932	11,655.8	7,412.0	2,837.4	629.6	393.2	237.9	52.5	57.9	35.2
1933	11,008.6	6,861.1	2,650.0	630.0	401.0	268.4	54.6	56.7	86.9
1934-1937									
1934	12,309.9	7,585.8	3,247.9	663.3	389.3	257.8	43.6	61.6	60.6
1935	14,583.4	8,629.7	3,971.9	854.1	528.1	341.9	85.0	92.1	80.6
1936	19,057.3	10,167.3	5,536.3	1,379.5	905.2	663.0	132.3	135.5	138.2
1937	21,144.3	12,305.4	5,729.6	1,327.7	848.0	589.2	135.8	116.6	91.9
1938-1941									
1938	18,846.3	11,999.6	4,749.1	875.1	492.1	343.8	98.1	108.1	180.3
1939	23,119.8	15,151.0	5,609.9	1,074.3	623.5	395.6	89.7	82.4	93.5
1940	36,492.8	27,400.6	6,322.9	1,243.5	716.9	487.2	112.1	101.7	108.1
1941	57,872.3[25]	46,418.4[25]	7,684.9	1,638.6	993.2	694.6	163.9	140.7	138.0
1942-1946									
1942	76,945.3[25]	62,668.7[25]	9,515.6	2,165.6	1,322.3	843.7	166.8	151.7	111.0
1943	97,984.9[25]	78,472.9[25]	13,220.2	2,956.9	1,739.0	1,082.7	193.5	190.8	129.1
1944[25]	104,687.0	80,478.5	17,499.4	3,250.2	1,875.4	1,101.0	194.7	169.0	118.6
1945[25]	108,900.9	80,937.9	19,671.8	4,016.2	2,276.0	1,351.4	261.5	222.8	163.4
1946[25]	122,738.2	87,721.6	24,850.3	4,896.6	2,704.5	1,652.9	316.9	311.8	283.7

	TOTAL[1]	Under 5	5-25	25-50	50-100	100-300	300-500	500-1,000	1,000 & over
				STATUTORY NET INCOME GROUP (thousands of dollars)[1]					
				PERCENTAGE DISTRIBUTION					
1917-1921									
1917	100.0	37.4	31.4	9.3	7.6	7.8	1.9	1.9	2.7
1918	100.0	59.0	24.4	6.1	4.3	3.7	0.9	0.8	0.9
1919	100.0	56.1	27.0	6.4	4.5	3.7	0.8	0.6	0.8
1920	100.0	64.4	23.7	5.5	3.4	2.0	0.4	0.3	0.3
1921	100.0	67.5	22.2	5.0	3.0	1.6	0.3	0.2	0.2
1922-1933									
1922	100.0	63.4	23.0	5.7	3.8	2.5	0.6	0.5	0.7
1923	100.0	66.6	21.0	5.4	3.4	2.2	0.5	0.4	0.6
1924	100.0	62.0	22.8	6.2	4.2	2.9	0.7	0.6	0.6
1925	100.0	41.6	32.0	9.3	6.5	5.6	1.6	1.5	1.9
1926	100.0	39.8	34.2	8.9	6.3	5.6	1.6	1.4	2.2
1927	100.0	37.6	33.9	9.1	6.8	6.3	1.9	1.7	2.7
1928	100.0	32.8	33.0	9.2	7.4	8.0	2.6	2.7	4.4
1929	100.0	32.7	34.3	8.8	6.6	7.5	2.5	2.7	4.9
1930	100.0	41.9	36.7	7.6	5.1	4.4	1.2	1.2	2.0
1931	100.0	49.0	35.4	6.0	3.9	3.0	0.8	0.8	1.2
1932	100.0	63.6	24.4	5.4	3.4	2.0	0.4	0.5	0.3
1933	100.0	62.3	24.1	5.7	3.6	2.4	0.5	0.5	0.8
1934-1937									
1934	100.0	61.6	26.4	5.4	3.2	2.1	0.4	0.5	0.5
1935	100.0	59.2	27.2	5.9	3.6	2.3	0.6	0.6	0.6
1936	100.0	53.4	29.1	7.2	4.7	3.5	0.7	0.7	0.7
1937	100.0	58.2	27.1	6.3	4.0	2.8	0.6	0.6	0.4
1938-1941									
1938	100.0	63.7	25.2	4.6	2.6	1.8	0.5	0.6	1.0
1939	100.0	65.5	24.3	4.6	2.7	1.7	0.4	0.4	0.4
1940	100.0	75.1	17.3	3.4	2.0	1.3	0.3	0.3	0.3
1941	100.0[25]	80.2[25]	13.3	2.8	1.7	1.2	0.3	0.2	0.2
1942-1946									
1942	100.0[25]	81.4[25]	12.4	2.8	1.7	1.1	0.2	0.2	0.1
1943	100.0[25]	80.1[25]	13.5	3.0	1.8	1.1	0.2	0.2	0.1
1944[25]	100.0	76.9	16.7	3.1	1.8	1.1	0.2	0.2	0.1
1945[25]	100.0	74.3	18.1	3.7	2.1	1.2	0.2	0.2	0.2
1946[25]	100.0	71.5	20.2	4.0	2.2	1.3	0.3	0.3	0.2

Based on Sources 1, 2, and 3.
For numbered notes see pp. 362-6.

II Sample Data for 1930, 1932, and 1933

Tables 42-65 summarize the capital gains and losses reported on samples of federal individual income tax returns for 1930, 1932, and 1933. Unlike the other tables in Appendix Two, they include information on gross as well as net capital gains and losses from sales of securities and other assets and on gross receipts from sales. The samples are described in more detail in Appendix One, Section F1.

Notes to Tables 42-65

[1] Includes gross receipts from sales of all assets. Gross receipts from sales of securities classified by income group not available.

[2] Negative indicates excess of gain over loss.

[3] Estimated cost equals gross receipts minus capital gain or plus capital loss. It may differ from original cost because such items as depreciation, cost of improvements and expenses in connection with sales of assets were taken into account by the taxpayer in computing realized net gain and loss.

[4] In 1930 includes one sale with gross receipts of about $20 million and with gain of about $17 million.

[5] In 1932 includes one sale with gross receipts of about $20 million and with loss of about $200,000.

[6] Data for 1933 cover sales of all assets; tabulations for sales of securities not available.

[7] 123 returns (8 classified as market traders and 115 other) with neither net capital gain nor loss are excluded in 1933, except Table 48, Section B, and Table 65, lines 1-6, 9, 13-18, and 21.

[8] Excludes sales with type of sale not stated.

[9] As reported on the face of the income tax return; differs slightly from corresponding figures taken from the back of the return.

[10] In 1932, gross loss from sales of securities as shown in Table 42, Section B.

[11] In 1933, gross loss from sales of assets as shown in Table 60.

[12] In 1932, from Table 48, Section A.

[13] In 1933, from Table 48, Section B.

[14] Col. 6 = $\dfrac{\text{Col. 1}}{1 - \text{Col. 4}}$ − Col. 1; Col. 7 = $\dfrac{\text{Col. 3}}{1 - \text{Col. 5}}$ − Col. 3.

[15] Excludes sales with month of sale not stated.

[16] Because of differences in the classification of securities held 12, 24, 60, and 120 months, the 5 holding periods do not correspond exactly with the detailed classification by number of months held in other tables.

[17] Includes short sales.

[18] 448 returns (43 classified as market traders and 405 other) reported over-all realized net gains; 1,456 (169 classified as market traders and 1,287 other) reported over-all realized net losses.

[19] 352 returns (31 classified as market traders and 321 other) reported over-all realized net gains; 3,052 (170 classified as market traders and 2,882 other) reported over-all realized net losses.

[20] Includes returns with net deficits.

[21] 742 returns (662 with net deficits or with net incomes under $50,000 and 80 with net incomes of $50,000 or more) reported over-all realized net gains; 1,299 (1,147 and 152 with net incomes under and over $50,000, respectively) reported over-all realized net losses. 123 sample returns with neither over-all net gain nor loss excluded.

[22] Includes sales with type of security not stated.

[23] In 1932, 59 returns were classified as market traders and 1,152 as 'other'. In 1930, 36 of the 59 and 122 of the 1,152 were classified as market traders, the remaining 1,053 as 'other'.

Table 42

Number of Returns, Gross Capital Gains and Losses, and Gross Receipts, by Statutory Net Income Groups, Sample Returns, 1930, 1932, and 1933 (dollar figures in thousands)

STATUTORY NET INCOME GROUP ($000)	NO. OF RETURNS	SALES OF ASSETS: GROSS RECEIPTS[1]	SALES OF SECURITIES			EXCESS OF LOSS AS % OF EST. COST[3]
			Gross gain	Gross loss	Excess of loss[2]	
A 1930 (1,904 RETURNS)						
Under 5	61	7,738	487	950	463	5.6
5- 25	631	84,632	6,115	11,180	5,064	5.6
25- 50	278	52,855	4,688	7,600	2,912	5.2
50-100	178	64,138	6,930	9,808	2,878	4.3
100-300	109	59,654	8,664	11,518	2,855	4.6
300 & over[4]	14	67,169	27,615	4,077	−23,538	−53.9[2]
Total[4]	1,271	336,187	54,500	45,134	−9,366	−2.9[2]
Net deficit	633	286,876	15,518	49,813	34,295	10.7
All returns[4]	1,904	623,063	70,017	94,947	24,930	3.8
Percentage Distribution						
Under 5	3.2	1.3	0.7	1.0	1.9	
5- 25	33.1	13.6	8.7	11.8	20.3	
25- 50	14.6	8.5	6.7	8.0	11.7	
50-100	9.3	10.3	9.9	10.3	11.5	
100-300	5.7	9.6	12.4	12.1	11.5	
300 & over[4]	0.7	10.8	39.4	4.3	−94.4	
Total[4]	66.8	54.0	77.8	47.5	−37.6	
Net deficit	33.2	46.0	22.2	52.5	137.6	
All returns[4]	100.0	100.0	100.0	100.0	100.0	
B 1932 (3,404 RETURNS)						
Under 5	565	25,414	913	5,089	4,176	14.1
5- 25	1,130	79,039	4,460	19,833	15,372	16.3
25- 50	476	48,940	2,864	17,328	14,464	22.8
50-100	330	58,427	3,653	25,437	21,785	27.2
100-300	121	57,994	3,356	24,002	20,645	26.3
300 & over[5]	9	32,153	835	8,108	7,274	18.4
Total[5]	2,631	301,964	16,080	99,797	83,717	21.7
Net deficit	773	75,405	4,354	38,582	34,228	31.2
All returns[6]	3,404	377,368	20,435	138,379	117,944	23.8
Percentage Distribution						
Under 5	16.6	6.7	4.5	3.7	3.5	
5- 25	33.2	20.9	21.8	14.3	13.0	
25- 50	14.0	13.0	14.0	12.5	12.3	
50-100	9.7	15.5	17.9	18.4	18.5	
100-300	3.6	15.4	16.4	17.3	17.5	
300 & over[5]	0.3	8.5	4.1	5.9	6.2	
Total[5]	77.3	80.0	78.7	72.1	71.0	
Net deficit	22.7	20.0	21.3	27.9	29.0	
All returns[6]	100.0	100.0	100.0	100.0	100.0	

STATUTORY NET INCOME GROUP ($000)	NO. OF RETURNS	Gross receipts	SALES OF ASSETS[6]			EXCESS OF LOSS AS % OF EST. COST[3]
			Gross gain	Gross loss	Excess of loss	
C 1933 (3,356 RETURNS)						
Under 5	504	43,407	2,559	4,329	1,770	3.9
5- 25	1,075	127,383	10,038	13,007	2,969	2.3
25- 50	472	98,718	9,283	18,178	8,895	8.3
50-100	285	100,813	9,205	17,590	8,385	7.7
100-300	99	134,217	8,545	18,221	9,676	6.7
300 & over	10	36,278	9,929	14,331	4,402	10.8
Total	2,445	540,816	49,560	85,656	36,096	6.3
Net deficit	788	109,959	8,739	30,245	21,506	16.4
All returns	3,233[7]	650,775	58,299	115,901	57,602	8.1
Percentage Distribution						
Under 5	15.6	6.7	4.4	3.7	3.1	
5- 25	33.3	19.6	17.2	11.2	5.2	
25- 50	14.6	15.2	15.9	15.7	15.4	
50-100	8.8	15.5	15.8	15.2	14.6	
100-300	3.1	20.6	14.7	15.7	16.8	
300 & over	0.3	5.6	17.0	12.4	7.6	
Total	75.6	83.1	85.0	73.9	62.7	
Net deficit	24.4	16.9	15.0	26.1	37.3	
All returns	100.0	100.0	100.0	100.0	100.0	

Based on Source 5.   For numbered notes see pp. 448-9

Table 43

Number of Sales of Securities by Statutory Net Income Groups, Sample Returns, 1930 and 1932

STATUTORY NET INCOME GROUP ($000)	ALL SALES		SALES WITH GAIN		SALES WITH LOSS	
	No.	%	No.	%	No.	%
A 1930 (1,904 RETURNS)						
Under 5	1,436	2.0	728	2.2	708	1.9
5- 25	17,368	24.6	8,799	26.8	8,569	22.7
25- 50	8,095	11.5	4,204	12.8	3,891	10.3
50-100	6,210	8.8	2,931	8.9	3,279	8.7
100-300	3,400	4.8	1,444	4.4	1,956	5.2
300 & over	784	1.1	421	1.3	363	1.0
Total	37,293	52.9	18,527	56.5	18,766	49.7
Net deficit	33,246	47.1	14,275	43.5	18,971	50.3
All returns	70,539	100.0	32,802	100.0	37,737	100.0
B 1932 (3,404 RETURNS)						
Under 5	11,407	13.8	5,178	16.9	6,229	11.9
5- 25	27,685	33.4	11,956	39.0	15,729	30.2
25- 50	11,777	14.2	4,112	13.4	7,665	14.7
50-100	7,645	9.2	2,112	6.9	5,533	10.6
100-300	3,498	4.2	683	2.2	2,815	5.4
300 & over	260	0.3	60	0.2	200	0.4
Total	62,272	75.2	24,101	78.6	38,171	73.2
Net deficit	20,563	24.8	6,565	21.4	13,998	26.8
All returns	82,835	100.0	30,666	100.0	52,169	100.0

Based on Source 5.

Table 44: Average Gross Capital Gain and Loss and Average Gross Receipts by Statutory Net Income Groups, Sample Returns, 1930, 1932, and 1933 (dollars)

	STATUTORY NET INCOME GROUP ($000)						TOTAL[4,5]	NET DEFICIT	ALL RETURNS[4,5]
	Under 5	5-25	25-50	50-100	100-300	300 & over[4,5]			
A 1930 (1,904 RETURNS)									
Sales of Securities									
Av. gross gains per									
Return	7,984	9,691	16,863	38,933	79,486	1,972,500	42,800	24,515	36,774
Sale with gain	669	695	1,115	2,364	6,000	65,594	2,942	1,087	2,135
Av. gross loss per									
Return	15,574	17,718	27,338	55,101	105,670	291,214	35,511	78,694	49,867
Sale with loss	1,342	1,305	1,953	2,991	5,889	11,231	2,405	2,626	2,516
Av. no. of sales per return	24	28	29	35	31	56	31	53	37
Sales of Assets									
Av. gross receipts[1] per									
Return	126,852	134,124	190,126	360,326	547,284	4,797,786	264,506	453,201	327,238
Sale	5,389	4,873	6,529	10,328	17,545	85,675	9,015	8,629	8,833
B 1932 (3,404 RETURNS)									
Sales of Securities									
Av. gross gain per									
Return	1,616	3,947	6,017	11,070	27,736	92,778	6,112	5,633	6,003
Sale with gain	176	373	696	1,730	4,914	13,917	667	663	666
Av. gross loss per									
Return	9,007	17,551	36,403	77,082	198,364	900,889	37,931	49,912	40,652
Sale with loss	817	1,261	2,261	4,597	8,526	40,540	2,614	2,756	2,653
Av. no of sales per return	20	24	25	23	29	29	24	27	24
Sales of Assets									
Av. gross receipts[1] per									
Return	44,981	69,946	102,815	177,052	479,289	3,572,556	114,772	97,549	110,860
Sale	2,228	2,855	4,156	7,643	16,579	123,665	4,849	3,667	4,556
C 1933 (3,356 RETURNS[7])									
Sales of Assets									
Av. per return									
Gross gain	5,077	9,338	19,667	32,298	86,313	992,900	20,270	11,090	18,032
Gross loss	8,589	12,100	38,513	61,719	184,050	1,433,100	35,033	38,382	35,849
Gross receipts[1]	86 125	118,496	209,148	353,730	1,355,727	3,627,800	221,193	139,542	201,291

Based on Source 5.

For numbered notes see pp. 448-9.

451

Table 45: Sales of Securities Reported on Returns Classified as Market Traders and on Other Returns: Gross Capital Gains and Losses, Gross Receipts, and Number of Sales, Sample Returns, 1930 and 1932

A 1930

	1,904 Returns			212 Market Traders			1,692 Other Returns		
	With gain[4]	With loss[5]	All[4,5]	With gain	With loss[5]	All[5]	With gain[4]	With loss	All[4]
Gain or loss, $000	70,017	−94,947	−24,930	22,790	−42,004	−19,214	47,227	−52,943	−5,716
Receipts, $000	334,471	277,048	611,519	166,098	157,569	323,667	168,373	119,479	287,852
No. of sales	32,802	37,737	70,539	10,874	12,023	22,897	21,928	25,714	47,642
Av. gain or loss ($) per Return	36,774	−49,867	−13,093	107,500	−198,132	−90,632	27,912	−31,290	−3,378
Sale	2,135	−2,516	−353	2,096	−3,494	−839	2,154	−2,059	−120
Av. receipts ($) per Return	175,668	145,508	321,175	783,481	743,250	1,526,731	99,511	70,614	170,125
Sale	10,197	7,342	8,669	15,275	13,106	14,136	7,678	4,646	6,042
Av. no. of sales per return	17	20	37	51	57	108	13	15	28

B 1932

	3,404 Returns			201 Market Traders			3,203 Other Returns		
	With gain[4]	With loss[5]	All[4,5]	With gain	With loss[5]	All[5]	With gain[4]	With loss	All[4]
Gain or loss, $000	20,435	−138,379	−117,944	9,720	−43,012	−33,292	10,715	−95,367	−84,652
Receipts, $000	140,354	222,822	363,176	66,377	112,576	178,953	73,977	110,246	184,223
No. of sales	30,666	52,169	82,835	6,309	8,516	14,825	24,357	43,653	68,010
Av. gain or loss ($) per Return	6,003	−40,652	−34,649	48,358	−213,990	−165,632	3,345	−29,774	−26,429
Sale	666	−2,653	−1,424	1,541	−5,051	−2,246	440	−2,185	−1,245
Av. receipts ($) per Return	41,232	65,459	106,691	330,234	560,080	890,313	23,096	34,420	57,516
Sale	4,577	4,271	4,384	10,521	13,219	12,071	3,037	2,526	2,709
Av. no. of sales per return	9	15	24	31	42	74	8	14	21

Based on Source 5.

For numbered notes see pp. 448-9.

Table 46

Capital Gains and Losses from Sales of Assets Segregated and Not Segregated at 12½ Percent, Sample Returns, 1930, 1932, and 1933, and Subject or Not Subject to Statutory Limitation on Losses, Sample Returns, 1932 and 1933

TYPE OF SALE	NET GAIN	NET LOSS	EXCESS OF GAIN	GROSS RECEIPTS	NET GAIN	NET LOSS	GROSS RECEIPTS	EXCESS OF GAIN AS % OF EST. COST[3]
	(thousands of dollars)				(percentages)			
A 1930								
1,904 Returns								
Segregated[4]	33,945	3,353	30,592	88,135	88.1	5.2	14.1	53.2
Other	4,569	60,943	−56,374	534,927	11.9	94.8	85.9	−9.5
Total[4]	38,514	64,296	−25,782	623,063	100.0	100.0	100.0	−4.0
212 Market Traders								
Segregated	6,246	1,236	5,010	21,004	82.9	4.6	6.4	31.3
Other	1,289	25,842	−24,553	309,658	17.1	95.4	93.6	−7.3
Total	7,536	27,078	−19,542	330,662	100.0	100.0	100.0	−5.6
1,692 Other Returns								
Segregated[4]	27,699	2,117	25,582	67,131	89.4	5.7	23.0	61.6
Other	3,280	35,101	−31,821	225,269	10.6	94.3	77.0	−12.4
Total[4]	30,979	37,218	−6,239	292,400	100.0	100.0	100.0	−2.1
B 1932								
3,404 Returns								
Segregated[5]	3,260	67,035	−63,775	101,642	55.0	52.2	26.9	−38.6
Other, total	2,666	61,411	−58,745	275,725	45.0	47.8	73.1	−17.6
Subject to limitation	1,864	24,810	−22,946	158,896	31.5	19.3	42.1	−12.6
Not subject	802	36,603	−35,801	116,829	13.5	28.5	31.0	−23.5
All sales[5]	5,926	128,448	−122,522	377,368	100.0	100.0	100.0	−24.5
201 Market Traders								
Segregated[5]	1,592	20,156	−18,564	59,223	67.1	54.3	31.9	−23.9
Other, total	780	16,979	−16,199	126,535	32.9	45.7	68.1	−11.3
Subject to limitation	497	8,127	−7,630	57,457	21.0	21.9	30.9	−11.7
Not subject	283	8,852	−8,569	69,078	11.9	23.8	37.2	−11.0
All sales[5]	2,372	37,135	−34,763	185,758	100.0	100.0	100.0	−15.8

453

TYPE OF SALE	GROSS GAIN	GROSS LOSS	EXCESS OF GAIN	GROSS RECEIPTS	GROSS GAIN	GROSS LOSS	GROSS RECEIPTS	EXCESS OF GAIN AS % OF EST. COST[3]
	(thousands of dollars)				(percentages)			
C 1933								
3,203 Other Returns								
Segregated	1,668	46,880	−45,212	42,419	46.9	51.3	22.1	−51.6
Other, total	1,886	44,432	−42,546	149,190	53.1	48.7	77.9	−22.2
Subject to limitation	1,367	16,681	−15,314	101,439	38.5	18.3	52.9	−13.1
Not subject	519	27,751	−27,232	47,751	14.6	30.4	24.9	−36.3
All sales	3,554	91,312	−87,758	191,609	100.0	100.0	100.0	−31.4
2,164 Returns[7]								
Segregated	11,822	36,848	−25,026	55,592	28.7	49.3	12.5	−31.0
Other, total	29,306	37,915	−8,609	390,278	71.3	50.7	87.5	−2.2
Subject to limitation	25,571	15,030	10,541	271,458	62.2	20.1	60.9	4.0
Not subject	3,735	22,885	−19,150	118,820	9.1	30.6	26.6	−13.9
All sales	41,128	74,763	−33,635	445,870	100.0	100.0	100.0	−7.0
322 Market Traders[7]								
Segregated	9,822	21,191	−11,369	38,407	39.8	59.5	13.6	−22.8
Other, total	14,851	14,453	398	243,268	60.2	40.5	86.4	0.2
Subject to limitation	13,106	8,311	4,795	157,643	53.1	23.3	56.0	3.1
Not subject	1,745	6,142	−4,397	85,625	7.1	17.2	30.4	−4.9
All sales	24,673	35,644	−10,971	281,675	100.0	100.0	100.0	−3.7
1,842 Other Returns[7]								
Segregated	2,000	15,657	−13,657	17,185	12.2	40.0	10.5	−44.3
Other, total	14,455	23,462	−9,007	147,010	87.8	60.0	89.5	−5.8
Subject to limitation	12,465	6,719	5,746	113,815	75.8	17.2	69.3	5.3
Not subject	1,990	16,743	−14,753	33,195	12.1	42.8	20.2	−30.8
All sales	16,455	39,119	−22,664	164,195	100.0	100.0	100.0	−12.1

Based on Source 5.

For numbered notes see pp. 448-9.

Table 47

Sales Subject and Not Subject to Statutory Limitation on Losses by Type of Sale, Sample Returns, 1932 and 1933

A 1932: SALES OF SECURITIES

TYPE OF SALE	SALES WITH GAIN			SALES WITH LOSS			PERCENTAGE DISTRIBUTION			
	Gross gain ($000)	No. of sales	Av. gain per sale ($)	Gross loss ($000)	No. of sales	Av. loss per sale ($)	Gross gain	No. of sales with gain	Gross loss	No. of sales with loss
				3,404 Returns						
Subject to limitation	7,928	26,425	300	30,374	26,750	1,135	38.8	86.2	21.9	51.3
Not subject	12,507	4,241	2,949	108,004	25,419	4,249	61.2	13.8	78.0	48.7
All sales	20,435	30,666	666	138,379	52,169	2,653	100.0	100.0	100.0	100.0
Subject to limitation, total[8]	6,939	24,610	282	25,590	25,107	1,019	100.0	100.0	100.0	100.0
Short sales of stocks	887	3,437	258	1,088	2,376	458	12.8	14.0	4.3	9.5
Long sales of stocks held 2 yr. or less	5,582	19,265	290	22,575	20,341	1,110	80.4	78.3	88.2	81.0
Bonds (except gov.) held 2 yr. or less	470	1,908	246	1,927	2,390	806	6.8	7.7	7.5	9.5
Not subject to limitation, total[8]	8,192	3,723	2,200	86,707	23,035	3,764	100.0	100.0	100.0	100.0
Held 2 yr. or less (gov. bonds)	277	978	283	1,697	1,074	1,580	3.4	26.2	2.0	4.7
Held over 2 yr.										
Stocks	7,198	1,413	5,094	67,301	12,941	5,201	87.9	38.0	77.6	56.2
Bonds	717	1,332	538	17,709	9,020	1,963	8.7	35.8	20.4	39.1
Not stated	5,304	2,333	2,273	26,081	4,027	6,477				
All sales	20,435	30,666	666	138,379	52,169	2,653				
				201 Market Traders						
Subject to limitation	2,919	5,346	546	10,169	4,977	2,043	30.0	84.7	23.6	58.4
Not subject	6,801	963	7,062	32,842	3,539	9,280	70.0	15.3	76.4	41.6
All sales	9,720	6,309	1,541	43,011	8,516	5,051	100.0	100.0	100.0	100.0

455

TYPE OF SALE	SALES WITH GAIN			SALES WITH LOSS			PERCENTAGE DISTRIBUTION			
	Gross gain ($000)	No. of sales	Av. gain per sale ($)	Gross loss ($000)	No. of sales	Av. loss per sale ($)	Gross gain	No. of sales with gain	Gross loss	No. of sales with loss
Subject to limitation, total[8]	2,495	5,169	483	8,456	4,754	1,779	100.0	100.0	100.0	100.0
Short sales of stocks	446	1,273	350	535	886	604	17.9	24.6	6.3	18.6
Long sales of stocks held 2 yr. or less	1,936	3,651	530	7,377	3,476	2,122	77.6	70.6	87.2	73.1
Bonds (except gov.) held 2 yr. or less	113	245	461	544	392	1,388	4.5	4.7	6.4	8.2
Not subject to limitation, total[8]	4,312	900	4,791	24,937	3,229	7,723	100.0	100.0	100.0	100.0
Held 2 yr. or less (gov. bonds)	187	330	567	1,133	428	2,647	4.3	36.7	4.5	13.3
Held over 2 yr.										
Stocks	3,706	251	14,765	17,624	1,217	14,482	86.0	27.9	70.7	37.7
Bonds	419	319	1,313	6,180	1,584	3,902	9.7	35.4	24.8	49.1
Not stated	2,913	240	12,138	9,618	533	18,045				
All sales	9,720	6,309	1,541	43,012	8,516	5,051				
				3,203 Other Returns						
Subject to limitation	5,009	21,079	238	20,205	21,773	928	46.7	86.5	21.2	49.9
Not subject	5,706	3,278	1,741	75,162	21,880	3,435	53.3	13.5	78.8	50.1
All sales	10,715	24,357	440	95,367	43,653	2,185	100.0	100.0	100.0	100.0
Subject to limitation, total[8]	4,444	19,441	229	17,134	20,353	842	100.0	100.0	100.0	100.0
Short sales of stocks	441	2,164	204	553	1,490	371	9.9	11.1	3.2	7.3
Long sales of stocks held 2 yr. or less	3,646	15,614	234	15,198	16,865	901	82.0	80.3	88.7	82.9
Bonds (except gov.) held 2 yr. or less	357	1,663	215	1,383	1,998	692	8.0	8.6	8.1	9.8
Not subject to limitation, total[8]	3,880	2,823	1,374	61,770	19,806	3,119	100.0	100.0	100.0	100.0
Held 2 yr. or less (gov. bonds)	90	648	139	564	646	873	2.3	23.0	0.9	3.3
Held over 2 yr.										
Stocks	3,492	1,162	3,005	49,677	11,724	4,237	90.0	41.2	80.4	59.2
Bonds	298	1,013	294	11,529	7,436	1,550	7.7	35.9	18.7	37.5
Not stated	2,391	2,093	1,142	16,463	3,494	4,712				
All sales	10,715	24,357	440	95,367	43,653	2,185				

B 1933: SALES OF ASSETS

TYPE OF SALE	Gross gain	Gross loss	Excess of gain	Gross receipts	PERCENTAGE DISTRIBUTION			Net gain as % of est. cost[3]
					Gross gain[7]	Gross loss	Gross receipts	
2,164 Returns[7]								
Subject to limitation	25,571	15,030	10,541	271,458	62.2	20.1	60.9	4.0
Not subject, total	15,557	59,733	−44,176	174,412	37.8	79.9	39.1	−20.2
Held 2 yr. or less	1,386	1,355	31	92,380	3.4	1.8	20.7	†
Segregated at 12½%	11,822	36,848	−25,026	55,592	28.7	49.3	12.5	−31.0
Other sales held over 2 yr.	2,349	21,530	−19,181	26,440	5.7	28.8	5.9	−42.0
All sales	41,128	74,763	−33,635	445,870	100.0	100.0	100.0	−7.0
322 Market Traders[7]								
Subject to limitation	13,106	8,311	4,795	157,643	53.1	23.3	56.0	3.1
Not subject, total	11,567	27,333	−15,766	124,032	46.9	76.7	44.0	−11.3
Held 2 yr. or less	905	843	62	77,937	3.7	2.4	27.7	0.1
Segregated at 12½%	9,822	21,191	−11,369	38,407	39.8	59.5	13.6	−22.8
Other sales held over 2 yr.	840	5,299	−4,459	7,688	3.4	14.9	2.7	−36.7
All sales	24,673	35,644	−10,971	281,675	100.0	100.0	100.0	−3.7
1,842 Other Returns[7]								
Subject to limitation	12,465	6,719	5,746	113,815	75.8	17.2	69.3	5.3
Not subject, total	3,990	32,400	−28,410	50,380	24.2	82.8	30.7	−36.1
Held 2 yr. or less	481	512	−31	14,443	2.9	1.3	8.8	−0.2
Segregated at 12½%	2,000	15,657	−13,657	17,185	12.2	40.0	10.5	−44.3
Other sales held over 2 yr.	1,509	16,231	−14,722	18,752	9.2	41.5	11.4	−44.0
All sales	16,455	39,119	−22,664	164,195	100.0	100.0	100.0	−12.1

Based on Source 5.
For numbered notes see pp. 448-9.

† Less than 0.05 percent.

Table 48

Disallowed Short Term Net Losses from Sales of Assets, by Statutory Net Income Groups: Amounts Reported on Sample Returns, 1932 and 1933 (dollar figures in thousands)

STATUTORY NET INCOME GROUP ($000)	NET LOSS NOT SEGREGATED AT 12½%			NET LOSS SEG. AT 12½% (4)	TOTAL NET LOSS (3)+(4) (5)	DISALLOWED NET LOSS AS % OF		
	Disallowed (1)	Statutory[9] (2)	Total (1)+(2) (3)			Total net loss except seg. (1)÷(3) (6)	Total net loss (1)÷(5) (7)	Total gross loss[10,11] (8)
A 1932 (3,404 RETURNS)								
Under 5	1,386	1,715	3,101	1,387	4,488	44.7	30.9	27.2
5- 25	5,627	3,038	8,665	8,063	16,728	64.9	33.6	28.4
25- 50	3,407	305	3,712	11,664	15,376	91.8	22.2	19.7
50-100	3,273	315	3,588	20,240	23,828	91.2	13.7	12.9
100-300	2,387	767	3,154	18,827	21,981	75.8	10.9	9.9
300 & over	817	275	1,092	6,854	7,946	74.8	10.3	10.1
Total	16,897	6,414	23,311	67,035	90,346	72.5	18.7	16.9
Net deficit	7,913	30,630	38,543		38,543	20.5	20.5	20.5
All returns	24,810	37,044	61,854	67,035	128,889	40.1	19.2	17.9
B 1933 (2,164 RETURNS)[7]								
Under 5	191	621	812		812	23.5	23.5	7.5
5- 25	551	960	1,511	2,333	3,844	36.5	14.3	6.4
25- 50	336	27	363	8,795	9,158	92.5	3.7	2.6
50-100	228	16	244	7,022	7,266	93.4	3.1	2.2
100-300	142	34	176 ⎱	13,243	13,497	80.7 ⎱	1.1	0.8
300 & over	3	75	78 ⎰			3.8 ⎰		
Total	1,451	1,733	3,184	31,393	34,577	45.6	4.2	2.7
Net deficit	853	15,474	16,327		16,327	5.2	5.2	3.9
All returns	2,304	17,207	19,511	31,393	50,904	11.8	4.5	3.1

Based on Source 5.

For numbered notes see pp. 448-9.

458

Table 49

Disallowed Short Term Net Losses from Sales of Assets, by Statutory Net Income Groups: Estimated Amount for All Returns, 1932 and 1933 (dollar figures in millions)

| STATUTORY NET INCOME GROUP ($000) | STAT. NET LOSS REPORTED ON ALL RETURNS | | | DISALLOWED NET LOSS AS % OF | | ESTIMATED DISALLOWED NET LOSS ON ALL RETURNS | |
	Not segregated at 12½% (1)	Segregated at 12½% (2)	Total (3)	Total loss except segregated at 12½%[12,13] (4)	Total loss[12,13] (5)	A[14] (6)	B[14] (7)
A 1932							
Under 5	200.8		200.8	44.7	30.9	162.3	89.8
5- 25	156.2	116.1	272.3	64.9	33.6	289.3	138.1
25- 50	7.9	241.1	249.0	91.8	22.2	88.0	71.0
50-100	4.8	219.0	223.8	91.2	13.7	49.6	35.6
100-300	3.5	169.9	173.4	75.8	10.9	10.8	21.1
300 & over	2.3	86.2	88.5	74.8	10.3	6.8	10.2
Total	375.4	832.4	1,207.8	72.5	18.7	606.8	365.8
Net deficit	835.3		835.3	20.5	20.5	215.8	215.8
All returns	1,210.7	832.4	2,043.1	40.1	19.2	822.6	581.6
B 1933							
Under 5	212.8		212.8	23.5	23.5	65.5	65.5
5- 25	138.7	69.4	208.1	36.5	14.3	79.6	34.8
25- 50	6.9	169.8	176.7	92.5	3.7	85.6	6.7
50-100	3.2	151.4	154.6	93.4	3.1	45.0	4.9
100-300	2.9	107.8	110.7	80.7 ⎫	1.1	12.1 ⎫	1.8
300 & over	1.3	55.4	56.7	3.8 ⎭		0.1 ⎭	
Total	365.8	553.8	919.6	45.6	4.2	287.9	113.7
Net deficit	773.9		773.9	5.2	5.2	42.6	42.6
All returns	1,139.7	553.8	1,693.5	11.8	4.5	330.5	156.3

Statutory net loss from Source 1; columns 4 and 5 based on Source 5.
For numbered notes see pp. 448-9.

Table 50: Sales of Stocks and of Bonds, Sample Returns, 1930 and 1932

TYPE OF SECURITY	GROSS GAIN OR LOSS (thousands of dollars)	GROSS RECEIPTS (thousands of dollars)	NO. OF SALES	AV. GAIN OR LOSS PER SALE (dollars)	AV. GROSS RECEIPTS PER SALE (dollars)	GROSS GAIN OR LOSS (percentages)	GROSS RECEIPTS (percentages)	NO. OF SALES (percentages)	GROSS GAIN OR LOSS AS % OF EST. COST[3]
A 1930									
1,904 Returns									
Sales with gain, total[4]	70,017	334,471	32,802	2,135	10,197	100.0	100.0	100.0	26.5
Stocks	33,770	236,350	27,279	1,238	8,664	94.4	89.4	90.8	16.7
Bonds	2,015	28,036	2,749	733	10,199	5.6	10.6	9.2	7.7
Not stated[4]	34,233	70,085	2,774	12,341	25,265				95.5
Sales with loss, total	−94,947	277,048	37,737	−2,516	7,342	100.0	100.0	100.0	−25.5
Stocks	−76,528	218,025	32,512	−2,354	6,706	97.4	90.3	91.6	−26.0
Bonds	−2,080	23,476	2,969	−701	7,907	2.6	9.7	8.4	−8.1
Not stated	−16,339	35,548	2,256	−7,242	15,757				−31.5
212 Market Traders									
Sales with gain, total	22,790	166,098	10,874	2,096	15,275	100.0	100.0	100.0	15.9
Stocks	17,487	146,760	9,689	1,805	15,147	93.8	94.1	94.2	13.5
Bonds	1,163	9,239	599	1,942	15,424	6.2	5.9	5.8	14.4
Not stated	4,141	10,099	586	7,067	17,234				69.5
Sales with loss, total	−42,004	157,569	12,023	−3,494	13,106	100.0	100.0	100.0	−21.0
Stocks	−36,110	136,612	10,926	−3,305	12,503	98.4	92.7	94.6	−20.9
Bonds	−597	10,701	618	−966	17,316	1.6	7.3	5.4	−5.3
Not stated	−5,297	10,257	479	−11,058	21,413				−34.1
1,692 Other Returns									
Sales with gain, total[4]	47,227	168,373	21,928	2,154	7,678	100.0	100.0	100.0	39.0
Stocks	16,283	89,590	17,590	926	5,093	95.0	82.7	89.1	22.2
Bonds	852	18,797	2,150	396	8,743	5.0	17.3	10.9	4.7
Not stated[4]	30,092	59,986	2,188	13,753	27,416				100.7
Sales with loss, total	−52,943	119,479	25,714	−2,059	4,646	100.0	100.0	100.0	−30.7
Stocks	−40,418	81,413	21,586	−1,872	3,772	96.5	86.4	90.2	−33.2
Bonds	−1,483	12,775	2,351	−631	5,434	3.5	13.6	9.8	−10.4
Not stated	−11,042	25,291	1,777	−6,214	14,232				−30.4

B 1932

3,404 Returns

Sales with gain, total	20,435	140,354	30,666	666	4,577	100.0	100.0	100.0	17.0
Stocks	13,667	76,869	24,115	567	3,188	90.3	66.3	85.1	21.6
Bonds	1,464	39,064	4,218	347	9,261	9.7	33.7	14.9	3.9
Not stated	5,304	24,421	2,333	2,273	10,468				27.7
Sales with loss, total[5]	−138,379	222,822	52,169	−2,653	4,271	100.0	100.0	100.0	−38.3
Stocks	−90,964	81,295	35,658	−2,551	2,280	81.0	46.3	74.1	−52.8
Bonds[5]	−21,333	94,371	12,484	−1,709	7,559	19.0	53.7	25.9	−18.4
Not stated	−26,081	47,156	4,027	−6,477	11,710				−35.6

201 Market Traders

Sales with gain, total	9,720	66,377	6,309	1,541	10,521	100.0	100.0	100.0	17.2
Stocks	6,088	31,908	5,175	1,176	6,166	89.4	54.8	85.3	23.6
Bonds	719	26,276	894	804	29,391	10.6	45.2	14.7	2.8
Not stated	2,913	8,193	240	12,138	34,138				55.2
Sales with loss, total[5]	−43,012	112,576	8,516	−5,051	13,219	100.0	100.0	100.0	−27.6
Stocks	−25,536	30,908	5,579	−4,577	5,540	76.5	32.0	69.9	−45.2
Bonds[5]	−7,857	65,581	2,404	−3,268	27,280	23.5	68.0	30.1	−10.7
Not stated	−9,618	16,087	533	−18,045	30,182				−37.4

3,203 Other Returns

Sales with gain, total	10,715	73,977	24,357	440	3,037	100.0	100.0	100.0	16.9
Stocks	7,579	44,961	18,940	400	2,374	91.0	77.9	85.1	20.3
Bonds	745	12,788	3,324	224	3,847	9.0	22.1	14.9	6.2
Not stated	2,391	16,228	2,093	1,142	7,753				17.3
Sales with loss, total	−95,367	110,246	43,653	−2,185	2,526	100.0	100.0	100.0	−46.4
Stocks	−65,428	50,387	30,079	−2,175	1,675	82.9	63.6	74.9	−56.5
Bonds	−13,476	28,790	10,080	−1,337	2,856	17.1	36.4	25.1	−31.9
Not stated	−16,463	31,069	3,494	−4,712	8,892				−34.6

Based on Source 5.

For numbered notes see pp. 448-9.

Table 51: Sales of Securities by Month of Sale: Gross Capital Gains and Losses, Gross Receipts, and Number of Sales Sample Returns, 1930 and 1932 (dollar figures in thousands)

A 1930
1,904 Returns

MONTH OF SALE	ALL SALES			SALES WITH GAIN			SALES WITH LOSS		
	Excess of loss[a]	Gross receipts	Number	Gross gain	Gross receipts	Number	Gross loss	Gross receipts	Number
January	1,017	37,319	4,463	3,091	22,747	2,600	4,108	14,572	1,863
February	−2,034	44,297	5,319	4,965	29,376	3,394	2,931	14,921	1,925
March	−3,650	70,388	7,474	7,222	50,193	5,103	3,572	20,195	2,371
April	−23,625[a]	95,234[a]	8,275	27,320[a]	72,421[a]	5,547	3,695	22,813	2,728
May	−571	50,426	6,295	4,918	26,347	3,162	4,347	24,079	3,133
June	5,634	63,304	6,803	4,041	25,553	2,266	9,675	37,751	4,537
July	1,228	30,663	3,679	2,326	16,705	1,985	3,554	13,958	1,694
August	1,255	31,242	3,372	1,729	15,082	1,514	2,984	16,160	1,858
September	2,713	31,663	4,292	2,095	13,720	1,732	4,808	17,943	2,560
October	9,605	43,385	6,435	3,110	16,064	1,944	12,715	27,321	4,491
November	8,561	33,841	4,883	2,480	11,394	1,407	11,041	22,447	3,476
December	22,874	45,481	7,562	2,095	15,381	1,338	24,969	30,100	6,224
Total	23,007	577,243	68,852	65,392	314,983	31,992	88,399	262,260	36,860
Not stated	1,920	34,275	1,687	4,626	19,487	810	6,546	14,788	877
Grand total	24,930	611,519	70,539	70,017	334,471	32,802	94,947	277,048	37,737

PERCENTAGE DISTRIBUTION

MONTH OF SALE	ALL SALES			SALES WITH GAIN			SALES WITH LOSS		
	Excess of loss[a]	Gross receipts	Number	Gross gain	Gross receipts	Number	Gross loss	Gross receipts	Number
January	4.4	6.5	6.5	4.7	7.2	8.1	4.6	5.6	5.1
February	−8.8	7.7	7.7	7.6	9.3	10.6	3.3	5.7	5.2
March	−15.9	12.2	10.9	11.0	15.9	16.0	4.0	7.7	6.4
April	−102.7[a]	16.5[a]	12.0	41.8[a]	23.0[a]	17.3	4.2	8.7	7.4
May	−2.5	8.7	9.1	7.5	8.5	9.9	4.9	9.2	8.5
June	24.5	11.0	9.9	6.2	8.1	7.1	10.9	14.4	12.3
July	5.3	5.3	5.3	3.6	5.3	6.2	4.0	5.3	4.6
August	5.5	5.4	4.9	2.6	4.8	4.7	3.5	6.2	5.0
September	11.8	5.5	6.2	3.2	4.4	5.4	5.4	6.8	6.9
October	41.7	7.5	9.3	4.8	5.1	6.1	14.4	10.4	12.2
November	37.2	5.9	7.1	3.8	3.6	4.4	12.5	8.6	9.4
December	99.4	7.9	11.0	3.2	4.9	4.2	28.2	11.5	16.9
Total	100.0	100.0	100.0	100.0	100.0	100.0	100.0	100.0	100.0

212 Market Traders

January	788	21,571	1,390	1,425	13,236	827	2,213	8,335	563
February	−1,192	25,598	1,569	2,678	17,107	1,009	1,486	8,491	560
March	−2,148	41,262	2,530	3,511	29,605	1,762	1,603	11,657	768
April	−1,677	38,861	2,546	3,751	25,646	1,702	1,834	13,215	844
May	−337	30,828	2,211	2,890	15,005	1,048	2,553	15,823	1,163
June	3,631	37,205	2,462	1,567	12,558	818	5,198	24,647	1,644
July	1,374	18,230	1,251	751	8,973	672	2,125	9,257	579
August	762	20,633	1,243	658	9,978	555	1,420	10,655	688
September	1,831	20,638	1,728	714	8,261	686	2,545	12,377	1,042
October	4,724	25,523	2,191	1,809	9,360	725	6,533	16,163	1,466
November	3,126	18,435	1,485	1,577	6,922	486	4,703	11,513	999
December	7,125	20,023	1,997	900	7,329	465	8,025	12,694	1,532
Total	18,007	318,807	22,603	22,231	163,980	10,755	40,238	154,827	11,848
Not stated	1,204	4,860	294	560	2,118	119	1,764	2,742	175
Grand total	19,214	323,667	22,897	22,790	166,098	10,874	42,004	157,569	12,023

PERCENTAGE DISTRIBUTION

January	4.4	6.8	6.1	6.4	8.1	7.7	5.5	5.4	4.8
February	−6.6	8.0	6.9	12.0	10.4	9.4	3.7	5.5	4.7
March	−11.9	12.9	11.2	16.9	18.1	16.4	4.0	7.5	6.5
April	−9.3	12.2	11.3	15.8	15.6	15.8	4.6	8.5	7.1
May	−1.9	9.7	9.8	13.0	9.2	9.7	6.3	10.2	9.8
June	20.2	11.7	10.9	7.0	7.7	7.6	12.9	15.9	13.9
July	7.6	5.7	5.5	3.4	5.5	6.2	5.3	6.0	4.9
August	4.2	6.5	5.5	3.0	6.1	5.2	3.5	6.9	5.8
September	10.2	6.5	7.6	3.2	5.0	6.4	6.3	8.0	8.8
October	26.2	8.0	9.7	8.1	5.7	6.7	16.2	10.4	12.4
November	17.4	5.8	6.7	7.1	4.2	4.5	11.7	7.4	8.4
December	39.6	6.3	8.8	4.0	4.5	4.3	19.9	8.2	12.9
Total[16]	100.0	100.0	100.0	100.0	100.0	100.0	100.0	100.0	100.0

MONTH OF SALE	Excess of loss[a]	ALL SALES		SALES WITH GAIN			SALES WITH LOSS		
		Gross receipts	Number	Gross gain	Gross receipts	Number	Gross loss	Gross receipts	Number
				1,692 Other Returns					
January	229	15,748	3,073	1,666	9,511	1,773	1,895	6,237	1,300
February	−842	18,699	3,750	2,287	12,269	2,385	1,445	6,430	1,365
March	−1,502	29,126	4,944	3,471	20,588	3,341	1,969	8,538	1,603
April	−21,948⁴	56,373⁴	5,729	23,809⁴	46,775⁴	3,845	1,861	9,598	1,884
May	−234	19,598	4,084	2,028	11,342	2,114	1,794	8,256	1,970
June	2,003	26,099	4,341	2,474	12,995	1,448	4,477	13,104	2,893
July	−146	12,433	2,428	1,575	7,732	1,313	1,429	4,701	1,115
August	493	10,609	2,129	1,071	5,104	959	1,564	5,505	1,170
September	882	11,025	2,564	1,381	5,459	1,046	2,263	5,566	1,518
October	4,881	17,862	4,244	1,301	6,704	1,219	6,182	11,158	3,025
November	5,435	15,406	3,398	903	4,472	921	6,338	10,934	2,477
December	15,749	25,458	5,565	1,195	8,052	873	16,944	17,406	4,692
Total	5,000	258,436	46,249	43,161	151,003	21,237	48,161	107,433	25,012
Not stated	716	29,415	1,393	4,066	17,369	691	4,782	12,046	702
Grand total	5,716	287,852	47,642	47,227	168,373	21,928	52,943	119,479	25,714

PERCENTAGE DISTRIBUTION

MONTH OF SALE	Excess of loss[a]	ALL SALES		SALES WITH GAIN			SALES WITH LOSS		
		Gross receipts	Number	Gross gain	Gross receipts	Number	Gross loss	Gross receipts	Number
January	4.6	6.1	6.6	3.9	6.3	8.3	3.9	5.8	5.2
February	−16.8	7.2	8.1	5.3	8.1	11.2	3.0	6.0	5.5
March	−30.0	11.3	10.7	8.0	13.6	15.7	4.1	7.9	6.2
April	−439.0⁴	21.8⁴	12.4	55.2⁴	31.0⁴	18.1	3.9	8.9	7.5
May	−4.7	7.6	8.8	4.7	7.5	10.0	3.7	7.7	7.9
June	40.0	10.1	9.4	5.7	8.6	6.8	9.3	12.2	11.6
July	−2.9	4.8	5.2	3.6	5.1	6.2	3.0	4.4	4.5
August	9.9	4.1	4.6	2.5	3.4	4.5	3.2	5.1	4.7
September	17.6	4.3	5.5	3.2	3.6	4.9	4.7	5.2	6.1
October	97.6	6.9	9.3	3.0	4.4	5.7	12.8	10.4	12.1
November	108.7	6.0	7.3	2.1	3.0	4.3	13.2	10.2	9.9
December	315.0	9.9	12.0	2.8	5.3	4.1	35.2	16.2	18.8
Total[16]	100.0	100.0	100.0	100.0	100.0	100.0	100.0	100.0	100.0

B 1932

3,404 Returns

January	4,169	24,090	5,444	2,770	10,832	2,160	6,939	13,258	3,284
February	5,725	19,220	5,383	1,052	7,513	2,078	6,777	11,707	3,305
March	8,238	23,585	5,198	983	9,887	1,854	9,221	13,698	3,344
April	9,437	42,166⁶	5,737	1,492	8,864	1,382	10,929	33,302⁶	4,355
May	8,080	20,728	5,017	811	8,750	1,070	8,891	11,978	3,947
June	9,181	20,372	4,709	740	5,116	1,222	9,921	15,256	3,487
July	7,172	15,564	4,325	589	5,774	1,494	7,761	9,790	2,831
August	8,964	38,305	12,804	2,641	22,074	7,257	11,605	16,231	5,547
September	2,075	36,194	9,674	3,157	18,601	5,396	5,232	17,593	4,278
October	4,290	20,001	5,630	867	8,456	1,844	5,157	11,545	3,786
November	8,339	21,675	5,088	803	7,480	1,720	9,142	14,195	3,368
December	33,746	32,583	9,377	1,639	9,246	1,419	35,385	23,337	7,958
Total	109,416	314,483	78,386	17,544	122,593	28,896	126,960	191,890	49,490
Not stated	8,527	48,692	4,449	2,892	17,760	1,770	11,419	30,932	2,679
Grand total	117,944	363,176	82,835	20,435	140,354	30,666	138,379	222,822	52,169

PERCENTAGE DISTRIBUTION

January	3.8	7.7	6.9	15.8	8.8	7.5	5.5	6.9	6.6
February	5.2	6.1	6.9	6.0	6.1	7.2	5.3	6.1	6.7
March	7.5	7.5	6.6	5.6	8.1	6.4	7.3	7.1	6.8
April	8.6	13.4⁶	7.3	8.5	7.2	4.8	8.6	17.4⁶	8.8
May	7.4	6.6	6.4	4.6	7.1	3.7	7.0	6.2	8.0
June	8.4	6.5	6.0	4.2	4.2	4.2	7.8	8.0	7.0
July	6.6	4.9	5.5	3.4	4.7	5.2	6.1	5.1	5.7
August	8.2	12.2	16.3	15.1	18.0	25.1	9.1	8.5	11.2
September	1.9	11.5	12.3	18.0	15.2	18.7	4.1	9.2	8.6
October	3.9	6.4	7.2	4.9	6.9	6.4	4.1	6.0	7.7
November	7.6	6.9	6.5	4.6	6.1	6.0	7.2	7.4	6.8
December	30.8	10.4	12.0	9.3	7.5	4.9	27.9	12.2	16.1
Total¹⁵	100.0	100.0	100.0	100.0	100.0	100.0	100.0	100.0	100.0

201 Market Traders

MONTH OF SALE	ALL SALES			SALES WITH GAIN			SALES WITH LOSS		
	Excess of loss[2]	Gross receipts	Number	Gross gain	Gross receipts	Number	Gross loss	Gross receipts	Number
January	419	11,788	1,143	2,024	5,770	483	2,443	6,018	660
February	1,763	5,965	977	276	2,461	371	2,039	3,504	606
March	3,750	12,790	1,067	470	5,678	476	4,220	7,112	591
April	2,287	31,154⁵	1,108	791	5,319	448	3,078	25,835⁵	660
May	1,584	12,204	962	412	6,483	357	1,996	5,721	605
June	2,355	12,253	1,019	430	2,270	374	2,785	9,983	645
July	2,672	8,661	885	264	3,133	268	2,936	5,528	617
August	3,383	18,266	2,357	864	10,012	1,393	4,247	8,254	964
September	−557	18,966	1,557	1,729	8,195	926	1,172	10,771	631
October	988	10,459	1,047	415	4,624	403	1,403	5,835	644
November	3,411	12,623	1,029	299	3,889	379	3,710	8,734	650
December	9,426	14,229	1,239	844	5,163	292	10,270	9,066	947
Total	31,481	169,358	14,390	8,818	62,997	6,170	40,299	106,361	8,220
Not stated	1,810	9,596	435	902	3,380	139	2,712	6,216	296
Grand total	33,292	178,953	14,825	9,720	66,377	6,309	43,012	112,576	8,516

PERCENTAGE DISTRIBUTION

MONTH OF SALE	ALL SALES			SALES WITH GAIN			SALES WITH LOSS		
	Excess of loss	Gross receipts	Number	Gross gain	Gross receipts	Number	Gross loss	Gross receipts	Number
January	1.3	7.0	7.9	23.0	9.2	7.8	6.1	5.7	8.0
February	5.6	3.5	6.8	3.1	3.9	6.0	5.1	3.3	7.4
March	11.9	7.6	7.4	5.3	9.0	7.7	10.5	6.7	7.2
April	7.3	18.4⁵	7.7	9.0	8.4	7.3	7.6	24.3⁵	8.0
May	5.0	7.2	6.7	4.7	10.3	5.8	5.0	5.4	7.4
June	7.5	7.2	7.1	4.9	3.6	6.1	6.9	9.4	7.8
July	8.5	5.1	6.2	3.0	5.0	4.3	7.3	5.2	7.5
August	10.7	10.8	16.4	9.8	15.9	22.6	10.5	7.8	11.7
September	−1.8	11.2	10.8	19.6	13.0	15.0	2.9	10.1	7.7
October	3.1	6.2	7.3	4.7	7.3	6.5	3.5	5.5	7.8
November	10.8	7.5	7.2	3.4	6.2	6.1	9.2	8.2	7.9
December	29.9	8.4	8.6	9.6	8.2	4.7	25.5	8.5	11.5
Total[12]	100.0	100.0	100.0	100.0	100.0	100.0	100.0	100.0	100.0

3,203 Other Returns

	(1)	(2)	(3)	(4)	(5)	(6)	(7)	(8)
January	4,301	12,302	746	5,062	1,677	4,496	7,240	2,624
February	4,406	13,255	776	5,052	1,707	4,738	8,203	2,699
March	4,131	10,795	513	4,209	1,378	5,001	6,586	2,753
April	4,629	11,012	701	3,545	934	7,851	7,467	3,695
May	4,055	8,524	399	2,267	713	6,895	6,257	3,342
June	3,690	8,119	310	2,846	848	7,136	5,273	2,842
July	3,440	6,903	325	2,641	1,226	4,825	4,262	2,214
August	10,447	20,039	1,777	12,062	5,864	7,358	7,977	4,583
September	8,117	17,228	1,428	10,406	4,470	4,060	6,822	3,647
October	4,583	9,542	452	3,832	1,441	3,754	5,710	3,142
November	4,059	9,052	504	3,591	1,341	5,432	5,461	2,718
December	8,138	18,354	795	4,083	1,127	25,115	14,271	7,011
Total	63,996	145,125	8,726	59,596	22,726	86,661	85,529	41,270
Not stated	4,014	39,096	1,990	14,380	1,631	8,707	24,716	2,383
Grand total	68,010	184,223	10,715	73,977	24,357	95,367	110,246	43,653

PERCENTAGE DISTRIBUTION

	(1)	(2)	(3)	(4)	(5)	(6)	(7)	(8)
January	6.7	8.5	8.5	8.5	7.4	5.2	8.5	6.4
February	6.9	9.1	8.9	8.5	7.5	5.5	9.6	6.5
March	6.5	7.4	5.9	7.1	6.1	5.8	7.7	6.7
April	7.2	7.6	8.0	5.9	4.1	9.0	8.7	9.0
May	6.3	5.9	4.6	3.8	3.1	8.0	7.3	8.1
June	5.8	5.6	3.6	4.8	3.7	8.2	6.2	6.9
July	5.4	4.8	3.7	4.4	5.4	5.6	5.0	5.4
August	16.3	13.8	20.4	20.2	25.8	8.5	9.3	11.1
September	12.7	11.9	16.4	17.5	19.7	4.7	8.0	8.8
October	7.2	6.6	5.2	6.4	6.3	4.3	6.7	7.6
November	6.3	6.2	5.8	6.0	5.9	6.3	6.4	6.6
December	12.7	12.6	9.1	6.9	5.0	29.0	16.7	17.0
Total[15]	100.0	100.0	100.0	100.0	100.0	100.0	100.0	100.0

Based on Source 5.

For numbered notes see pp. 448-9.

Table 52: Sales of Securities by Number of Months Held: Gross Capital Gains and Losses, Gross Receipts, and Number of Sales, Sample Returns, 1930 and 1932 (dollar figures in thousands)

A 1930

1,904 Returns

TYPE OF SECURITY AND MONTHS HELD	ALL SALES			SALES WITH GAIN			SALES WITH LOSS		
	Excess of loss[a]	Gross receipts	Number	Gross gain	Gross receipts	Number	Gross loss	Gross receipts	Number
Stocks, total	42,758	454,375	59,791	33,770	236,350	27,279	76,528	218,025	32,512
Short sales	−68	32,694	3,395	1,051	19,066	2,134	983	13,628	1,261
Long sales									
0 months	−375	141,281	16,550	3,854	90,054	10,357	3,479	51,227	6,193
1	1,300	67,608	8,803	2,920	37,738	4,630	4,220	29,870	4,173
2	2,395	29,762	4,239	1,502	13,067	1,849	3,897	16,695	2,390
3	2,378	21,781	3,056	1,375	10,064	1,269	3,753	11,717	1,787
4	2,135	15,873	2,273	1,089	5,314	880	3,224	10,559	1,393
5	2,257	13,150	1,973	1,003	4,608	619	3,260	8,542	1,354
6- 9	10,164	27,530	4,560	1,753	7,278	961	11,917	20,252	3,599
9- 12	7,751	17,229	2,838	984	3,908	523	8,735	13,321	2,315
12- 15	8,459	15,685	2,876	890	4,465	533	9,349	11,220	2,343
15- 18	5,802	11,395	1,780	867	2,838	349	6,669	8,557	1,431
18- 24	5,872	13,373	2,171	1,271	5,510	467	7,143	7,863	1,704
24- 36	2,623	14,857	2,009	2,544	7,591	727	5,167	7,266	1,282
36- 48	−1,633	9,497	931	2,958	6,331	511	1,325	3,166	420
48- 60	−147	3,983	586	1,114	2,817	328	967	1,166	258
60-120	−4,153	12,038	1,290	5,473	9,733	858	1,320	2,305	432
120 & over	−1,998	6,637	461	3,121	5,966	284	1,123	671	177
Bonds, total	65	51,512	5,718	2,015	28,036	2,749	2,080	23,476	2,969
0- 6 months	7	9,925	1,007	114	5,480	593	121	4,445	414
6- 12	130	2,888	524	74	1,618	255	204	1,270	269
12- 24	208	4,285	725	58	1,677	319	266	2,608	406
24- 36	387	7,267	885	54	1,697	276	441	5,570	609
36- 48	−706	4,672	562	952	2,635	235	246	2,037	347
48- 60	26	3,839	467	146	1,920	217	172	1,919	250
60-120	50	14,604	1,224	391	9,608	674	441	4,996	550
120 & over	−35	4,032	304	225	3,402	180	190	630	124
Not stated	−17,894[a]	105,633[a]	5,030	34,233[a]	70,085[a]	2,774	16,339	35,548	2,256
Total	24,930[a]	611,519[a]	70,539	70,017[a]	334,471[a]	32,802	94,947	277,048	37,737

| | 212 MARKET TRADERS | | | | | | 1,692 OTHER RETURNS | | | | | |
| | SALES WITH GAIN | | | SALES WITH LOSS | | | SALES WITH GAIN | | | SALES WITH LOSS | | |
	Gross gain	Gross receipts	Number	Gross loss	Gross receipts	Number	Gross gain	Gross receipts	Number	Gross loss	Gross receipts	Number
Stocks, total	17,487	146,760	9,689	36,110	136,612	10,926	16,283	89,590	17,590	40,418	81,413	21,586
Short sales	705	13,564	1,044	620	10,765	648	346	5,502	1,090	363	2,863	613
Long sales												
0 months	2,417	61,823	4,291	2,466	37,923	2,781	1,437	28,231	6,066	1,013	13,304	3,412
1	1,795	24,339	1,565	2,732	20,711	1,682	1,125	13,399	3,065	1,488	9,159	2,491
2	785	7,347	494	2,398	11,224	835	717	5,720	1,355	1,499	5,471	1,555
3	735	5,697	388	2,233	7,157	554	640	4,367	881	1,520	4,560	1,233
4	555	2,828	264	1,517	5,741	392	534	2,486	616	1,707	4,818	1,001
5	526	2,381	163	1,661	4,859	354	477	2,227	456	1,599	3,683	1,000
6- 9	888	3,435	273	5,003	9,424	983	865	3,843	688	6,914	10,828	2,616
9- 12	577	2,052	156	4,181	7,439	688	407	1,856	367	4,554	5,882	1,627
12- 15	553	2,800	135	4,490	5,593	638	337	1,665	398	4,859	5,627	1,705
15- 18	565	1,719	114	2,564	5,189	350	302	1,119	235	4,105	3,368	1,081
18- 24	615	3,533	125	2,546	3,579	427	656	1,977	342	4,597	4,284	1,277
24- 36	1,127	3,685	230	2,013	3,336	339	1,417	3,906	497	3,154	3,930	943
36- 48	1,760	3,409	134	487	1,823	96	1,198	2,922	377	838	1,343	324
48- 60	508	1,155	67	185	399	47	606	1,662	261	782	767	211
60-120	2,025	3,795	169	465	1,141	76	3,448	5,938	689	855	1,164	356
120 & over	1,351	3,198	77	551	309	36	1,770	2,768	207	572	362	141
Bonds, total	1,163	9,239	599	597	10,701	618	852	18,797	2,150	1,483	12,775	2,351
0- 6	58	3,551	223	49	3,337	133	56	1,929	370	72	1,108	281
6- 12	24	526	36	24	300	37	50	1,092	219	180	970	232
12- 24	21	611	81	55	948	79	37	1,066	238	211	1,660	327
24- 36	8	576	95	176	2,906	132	46	1,121	181	265	2,664	477
36- 48	902	1,457	37	44	793	66	50	1,178	198	202	1,244	281
48- 60	90	1,128	48	41	914	46	56	792	169	131	1,005	204
60-120	50	1,263	69	113	1,406	110	341	8,345	605	328	3,590	440
120 & over	9	127	10	95	96	15	216	3,275	170	95	534	109
Not stated	4,141	10,099	586	5,297	10,257	479	30,092*	59,986*	2,188	11,042	25,291	1,777
Total	22,790	166,098	10,874	42,004	157,569	12,023	47,227*	168,373*	21,928	52,943	119,479	25,714

B 1932

3,404 Returns

TYPE OF SECURITY AND MONTHS HELD	Excess of loss²	ALL SALES Gross receipts	ALL SALES Number	SALES WITH GAIN Gross gain	SALES WITH GAIN Gross receipts	SALES WITH GAIN Number	SALES WITH LOSS Gross loss	SALES WITH LOSS Gross receipts	SALES WITH LOSS Number
Stocks, total	77,297	158,164	59,773	13,667	76,869	24,115	90,964	81,295	35,658
Short sales	201	21,492	5,812	887	13,006	3,436	1,088	8,486	2,376
Long sales									
0 months	−551	44,281	15,644	1,888	29,356	10,167	1,337	14,925	5,477
1	154	15,062	6,445	1,074	8,806	3,585	1,228	6,256	2,860
2	232	6,498	2,934	609	3,636	1,536	841	2,862	1,398
3	162	4,672	2,035	537	2,675	1,038	699	1,997	997
4	315	3,436	1,556	336	1,554	788	651	1,882	768
5	358	2,120	1,112	246	1,056	480	604	1,064	632
6- 9	1,711	4,437	2,622	328	1,676	846	2,039	2,761	1,776
9- 12	1,837	3,223	1,979	205	931	439	2,042	2,292	1,540
12- 15	2,438	2,977	1,424	128	564	178	2,566	2,413	1,246
15- 18	2,601	2,008	1,169	18	87	77	2,619	1,921	1,092
18- 24	5,453	3,577	2,011	76	244	106	5,529	3,333	1,905
24- 36	26,908	12,141	5,808	379	898	215	27,287	11,243	5,593
36- 48	20,604	9,500	3,663	833	1,667	237	21,437	7,833	3,426
48- 60	7,704	5,222	1,608	818	1,424	112	8,522	3,798	1,496
60-120	6,227	10,699	2,697	2,820	4,983	471	9,047	5,716	2,226
120 & over	943	6,825	1,253	2,486	4,311	403	3,429	2,514	850
Bonds, total	19,869	133,435⁵	16,702	1,464	39,064	4,218	21,333	94,371⁵	12,484
0- 6 months	−198	34,315	3,430	564	20,768	2,227	366	13,547	1,203
6- 12	803	13,694	1,290	155	6,193	514	958	7,501	776
12- 24	2,048	10,110	1,544	26	1,539	132	2,074	8,571	1,412
24- 36	3,872	29,660⁵	1,955	49	1,979	155	3,921	27,681⁵	1,800
36- 48	3,114	7,400	1,630	21	902	139	3,135	6,498	1,491
48- 60	3,274	7,008	1,699	194	1,036	126	3,468	5,972	1,573
60-120	5,964	22,886	3,877	247	3,846	523	6,211	19,040	3,354
120 & over	992	8,359	1,277	207	2,800	402	1,199	5,559	875
Not stated	20,777	71,577	6,360	5,304	24,421	2,333	26,081	47,156	4,027
Total	117,944	363,176⁵	82,835	20,435	140,354	30,666	138,379	222,822⁵	52,169

201 MARKET TRADERS — 3,203 OTHER RETURNS

	201 MARKET TRADERS						3,203 OTHER RETURNS					
	SALES WITH GAIN			SALES WITH LOSS			SALES WITH GAIN			SALES WITH LOSS		
	Gross gain	Gross receipts	Number	Gross loss	Gross receipts	Number	Gross gain	Gross receipts	Number	Gross loss	Gross receipts	Number
Stocks, total	6,088	31,908	5,175	25,536	30,908	5,579	7,579	44,961	18,940	65,428	50,387	30,079
Short sales	446	6,724	1,273	535	4,768	886	441	6,282	2,163	553	3,718	1,490
Long sales												
0 months	692	11,576	2,297	496	6,712	1,298	1,196	17,780	7,870	841	8,213	4,179
1	332	3,002	549	436	2,522	546	742	5,804	3,036	792	3,734	2,314
2	193	1,364	227	255	1,028	250	416	2,272	1,309	586	1,834	1,148
3	211	1,205	186	217	888	176	326	1,470	852	482	1,109	821
4	77	443	106	256	1,000	121	259	1,111	682	395	882	647
5	63	293	61	193	275	102	183	763	419	411	789	530
6- 9	95	442	85	674	901	221	233	1,234	761	1,365	1,860	1,555
9- 12	35	194	48	575	693	213	170	737	391	1,467	1,599	1,327
12- 15	88	344	59	1,032	896	193	40	220	119	1,534	1,517	1,053
15- 18	8	17	14	664	618	111	10	60	63	1,955	1,303	981
18- 24	47	95	15	1,906	1,256	181	29	149	91	3,621	2,077	1,724
24- 36	109	300	14	6,843	3,254	385	270	598	201	20,444	7,989	5,208
36- 48	472	756	24	6,184	2,570	336	361	911	213	15,253	5,263	3,090
48- 60	463	673	32	1,914	1,177	150	355	751	80	6,608	2,621	1,346
60-120	1,378	2,383	95	2,424	1,500	322	1,442	2,600	376	6,623	4,216	1,904
120 & over	1,379	2,095	90	932	849	88	1,107	2,216	313	2,497	1,665	762
Bonds, total	719	26,276	894	7,857	65,581[5]	2,404	745	12,788	3,324	13,476	28,790	10,080
0- 6	218	15,252	451	149	11,206	289	346	5,516	1,776	217	2,341	914
6- 12	73	4,342	92	602	5,635	213	82	1,851	422	356	1,866	563
12- 24	8	1,007	30	810	5,250	298	18	532	102	1,264	3,321	1,114
24- 36	22	1,421	40	1,365	23,659[5]	219	27	558	115	2,556	4,022	1,581
36- 48	6	446	41	660	3,300	210	15	456	98	2,475	3,198	1,281
48- 60	183	561	46	1,152	3,063	255	11	475	80	2,316	2,909	1,318
60-120	151	2,079	108	2,601	10,443	686	96	1,767	415	3,610	8,600	2,668
120 & over	57	1,167	86	517	3,024	234	150	1,633	316	682	2,535	641
Not stated	2,913	8,193	240	9,618	16,087	533	2,391	16,228	2,093	16,463	31,069	3,494
Total	9,720	66,377	6,309	43,012	112,576[5]	8,516	10,715	73,977	24,357	95,367	110,246	43,653

Based on Source 5.

For numbered notes see pp. 448-9.

Table 53

Sales of Stocks by Number of Months Held: Percentage Distribution of Gross Capital Gains and Losses, Sample Returns, 1930 and 1932

A 1930

	SALES WITH GAIN IN 1930				SALES WITH LOSS IN 1930			
MONTHS HELD	Year	March	June	Dec.	Year	March	June	Dec.
212 Market Traders								
Short sales	4.0	0.7	12.3	3.4	1.7	6.4	0.9	0.5
Long sales								
0 months	13.8	16.3	13.2	4.6	6.8	7.7	9.9	0.7
1	10.3	17.9	2.0	1.5	7.6	4.8	16.3	1.3
2	4.5	5.2	4.4	0.1	6.6	9.9	21.4	3.0
3	4.2	8.9	2.8	†	6.2	3.6	14.3	5.4
4	3.2	4.9	0.9	1.6	4.2	7.5	3.9	2.7
5	3.0	0.7	1.5	1.5	4.6	19.4	2.4	2.3
6- 12	8.4	10.7	10.3	6.6	25.4	26.6	12.3	24.9
12- 24	9.9	4.3	21.2	14.1	26.6	7.7	12.6	38.1
24- 60	19.4	16.3	18.0	30.6	7.4	5.4	5.3	12.8
60-120	11.6	12.5	7.0	13.6	1.3	0.7	0.4	1.4
120 & over	7.7	1.5	6.5	22.0	1.5	0.3	0.2	7.1
Total stocks	100.0	100.0	100.0	100.0	100.0	100.0	100.0	100.0
1,692 Other Returns								
Short sales	2.1	1.1	3.8	1.2	0.9	1.8	0.8	0.1
Long sales								
0 months	8.8	8.2	5.9	6.1	2.5	3.2	5.8	0.7
1	6.9	10.4	1.6	1.6	3.7	5.0	9.2	0.7
2	4.4	4.8	1.2	0.7	3.7	2.1	12.6	0.9
3	3.9	7.0	1.0	†	3.8	3.7	7.4	3.1
4	3.3	6.2	1.5	0.4	4.2	2.2	2.5	1.8
5	2.9	5.7	2.5	0.3	4.0	7.1	1.1	1.4
6- 12	7.8	10.9	11.1	5.9	28.4	28.3	27.8	31.4
12- 24	8.0	7.7	5.3	5.4	33.6	22.0	23.4	42.2
24- 60	19.8	17.5	28.9	23.8	11.8	13.3	8.4	14.2
60-120	21.2	15.7	18.2	49.0	2.1	0.3	0.6	2.2
120 & over	10.9	4.7	19.2	5.6	1.4	10.8	0.4	1.3
Total stocks	100.0	100.0	100.0	100.0	100.0	100.0	100.0	100.0

B 1932

	SALES WITH GAIN IN 1932				SALES WITH LOSS IN 1932			
	Year	Aug.	Sept.	Dec.	Year	Aug.	Sept.	Dec.
201 Market Traders								
Short sales	7.3	4.2	3.5	1.0	2.1	1.6	4.0	0.2
Long sales								
0 months	11.4	37.0	11.9	1.3	1.9	1.9	18.4	0.3
1	5.5	9.4	7.2	0.9	1.7	0.1	5.0	0.7
2	3.2	6.2	1.7	0.3	1.0	†	0.5	0.3
3	3.5	21.6	0.9	0.6	0.8	0.1	3.8	0.9
4	1.3	4.9	1.2	0.9	1.0	0.8		0.8
5	1.0	0.9	1.3	3.7	0.8	0.5	0.2	†
6- 12	2.1	4.7	2.3	1.8	4.9	5.8	2.6	0.6
12- 24	2.3	2.8	0.7	0.6	14.1	8.8	15.8	1.4
24- 60	17.1	0.4	5.2	6.8	58.5	76.1	41.4	72.8
60-120	22.6	1.3	60.8	6.6	9.5	3.0	8.2	17.3
120 & over	22.7	6.5	3.4	75.5	3.6	1.4	0.3	4.8
Total stocks	100.0	100.0	100.0	100.0	100.0	100.0	100.0	100.0

472

	SALES WITH GAIN IN 1932				SALES WITH LOSS IN 1932			
	Year	Aug.	Sept.	Dec.	Year	Aug.	Sept.	Dec.
				3,203 Other Returns				
Short sales	5.8	2.2	5.6	0.8	0.8	1.6	0.8	†
Long sales								
0 months	15.8	26.8	24.9	4.9	1.3	1.6	7.6	0.2
1	9.8	13.7	19.9	2.4	1.2	0.1	2.3	0.2
2	5.5	11.3	6.9	2.0	0.9	0.1	0.1	0.2
3	4.3	10.3	6.9	0.8	0.7	0.1	†	0.5
4	3.4	6.9	6.0	2.2	0.6	0.6	†	0.4
5	2.4	5.3	5.1	1.4	0.6	1.0	0.1	†
6- 12	5.3	7.1	10.2	6.3	4.3	5.6	2.0	0.2
12- 24	1.0	0.3	2.1	1.2	10.9	13.9	16.5	2.1
24- 60	13.0	4.3	2.6	16.1	64.7	64.1	62.8	75.3
60-120	19.0	2.2	3.6	15.1	10.1	9.0	5.4	14.8
120 & over	14.6	9.7	6.2	46.9	3.8	2.4	2.4	6.2
Total stocks	100.0	100.0	100.0	100.0	100.0	100.0	100.0	100.0

Based on Source 5.   † Less than 0.05 percent.

Table 54

Sales of Stocks by Number of Months Held: Gross Capital Gains and Losses as Percentages of Estimated Cost, Sample Returns, 1930 and 1932

	SALES WITH GAIN Gross Gain as % of Estimated Cost[3]			SALES WITH LOSS Gross Loss as % of Estimated Cost[3]		
			A 1930			
MONTHS HELD	*1,904 returns*	*212 market traders*	*1,692 other returns*	*1,904 returns*	*212 market traders*	*1,692 other returns*
Short sales	5.8	5.5	6.7	6.7	5.4	11.3
Long sales						
0 months	4.5	4.1	5.4	6.4	6.1	7.1
1	8.4	8.0	9.2	12.4	11.7	14.0
2	13.0	12.0	14.3	18.9	17.6	21.5
3	15.8	14.8	17.2	24.3	23.8	25.0
4	25.8	24.4	27.4	23.4	20.9	26.2
5	27.8	28.4	27.3	27.6	25.5	30.3
6- 9	31.7	34.9	29.0	37.0	34.7	39.0
9- 12	33.7	39.1	28.1	39.6	36.0	43.6
12- 15	24.9	24.6	25.4	45.5	44.5	46.3
15- 18	44.0	49.0	37.0	43.8	33.1	54.9
18- 24	30.0	21.1	49.7	47.6	41.6	51.8
24- 36	50.4	44.1	56.9	41.6	37.6	44.5
36- 48	87.7	106.7	69.5	29.5	21.1	38.4
48- 60	65.4	78.5	57.4	45.3	31.7	50.5
60-120	128.5	114.4	138.5	36.4	29.0	42.3
120 & over	109.7	73.1	177.4	62.6	64.1	61.2
Total stocks	16.7	13.5	22.2	26.0	20.9	33.2

SALES WITH GAIN
Gross Gain as % of
Estimated Cost[3]

SALES WITH LOSS
Gross Loss as % of
Estimated Cost[3]

B 1932

	3,404 returns	201 market traders	3,203 other returns	3,404 returns	201 market traders	3,203 other returns
Short sales	7.3	7.1	7.6	11.4	10.1	12.9
Long sales						
0 months	6.9	6.4	7.2	8.2	6.9	9.3
1	13.9	12.4	14.7	16.4	14.7	17.5
2	20.1	16.5	22.4	22.7	19.9	24.2
3	25.1	21.2	28.5	25.9	19.6	30.3
4	27.6	21.0	30.4	25.7	20.4	30.9
5	30.4	27.4	31.6	36.2	41.2	34.3
6- 9	24.3	27.4	23.3	42.5	42.8	42.3
9- 12	28.2	22.0	30.0	47.1	45.3	47.8
12- 15	29.4	34.4	22.5	51.5	53.5	50.3
15- 18	26.1	88.9	20.0	57.7	51.8	60.0
18- 24	45.2	97.9	24.2	62.4	60.3	63.5
24- 36	73.0	57.1	82.3	70.8	67.8	71.9
36- 48	99.9	166.2	65.6	73.2	70.6	74.3
48- 60	135.0	220.5	89.6	69.2	61.9	71.6
60-120	130.4	137.1	124.5	61.3	61.8	61.1
120 & over	136.2	192.6	99.8	57.7	52.3	60.0
Total stocks	21.6	23.6	20.3	52.8	45.2	56.5

Based on Source 5.

For numbered notes see pp. 448-9.

Table 55

Sales of Stocks by Number of Months Held: Average Gross Capital Gain or Loss and Average Gross Receipts, Sample Returns, 1930 and 1932

	SALES WITH GAIN		SALES WITH LOSS	
MONTHS HELD	Av. gain per sale	Av. receipts per sale	Av. loss per sale	Av. receipts per sale
A 1930 (1,904 RETURNS)				
Short sales	$493	$8,934	$780	$10,807
Long sales				
0 months	372	8,695	562	8,272
1	631	8,151	1,011	7,158
2	812	7,067	1,631	6,985
3	1,084	7,931	2,100	6,557
4	1,238	6,039	2,314	7,580
5	1,620	7,444	2,408	6,309
6- 12	1,844	7,538	3,492	5,677
12- 24	2,245	9,498	4,228	5,046
24- 60	4,225	10,689	3,806	5,917
60-120	6,379	11,344	3,056	5,336
120 & over	10,989	21,007	6,345	3,791
Total stocks	1,238	8,664	2,354	6,706

	SALES WITH GAIN		SALES WITH LOSS	
	Av. gain per sale	Av. receipts per sale	Av. loss per sale	Av. receipts per sale
	B 1932 (3,404 Returns)			
Short sales	$258	$3,785	$458	$3,572
Long sales				
0 months	186	2,887	244	2,725
1	300	2,456	429	2,187
2	396	2,367	602	2,047
3	517	2,577	701	2,003
4	426	1,972	848	2,451
5	513	2,200	956	1,684
6- 12	415	2,029	1,231	1,524
12- 24	615	2,479	2,525	1,807
24- 60	3,599	7,073	5,444	2,175
60-120	5,987	10,580	4,064	2,568
120 & over	6,169	10,697	4,034	2,958
Total stocks	567	3,188	2,551	2,280

Based on Source 5.

Table 56

Sales of Securities by 5 Holding Periods: Gross Capital Gains and Losses by Statutory Net Income Groups, Sample Returns, 1930 and 1932

STATUTORY NET INCOME GROUP ($000)	TOTAL	YEARS HELD [16]					
		1 or less[17]	1- 2	2- 5	5- 10	Over 10	Not stated
		A 1930 (1,904 Returns)					
		GROSS GAIN ($000)					
Under 5	487	254	13	68	59	2	91
5- 25	6,115	3,104	370	631	631	289	1,091
25- 50	4,688	1,805	285	679	798	189	932
50-100	6,930	1,311	566	900	1,494	366	2,293
100 & over	36,279[4]	1,615	570	3,415	1,459	1,872	27,347[4]
Total	54,500[4]	8,090	1,805	5,693	4,441	2,717	31,754[4]
Net deficit	15,518	7,862	1,578	1,675	1,313	611	2,479
All returns	70,017[4]	15,952	3,383	7,369	5,754	3,328	34,232[4]
		Percentage Distribution					
Under 5	100.0	52.2	2.7	14.0	12.1	0.4	18.7
5- 25	100.0	50.8	6.1	10.3	10.3	4.7	17.8
25- 50	100.0	38.5	6.1	14.5	17.0	4.0	19.9
50-100	100.0	18.9	8.2	13.0	21.6	5.3	33.1
100 & over	100.0[4]	4.5	1.6	9.4	4.0	5.2	75.4[4]
Total	100.0[4]	14.8	3.3	10.4	8.1	5.0	58.3[4]
Net deficit	100.0	50.7	10.2	10.8	8.5	3.9	16.0
All returns	100.0[4]	22.8	4.8	10.5	8.2	4.8	48.9[4]

STATUTORY NET INCOME GROUP ($000)	TOTAL	YEARS HELD[16]					
		1 or less[17]	1- 2	2- 5	5- 10	Over 10	Not stated

GROSS LOSS ($000)

STATUTORY NET INCOME GROUP ($000)	TOTAL	1 or less[17]	1- 2	2- 5	5- 10	Over 10	Not stated
Under 5	950	525	129	106	1	*	190
5- 25	11,180	6,077	2,621	969	192	78	1,242
25- 50	7,600	3,241	2,152	822	263	99	1,022
50-100	9,808	4,376	2,385	1,240	226	49	1,532
100 & over	15,595	4,617	3,362	1,391	407	469	5,349
Total	45,134	18,836	10,650	4,529	1,089	695	9,335
Net deficit	49,813	27,742	10,762	3,174	523	607	7,005
All returns	94,947	46,578	21,412	7,703	1,612	1,302	16,339

Percentage Distribution

Under 5	100.0	55.3	13.6	11.2	0.1	†	20.0
5- 25	100.0	54.4	23.4	8.7	1.7	0.7	11.1
25- 50	100.0	42.6	28.3	10.8	3.5	1.3	13.4
50-100	100.0	44.6	24.3	12.6	2.3	0.5	15.6
100 & over	100.0	29.6	21.6	8.9	2.6	3.0	34.3
Total	100.0	41.7	23.6	10.0	2.4	1.5	20.7
Net deficit	100.0	55.7	21.6	6.4	1.0	1.2	14.1
All returns	100.0	49.1	22.6	8.1	1.7	1.4	17.2

EXCESS OF LOSS OVER GAIN[2] ($000)

Under 5	463	270	116	38	−58	−2	99
5- 25	5,064	2,973	2,252	338	−440	−211	151
25- 50	2,912	1,437	1,867	143	−535	−90	91
50-100	2,878	3,064	1,819	340	−1,267	−317	−761
100 & over	−20,683[4]	3,002	2,792	−2,023	−1,052	−1,403	−21,999[4]
Total	−9,366[4]	10,746	8,845	−1,164	−3,352	−2,022	−22,419[4]
Net deficit	34,295	19,880	9,184	1,498	−790	−3	4,526
All returns	24,930[4]	30,627	18,029	334	−4,142	−2,026	−17,893[4]

Percentage Distribution

Under 5	100.0	58.3	25.1	8.2	−12.5	−0.4	21.4
5- 25	100.0	58.7	44.5	6.7	−8.7	−4.2	3.0
25- 50	100.0	49.3	64.1	4.9	−18.4	−3.1	3.1
50-100	100.0	106.5	63.2	11.8	−44.0	−11.0	−26.4
100 & over	100.0[4]	−14.5	−13.5	9.8	5.1	6.8	106.4[4]
Total	100.0[4]	−114.7	−94.4	12.4	35.8	21.6	239.4[4]
Net deficit	100.0	58.0	26.8	4.4	−2.3	−0.1	13.2
All returns	100.0[4]	122.9	72.3	1.3	−16.6	−8.1	−71.8[4]

B 1932 (3,404 RETURNS)

GROSS GAIN ($000)

Under 5	913	700	5	39	37	70	62
5- 25	4,460	2,688	47	344	305	338	738
25- 50	2,864	1,117	113	235	322	354	721
50-100	3,653	774	6	833	686	706	647
100 & over	4,191	290	28	645	1,041	905	1,281
Total	16,080	5,570	199	2,098	2,392	2,373	3,449
Net deficit	4,354	1,292	156	285	479	288	1,855
All returns	20,435	6,862	354	2,383	2,870	2,661	5,304

Percentage Distribution

Under 5	100.0	76.7	0.5	4.3	4.1	7.7	6.8
5- 25	100.0	60.3	1.1	7.7	6.8	7.6	16.5
25- 50	100.0	39.0	3.9	8.2	11.2	12.4	25.2
50-100	100.0	21.2	0.2	22.8	18.8	19.3	17.7
100 & over	100.0	6.9	0.7	15.4	24.8	21.6	30.6
Total	100.0	34.6	1.2	13.0	14.9	14.8	21.4
Net deficit	100.0	29.7	3.6	6.5	11.0	6.6	42.6
All returns	100.0	33.6	1.7	11.7	14.0	13.0	26.0

STATUTORY NET INCOME GROUP ($000)	TOTAL	YEARS HELD[16]					
		1 or less[17]	1-2	2-5	5-10	Over 10	Not stated
GROSS LOSS ($000)							
Under 5	5,089	1,045	650	1,983	289	157	964
5- 25	19,833	4,284	3,069	8,090	1,758	406	2,225
25- 50	17,328	2,256	1,750	8,343	2,057	794	2,128
50-100	25,437	968	2,046	12,706	3,707	981	5,030
100 & over	32,110	776	2,567	14,192	4,059	1,137	9,378
Total	99,797	9,330	10,082	45,315	11,870	3,475	19,725
Net deficit	38,582	3,623	4,252	20,468	2,834	1,046	6,357
All returns	138,379	12,953	14,334	65,783	14,705	4,522	26,082
Percentage Distribution							
Under 5	100.0	20.5	12.8	39.0	5.7	3.1	18.9
5- 25	100.0	21.6	15.5	40.8	8.9	2.0	11.2
25- 50	100.0	13.0	10.1	48.1	11.9	4.6	12.3
50-100	100.0	3.8	8.0	50.0	14.6	3.9	19.8
100 & over	100.0	2.4	8.0	44.2	12.6	3.5	29.2
Total	100.0	9.3	10.1	45.4	11.9	3.5	19.8
Net deficit	100.0	9.4	11.0	53.1	7.3	2.7	16.5
All returns	100.0	9.4	10.4	47.5	10.6	3.3	18.8
EXCESS OF LOSS OVER GAIN ($000)							
Under 5	4,176	345	645	1,943	253	88	902
5- 25	15,372	1,596	3,022	7,746	1,453	68	1,487
25- 50	14,464	1,139	1,637	8,108	1,734	440	1,407
50-100	21,785	194	2,040	11,873	3,020	275	4,383
100 & over	27,919	486	2,539	13,547	3,018	232	8,097
Total	83,717	3,760	9,883	43,217	9,479	1,102	16,276
Net deficit	34,228	2,332	4,097	20,183	2,356	758	4,502
All returns	117,944	6,091	13,980	63,400	11,834	1,861	20,778
Percentage Distribution							
Under 5	100.0	8.3	15.4	46.5	6.1	2.1	21.6
5- 25	100.0	10.4	19.7	50.4	9.5	0.4	9.7
25- 50	100.0	7.9	11.3	56.1	12.0	3.0	9.7
50-100	100.0	0.9	9.4	54.3	13.9	1.3	20.1
100 & over	100.0	1.7	9.1	48.5	10.8	0.8	29.0
Total	100.0	4.5	11.8	51.6	11.3	1.3	19.4
Net deficit	100.0	6.8	12.0	59.0	6.9	2.2	13.2
All returns	100.0	5.2	11.9	53.8	10.0	1.6	17.6

Based on Source 5. * Less than $500. † Less than 0.05 percent.
For numbered notes see pp. 448-9.

478

Table 57

Capital Gains and Losses from Sales of Assets Segregated and Not Segregated at 12½ Percent, 1930, 1932, and 1933, and Subject or Not Subject to Statutory Limitation on Losses, 1932 and 1933 (dollar figures in thousands) Sample Returns with Over-all Realized Net Capital Gains or Losses

A 1930

Type of sale	1,904 Returns					212 Market Traders		1,692 Other Returns	
	Net gain	Net loss	Excess of gain	Gross receipts	Excess as % of est. cost[3]	Excess of gain	Excess as % of est. cost[3]	Excess of gain	Excess as % of est. cost[3]
Returns with Over-all Realized Net Gains[28]									
Segregated	32,287	29	32,258	66,936	93.0	5,958	78.0	26,300	97.3
Other	4,457	4,106	351	99,863	0.4	−1,216	−2.5	1,567	3.1
Total	36,745	4,135	32,610	166,800	24.3	4,742	8.4	27,867	35.8
Returns with Over-all Realized Net Losses[28]									
Segregated	1,658	3,324	−1,666	21,199	−7.3	−948	−11.3	−718	−4.9
Other	112	56,837	−56,725	435,064	−11.5	−23,337	−8.2	−33,388	−16.2
Total	1,770	60,160	−58,390	456,263	−11.3	−24,284	−8.3	−34,106	−15.4

B 1932

	3,404 Returns			201 Market Traders			3,203 Other Returns		
	Net gain	Net loss	Excess of gain	Net gain	Net loss	Excess of gain	Net gain	Net loss	Excess of gain
Returns with Over-all Realized Net Gains[29]									
Segregated	2,754	91	2,663	1,592	28	1,564	1,162	63	1,099
Other, total	1,667	690	977	575	416	159	1,092	274	818
Subject to limitation	1,066	408	658	372	259	113	694	149	545
Not subject	601	282	319	203	157	46	398	125	273
All sales	4,421	781	3,640	2,167	444	1,723	2,254	337	1,917

Returns with Over-all Realized Net Losses[19]

Segregated	506	66,945	−66,439		20,128	−20,128	506	46,817	−46,311
Other, total	999	60,721	−59,722	205	16,563	−16,358	794	44,158	−43,364
Subject to limitation	798	24,401	−23,603	125	7,868	−7,743	673	16,532	−15,859
Not subject	201	36,321	−36,120	80	8,695	−8,615	121	27,626	−27,505
All sales	1,505	127,666	−126,161	205	36,691	−36,486	1,300	90,975	−89,675

C 1 9 3 3

	2,164 Returns[7]					1,809 Returns with Net Incomes under $50,000[20]		232 Returns with Net Incomes of $50,000 & over	
	Gross gain	Gross loss	Excess of gain	Gross receipts	Excess as % of est. cost[a]	Excess of gain	Excess as % of est. cost[a]	Excess of gain	Excess as % of est. cost[a]
Returns with Over-all Realized Net Gains[21]									
Segregated	9,055	3,434	5,621	18,330	44.2	−286	−8.8	5,907	62.4
Other									
Subject to limitation	12,079	4,954	7,125	117,415	6.5	5,733	6.7	1,392	5.5
Not subject									
Held 2 yr. or less	993	491	502	62,536	0.8	289	1.9	213	0.5
Held over 2 yr.	1,111	1,536	−425	3,858	−9.9	−425	−9.9		
All sales	23,238	10,415	12,823	202,139	6.8	5,311	4.9	7,512	9.2
Returns with Over-all Realized Net Losses[21]									
Segregated	2,767	33,414	−30,647	37,262	−45.1	−10,778	−45.1	−19,869	−45.1
Other									
Subject to limitation	13,492	10,076	3,416	154,043	2.3	1,319	1.2	2,097	5.4
Not subject									
Held 2 yr. or less	393	864	−471	29,844	−1.6	−349	−1.6	−122	−1.5
Held over 2 yr.	1,238	19,994	−18,756	22,582	−45.4	−18,756	−45.4		
All sales	17,890	64,348	−46,458	243,731	−16.0	−28,564	−14.3	−17,894	−19.7

Based on Source 5.

For numbered notes see pp. 448-9.

Table 58: Net Capital Gains and Losses from Sales of Assets by Gross Receipts: 1,904 Returns with Over-all Realized Net Capital Gains or Losses, 1930

GROSS RECEIPTS FROM SALES GROUP ($000)	NO. OF RETURNS	NET GAIN OR LOSS (thousands of dollars)	GROSS RECEIPTS (thousands of dollars)	NET GAIN OR LOSS AS % OF EST. COST[3]	NUMBER OF SALES Total	NUMBER OF SALES Av. no. per return	AVERAGE PER SALE (dollars) Net gain or loss	AVERAGE PER SALE (dollars) Gross receipts
Returns with Over-all Realized Net Gains								
Under 50	125	331	3,732	9.7	1,934	15	171	1,930
50-100	83	583	5,766	11.2	1,851	22	315	3,115
100-200	109	1,476	15,760	10.3	3,031	28	487	5,200
200-300	41	982	10,195	10.7	1,551	38	633	6,573
300-400	17	620	6,083	11.3	686	40	904	8,867
400-500	17	565	7,734	7.9	978	58	578	7,908
500 & over, total[4]	56	28,053	117,529	31.4	3,752	67	7,477	31,324
Market traders	43	4,742	61,186	8.4	3,130	73	1,515	19,548
Other returns[4]	13	23,312	56,344	70.6	622	48	37,479	90,585
Total[4]	448	32,610	166,800	24.3	13,783	31	2,366	12,102
Total excl. market traders[4]	405	27,867	105,614	35.8	10,653	26	2,616	9,914
Returns with Over-all Realized Net Losses								
Under 50	423	−3,782	11,767	−24.3	7,155	17	−529	1,645
50-100	310	−4,537	22,153	−17.0	7,054	23	−643	3,140
100-200	287	−8,131	40,702	−16.7	9,938	35	−818	4,096
200-300	123	−5,498	30,273	−15.4	5,337	43	−1,030	5,672
300-400	69	−3,948	23,516	−14.4	3,451	50	−1,144	6,814
400-500	55	−4,866	24,269	−16.7	3,695	67	−1,317	6,568
500 & over, total	189	−27,628	303,583	−8.3	20,588	109	−1,342	14,746
Market traders	169	−24,284	269,476	−8.3	19,844	117	−1,224	13,580
Other returns	20	−3,344	34,107	−8.9	744	37	−4,495	45,843
Total	1,456	−58,390	456,263	−11.3	57,218	39	−1,020	7,974
Total excl. market traders	1,287	−34,106	186,787	−15.4	38,118	30	−895	4,900

Based on Source 5.

For numbered notes see pp. 448-9.

Table 59

Net Capital Gains and Losses from Sales of Assets by Realized Net Gain or Loss Classes: 1,904 Returns with Over-all Realized Net Capital Gains or Losses, 1930

REALIZED NET GAIN OR LOSS GROUP ($000)	NO. OF RETURNS	NET GAIN OR LOSS (thousands of dollars)	GROSS RECEIPTS (thousands of dollars)	NET GAIN OR LOSS AS % OF EST. COST[3]	NUMBER OF SALES Total	NUMBER OF SALES Av. no. per return	AVERAGE PER SALE Net gain or loss (dollars)	AVERAGE PER SALE Gross receipts (dollars)
Returns with Over-all Realized Net Gains								
Under 5	204	389	23,984	1.6	5,428	27	72	4,419
5- 10	88	692	14,101	5.2	2,251	26	307	6,264
10- 25	69	1,074	16,246	7.1	2,348	34	457	6,919
25- 50	38	1,395	13,135	11.9	1,384	36	1,008	9,491
50-100	21	1,443	19,997	7.8	861	41	1,676	23,225
100-300	22	3,450	20,815	19.8	893	41	3,863	23,309
300-500	2	842	2,568	48.8	81	40	10,395	31,704
500 & over[4]	4	23,324	55,953	71.5	537	134	43,434	104,196
Total[4]	448	32,610	166,800	24.3	13,783	31	2,366	12,102
Returns with Over-all Realized Net Losses								
Under 5	370	−832	34,606	−2.3	9,065	24	−92	3,818
5- 10	252	−1,774	25,527	−6.5	6,994	28	−254	3,650
10- 25	359	−5,813	67,482	−7.9	12,400	35	−469	5,442
25- 50	194	−6,672	57,399	−10.4	9,333	48	−715	6,150
50-100	105	−7,307	42,620	−14.6	4,747	45	−1,539	8,978
100-300	151	−24,400	163,680	−13.0	12,027	80	−2,029	13,609
300-500	17	−6,597	31,450	−17.3	1,785	105	−3,696	17,619
500 & over	8	−4,996	33,498	−13.0	867	108	−5,762	38,637
Total	1,456	−58,390	456,263	−11.3	57,218	39	−1,020	7,974

Based on Source 5.

For numbered notes see pp. 448-9.

Table 60

Net Capital Gains and Losses from Sales of Assets by Statutory Net Income Groups: 2,164 Returns with Over-all Realized Net Capital Gains or Losses,[7] 1933

STATUTORY NET INCOME GROUP ($000)	NO. OF RETURNS	GROSS GAIN	GROSS LOSS	NET GAIN OR LOSS	GROSS RECEIPTS	NET GAIN OR LOSS AS % OF EST. COST[8]	AV. NET GAIN OR LOSS PER RETURN (dollars)	GROSS LOSS AS % OF GROSS GAIN[a]
			(thousands of dollars)					
Returns with Over-all Realized Net Gains								
Under 5	100	840	517	323	11,513	2.9	3,230	61.5
5- 25	388	5,069	2,837	2,232	55,365	4.2	5,753	56.0
25- 50	133	4,055	2,086	1,969	36,092	5.8	14,805	51.4
50-100	64	2,952	1,414	1,538	26,817	6.1	24,031	47.9
100 & over	16	8,702	2,728	5,974	62,211	10.6	373,375	31.3
Total	701	21,618	9,582	12,036	191,998	6.7	17,170	44.3
Net deficit	41	1,620	833	787	10,141	8.4	19,195	51.4
All returns	742	23,238	10,415	12,823	202,139	6.8	17,282	44.8
Returns with Over-all Realized Net Losses								
Under 5	163	929	2,035	−1,106	16,159	−6.4	−6,785	45.7
5- 25	294	2,218	5,791	−3,573	40,774	−8.1	−11,905	38.3
25- 50	196	3,369	10,814	−7,445	39,948	−15.7	−37,985	31.2
50-100	105	3,102	8,915	−5,813	35,317	−14.1	−55,371	34.8
100 & over	47	3,697	15,778	−12,081	37,642	−24.3	−257,043	23.4
Total	805	13,315	43,333	−30,018	169,840	−15.0	−37,200	30.7
Net deficit	494	4,575	21,015	−16,440	73,891	−18.2	−33,279	21.8
All returns	1,299	17,890	64,348	−46,458	243,731	−16.0	−35,709	27.8
Market Traders with Over-all Realized Net Gains								
Under 5	7	222	172	50	4,709	1.1	7,143	77.5
5- 25	42	1,462	1,024	438	23,662	1.9	10,429	70.0
25- 50	33	1,792	964	828	22,695	3.8	25,091	54.0
50-100	29	1,889	945	944	20,731	4.8	32,552	50.0
100 & over	11	8,366	2,629	5,737	61,272	10.3	521,545	31.4
Total	122	13,731	5,734	7,997	133,069	6.4	65,549	41.8
Net deficit	6	1,165	576	589	6,854	9.4	98,167	49.4
All returns	128	14,896	6,310	8,586	139,923	6.5	67,078	42.4
Market Traders with Over-all Realized Net Losses								
Under 5	9	274	355	−81	5,482	−1.5	−9,000	77.2
5- 25	26	503	1,060	−557	18,463	−2.9	−21,423	47.5
25- 50	36	1,605	3,944	−2,339	21,659	−9.7	−64,972	40.7
50-100	37	2,106	4,671	−2,565	26,988	−8.7	−69,324	45.1
100 & over	25	3,400	13,153	−9,753	34,169	−22.2	−390,120	25.8
Total	133	7,888	23,183	−15,295	106,761	−12.5	−115,000	34.0
Net deficit	53	1,889	6,151	−4,262	34,991	−10.9	−80,415	30.7
All returns	186	9,777	29,334	−19,557	141,752	−12.1	−105,145	33.3

Based on Source 5.
[a] For returns with over-all realized net losses, gross gain as a percentage of gross loss.
For numbered notes see pp. 448-9.

Table 61

Percentage Distribution of Net Capital Gains and Losses from Sales of Assets by Statutory Net Income Groups: 2,164 Returns with Over-all Realized Net Capital Gains or Losses,[7] 1933

STATUTORY NET INCOME GROUP ($000)	NUMBER OF RETURNS	GROSS GAIN	GROSS LOSS	NET GAIN OR LOSS	GROSS RECEIPTS
Returns with Over-all Realized Net Gains					
Under 5	13.5	3.6	5.0	2.5	5.7
5- 25	52.3	21.8	27.2	17.4	27.4
25- 50	17.9	17.4	20.0	15.4	17.9
50-100	8.6	12.7	13.6	12.0	13.3
100 & over	2.2	37.4	26.2	46.6	30.8
Total	94.5	93.0	92.0	93.9	95.0
Net deficit	5.5	7.0	8.0	6.1	5.0
All returns	100.0	100.0	100.0	100.0	100.0
Returns with Over-all Realized Net Losses					
Under 5	12.5	5.2	3.2	2.4	6.6
5- 25	22.6	12.4	9.0	7.7	16.7
25- 50	15.1	18.8	16.8	16.0	16.4
50-100	8.1	17.3	13.9	12.5	14.5
100 & over	3.6	20.7	24.5	26.0	15.4
Total	62.0	74.4	67.3	64.6	69.7
Net deficit	38.0	25.6	32.7	35.4	30.3
All returns	100.0	100.0	100.0	100.0	100.0
Market Traders with Over-all Realized Net Gains					
Under 5	5.5	1.5	2.7	0.6	3.4
5- 25	32.8	9.8	16.2	5.1	16.9
25- 50	25.8	12.0	15.3	9.6	16.2
50-100	22.7	12.7	15.0	11.0	14.8
100 & over	8.6	56.2	41.7	66.8	43.8
Total	95.3	92.2	90.9	93.1	95.1
Net deficit	4.7	7.8	9.1	6.9	4.9
All returns	100.0	100.0	100.0	100.0	100.0
Market Traders with Over-all Realized Net Losses					
Under 5	4.8	2.8	1.2	0.4	3.9
5- 25	14.0	5.1	3.6	2.8	13.0
25- 50	19.4	16.4	13.4	12.0	15.3
50-100	19.9	21.5	15.9	13.1	19.0
100 & over	13.4	34.8	44.8	49.9	24.1
Total	71.5	80.7	79.0	78.2	75.3
Net deficit	28.5	19.3	21.0	21.8	24.7
All returns	100.0	100.0	100.0	100.0	100.0

Based on Source 5.
For numbered notes see pp. 448-9.

Table 62

Sales of Securities Reported on Matched Groups of Sample Returns: Gross Capital Gains and Losses, and Gross Receipts, 1930, 1932, and 1933

TYPE OF SALE	GROSS GAIN OR LOSS (thousands of dollars)	GROSS RECEIPTS (thousands of dollars)	NUMBER OF SALES	GAIN OR LOSS AS % OF ESTIMATED COST[3]	AVERAGE GAIN OR LOSS PER (dollars) Return	Sale	AVERAGE RECEIPTS PER Return	Sale	AVERAGE NUMBER OF SALES PER RETURN
				1930 (1,904 Returns)					
With gain[4]	70,017	334,471	32,802	26.5	36,774	2,135	175,668	10,197	17
With loss	−94,947	277,048	37,737	−25.5	−49,867	−2,516	145,508	7,342	20
All	−24,930	611,519	70,539	−3.9	−13,093	−353	321,175	8,669	37
				1932 (1,211 Returns included in the 1930 Sample)[23]					
With gain	6,707	51,079	6,982	15.1	5,538	961	42,179	7,316	6
With loss[5]	−50,313	103,805	12,974	−32.6	−41,547	−3,878	85,718	8,001	11
All	−43,606	154,884	19,956	−22.0	−36,008	−2,185	127,898	7,761	16
				1933 (1,192 Returns included in the 1930 Sample)[6]					
With gain	17,171				14,405				
With loss	−41,138				−34,512				
All	−23,967	204,905		−10.5	−20,107		171,900		

Based on Source 5.
For numbered notes see pp. 448-9.

484

Table 63

Sales of Securities Reported on Matched Groups of Sample Returns: Gross Capital Gains and Losses and Gross Receipts by Statutory Net Income Groups, 1930, 1932, and 1933

STATUTORY NET INCOME GROUP	NUMBER OF RETURNS	GROSS GAIN	GROSS LOSS	GROSS RECEIPTS[1]	EXCESS OF GAIN AS % OF ESTIMATED COST[3]	NO. OF RETURNS	GROSS GAIN	GROSS LOSS	GROSS RECEIPTS
		(thousands of dollars)					(percentages)		
				1930 (1,904 Returns)					
Under $50,000[20]	1,603	26,808	69,543	432,101	−9.0	84.2	38.3	73.3	69.4
$50,000 & over[4]	301	43,209	25,403	190,961	10.3	15.8	61.7	26.7	30.7
Total	1,904	70,017	94,947	623,063	−3.8	100.0	100.0	100.0	100.0
				1932 (1,211 Returns included in the 1930 Sample)[28]					
Under $50,000[20]	1,059	5,009	29,040	84,065	−22.2	87.4	74.7	57.7	51.9
$50,000 & over[5]	152	1,697	21,272	77,971	−20.1	12.6	25.3	42.2	48.1
Total	1,211	6,707	50,313	162,036	−21.2	100.0	100.0	100.0	100.0
				1933 (1,192 Returns included in the 1930 Sample)[6]					
Under $50,000[20]	1,030	7,944	19,831	95,584	−11.1	86.4	46.2	48.1	46.7
$50,000 & over	162	9,227	21,307	109,321	−10.0	13.6	53.8	51.8	53.4
Total	1,192	17,171	41,138	204,905	−10.5	100.0	100.0	100.0	100.0

Based on Source 5.
For numbered notes see pp. 448-9.

Table 64

Sales of Securities Reported on Matched Groups of Sample Returns: Sales of Stocks and of Bonds, 1930 and 1932

TYPE OF SECURITY	GROSS GAIN OR LOSS (thousands of dollars)	GROSS RECEIPTS (thousands of dollars)	NUMBER OF SALES	GAIN OR LOSS AS % OF ESTIMATED COST[3]	AVERAGE GAIN OR LOSS PER (dollars) Return	Sale	AVERAGE RECEIPTS PER Return	Sale	AVERAGE NUMBER OF SALES PER RETURN
				1930 (1,904 Returns)					
Sales with gain[22,4]	70,017	334,471	32,802	26.5	36,774	2,135	175,668	10,197	17
Stocks	33,770	236,350	27,279	16.7	17,736	1,238	124,133	8,664	14
Bonds	2,015	28,036	2,749	7.7	1,058	733	14,725	10,199	1
Sales with loss[22]	−94,947	277,048	37,737	−25.5	−49,867	−2,516	145,508	7,342	20
Stocks	−76,528	218,025	32,512	−26.0	−40,193	−2,354	114,509	6,706	17
Bonds	−2,080	23,476	2,969	−8.1	−1,092	−701	12,330	7,907	2
				1932 (1,211 Returns included in the 1930 Sample)[23]					
Sales with gain[22]	6,707	51,079	6,982	15.1	5,538	961	42,179	7,316	6
Stocks	3,482	17,336	4,664	25.1	2,875	747	14,315	3,717	4
Bonds	414	19,195	1,015	2.2	342	408	15,851	18,911	1
Sales with loss[22]	−50,313	103,805	12,974	−32.6	−41,547	−3,878	85,718	8,001	11
Stocks	−32,558	25,003	8,215	−56.6	−26,885	−3,963	20,647	3,044	7
Bonds[5]	−6,357	47,879	2,708	−11.7	−5,249	−2,347	39,537	17,681	2

Based on Source 5.

For numbered notes see pp. 448-9.

Table 65: Overstatement in Over-all Net Capital Gains and Losses due to Adding Components, by Statutory Net Income Groups, 2,164 Returns,[7] 1933 (thousands of dollars)

		ALL RETURNS WITH NET INCOMES	STATUTORY NET INCOME GROUP ($000)					RETURNS WITH NET DEFICITS	ALL RETURNS
			Under 5	5-25	25-50	50-100	100 & over		
	NET CAPITAL GAINS FROM SALES OF ASSETS								
1	Sales subject to loss limitation	10,790	640	3,079	3,155	2,294	1,622	2,316	13,106
2	Other assets held 2 years or less	948	60	207	262	172	247	161	1,109
3	Assets held over 2 years except seg.	362	32	218	112			22	384
4	Total not segregated	12,100	732	3,504	3,529	2,466	1,869	2,499	14,599
5	Segregated at 12½%	6,526		20	258	559	5,689		6,526
6	Total (lines 4 & 5)	18,626	732	3,524	3,787	3,025	7,558	2,499	21,125
7	Over-all net gain from all sales	12,036	323	2,232	1,969	1,538	5,974	787	12,823
8	Ratio: line 6 to line 7	1.55	2.27	1.58	1.92	1.97	1.26	3.18	1.65
9	Over-all net gain except seg.	10,403	323	2,549	3,408	2,435	1,688	787	11,190
10	Ratio: line 4 to line 9	1.16	2.27	1.38	1.04	1.01	1.11	3.18	1.30
11	Sum: lines 5 & 9	16,929	323	2,569	3,666	2,994	7,377	787	17,716
12	Ratio: line 11 to line 7	1.41	1.00	1.15	1.86	1.95	1.24	1.00	1.38
	NET CAPITAL LOSSES FROM SALES OF ASSETS								
13	Sales subject to loss limitation	1,451	191	551	336	228	145	853	2,304
14	Other assets held 2 years or less	717	103	212	74	51	277	364	1,081
15	Assets held over 2 years except seg.	2,972	1,218	1,696	58			16,935	19,907
16	Total not segregated	5,140	1,512	2,459	468	279	422	18,152	23,292
17	Segregated at 12½%	31,393		2,333	8,795	7,022	13,243	18,152	31,393
18	Total (lines 16 & 17)	36,533	1,512	4,792	9,263	7,301	13,665	18,152	54,685
19	Over-all net loss from all sales	30,018	1,106	3,573	7,445	5,813	12,081	16,440	46,458
20	Ratio: line 18 to line 19	1.22	1.37	1.34	1.24	1.26	1.13	1.10	1.18
21	Over-all net loss except seg.	3,446	1,106	1,504	347	248	241	16,440	19,886
22	Ratio: line 16 to line 21	1.49	1.37	1.64	1.35	1.12	1.75	1.10	1.17
23	Sum: lines 17 & 21	34,839	1,106	3,837	9,142	7,270	13,484	16,440	51,279
24	Ratio: line 23 to line 19	1.16	1.00	1.07	1.23	1.25	1.12	1.00	1.10

Based on Source 5. See Appendix One, Section E1, note 22. For numbered notes see pp. 448-9.

III ADDITIONAL DATA FOR 1936

Tables 66-81 summarize data compiled from special tabulations of federal individual and taxable fiduciary income tax returns for 1936. They differ from those presented elsewhere, first by including other types of net income classification in addition to statutory net income groupings, and second by classifying net capital gains and losses by type of assets sold. See Appendix One, Section F2.

Notes to Tables 66-81

[1] Represents realized net capital gain and loss before the application of statutory percentages and before the $2,000 limitation on net loss. In tables where data are not classified by holding period or type of asset, realized net capital gain is the sum of the realized net gains reported on returns with over-all realized net capital gains minus the sum of the realized net losses reported on such returns; realized net loss is the corresponding figure reported on returns with over-all realized net capital losses; the net gain or loss reported on all returns with capital transactions is labeled 'excess'. In tables where data are classified by holding period or type of asset, realized net gain is the net gain in the given holding period or from sales of the given type of asset reported on the designated group of returns before offsetting against such gain the net loss in that holding period or from that type of asset reported on other returns in the same group; realized net loss is defined similarly.

[2] Returns are classified according to whether they reported an over-all realized net capital gain or loss for all holding periods combined.

[3] From Source 4d, as reported on all individual and taxable fiduciary income tax returns, regardless whether any capital transactions are reported; see Appendix One, Section B.

[4] Realized net gain from stocks and bonds is the net gain reported on returns that realized a net gain from sales of stocks and bonds; statutory net gain, the net gain from stocks and bonds reported on returns that realized a net gain from sales of all types of asset. Realized and statutory net loss from stocks and bonds are similarly differentiated. Total realized net gain from stocks and bonds reported on returns with realized net gain from sales of all types of asset was $959.0 million; realized net loss, $429.0 million.

[5] Statutory net gain exceeds statutory net loss.

[6] This total, i.e., the sum of net gains in the various holding periods, overstates the over-all realized net gain from transactions in all holding periods combined, because net gains in any one holding period were not reduced by net losses in other holding periods realized by the same individuals. A similar overstatement appears in the sum of net losses in the various holding periods. and the same difficulty arises when the net gains (or losses) from 2 or more holding periods are added.

[7] The total for net gain from sales of securities, assets other than securities, or all assets — in each case the sum of net gains from the component types of asset — overstates the over-all net gain from all transactions because the net

gains from sales of any one type of asset were not reduced by net losses from sales of other types of asset realized by the same individuals. A similar over-statement appears in the totals for the corresponding loss items. The total number of returns is also overstated in each case because the same return may have had net gains from more than one type of asset or net gains from one type and net losses from another. The number of returns with over-all net gains from sales of all assets in 1936 was 57,652 in New York, 22,496 in Pennsylvania, and 16,983 in Illinois; the number with over-all net losses from sales of all assets was 30,796 in New York, 12,372 in Pennsylvania, and 10,591 in Illinois.

[8] Estimated cost, gross receipts minus realized net capital gain or plus realized net capital loss, may differ from original cost because such items as deprecia-tion, cost of improvements, and expenses in connection with sales of assets were taken into account by the taxpayer in computing realized net capital gain and loss.

[9] The sum of the positive items of income reported on the face of the income tax return.

[10] For returns with 4 or more sources of income, the 3 main sources are shown.

[11] The classification by statutory net capital gain or loss refers to all holding periods combined.

Table 66

Realized and Statutory Net Capital Gains and Losses and Net Income Reported on Returns with Capital Transactions by 3 Types of Net Income Group, 1936 (dollar figures in millions)

| | | RETURNS WITH NET | | NET INCOME GROUPS AS DEFINED IN SECTIONS A, B, AND C ($000) | | | | | | | |
	TOTAL	Deficits	Incomes	Under 5	5–30	30–50	50–100	100–300	300–500	500–1,000	1,000 & over
A Statutory Net Income											
No. of returns with net capital gains or losses	482,622	17,010	465,612	224,072	213,162	15,922	9,067	2,954	255	136	44
Stat. net income	4,750.7	−124.4	4,875.1	623.5	2,332.2	605.1	611.3	439.7	94.7	93.1	75.6
Excess of gain over loss											
Realized[1]	579.6	−62.7	642.3	−49.0	278.8	109.2	113.4	106.0	21.1	20.7	42.1
Statutory	707.1	5.5	701.6	64.8	335.9	98.6	96.9	67.5	12.2	11.5	14.2
Excl. gain or loss	−127.5	−68.2	−59.3	−113.8	−57.1	10.6	16.5	38.5	8.9	9.2	27.9
B Net Income Excluding Statutory Net Capital Gain and Loss											
No. of returns with net capital gains or losses	482,622	23,937	458,685	246,404	189,667	12,818	7,133	2,305	208	113	37
Net income excl. stat. net gain & loss	4,043.6	−161.6	4,205.8	635.3	2,045.2	486.9	480.1	344.5	76.9	76.8	59.6
Excess of gain over loss											
Realized[1]	579.6	161.3	418.3	165.5	123.8	49.8	35.7	31.5	5.8	3.3	2.8
Statutory	707.1	124.2	582.9	213.1	243.3	53.2	39.7	25.3	3.5	2.6	2.2
Excl. gain or loss	−127.5	37.1	−164.6	−47.6	−119.5	−3.4	−4.0	6.2	2.3	0.7	0.6
C Net Income Including Realized but Excluding Statutory Net Capital Gain and Loss											
No. of returns with net capital gains or losses	482,622	37,716	444,906	209,086	206,184	16,097	9,618	3,372	320	171	58
Net income incl. realized but excl. stat. net gain & loss	4,623.2	−368.8	4,992.1	579.4	2,278.3	612.3	650.4	506.1	119.9	118.7	126.9
Excess of gain over loss											
Realized[1]	579.6	−362.2	941.9	5.4	380.7	127.0	152.5	135.1	38.9	34.8	67.5
Statutory	707.1	−29.7	736.8	61.3	338.4	98.2	105.6	77.4	18.0	16.9	21.0
Excl. gain or loss	−127.5	−332.5	205.1	−55.9	42.3	28.8	46.9	57.7	20.9	17.9	46.5

490

Percentage Distribution

A STATUTORY NET INCOME

No. of returns with net capital gains or losses	100.0	3.5	96.5	46.4	44.2	3.3	1.9	0.6	0.1	†	†
Stat. net income	100.0	−2.6	102.6	13.1	49.1	12.7	12.9	9.3	2.0	2.0	1.6
Excess of gain over loss											
Realized[1]	100.0	−10.8	110.8	−8.5	48.1	18.8	19.6	18.3	3.6	3.6	7.3
Statutory	100.0	0.8	99.2	9.2	47.5	13.9	13.7	9.5	1.7	1.6	2.0

B NET INCOME EXCLUDING STATUTORY NET CAPITAL GAIN AND LOSS

No. of returns with net capital gains or losses	100.0	5.0	95.0	51.1	39.3	2.7	1.5	0.5	†	†	†
Net income excl. stat. net gain & loss	100.0	−4.0	104.0	15.7	50.6	12.0	11.9	8.5	1.9	1.9	1.5
Excess of gain over loss											
Realized[1]	100.0	27.8	72.2	28.6	21.4	8.6	6.2	5.4	1.0	0.6	0.5
Statutory	100.0	17.6	82.4	30.1	34.4	7.5	5.6	3.6	0.5	0.4	0.3

C NET INCOME INCLUDING REALIZED BUT EXCLUDING STATUTORY NET CAPITAL GAIN AND LOSS

No. of returns with net capital gains or losses	100.0	7.8	92.2	43.3	42.7	3.3	2.0	0.7	0.1	†	†
Net income incl. realized but excl. stat. net gain & loss	100.0	−8.0	108.0	12.5	49.3	13.2	14.1	10.9	2.6	2.6	2.7
Excess of gain over loss											
Realized[1]	100.0	−62.5	162.5	0.9	65.7	21.9	26.3	23.3	6.7	6.0	11.6
Statutory	100.0	−4.2	104.2	8.7	47.9	13.9	14.9	10.9	2.5	2.4	3.0

Based on Source 4.
† Less than 0.05 percent.
For numbered notes see pp. 488-9.

Table 67: Number of Returns with Capital Transactions by 3 Types of Net Income Group, 1936

NET INCOMB GROUP ($000)	TOTAL	RETURNS WITH NET		NET INCOME GROUPS AS DEFINED IN SECTIONS A, B, AND C ($000)							
		Deficits	Incomes	Under 5	5- 30	30- 50	50- 100	100- 300	300- 500	500- 1,000	1,000 & over
A		**NET INCOME EXCLUDING STATUTORY NET CAPITAL GAIN AND LOSS**									
Statutory											
Under 5	224,072	8,419	215,653	205,707	9,946						
5- 30	213,162	3,061	210,101	35,306	174,389	406					
30- 50	15,922	208	15,714	348	4,440	10,786	140				
50- 100	9,067	118	8,949	89	806	1,507	6,517	30			
100- 300	2,954	47	2,907	20	82	115	471	2,217	2		
300- 500	255	2	253	1	3	2	4	49	194		
500-1,000	136	1	135		1	1	1	9	12	111	
1,000 & over	44	4	40			1	1			2	37
Total with net incomes	465,612	11,860	453,752	241,471	189,667	12,818	7,133	2,305	208	113	37
With net deficits	17,010	12,077	4,933	4,933							
Total	482,622	23,937	458,685	246,404	189,667	12,818	7,133	2,305	208	113	37
B		**NET INCOME EXCLUDING STATUTORY BUT INCLUDING REALIZED NET CAPITAL GAIN AND LOSS**									
Statutory											
Under 5	224,072	17,708	206,364	195,427	10,921	9	6	1			
5- 30	213,162	3,929	209,233	12,656	193,582	2,602	376	17			
30- 50	15,922	142	15,780	43	1,379	12,921	1,326	111			
50- 100	9,067	80	8,987	9	105	548	7,761	559	5		
100- 300	2,954	14	2,940	1	9	9	136	2,661	99	23	2
300- 500	255	1	254					14	210	27	3
500-1,000	136		136						5	118	13
1,000 & over	44	1	43							3	40
Total with net incomes	465,612	21,875	443,737	208,136	205,996	16,089	9,605	3,363	319	171	58
With net deficits	17,010	15,841	1,169	950	188	8	13	9	1		
Total	482,622	37,716	444,906	209,086	206,184	16,097	9,618	3,372	320	171	58
C		**NET INCOME EXCLUDING STATUTORY BUT INCLUDING REALIZED NET CAPITAL GAIN AND LOSS**									
Net income group excl. stat. net capital gain & loss											
Under 5	246,404	19,497	226,907	183,153	42,759	634	271	81	8	4	1
5- 30	189,667	6,682	182,985	18,010	157,793	5,436	1,466	264	11	7	1
30- 50	12,818	154	12,664	47	1,462	9,131	1,771	225	20	4	1
50- 100	7,133	74	7,059	13	103	542	5,746	621	29	21	5
100- 300	2,305	14	2,291		10	6	140	2,049	60	16	4
300- 500	208	1	207					15	172	103	5
500-1,000	113		113						5	3	33
1,000 & over	37	1	36								1
Total with net incomes	458,685	26,423	432,262	201,223	202,127	15,749	9,394	3,255	305	158	51
With net deficits	23,937	11,293	12,644	7,863	4,057	348	224	117	15	13	7
Total	482,622	37,716	444,906	209,086	206,184	16,097	9,618	3,372	320	171	58

Based on Source 4.

Table 68

Returns with Realized Net Capital Gains or Losses: Realized and Statutory Net Gains and Losses, Number of Returns, and Net Income Reported on Returns with Capital Transactions, by Net Income Groups Defined to Exclude Statutory Gain and Loss, 1936 (dollar figures in million)

	TOTAL	RETURNS WITH NET Deficits	RETURNS WITH NET Incomes	NET INCOME GROUP EXCL. STATUTORY NET CAPITAL GAIN & LOSS ($000) Under 5	5-30	30-50	50-100	100-300	300-500	500-1,000	1,000 & over
				Returns with Over-all Realized Net Capital Gains[2]							
No. of returns	316,502	17,949	298,553	169,041	115,367	8,054	4,448	1,424	135	64	20
Net income excl. stat. net capital gain	2,502.7	−111.3	2,614.0	414.4	1,252.2	306.1	298.4	212.5	49.3	45.0	36.0
Net capital gain											
Realized[1]	1,224.9	218.6	1,006.3	362.1	418.9	89.3	69.1	46.0	8.4	5.0	7.5
Statutory	820.5	129.3	691.2	261.8	297.6	56.6	41.2	25.6	3.5	2.7	2.2
Excluded	404.4	89.3	315.1	100.3	121.3	32.7	27.9	20.4	4.9	2.3	5.3
Excl. as % of realized gain	33.0	40.9	31.3	27.7	29.0	36.6	40.4	44.3	58.3	46.0	70.7
Realized gain as % of net income excl. gain			38.5	87.4	33.5	29.2	23.2	21.6	17.0	11.1	20.8
				Returns with Over-all Realized Net Capital Losses[2]							
No. of returns	166,120	5,988	160,132	77,363	74,300	4,764	2,685	881	73	49	17
Net income excl. stat. net capital loss	1,540.8	−50.4	1,591.2	220.9	792.9	180.8	181.7	132.0	27.6	31.8	23.6
Net capital loss											
Realized[1]	645.3	57.3	588.0	196.6	295.1	39.5	33.4	14.4	2.6	1.7	4.7
Statutory	113.4	5.1	108.3	48.7	54.2	3.5	1.5	0.3	*	*	*
Disallowed	531.9	52.2	479.7	147.9	240.9	36.0	31.9	14.1	2.6	1.7	4.7
Disallowed as % of realized loss	82.4	91.1	81.6	75.2	81.6	91.1	95.5	97.9	100.0	100.0	100.0
Realized loss as % of net income excl. loss			37.0	89.0	37.2	21.8	18.4	10.9	9.4	5.3	19.9

493

		NET INCOME GROUP EXCL. STATUTORY NET CAPITAL GAIN & LOSS ($000)								
	TOTAL	RETURNS WITH NET Deficits	Under 5	5- 30	30- 50	50- 100	100- 300	300- 500	500- 1,000	1,000 & over
All Returns										
Stat. net income excl. stat. net capital gain & loss reported on all income tax returns[3]	18,163.0		10,095.1	5,674.1	849.5	751.0	506.5	102.2	184.6	184.6
Realized net capital gain as % of net income reported on all returns	5.5		3.6	7.4	10.5	9.2	9.1	8.2	6.8	6.8
Realized net capital loss as % of net income reported on all returns	3.2		1.9	5.2	4.6	4.4	2.8	2.5	2.9	3.5
Ratio: realized gain to loss	1.7	3.8	1.8	1.4	2.3	2.1	3.2	3.2		1.6
PERCENTAGE DISTRIBUTION										
Returns with Over-all Realized Net Capital Gains[2]										
No. of returns	100.0		56.6	38.6	2.7	1.5	0.5	†	†	†
Net income excl. stat. gain	100.0		15.9	47.9	11.7	11.4	8.1	1.9	1.7	1.4
Net capital gain										
Realized[1]	100.0		36.0	41.6	8.9	6.9	4.6	0.8	0.5	0.7
Statutory	100.0		37.9	43.1	8.2	6.0	3.7	0.5	0.4	0.3
Excluded	100.0		31.8	38.5	10.4	8.9	6.5	1.6	0.7	1.7
Returns with Over-all Realized Net Capital Losses[2]										
No. of returns	100.0		48.3	46.4	3.0	1.7	0.6	†	†	†
Net income excl. stat. loss	100.0		13.9	49.8	11.4	11.4	8.3	1.7	2.0	1.5
Net capital loss:										
Realized[1]	100.0		33.4	50.2	6.7	5.7	2.4	0.4	0.3	0.8
Statutory	100.0		45.0	50.0	3.2	1.4	0.3	†	†	†
Disallowed	100.0		30.8	50.2	7.5	6.6	2.9	0.5	0.4	1.0

Based on Source 4, except 'statutory net income excluding statutory gain and loss reported on all income tax returns', which is based on Source 4d.

✕ Less than $50,000.
† Less than 0.05 percent.
For numbered notes see pp. 488-9.

Table 69

Returns with Realized Net Capital Gains or Losses: Realized and Statutory Net Gains and Losses from Stocks and Bonds and from All Assets, by Net Income Groups Defined to Exclude Statutory Gain and Loss, 1936 (dollar figures in millions)

	TOTAL	RETURNS WITH NET Deficits	RETURNS WITH NET Incomes	NET INCOME GROUP EXCL. STATUTORY NET CAPITAL GAIN & LOSS ($000) Under 5	5–30	30–50	50–100	100–300	300–500	500–1,000	1,000 & over
Returns with Over-all Realized Net Capital Gains[2]											
Realized net gain[1] from											
All capital assets	1,224.9	218.6	1,006.3	362.1	418.9	89.3	69.1	46.0	8.4	5.0	7.5
Stocks & bonds[4]	967.4	170.7	796.7	266.3	341.9	76.2	56.9	36.4	8.3	3.3	7.4
Stocks & bonds as % of total	79.0	78.1	79.2	73.5	81.6	85.3	82.3	79.1	98.8	66.0	98.7
Stat. net gain from											
All capital assets	820.5	129.3	691.2	261.8	297.6	56.6	41.2	25.6	3.5	2.7	2.2
Stocks & bonds[4]	633.6	95.2	538.4	193.5	238.1	47.0	32.9	19.9	3.4	1.5	2.1
Stocks & bonds as % of total	77.2	73.6	77.9	73.9	80.0	83.0	79.9	77.7	97.1	55.6	95.5
No. of returns with realized net gain from											
All capital assets	316,502	17,949	298,553	169,041	115,367	8,054	4,448	1,424	135	64	20
Stocks & bonds	240,231	11,822	228,409	122,682	93,552	6,927	3,833	1,216	124	56	19
Stocks & bonds as % of total	75.9	65.9	76.5	72.6	81.1	86.0	86.2	85.4	91.9	87.5	95.0
Returns with Over-all Realized Net Capital Losses[2]											
Realized net loss[1] from											
All capital assets	645.3	57.3	588.0	196.6	295.1	39.5	33.4	14.4	2.6	1.7	4.7
Stocks & bonds[4]	437.5	31.6	405.9	113.7	214.9	31.3	25.0	11.8	2.3	1.7	5.2
Stocks & bonds as % of total	67.8	55.1	69.0	57.8	72.8	79.2	74.9	81.9	88.5	100.0	110.6
Stat. net loss from											
All capital assets	113.4	5.1	108.3	48.7	54.2	3.5	1.5	0.3	*	*	*
Stocks & bonds[4]	64.0	1.7	62.3	26.1	33.0	1.9	1.4	*[5]	*	-0.1[5]	*
Stocks & bonds as % of total	56.4	33.3	57.5	53.6	60.9	54.3	93.3				
No. of returns with realized net loss from											
All capital assets	166,120	5,988	160,132	77,363	74,300	4,764	2,685	881	73	49	17
Stocks & bonds	111,928	3,348	108,580	48,144	53,628	3,785	2,158	744	60	45	16
Stocks & bonds as % of total	67.4	55.9	67.8	62.2	72.2	79.5	80.4	84.4	82.2	91.8	94.1
All Returns with Capital Transactions											
No. of returns with transactions in											
All capital assets	482,622	23,937	458,685	246,404	189,667	12,818	7,133	2,305	208	113	37
Stocks & bonds	352,159	15,170	336,989	170,826	147,180	10,712	5,991	1,960	184	101	35
Stocks & bonds as % of total	73.0	63.4	73.5	69.3	77.6	83.6	84.0	85.0	88.5	89.4	94.6

* Less than $50,000.

Based on Sources 4 and 4a.

For numbered notes see pp. 488–9.

Table 70

Returns with Realized Net Capital Gains or Losses by Size and by Gross Receipts, 1936

Federal income tax returns filed in New York State

GROSS RECEIPTS ($000)	TOTAL	Under 0.5	REALIZED NET CAPITAL GAIN OR LOSS (thousands of dollars)[1]								
			0.5-1	1-2	2-5	5-10	10-30	30-50	50-100	100-500	500 & over
Returns with Over-all Realized Net Capital Gains[a]											
Under 1	5,367	5,136	231								
1-2	5,223	3,874	1,048	301							
2-5	9,801	4,884	2,488	1,757	672						
5-10	9,064	2,762	2,153	2,220	1,638	291					
10-25	11,071	1,692	1,818	2,800	3,363	1,125	273				
25-50	6,818	451	536	1,184	2,482	1,418	700	47			
50-100	4,707	194	210	481	1,355	1,223	1,069	116	59		
100-500	4,701	98	130	250	756	1,011	1,701	409	263	83	
500-1,000	570	5	9	9	47	66	200	109	83	42	
1,000 & over	330	4	2	11	22	35	89	51	64	47	5
Total	57,652	19,100	8,625	9,013	10,335	5,169	4,032	732	469	172	5
Returns with Over-all Realized Net Capital Losses[a]											
Under 1	6,386	2,970	1,200	989	843	302	70	9	3		
1-2	3,363	1,223	512	650	661	239	72	5	1		
2-5	5,570	1,749	762	1,025	1,297	565	161	8	2	1	
5-10	4,525	1,143	563	749	1,192	608	247	16	6	1	
10-25	4,915	999	532	686	1,243	857	525	51	20	2	
25-50	2,596	324	238	347	588	574	420	67	34	3	1
50-100	1,782	187	147	179	375	370	399	73	31	20	1
100-500	1,422	86	65	127	245	268	415	119	53	43	1
500-1,000	145	7	6	12	23	8	24	23	24	17	1
1,000 & over	92	3	3	4	10	12	14	14	8	22	1[a]
Total	30,796	8,691	4,028	4,768	6,477	3,803	2,347	385	182	109	5

Based on Source 4b. Includes returns with statutory net incomes or deficits. [a] Reported a realized net capital loss of over $1 million. For numbered notes see pp. 488-9.

Table 71

Realized Net Capital Gains and Losses[1] in 5 Holding Periods: Gains and Losses, Number of Returns, and Average Gain or Loss per Return, 1936 (aggregates in millions of dollars)

	1 or less	1-2	2-5	5-10	Over 10	Not stated
			YEARS HELD			
Returns with Over-all Realized Net Capital Gains[a]						
No. with gain[a]	177,480	87,902	114,974	66,766	48,201	19,964
Gain	404.1	153.7	271.3	143.2	342.6	26.2
Av. gain per return ($)[b]	2,300	1,700	2,400	2,100	7,100	1,300
No. with loss[c]	13,346	10,365	14,033	34,073	10,091	884
Loss	9.2	5.1	10.7	76.2	13.8	1.0
Av. loss per return ($)[b]	700	500	800	2,200	1,400	1,200
Returns with Over-all Realized Net Capital Losses[a]						
No. with gain[a]	38,992	21,686	26,649	5,411	8,307	2,663
Gain	60.0	28.6	45.1	4.7	14.0	1.3
Av. gain per return ($)[b]	1,500	1,300	1,700	900	1,700	500
No. with loss[c]	28,456	12,550	31,219	97,785	41,530	5,459
Loss	25.4	12.8	56.0	491.0	197.6	16.1
Av. loss per return ($)[b]	900	1,000	1,800	5,000	4,800	2,900
All Returns with Capital Transactions						
No. with gain[a]	216,472	109,588	141,623	72,177	56,508	22,627
Gain	464.1	182.2	316.3	147.9	356.5	27.5
Av. gain per return ($)[b]	2,100	1,700	2,200	2,000	6,300	1,200
No. with loss[c]	41,802	22,915	45,252	131,858	51,621	6,343
Loss	34.6	17.9	66.7	567.2	211.4	17.1
Av. loss per return ($)[b]	800	800	1,500	4,300	4,100	2,700

Based on Sources 4 and 4a.

Includes returns with statutory net incomes or deficits.

[a] Number of returns with realized net gain in holding period.

[b] Average net gain per return with realized net gain in holding period; and average net loss per return with realized net loss in holding period.

[c] Number of returns with realized net loss in holding period.

For numbered notes see pp. 488-9.

Table 72

Realized Net Capital Gains and Losses in 5 Holding Periods by Net
Income Groups Defined to Exclude Statutory Gain and Loss, 1936
(dollar figures in millions)

NET INCOME GROUP EXCL. STATUTORY NET CAPITAL GAIN AND LOSS ($000)	1 or less	1-2	2-5	5-10	Over 10	Not stated	TOTAL[6]
			YEARS HELD				

A GAINS AND LOSSES FROM SALES OF ALL ASSETS

Realized Net Capital Gain[1]

	1 or less	1-2	2-5	5-10	Over 10	Not stated	TOTAL[6]
Total	464.1	182.2	316.3	147.9	356.5	27.5	1,494.6
With net deficits	60.2	20.8	37.3	21.6	95.1	6.5	241.5
With net incomes	403.9	161.4	279.0	126.3	261.5	21.0	1,253.1
Under 5	150.6	53.8	91.7	40.2	68.8	11.1	416.2
5- 30	181.7	72.5	122.3	51.9	95.5	7.5	531.5
30- 50	32.2	14.3	25.3	13.3	30.7	1.2	117.0
50- 100	23.1	11.6	22.3	12.5	27.8	0.9	98.4
100- 300	13.8	6.4	12.1	6.5	22.5	0.2	61.5
300- 500	0.7	1.7	2.3	1.1	5.2	*	11.0
500-1,000	1.4	0.8	2.2	0.6	3.5	*	8.4
1,000 & over	0.2	0.2	0.9	*	7.5	*	9.0

Realized Net Capital Loss[1]

	1 or less	1-2	2-5	5-10	Over 10	Not stated	TOTAL[6]
Total	34.6	17.9	66.7	567.2	211.4	17.1	915.0
With net deficits	3.2	1.6	6.4	43.3	21.7	4.1	80.3
With net incomes	31.4	16.3	60.3	524.0	189.7	13.0	834.7
Under 5	9.7	5.6	21.3	144.0	63.7	6.3	250.7
5- 30	14.0	7.2	27.0	264.5	89.9	5.1	407.7
30- 50	2.3	1.1	4.2	44.4	14.0	1.2	67.2
50- 100	3.6	1.3	4.6	38.8	14.1	0.4	62.7
100- 300	1.2	0.7	2.2	19.4	6.5	0.1	30.0
300- 500	0.1	0.2	0.3	4.2	0.3	*	5.1
500-1,000	0.2	0.1	0.2	3.9	0.8	*	5.1
1,000 & over	0.4	*	0.4	4.9	0.4	*	6.2

Excess of Realized Gain over Loss

	1 or less	1-2	2-5	5-10	Over 10	Not stated	TOTAL[6]
Total	429.5	164.3	249.6	−419.3	145.1	10.3	579.6
With net deficits	57.1	19.2	30.9	−21.7	73.4	2.4	161.3
With net incomes	372.5	145.1	218.7	−397.6	71.7	7.9	418.3
Under 5	140.9	48.2	70.3	−103.7	5.0	4.8	165.5
5- 30	167.8	65.3	95.3	−212.6	5.6	2.5	123.8
30- 50	29.9	13.2	21.1	−31.0	16.8	*	49.8
50- 100	19.6	10.4	17.7	−26.2	13.7	0.5	35.7
100- 300	12.7	5.7	9.9	−12.8	16.0	0.1	31.5
300- 500	0.6	1.5	1.9	−3.1	4.9	*	5.8
500-1,000	1.2	0.7	1.9	−3.3	2.7	*	3.3
1,000 & over	−0.2	0.2	0.5	−4.9	7.1	*	2.8

NET INCOME GROUP EXCL. STATUTORY NET CAPITAL GAIN AND LOSS ($000)	1 or less	1-2	YEARS HELD 2-5	5-10	Over 10	Not stated	TOTAL[6]

PERCENTAGE DISTRIBUTION

Realized Net Capital Gain[1]

Total	31.1	12.2	21.2	9.9	23.9	1.8	100.0
With net deficits	24.9	8.6	15.5	8.9	39.4	2.7	100.0
With net incomes	32.2	12.9	22.3	10.1	20.9	1.7	100.0
Under 5	36.2	12.9	22.0	9.7	16.5	2.7	100.0
5- 30	34.2	13.6	23.0	9.8	18.0	1.4	100.0
30- 50	27.5	12.2	21.6	11.4	26.3	1.0	100.0
50- 100	23.5	11.8	22.7	12.8	28.2	0.9	100.0
100- 300	22.5	10.4	19.7	10.6	36.5	0.3	100.0
300- 500	6.7	15.0	20.6	10.4	47.2	0.1	100.0
500-1,000	16.3	9.6	25.7	6.7	41.3	0.4	100.0
1,000 & over	2.7	2.8	10.4	0.4	83.8	†	100.0

Realized Net Capital Loss[1]

Total	3.8	2.0	7.3	62.0	23.1	1.9	100.0
With net deficits	3.9	2.0	8.0	53.9	27.0	5.1	100.0
With net incomes	3.8	2.0	7.2	62.8	22.7	1.6	100.0
Under 5	3.9	2.3	8.5	57.4	25.4	2.5	100.0
5- 30	3.4	1.8	6.6	64.9	22.1	1.2	100.0
30- 50	3.5	1.6	6.3	66.1	20.8	1.7	100.0
50- 100	5.7	2.1	7.4	61.8	22.4	0.6	100.0
100- 300	3.9	2.4	7.3	64.5	21.7	0.3	100.0
300- 500	1.8	3.7	6.1	82.2	5.6	0.5	100.0
500-1,000	3.4	1.8	4.6	75.2	15.0		100.0
1,000 & over	6.7	0.5	6.4	79.0	7.1	0.2	100.0

B GAINS AND LOSSES FROM STOCKS AND BONDS

Realized Net Capital Gain[1]

Total	354.2	147.0	255.8	116.3	291.2	15.7	1,180.3
With net deficits	41.7	15.8	29.0	15.7	82.0	2.7	186.9
With net incomes	312.6	131.3	226.7	100.6	209.2	13.0	993.4
Under 5	112.9	42.1	69.9	28.4	46.8	6.7	306.8
5- 30	144.6	59.6	101.0	42.4	79.8	4.9	432.4
30- 50	25.8	12.3	22.1	12.0	26.4	0.5	99.2
50- 100	17.4	9.6	18.8	10.2	24.0	0.6	80.6
100- 300	10.3	5.5	10.1	6.2	17.2	0.1	49.3
300- 500	0.6	1.5	2.0	1.1	5.3	*	10.6
500-1,000	0.7	0.6	1.9	0.2	2.2	*	5.7
1,000 & over	0.2	0.2	0.9	*	7.5	*	8.9

Realized Net Capital Loss[1]

Total	21.5	10.1	41.5	435.2	130.7	11.4	650.5
With net deficits	1.6	0.6	3.3	29.4	10.7	2.2	47.9
With net incomes	19.8	9.5	38.2	405.9	120.0	9.2	602.6
Under 5	5.1	2.6	10.7	100.6	30.9	4.3	154.3
5- 30	8.5	4.3	18.0	209.5	61.6	3.5	305.4
30- 50	1.5	0.8	3.2	37.0	10.8	0.9	54.3
50- 100	3.2	0.9	3.8	31.0	9.4	0.3	48.7
100- 300	1.0	0.6	1.8	16.0	5.3	0.1	24.6
300- 500	0.1	0.1	0.2	4.0	0.1	*	4.6
500-1,000	0.1	0.1	0.1	3.0	0.7		4.1
1,000 & over	0.4	*	0.4	4.7	1.1	*	6.7

NET INCOME GROUP EXCL. STATUTORY NET CAPITAL GAIN AND LOSS ($000)	1 or less	1-2	2-5	5-10	Over 10	Not stated	TOTAL[6]
Excess of Realized Gain over Loss							
Total	332.7	136.9	214.3	−318.9	160.5	4.3	529.9
With net deficits	40.0	15.2	25.7	−13.7	71.3	0.5	139.0
With net incomes	292.7	121.8	188.5	−305.3	89.2	3.8	390.8
Under 5	107.9	39.5	59.2	−72.2	15.8	2.4	152.6
5- 30	136.1	55.3	83.0	−167.1	18.2	1.4	127.0
30- 50	24.3	11.5	18.9	−25.0	15.6	−0.4	44.9
50- 100	14.2	8.6	15.0	−20.8	14.5	0.3	31.9
100- 300	9.3	4.9	8.3	−9.8	11.9	0.1	24.7
300- 500	0.6	1.4	1.8	−2.9	5.2	*	6.0
500-1,000	0.6	0.5	1.8	−2.8	1.5	*	1.6
1,000 & over	−0.2	0.2	0.5	−4.7	6.4	*	2.2

PERCENTAGE DISTRIBUTION

	1 or less	1-2	2-5	5-10	Over 10	Not stated	TOTAL[6]
Realized Net Capital Gain[1]							
Total	30.0	12.5	21.7	9.9	24.7	1.3	100.0
With net deficits	22.3	8.4	15.5	8.4	43.9	1.4	100.0
With net incomes	31.5	13.2	22.8	10.1	21.1	1.3	100.0
Under 5	36.8	13.7	22.8	9.3	15.2	2.2	100.0
5- 30	33.4	13.8	23.4	9.8	18.5	1.1	100.0
30- 50	26.0	12.4	22.3	12.1	26.7	0.5	100.0
50- 100	21.6	11.8	23.4	12.7	29.7	0.8	100.0
100- 300	20.9	11.1	20.4	12.5	34.8	0.2	100.0
300- 500	6.0	14.4	18.7	10.7	50.0	0.1	100.0
500-1,000	12.8	9.7	33.7	4.3	39.0	0.4	100.0
1,000 & over	2.2	2.6	10.4	0.4	84.4	†	100.0
Realized Net Capital Loss[1]							
Total	3.3	1.6	6.4	66.9	20.1	1.8	100.0
With net deficits	3.4	1.2	7.0	61.3	22.3	4.7	100.0
With net incomes	3.3	1.6	6.3	67.4	19.9	1.5	100.0
Under 5	3.3	1.7	6.9	65.2	20.1	2.8	100.0
5- 30	2.8	1.4	5.9	68.6	20.2	1.1	100.0
30- 50	2.8	1.5	5.9	68.2	20.0	1.7	100.0
50- 100	6.6	1.9	7.9	63.6	19.3	0.7	100.0
100- 300	4.0	2.4	7.1	64.8	21.4	0.3	100.0
300- 500	1.6	3.0	4.6	87.6	2.7	0.5	100.0
500-1,000	3.4	2.2	2.8	74.0	17.6		100.0
1,000 & over	6.2	0.5	5.9	70.6	16.6	0.2	100.0

Based on Source 4.

Includes all returns with capital transactions.

* Less than $50,000.

† Less than 0.05 percent.

For numbered notes see pp. 488-9.

Table 73: Number of Returns with Realized Net Capital Gains or Losses[1] in 5 Holding Periods and Average Realized Net Capital Gain or Loss per Return, by Net Income Groups Defined to Exclude Statutory Gain and Loss, 1936

NET INCOME EXCL. STATUTORY NET CAPITAL GAIN AND LOSS ($000)	YEARS HELD					
	1 or less	1-2	2-5	5-10	Over 10	Not Stated

A NUMBER OF RETURNS
Returns with Realized Net Gains in Holding Period

	1 or less	1-2	2-5	5-10	Over 10	Not Stated
Total	216,472	109,588	141,623	72,177	56,508	22,627
With net deficits	11,361	5,928	6,860	3,247	3,294	1,888
With net incomes	205,111	103,660	134,763	68,930	53,214	20,739
Under 5	106,551	51,001	67,079	35,179	25,496	12,301
5- 30	86,823	45,063	58,263	29,299	23,141	7,418
30- 50	6,627	4,133	5,146	2,434	2,409	563
50- 100	3,757	2,534	3,083	1,472	1,526	333
100- 300	1,167	799	1,022	468	517	110
300- 500	111	74	93	49	75	6
500-1,000	56	44	57	23	39	7
1,000 & over	19	12	20	6	11	1

Returns with Realized Net Losses in Holding Period

	1 or less	1-2	2-5	5-10	Over 10	Not Stated
Total	41,802	22,915	45,252	131,858	51,621	6,343
With net deficits	1,514	1,082	1,941	5,024	2,390	515
With net incomes	40,288	21,833	43,311	126,834	49,231	5,828
Under 5	18,321	9,870	20,705	57,598	22,884	3,142
5- 30	18,966	10,073	19,703	61,045	22,462	2,456
30- 50	1,640	975	1,573	4,532	2,001	136
50- 100	961	629	922	2,629	1,295	68
100- 300	340	236	350	884	508	21
300- 500	26	33	34	79	39	4
500-1,000	25	10	17	48	30	
1,000 & over	9	7	7	19	12	1

B AVERAGE REALIZED NET CAPITAL GAIN OR LOSS PER RETURN[a]
Average Realized Net Gain[1]

	1 or less	1-2	2-5	5-10	Over 10	
Total	2,100	1,700	2,200	2,000	6,300	
With net deficits	5,300	3,500	5,400	6,600	28,900	
With net incomes	2,000	1,600	2,100	1,800	4,900	
Under 5	1,400	1,100	1,400	1,100	2,700	
5- 30	2,100	1,600	2,100	1,800	4,100	
30- 50	4,900	3,500	4,900	5,500	12,800	
50- 100	6,200	4,600	7,200	8,500	18,200	
100- 300	11,900	8,000	11,800	14,000	43,500	
300- 500	6,700	22,300	24,300	23,300	69,100	
500-1,000	24,600	18,300	38,000	24,700	89,200	
1,000 & over	12,600	20,700	46,900	5,800	685,500	

Average Realized Net Loss[1]

	1 or less	1-2	2-5	5-10	Over 10	
Total	800	800	1,500	4,300	4,100	
With net deficits	2,100	1,500	3,300	8,600	9,100	
With net incomes	800	700	1,400	4,100	3,900	
Under 5	500	600	1,000	2,500	2,800	
5- 30	700	700	1,400	4,300	4,000	
30- 50	1,400	1,100	2,700	9,800	7,000	
50- 100	3,700	2,100	5,000	14,700	10,900	
100- 300	3,400	3,000	6,300	21,900	12,800	
300- 500	3,700	5,800	9,300	53,500	7,400	
500-1,000	7,100	9,100	14,000	80,500	25,700	
1,000 & over	46,300	4,900	56,700	258,200	36,700	

Based on Source 4. Includes all returns with capital transactions.
[a] Average net gain per return with realized net gain in holding period; and average net loss per return with realized net loss in holding period.
For numbered notes see pp. 488-9.

Table 74

Realized Net Capital Gains and Losses, Number of Returns and Sales, and Gross Receipts by 10 Types of Asset, 1936 (dollar figures in millions)

Federal income tax returns filed in New York, Pennsylvania, and Illinois

	NUMBER OF SALES	GROSS RECEIPTS	RETURNS WITH REALIZED NET GAINS OR LOSSES FROM SALES OF SPECIFIED TYPE OF ASSET			
			No. with gains	Real-ized gain[1]	No. with losses	Real-ized loss[1]
New York						
Securities, total[7]	765,742	3,041.1	66,302	221.9	29,285	123.2
Tax exempt	13,945	146.8	3,883	4.4	1,154	1.3
Other bonds, notes, debentures	121,313	390.6	18,857	28.0	6,881	17.2
Stocks	598,964	2,150.8	40,185	175.3	19,481	97.6
Unclassified	31,520	352.9	3,377	14.2	1,769	7.1
Other assets, total[7]	10,298	111.7	2,206	7.4	3,483	20.0
Real estate & improvements	4,909	45.1	1,291	4.4	2,362	14.6
Mortgages, loans, etc.	1,208	6.1	164	0.4	723	3.2
Commodities	3,273	47.9	479	1.1	197	0.3
Other tangible assets	753	10.7	214	1.3	163	1.6
Intangible assets	155	1.9	58	0.2	38	0.3
Unclassified	31,325	906.3	9,153	41.8	5,301	22.4
Total[7]	807,365	4,059.1	77,661	271.1	38,069	165.6
Pennsylvania						
Securities, total[7]	225,996	646.4	25,128	70.4	12,239	44.0
Tax exempt	4,547	36.1	1,392	1.0	452	0.5
Other bonds, notes, debentures	48,964	145.6	8,039	11.6	3,280	8.6
Stocks	167,395	445.5	14,993	55.7	7,980	33.2
Unclassified	5,090	19.2	704	2.1	527	1.6
Other assets, total[7]	4,366	31.2	949	2.5	1,404	5.5
Real estate & improvements	2,656	16.7	703	1.9	1,123	4.9
Mortgages, loans, etc.	287	0.9	36	*	176	0.5
Commodities	1,163	12.1	96	0.2	48	0.1
Other tangible assets	195	1.0	76	0.2	41	0.1
Intangible assets	65	0.6	38	0.2	16	*
Unclassified	11,359	67.1	3,483	7.9	2,015	6.1
Total[7]	241,721	744.7	29,560	80.8	15,658	55.7
Illinois						
Securities, total[7]	164,181	472.2	18,397	54.9	9,213	26.5
Tax exempt	5,057	32.9	1,324	1.2	474	0.5
Other bonds, notes, debentures	32,040	77.0	4,789	5.5	2,875	6.3
Stocks	121,913	338.4	11,674	46.0	5,561	18.8
Unclassified	5,171	23.9	610	2.1	303	0.9
Other assets, total[7]	7,955	58.0	1,276	3.5	2,192	10.2
Real estate & improvements	3,103	21.8	748	1.7	1,461	8.5
Mortgages, loans, etc.	738	3.1	74	0.5	439	1.2
Commodities	3,821	32.0	359	0.9	221	0.3
Other tangible assets	208	0.8	61	0.2	55	0.1
Intangible assets	85	0.4	34	0.2	16	0.1
Unclassified	9,490	61.4	2,703	6.3	2,056	6.0
Total[7]	181,626	591.6	22,376	64.6	13,461	42.8

For numbered notes see pp. 458-9.

	NUMBER OF SALES	GROSS RECEIPTS	No. with gains	Real- ized gain[1]	No. with losses	Real- ized loss[1]
			PERCENTAGE DISTRIBUTION			
			New York			
Securities, total[7]	94.8	74.9	85.4	81.8	76.9	74.4
Tax exempt	1.7	3.6	5.0	1.6	3.0	0.8
Other bonds, notes, debentures	15.0	9.6	24.3	10.3	18.1	10.4
Stocks	74.2	53.0	51.7	64.7	51.2	58.9
Unclassified	3.9	8.7	4.3	5.2	4.6	4.3
Other assets, total[7]	1.3	2.8	2.8	2.7	9.1	12.1
Real estate & improvements	0.6	1.1	1.7	1.6	6.2	8.8
Mortgages, loans, etc.	0.1	0.2	0.2	0.1	1.9	1.9
Commodities	0.4	1.2	0.6	0.4	0.5	0.2
Other tangible assets	0.1	0.3	0.3	0.5	0.4	1.0
Intangible assets	†	†	0.1	0.1	0.1	0.2
Unclassified	3.9	22.3	11.8	15.4	13.9	13.5
Total[7]	100.0	100.0	100.0	100.0	100.0	100.0
			Pennsylvania			
Securities, total[7]	93.5	86.8	85.0	87.1	78.2	79.1
Tax exempt	1.9	4.8	4.7	1.3	2.9	1.0
Other bonds, notes, debentures	20.3	19.6	27.2	14.3	20.9	15.5
Stocks	69.3	59.8	50.7	68.9	51.0	59.7
Unclassified	2.1	2.6	2.4	2.6	3.4	2.9
Other assets, total[7]	1.8	4.2	3.2	3.2	9.0	9.9
Real estate & improvements	1.1	2.2	2.4	2.3	7.2	8.8
Mortgages, loans, etc.	0.1	0.1	0.1	†	1.1	0.8
Commodities	0.5	1.6	0.3	0.2	0.3	0.1
Other tangible assets	0.1	0.1	0.3	0.2	0.3	0.1
Intangible assets	†	0.1	0.1	0.3	0.1	†
Unclassified	4.7	9.0	11.8	9.7	12.9	11.0
Total[7]	100.0	100.0	100.0	100.0	100.0	100.0
			Illinois			
Securities, total[7]	90.4	79.8	82.2	84.9	68.4	61.9
Tax exempt	2.8	5.6	5.9	1.9	3.5	1.1
Other bonds, notes, debentures	17.6	13.0	21.4	8.5	21.4	14.8
Stocks	67.1	57.2	52.2	71.2	41.3	43.8
Unclassified	2.8	4.0	2.7	3.3	2.3	2.2
Other assets, total[7]	4.4	9.8	5.7	5.4	16.3	23.9
Real estate & improvements	1.7	3.7	3.3	2.7	10.9	19.9
Mortgages, loans, etc.	0.4	0.5	0.3	0.8	3.3	2.8
Commodities	2.1	5.4	1.6	1.3	1.6	0.7
Other tangible assets	0.1	0.1	0.3	0.3	0.4	0.3
Intangible assets	†	0.1	0.2	0.3	0.1	0.1
Unclassified	5.2	10.4	12.1	9.7	15.3	14.1
Total[7]	100.0	100.0	100.0	100.0	100.0	100.0

Based on Source 4b. For numbered notes see pp. 488-9.
Includes all returns with capital transactions, with statutory net incomes or deficits.
* Less than $50,000. † Less than 0.05 percent.

Table 75: Average Realized Net Capital Gain or Loss[1] per Return, Average Gross Receipts per Sale, and Net Gain or Loss as a Percentage of Estimated Cost, by 10 Types of Asset, 1936
Federal income tax returns filed in New York, Pennsylvania, and Illinois

	AVERAGE GAIN[a]	AVERAGE LOSS[a]	AVERAGE GROSS RECEIPTS PER SALE	EXCESS OF REALIZED GAIN AS % OF ESTIMATED COST[8]
	(d o l l a r s)			
New York				
Securities, total[7]	3,346	4,207	3,971	3.4
Tax exempt	1,128	1,121	10,529	2.1
Other bonds, notes, debentures	1,485	2,502	3,220	2.8
Stocks	4,363	5,010	3,591	3.7
Unclassified	4,202	4,007	11,196	2.1
Other assets, total[7]	3,367	5,749	10,843	−10.1
Real estate & improvements	3,405	6,194	9,182	−18.5
Mortgages, loans, etc.	2,445	4,422	5,084	−31.3
Commodities	2,376	1,289	14,632	1.9
Other tangible assets	6,000	9,908	14,194	−3.0
Intangible assets	3,603	8,605	12,071	−5.9
Unclassified	4,565	4,228	28,932	2.2
Total[7]	3,491	4,351	5,028	2.7
Pennsylvania				
Securities, total[7]	2,803	3,599	2,860	4.3
Tax exempt	754	1,175	7,935	1.5
Other bonds, notes, debentures	1,439	2,633	2,974	2.1
Stocks	3,714	4,165	2,661	5.3
Unclassified	3,028	3,112	3,778	2.6
Other assets, total[7]	2,686	3,927	7,156	−8.7
Real estate & improvements	2,684	4,357	6,274	−15.3
Mortgages, loans, etc.	833	2,688	3,010	−33.9
Commodities	2,000	1,146	10,374	1.1
Other tangible assets	2,658	1,634	5,292	15.1
Intangible assets	6,263	1,625	9,477	52.5
Unclassified	2,260	3,032	5,907	2.7
Total[7]	2,735	3,555	3,081	3.5
Illinois				
Securities, total[7]	2,983	2,878	2,876	6.4
Tax exempt	912	1,021	6,497	2.3
Other bonds, notes, debentures	1,151	2,202	2,402	−1.1
Stocks	3,943	3,376	2,776	8.8
Unclassified	3,500	3,079	4,628	5.3
Other assets, total[7]	2,721	4,675	7,297	−10.5
Real estate & improvements	2,324	5,845	7,039	−23.7
Mortgages, loans, etc.	6,838	2,743	4,187	−18.4
Commodities	2,376	1,439	8,372	1.7
Other tangible assets	3,279	2,345	3,702	10.2
Intangible assets	5,147	3,625	4,188	49.0
Unclassified	2,314	2,940	6,471	3.4
Total[7]	2,888	3,180	3,257	3.8

Based on Source 4b.   For numbered notes see pp. 488-9.
Includes all returns with capital transactions, with statutory net incomes or deficits.
[a] Average net gain per return with realized net gain from sales of specified type of asset; average net loss per return with realized net loss from sales of specified type of asset.

Table 76

Realized Net Capital Gains and Losses, Number of Returns with Gains or Losses, Number of Sales, Gross Receipts, and Average Realized Gain or Loss per Return, by 10 Types of Asset and by Net Income Groups Defined to Exclude Statutory Gain and Loss, 1936

Federal income tax returns filed in New York State

REALIZED NET CAPITAL GAIN[1] (thousands of dollars)

	TOTAL	RETURNS WITH NET Deficits	RETURNS WITH NET Incomes	NET INCOME GROUP EXCLUDING STATUTORY NET CAPITAL GAIN AND LOSS[1] ($000) Under 5	5-30	30-50	50-100	100-300	300-500	500-1,000
Securities										
Tax exempt	4,381	267	4,113	559	1,421	776	635	348	16	359
Other bonds, notes, debentures	27,997	2,918	25,079	6,255	11,712	2,615	2,557	1,499	370	71
Stocks	175,316	22,948	152,369	43,505	66,946	17,565	14,779	7,908	944	723
Unclassified	14,187	1,565	12,622	3,578	5,627	1,437	1,360	324	130	165
Other Assets										
Real estate & improvements	4,396	1,618	2,778	1,236	979	171	344	46	2	
Mortgages, loans, etc.	401	109	292	73	129	19	71			
Commodities	1,138	181	957	351	339	80	113	65	5	10
Other tangible assets	1,284	143	1,141	214	580	339	2	*		
Intangible assets	209	65	144	77	64	1	2			
Unclassified	41,781	6,153	35,629	12,104	14,851	3,218	3,348	1,924	168	15
Total[r]	271,090	35,966	235,124	67,952	102,647	26,222	23,210	12,115	1,635	1,343

Percentage Distribution

	TOTAL	Deficits	Incomes	Under 5	5-30	30-50	50-100	100-300	300-500	500-1,000
Securities										
Tax exempt	100.0	6.1	93.9	12.8	32.4	17.7	14.5	7.9	0.4	8.2
Other bonds, notes, debentures	100.0	10.4	89.6	22.3	41.8	9.3	9.1	5.4	1.3	0.3
Stocks	100.0	13.1	86.9	24.8	38.2	10.0	8.4	4.5	0.5	0.4
Unclassified	100.0	11.0	89.0	25.2	39.7	10.1	9.6	2.3	0.9	1.2
Other Assets										
Real estate & improvements	100.0	36.8	63.2	28.1	22.3	3.9	7.8	1.0	†	
Mortgages, loans, etc.	100.0	27.2	72.8	18.2	32.2	4.7	17.7			
Commodities	100.0	15.9	84.1	30.8	29.8	7.0	9.9	5.7	0.4	0.9
Other tangible assets	100.0	11.1	88.9	16.7	45.2	26.4	0.2	†		
Intangible assets	100.0	31.1	68.9	36.8	30.6	0.5	1.0			
Unclassified	100.0	14.7	85.3	29.0	35.5	7.7	8.0	4.6	0.4	†

505

NET INCOME GROUP

EXCLUDING STATUTORY NET CAPITAL LOSS[1] ($000)

REALIZED NET CAPITAL GAIN AND LOSS (thousands of dollars)

	TOTAL	RETURNS WITH NET Deficits	RETURNS WITH NET Incomes	Under 5	5-30	30-50	50-100	100-300	300-500	500-1,000
Securities										
Tax exempt	1,294	36	1,258	118	472	133	149	364	18	5
Other bonds, notes, debentures	17,218	1,310	15,908	5,211	7,558	1,003	1,204	848	7	76
Stocks	97,597	6,606	90,991	21,314	47,782	7,794	7,053	4,894	650	1,505
Unclassified	7,089	410	6,679	1,551	3,790	696	321	321		1
Other Assets										
Real estate & improvements	14,630	2,825	11,805	5,190	5,157	875	340	32	189	22
Mortgages, loans, etc.	3,197	645	2,552	1,120	1,187	164	47	33	7	
Commodities	254	13	242	62	117	18	22	1		14
Other tangible assets	1,615	830	785	205	136	358	57	28		
Intangible assets	327	8	319	104	177	32		6		
Unclassified	22,413	1,393	21,020	8,337	8,522	1,418	1,495	1,069	5	174
Total[r]	165,634	14,076	151,558	43,211	74,898	12,492	10,688	7,598	876	1,795

Percentage Distribution

	TOTAL	RETURNS WITH NET Deficits	RETURNS WITH NET Incomes	Under 5	5-30	30-50	50-100	100-300	300-500	500-1,000
Securities										
Tax exempt	100.0	2.8	97.2	9.1	36.5	10.3	11.5	28.1	1.4	0.4
Other bonds, notes, debentures	100.0	7.6	92.4	30.3	43.9	5.8	7.0	4.9	†	0.4
Stocks	100.0	6.8	93.2	21.8	49.0	8.0	7.2	5.0	0.7	1.5
Unclassified	100.0	5.8	94.2	21.9	53.5	9.8	4.5	4.5		†
Other Assets										
Real estate & improvements	100.0	19.3	80.7	35.5	35.2	6.0	2.3	0.2	1.3	0.2
Mortgages, loans, etc.	100.0	20.2	79.8	35.0	37.1	5.1	1.5	1.0		
Commodities	100.0	5.1	95.3	24.4	46.1	7.1	8.7	0.4	2.8	5.5
Other tangible assets	100.0	51.4	48.6	12.7	8.4	22.2	3.5	1.7		
Intangible assets	100.0	2.4	97.6	31.8	54.1	9.8		1.8		
Unclassified	100.0	6.2	93.8	37.2	38.0	6.3	6.7	4.8	†	0.8

Securities										
Tax exempt	3,883	159	3,724	1,191	1,806	333	245	132	9	8
Other bonds, notes, debentures	18,857	748	18,109	7,466	8,808	990	584	229	21	11
Stocks	40,185	2,106	38,079	18,782	16,473	1,499	940	334	34	17
Unclassified	3,377	186	3,191	1,529	1,452	112	73	22	2	1
Other Assets										
Real estate & improvements	1,291	181	1,110	687	354	37	21	9	2	
Mortgages, loans, etc.	164	24	140	68	64	5	3			
Commodities	479	45	434	181	192	28	24	8	1	1
Other tangible assets	214	39	175	101	61	8	2	2	1	
Intangible assets	58	12	46	23	19	2	2			
Unclassified	9,153	674	8,479	4,765	3,216	254	174	61	7	2
Total[7]	77,661	4,174	73,487	34,793	32,445	3,268	2,068	797	76	40

Percentage Distribution

Securities										
Tax exempt	100.0	4.1	95.9	30.7	46.5	8.6	6.3	3.4	0.2	0.2
Other bonds, notes, debentures	100.0	4.0	96.0	39.6	46.7	5.3	3.1	1.2	0.1	0.1
Stocks	100.0	5.2	94.8	46.7	41.0	3.7	2.3	0.8	0.1	†
Unclassified	100.0	5.5	94.5	45.3	43.0	3.3	2.2	0.7	0.1	†
Other Assets										
Real estate & improvements	100.0	14.0	86.0	53.2	27.4	2.9	1.6	0.7	0.2	
Mortgages, loans, etc.	100.0	14.6	85.4	41.5	39.0	3.0	1.8			
Commodities	100.0	9.4	90.6	37.8	40.1	5.8	5.0	1.7	0.2	0.2
Other tangible assets	100.0	18.2	81.8	47.2	28.5	3.7	0.9	0.9	0.5	
Intangible assets	100.0	20.7	79.3	39.7	32.8	3.4	3.4			
Unclassified	100.0	7.4	92.6	52.1	35.1	2.8	1.9	0.7	0.1	†

NET INCOME GROUP

EXCLUDING STATUTORY NET CAPITAL GAIN AND LOSS ($000)

NUMBER OF RETURNS WITH REALIZED NET LOSSES FROM SALES OF EACH TYPE OF ASSET

	TOTAL	RETURNS WITH NET Deficits	Incomes	Under 5	5-30	30-50	50-100	100-300	300-500	500-1,000
Securities										
Tax exempt	1,154	44	1,110	247	531	125	117	78	10	2
Other bonds, notes, debentures	6,881	209	6,672	2,863	3,207	290	206	97	4	5
Stocks	19,481	528	18,953	7,969	9,430	821	491	208	19	15
Unclassified	1,769	56	1,713	696	896	67	28	24		2
Other Assets										
Real estate & improvements	2,362	201	2,161	1,085	946	70	42	13	4	1
Mortgages, loans, etc	723	54	669	334	302	21	10	2		
Commodities	197	10	187	63	99	12	9	1	2	1
Other tangible assets	163	14	149	80	48	12	5	4		
Intangible assets	38	3	35	14	17	2		2		
Unclassified	5,301	189	5,112	2,636	2,209	140	86	37	2	2
Total	38,069	1,308	36,761	15,987	17,685	1,560	994	466	41	28

Percentage Distribution

	TOTAL	RETURNS WITH NET Deficits	Incomes	Under 5	5-30	30-50	50-100	100-300	300-500	500-1,000
Securities										
Tax exempt	100.0	3.8	96.2	21.4	46.0	10.8	10.1	6.8	0.9	0.2
Other bonds, notes, debentures	100.0	3.0	97.0	41.6	46.6	4.2	3.0	1.4	0.1	0.1
Stocks	100.0	2.7	97.3	40.9	48.4	4.2	2.5	1.1	0.1	0.1
Unclassified	100.0	3.2	96.8	39.3	50.6	3.8	1.6	1.4		0.1
Other Assets										
Real estate & improvements	100.0	8.5	91.5	45.9	40.1	3.0	1.8	0.6	0.2	†
Mortgages, loans, etc.	100.0	7.5	92.5	46.2	41.8	2.9	1.4	0.3		
Commodities	100.0	5.1	94.9	32.0	50.3	6.1	4.6	0.5	1.0	0.5
Other tangible assets	100.0	8.6	91.4	49.1	29.4	7.4	3.1	2.5		
Intangible assets	100.0	7.9	92.1	36.8	44.7	5.3		5.3		
Unclassified	100.0	3.6	96.4	49.7	41.7	2.6	1.6	0.7	†	†

GROSS RECEIPTS FROM SALES (thousands of dollars)

Securities										
Tax exempt	146,820	8,708	138,112	17,710	40,477	19,552	23,736	26,218	2,048	8,371
Other bonds, notes, debentures	390,630	37,379	353,251	78,239	183,275	35,672	31,199	17,417	4,843	2,604
Stocks	2,150,776	258,429	1,892,347	515,913	826,420	232,398	186,105	108,750	10,763	11,999
Unclassified	352,886	72,662	280,223	64,444	152,930	28,764	25,081	7,360	198	1,446
Other Assets										
Real estate & improvements	45,075	10,067	35,008	15,720	13,659	2,637	2,516	376	87	11
Mortgages, loans, etc.	6,141	1,483	4,658	1,841	2,363	216	181	56		
Commodities	47,891	3,470	44,421	13,534	12,130	3,416	6,350	4,039	3,632	1,319
Other tangible assets	10,688	1,438	9,250	3,782	2,955	2,096	256	157	5	
Intangible assets	1,871	132	1,739	277	1,006	294	151	11		
Unclassified	906,286	137,233	769,052	250,116	327,272	69,706	83,155	31,124	4,279	3,401
Total	4,059,064	531,001	3,528,063	961,577	1,562,487	394,752	358,729	195,510	25,856	29,151

Percentage Distribution

Securities										
Tax exempt	100.0	5.9	94.1	12.1	27.6	13.3	16.2	17.9	1.4	5.7
Other bonds, notes, debentures	100.0	9.6	90.4	20.0	46.9	9.1	8.0	4.5	1.2	0.7
Stocks	100.0	12.0	88.0	24.0	38.4	10.8	8.7	5.1	0.5	0.6
Unclassified	100.0	20.6	79.4	18.3	43.3	8.2	7.1	2.1	0.1	0.4
Other Assets										
Real estate & improvements	100.0	22.3	77.7	34.9	30.3	5.9	5.6	0.8	0.2	†
Mortgages, loans, etc.	100.0	24.1	75.9	30.0	38.5	3.5	2.9	0.9		
Commodities	100.0	7.2	92.8	28.3	25.3	7.1	13.3	8.4	7.6	2.8
Other tangible assets	100.0	13.5	86.5	35.4	27.6	19.6	2.4	1.5	†	
Intangible assets	100.0	7.1	92.9	14.8	53.8	15.7	8.1	0.6		
Unclassified	100.0	15.1	84.9	27.6	36.1	7.7	9.2	3.4	0.5	0.4

NET INCOME GROUP
EXCLUDING STATUTORY NET CAPITAL GAIN AND LOSS ($000)

	TOTAL	RETURNS WITH NET		Under 5	5-30	30-50	50-100	100-300	300-500	500-1,000
		Deficits	Incomes							

NUMBER OF SALES

Securities										
Tax exempt	13,945	613	13,332	2,998	5,985	1,468	1,651	1,047	81	97
Other bonds, notes, debentures	121,313	6,480	114,833	37,986	63,810	6,701	4,318	1,835	106	77
Stocks	598,964	52,622	546,342	236,903	243,217	32,099	24,179	8,807	626	511
Unclassified	31,520	2,277	29,243	12,082	14,690	1,197	949	276	4	45
Other Assets										
Real estate & improvements	4,909	646	4,263	2,250	1,731	172	78	24	7	1
Mortgages, loans, etc.	1,208	113	1,095	525	488	54	26	2		
Commodities	3,273	340	2,933	1,221	1,218	148	276	37	28	5
Other tangible assets	753	275	478	243	174	42	8	10	1	
Intangible assets	155	31	124	62	50	7	2	3		
Unclassified	31,325	2,328	28,997	14,283	12,384	1,064	792	340	23	111
Total	807,365	65,725	741,640	308,553	343,747	42,952	32,284	12,381	876	847

Percentage Distribution

Securities										
Tax exempt	100.0	4.4	95.6	21.5	42.9	10.5	11.8	7.5	0.6	0.7
Other bonds, notes, debentures	100.0	5.3	94.7	31.3	52.6	5.5	3.6	1.5	0.1	0.1
Stocks	100.0	8.8	91.2	39.6	40.6	5.4	4.0	1.5	0.1	0.1
Unclassified	100.0	7.2	92.8	38.3	46.6	3.8	3.0	0.9	†	0.1
Other Assets										
Real estate & improvements	100.0	13.2	86.8	45.8	35.3	3.5	1.6	0.5	0.1	†
Mortgages, loans, etc.	100.0	9.4	90.6	43.5	40.4	4.5	2.2	0.2		
Commodities	100.0	10.4	89.6	37.3	37.2	4.5	8.4	1.1	0.9	0.2
Other tangible assets	100.0	36.5	63.5	32.3	23.1	5.6	1.1	1.3	0.1	
Intangible assets	100.0	20.0	80.0	40.0	32.3	4.5	1.3	1.9		
Unclassified	100.0	7.4	92.6	45.6	39.5	3.4	2.5	1.1	0.1	0.4

510

REALIZED NET GAIN FROM EACH TYPE OF ASSET AS % OF TOTAL NET GAIN

Securities										
Tax exempt	1.6	0.7	1.7	0.8	1.4	3.0	2.7	2.9	1.0	26.7
Other bonds, notes, debentures	10.3	8.1	10.7	9.2	11.4	10.0	11.0	12.4	22.6	5.3
Stocks	64.7	63.8	64.8	64.0	65.2	67.0	63.7	65.3	57.7	53.8
Unclassified	5.2	4.4	5.4	5.3	5.5	5.5	5.9	2.7	8.0	12.3
Other Assets										
Real estate & improvements	1.6	4.5	1.2	1.8	1.0	0.7	1.5	0.4	0.1	
Mortgages, loans, etc.	0.1	0.3	0.1	0.1	0.1	0.1	0.3			
Commodities	0.4	0.5	0.4	0.5	0.3	0.3	0.5	0.5		0.7
Other tangible assets	0.5	0.4	0.5	0.3	0.6	1.3	†	†	0.3	
Intangible assets	0.1	0.2	0.1	0.1	0.1	†	†			
Unclassified	15.4	17.1	15.2	17.8	14.5	12.3	14.4	15.9	10.3	1.1
Total[T]	100.0	100.0	100.0	100.0	100.0	100.0	100.0	100.0	100.0	100.0

REALIZED NET LOSS FROM EACH TYPE OF ASSET AS % OF TOTAL NET LOSS

Securities										
Tax exempt	0.8	0.3	0.8	0.3	0.6	1.1	1.4	4.8	2.1	0.3
Other bonds, notes, debentures	10.4	9.3	10.5	12.1	10.1	8.0	11.3	11.2	0.8	4.2
Stocks	58.9	46.9	60.0	49.3	63.8	62.4	66.0	64.4	74.2	83.3
Unclassified	4.3	2.9	4.4	3.6	5.1	5.6	3.0	4.2		0.1
Other Assets										
Real estate & improvements	8.8	20.1	7.8	12.0	6.9	7.0	3.2	0.4	21.6	1.2
Mortgages, loans, etc.	1.9	4.6	1.7	2.6	1.6	1.3	0.4	0.4		
Commodities	0.2	0.1	0.2	0.1	0.2	0.1	0.2	†	0.8	0.8
Other tangible assets	1.0	5.9	0.5	0.5	0.2	2.9	0.5	0.4		
Intangible assets	0.2	0.1	0.2	0.2	0.2	0.3		0.1		
Unclassified	13.5	9.9	13.9	19.3	11.4	11.4	14.0	14.1	0.6	9.7
Total[T]	100.0	100.0	100.0	100.0	100.0	100.0	100.0	100.0	100.0	100.0

NET INCOME GROUP

EXCLUDING STATUTORY NET CAPITAL GAIN AND LOSS ($000)

	TOTAL	RETURNS WITH NET		Under 5	5- 30	30- 50	50- 100	100- 300	300- 500	500- 1,000
		Deficits	Incomes							
AVERAGE REALIZED NET GAIN[a] (dollars)										
Securities										
Tax exempt	1,128	1,679	1,104	469	787	2,330	2,592	2,636	1,778	44,875
Other bonds, notes, debentures	1,485	3,901	1,385	838	1,330	2,641	4,378	6,546	17,619	6,455
Stocks	4,363	10,896	4,001	2,316	4,064	11,718	15,722	23,677	27,765	42,529
Unclassified	4,201	8,414	3,955	2,340	3,875	12,830	18,630	14,727	65,000	165,000
Other Assets										
Real estate & improvements	3,405	8,939	2,503	1,799	2,766	4,622	16,381	5,111	1,000	
Mortgages, loans, etc.	2,445	4,542	2,086	1,074	2,016	3,800	23,667			
Commodities	2,376	4,022	2,205	1,939	1,766	2,857	4,708	8,125	5,000	10,000
Other tangible assets	6,000	3,667	6,520	2,119	9,508	42,375	1,000	*		
Intangible assets	3,603	5,417	3,130	3,348	3,368	500	1,000			
Unclassified	4,565	9,129	4,202	2,540	4,618	12,669	19,241	31,541	24,000	7,500
AVERAGE REALIZED NET LOSS[a] (dollars)										
Securities										
Tax exempt	1,121	818	1,133	478	889	1,064	1,274	4,667	1,800	2,500
Other bonds, notes, debentures	2,502	6,268	2,384	1,820	2,357	3,459	5,845	8,742	1,750	15,200
Stocks	5,010	12,511	4,801	2,675	5,067	9,493	14,365	23,529	34,211	100,333
Unclassified	4,007	7,321	3,899	2,228	4,230	10,388	11,464	13,375		500
Other Assets										
Real estate & improvements	6,194	14,055	5,463	4,783	5,451	12,500	8,095	2,462	47,250	22,000
Mortgages, loans, etc.	4,422	11,944	3,815	3,353	3,930	7,810	4,700	16,500		
Commodities	1,289	1,300	1,294	984	1,182	1,500	2,444	1,000	3,500	14,000
Other tangible assets	9,908	59,286	5,268	2,562	2,833	29,833	11,400	7,000		
Intangible assets	8,605	2,667	9,114	7,429	10,412	16,000		3,000		
Unclassified	4,228	7,370	4,112	3,163	3,858	10,129	17,384	28,892	2,500	87,000

† Less than 0.05 percent.
For numbered notes see pp. 488-9.

Based on Source 4b.
Includes all returns with capital transactions.
* Less than $500.
[a] Average net gain per return with realized net gain from sales of specified type of asset; average net loss per return with realized net loss from sales of specified type of asset.

Table 77

Returns with Statutory Net Capital Gains by Number and Type of Other Sources of Income, 1936

| | RETURNS REPORTING STATUTORY NET CAPITAL GAINS | | | |
| | *All* | | *With total incomes*[9] *of $50,000 & over* | |
SOURCE OF INCOME[a]	Number	%	Number	%
Capital gain & no other source	6,996		93	
Capital gain & 1 other source				
Dividends	12,821	26.9	218	69.2
Salaries	21,294	44.7	30	9.5
Interest	2,873	6.0	12	3.8
Business	5,960	12.5	6	1.9
Rent	1,761	3.7	4	1.3
Other sources	2,903	6.1	45	14.3
Total	47,612	100.0	315	100.0
Capital gain & 2 other sources				
Dividends & salaries	53,036	40.2	559	30.7
Dividends & interest	33,475	25.4	817	44.9
Dividends & business	7,759	5.9	46	2.5
Dividends & rent	2,906	2.2	32	1.8
Dividends & other sources	5,445	4.1	196	10.8
Salaries & interest	9,605	7.3	38	2.1
Salaries & rent	3,680	2.8	2	0.1
Business & rent	2,391	1.8	2	0.1
Other combinations	13,540	10.3	126	6.9
Total	131,837	100.0	1,818	100.0
Capital gain & 3 or more other sources[10]				
Dividends & salaries	60,807	36.2	2,829	36.8
Dividends & interest	22,241	13.2	1,484	19.3
Dividends & business	9,643	5.7	250	3.2
Dividends & rent	5,457	3.2	243	3.2
Dividends & other sources	14,133	8.4	1,893	24.6
Salaries & interest	13,878	8.3	120	1.6
Salaries & rent	8,115	4.8	46	0.6
Business & rent	3,333	2.0	28	0.4
Other combinations	30,370	18.1	802	10.4
Total	167,977	100.0	7,695	100.0

Based on Source 4c.

Includes returns with statutory net incomes.

[a] The total number of returns showing 1, 2, 3, and 4 or more sources, respectively, were 2,944,660; 1,176,212; 682,863; 482,973.

For numbered notes see pp. 488-9.

Table 78

Realized and Statutory Net Capital Gains and Losses, 1936: Estimates Based on *Statistics of Income* and on *Statistics of Income Supplement for 1936* (millions of dollars)

	Statistics of Income & Source Book RETURNS WITH STAT. NET CAPITAL			Statistics of Income Supplement RETURNS WITH OVER-ALL REALIZED NET CAPITAL		
	Gains[11] (1)	Losses[11] (2)	Total (3)	Gains[2] (4)	Losses[2] (5)	Total (6)
Realized net gain[1]				1,224.9		1,224.9
Realized net loss[1]					645.3	645.3
Excess	1,416.8	−828.1	588.7	1,224.9	−645.3	579.6
Statutory net gain	996.3		996.3	821.1	16.4	837.5
Statutory net loss		144.6	144.6	0.6	129.8	130.4
Excess	996.3	−144.6	851.7	820.5	−113.4	707.1
Realized net gain: sum of net gains in 5 holding periods[6]	1,686.9	161.8	1,848.7	1,341.0	153.6	1,494.6
Realized net loss: sum of net losses in 5 holding periods[6]	270.2	990.0	1,260.1	116.1	798.9	915.0
Excess	1,416.8	−828.1	588.7	1,224.9	−645.3	579.6

Columns 1-3 based on Sources 1 and 2; columns 4-6 on Sources 4 and 4a.
For discussion, see Appendix One, Section F2.
Includes returns with statutory net incomes or deficits.
For numbered notes see pp. 488-9.

Table 79

Percentage of Returns with Net Capital Gains and Average Gain per Return, by Statutory Net Income Groups Including and Excluding Statutory Net Capital Gain and Loss, 1936

NET INCOME GROUP (thousands of dollars)

Including Statutory Net Capital Gain and Loss

	5-25	25-50	50-100	100-300	300-500	500-1,000	1,000 & over
Returns with net gains as % of all returns filed	26.7	49.9	57.0	60.9	63.3	63.5	59.0
Av. realized net gain[1,a]	3,300	10,300	20,400	54,700	125,700	281,900	1,458,900

Excluding Statutory Net Capital Gain and Loss

	5-30	30-50	50-100	100-300	300-500	500-1,000	1,000 & over
Returns with net gains as % of all returns filed	19.0	35.9	39.6	42.2	49.8	43.1	
Av. realized net gain[1,a]	3,600	11,100	15,500	32,300	62,200	78,100	375,000

Top section based on Sources 1 and 2; lower section on Source 4 and, for all returns filed, on Source 4d.
a In top section, average per return with statutory net capital gain;[11] in lower section, average per return with over-all realized net capital gain.[2]
For numbered notes see pp. 488-9.

Table 80

Average Realized Net Capital Gain per Return[1] by 5 Holding Periods and by Statutory Net Income Groups Including and Excluding Statutory Net Capital Gain and Loss, 1936 (dollars)

NET INCOME GROUP ($000)	1 or less	YEARS HELD			Over 10
		1-2	2-5	5-10	
Statutory Net Income including Statutory Net Capital Gain and Loss					
5- 25	2,400	1,800	2,300	2,500	5,300
25- 50	7,300	5,200	5,800	6,200	9,800
50- 100	13,600	7,900	12,900	12,900	25,200
100- 300	18,500	11,200	18,000	29,100	66,600
300- 500	30,200	26,500	38,300	45,800	168,200
500-1,000	69,400	45,600	90,100	102,200	251,900
1,000 & over	17,700	24,900	160,300	139,500	2,588,100
Statutory Net Income excluding Statutory Net Capital Gain and Loss					
5- 30	2,100	1,600	2,100	1,800	4,100
30- 50	4,900	3,500	4,900	5,500	12,800
50- 100	6,200	4,600	7,200	8,500	18,200
100- 300	11,900	8,000	11,800	14,000	43,500
300- 500	6,700	22,300	24,300	23,300	69,100
500-1,000	24,600	18,300	38,000	24,700	89,200
1,000 & over	12,600	20,700	46,900	5,800	685,500

Includes all returns with capital transactions. Top section based on Sources 1 and 2; lower section on Source 4. Average net gain per return with realized net gain in the holding period.

For numbered notes see pp. 488-9.

515

Table 81

Excluded Net Capital Gain and Disallowed Net Capital Loss by Statutory Net Income Groups Including and Excluding Statutory Net Capital Gain and Loss, 1936

NET INCOME GROUP ($000)	EXCLUDED GAIN[a] Millions of dollars	% of total real-ized net gain	DISALLOWED LOSS[b] Millions of dollars	% of total real-ized net loss	EXCESS OF EXCLUDED GAIN OVER DISALLOWED LOSS ($ mil.)	EXCL. GAIN (percentages)	DIS-AL-LOWED LOSS (percentages)
Statutory Net Income including Statutory Net Capital Gain and Loss							
Under 5	52.8	24.0	231.0	77.6	−178.2	13.1	39.4
5- 25	141.9	26.3	212.1	80.8	−70.2	35.1	36.2
25- 50	47.7	22.5	68.7	89.8	−21.0	11.8	11.7
50- 100	43.4	27.4	51.7	94.0	−8.3	10.7	8.8
100- 300	55.9	40.4	12.0	90.9	43.8	13.8	2.1
300- 500	12.4	47.4	4.6	97.7	7.8	3.1	0.8
500-1,000	14.3	44.8	1.6	95.2	12.7	3.5	0.3
1,000 & over	35.5	67.5	4.8	99.3	30.6	8.8	0.8
Total with net income	403.9	29.3	586.6	81.9	−182.8	100.0	100.0
Statutory Net Income excluding Statutory Net Capital Gain and Loss							
Under 5	100.3	27.7	147.9	75.2	−47.6	31.8	30.8
5- 30	121.3	29.0	240.9	81.6	−119.5	38.5	50.2
30- 50	32.7	36.6	36.0	91.1	−3.4	10.4	7.5
50- 100	27.9	40.4	31.9	95.5	−4.0	8.9	6.6
100- 300	20.4	44.3	14.1	97.9	6.2	6.5	2.9
300- 500	4.9	58.3	2.6	100.0	2.3	1.6	0.5
500-1,000	2.3	46.0	1.7	100.0	0.7	0.7	0.4
1,000 & over	5.3	70.7	4.7	100.0	0.6	1.7	1.0
Total with net income	315.1	31.3	479.7	81.6	−164.6	100.0	100.0

Top section based on Sources 1 and 2; lower section on Source 4.

[a] Top section covers returns with statutory net capital gains;[11] lower section returns with over-all realized net capital gains.[2]

[b] Top section covers returns with statutory net capital losses;[11] lower section returns with over-all realized net capital losses.[2]

For numbered notes see pp. 488-9.

IV Individuals with Highest Incomes, Selected Years

Tables 82-86 summarize the capital gains and losses over a period of years of groups of persons with high incomes, as reported on federal income tax returns.

Notes to Tables 82-86

[1] Includes net deficit.

[2] Excludes disallowed short term net loss from stocks and bonds (other than government bonds) in 1932 and 1933.

[3] Net capital gain is the sum of the annual net gains reported on each group of returns; net capital loss, the sum of annual net losses.

[4] The sum of the positive items of net income reported on the returns.

[5] Standard and Poor's December average of the daily prices of 90 stocks (1926 average: 100).

[6] This income classification differs from the one used in other tables in that capital net loss segregated for tax credit at 12½ percent was deducted in determining net income.

[7] Net gain for the net deficit group included with total for lowest net income group.

Table 82

400 Persons with Net Incomes of $100,000 and Over in 1916 Capital Gains and Losses by Type of Asset, 1917-1922

TYPE OF ASSET	GAIN	LOSS	GAIN	LOSS
	($ million)		(percentages)	
Total stock transactions	30.5	65.2	89.2	70.7
Railroad & public utility	1.2	17.4	3.5	18.9
All other stock	29.3	47.8	85.7	51.8
Total bond transactions	1.7	19.0	4.9	20.6
Railroad & public utility	0.3	6.4	0.9	6.9
All other bond	1.4	12.7	4.1	13.8
Real estate sales	2.0	3.3	5.9	3.6
Loss on worthless stocks & bonds		4.7		5.2
Total	34.2	92.3	100.0	100.0

Based on Source 6d.

Table 83

45 Persons with Net Incomes of $1,000,000 and Over in 1924 by Statutory Net Income Groups, 1917-1933

	TOTAL[1]	STATUTORY NET INCOME GROUP (thousands of dollars)						
		Under 50[1]	50- 100	100- 300	300- 500	500- 1,000	1,000- 5,000	5,000 & over
1917	45	4	2	9	1	6	22	1
1918	45	5	2	5	8	7	18	
1919	45	5	3	9	4	13	8	3
1920	45	6	6	12	5	7	6	3
1921	45	4	8	5	8	10	9	1
1922	45	1		7	3	9	22	3
1923	45	1	3	5	5	10	18	3
1924	45						42	3
1925	45			2	1	4	34	4
1926	45			3		8	28	6
1927	45			2	1	5	30	7
1928	45	1		2		4	31	7
1929	45	2		4	2	2	23	12
1930	45	6		8	1	8	18	4
1931	45	10	1	8	3	9	11	3
1932	45	15	3	9	3	8	7	
1933	45	9	2	12	6	11	4	1

Based on Source 6b.
For numbered notes see p. 517.

Table 84

45 Persons with Net Incomes of $1,000,000 and Over in 1924: Net Capital Gains and Losses,[2] 1917-1933 as a Whole, by Groups Realizing an Over-all Net Capital Gain or Loss

	NET GAIN IN YEARS WITH NET GAIN[3]	NET LOSS IN YEARS WITH NET LOSS[3]	EXCESS OF GAIN	TOTAL INCOME[4]	NET GAIN OR LOSS AS % OF TOTAL INCOME		
					Gain	Loss	Excess
	(thousands of dollars)						
27 returns with excess of gain, 1917-33	341,299	88,480	252,819	1,434,457	23.8	6.2	17.6
18 returns with excess of loss, 1917-33	47,555	113,825	−66,270	692,213	6.9	16.4	−9.5
All 45 returns	388,854	202,305	186,549	2,126,670	18.3	9.5	8.8
27 returns with excess of gain							
Excess of gain as % of total income							
Less than 5% (3 returns)	18,150	14,386	3,764	189,768	9.6	7.6	2.0
5-15% (10 returns)	116,189	34,118	82,071	822,350	14.1	4.1	10.0
15-25% (3 returns)	32,760	16,704	16,056	84,100	39.0	19.9	19.1
25-50% (7 returns)	92,473	16,176	76,297	207,732	44.5	7.8	36.7
50% & over (4 returns)	81,727	7,096	74,631	130,507	62.6	5.4	57.2
18 returns with excess of loss							
Excess of loss as % of total income							
Less than 5% (6 returns)	13,575	21,063	−7,488	241,960	5.6	8.7	−3.1
5-15% (7 returns)	19,695	40,570	−20,875	263,226	7.5	15.4	−7.9
15-25% (5 returns)	14,285	52,192	−37,907	187,027	7.6	27.9	−20.3

Based on Source 6b.
For numbered notes see p. 517.

519

Table 85

45 Persons with Net Incomes of $1,000,000 and Over in 1924
Net Capital Gains and Losses, 1917-1933

	NET GAIN	NET LOSS	EXCESS OF GAIN	STOCK PRICE INDEX[5]
		(millions of dollars)		
1917	0.8	0.7	0.1	55.3
1918	1.7	4.3	−2.6	63.8
1919	2.8	11.2	−8.5	66.0
1920	1.2	19.1	−17.9	53.7
1921	0.1	15.8	−15.8	58.0
1922	9.0	9.8	−0.8	68.2
1923	10.9	8.0	2.9	67.6
1924	21.6	0.6	20.9	82.4
1925	41.1	5.1	36.0	101.2
1926	29.5	1.0	28.5	107.1
1927	47.2	1.6	45.6	138.7
1928	65.5	1.2	64.3	183.8
1929	89.0	4.0	85.0	170.0
1930	54.8	16.4	38.4	123.2
1931	3.5	40.6	−37.2	67.0
1932[2]	0.7	34.1	−33.4	54.2
1933[3]	9.6	28.5	−19.0	79.2

Based on Source 6b.
For numbered notes see p. 517.

Table 86: 141 Persons with Largest Net Incomes in 1929: Net Capital Gains and Losses by Net Income Groups, 1929, 1932, and 1937 (dollar figures in thousands)

A By Net Income Groups including Net Capital Gain & Loss[6]

Net Income Groups as defined in A & B ($000)	NUMBER OF RETURNS	RETURNS WITH NET CAP. GAINS No.	Gain	RETURNS WITH NET CAP. LOSSES No.	Loss
1929					
Under 50	2			2	2,859
50- 100	27	12	528	11	1,394
100- 300	100	72	89,668	18	3,704
300- 500	5	5	23,368		
500- 1,000	7	7	84,157		
1,000- 5,000					
5,000-10,000					
10,000 & over					
Total	141	96	197,721	31	7,957
Net deficit					
All returns	141	96	197,721	31	7,957
1932[2]					
Under 50	12	1	180	11	1,633
50- 100	4			3	111
100- 300	21	2 }	594	16	2,896
300- 500	23	7 }		10	893
500- 1,000	22	9	2,478	10	1,073
1,000- 5,000	8			5	3,445
Total	90	19	3,252	55	10,051
Net deficit	51			49	40,507
All returns	141	19	3,252	104	50,558
1937					
Under 50	1			1 }	145
50- 100	4			3 }	
100- 300	46	19	296	23	636
300- 500	20	11	744	5	59
500- 1,000	35	16	1,640	17	162
1,000- 5,000	32	15 }	11,534	11	3,319
5,000-10,000	1 }	1 }			
Total	139	62	14,214	60	4,321
Net deficit	2			2	928
All returns	141	62	14,214	62	5,249

B By Net Income Groups excluding Net Capital Gain & Loss

Net Income Groups	NUMBER OF RETURNS	RETURNS WITH NET CAP. GAINS No.	Gain	RETURNS WITH NET CAP. LOSSES No.	Loss
1929					
Under 50	4	4	9,449[r]		
50- 100	2	2	6,063		
100- 300	16	16	30,142		
300- 500	12	12	26,525		
500- 1,000	38	24	13,163	10	1,601
1,000- 5,000	66	35	105,926	21	6,356
5,000-10,000	1	1 }	6,453		
10,000 & over	1 }	1 }			
Total	140	95	197,721[r]	31	7,957
Net deficit	1	1			
All returns	141	96	197,721	31	7,957
1932					
Under 50	5	2	918[r]	3	150
50- 100	10	2	603	7	742
100- 300	43	5	1,534	35	10,064
300- 500	27	4	32	17	8,776
500- 1,000	35	5	165	27	22,356
1,000- 5,000	11			8	7,969
Total	131	18	3,252[r]	97	50,057
Net deficit	10	1		7	501
All returns	141	19	3,252	104	50,558
1937					
Under 50					
50- 100	1				
100- 300	52	24	2,069[r]	24	1,544
300- 500	19	7	188	8	57
500- 1,000	36	16	5,783	18	329
1,000- 5,000	31	14	6,174	11 }	3,319
5,000-10,000	1			1 }	
Total	140	61	14,214[r]	62	5,249
Net deficit	1	1			
All returns	141	62	14,214	62	5,249

Based on Source 6g.

For numbered notes see p. 517.

V Tax Rates and Revenues

Tables 87-90 present tax rates applicable to gains received from sales of capital assets and estimated net revenue from the tax treatment of capital gains and losses.

Table 87

Effective Tax Rate on Additional Dollar of Long Term Capital Gains and of Ordinary Income or Short Term Capital Gains: Individuals at 6 Levels of Statutory Net Income, 1917-1950

Married person with 2 dependents besides his wife and with maximum earned income credit

	STATUTORY NET INCOME (thousands of dollars)					
	5	10	25	50	100	1,000
			(tax rates, percentages)			
A LONG TERM CAPITAL GAINS						
1917	5	7	12	16	31	65
1918	7	16	23	36	64	77
1919-21	5	12	19	32	60	73
1922	4	10	12.5	12.5	12.5	12.5
1923	3	7.5	12.5	12.5	12.5	12.5
1924	2	5	12.5	12.5	12.5	12.5
1925-28	1.5	4	12	12.5	12.5	12.5
1929	.5	3	11	12.5	12.5	12.5
1930-31	1.5	4	12	12.5	12.5	12.5
1932-33	4	10	12.5	12.5	12.5	12.5
1934-35	2.4	5.4	11.4	18.6	32.4	37.2
1936-37	2.4	5.4	11.4	18.6	35.4	45.6
1938-39	2	4.5	9.5	15	15	15
1940[a]	2.2	5.5	16.5	16.5	16.5	18.5
1941	6.5	10.5	15	15	15	15
1942-43	11	17	25	25	25	25
1944-45	12.5	18.5	25	25	25	25
1946-47	10.5	16.2	25	25	25	25
1948-49[b]	8.3	9.7	16.7	25	25	25
1950[b]	8.7	10.0	17.3	25	25	25

In 1917-21 long term gains were not differentiated from short term gains or ordinary income; in 1922-33 they comprise those from capital assets held longer than 2 years; in 1934-37 they were of several classes, of which that consisting of assets held over 2 but not over 5 years is referred to here; in 1938-41 they were of two classes of which the longer — those from capital assets held more than 24 months — is referred to here; and in 1942-50, they were defined as gains from capital assets held more than 6 months.

EFFECTIVE TAX RATES ON AN ADDITIONAL DOLLAR OF CAPITAL GAINS FROM ASSETS HELD OVER 1 BUT NOT OVER 2 YEARS, FROM ASSETS HELD OVER 5 BUT NOT OVER 10 YEARS, AND FROM ASSETS HELD OVER 10 YEARS, 1934-1937

	STATUTORY NET INCOME (thousands of dollars)					
	5	10	25	50	100	1,000
			(tax rates, percentages)			
From assets held more than 1 but not over 2 years						
1934-35	3.2	7.2	15.2	24.8	43.2	49.6
1936-37	3.2	7.2	15.2	24.8	47.2	60.8
From assets held more than 5 but not over 10 years						
1934-35	1.6	3.6	7.6	12.4	21.6	24.8
1936-37	1.6	3.6	7.6	12.4	23.6	30.4
From assets held more than 10 years						
1934-35	1.2	2.7	5.7	9.3	16.2	18.6
1936-37	1.2	2.7	5.7	9.3	17.7	22.8

EFFECTIVE TAX RATES ON AN ADDITIONAL DOLLAR OF CAPITAL GAINS FROM ASSETS HELD MORE THAN 18 BUT NOT OVER 24 MONTHS, 1938-1941

	STATUTORY NET INCOME (thousands of dollars)					
	5	10	25	50	100	1,000
	(tax rates, percentages)					
1938-39	2.7	6.0	12.7	20	20	20
1940[a]	2.9	7.3	22	22	22	24.7
1941	8.7	14.0	20	20	20	20

B ORDINARY INCOME OR SHORT TERM CAPITAL GAINS

	5	10	25	50	100	1,000
1917	5	7	12	16	31	65
1918	7	16	23	36	64	77
1919-21	5	12	19	32	60	73
1922	4	10	18	31	56	58
1923	3	7.5	13.5	23.3	42	43.5
1924	2	5	13	24	43	46
1925-28	1.5	4	12	18	25	25
1929	0.5	3	11	17	24	24
1930-31	1.5	4	12	18	25	25
1932-33	4	10	18	31	56	63
1934-35	4	9	19	31	54	62
1936-39	4	9	19	31	59	76
1940[a]	4.4	11	34.1	48.4	66	78.4
1941	13	21	48	59	68	78
1942	22	34	58	69	83	88
1943[c]	24.8	36.8	60.8	71.8	88	90[d]
1944-45	25	37	62	75	90	90[d]
1946-47	20.9	32.3	56.1	68.4	82.7	86.5
1948-49[b]	16.6	19.4	33.4	51.9	63.4	82.1
1950[b]	17.4	20.0	34.6	53.7	65.5	84.4

In 1917-21 short term capital gains were not differentiated from long term gains or ordinary income; in 1922-33 they comprise gains from assets held 2 years or less; in 1934-37 they were of several classes, the shortest of which — gains from assets held 1 year or less — is referred to here; in 1938-41 they were defined as those from assets held 18 months or less; and in 1942-50, as those from assets held 6 months or less. These rates would apply to any additional 'unearned' income up to the point at which a higher surtax bracket is reached.

[a] Includes Defense Tax, which was 10 percent of the total income tax liability as otherwise determined, except that it was limited to no more than 10 percent of the net income in excess of the total tax computed without regard to the Defense Tax, a limitation that was operative for net income of $1 million.

[b] Rates are for joint return.

[c] Includes Victory Tax. Effective rates computed on assumption that Victory Tax net income equals regular net income. For any given return, unless a major share of the income was from specified types of government obligations, this assumption probably understates the actual Victory Tax net income because certain categories of deductions, included in regular net income, were excluded from Victory Tax net income. The result may be some understatement in effective rates for any given return with net income of $50,000 or below. At net income levels above $50,000 the full Victory Tax rate is applied.

The rates in Section B apply to an additional dollar of ordinary net income only, inasmuch as capital gains were not subject to the Victory Tax. In 1943 the effective tax rates on an additional dollar of short term capital gains were as follows for the stated amounts of statutory net income: $5,000, 22%; $10,000, 34%; $25,000, 58%; $50,000, 69%; $100,000, 83%; $1,000,000, 88%.

[d] Taking into account the statutory limitation of the maximum effective rate to 90 percent.

Table 88

Effective Tax Rate on First Dollar of Long Term Capital Gains as a Percentage of Tax Rate on Ordinary Income: 6 Levels of Statutory Net Income, 1922-1950

Married person with 2 dependents besides his wife and with maximum earned income credit

| | STATUTORY NET INCOME (thousands of dollars) | | | | | |
	5	10	25	50	100	1,000
1922	100.0	100.0	69.4	40.3	22.3	21.6
1923	100.0	100.0	92.6	53.6	29.8	28.7
1924	100.0	100.0	96.2	52.1	29.1	27.2
1925-28	100.0	100.0	100.0	69.4	50.0	50.0
1929	100.0	100.0	100.0	73.5	52.1	52.1
1930-31	100.0	100.0	100.0	69.4	50.0	50.0
1932-33	100.0	100.0	69.4	40.3	22.3	19.8
1934-37	60.0	60.0	60.0	60.0	60.0	60.0
1938-39	50.0	50.0	50.0	48.4	25.4	19.7
1940	50.0	50.0	48.4	34.1	25.0	23.6
1941	50.0	50.0	31.3	25.4	22.1	19.2
1942	50.0	50.0	43.1	36.2	30.1	28.4
1943	44.4	46.2	41.1	34.8	28.4	27.8
1944-45	50.0	50.0	40.3	33.3	27.8	27.8
1946-47	50.0	50.0	44.6	36.5	30.2	28.9
1948-49	50.0	50.0	50.0	48.2	39.5	30.4
1950	50.0	50.0	50.0	46.6	38.2	29.6

See Table 87, note to Section A. In 1934-37 the effective tax rate on an additional dollar of capital gains from capital assets held over 1 but not over 2 years was 80 percent of the ordinary rate at all income levels; from capital assets held over 5 but not over 10 years, 40 percent; and from capital assets held more than 10 years, 30 percent. For capital assets held 1 year or less, it was 100 percent of the ordinary rate at all income levels.

Table 89

Effective Rate of Tax and of Tax Credit for Long Term Net Capital Gains and Losses, respectively, of Specified Sizes under Present Law and if Prorated over 3, 5, 10, and 20 Years and Taxed in Full at Ordinary Rates

Married persons without dependents; i.e., one spouse is assumed to possess the entire income

A GAINS (tax rates, percentages)

	ORDINARY NET INCOME BEFORE PERSONAL EXEMPTIONS (thousands of dollars)							
	5	10	15	25	50	75	100	250
$5,000 Long Term Net Capital Gain								
TAX RATE								
Present[a]	9.6	11.4	13.4	18.7	25.0	25.0	25.0	25.0
If prorated over								
3 years	19.0	22.9	26.4	37.3	51.9	57.2	64.1	78.3
5 years	18.8	22.9	26.4	37.0	51.9	57.2	63.4	78.3
10 years	18.3	22.9	26.4	36.1	51.9	57.2	63.4	78.3
20 years	17.2	22.9	26.4	34.3	51.9	57.2	63.4	78.3
$10,000 Long Term Net Capital Gain								
Present[a]	9.9	12.1	14.2	19.1	25.0	25.0	25.0	25.0
If prorated over								
3 years	19.2	23.0	27.6	37.6	52.0	58.4	65.0	78.3
5 years	19.1	22.9	26.4	37.4	51.9	57.2	64.4	78.3
10 years	18.8	22.9	26.4	37.0	51.9	57.2	63.4	78.3
20 years	18.3	22.9	26.4	36.1	51.9	57.2	63.4	78.3
$25,000 Long Term Net Capital Gain								
Present[a]	11.5	13.7	15.9	20.5	25.0	25.0	25.0	25.0
If prorated over								
3 years	21.1	25.5	29.9	39.5	53.5	59.8	65.6	78.3
5 years	19.8	24.1	28.4	38.2	52.9	59.2	65.4	78.3
10 years	19.1	22.9	26.8	37.5	51.9	57.6	64.7	78.3
20 years	18.9	22.9	26.4	37.1	51.9	57.2	63.5	78.3
$50,000 Long Term Net Capital Gain								
Present[a]	14.3	16.6	18.7	22.6	25.0	25.0	25.0	25.0
If prorated over								
3 years	24.8	29.3	33.9	42.5	54.3	60.6	65.8	78.3
5 years	22.0	26.3	30.5	40.3	53.7	59.9	65.7	78.3
10 years	19.8	24.1	28.4	38.2	52.9	59.2	65.4	78.3
20 years	19.1	22.9	26.8	37.5	51.9	57.6	64.7	78.3

[a] Tax rate under 1949 law, taking into account the 50 percent exclusion and the maximum effective rate limitation on long term gains.

B LOSSES (tax credits, percentages)

ORDINARY NET INCOME BEFORE PERSONAL EXEMPTIONS
(thousands of dollars)

	5	10	15	25	50	75	100	250
				$5,000 Long Term Net Capital Loss				
TAX CREDIT								
Present[b]	8.3	11.2	13.2	16.7	26.0	28.6	31.7	39.2
If prorated over								
3 years	16.6	21.0	26.4	33.4	51.9	57.2	63.4	78.3
5 years	16.6	22.2	26.4	33.4	51.9	57.2	63.4	78.3
10 years	16.6	22.9	26.4	33.4	51.9	57.2	63.4	78.3
20 years	16.6	22.9	26.4	33.4	51.9	57.2	63.4	78.3
				$10,000 Long Term Net Capital Loss				
Present[b]	8.3	11.1	13.2	16.7	26.0	28.6	31.7	39.2
If prorated over								
3 years	16.6	20.2	24.8	33.4	51.9	57.2	63.4	78.3
5 years	16.6	20.8	26.0	33.4	51.9	57.2	63.4	78.3
10 years	16.6	22.2	26.4	33.4	51.9	57.2	63.4	78.3
20 years	16.6	22.9	26.4	33.4	51.9	57.2	63.4	78.3
				$25,000 Long Term Net Capital Loss				
Present[b]	4.0	5.3	6.3	8.0	12.5	13.7	15.2	18.8
If prorated over								
3 years	7.6	18.5	22.6	31.3	50.8	57.2	63.4	78.3
5 years	12.6	19.8	24.1	32.6	51.8	57.2	63.4	78.3
10 years	16.6	20.5	25.4	33.4	51.9	57.2	63.4	78.3
20 years	16.6	21.6	26.4	33.4	51.9	57.2	63.4	78.3
				$50,000 Long Term Net Capital Loss				
Present[b]	2.0	2.7	3.2	4.0	6.2	6.9	7.6	9.4
If prorated over								
3 years	3.8	9.7	17.0	27.6	48.2	56.1	62.4	78.3
5 years	6.3	16.2	22.0	30.5	50.2	57.1	63.4	78.3
10 years	12.6	19.8	24.1	32.6	51.8	57.2	63.4	78.3
20 years	16.6	20.5	25.4	33.4	51.9	57.2	63.4	78.3

[b] Tax credit under 1949 law, taking into account the 50 percent exclusion, the maximum $1,000 offset of capital losses against ordinary income, and the 5 year carryover of losses.

Table 90

Estimated Net Revenue from Tax Treatment of Capital Gains and Losses, 1926-1947

Individual and Taxable Fiduciary Income Tax Returns

	ESTIMATED NET REVENUE FROM CAPITAL GAINS AND LOSSES	ESTIMATED TAX LIABILITY ON OTHER INCOME	TOTAL TAX LIABILITY	NET REVENUE FROM GAINS AND LOSSES AS % OF TOTAL TAX LIABILITY
	(millions of dollars)			
1926	225	507	732	30.7
1927	297	534	831	35.7
1928	576	588	1,164	49.4
1929	421	581	1,002	42.0
1930	−15	492	477	−3.1
1931	−89	335	246	−36.2
1932	−80	410	330	−24.2
1933	16	358	374	4.3
1934	17	494	511	3.3
1935	72	585	657	11.0
1936	171	1,043	1,214	14.1
1937	41	1,100	1,142	3.6
1938	12	753	766	1.6
1939	4	924	929	0.4
1940	−7	1,504	1,496	−0.5
1941	−86	3,994	3,908	−2.2
1942	68	8,859	8,927	0.8
1943	266	14,324	14,590[a]	1.8
1944	354	15,993	16,347	2.2
1945	721	16,505	17,226	4.2
1946	850	15,431	16,281	5.2
1947	500	17,749	18,249	2.7

Sources 1926-34: Treasury Department, Division of Research and Statistics: *Revenue Revision Hearings before the Committee on Ways and Means,* House of Representatives (77 Cong., 2 sess., Revised, II, 1637, Government Printing Office, 1942); 1935-45: Treasury Department, Technical Staff: *Ibid.* (81 Cong., 2 sess., II, 2943, Government Printing Office, 1950); 1946-47: figures for total tax liability from Bureau of Internal Revenue; those for net revenue from capital gains and losses estimated by us.

Estimated net revenue from capital gains and losses is the difference between 1) total tax liability under the provisions of the particular revenue act applicable to each specified income year and 2) estimated tax liability on other income if capital gains and losses had been entirely excluded from the tax computation.

Estimates of net revenue from capital gains and losses for 1926-34 are overstated as compared with those for 1935-47 because returns reporting net deficits were excluded in the earlier period and cruder statistical procedures were used.

[a] Excludes additions to liability under the Current Tax Payment Act of 1943 amounting to $2,555,894,000.

Table 91 summarizes changes in the assessed values of various groundsites in New York City, 1909-42, and in Cleveland, 1910-42.

Table 91

Percentage Change in Assessed Values of Various Groundsites, New York City, 1909-1942; Cleveland, 1910-1942

A New York City (manhattan)

Location	Block	1909-42	1909-31	1931-42
6th Ave.	821	−74.6	−48.8	−50.5
5th Ave.	850	−70.8	−40.0	−51.3
14th St.	816	−33.3	−8.3	−27.3
5th Ave.	1380	−28.6	14.3	−37.5
Times Sq.	996	10.0	56.7	−29.8
8th Ave.	754	17.2	118.8	−46.4
6th Ave.	573	20.0	32.0	−9.8
Greeley Sq.	810	30.0	42.0	−8.5
Broadway	46	38.9	55.6	−10.7
Greeley Sq.	808	39.7	63.8	−14.7
14th St.	571	50.0	38.9	8.0
5th Ave.	550	50.0	120.0	−31.8
8th Ave.	763	77.1	181.3	−37.0
5th Ave.	1285	81.3	175.0	−34.1
8th Ave.	1033	87.5	216.7	−40.8
Greeley Sq.	809	96.8	122.6	−11.6
Times Sq.	995	103.8	162.5	−22.4
Times Sq.	997	116.7	186.7	−24.4
8th Ave.	784	212.5	303.4	−22.5
7th Ave.	786	225.0	291.7	−17.0
6th Ave.	259	227.4	429.8	−38.2
Beekman Pl.	1361	313.3 (1913-42)	466.7 (1913-31)	−27.1
Beekman Pl.	1361E	406.7 (1913-42)	566.7 (1913-31)	−24.0
Sutton Pl.	1367	466.7	633.3	−22.7

B Cleveland

	1910-42	1910-24	1924-42
E. 55th N. Euclid	−64.6	32.6	−73.3
Euclid N.E. 65th	−50.0	300.0	−87.5
Euclid N.E. 40th	−8.1	568.6	−86.3
Cuyahoga County	76.4	325.7	−58.6
Euclid N.E. 3d	100.0	152.5	−20.8
Euclid N.E. 105th	340.0	700.0	−45.0

Sources: New York, land value maps of Surveyors Bureau of New York City Tax Department.
Cleveland, data supplied by John A. Zangerle, Auditor of Cuyahoga County.
Negative figures indicate percentage decrease.

VII Basic Data for Corporations, 1928-1947

Tables 92-98 summarize the capital gains and losses reported on federal income tax returns filed by corporations for 1928-47. The statutory provisions with respect to corporate capital gains and losses and the lack of comparability of the data for various years are discussed in Appendix One, Part II.

Table 92

Net Capital Gains and Losses of All Corporations and of Financial and Nonfinancial Corporations, by Groups Reporting Net Incomes or Deficits, 1928-1947 (millions of dollars)

All Corporations

| | NET GAIN | | | NET LOSS | | | EXCESS OF GAIN | | |
| | Returns with Net | | All returns | Returns with Net | | All returns | Returns with Net | | All returns |
	Incomes	Deficits		Incomes	Deficits		Incomes	Deficits	
1928	606.9	115.1	721.9						
1929	1,165.4	150.0	1,315.4						
1930	490.3	155.5	645.8	160.4	775.4	935.7	329.9	−619.9	−289.9
1931	157.4	141.2	298.6	153.8	1,548.5	1,702.3	3.7	−1,407.3	−1,403.6
1932	47.6	94.8	142.5	110.9	1,594.3	1,705.2	−63.2	−1,499.5	−1,562.7
1933	115.7	146.7	262.5	171.3	1,514.6	1,685.9	−55.6	−1,367.8	−1,423.4
1934	104.2	138.3	242.6	21.7	275.7	297.4	82.5	−137.4	−54.8
1935	297.6	172.3	469.9	16.2	222.8	239.0	281.4	−50.5	230.9
1936	481.8	99.4	581.2	24.1	118.4	142.4	457.7	−19.0	438.8
1937	214.7	90.6	305.3	34.8	129.7	164.5	179.9	−39.1	140.8
1938	209.9	92.1	302.0	41.5	185.3	226.8	168.4	−93.2	75.2
1939	249.8	77.1	326.9	56.9	194.1	251.1	192.9	−117.0	75.8
1940	294.0	72.6	366.6	311.9	726.8	1,038.7	−17.9	−654.2	−672.1
1941	284.6	62.5	347.1	672.6	630.0	1,302.6	−388.0	−567.5	−955.5
1942[a]	266.4	43.9	310.3	205.4	281.1	486.5	61.0	−237.1	−176.2
1943[a]	385.6	39.1	424.7	264.5	319.4	583.9	121.0	−280.2	−159.2
1944[a]	528.2	39.3	567.5	249.9	254.3	504.2	278.3	−215.0	63.3
1945[a]	1,046.5	59.0	1,105.5	214.6	249.5	464.1	831.9	−190.5	641.4
1946[a]			1,508.9			239.6			1,269.3
1947[a]			1,248.4			324.8			923.6

Financial Corporations

	NET GAIN			NET LOSS			EXCESS OF GAIN		
	Returns with Net			Returns with Net			Returns with Net		
	Incomes	Deficits	All returns	Incomes	Deficits	All returns	Incomes	Deficits	All returns
1928	334.5	65.8	400.3	45.3	537.8	583.2	224.1	−440.5	−216.4
1929	788.6	98.8	887.4	53.8	1,034.7	1,088.5	21.8	−969.4	−947.6
1930	269.4	97.3	366.7	50.1	1,054.5	1,104.6	−24.3	−1,008.4	−1,032.7
1931	75.6	65.3	140.9	66.8	1,003.3	1,070.2	−0.6	−911.7	−912.4
1932	25.8	46.1	71.9	6.6	190.5	197.1	44.5	−98.2	−53.6
1933	66.2	91.6	157.8	6.5	151.9	158.4	211.4	−21.1	190.3
1934	51.1	92.3	143.5	12.8	87.4	100.1	372.4	−27.2	345.3
1935	217.9	130.8	348.7	23.3	99.9	123.3	102.6	−45.1	57.4
1936	385.2	60.2	445.4	22.2	114.1	136.3	131.0	−58.2	72.8
1937	125.9	54.8	180.7	26.6	126.8	153.3	157.6	−77.4	80.2
1938	153.2	55.9	209.1	145.6	487.5	633.1	38.9	−437.6	−398.7
1939	184.1	49.4	233.5	178.8	453.7	632.5	−24.4	−409.6	−434.0
1940	184.5	49.9	234.4	76.6	187.4	264.0	22.5	−158.0	−135.5
1941	154.4	44.1	198.5	94.5	172.6	267.1	85.0	−150.1	−65.1
1942[a]	99.1	29.4	128.5	74.5	147.0	221.6	224.0	−126.5	97.6
1943[a]	179.5	22.4	202.0	37.8	125.7	163.5	602.6	−98.1	504.5
1944[a]	298.5	20.6	319.1			117.6			748.0
1945[a]	640.4	27.6	668.0			110.5			463.9
1946[a]			865.6						
1947[a]			574.3						

Nonfinancial Corporations

Year									
1928	272.4	49.3	321.6	115.1	237.6	352.7	105.8	−179.4	−73.5
1929	376.8	51.2	428.0	100.0	513.8	613.8	−18.1	−437.9	−456.0
1930	220.9	58.2	279.1	60.8	539.8	600.6	−38.9	−491.1	−530.0
1931	81.8	75.9	157.7	104.5	511.3	615.7	−55.0	−456.1	−511.0
1932	21.8	48.7	70.6	15.1	85.2	100.3	38.0	−39.2	−1.2
1933	49.5	55.1	104.7	9.7	70.9	80.6	70.0	−29.4	40.6
1934	53.1	46.0	99.1	11.3	31.0	42.3	85.3	8.2	93.5
1935	79.7	41.5	121.2	11.5	29.8	41.2	77.3	6.0	83.4
1936	96.6	39.2	135.8	19.3	71.2	90.5	37.4	−35.0	2.4
1937	88.8	35.8	124.6	30.4	67.3	97.8	35.3	−39.6	−4.4
1938	56.7	36.2	92.9	166.3	239.3	405.6	−56.8	−216.6	−273.4
1939	65.7	27.7	93.4	493.8	176.3	670.1	−363.6	−157.9	−521.5
1940	109.5	22.7	132.2	128.8	93.7	222.5	38.5	−79.1	−40.7
1941	130.2	18.4	148.6	170.1	146.8	316.8	36.0	−130.1	−94.1
1942ᵃ	167.3	14.5	181.8	175.4	107.2	282.7	54.2	−88.5	−34.3
1943ᵃ	206.0	16.7	222.7	176.8	123.7	300.6	229.2	−92.4	136.9
1944ᵃ	229.7	18.7	248.4			122.0			521.3
1945ᵃ	406.1	31.4	437.4			214.4			459.7
1946ᵃ			643.3						
1947ᵃ			674.1						

Based on Source 1, supplemented for 1928 by *Source Book of Statistics of Income*. For differences in the data for various years see Appendix One, Part II.

ᵃ Net loss excludes all loss except net loss on sales of depreciable assets.

Table 93

Statutory Net Income and Deficit of All Corporations and of Financial and Nonfinancial Corporations, and Number of Returns with Statutory Net Incomes or Deficits, 1928-1947

	STAT. NET INCOME OR DEFICIT ($ mil.)			NUMBER OF RETURNS		
	Returns with Net		All	*Returns with Net*		All
	Incomes	Deficits	returns	Incomes	Deficits	returns
All Corporations						
1928	10,617.7	2,391.1	8,226.6	268,783	174,828	443,611
1929	11,653.9	2,914.1	8,739.8	269,430	186,591	456,021
1930	6,428.8	4,877.6	1,551.2	221,420	241,616	463,036
1931	3,683.4	6,970.9	−3,287.5	175,898	283,806	459,704
1932	2,153.1	7,796.7	−5,643.6	82,646	369,238	451,884
1933	2,986.0	5,533.3	−2,547.4	109,786	337,056	446,842
1934	4,275.2	4,181.0	94.2	145,101	324,703	469,804
1935	5,164.7	3,468.8	1,696.0	164,231	312,882	477,113
1936	9,478.2	2,152.0	7,326.2	203,161	275,696	478,857
1937	9,634.8	2,280.8	7,354.0	192,028	285,810	477,838
1938	6,526.0	2,853.1	3,672.9	169,884	301,148	471,032
1939	8,826.7	2,092.1	6,734.6	199,479	270,138	469,617
1940	11,203.2	2,283.8	8,919.4	220,977	252,065	473,042
1941	18,111.1	1,778.6	16,332.5	264,628	204,278	468,906
1942	24,052.4	1,000.7	23,051.6	269,942	172,723	442,665
1943	28,718.0	898.7	27,819.2	283,735	136,786	420,521
1944	27,123.7	819.3	26,304.5	288,904	123,563	412,467
1945	22,165.2	1,026.3	21,139.0	303,019	118,106	421,125
1946	27,184.6	−1,991.7	25,192.9	359,310	131,842	491,152
1947	33,381.3	−1,958.6	31,422.7	382,531	169,276	551,807
Financial Corporations						
1928	1,971.3	566.2	1,405.1	80,315	48,824	129,139
1929	2,197.5	1,008.8	1,188.7	80,260	53,677	133,937
1930	1,064.8	1,566.7	−501.9	72,102	64,477	136,579
1931	570.5	2,256.8	−1,686.3	59,129	75,434	134,563
1932	288.0	2,335.5	−2,047.5	26,395	98,725	125,120
1933	260.6	2,273.8	−2,013.2	22,369	99,314	121,683
1934	452.4	1,657.2	−1,204.8	27,257	98,839	126,096
1935	603.3	1,381.6	−778.3	33,231	91,702	124,933
1936	2,219.9	771.5	1,448.4	43,866	71,828	115,694
1937	2,143.8	802.6	1,341.2	43,581	73,498	117,079
1938	1,704.1	815.8	888.3	51,806	88,631	140,437
1939	1,776.5	840.4	936.1	55,646	86,686	142,332
1940	2,030.9	1,162.5	868.4	58,988	83,614	142,602
1941	2,196.6	1,084.0	1,112.7	66,304	77,190	143,494
1942	2,529.5	486.2	2,043.3	68,489	68,393	136,882
1943	2,786.7	409.4	2,377.4	74,956	58,699	133,655
1944	3,200.2	304.8	2,895.4	82,837	51,042	133,879
1945	3,756.0	262.1	3,493.9	90,568	45,005	135,573
1946			4,004.5			144,373
1947			3,841.5			151,043

	STAT. NET INCOME OR DEFICIT ($ mil.)			NUMBER OF RETURNS		
	Returns with Net		All	*Returns with Net*		All
	Incomes	Deficits	returns	Incomes	Deficits	returns
		Nonfinancial Corporations				
1928	8,646.4	1,825.0	6,821.5	188,468	126,004	314,472
1929	9,456.4	1,905.3	7,551.1	189,170	132,914	322,084
1930	5,364.0	3,310.9	2,053.1	149,318	177,139	326,457
1931	3,112.9	4,714.1	−1,601.2	116,769	208,372	325,141
1932	1,865.1	5,461.2	−3,596.1	56,251	270,513	326,764
1933	2,725.4	3,259.5	−534.2	87,417	237,742	325,159
1934	3,822.8	2,523.8	1,299.0	117,844	225,864	343,708
1935	4,561.4	2,087.2	2,474.3	131,000	221,180	352,180
1936	7,258.5	1,380.5	5,877.8	159,295	203,868	363,163
1937	7,491.0	1,478.2	6,012.8	148,447	212,312	360,759
1938	4,821.9	2,037.3	2,784.6	118,078	212,517	330,595
1939	7,050.2	1,251.7	5,798.5	143,835	183,452	327,285
1940	9,172.3	1,121.3	8,051.0	161,989	168,451	330,440
1941	15,914.5	694.6	15,219.8	198,324	127,088	325,412
1942	21,522.9	514.6	21,008.3	201,453	104,330	305,783
1943	25,931.2	489.3	25,441.9	208,779	78,087	286,866
1944	23,923.5	514.5	23,409.1	206,067	72,521	278,588
1945	18,409.2	764.1	17,645.1	212,451	73,101	285,552
1946			21,188.4			346,779
1947			27,581.2			400,764

Source 1. For differences in the data for various years see Appendix One, Part II.

Table 94

Net Capital Gains and Losses of All Corporations and of Financial and Nonfinancial Corporations as Percentages of Statutory Net Incomes or Deficits, 1928-1945

	NET GAIN		NET LOSS	
	Returns with Net		*Returns with Net*	
	Incomes	Deficits	Incomes	Deficits
		All Corporations		
1928	5.7	4.8		
1929	10.0	5.1		
1930	7.6	3.2	2.5	15.9
1931	4.3	2.0	4.2	22.2
1932	2.2	1.2	5.2	20.4
1933	3.9	2.7	5.7	27.4
1934	2.4	3.3	0.5	6.6
1935	5.8	5.0	0.3	6.4
1936	5.1	4.6	0.3	5.5
1937	2.2	4.0	0.4	5.7
1938	3.2	3.2	0.6	6.5
1939	2.8	3.7	0.6	9.3
1940	2.6	3.2	2.8	31.8
1941	1.6	3.5	3.7	35.4
1942	1.1	4.4	0.9	28.1
1943	1.3	4.4	0.9	35.5
1944	1.9	4.8	0.9	31.0
1945	4.7	5.7	1.0	24.3

	NET GAIN *Returns with Net*		NET LOSS *Returns with Net*	
	Incomes	Deficits	Incomes	Deficits

Financial Corporations

	Incomes	Deficits	Incomes	Deficits
1928	17.0	11.6		
1929	35.9	9.8		
1930	25.3	6.2	4.3	34.3
1931	13.3	2.9	9.4	45.8
1932	9.0	2.0	17.4	45.1
1933	25.4	4.0	25.6	44.1
1934	11.3	5.6	1.5	11.5
1935	36.1	9.5	1.1	11.0
1936	17.3	7.8	0.6	11.3
1937	5.9	6.8	1.1	12.4
1938	9.0	6.9	1.3	14.0
1939	10.4	5.9	1.5	15.1
1940	9.1	4.3	7.2	41.9
1941	7.0	4.1	8.1	41.9
1942	3.9	6.1	3.0	38.6
1943	6.4	5.5	3.4	42.2
1944	9.3	6.8	2.3	48.2
1945	17.1	10.5	1.0	48.0

Nonfinancial Corporations

	Incomes	Deficits	Incomes	Deficits
1928	3.2	2.7		
1929	4.0	4.7		
1930	4.1	1.8	2.1	7.2
1931	2.6	1.6	3.2	10.9
1932	1.2	0.9	3.3	9.9
1933	1.8	1.7	3.8	15.7
1934	1.4	1.8	0.4	3.4
1935	1.7	2.0	0.2	3.4
1936	1.3	2.8	0.2	2.2
1937	1.2	2.4	0.2	2.0
1938	1.2	1.8	0.4	3.4
1939	0.9	2.2	0.4	5.4
1940	1.2	2.0	1.8	21.3
1941	0.8	2.6	3.1	25.4
1942	0.8	2.8	0.6	18.2
1943	0.8	3.4	0.7	30.0
1944	1.0	3.6	0.7	20.8
1945	2.2	4.1	1.0	16.2

See Table 92, source note.

Table 95

Financial Corporations as Percentages of Total: Net Capital Gains and Losses, Statutory Net Income or Deficit, and Number of Returns with Statutory Net Incomes or Deficits, 1928-1947

| | NET GAIN OF FINANCIAL CORPORATIONS AS % OF TOTAL CORP. NET GAIN | | | NET LOSS OF FINANCIAL CORPORATIONS AS % OF TOTAL CORP. NET LOSS | | | FINANCIAL CORPORATION RETURNS AS % OF ALL CORPORATE RETURNS | | | STAT. NET INC. OR DEF. OF FIN. CORP. AS % OF TOTAL FOR ALL CORPORATIONS | |
| | *Returns with Net* | | | *Returns with Net* | | | *Returns with Net* | | | *Returns with Net* | |
	Incomes	Deficits	All returns	Incomes	Deficits	All returns	Incomes	Deficits	All returns	Incomes	Deficits
1928	55.1	57.2	55.5	28.2	69.4	62.3	29.9	27.9	29.1	18.6	23.7
1929	67.7	65.9	67.5	35.0	66.8	63.9	29.8	28.8	29.4	18.9	34.6
1930	54.9	62.6	56.8	45.2	66.1	64.8	32.6	26.7	29.5	16.6	32.1
1931	48.0	46.2	47.2	39.0	66.2	63.5	33.6	26.6	29.3	15.5	32.4
1932	54.2	48.6	50.5	30.4	69.1	66.3	31.9	26.7	27.7	13.4	30.0
1933	57.2	62.4	60.1	40.1	68.2	66.3	20.4	29.5	27.2	8.7	41.1
1934	49.0	66.7	59.2	53.1	73.8	70.3	18.8	30.4	26.8	10.6	39.6
1935	73.2	75.9	74.2	67.0	77.0	75.0	20.2	29.3	26.2	11.7	39.8
1936	80.0	60.6	76.6	53.5	61.6	60.1	21.6	26.1	24.2	23.4	35.8
1937	58.6	60.5	59.2	46.6	65.3	61.1	22.7	25.7	24.5	22.2	35.2
1938	73.0	60.7	69.2	46.7	67.1	61.0	30.5	29.4	29.8	26.1	28.6
1939	73.7	64.1	71.4	26.6	72.0	48.6	27.9	32.1	30.3	20.1	40.2
1940	62.8	68.7	63.9	37.3	66.7	54.3	26.7	33.2	30.1	18.1	50.9
1941	54.3	70.6	57.2	35.7	54.0	45.7	25.1	37.8	30.6	12.1	60.9
1942[a]	37.2	67.0	41.4	29.8	57.8	43.9	25.4	39.6	30.9	10.5	48.6
1943[a]	46.6	57.3	47.6	17.6	50.4	35.2	26.4	42.9	31.8	9.7	45.6
1944[a]	56.5	52.3	56.2			49.1	28.7	41.3	32.5	11.8	37.2
1945[a]	61.2	46.8	60.4			34.0	29.9	38.1	32.2	16.9	25.5
1946[a]			42.6						29.4		
1947[a]			46.0						27.4		

See Table 92, source note.

[a] See Table 92, note a.

Table 96

Net Capital Gains and Losses: Financial Corporations by Type,
1939-1947

	NET GAIN	NET LOSS	EXCESS OF GAIN	NET GAIN	NET LOSS	EXCESS OF GAIN
TYPE OF COMPANY	(millions of dollars)			(percentages)		
1939						
Banks & trust companies	110.7	55.0	55.8	47.4	35.8	69.5
Invest. trusts & invest. cos.	12.2	1.0	11.2	5.2	0.7	14.0
Other invest. cos. incl. holding cos.	10.8	4.8	6.0	4.6	3.2	7.5
Security & commodity exchange brokers & dealers	43.5	6.7	36.8	18.6	4.3	45.9
Ins. carriers, agents, etc.	3.9	4.1	−0.2	1.7	2.7	−0.3
Real estate & build. lessors	37.4	61.7	−24.3	16.0	40.2	−30.2
Other	15.0	20.1	−5.1	6.4	13.1	−6.4
Total	233.5	153.3	80.2	100.0	100.0	100.0
1940						
Banks & trust companies	92.2	97.6	−5.4	39.4	15.4	1.4
Invest. trusts & invest. cos.	12.3	122.4	−110.1	5.3	19.3	27.6
Other invest. cos. incl. holding cos.	7.7	176.2	−168.5	3.3	27.8	42.3
Security & commodity exchange brokers & dealers	53.1	5.2	47.9	22.6	0.8	−12.0
Ins. carriers, agents, etc.	4.6	66.4	−61.8	2.0	10.5	15.5
Real estate & build. lessors	53.2	119.0	−65.7	22.7	18.8	16.5
Other	11.2	46.3	−35.1	4.8	7.3	8.8
Total	234.4	633.1	−398.7	100.0	100.0	100.0
1941						
Banks & trust companies	66.9	131.2	−64.3	33.7	20.8	14.8
Invest. trusts & invest. cos.	8.9	98.6	−89.8	4.5	15.6	20.7
Other invest. cos. incl. holding cos.	12.0	148.0	−136.0	6.1	23.4	31.3
Security & commodity exchange brokers & dealers	42.3	3.8	38.5	21.3	0.6	−8.9
Ins. carriers, agents, etc.	7.3	62.4	−55.1	3.7	9.9	12.7
Real estate & build. lessors	49.0	137.6	−88.6	24.7	21.8	20.4
Other	12.0	50.8	−38.8	6.0	8.0	8.9
Total	198.5	632.5	−434.0	100.0	100.0	100.0
1942[a]						
Banks & trust companies	14.3	125.5	−111.2	11.2	47.5	82.1
Invest. trusts & invest. cos.	5.5	1.2	4.2	4.3	0.5	−3.1
Other invest. cos. incl. holding cos.	4.9	4.5	0.4	3.8	1.7	−0.3
Security & commodity exchange brokers & dealers	33.7	4.5	29.2	26.3	1.7	−21.6
Ins. carriers, agents, etc.	2.7	7.7	−5.1	2.1	2.9	3.8
Real estate & build. lessors	58.8	91.8	−32.9	45.8	34.8	24.3
Other	8.5	28.7	−20.1	6.6	10.9	14.9
Total	128.5	264.0	−135.5	100.0	100.0	100.0

TYPE OF COMPANY	NET GAIN	NET LOSS	EXCESS OF GAIN	NET GAIN	NET LOSS	EXCESS OF GAIN
	(millions of dollars)			(percentages)		
1943[a]						
Banks & trust companies	36.2	100.0	−64.5	17.9	37.7	99.0
Invest. trusts & invest. cos.	18.9	1.6	17.3	9.4	0.6	−26.7
Other invest. cos. incl. holding cos.	10.8	9.2	1.6	5.3	3.4	−2.4
Security & commodity exchange brokers & dealers	50.6	9.6	41.0	25.1	3.6	−63.0
Ins. carriers, agents, etc.	5.7	9.8	−4.1	2.8	3.7	6.3
Real estate & build. lessors	65.2	110.7	−45.4	32.3	41.4	69.8
Other	14.6	25.6	−11.0	7.2	9.6	16.9
Total	202.0	267.1	−65.1	100.0	100.0	100.0
1944[a]						
Banks & trust companies	85.0	71.5	13.4	26.6	32.3	13.8
Invest. trusts & invest. cos.	55.7	0.9	54.7	17.5	0.4	56.1
Other invest. cos. incl. holding cos.	12.7	5.2	7.5	4.0	2.3	7.7
Security & commodity exchange brokers & dealers	51.2	1.5	49.7	16.0	0.7	51.0
Ins. carriers, agents, etc.	9.2	7.1	2.1	2.9	3.2	2.1
Real estate & build. lessors	88.1	103.6	−15.4	27.6	46.7	−15.8
Other	17.2	31.8	−14.6	5.4	14.4	−15.0
Total	319.1	221.6	97.6	100.0	100.0	100.0
1945[a]						
Banks & trust companies	234.8	31.2	203.6	35.1	19.1	40.4
Invest. trusts & invest. cos.	122.7	3.2	119.5	18.4	1.9	23.7
Other invest. cos. incl. holding cos.	28.1	3.9	24.2	4.2	2.4	4.8
Security & commodity exchange brokers & dealers	85.4	1.0	84.4	12.8	0.6	16.7
Ins. carriers, agents, etc.	34.8	6.3	28.5	5.2	3.9	5.6
Real estate & build. lessors	134.4	98.2	36.2	20.1	60.1	7.2
Other	27.8	19.6	8.2	4.2	12.0	1.6
Total	668.0	163.5	504.5	100.0	100.0	100.0
1946[a]						
Banks & trust companies	190.2	20.6	169.6	22.0	17.5	22.7
Invest. trusts & invest. cos.	145.0	1.1	143.9	16.7	0.9	19.2
Other invest. cos. incl. holding cos.	44.0	3.3	40.7	5.1	2.8	5.4
Security & commodity exchange brokers & dealers	78.9	2.0	76.9	9.1	1.7	10.3
Ins. carriers, agents, etc.	60.1	2.7	57.4	6.9	2.3	7.7
Real estate & build. lessors	309.1	75.4	233.7	35.7	64.1	31.2
Other	38.3	12.5	25.8	4.4	10.6	3.5
Total	865.6	117.6	748.0	100.0	100.0	100.0
1947[a]						
Banks & trust companies	79.2	38.0	41.2	13.8	34.4	8.9
Invest. trusts & invest. cos.	60.1	1.0	59.0	10.5	0.9	12.7
Other invest. cos. incl. holding cos.	22.7	5.3	17.4	3.9	4.8	3.7
Security & commodity exchange brokers & dealers	56.6	2.6	54.0	9.9	2.3	11.6
Ins. carriers, agents, etc.	23.5	1.9	21.7	4.1	1.7	4.7
Real estate & build. lessors	296.3	51.5	244.8	51.6	46.6	52.8
Other	36.0	10.3	25.7	6.3	9.3	5.5
Total	574.3	110.5	463.9	100.0	100.0	100.0

See Table 93, source note. [a] See Table 92, note a.

Table 97

Net Capital Gains and Losses and Statutory Net Income: All Corporations and Corporations Submitting and not Submitting Balance Sheets, 1931-1947 (millions of dollars)

	ALL CORPORATIONS			SUBMITTING BALANCE SHEETS			NOT SUBMITTING BALANCE SHEETS		
	Gain	Loss	Income	Gain	Loss	Income	Gain	Loss	Income
1931	298.6	1,702.3	−3,287.5	283.5	1,538.5	−2,924.9	15.1	163.8	−362.6
1932	142.5	1,705.2	−5,643.6	136.3	1,538.1	−5,262.1	6.2	167.1	−381.5
1933	262.5	1,685.9	−2,547.4	253.2	1,488.1	−2,183.1	9.3	197.8	−364.3
1934	242.6	297.4	94.2	233.3	257.7	258.3	9.3	39.7	−164.1
1935	469.9	239.0	1,696.0	452.3	179.3	1,883.5	17.6	59.7	−187.5
1936	581.2	142.4	7,326.2	552.6	123.5	7,177.9	28.6	18.9	148.3
1937	305.3	164.5	7,354.0	270.6	144.3	7,306.1	34.7	20.2	47.9
1938	302.0	226.8	3,672.9	290.6	193.1	3,691.9	11.4	33.7	−19.0
1939	326.9	251.1	6,734.6	313.8	206.6	6,798.8	13.1	44.5	−64.2
1940	366.6	1,038.7	8,919.4	348.3	872.2	9,048.2	18.3	166.5	−128.8
1941	347.1	1,302.6	16,332.5	315.2	1,155.3	16,253.6	31.9	147.3	78.9
1942[a]	310.3	486.5	23,051.6	292.2	406.5	22,945.8	18.1	80.0	105.8
1943[a]	424.7	583.9	27,819.2	402.8	524.1	27,627.3	21.9	59.8	192.0
1944[a]	567.5	504.2	26,304.5	540.9	435.0	26,212.8	26.6	69.3	91.7
1945[a]	1,105.5	464.1	21,139.0	1,053.6	415.0	21,014.0	51.8	49.0	125.0
1946[a]	1,508.9	239.6	25,192.9	1,419.4	199.9	24,820.5	89.5	39.7	372.4
1947[a]	1,248.4	324.8	31,422.7	1,140.3	264.4	31,015.3	108.2	60.4	407.4

See Table 93, source note.

[a] See Table 92, note a

540

Table 98

Net Capital Gains and Losses of Corporations Submitting Balance Sheets, by Size of Total Assets, 1931-1947

				TOTAL ASSETS (thousands of dollars)						
	Under 50	50-100	100-250	250-500	500-1,000	1,000-5,000	5,000-10,000	10,000-50,000	50,000 & over	Total
A. NET CAPITAL GAINS (millions of dollars)										
1931	13.1	9.8	20.5	17.6	21.3	47.0	17.6	34.1	102.4	283.5
1932	9.0	6.1	11.6	10.0	9.5	25.8	11.8	15.8	36.7	136.3
1933	10.3	6.6	16.1	15.0	18.1	56.5	23.9	50.4	56.2	253.2
1934	10.5	6.2	15.5	14.2	17.0	42.0	24.1	35.6	68.2	233.3
1935	14.8	15.7	31.4	34.1	37.1	91.5	42.7	72.6	112.4	452.3
1936	16.2	12.3	32.1	40.0	43.0	128.3	48.8	95.2	136.8	552.6
1937	15.2	10.2	20.1	25.7	27.0	65.5	23.6	40.1	43.1	270.6
1938	16.2	9.9	18.0	20.0	24.2	58.1	23.7	48.9	71.6	290.6
1939	17.3	10.8	18.3	22.7	25.3	61.0	26.5	43.3	88.7	313.8
1940	23.0	17.7	29.9	27.4	26.0	69.1	24.4	54.8	76.1	348.3
1941	20.8	14.1	27.7	27.5	28.7	67.1	21.7	49.1	58.5	315.2
1942	24.1	19.1	29.8	26.1	26.1	54.5	17.1	47.5	47.9	292.2
1943	28.4	19.3	33.5	36.4	32.5	79.9	42.4	63.6	66.9	402.8
1944	32.8	23.6	42.9	40.3	49.4	104.3	44.9	93.4	109.4	540.9
1945	43.9	37.2	65.0	57.8	67.0	182.3	95.7	204.0	300.7	1,053.6
1946	79.5	67.8	118.1	102.2	104.4	255.4	118.3	269.7	304.0	1,419.4
1947	70.0	62.8	114.5	101.4	104.9	230.4	95.5	161.2	199.6	1,140.3
Percentage Distribution										
1931	4.6	3.5	7.2	6.2	7.5	16.6	6.2	12.0	36.1	100.0
1932	6.6	4.5	8.5	7.3	7.0	18.9	8.7	11.6	26.9	100.0
1933	4.1	2.6	6.4	5.9	7.1	22.3	9.4	19.9	22.2	100.0
1934	4.5	2.7	6.6	6.1	7.3	18.0	10.3	15.3	29.2	100.0
1935	3.3	3.5	6.9	7.5	8.2	20.2	9.4	16.1	24.9	100.0
1936	2.9	2.2	5.8	7.2	7.8	23.2	8.8	17.2	24.8	100.0

Total Assets (thousands of dollars)

	Under 50	50-100	100-250	250-500	500-1,000	1,000-5,000	5,000-10,000	10,000-50,000	50,000 & over	Total
A					*Percentage Distribution*					
1937	5.6	3.8	7.4	9.5	10.0	24.2	8.7	14.8	15.9	100.0
1938	5.6	3.4	6.2	6.9	8.3	20.0	8.2	16.8	24.6	100.0
1939	5.5	3.4	5.8	7.2	8.1	19.4	8.4	13.8	28.3	100.0
1940	6.6	5.1	8.6	7.9	7.5	19.8	7.0	15.7	21.8	100.0
1941	6.6	4.5	8.8	8.7	9.1	21.3	6.9	15.6	18.6	100.0
1942	8.2	6.5	10.2	8.9	8.9	18.7	5.9	16.3	16.4	100.0
1943	7.1	4.8	8.3	9.0	8.1	19.8	10.5	15.8	16.6	100.0
1944	6.1	4.4	7.9	7.4	9.1	19.3	8.3	17.3	20.2	100.0
1945	4.2	3.5	6.2	5.5	6.4	17.3	9.1	19.4	28.5	100.0
1946	5.6	4.8	8.3	7.2	7.4	18.0	8.3	19.0	21.4	100.0
1947	6.1	5.5	10.0	8.9	9.2	20.2	8.4	14.1	17.5	100.0
B					Net Capital Losses (millions of dollars)					
1931	72.2	29.2	72.6	76.5	90.9	316.6	169.6	292.4	418.4	1,538.5
1932	75.7	46.7	73.3	74.8	103.2	293.9	195.9	342.1	332.6	1,538.1
1933	77.1	28.6	61.3	62.3	76.1	314.1	208.8	392.5	267.3	1,488.1
1934	29.2	10.8	16.3	20.9	21.6	68.3	43.2	30.2	17.0	257.7
1935	17.2	8.6	14.8	12.3	12.7	40.6	17.3	40.9	14.9	179.3
1936	13.1	6.4	10.5	11.1	18.5	32.5	8.2	14.4	8.9	123.5
1937	17.2	5.0	7.3	10.3	11.9	24.6	8.7	44.7	14.6	144.3
1938	34.8	8.7	14.2	14.4	22.3	37.9	19.7	21.9	19.3	193.1
1939	22.0	11.1	19.1	20.9	18.5	50.0	19.0	30.3	15.7	206.6
1940	45.0	29.6	32.2	39.1	47.8	153.9	117.0	160.5	247.2	872.2
1941	42.4	19.7	49.7	43.0	63.4	195.6	74.6	227.4	439.6	1,155.3
1942[a]	29.0	9.7	17.2	19.5	21.8	87.1	27.8	73.6	120.6	406.5
1943[a]	34.1	14.3	24.1	20.9	22.1	68.4	36.2	74.5	229.4	524.1
1944[a]	33.5	11.3	20.3	20.7	29.2	60.0	48.7	71.5	139.7	435.0
1945[a]	28.9	12.8	26.4	19.6	24.0	69.5	24.0	63.1	146.6	415.0
1946[a]	20.9	11.1	15.7	14.3	12.5	33.4	15.8	24.1	52.1	199.9
1947[a]	23.9	11.1	15.3	10.7	13.6	28.0	15.9	85.1	60.9	264.4

Percentage Distribution

Year										Total
1931	4.7	1.9	4.7	5.0	5.9	20.6	11.0	19.0	27.2	100.0
1932	4.9	3.0	4.8	4.9	6.7	19.1	12.7	22.2	21.6	100.0
1933	5.2	1.9	4.1	4.2	5.1	21.1	14.0	26.4	18.0	100.0
1934	11.3	4.2	6.3	8.1	8.5	26.5	16.8	11.7	6.6	100.0
1935	9.6	4.8	8.3	6.9	7.1	22.6	9.6	22.8	8.3	100.0
1936	10.6	5.2	8.5	9.0	15.0	26.3	6.6	11.7	7.2	100.0
1937	11.9	3.5	5.1	7.1	8.2	17.0	6.0	31.0	10.1	100.0
1938	18.0	4.5	7.4	7.5	11.5	19.6	10.2	11.3	10.0	100.0
1939	10.6	5.4	9.2	10.1	9.0	24.2	9.2	14.7	7.6	100.0
1940	5.2	3.4	3.7	4.5	5.5	17.6	13.4	18.4	28.3	100.0
1941	3.7	1.7	4.3	3.7	5.5	16.9	6.5	19.7	38.1	100.0
1942a	7.1	2.4	4.2	4.8	5.4	21.4	6.8	18.1	29.7	100.0
1943a	6.5	2.7	4.6	4.0	4.2	13.1	6.9	14.2	43.8	100.0
1944a	7.7	2.6	4.7	4.8	6.7	13.8	11.2	16.4	32.1	100.0
1945a	7.0	3.1	6.4	4.7	5.8	16.8	5.8	15.2	35.3	100.0
1946a	10.5	5.5	7.8	7.1	6.3	16.7	7.9	12.1	26.1	100.0
1947a	9.0	4.2	5.8	4.0	5.1	10.6	6.0	32.2	23.0	100.0

C   EXCESS OF CAPITAL GAINS OVER LOSSES (millions of dollars)

Year										Total
1931	−59.1	−19.4	−52.1	−58.9	−69.6	−269.6	−152.0	−258.3	−316.0	−1,255.0
1932	−66.7	−40.6	−61.7	−64.8	−93.7	−268.1	−184.1	−326.3	−295.9	−1,401.8
1933	−66.8	−22.0	−45.2	−47.3	−58.0	−257.6	−184.9	−342.1	−211.1	−1,234.9
1934	−18.7	−4.6	−0.8	−6.7	−4.6	−26.3	−19.1	5.4	51.2	−24.4
1935	−2.4	7.1	16.6	21.8	24.4	50.9	25.4	31.7	97.5	273.0
1936	3.1	5.9	21.6	28.9	24.5	95.8	40.6	80.8	127.9	429.1
1937	−2.0	5.2	12.8	15.4	15.1	40.9	14.9	−4.6	28.5	126.3
1938	−18.6	1.2	3.8	5.6	1.9	20.2	4.0	27.0	52.3	97.5
1939	−4.7	−0.3	−0.8	1.8	6.8	11.0	7.5	13.0	73.0	107.2
1940	−22.0	−11.9	−2.3	−11.7	−21.8	−84.8	−92.6	−105.7	−171.1	−523.9
1941	−21.6	−5.6	−22.0	−15.5	−34.7	−128.5	−52.9	−178.3	−381.1	−840.1
1942a	−4.9	9.4	12.6	6.6	4.3	−32.6	−10.7	−26.1	−72.7	−114.3
1943a	−5.7	5.0	9.3	15.6	10.5	11.4	6.2	−11.0	−162.5	−121.3
1944a	−0.7	12.3	22.5	19.6	20.2	44.3	−3.8	21.9	−30.3	105.9
1945a	15.0	24.4	38.6	38.2	43.0	112.8	71.7	140.9	154.1	638.6
1946a	58.6	56.7	102.5	87.9	91.9	222.0	102.5	245.5	251.9	1,219.6
1947a	46.1	51.7	99.2	90.8	91.3	202.5	79.6	76.1	138.7	875.8

TOTAL ASSETS (thousands of dollars)

Percentage Distribution

	Under 50	50-100	100-250	250-500	500-1,000	1,000-5,000	5,000-10,000	10,000-50,000	50,000 & over	Total
1931	4.7	1.5	4.2	4.7	5.5	21.5	12.1	20.6	25.2	100.0
1932	4.8	2.9	4.4	4.6	6.7	19.1	13.1	23.3	21.1	100.0
1933	5.4	1.8	3.7	3.8	4.7	20.9	15.0	27.7	17.1	100.0
1934	76.6	18.9	3.3	27.5	18.9	107.8	78.3	-22.1	-209.8	100.0
1935	-0.9	2.6	6.1	8.0	8.9	18.6	9.3	11.6	35.7	100.0
1936	0.7	1.4	5.0	6.7	5.7	22.3	9.5	18.8	29.8	100.0
1937	-1.6	4.1	10.1	12.2	12.0	32.4	11.8	-3.6	22.6	100.0
1938	-19.1	1.2	3.9	5.7	1.9	20.7	4.1	27.7	53.6	100.0
1939	-4.4	-0.2	-0.7	1.7	6.3	10.3	7.0	12.1	68.1	100.0
1940	4.2	2.3	0.4	2.2	4.2	16.2	17.7	20.2	32.7	100.0
1941	2.6	0.7	2.6	1.8	4.1	15.3	6.3	21.2	45.4	100.0
1942a	4.3	-8.2	-11.0	-5.8	-3.8	28.5	9.4	22.8	63.6	100.0
1943a	4.7	-4.1	-7.7	-12.8	-8.6	-9.4	-5.1	9.1	134.0	100.0
1944a	-0.7	11.6	21.3	18.5	19.1	41.8	-3.6	20.6	-28.6	100.0
1945a	2.4	3.8	6.0	6.0	6.7	17.7	11.2	22.1	24.1	100.0
1946a	4.8	4.7	8.4	7.2	7.5	18.2	8.4	20.1	20.7	100.0
1947a	5.3	5.9	11.3	10.4	10.4	23.1	9.1	8.7	15.8	100.0

D STATUTORY NET INCOME OR DEFICIT

	Under 50	50-100	100-250	250-500	500-1,000	1,000-5,000	5,000-10,000	10,000-50,000	50,000 & over	Total
1931	-417.8	-219.4	-361.5	-289.8	-311.1	-788.7	-281.2	-434.6	179.1	-2,924.9
1932	-612.3	-317.8	-502.0	-405.7	-442.8	-1,035.6	-452.8	-781.6	-711.6	-5,262.1
1933	-382.6	-134.8	-205.2	-156.6	-145.3	-435.5	-214.6	-357.3	-151.1	-2,183.1
1934	-256.8	-52.6	-49.8	-12.6	-4.4	27.3	11.3	274.3	321.6	258.3
1935	-189.4	-15.5	47.4	92.2	109.3	332.1	155.1	605.2	747.1	1,883.5
1936	-102.0	55.8	223.7	275.8	351.5	1,118.1	580.3	1,464.0	3,210.6	7,177.9
1937	-131.7	37.5	176.3	235.0	303.8	1,055.6	517.0	1,565.0	3,547.5	7,306.1
1938	-204.3	-21.7	48.2	100.3	149.0	512.1	277.0	893.4	1,937.8	3,691.9
1939	-120.5	40.3	191.7	242.5	303.7	1,057.1	518.1	1,505.3	3,060.5	6,798.8
1940	-96.3	56.6	273.3	339.7	416.3	1,357.6	666.4	1,795.6	4,238.9	9,048.2
1941	43.3	199.8	559.3	686.1	880.4	2,610.9	1,347.7	3,022.3	6,903.8	16,253.6
1942	131.6	270.0	728.1	890.3	1,176.5	3,549.8	1,747.2	4,431.6	10,020.6	22,945.8
1943	225.1	338.5	850.0	1,012.6	1,345.2	4,103.4	2,133.2	5,053.0	12,566.3	27,627.3
1944	256.9	350.3	847.4	993.3	1,300.6	3,992.2	2,057.1	4,730.5	11,684.4	26,212.8
1945	267.6	376.4	837.1	913.6	1,193.7	3,427.4	1,704.2	3,868.1	8,425.9	21,014.0
1946	362.9	649.2	1,494.8	1,583.6	1,837.4	4,605.0	2,118.6	4,084.3	8,084.7	24,820.5
1947	177.6	589.4	1,574.2	1,700.6	2,026.5	5,312.4	2,509.0	5,158.4	11,967.3	31,015.3

Percentage Distribution

Year										
1931	14.3	7.5	12.4	9.9	10.6	27.0	9.6	14.9	−6.1	100.0
1932	11.6	6.0	9.5	7.7	8.4	19.7	8.6	14.9	13.5	100.0
1933	17.5	6.2	9.4	7.2	6.7	19.9	9.8	16.4	6.9	100.0
1934	−99.4	−20.3	−19.3	−4.9	−1.7	10.6	4.4	106.2	124.5	100.0
1935	−10.1	−0.8	2.5	4.9	5.8	17.6	8.2	32.1	39.7	100.0
1936	−1.4	0.8	3.1	3.8	4.9	15.6	8.1	20.4	44.7	100.0
1937	−1.8	0.5	2.4	3.2	4.2	14.4	7.1	21.4	48.6	100.0
1938	−5.5	−0.6	1.3	2.7	4.0	13.9	7.5	24.2	52.5	100.0
1939	−1.8	0.6	2.8	3.6	4.5	15.5	7.6	22.1	45.0	100.0
1940	−1.1	0.6	3.0	3.8	4.6	15.0	7.4	19.8	46.8	100.0
1941	0.3	1.2	3.4	4.2	5.4	16.1	8.3	18.6	42.5	100.0
1942	0.6	1.2	3.2	3.9	5.1	15.5	7.6	19.3	43.7	100.0
1943	0.8	1.2	3.1	3.7	4.9	14.9	7.7	18.3	45.5	100.0
1944	1.0	1.3	3.2	3.8	5.0	15.2	7.8	18.0	44.6	100.0
1945	1.3	1.8	4.0	4.3	5.7	16.3	8.1	18.4	40.1	100.0
1946	1.5	2.6	6.0	6.4	7.4	18.6	8.5	16.5	32.6	100.0
1947	0.6	1.9	5.1	5.5	6.5	17.1	8.1	16.6	38.6	100.0

E NUMBER OF CORPORATIONS SUBMITTING BALANCE SHEETS

Year										
1931	182,447	61,144	63,428	31,052	19,335	18,345	2,588	2,117	632	381,088
1932	206,477	58,320	59,500	28,422	17,590	16,705	2,442	1,947	618	392,021
1933	211,586	56,205	56,745	26,773	16,592	15,840	2,344	1,885	594	388,564
1934	223,073	57,840	58,186	28,673	18,339	18,499	2,844	2,411	761	410,626
1935	227,545	58,434	58,208	28,605	18,102	18,407	2,769	2,393	742	415,205
1936	227,343	59,528	58,442	28,342	17,941	18,277	2,719	2,311	751	415,654
1937	228,721	60,238	58,817	27,992	17,587	17,897	2,620	2,281	749	416,902
1938	227,491	59,582	57,733	27,371	17,079	17,187	2,542	2,213	743	411,941
1939	226,877	60,256	58,119	27,447	17,232	17,337	2,537	2,217	737	412,759
1940	225,000	61,053	59,059	27,832	17,505	17,627	2,603	2,266	771	413,716
1941	213,086	61,525	60,386	28,751	18,424	18,832	2,812	2,411	826	407,053
1942	196,642	58,338	57,365	27,300	18,109	19,582	2,905	2,467	826	383,534
1943	181,961	56,579	56,105	26,757	17,893	20,737	3,232	2,719	887	366,870
1944	176,212	56,831	56,782	26,496	17,625	21,590	3,646	2,942	932	363,056
1945	177,788	61,431	60,308	27,583	17,669	22,057	3,948	3,197	969	374,950
1946	199,076	76,821	76,592	34,264	20,803	24,618	4,241	3,341	994	440,750
1947	218,623	89,002	90,709	39,571	23,258	26,447	4,576	3,565	1,070	496,821

			TOTAL ASSETS (thousands of dollars)							
	Under 50	50-100	100-250	250-500	500-1,000	1,000-5,000	5,000-10,000	10,000-50,000	50,000 & over	Total
				Percentage Distribution						
1931	47.9	16.0	16.6	8.1	5.1	4.8	0.7	0.6	0.2	100.0
1932	52.7	14.9	15.2	7.2	4.5	4.3	0.6	0.5	0.2	100.0
1933	54.5	14.5	14.6	6.9	4.3	4.1	0.6	0.5	0.2	100.0
1934	54.3	14.1	14.2	7.0	4.5	4.5	0.7	0.6	0.2	100.0
1935	54.8	14.1	14.0	6.9	4.4	4.4	0.7	0.6	0.2	100.0
1936	54.7	14.3	14.1	6.8	4.3	4.4	0.7	0.6	0.2	100.0
1937	54.9	14.4	14.1	6.7	4.2	4.3	0.6	0.5	0.2	100.0
1938	55.2	14.5	14.0	6.6	4.1	4.2	0.6	0.5	0.2	100.0
1939	55.0	14.6	14.1	6.6	4.2	4.2	0.6	0.5	0.2	100.0
1940	54.4	14.8	14.3	6.7	4.2	4.3	0.6	0.5	0.2	100.0
1941	52.3	15.1	14.8	7.1	4.5	4.6	0.7	0.6	0.2	100.0
1942	51.3	15.2	15.0	7.1	4.7	5.1	0.8	0.6	0.2	100.0
1943	49.6	15.4	15.3	7.3	4.9	5.7	0.9	0.7	0.2	100.0
1944	48.5	15.7	15.6	7.3	4.9	5.9	1.0	0.8	0.3	100.0
1945	47.4	16.4	16.1	7.4	4.7	5.9	1.1	0.9	0.3	100.0
1946	45.2	17.4	17.4	7.8	4.7	5.6	1.0	0.8	0.2	100.0
1947	44.0	17.9	18.3	8.0	4.7	5.3	0.9	0.7	0.2	100.0

See Table 93, source note.
ª See Table 92, note a.

546

INDEX

Manhattan real estate, 1, 2, 148, 151
Marainanga Estates Co. Ltd. v. Commissioner, 266
Market effects of tax treatment, 313-7; *see also* Mobility of capital
Market traders, definition of in data, 351
Market value of capital assets
and reinvested profits, 222-5
changes in, and speculation, 64-7
effect of earnings on, 56-8
relation between book and, 74-5
Marr v. U. S., 42
Martin v. Lowry, 257
Mathematical expectation of gains, 54-8, 64, 67-71, 75-82
Martin, E. M., 51
May, George O., 28, 29, 176, 256, 292
McGrath, J. Y., 264
Means, G. C., 167
Merchant's Loan and Trust Co. v. Smietanka, 35
Mobility of capital assets, effect of tax on, 16-8, 156, 283-4, 287-8; *see also* Property transfers
Monsanto Chemical Co., 74
Morgenstern, Oskar, 70
Motion picture industry, collapsible corporations in, 234-5
Myrdal, Gunnar, 47

National Association of Manufacturers, 22
National income
analysis of, and capital gains, 49-51, 92-3
and capital gains realization, 174, 175
National Industrial Conference Board, 146
National Steel Corp., 65
Net capital gains and losses; *see* Capital gains and losses
Net deficits, classification of returns with, 323
Net income
and size of gain or loss, 142-4
classification, 122, 172, 353-6
definition of, 34-5
gain and loss as proportion of, 7-9, 119, 122-4, 128-30
Net income groups, shares of gains received by, 124-5
Net receipts, change in expected, 54-60
Net worth tax
Belgium, 270
Denmark, 274

Finland, 275
Germany, 277
Hungary, 279
Netherlands, 271
Norway, 274
Switzerland, 275-6
Netherlands, 13, 271-2
Neubert, Reinhard, 276
New investments, effect of
capital gains tax on, 107-8, 156
capital loss allowance on, 183-4
New York State, 145, 148
New Zealand, 265-6
Nicholson, John R., 245
Nonprofessional authors, 245-6
Nontax factors
in gains realization, 162-5, 171, 174-5, 180
in loss realization, 189-90, 195
Northern States Power Co., 1, 2
Norway, 13, 273-4

Odds, balancing of through loss allowance, 181-3
Offsets, gain and loss, 197
Oil and gas industry, future leasal incomes in, 250
Oil Shares, Inc., 21
Operating profits, capital gains included in, 79-82
Optional inventorying, 46
Optional periodic averaging of capital gains and losses, 306
Options
as device for extending holding period of real estate, 202
stock purchase, 237-41
Ordinary income
in conventional capital gains, 67-71
sources of, 3
see also Profits
Ordinary income tax rates, capital gains subject to, 161-2
Ordinary profits and losses and capital gains, 3-5, 8-12, 75-82; *see also* Ordinary income
Original cost, gain and loss as percentage of, 144-5

Partnership liquidations, 237
Partnerships, tabulation of gains and losses of, 345
Paul, Randolf E., 45
Peabody v. Eisner, 41
Penny (J. C.) Co., 74
Pennsylvania, 145
Pennsylvania Railroad, 167
Pensions, 241-5
Pepsi Cola Co., 1, 74

under annual accrual tax, 290-1

Risks
 appraisal of, 64
 compensation for in capital gains, 61-2, 68
 compensation for in profits, 80
 disposition to face, 18, 61-2, 156
 diversification of real estate, 149
 effect of loss allowance on, 183-4, 188
 tax incentive to reduction of, 177-8

Robbins, Lionel, 50
Rockefeller v. U. S., 42
Roosevelt, Franklin D., 229, 230
Rosendorff, Richard, 255
Rottschaefer, Henry, 294
Rudick, Harry J., 176, 245
Rutledge v. C. A. R., 257

Savings compared with capital gains, 87-9
Schanz, Georg, 40, 41
Schwinn, Ignaz, v. Commissioner, 21, 24
Securities
 and physical concept of income, 27-9
 switching out of, 248-9
 see also Stocks and bonds
Security price fluctuations and capital gains tax, 16-8
Security redemption and distribution of corporate earnings, 233-4
Seidman, J. S., 31, 43
Seligman, Eustace, 176, 178, 302
Seltzer, Lawrence H., 176, 223
Short selling as device for extending holding period, 202
Short term gains and losses
 and stock market fluctuations, 136-9
 description of data, 345-9
 disallowance of loss, 21, 335
 reason for taxing differently, 131-4
 relative importance of, 134-6, 140-2, 198-200
 tax treatment of, 159-62, 197-202, 316-7
Shoup, Carl S., 51
Silkin, Lewis, 262
Silverstein, Harry, 245
Simons, Henry, 40, 41, 50, 102, 302, 305, 306
Sinclair, Harry F., 238
Sixteenth Amendment, 13, 34-6
Sloss-Sheffield Steel Co., 74
Small investors, effect of capital loss allowance on, 184-5
Social income, capital gains as, 91-3
Socony-Vacuum Oil Co. Inc., 74
Sources of data, 321-2

South Africa, 12, 266-7
Speculation
 and price movements, 58, 64-7
 and stock market boom, 163-4
Spengler, Edwin H., 148
Springford, Herbert H., 239
Stability of revenue yield and capital gains tax, 204-6
Standard Gas and Electric Co., 2
Standard Oil Co. of Indiana, 74
Stock bonuses, 241-5
Stock dividends, 36-8, 222
 Canada, 263
Stock market boom, 156, 159, 162-7
Stock ownership, diffusion of, 167
Stock prices and
 net capital gain and loss, 119-22, 180
 reinvested earnings, 222-5
 short term transactions, 136-9, 198-200
 tax treatment, 167
Stock purchase options as personal compensation, 237-241
Stocks
 as source of gain and loss, 1-3, 145
 price fluctuations of, 1-3, 119-22, 136-9
 volume of trading, 137
Stocks and bonds
 as source of capital gains, 4
 disallowance of losses from, 21, 325, 358
Stratton's Independence, Ltd. v. Howbert, 33
Surrey, S. S., 302
Sweden, 5, 13, 79, 272-3
Swift and Co., 74
Switzerland, 275-6

Tarleau, Thomas N., 176
Tax avoidance
 and federal revenues, 208-9
 and gifts, 111, 299-304
 and inheritances, 110, 299-304
 and loss allowance limitation, 185-8
 and realization, 41-2
 through closely held operating corporations, 231-3
 through collapsible corporations, 234-7
 through corporate reorganizations, 44-5
 through deferred compensation plans, 241-5
 through loans, 252-3
 through partnership liquidations, 237
 through personal holding companies, 217-21